WHELDON'S
COST ACCOUNTING AND COSTING METHODS

WHELDON'S
COST ACCOUNTING
AND COSTING METHODS

TENTH EDITION

Completely revised by

L. W. J. OWLER, F.C.I.S., F.H.A., A.C.W.A.

and

J. L. BROWN, A.C.W.A., F.Comm.A.

MACDONALD & EVANS
8 John Street, London W.C.1
1960

First published August, 1932
Second edition May, 1934
Third edition March, 1936
Fourth edition August, 1937
Fifth edition September, 1938
Sixth edition August, 1940
Seventh edition January, 1942
Reprinted February, 1943
Eighth edition January, 1944
Reprinted April, 1945
Reprinted September, 1945
Reprinted February, 1946
Reprinted July, 1946
Reprinted January, 1947
Ninth edition April, 1948
Reprinted July, 1949
Reprinted September, 1951
Reprinted October, 1952
Reprinted September, 1953
Reprinted May, 1955
Reprinted April, 1956
Reprinted August, 1957
Reprinted July, 1958
Reprinted January, 1959
Tenth edition August, 1960
Reprinted September, 1960
Reprinted July, 1962
Reprinted July, 1963
Reprinted April, 1965

©

MACDONALD & EVANS LTD.
1960

Printed in Great Britain by Richard Clay (The Chaucer Press), Ltd., Bungay, Suffolk

PREFACE TO TENTH EDITION

THE industrial scene today affords many opportunities to the qualified cost accountant. The long struggle for recognition of the value and importance of cost accountancy is now over. It has proved itself in practice, and manufacturers are becoming more and more cost-conscious.

Since 1932, when the late Mr. Wheldon penned his first preface, the changes and developments in the subject have been profound and far-reaching: indeed, one of the factors which make cost accountancy so interesting and rewarding a field of study is that it is so alive. Mr. Wheldon himself revised his work several times to keep abreast of new thought, and this present edition, which was undertaken as a further revision of his book, has inevitably taken on more and more the character of a new one.

Nevertheless, the groundwork is still there, and the revisers gratefully acknowledge the debt which they and countless others owe to the late Mr. Wheldon. For nearly thirty years his book has been the basis of much of the costing student's knowledge of the subject, and it is hoped that in its new format it will long continue to enjoy the same prestige.

Acknowledgments are due for assistance afforded by the following:

> James Pascall Ltd.
> Harlow Printing Works
> Kalamazoo Ltd.
> National Cash Register Co. Ltd.
> Logabax Ltd.
> Copeland Chatterson Co. Ltd.
> Burroughs Adding Machine Ltd.
> I.B.M. (United Kingdom) Ltd.
> Remington Rand Ltd.
> Shannon Ltd.

and a special word of thanks is due to Mr. A. A. McPhie, of International Computers and Tabulators, for his contribution on Punched Card Accounting for use with Sorters and Tabulators.

All the professional bodies approached readily gave their consent to the use of past examination papers, and questions have been included which in the opinion of the revisers are considered to be most helpful to the student, and which reflect present tendencies of thought.

The following coding will indicate the sources from which they have been taken:

I.C.W.A.	The Institute of Cost and Works Accountants.
C.A.	The Institute of Chartered Accountants in England and Wales.
C.A.A.	The Cost Accountants' Association.
C.C.A.	The Association of Certified and Corporate Accountants.
C.I.S.	The Chartered Institute of Secretaries.
C.C.S.	The Corporation of Secretaries.
A.I.A.	The Association of International Accountants.
Comm. A.	The Society of Commercial Accountants.
I.A.	The Society of Incorporated Accountants.
R.S.A.	Royal Society of Arts.

The Institute of Cost and Works Accountants also kindly gave permission for reference and quotations to be made to any of their publications, and much use has been made of the *Terminology of Cost Accountancy*. For convenience this has been reprinted again in full at the end of the book.

Both of the revisers have had industrial costing experience, but this book has been revised from the point of view of full-time teachers in Cost Accountancy, and bearing in mind the special needs of the student for examination purposes.

L. W. J. OWLER
J. L. BROWN

25 June 1960

CONTENTS

LIST OF ILLUSTRATIONS

LIST OF ILLUSTRATIONS   xiii

CHAPTER 1

INTRODUCTION

DEFINITION OF COSTING

The *Terminology of Cost Accountancy* published by the Institute of Cost and Works Accountants gives the following definitions:

Cost Accountancy

The science, art, and practice of a cost accountant.

Costing

The technique and process of ascertaining costs.

Expanding the ideas contained in these definitions, it may be said that costing is

"The classifying, recording, and appropriate allocation of expenditure for the determination of the costs of products or services."

These costs may be ascertained

(*a*) historically, *i.e.* after they have been incurred, or

(*b*) by predetermined standards, combined with subsequent analysis of variances between those standards, and the actual cost incurred, and

(*c*) by the use of marginal methods of presentation for either (*a*) or (*b*), involving the differentiation between "fixed" and "variable" costs.

COSTING AS AN AID TO MANAGEMENT

Although manufacturers are now willing to accept as a principle that costing is of value, there is still a considerable lack of appreciation by many of them as to where the value lies.

Costing enables a business not only to find out what various jobs or processes have cost but also what they should have cost: it indicates where losses and waste are occurring before the work is finished, therefore immediate action may be taken, if possible, to avoid such loss or waste.

Business policy may require the consideration of alternative methods and procedures, and this is facilitated by cost information correctly presented. For example, by the aid of cost reports management can decide whether the manufacture of certain products increases overhead expenditure disproportionately; whether to treat by-products, even if at a loss, to make possible a more important trade in another product; whether the plant and machinery could be used more advantageously by concentrating on particular products to the exclusion of less profitable ones; or whether prices could or should be adjusted.

It was stated in *Target*

"Probably the greatest scope for increasing efficiency and cutting costs is at the design stage. The cost accountant and the design staff should work in close collaboration, not only on new products but on old lines as well, seeking ways and means of reducing the material costs by simplification of design, the elimination of unnecessary parts or features, and by the use, where possible, of cheaper but equally suitable materials. It is the designers who are concerned with the technical points—the cost accountant supplies the figures which measure the value of each idea and the estimates of costs of new products. One of the Productivity Teams which visited the U.S.A. found a system called 'Value Analysis' in use, which reviews the design of component and assembly items by asking a series of questions, for example, of any component:

(*a*) does its use contribute value?
(*b*) is its cost proportionate to its usefulness?
(*c*) does it need all of its features?
(*d*) is there anything better?
(*e*) can it be made by a better method?
(*f*) can a standard part replace it?
(*g*) will another supplier provide it for less?
(*h*) is anyone buying it for less?"

COSTING ESSENTIAL TO INDUSTRIAL CONTROL

An efficient system of costing is an essential factor for industrial control under modern conditions of business, and as such may be regarded as an important part in the efforts of any management to secure business stability. The organisation of an undertaking has to be so controlled that the desired volume of production is secured at the least possible cost in relation to the scheduled quantity of the product. Cost accounting provides the measurement of the degree to which this objective is attained, and thus has a definite place in the organisation of the business. All expense is localised, and thereby controlled, in the light of information provided by the cost records.

COSTING IN PERIODS OF TRADE COMPETITION

When business is not difficult to secure, many manufacturers are able to show a profit notwithstanding the leakages which pass unchecked, but in periods of trade competition concealed inefficiencies have to be tracked down, and rigorous control must be exercised to ensure even modest margins of profit. Failure to maintain normal output results in overhead expenses not being recovered in full. The value of a costing system is thus seen, since by indicating where economies may be sought, waste eliminated, and efficiency increased, some of the loss occasioned by reduced turn-over and falling prices may be avoided. Further, knowing the real cost of production, a manufacturer, when tendering, can fix the lowest possible price on the reduced output so that he may continue to enjoy a share of the market; and the importance of making use of idle capacity is pressed upon him. The probable effects of reducing prices with the object of increasing turnover can also be presented to him; and in many other ways the Cost Accounts provide essential data for management decisions.

ESTIMATES

Estimates, it should be observed, are not costs, from which they differ in several ways. Usually, estimates are based on present or pro-spective market prices of materials and labour and, while previously ascertained costs may be used as a guide in fixing prices, it is sometimes necessary to prepare estimates on a competitive basis, making quota-tions even below cost to avoid greater loss where there is a costly plant and fixed overhead expense is heavy.

Cost Accounts, however, record the actual or maybe standard costs of materials, wages, and overhead. It has been said very aptly, that "an estimate is an opinion, price is a policy, and cost is a fact."

The ascertained costs, whether actual or standard, provide a measure for estimates, a guide to policy, and a control over current production.

DESIRABLE CONDITIONS FOR A COSTING SYSTEM

The following general conditions should be observed as far as possible when installing a costing system:

1. The arrangement of the system should be adapted to suit the general organisation of the particular business, subject to such alterations as may be unavoidable. Usually, any scheme to alter the plan of the business to adapt it to a costing system will be un-satisfactory, and, owing to resentment of officials, there is the probability that the fullest co-operation will not be forthcoming.

2. The technical aspects of the business should be carefully studied, and an effort made to secure the sympathetic assistance and sup-port of the principal members of the works staff and of the workers generally.

3. The minimum amount of detail in which records are to be com-piled should be arranged. Complete analyses are desirable, but

over-elaboration must be avoided. The compilation of schedules and analyses with unnecessary details involving undue clerical work will make the system costly, and disproportionate to the benefits received. Nevertheless, the costing system should, without exception, cover the whole work of production and services.

4. The records to be made by foremen and workers should involve as little clerical work as possible. Printed forms should be provided, and all instructions written or printed. It is advantageous to provide written or printed instructions as to the origin, use, and disposition of each form.

5. To ensure reliable statistics, every original entry on factory forms should be supported by an examiner's signature, or by counter-checks.

6. Promptitude, frequency, and regularity in the presentation of costs and statistics must be arranged for.

7. The Cost Accounts and the Financial Accounts should be either interlocked in one integral accounting scheme or be so arranged that the results of the two sets of accounts are reconciled by means of Control Accounts.

SUMMARY OF PURPOSES OF COST ACCOUNTS

The following summary may be useful to the student:

1. To analyse and classify with reference to the cost of products and operations the same expenditure which, in the Financial Accounts, has been recorded and summarised under Nominal Account headings.

2. To arrive at the cost of production of every unit, job, operation, process, department, or service, and to develop cost standards.

3. To indicate to the management any inefficiencies, and the extent of various forms of waste, whether of materials, time, expense, or in the use of machinery, equipment, and tools. Analysis of the causes of unsatisfactory results may indicate remedial action.

4. To provide data for periodical Profit and Loss Accounts and Balance Sheets at such intervals, *e.g.* weekly, monthly, or quarterly, as may be desired during the financial year, not only for the whole business but also by departments or individual products.

5. To reveal sources of economies in production, having regard to methods, types of equipment, design, output, and layout. Daily, weekly, monthly, or quarterly information may be necessary to ensure prompt constructive action.

6. To provide actual figures of cost for comparison with estimates, and to serve as a guide for future estimates, or quotations, and to assist the management in their price-fixing policy.

7. To show, where Standard Costs are prepared, what the cost of production is to be, and with which the actual costs which are eventually recorded may be compared.
8. To present comparative cost data for different periods and various volumes of production output, and to provide guidance in the development of the business. This is valuable in connection with budgetary control.
9. To indicate whether the cost of certain articles or components made in the factory is such that it would be more economical to buy from outside sources.
10. To record the relative production results of each unit of plant and machinery in use as a basis for examining its efficiency. A comparison with the performance of other types of machines may suggest the necessity for replacement.
11. To provide a perpetual inventory of stores and other materials, so that

   (a) interim Profit and Loss Accounts and Balance Sheets can be prepared without stock-taking, and
   (b) checks on stores and adjustments are made at frequent intervals.

12. To explain in detail the sources of profit or loss revealed in total in the Profit and Loss Account.

PRACTICAL EXAMPLE OF THE VALUE OF COST ACCOUNTS

In order that it may be clearly seen how valuable the presentation of cost accounting information may be, the following illustration is given, showing Final Accounts drawn up both on ordinary accounting lines and also by costing methods.

The Financial Accountant has prepared a simple account for the year as follows:

	£		£
Materials consumed	15,000	Sales	30,000
Wages	7,000		
Production expenses	2,000		
Gross Profit (20%)	6,000		
	£30,000		£30,000
Administration expenses	2,000	Gross Profit	6,000
Selling and Distribution expenses	1,000		
Net Profit (10%)	3,000		
	£6,000		£6,000

This reveals an apparently satisfactory net profit of £3000, which represents 10% of turnover. However, the information is too general to be of great use to management, who need to know the profit or loss on each product, so that policy decisions can be made.

The allocation of costs to each product is one of the main functions of a cost accounting system, so that reasonably reliable production costs can be ascertained. The Cost Accountant may produce a simple cost statement, which may look like this:

	A.	B.	C.	Total
	£	£	£	£
Materials consumed	4,800	3,700	6,500	15,000
Wages	1,500	2,500	3,000	7,000
Production Overhead	500	600	900	2,000
	6,800	6,800	10,400	24,000
Administration Overhead	700	800	500	2,000
Selling and Distribution Overhead	300	400	300	1,000
Total Cost	£7,800	£8,000	£11,200	£27,000
Sales	10,240	10,800	8,960	30,000
Profit	2,440	2,800	—	3,000
Loss	—	—	2,240	—
Profit (%)	24	26	—	10

This statement clearly reveals to management that products A and B are obtaining approximately 25% profit, but that product C is pulling down the total profit to 10%. Ignoring such items as plant capacity, plant utilisation, volume of sales, etc., there are four possible courses which management may follow:

1. Investigate thoroughly product C to find possible economies.
2. Stop production of C.
3. Increase selling price of C.
4. Produce C as a "loss-leader," i.e. produce and sell C in the hope of encouraging consumers to buy also A or B.

The Cost Accountant points out the facts and, where possible, suggests remedies; management must make the final decisions on policy.

CHAPTER 2

THE ELEMENTS OF COST

THE ANALYSIS AND CLASSIFICATION OF COST

If management is to be provided with the data required for cost control it is necessary to analyse and classify costs.

A classification has to be made to arrive at the detailed costs of departments, processes, production orders, jobs, or other cost units. The total cost of production can be found without such analysis, and in most instances an average unit cost could be obtained, but none of the advantages of an analysed cost would be available.

Generally speaking, all expenditure may be divided into groups corresponding to the activities of a manufacturing concern, namely:

1. Producing Departments or Shops.
2. Service Departments.
3. Works Expenses.
4. Administration Expenses.
5. Selling Expenses.
6. Distribution Expenses.

} Expenditure of Manufacturing.

Again, total cost can be separated under three broad headings, namely, Materials, Labour, and Overhead, and these three groups of expenditure are known as the elements of cost.

THE ANALYSIS OF TOTAL COST

The total expenditure incidental to production, administration, selling, and distribution may be analysed by the Cost Accountant as follows:

1. Direct Materials.
2. Direct Labour.
3. Direct Expenses (if any).
4. Overhead Expenses.

   (a) Factory.

      (i) Departmental.
      (ii) General.
      (iii) Services.

   (b) Administration.
   (c) Selling and Distribution.

Works or Factory Cost.

Total Costs of Sales.

The first three items constitute Prime Cost, so that the elements of cost may be said to comprise Prime Cost and overhead. Each item is defined and explained below.

DIRECT LABOUR

Direct labour is all labour expended in altering the construction, composition, conformation, or condition of the product. The wages paid to skilled and unskilled workers for this labour can be allocated specifically to the particular cost accounts concerned—hence the term "Direct Wages," which may be defined as the measure of direct labour in terms of money.

Other descriptions sometimes used are: Process Labour; Productive Labour; Operating Labour. Indirect Labour is dealt with on p. 11.

In practice there are often circumstances which permit of wages of certain classes of labour being included under the heading of direct wages which are more commonly regarded as indirect wages. This could be the case when labour, whilst not directly expended in altering the material or condition of the product, is specifically connected with such activity and can be accurately so identified for costing purposes. In such circumstances the wages of those directly involved in handling a particular product to the finished store or despatch may be regarded as direct. The particular circumstances within certain industries make this practicable.

In a few exceptional circumstances wages in respect of the following may be treated as direct wages: general labour, foremen, charge hands, inspection, shop clerks, internal transport, and trainees; they are, however, normally indirect wages.

DIRECT MATERIAL

Direct material is all material that becomes a part of the product, the costs of which are directly charged as part of the Prime Cost. In other words, it is the material which can be measured and charged directly to the cost of the product. The following groups of materials fall within the definition:

1. All material specially purchased for a particular job, order, or process.
2. All materials (including primary materials and raw materials) acquired and subsequently requisitioned from the stores for particular production orders.
3. Components purchased or produced, and similarly requisitioned from the finished parts store.
4. Material passing from one operation or process to another, *e.g.*

produced, converted, or part-manufactured material which is intended for further treatment or operations.

5. Primary packing materials (*e.g.* cartons, wrappings, cardboard boxes, etc.).

The following descriptions are used in the same sense as Direct Materials: Process Material; Prime Cost Material; Production Material; Stores Material; Constructional Material.

Items such as import duties, dock charges, transport of materials, storing of materials, cost of purchasing and receiving materials, cost of rectifying materials, are proper additions to their invoiced price, and when this course is followed the materials are charged out at this augmented initial cost. Indirect Material is covered on p. 11.

Raw Material.—Reference may be usefully made here to the term "Raw Material." In the majority of instances the finished product of one industry is the raw material of another. Thus sheet steel may be the finished product of the steel rolling-mill, but the raw material of a metal-cutting works. The finished product of a wool-spinning mill becomes the raw material of the weaving-mill. Pulp board is the finished product of mills which pulp timber, but this is part of the raw material of the paper-mill.

Circumstances arise when some direct materials are used in comparatively small quantities, and it would be a futile elaboration to make an analysis of them for the purpose of a direct charge. In the manufacture of hats or sewn boots it would be absurd to measure the value of the thread; or in making cardboard boxes, to determine the glue cost for fixing strips of linen used for binding the corners. Such direct material as this should be treated as a production expense item.

DIRECT EXPENSES

Direct expense includes any expenditure other than direct material or direct labour directly incurred on a specific cost unit. Such special necessary expense is charged directly to the particular cost account concerned, as part of the Prime Cost. Examples of direct expenses (sometimes also known as "Chargeable Expenses") are as follows:

1. Hire of special or single purpose tools or equipment for a particular production order or product.
2. Costs of special layout, designs, or drawings.
3. Maintenance costs of such equipment.

OVERHEAD EXPENSES

The three elements of cost just described constitute Prime Cost, and all expense over and above Prime Cost is Overhead. Prime Cost plus Factory Overhead represents Works, or Factory Cost.

"Overhead" may be defined as the cost of indirect material, indirect labour, and such other expenses, including Services, as cannot conveniently be charged direct to specific cost units. Alternatively, overheads are all expenses other than direct expenses.

In general terms overhead comprises all expenses incurred for, or in connection with, the general organisation of the whole or part of the undertaking. In other words, the general costs of operating supplies and services used by the undertaking, and including the maintenance of capital assets.

The main groups into which overhead may be subdivided are:

1. Production or Factory Expense, including Services.
2. Administration Expense.
3. Selling Expense. ⎫
4. Distribution Expense. ⎭ Sometimes combined.

Overhead may also be classified as Fixed Overhead and Variable Overhead and this aspect of expense analysis is discussed on pp. 278 and 296.

PRODUCTION (OR FACTORY) EXPENSE

This category covers all indirect expenditure incurred by the undertaking from the receipt of the order until its completion ready for despatch, either to the customer or to Finished Goods Store. Any expenses not taken to account as a direct expense are known as overhead. Other terms used are: Factory Overhead; Factory Oncost; Production Overhead; Works Overhead; Works Oncost; Mill Oncost.

Examples of Production Overhead are:

1. Rent, rates, and insurance chargeable against the works, excluding any which can be apportioned to the general administration offices, selling departments, warehouse, and distribution.
2. Indirect labour, *e.g.* supervision, such as salary of works managers, wages of foremen, etc.; shop clerical work; testing, gauging, and examining; indirect labour in connection with production shops.
3. Power (steam, gas, electric, hydraulic, compressed air) and other services in aid of production; process fuel; internal transport; canteens, etc.
4. Consumable stores, and all forms of indirect material, *i.e.* material which cannot be traced as part of the finished product, such as cotton waste, grease and oil, small tools, etc.
5. Depreciation, maintenance, and repairs of buildings, plant, machinery, tools, etc.
6. Sundry expenses *re* personnel, such as employment office, works

police, rewards for suggestions and all forms of welfare, such as canteens, recreation, first aid, works entertainments, works newspapers, radio music, and safety first.

Indirect Material.—In its strict sense, indirect material is material that cannot be traced as part of the product. It usually comprises materials required for operating and maintaining the plant and equipment, commonly called "consumable stores" (*e.g.* lubricants, cotton waste, belt fasteners) and items like hand tools and works stationery. Sometimes minor items of material which enter into production are treated as indirect material because of the futility of attempting minute analysis, as mentioned above in the last paragraph of the section dealing with direct materials (p. 9). Synonyms are: "Oncost Materials," "Expense Materials."

Indirect Labour.—This may be defined as labour expended that does not alter the construction, conformation, composition, or condition of the product, but which contributes generally to such work and to the completion of the product and its progressive movement and handling up to the point of despatch. It is sometimes referred to as "nonproductive" labour, but this is an inaccurate description, and one which has fallen into disuse as being contrary to modern conception. Other synonyms are: "Oncost Labour," "Auxiliary Labour," "Ancillary Labour."

Indirect Wages.—This term may be defined as the measure of indirect labour expressed in terms of remuneration paid. Under this heading are included:

Supervisors, Foremen, and Charge-hands.
Inspection.
Labourers and general handling of work and materials.
Storekeepers.
Work checkers and Recorders.
Maintenance Services, Oilers, Cleaners, and Repairers.
Instructors.
Transport.
Drawing Office.
Tool Room.
Works Clerical Staff.
Idle time of operatives.
Works Police, Gatemen, etc.
Welfare Services.
Any wages which cannot be identified as directly chargeable to Prime
   Cost as Direct Wages.

Whether materials or labour are indirect or otherwise largely depends on circumstances obtaining in particular businesses.

ADMINISTRATION EXPENSE

This consists of all expense incurred in the direction, control, and administration (including secretarial, accounting, and financial control) of an undertaking.

Examples are: The expenses in running the general offices, *e.g.* office rent, light, heat, salaries and wages of clerks, secretaries, accountants, credit approval, cash collection and treasurer's department, general managers, directors, executives; legal and accounting machine services; investigations and experiments; and miscellaneous fixed charges.

SELLING AND DISTRIBUTION EXPENSE

Selling Expense

This portion of the overhead comprises the cost to producers or distributors of soliciting and securing orders for the articles or commodities dealt in, and of efforts to find and retain customers. It includes advertising; salaries and commission of sales manager, travellers, and agents; training of salesmen and sales correspondents; the cost of preparing tenders and estimates for special selling projects; sales stock shortages; rent of sale rooms and offices; consumer service and service after sales, etc.; demonstrators and technical advisers to customers or prospective customers.

Distribution Expense

This comprises all expenditure incurred from the time the product is completed in the works until it reaches its destination. Under this heading would be included Warehouse or Finished Stock Store charges, and the cost of transporting goods thereto, packing-cases, loading, carriage outwards, and of goods on sale or return, upkeep and running of delivery vehicles, despatch clerks and labourers, and other items of like nature.

Selling and Distribution Expenses are collected and analysed:

1. According to the nature of the expense, and also by function, *e.g.* advertising, salesmen, showrooms, storage, etc.
2. By location, *e.g.* representatives' territories, agents, markets, counties, countries, etc.; by departments, depots, etc.; or by type or grade of products. For the distribution of such costs various factors may be used, according to which is most suitable as regards incidence. Suggested factors are units of product, weights, values by selling turnover, time, distance, cubic capacity, invoices, and so on. The object is to show the relationship of sales turnover to costs, and the relationship of sales turnover to the potential market.

Hence the analysis of sales turnover and of these costs must be on the same basis. The effectiveness of these expenses towards profit earning can then be measured.

THE METHODS OF COST ACCOUNTING

The general fundamental principles of cost ascertainment are the same in every system of cost accounting, but the methods of collating and presenting the costs vary with the type of production to be costed.

Seven methods of costing for the ascertainment of *actual* costs may be identified, although basically there are two major groupings: (*a*) Job Costing, (*b*) Unit or Process Costing. The names given to the seven methods are used as a convenient means of referring to the variations of procedure for different types of production.

The methods are:

1. *Unit Costing*, formerly known as "Output" or "Single Output" Costing; originally the term referred to the costing of goods.
2. *Operating Costing*. Actually this is Unit Costing as applied to the costing of services. Unit costs may be presented in a variety of aspects in respect of the same expenditure.
3. *Job Costing*, sometimes referred to as "Terminal" Costing. It also includes "Contract Costing."
4. *Batch Costing*, which is a form of Job Costing, a convenient batch of production being treated as a "Job." The batch cost is then used to determine the unit cost of the articles produced.
5. *Process Costing*.
6. *Operation Costing*, a method of Unit Costing by operation connected with mass production and repetitive production.
7. *Multiple or Composite Costing*, used when there are a variety of components separately produced, and subsequently assembled in a complex production (*e.g.* motor cars, aeroplanes).

In addition to costs found by the above methods, mention should be made of two other kinds of cost determined for special purposes of control and policy, namely:

(*a*) Standard or Predetermined Costs.
(*b*) Marginal Costs.

Any of the above-mentioned methods may be the basis of a *Uniform System of Costing*.

CHAPTER 3

FACTORY ORGANISATION IN CONJUNCTION WITH THE COSTING SYSTEM

PRODUCTION EFFICIENCY

The organisation of a factory or workshop has for its aim efficient production—this efficiency being measured by the number of articles produced, the quality and price of the production, and the quickness of delivery. The requirements for successful competition are that production must be expeditious, correct, and at a minimum cost.

The attainment of these objectives demands careful organisation, good management, and the fullest use of plant and the other agents of production. The inclusion of a system of costing provides a reliable means of measuring the extent to which the management succeeds in achieving these objectives.

THE NEED FOR CO-OPERATION

It is essential that the works system and routine should include arrangements for providing the cost accountant with the figures and information necessary for preparing the cost data. A costing system, however good, cannot function properly if the works organisation is unsatisfactory, and, therefore, it is desirable that the system should be drawn up in collaboration with the Works Manager, and, probably, departmental heads, so that full co-operation of all concerned may be secured. Every effort should be made to eliminate friction and departmental jealousy, and to adopt all suggestions which will tend to make the arrangements run smoothly with the least possible trouble in the workshops.

THE SCHEME OF ADMINISTRATION AND MANAGEMENT

Particular and varying conditions in different industries and works make it impracticable to describe a standard system of works organisation which would be universally suitable, but the principles of works management and organisation can be outlined. For present purposes it will be sufficient to describe the functions of the various departments and officials in a representative works. Others are referred to in later chapters dealing with systems in specific industries. In large works the duties and responsibilities are shared by more officials than in a small factory; hence, when studying the functions outlined below, it should be noted that in a smaller organisation one individual may combine several such functions within his sphere of responsibility. The main principle to observe is that each person should have his authority and responsibility well defined, so that overlapping of duties does not occur. Provision has to be made for fullest co-ordination and liaison.

THE MAIN DIVISIONS OF MANAGEMENT

The administration of a manufacturing business is usually controlled by a Managing Director, or General Manager, and the main division of managerial responsibility can be identified, viz.:

1. Secretarial and Financial.
2. Sales and Distribution of the products.
3. Production and Production Services.
4. Design and Research, in large concerns.

The Secretarial and Financial Management is usually the responsibility of the Secretary, or a director of a company, or, in many instances, of the Chief Accountant, or Chief Clerk. The functions usually include:

1. Secretarial work, and control of the general office staff.
2. The control of financing operations and the ordinary financial books of account.
3. Collaboration with the Works Manager in regard to the financing aspect of equipment and production.

The Sales Manager is responsible for sales promotion in its various forms. He devises selling and advertising campaigns, controls the salesmen, submits estimates and tenders, and is responsible for all statistics relating to sales. He must collaborate with the Works Manager, or Planning Department, as to types and quantities of various goods likely to be required. For estimates and tenders he will consult the Cost Accountant, or, in some cases, the Ratefixer, who often functions as an estimator.

The third division—that of Production Management—is the most important from the point of view of this book, and will be considered in greater detail, using for purposes of illustration a large engineering works.

PRODUCTION MANAGEMENT

The organisation or production management is co-ordinated by the Works Manager, and the technical control is exercised by the Chief Engineer or Chemist.

WORKS MANAGER

The Works Manager supervises all who are in the chain of control of production, the main sections of which are:

1. Production Control.
2. The Production Departments, including Stores, Labour Engagement, and Welfare.
3. The Purchasing Department.
4. The Service Departments.

Much of his time is spent in smoothing out the difficulties of his subordinates, and giving decisions when special matters arise in respect of production. He must keep himself well informed of all that takes place in the works, and act as general controller in all matters relating to production.

1. *Production Control*

Production Control is responsible for:

1. Planning—arranging how and where the work is to be done and the issue of instructions.
2. Control—which regulates the work in accordance with the time-table set by the Planning Section. Sometimes that department determines the sequence of operations, the Control Section being responsible for the detailed arrangements.
3. The Tool-drawing Office.
4. The Ratefixing and Time-study Department.
5. The Tool-room, and, sometimes,
6. The Tool Stores. The Tool-room and Store sometimes come under the control of the Production Department.

These are now dealt with in more detail below.

The Planning Section.—This relieves the foremen of many responsibilities, and co-ordinates production by providing the plan of procedure and time-table for the whole works. Arrangements are made for the passing of each order through the shops. Not only the route but also the machines to be used are specified, and the supply of requisite materials is ensured. Attention has to be paid to machining and handling methods, and to the volume of production which can be coped with by each department or shop. In matters of cost, the Cost Accountant has to be consulted, particularly in regard to alterations in procedure.

The Control Section.—This is responsible for the details of manufacture which have been arranged by the Planning Section. The latter will plan the sequence of operations, and the Control Section details the particular machines to be used, regulates the work, and "progresses" its movement to time through every stage of manufacture. The Control Section makes sure that materials required are in stock, or that specially purchased material is delivered to time. It obtains the specifications of materials and drawings from the Drawing Office, and sees that any necessary jigs or tools are available. Where special tools are required, drawings will be made and orders given for the making of the tools. Schedules are prepared for every movement of the work, so that the progress man knows what work is on each machine, and can be making preparations for the next job to follow. Graphic charts are often used, the Gantt Charts being particularly appropriate.

The Tool-drawing Office.—This is another part of Production Control, which is generally separate from the main Drawing Office. The jigs, gauges, and tools required by the Planning Section are designed in the Tool-drawing Office.

The Ratefixer.—In some works this official may perform some of his functions under supervision of Production Control. He may decide whether day- or piece-work is to be used, indicate the time allowed, and is responsible for fixing time or piece rates for each piece or operation not produced or paid by ordinary time-work rates. A careful investigation is made in detail for every operation; timing is made with the aid of a stop-watch, and a reliable average time fixed, and, finally, the piece-work or premium-bonus rate. All factors which affect the work are considered, including the type of machine, its speed, and the kind of material to be worked upon. It is apparent that the Ratefixer must have a practical working knowledge of every machine, and thoroughly understand tool design. Careful enquiry into motion-study methods, advised by industrial psychologists, may lead to better results.

The Tool-room.—This produces the jigs, gauges, and tools required by Production Control. It examines tools returned from the shops, and reconditions them if this is necessary. The foreman in charge is usually a highly skilled man, and he is provided with machine tools, special furnaces for hardening, etc., and various instruments for measuring accurately. All tools made or returned from the shops are passed to the Tool Store, from which they are issued only on presentation of formal requisitions.

2. *The Production Department*

This department, like that of Production Control, also comes directly under the jurisdiction of the Works Manager. It controls:

1. Shop Superintendents, and through them the Foremen and Charge Hands.
2. Stores Departments,* *e.g.*:

---

* The Stores are sometimes under the control of the Cost Accountant, or Financial Officer. The control is twofold: (*a*) financial, (*b*) physical.

(i) Main Stores of Materials.
(ii) Part Finished Stores.
(iii) Finished Stores.
(iv) Tool Stores, if not supervised by the Planning Department.
(v) Consumable Stores.

3. Despatch Packing.
4. Transport.
5. Labour Engagements and Records, and Welfare.

Immediately responsible to the Works Manager are the:

Works or Shop Superintendents.—Each has one or more producing shops under his supervision and control.

Where there is a Personnel Department, the Works Superintendent may be responsible for authorising the engagement of workers requisitioned by foremen. His chief duties are: representing the Works Manager, attending to matters delegated to him, and supervising the conduct of the shops for which he is responsible.

The Foreman.—He is mainly concerned with supervision of the men and work in his shop. Through him all instructions and works orders pass to the workers, and his duty is to see these are duly and correctly carried out.

The foreman will see that proper shop records are kept of orders handed to the workers, and that time spent on each is correctly booked. The modern practice is to have this work done by a clerk assisting the foreman.

The work done in his shop will generally be inspected by him or his assistant, and he will see that machines are kept running, reporting defects to the Repair Department. In large shops charge-hands may assist the foreman.

The Storekeeper.—He is responsible for the care and custody of materials, and sometimes of finished stock. He must see that all materials are kept in an orderly manner, and that quantities are maintained in accordance with the maxima and minima which have been fixed by the management. Proper records of receipts and issues must be kept by him. He must see that nothing is issued, except on presentation of a duly authorised requisition. He is responsible for these requisitions being sent daily to the Cost Office.

If departmental stores are kept, in addition to the main stores, an Assistant Storekeeper will be in charge of each. Stores procedure and organisation will be dealt with in a separate chapter.

Stores Audit.—It is usual to have a continuous check on the records and physical stock, a portion being done each day or week in a large works.

The Despatch Department.—This department is responsible for the packing and despatch of goods; for the checking of the quantity and weight of packages; and for the careful execution of delivery instructions given by customers.

Transport.—This is dealt with later in more detail. (*See* Chapter 19.)

3. The Purchasing Department

This is the third major department under the direct control of the Works Manager. It is responsible for dealing with replenishment requisitions from the Stores; and for the securing of special direct material.

The Buyer purchases materials for all purposes. Generally, materials have to be bought to specification. The requisitions upon which the Buyer acts emanate from the Storekeeper for replenishment of standard materials, and from the Engineer's Office or Drawing Office for special materials for a particular job or order.

The department must see that delivery is made within the time required for use. The most suitable markets must be known, quotations secured and orders placed. Good indexes should be kept, and constantly revised, showing: (*a*) the goods used by the factory; (*b*) suppliers, with their latest prices for such goods, time required for delivery, and other useful particulars. Purchasing procedure is detailed in the next chapter.

4. The Service Department

Production Department is the term used to connote the department in which the actual product for sale is manufactured or produced, in contradistinction to the service departments which are ancillary.

A Production Service is a facility available to a production department. Examples are: Repair and Maintenance, and Power Services: Electricity, Gas, Water, Hydraulic Pressure, Compressed Air, Vacuum, and Steam. Some pharmaceutical factories have a service of distilled water to all departments.

Preventive Maintenance includes routine inspection of plant, tools, and equipment at regular intervals for avoidance of breakdown by prompt replacement and repairs at convenient times instead of when emergencies arise.

CHIEF ENGINEER

The Chief Engineer supervises the technical side of the works, and acts as technical consultant to almost every section. He designs the articles to be made and any variations arising out of special specifications. It is his duty to study the latest technical information, and to propose improvement in design and materials, after proper research and experiment, if necessary in conjunction with the Works Chemist.

B

The departments he is responsible for are:

The Drawing Office

Under the instructions of the Engineer, working drawings are pre-pared, and the necessary blue-prints for use in the shops. A carefully indexed file of drawings and blue-prints is kept. The Tracers and Blue-print Room are supervised by the Chief Draughtsman.

Specifications of Material (sometimes called Bills of Material) suggested by the Engineer are prepared, and orders pass from the Engineer's Department to the Drawing Office and Planning Department for the issue of instructions.

Experiment and Research Department

New designs, improvements, and new methods are tried out in this department. It is also responsible for testing materials and examining them to ascertain whether they conform to specification. Various physical and chemical tests may be necessary, especially where metals and chemicals are used in the process of manufacture.

INSPECTION DEPARTMENT

The Chief Inspector must of necessity be a technical man who understands all manufacturing operations to enable him to trace reasons for defective work. Inspection duties can be divided into four sections:

1. Inspection of purchased raw materials. Examination is made as to dimensions, tensile strength, chemical composition, finish, or other factors mentioned in the purchase specification. It should be noticed that the finished product of one industry, or department, may be the raw material of another.
2. Inspection of goods purchased in a partly finished or machined condition. The examination is made to see that the articles agree with the specification. Where gauges have been supplied, copies will be used to test the articles, in addition to inspection of the general finish.
3. Inspection of finished parts, or components, made in the factory. This may be conducted after every operation or process; but if this cannot be done without unduly large expense, the finished part is examined on completion. Each person examining will stamp or otherwise impress the articles with his own identification mark.
4. Inspection of finished products for stock or despatch. Each part assembled is examined, e.g. the painting, polish, and general appearance, the fit if applicable, and the correct components or accessories. Quantities are also usually certified by the Inspection Department, showing the number of rejects.

THE COSTING DEPARTMENT

The Cost Accountant should be directly responsible to the General Manager, but must work in close collaboration with the Engineer, and the Planning and Production Departments. The department is responsible for the preparation of the Cost Accounts, returns for the guidance of the management, and particularly for indicating where loss, waste, inefficiency, and possibility of saving occur.

Particulars of expenditure of all kinds must be transmitted to it from the General Office, and, as both the Cost and Financial Accounts are based on the same original data, the scheme of accounts must be made to reconcile with those of the Financial Accountant's department. No attempt should be made to effect agreement in details, so long as the final results and main sectional totals are reconciled. Over-elaboration makes the department unnecessarily costly, and may even obscure rather than elucidate results. Whatever cost reports are prepared, they should be in a form readily understood by those managers for whom they are prepared.

The Cost Office is responsible for recording particulars of requisitions and prices for materials. These requisitions received from the Storekeeper must be checked against the shop requisition book counterfoils or duplicates to ensure none is missing. Prices and variations thereof are dealt with.

The Wages and Timekeeper's offices are usually under the control of the Cost Accountant, at least in so far as the calculation of times and amounts payable are concerned and the form in which records are entered up. The Timekeeper is directly responsible for the recording of the times of workers, computing time and overtime, and the operation of attendance-time recording devices. The Wages Office, from details supplied by the Timekeeper, or from work tickets, makes up the payroll from which the Cashier pays. The detailed procedure of these departments is described later.

The organisation in other types of industry will naturally vary, particularly as regards production management. Thus, in the chemical and certain food-manufacturing factories the works manager is a chemist, while inspection assumes the form of laboratory analysis and various kinds of testing at successive stages of production, and of the final product. Research for new chemicals, drugs, and combinations of ingredients; for new processes and methods; or for improvement of existing lines, or of plant is a continuous and costly part of the organisation. There are also special features as regards the control of stores materials, particularly when costly, and sometimes dangerous, chemicals and drugs are concerned.

CHAPTER 4

PURCHASING PROCEDURE

IN each industry, and in different works within an industry, the detailed organisation will vary according to particular conditions and ideas, but the general procedure and principles outlined in this chapter may be regarded as typical, although particularly suitable for an engineering or similar factory. The forms used as illustrations are based on some actually in use, but again will vary in ruling and wording to suit particular needs.

A large engineering firm will require an efficient Purchasing Department, while, on the other hand, a small concern may have all functions, including purchasing, carried out by the owner. However, it is essential that in any firm, whether large or small, only one person or one department should be authorised to place orders with suppliers, otherwise purchase orders may be duplicated.

ORGANISATION OF THE PURCHASING DEPARTMENT

The Buyer in a manufacturing business has considerable responsibility, and in a large concern much money can be lost or saved by his department. He requires a good technical knowledge of the industry, and a large measure of administrative and organising ability; he must keep in constant touch with market prices, reports, and market tendencies, and have a working knowledge of contract law and procedure, together with a practical understanding of the principles of economic laws.

The Buyer should be provided with a schedule of technical specifications of the materials usually employed, each item having a code number which will be quoted by those issuing Purchase Requisitions.

The department should keep files suitably indexed, both under the names of suppliers and materials. Records of prices and quotations for all materials should be kept in schedule form, arranged to show the seasonal and other movements of prices (*see* Fig. 1).

No purchases should be permitted except on receipt of duly authorised Purchase Requisitions but, in the case of materials largely and regularly used, forward contracts may be made after consultation with the management. Where purchase contracts are placed, a record of orders issued against them and deliveries made should be kept (Fig. 2).

SCHEDULE OF QUOTATIONS

Material: 1″ Copper Tube   **Date:** 20 June, 19...   **File No.:** 32

	Rate £	Amount £ s. d.	Time of Delivery	Terms	Delivery	Remarks
Estimated cost or part price.	76	1520 0 0				
1. Hall & Co.	75	1500 0 0	7 days	Net monthly	Free	
2. Tube Mfg. Co.	72	1440 0 0	14 days	,,	,,	Accepted
3. Copper & Co. Ltd.	76	1520 0 0	4 weeks	,,	,,	
4. F. White & Co.	80	1600 0 0	10 days	,,	,,	
5.						

FIG. 1.—*Schedule of Quotations*

These schedules are filed under type of material and form a valuable guide to the prices to be expected.

PURCHASE CONTRACT RECORD

File No.: 87

Material: 1″ Copper Tubes.
Suppliers: Tube Mfg. Co.
Contract No.: 261/22 June, 19...
Completed: 25 Sept., 19...

Quantity: 20 tons.
Price: £72 per ton.
Free delivered.
Net monthly.
Total Cost: £1440

Ordered			Delivered				
Date	Quantity (tons)	Balance to Order (tons)	Date	Quantity (tons)	Current Price (per (ton) £	Value £	Balance to Deliver (tons)
19...			19...				
June 22	5	15	July 7	5	73	365	15
July 10	4	11	,, 12	2	73	146	13
Aug. 20	11	—	,, 30	2	74	148	11
			Aug. 14	5	73	365	6
			,, 21	2	75	150	4
			Sept. 8	4	74	296	—
	20			20		£1470	

FIG. 2.—*Purchase Contract Record*

This record gives a continuous check on the position of an order, the delivery of which is spread over a period.

PROCEDURE IN THE PURCHASING DEPARTMENT

On receipt of purchase requisitions the Buyer will obtain quotations or, for important requirements, may invite tenders for the supply of the materials required. Consideration has to be given to factors other than price—namely, to specifications, conditions of delivery, various charges, times of delivery, terms of payment and discount (*see also* Fig. 1).

After the Buyer has decided which quotation is most acceptable, a Purchase Order (Fig. 3) is prepared, which is evidence of the contract between the buyer and the supplier. The number of copies of the Pur-

---

ORDER

No. 4721

To Messrs. Smith, Jones & Co.,
Birmingham.

From A. Maker & Co., Ltd., Star Works, London, N.W.

Our ref.: Req. 284.   **Date:** 28/2/19...
   Please supply, in accordance with the instructions herein, the following:

Particulars	Price	per	Delivery
2 tons $\frac{7}{8}''$ Mild Steel Bars, round.	£x	ton	At once

Delivery free at our Works.
Mark Order No. on invoice and advice note.
Terms: 5% Monthly Account.

For A. Maker & Co., Ltd.
C. Davis.

Fig. 3.—*Purchase Order*

Care should be taken to see that the Purchase Order specifies the date and terms of delivery, the price, and the cash discount available if payment is made within the stipulated period.

chase Order depends on the organisation of the business: a small firm may require three copies, while a large concern may require five copies. A possible routing of Purchase Order copies is as follows:

1. To the supplier.
2. To the Receiving Department.
3. To the Accounting Department.

4. To the department which initiated the Purchase Requisition.
5. Retained in the Purchasing Department.

The following up of deliveries on or before due date is important and necessitates the prompt marking off of deliveries from the Goods Received Note. If deliveries are not made on the expected day, and no advice of despatch has been received from the supplier, the receiving clerk must inform the Buyer, who will urge delivery.

PURCHASE REQUISITIONING

The Purchasing Department places all orders for materials and supplies in accordance with requisitions received from:

1. The Storekeeper for all standard materials, the stocks of which require replenishment (*see* Fig. 4).
2. The Production Control Department for all special materials which are required for direct delivery to work in progress.
3. The Plant Engineer for materials required for capital expenditure or special maintenance projects.
4. The Head of the department requiring special indirect material: for example, the Accountant may require a new filing basket.

PURCHASE REQUISITION FOR STOCK				
Date: 16 June, 19...				No. 86
Quantity	Description	Stock Code No.	Purchase Order No.	Supplier
1 cwt.	1½″ Copper Nails, Sq.	B. 36	M.S. 681	C. Hall & Co.

Signed
Storekeeper: J. Stockwell.   Approved: T. S. Shaw.

FIG. 4.—*Purchase Requisition for Stock*

Requisitions for materials kept in regular stock might be initiated by the Storekeeper; others by the Department concerned.

NOTE.—Sometimes an additional column is included for the storekeeper to state the balance of material in stock, for the guidance of the manager and buyer. The last two columns are filled in by the buyer.

The procedure would then be for the department concerned to prepare each Purchase Requisition (*see* Fig. 4) in triplicate; these are then routed

(a) to the Buyer,
(b) to the Production Control Department,
(c) retained in the Department.

Requisitions received from the Production Control Department and the Plant Engineer may be based on the specification of material prepared by the Drawing Office.

A SPECIFICATION OF MATERIAL

Such a specification is a complete schedule of parts and materials required for a particular order, prepared by the Drawing Office, and issued by it, together with the necessary blue-prints of drawings. For standard products, printed copies of the Specification of Material may be kept in stock, with blank spaces for any special details of modifications for a particular job. The schedule details everything required, even to nuts, bolts, and screws, as well as weights and sizes.

Suggested routing is

(a) Purchasing Department,
(b) Planning Department,
(c) Foreman of the Department concerned,
(d) Drawing Office—copy retained.

An example of a Specification of Materials is shown in Fig. 5.

Classification code for materials

The use of material specification code numbers is an advantage, not only to the Purchasing Department and Drawing Office but also to the pricing clerk in the Cost Department, in that ambiguity is eliminated. The code may consist of symbols and numbers, the symbol indicating a material or an item, and the number the size, pattern, etc.

A simple example will make this clear. Screws, brass and steel, could be given the symbols B.S. and S.S. respectively, a number being added for each size, the first in sixteenths, the next two being length in eighths:

B.S. 403 = Brass Screw $\frac{1}{4}$ in. $\times$ $\frac{3}{8}$ in.	S.S. 403	
B.S. 504 = ,, $\frac{5}{16}$ in. $\times$ $\frac{1}{2}$ in.	S.S. 504	Steel screws of the
B.S. 707 = ,, $\frac{7}{16}$ in. $\times$ $\frac{7}{8}$ in.	S.S. 707	same sizes as stated
B.S. 414 = ,, $\frac{1}{4}$ in. $\times$ $1\frac{3}{4}$ in.	S.S. 414	for brass.
B.S. 418 = ,, $\frac{1}{4}$ in. $\times$ $2\frac{1}{4}$ in.	S.S. 418	

All standard articles will have identifying symbols and numbers, and, although the system may appear complicated, it will be found in

SPECIFICATION OF MATERIAL

For Order No. PO. 296.   Electric Motor No. 7.   Assembly Drawing No. 39.   Date: 26 February, 19...   No. 268

Symbol No. of parts	Description	No. per set	Total No.	Materials				For Purchase Department			
				Code No.	Description	Quantity	Remarks	Reqn. No.	Date	Deliveries specified	Order No.
E.M. 3 C.	Iron casing	2	2	M. 16	Standard Slotted open type	20	Stock				
E.M. 3 B.	Core plates	10		P. 14		2	Japanned wrought iron				
E.M. 3 F.	Frame	1		M. 15	Cast Iron	1	Stock				
F.C. 7	End rings	1		S. 27	Stardard	4	Ref. 276				
	Iron cylinder, etc.	1		B. 9	Parkinson Stardard	8	Stock				
	Ring bolts	4		S.N. 4	Stardard	16					
	Nuts, 5/8"	4		S.N. 5	"	2					
	Nuts, 5/8"	4		B.O. 2	"	2					
P.M. 81	Nuts, 5/8"	2		—	Thompson	12	St. 243	72	28/2	28/2	273
	Brass cups	2						72	5/3	5/3	274
	Brush holders, etc.	3	12								

Drawing Office Copy.	
Date Order: Feb. 24, 19... Delivery: Mar. 19, ... No. of Sheets: 4, ...	Prepared by: J. H. Ross. Checked by: C. F. Davis.
	Dated to stores: Feb. 26, 19... from stores: 28, 19... to shops: Mar. 7, 19...

FIG. 5.—*Specification of Material*

This schedule is often referred to as a Bill of Material, and shows the complete requirements of raw material and component parts to complete a particular job.

practice that storemen, clerks and draughtsmen find these codes easy to work with, since the code numbers of the more frequently used materials are readily memorised. In the Cost Department the pricing of issued material is facilitated and uncertainty as to size and kind of material is avoided. In the Bills of Material, stock materials will be indicated by the appropriate code number, but full details will have to be specified for special parts and materials which have to be manufactured or purchased outside.

PURCHASE PRICE

The purchase price per unit of quantity of the material to be ordered will be agreed between the Buyer and the Supplier. Frequently, however, calculations may be required in respect of the following items:

1. QUANTITY DISCOUNT

Quantity discount is an allowance made by the supplier to the purchaser, to encourage large orders. The larger the quantity ordered, the lower becomes the price per unit—within fixed limits. The producer hopes to enjoy larger production runs, thus reducing production costs, while the expense of delivering one or two large orders is much less than that of innumerable small orders, so packing and distribution costs are reduced. Part of the savings enjoyed by the supplier is passed on to the purchaser by means of this quantity discount. The Buyer will try to take advantage of this discount where production requirements, storage, and financial facilities permit.

2. TRADE DISCOUNT

Trade discount is an allowance made by the supplier to a purchaser who has to re-sell the article, for example a manufacturer may allow a wholesaler 20% trade discount. This allowance is to compensate the purchaser for his costs of storage, breaking bulk, re-packing articles, selling, and delivering small quantities.

3. CASH DISCOUNT

Cash discount is an allowance made by the supplier to a purchaser to encourage prompt payments of invoices; for example, a 5% discount may be allowed if payment is received within seven days of the date of the invoice.

NOTE.—This discount is allowed only if payment is received in the stipulated time, so it is a question of managerial policy whether or not the Buyer takes advantage of the offer. It is thus a financial item, and should not appear in the Cost Accounts.

4. TRANSPORT AND STORAGE CHARGES

Sometimes the purchase price quoted by the supplier includes the cost of transporting the commodities to the purchaser and any storage charges incurred. Where, however, the price does not include these charges and the purchaser has to bear the cost, the charges should if possible be added to the purchase price. Frequently it is impracticable to add these charges to the purchase price, in which case the charges should be absorbed in Factory Overhead.

5. CONTAINERS

Containers may or may not be charged by the supplier. If they are not charged, then no accounting entry will be necessary in the books of the purchaser. However, if containers are separately charged the treatment may be as follows:

Non-returnable containers

The cost of the container will be added to the purchase price of materials.

Returnable containers credited at full value on return

The cost of the container will not be included in the purchase price, assuming the container is returned to the supplier.

Returnable containers credited at reduced value on return

The difference between the cost of the container and the amount credited by the supplier will be added to the purchase price of the material, assuming the container is returned to the supplier:

EXAMPLE

A supplier quotes for material "A" as follows:

Lot Price	100 units	5s. each.
	500 „	4s. 9d. each.
	1000 „	4s. 6d. „

Trade discount 20%. Cash discount 5% in seven days.
Containers charged at 10s. each; 7s. 6d. credited on return.
1 container required for every 100 units.
The purchaser decides to buy 600 units.
Transport charges amounting to £3 7s. 6d. and Storage 12s. 6d., were charged by the supplier.

Calculation of Purchase Price

	Amount £ s. d.	Cost per Unit £ s. d.
Material A: 600 units at 4s. 9d. each	142 10 0	4 9·0
Less Trade Discount at 20%	28 10 0	11·4
	114 0 0	3 9·6

Returnable containers:	£ s. d.		
6 Containers at 10s. each	3 0 0		
Less Credited on Return at 7s. 6d.	2 5 0		
		15 0	0·3
		114 15 0	3 9·9
Transport	3 7 6		
Storage	12 6		
		4 0 0	1·6
		£118 15 0	3 11·5

NOTE.—Cash discount of £5 18s. 9d. would be received if payment made within 7 days, but would not affect Cost Accounts.

PROCEDURE ON RECEIPT OF MATERIALS

Suppliers usually send a Delivery Note, or an Advice of Despatch, which is passed to the receiving clerk. Invoices received are passed direct to the Accounts Department.

Materials entering the factory should be unloaded at special receiving centres. These should be situated as near to the road, railway siding, canal, or wharf as possible, yet at the same time be accessible from any part of the factory, so as to reduce handling charges to a minimum.

The Receiving Department should have a copy of the Purchase Order so that, if necessary, arrangements can be made to unload the materials—special apparatus may be necessary to handle heavy or bulky materials. The goods received can be checked with the details on the Purchase Order and entered on a Goods Received Note (*see* Fig. 6).

THE GOODS RECEIVED NOTE

The Goods Received Note will have additional copies, the number depending on the organisation of the firm; a suggested routing is:

1. To the Purchasing Department.
2. To the Accounting Department.
3. To the Department which initiated the Purchase Requisition.
4. To the Stores Department.
5. One copy held in the Receiving Department for reference purposes.

The advantage of Goods Received Notes is that, after being filled in with particulars as to quantities and other information, they can be passed to the official responsible for approving the goods, who signs the notes, and sends them with the goods to the Storekeeper. The receiving and approving of goods is sometimes the duty of the Storekeeper himself, in which case he will prepare the Goods Received Notes.

GOODS RECEIVED NOTE								
From: Smith, Jones & Co., Birmingham.					G.R. No. 59 Date: 5 Mar., 19...			
				Order No.	For Office Use			
Goods	Quantity	Packages			Rate	£	s.	d.
				4721				
Carrier BR	Received by A. Jones	Goods Inspection Report Correct. B. Hall						
Purchase Requisition No. 284	Noted on Progress Chart 5/621	Bin No. 72		Stores Ledger 212	Invoice No. 360		A/cs. Ref. P.J. 84	

FIG. 6.—*Goods Received Note*

This is made out by the Receiving Department when materials are received and is priced by the Cost Department from copy Orders. It forms the basis of entries to the Stores Ledger made in advance of Invoices, with which they are later agreed.

When the Purchasing Department receive their copy of the Goods Received Note, together with the receiving clerk's copy of the Purchase Order, the order can be marked off in the Order Book.

Goods should be inspected for quality to ensure that they comply with any specification which may have been stated on the Purchase Order. In many large firms an Inspection staff is attached to the Receiving Department, while in small firms the Storekeeper is responsible for inspection. If any goods are rejected, the Inspector will enter the reason for rejection on a special Rejection Report, so that the Buyer is immediately informed and can contact the supplier.

CHECKING INWARD INVOICES

When invoices are received it is useful to impress each with a rubber stamp, as shown in Fig. 7.

Invoices are numbered consecutively on entry into the Invoice

Register. The Purchasing Department clerk enters the Order Number, Goods Received Note Number, and signs for the correctness of the particulars, which he is able to check with the Order and the certified Goods Received Note. The Order Book should be marked with the invoice number to preclude the passing of a duplicate invoice.

Regist. No. 360	Goods Correct A. Buyer	Checked	Noted Works Office	Bought Jrl. Fo. 84	Passed for Payment
Order No. 472	G.R. No. 59	With order: A.B. Prices: A.B. Extens.: R.S.	Charged to: Stores Initials: R.C.	Charged to: Stores A/c	C. Davis

FIG. 7—*Invoice Stamp*

Usually a rubber stamp is used on the bottom corner of the Invoice so that the signatures authorising its payment are found in a convenient position.

If the invoice is in order the Buyer will sign and pass it to the Accounts Department for payment. There it will be checked by a clerk or preferably a calculating-machine operator, to ensure that the calculations are correct. The invoice is entered in the Purchase Journal, from which the supplier's account is credited in the Purchase Ledger. The total of the Purchase Journal is debited to Purchases Account in the General Ledger and credited to Total Creditors. The detailed procedure for cost accounting and specimen entries are given in Chapter 14.

RECONCILIATION OF COST AND FINANCIAL ACCOUNTS

The Goods Received Note is priced from the copy Purchase Order or the Invoice, and then the appropriate material account is debited in the Stores Ledger, except in the case of material purchased for a specific job, when the debit is made to the Cost Account for that job. Thus entries in the Cost Accounts are entered in the first place from the Goods Received Notes, while as mentioned above, the Financial Accounts are entered from the Invoices.

It is essential to reconcile the Cost Accounts with the Financial Accounts; this will be discussed in greater detail in Chapter 15.

CHAPTER 5

STORES ROUTINE

THE Stores Department in many small firms is often neglected, and it is not realised that materials represent an equivalent amount of cash. Material pilferage, deterioration of materials, and careless handling of stores lead to reduced profits, or even losses, so it is essential that to obtain the maximum advantage of a cost-accounting system an efficient, well-equipped Stores Department be maintained.

ORGANISATION OF STORES

TYPE OF ORGANISATION

In large manufacturing concerns the problem often arises as to the type of organisation which should be adopted in the storage department. There are three main types:

1. Central Stores: centralised buying and handling of stores.
2. Central Stores with sub-stores: centralised buying, but handling of stores undertaken by the sub-storekeeper.
3. Independent Stores situated in various departments: buying and handling of stores is undertaken by the buyer and storekeeper in each department.

Consideration must, of course, be given to the particular circumstances prevailing in the factory, but in general the first or second course will be adopted.

CENTRALISED BUYING

The advantages of centralised buying are four, namely:

1. A firm policy can be initiated with regard to conditions of purchasing, *e.g.* terms of payment.
2. Standardisation of articles is facilitated.
3. Expert buying staff is concentrated in one department.
4. Combined purchasing power may result in reduced prices of commodities.

These must be set against the disadvantage that the creation of a special department may lead to high administration costs. Nevertheless, it would appear from the above points that centralised buying is normally to be preferred to de-centralised buying.

CENTRALISED STORAGE

On the question of centralised handling of stores, it is much more difficult to generalise, because even though central Stores may be preferred, it is very much a matter of circumstance whether or not sub-stores will be maintained (see below). The advantages and disadvantages of purely central storage may be set out as follows:

Advantages

1. Economy in staff and concentration of experts in one department.
2. Reduced clerical costs and economy in records and stationery.
3. Better supervision is possible.
4. Staff become acquainted with different types of stores, which is very useful if anyone is absent from work.
5. Better layout of Stores.
6. Inventory checks facilitated.
7. Stocks are kept to a minimum, thus reducing storage space.
8. Fewer obsolete articles.
9. The amount of capital invested in stock is minimised.

Disadvantages

1. Increased transportation costs.
2. Stores may be situated at some distance from many departments which draw from them, thus causing inconvenience and delay.
3. Breakdowns in transport or hold-ups in central store may cause production stoppages in departments.
4. Greater risk of loss by fire.

It is sometimes the practice to use the *imprest system* of Stores control, which operates in rather a similar way to a petty-cash system. For each item in stock a quantity will be determined which represents the number of articles which should be in stock at the beginning of any period. Consequently, at the end of a period the Storekeeper will requisition for the number of articles required to bring the physical stock up to the predetermined quantity.

STORES LOCATION AND LAYOUT

The location of the Stores Department should be carefully planned so as to ensure maximum efficiency. It should be as near to the Receiving Department as possible so that handling charges are at a minimum. There should be easy access to all departments, especially to those in which heavy or bulky materials are to be delivered.

In large factories, where there are many departments, the Stores Department could not be situated where it is convenient to deliver to all departments and at the same time be near the Receiving Department, so it is often necessary to set up sub-stores conveniently situated to serve a particular part of the organisation. The central Stores Department will then issue to the sub-stores the materials specially required for the department or departments serviced by the sub-store. It is strongly recommended that the storekeeper of each sub-store should be responsible to the Chief Storekeeper. This will ensure that a uniform policy of buying, storing, and issuing is followed.

The layout of the department requires careful thought. Shelves, racks, bins, etc., should be situated in clearly defined lanes, so that easy access is provided. In many cases it may be necessary to allow enough room for the passage of trucks, so that white lines should be painted on the floor, determining the position of storage containers.

Special attention must be paid to storage of materials which are affected by atmospheric conditions, because substantial losses may be incurred due to evaporation, deterioration, etc.

THE STOREKEEPER

The Department should be under the control of one person, who may be known as the Storekeeper, Chief Storekeeper, or Stores Superintendent. He should be a man of wide experience in Stores routine, able to organise the operation of the Stores, of undoubted integrity, and capable of controlling the men under his charge.

His duties and responsibilities may be as follows:

1. Maintaining the Stores in a tidy manner.
2. Accepting materials into the Stores, after having ascertained that the delivery complies with instructions detailed on the Purchase Order and Goods Received Note.
3. Correct positioning of all materials in store.
4. Checking the Bin Card balances with the physical quantities in the bins.
5. Requisitioning further supplies from the Purchasing Department when the re-order level is reached on any material (see below).
6. Preventing unauthorised persons entering the Stores.

RECEIPT AND ISSUE OF MATERIALS

REQUISITION FOR STOCK

The Storekeeper is guided, when requisitioning for stock as outlined on p. 25, by the maximum and minimum quantity which he is authorised to store in respect of each kind of material, and the re-order level. These items are shown on the Bin Card (*see* Fig. 11).

The maximum stock is fixed by taking into account such aspects as:

1. Rate of consumption of the material.
2. Time necessary to obtain new deliveries.
3. Amount of capital necessitated and available.
4. Keeping qualities, *e.g.* risk of deterioration, evaporation.
5. Storage space available.
6. Cost of storage, particularly if cold storage is necessary.
7. Extent to which price fluctuations may be important.
8. Risks of changing specifications or of obsolescence.
9. Seasonal considerations as to both price and availability of supplies, *e.g.* market shortage.
10. Economic ordering quantities.
11. The incidence of insurance costs, which may be important for some materials.
12. Any restrictions imposed by local or national authority in regard to materials in which there are inherent risks, *e.g.* fire and explosion.

The minimum stock is fixed by taking into account:

1. Rate of consumption of the material.
2. Time necessary to obtain delivery of the new materials.

The re-ordering level is the point fixed between maximum and minimum stock figures, at which time it is essential to initiate purchase requisitions for fresh supplies of the material. This point will usually be slightly higher than the minimum stock, to cover such emergencies as abnormal usage of the material or unexpected delay in delivery of fresh supplies.

RECEIPT OF MATERIALS

Purchased materials are passed into the custody of the Storekeeper when they have been examined and approved. Some articles or parts for stock are not purchased from outside suppliers but made in the works. These will be inspected in the usual course, and then passed into the Stores. In order to keep the accounting uniform, it is desirable that a Goods Received Note be prepared for these articles. The necessary debits and credits, as between production and stores, will be dealt with by the Cost Office.

ISSUE OF MATERIALS

It is essential that all stores issued should be promptly recorded, so that accurate material costs may be obtained. Materials should be issued by the Storekeeper only on presentation of an authorised document—usually called a Stores Requisition Note.

Material Requisition

This form (Fig. 8) is an authorisation to the Storekeeper to issue raw material, finished parts, or other stores. It is usually signed by the foreman, but in some cases when a greater authority is required, for example when extra large quantities are needed for production, the

---

MATERIAL REQUISITION

No. 76

Materials Required for: Job. E 513
(Job or Process)
Department: Engines
Shop: E3   **Date:** 20 July, 19...

Quantity	Description	Code No.	Weight	Rate	£	s.	d.	Notes
10 ft.	¼″ Brass X.E.D.	B 102	12 lb	1s. lb		12	0	

Workman: F. Simpson   **Stores Ledger Fo.:** 218   **Cost Office ref.:** MA 364
                         Bin No.: 975
Foreman: E. Barry   **Storekeeper:** A.S.   **Priced by:** G.B.

FIG. 8.—*Material Requisition*

This illustrates the request for materials from Stores for a job about to be commenced. It is priced by the Cost Office according to one of the agreed methods, and posted to the credit of the Stores Ledger Account.

manager's signature may be necessary. Frequently the Planning or Progress Department issue these requisitions to the foreman, who presents them to the Storekeeper as and when required.

Any materials ordered for a specific job will be marked with the job number, and kept apart ready for issue. The foreman will be informed that the material is available.

The Storekeeper will enter the details of the Material Requisition on to the Bin Cards, and adjust the balances in the Stock Column. The note will then be routed to the Cost Department, where it will be evaluated, the Stores Ledger credited, and an entry made on the Materials Abstract for posting to the debit of the Cost Ledger.

THE RECEIPT AND ISSUE OF SPECIAL MATERIALS

Materials ordered for a specific job will be marked with the job number, and kept apart ready for issue. The foreman will be informed that the material is available. A good plan for this is for the Production Department to prepare a Stores Requisition Note, and send it to the foreman, who can sign it, and present it at the Stores when he is ready to use the material.

STORES RECORDS

Two records are usually kept of materials received, issued, or transferred—namely on the Bin Cards and in the Stores Ledger. The Bin Cards are written up in the Stores, but the Stores Ledger is sometimes kept by the Cost Department or Stores Office.

There is considerable advantage in this procedure, as it leaves the Storekeeper with the minimum amount of clerical work, and the Stores accounting records are kept cleaner and more accurately by an experienced stores clerk.

Stores Appropriation Record

A Stores Appropriation Record is often kept when it is not convenient to work to definite maxima and minima of certain types of materials which may be required to meet orders. It may be used in connection with Stores materials, or components which are made in the works or ordered from outside, and is of great value to the Planning Department, in that it shows the quantity in stock and on order. The record may be combined in the ordinary Bin Card by providing a special column for the purpose, or a separate Stores Appropriation Ledger may be used. When the latter is adopted the procedure is to debit each account with the quantities in stock and ordered. As a quantity is appropriated it is credited, and the balance represents the quantity in stock and on order.

FINISHED PARTS OR COMPONENTS STORE

Items or sub-assemblies awaiting final assembly or sale as spares are sometimes kept in a separate store, under the control of the Progress or Planning Department. It is usual to keep a Finished Parts Stock Record indicating the quantity and also in some cases the value of each class of finished part and its location in the stores. Stock orders for quantities of standard parts will be issued in batches convenient for economical manufacture. A Stores Appropriation Record is useful for the control. The cost, ascertained from the Works Order for the production of these stock orders, will ordinarily be the charging-out price, when components are issued on requisition for assembly on various Works Orders.

TRANSFER OF MATERIALS

Transfers of materials from one departmental store to another should be recorded by means of a Stores Requisition signed by the Storekeeper and marked "Transfer." This memorandum can then be used in the office for the making of the necessary credit and debit.

Where transfers are numerous it is sometimes the practice to have special columns in the Stock Record Sheets or Bin Cards for recording the details of the transfers.

Material Transfer Note

The transfer of material from one job to another in the Works should be strictly prohibited unless the procedure is adequately recorded on the Material Transfer Note (Fig. 9), showing all necessary data for crediting and debiting the Cost Accounts affected, as otherwise the records and Cost Accounts concerned would be incorrect. Such transfers occur where an urgent order has to be made, and work started on a less-urgent order may be appropriated. In such a case there must be provision for the re-issue of material to the job from which material already issued has been transferred. Any excess material should be returned to the Stores, when a Shop Credit Note can be made out.

Considerable care must be taken to ensure that excess material is not left lying around departments, because this will lead to deterioration in the value of the materials as well as to congestion in the departments. Scrutiny of the Cost Accounts may reveal excess material in any department, where the material charge is higher than expected. Action should then be taken to return the material to the Stores and the Department concerned credited with the value of material.

MATERIAL ISSUED IN EXCESS OF REQUIREMENTS

Bulk material has to be issued at times in excess of the needs for a particular job. This is the case with sheet iron or steel bars, which in some instances cannot be cut off in the Stores to the exact size required, and which can be more advantageously operated upon in the works when full size. The procedure is to charge out the full quantity issued and, when the excess is returned to store, a Stores Debit Note is filled in, signed by the foreman, and handed to the Storekeeper.

Material Return Note

This Note (Fig. 10) is an authorisation to return to the Storekeeper raw material, finished parts, or other stores no longer required by the

MATERIAL TRANSFER NOTE

Issuing Dept.: Engines   No. 57
Receiving Dept.: Tools   Date: 31 July, 19...

Quantity	Description	Code No.	Weight	Rate	Amount			Notes
					£	s.	d.	
5 ft.	½″ Brass X.E.D.	B102	6 lb	1s. lb.	–	6	–	

Authorised by: F.S.   Received by: E.R.   Cost Office ref.: MA 364
From Job No.: E513   To Job No.: T27   Priced by: G.B.

FIG. 9.—*Material Transfer Note*

A form like this is necessary to cover the transfer of material from one job to another and from one Department to another; otherwise the costs will be wrongly charged.

NOTE.—The pricing out is done in the Cost Office.

MATERIAL RETURN NOTE

                                No. 7
Issuing Dept.: Engines   Date: 20 July, 19...

Quantity	Description	Code No.	Weight	Rate	Amount			Notes
					£	s.	d.	
5 ft.	½″ Brass X.E.D.	B102	6 lb	1s. lb	–	6	–	

Authorised by: E.B.   Received by: A.S.   Cost Office ref.: MA 364
                     To Bin No.: 975
From Job No.: E513   Stores Ledger Fo.: 218   Priced by: G.B.

FIG. 10.—*Material Return Note*

When excess material is returned to Stores a form like this is used to ensure that the job concerned receives credit for the material, and that the Stores can keep its records correctly.

NOTE.—The pricing out is done in the Cost Office.

factory. It is sometimes referred to as a Stores Debit Note or Shop Credit Slip. The various stock records and cost accounts are adjusted in due course from the details given on this form. These debit notes may be drawn up in the same form as a Stores Requisition, but printed in red to distinguish them.

MATERIAL RECORDS

Bin Cards

Materials are kept in appropriate bins, drawers, or other receptacles; some are stacked, others racked. For each kind of material or article, a separate record is kept on a Bin Card (Fig. 11), showing in detail all

BIN CARD

Description: ....

Bin No.: ....
Code No.: ....

Normal Quantity
  to Order: ....
Stores Ledger Fo.: ....

Maximum: ....
Minimum: ....
Re-order Level: ......

Receipts			Issues			Balance	Remarks
Date	G.R. No.	Quan-tity	Date	Req. No.	Quan-tity	Quantity	Goods on Order and Audit Notes

FIG. 11.—*Bin Card*

This is the storekeeper's record of the movement "In" and "Out" of the materials under his control. It should show in the Balance column the actual quantity of the particular material in stock at that time.

NOTE.—The columns headed "quantity" may be ruled for tons, cwt, qrs, lb; cwt, qrs, lb, oz; gross, doz., units; or simply for units; yards, ft, in; gallons, qts, pts, oz as may be necessary.

receipts and issues. The Bin Cards are used not only for detailing receipts and issues of materials but also to assist the Storekeeper to control the stock. For each material, the maximum and minimum to be carried are stated on the card—these limits having been determined by the Production Department in the first instance as illustrated on p. 36. From time to time these maxima and minima may be altered to suit current requirements.

To facilitate ordering of further supplies, the normal quantity to

STORES MATERIAL CONTROL RECORD

Description: ....

Code No.: ....

Ordering Level: ....

LIMITS

Maximum: ....

Minimum: ....

Quantity to Order: ....

Bin No.: ....

Unit: ....

Receipts			Issues		Balance	On Order				Remarks and Stock Counts	
Date	G.R. No.	Quantity	Date	Req. No.	Quantity	Quantity	Date	Pur. Req. No.	Supplier	Quantity	Delivered

Fig. 12.—*Stores Material Control Record*

This is a more detailed stores record card, and is helpful for Production Control purposes, since it shows not only the present balance, but what is on order.

order is sometimes stated at the head of the card. When materials are of a kind requiring advance ordering, an Ordering Level may be specified on the Bin Card. The various receptacles in which materials are kept are numbered, the Bin Card for each being similarly numbered. Where identifying code numbers are used for materials, it is advantageous to attach these to the bin, and to quote them on the Bin Card.

Stores Material Control Record

An alternative to Bin Cards is a Stores Material Control Record (Fig. 12) written up in the Stores and/or by Production Control in a loose-leaf book or card file. On this record, as on the Bin Cards, quantities only are recorded, all money values being shown only in the Stores Ledger in the Office. An advantage of this record is that the Storekeeper has all details close at hand and can note in it such information as quantities ordered, probable requirements for particular contracts, and other details. Where transfers between inter-departmental stores are numerous, an additional section may be included on the Stock Record Sheets for details of the transfers as distinct from issues to the shops.

Stores Ledger

The Stores Ledger is kept in the Cost Department and is identical with the Bin Cards, except that money values are shown. Correct stores accounting is as important as accounting for cash, hence the separation of this clerical work from the actual handling of the materials. The Ledger is usually of the loose-leaf or card type, each account representing an item of material in store. The ruling of the accounts may be as shown in Figs. 13 or 14.

It can be seen from Fig. 14 that in addition to the stores available, the materials ordered from suppliers and the materials reserved for special jobs can be ascertained. The debit side is prepared either from the Goods Received Notes or Invoices, and from Stores Debit Notes; the credit side either directly from the Stores Requisition Notes or from an abstract summary compiled from them.

STORES CONTROL

THE PERPETUAL INVENTORY SYSTEM

This may be defined as a method of recording Stores balances after every receipt and issue, to facilitate regular checking and to obviate closing down for stock-taking. It is sometimes termed "Continuous Inventory".

The balance of any account in the Stores Ledger should agree with the balance shown on the Bin Card, or Stock Control Record, for the

STORES LEDGER ACCOUNT

Material: ....   Code: ....   Maximum Quantity: ....   Folio: ....
Minimum Quantity: ....   Location: ....

Date	Receipts				Issues				Stock		
	G.R. No.*	Quantity	Price	Amount £	S.R. No.†	Quantity	Price	Amount £	Quantity	Price	Amount £

Fig. 13.—*Stores Ledger Account (1)*

The receipts and issues columns are entered from the Goods Received Notes and Stores Requisition Notes, the totals of which are posted in the main books of account to Stores Ledger Control Account.

NOTE.—The Receipts and Issues columns are part of the double-entry accounting system; the Stock column is memorandum only.
* Goods Received Note number.   † Stores Requisition number.

STORES LEDGER ACCOUNT

MATERIAL: ....   Code: ....   Maximum Quantity: ....   Folio: ....
Minimum Quantity: ....   Location: ....
Re-order Level: ....

Ordered			Reserved			Received					Issued				Stock			Stock Checked		
Date	Ref.	Quantity	Date	Ref.	Quantity	Date	G.R. No.	Quantity	Price	Amount	S.R. No.	Quantity	Price	Amount	Quantity	Price	Amount	Date	Initials	Remarks

Fig. 14.—*Stores Ledger Account (2)*

In this form of account, the "reserved" stores show the amounts earmarked for production soon to commence. It helps to disclose the approach of the re-order level, and thus to prevent shortages of vital materials.

NOTE.—The Receipts and Issues columns are part of the double-entry accounting system; the Ordered, Reserved, and Stock columns are memoranda only. Stock Checked column is used when the stock checkers have physically counted the items in stock.

same item of material, and a frequent checking of these dual records should be made, as well as of the actual quantity in stock.

An essential feature of the perpetual inventory system is the continuous checking of the stock. A number of items are counted daily or at frequent intervals, and compared with the Bin Cards and Stores Ledger by a Stores Audit Clerk. Discrepancies are investigated; many may be clerical errors, which will be corrected. When, however, the stock is incorrect, an enquiry is made, after which any shortage or surplus is adjusted in the records to make them correspond with the physical count. This may be done conveniently by making out a Credit Note or Debit Note, as the case may be, for the difference, and then, after obtaining authority to pass for adjustment through the Cost Journal, debiting (or crediting) a Stock Adjustment Account. The balance on that account is written off direct to Profit and Loss Account at appropriate times.

The usual causes of differences are: incorrect entries, breakage, pilferage, evaporation, breaking bulk, short or over issues, absorption of moisture, price approximation or pricing method, and placing of stores in the wrong bin.

The advantages of the Perpetual Inventory system are as follows:

1. The long and costly work of a stocktaking count is avoided, and the stock of materials, as shown by the Stores Ledger (but not the work in progress), can be obtained quickly for the preparation of a Profit and Loss Account and Balance Sheet at interim periods if required.
2. A detailed, reliable check on the stores is obtained.
3. Experienced men can be employed to check the stock at regular intervals.
4. It is not necessary to stop production so as to carry out a complete physical stocktaking, except possibly at the end of each year.
5. Discrepancies are readily localised and discovered, giving an opportunity for preventing a recurrence in many cases.
6. The moral effect on the staff tends to greater care, and serves as a deterrent to dishonesty.
7. The audit extends to comparing the actual stock with the authorised maxima and minima, thus ensuring that adequate stocks are maintained within the prescribed limits.
8. The storekeeper's duty of attending to replenishments is facilitated, as he is kept informed of the stock of every kind of material, thus ensuring uninterrupted and safe manufacturing stocks.
9. The stock being kept within the limits decided upon by the management, the working capital sunk in stores materials cannot exceed the amount arranged for.

10. The disadvantages of excessive stocks are avoided, as, for example:

   (a) Loss of interest on capital locked up in stock.
   (b) Loss through deterioration.
   (c) Danger of depreciation in market values.
   (d) Risks of obsolescence.

TURNOVER OF STORES MATERIAL

It is an advantage to compare the turnover of different grades and kinds of material as a means of detecting stock which does not move regularly, thus enabling management to avoid keeping capital locked up in undesirable stocks. It is not an infrequent occurrence for a particular item of stock to be overlooked for considerable periods, unless means are taken to prevent such accumulations.

The balance of stores, compared with the total withdrawals, indicates how many times a year the stock is renewed.

SCRAP MATERIALS

Scrap materials generally fall into three categories:

1. Some manufacturing operations create trimmings, off-cuts, and other waste which is too small or otherwise unsuitable to treat as (2) and (3) below. Such waste will have to be collected for sale as scrap, destroyed, or dumped.
2. In some cases off-cuts may be suitable for making other things, and this material is returned to store. It is usually taken on charge in the Stores Ledger at a lower value than the original price; a corresponding credit is given to the operation in which it arose.
3. Other scrap consists of rejected products arising from inspection, or which have been spoiled or damaged and are not capable of being made good. There is often some salvage or sales value.

All saleable or usable scrap should be passed to the care of the Storekeeper, so that usual Stores records and control can be ensured. The treatment of scrap materials is discussed in more detail in Chapter 20.

MATERIALS ISSUED AT AN INFLATED PRICE

Wastage of materials frequently occurs in a store due to evaporation, deterioration in quality, or some similar cause. When this occurs, it is necessary to charge materials to production at an inflated price to ensure that the true cost is recovered. For example, if 1000 lb of material are bought at 2s. per lb, and it is known from past experience that the normal wastage of this material is 5%, the charge to production should be: $\dfrac{£100}{950} = 2s.\ 1\tfrac{1}{4}d.$ per lb.

SMALL TOOLS

In a general engineering factory such tools form a large and valuable stock, consisting as they do of such items as turning tools and bits, milling cutters, reamers, drills, taps, dies, and many other items of small

RECORDING
MATERIAL NOTES

GOODS RECEIVED NOTES ARE PRICED FROM ORDERS OR INVOICES

STORES REQUISITIONS ARE PRICED FROM THE STORES LEDGER

MATERIAL TRANSFER NOTES ARE PRICED FROM THE COST LEDGER OR COST CARD

BIN CARD

IN	OUT
GOODS RECEIVED NOTES	STORES REQUISITIONS
STORES DEBIT NOTES	

STORES LEDGER		COST LEDGER	
DR	CR	DR	CR
GOODS RECEIVED NOTES	STORES REQUISITIONS	STORES REQUISITIONS	STORES DEBIT NOTES
STORES DEBIT NOTES		MATERIAL TRANSFER NOTES	

Fig. 15.—*Accounting for Material*

equipment. Storage, inspection, and maintenance of such tools involves considerable expense and careful control. This control is effected by the use of check discs, foremen's requisitions, or both.

Tool-store Procedure is described in Chapter 18.

CATEGORIES OF STOCK

It is usual to keep separate stores for part-finished stocks, finished stocks, raw materials, and indirect materials. The definitions of the kinds of stock are:

Raw materials

Primary materials purchased or produced either in a natural or manufactured condition. Manufactured materials of one industry are often the raw materials of another.

Bulk material

This is a term often used to describe material not in unit form directly suited to the work in hand, as for example, material not measurable except by weight or volume, e.g. sheets, bars, tubes, and bales.

Part-finished stock

This is work in progress that has not reached the stage of completion as a part or component. In the case of some chemical or food-manufacturing processes the work in progress often consists of quantities of part-processed material or intermediate products.

Finished parts

These are items, or sub-assemblies, put into store awaiting final assembly, or sale as spares.

Finished stock

This is the completed product awaiting sale or despatch. Stock is so named after transfer from work in progress, physically and by entry in the accounts.

Stores expenses

If of a general nature Stores expenses are included in Stores Overhead, but expenses particular to a specific order may be charged thereto in addition to the price of the material, as may the cost of carriage inwards and handling.

CHAPTER 6

METHODS OF VALUING MATERIAL ISSUES

THERE are many methods of valuing material issues, the most important being:

1. F.I.F.O. (First in, first out).
2. L.I.F.O. (Last in, first out).
3. Base Stock.
4. Simple Average.
5. Weighted Average.
6. Periodic Simple Average.
7. Periodic Weighted Average.
8. Standard Price.

The use, advantages, and disadvantages of these methods may be illustrated by the following Stores Ledger Accounts compiled from these transactions:

Jan.	1	Received	1000	Units at	20s.	per unit.	
„	10	Received	260	„		21s.	„
„	20	Issued	700	„			
Feb	4	Received	400	„		23s.	„
„	21	Received	300	„		25s.	„
March	16	Issued	620	„			
April	12	Issued	240	„			
May	10	Received	500	„		22s.	„
„	25	Issued	380	„			

NOTE.—For simplicity, the amounts columns in the following accounts have been calculated to the nearest £1; in practice, calculations would show shillings and pence.

1. F.I.F.O. (Fig. 16)

This method ensures that materials are issued at actual cost, so no profits or losses will be incurred merely by adopting this price; it will be seen later in this chapter that when estimates or approximations are used a profit or loss on issue may be obtained.

It is assumed that the materials purchased are issued in strict chronological order. F.I.F.O. is easy to operate, but if the price of the materials purchased fluctuates considerably it involves a number of tedious calculations, which may increase the possibility of errors.

Comparison of the costs of one job with another may be difficult

STORES LEDGER ACCOUNT

Material: .... Code: ....

Maximum Quantity: .... Folio: ....

Minimum Quantity: .... Location: ....

Date	G.R. No.	Receipts			S.R. No.	Issues			Stock		
		Quantity	Price	Amount £		Quantity	Price	Amount £	Quantity	Price	Amount £
Jan. 1		1000	20s.	1000					1000	20s.	1000
10		260	21s.	273					1260		1273
20						700	20s.	700	560		573
Feb. 4		400	23s.	460					960		1033
21		300	25s.	375					1260		1408
Mar. 16						620	20s.	300			
						300	21s.	273	640		766
						260	23s.	69	400		490
						60	23s.	276	900		1040
						240					
Apr. 12		500	22s.	550							
May 10						380	23s.	115			
25						100	25s.	350	520		575
						280					

Fig. 16.—*Stores Ledger Account* (3)

This account has been entered on the First-in First-out principle, which has the same effect as if materials were issued in strict chronological order.

NOTE.—The closing stock represents:

$$20 \text{ units at } 25s. \text{ per unit} = 25$$
$$500 \quad „ \quad 22s. \quad „ \quad = 550$$
$$\underline{520} \qquad\qquad \underline{\underline{£575}}$$

STORES LEDGER ACCOUNT

Material: .... Code: .... Folio: ....
Maximum Quantity: .... Location: ....
Minimum Quantity: ....

Date	G.R. No.	Receipts			S.R. No.	Issues			Stock		
		Quantity	Price	Amount £		Quantity	Price	Amount £	Quantity	Price	Amount £
Jan. 1		1000	20s.	1000					1000	20s.	1000
10		260	21s.	273					1260		1273
20						700 { 260 / 440	21s. / 20s.	273 / 440	560		560
Feb. 4		400	23s.	460					960		1020
21		300	25s.	375					1260		1395
Mar. 16						620 { 300 / 320	25s. / 23s.	375 / 368	640		652
Apr. 12						240 { 80 / 160	23s. / 20s.	92 / 160	400		400
May 10		500	22s.	550					900		950
25						380	22s.	418	520		532

FIG. 17.—*Stores Ledger Account (4)*

This records the same facts as in Fig. 16, but on the Last-in First-out principle. This tends to charge current production with current prices.

NOTE.—The closing stock represents:

400 units at 20s. per unit	=	400	
120 ,, 22s. ,,	=	132	
520		£532	

C

STORES LEDGER ACCOUNT

Material: ....   Code: ....   Maximum Quantity: ....   Folio:....................

Minimum Quantity: ....   Location: ....

Date		Receipts				Issues				Stock		
	G.R. No.	Quantity	Price	Amount £	S.R. No.		Quantity	Price	Amount £	Quantity	Price	Amount £
Jan. 1		1000	20s.	1000						1000	20s.	1000
10		260	21s.	273						1260		1273
20							700	20s.	700	560		573
Feb. 4		400	23s.	460						960		1033
21		300	25s.	375						1260		1408
Mar. 16						620	200	20s.	200			
							260	21s.	273			
							160	23s.	184	640		751
							240	23s.	276	400		475
Apr. 12												
May 10		500	22s.	550						900		1025
25						380	300	25s.	375			
							80	22s.	88	520		562

Fig. 18.—*Stores Ledger Account* (5)

    The entries shown here conform to the Base Stock method of keeping stores. This supposes that each stores account carries a fixed minimum stock below which it must not be allowed to fall, and which is therefore never issued.

    NOTE.—The closing stock represents:

$$
\begin{array}{lll}
100 \text{ units at } 20s. \text{ per unit} & = & 100 \text{ (BASE)} \\
420 \quad\quad\,, \quad\, 22s. \quad\quad\,, & = & 462 \\
\hline
520 & & \pounds562 \\
\end{array}
$$

because issues to one job may be at, for example, 20s., while the next job may be priced at 18s. or 22s., if the stock at 20s. has been exhausted. In stock valuation a great advantage of F.I.F.O. is that not only is stock at cost but is as closely representative of current prices as possible. When prices are falling the material charge to production is high, while the cost of stock replacement will be low. Conversely, when prices are rising the charge to production will be low, while the replacement cost will be high.

2. L.I.F.O. (Fig. 17)

This method also ensures that materials are issued at actual cost. It is assumed that the materials purchased are issued in the reverse order to F.I.F.O., *i.e.* the last receipt is the first issue.

L.I.F.O. suffers from the disadvantages mentioned in F.I.F.O., concerning tedious calculations and unfair comparisons of job costs. In addition, although stock is at cost, the price is that of the oldest material in store, so does not represent current price levels. Consequently it may be necessary to write off stock losses during periods of falling prices, as the book values of the materials will exceed market values.

A great advantage of this method is that the charge to production is as closely related to current price levels as possible. Assuming the purchase of materials was in recent times, it will not be necessary to ascertain market values.

3. BASE STOCK (Fig. 18)

This method also ensures that materials are issued at actual cost. It is assumed that a fixed minimum stock of the material is always carried at original cost. On p. 36 it was mentioned that a minimum stock is calculated for each item of material in stock below which the stock is not allowed to fall. In effect, this minimum stock is always in store, and cannot be released unless an emergency arises, for instance when supplies of the material are delayed and production must continue, or the business ceases to continue, when the stock will be sold. This minimum stock is therefore regarded as being in the nature of a fixed asset.

Base stock is rather similar to F.I.F.O. in operation, and suffers from the same disadvantages, namely, tedious calculations and unfair comparisons of job costs.

In stock valuation the stock will normally contain the minimum stock plus any of the latest purchases which have not been issued to production. Fig. 18 assumes that a minimum stock of 100 units was to be carried.

4. SIMPLE AVERAGE (Fig. 19)

Under this method an approximated figure is obtained, due to the fact that the total of the prices paid for the material is divided by the number of prices used in the calculation. Materials are not therefore charged out at actual cost, so a profit or loss may be incurred merely by adopting this price when evaluating materials charged to production.

The Simple Average is very easy to operate, and when prices of purchases do not fluctuate very much can give reasonably accurate results.

It will be noticed that in this illustration the design of the account has been changed slightly. Cumulative quantity columns have been introduced so that comparisons one with another can be made to ascertain which materials have been fully issued from stock. It is recommended that the cumulative issues column is not entered until after the price has been calculated. Thus

In the first issue:

Cumulative Receipts 1260; Cumulative Issues NIL, so price is

$$(20s. + 21s.) \div 2 = 20s.\ 6d.$$

In the second issue:

Cumulative Receipts 1960; Cumulative Issues 700, so price is

$$(20s. + 21s. + 23s. + 25s.) \div 4 = 22s.\ 3d.$$

In the third issue:

Cumulative Receipts 1960; Cumulative Issues 1320

1320 exceeds Cum. Receipt to January 10 (1260), so price is
$$(23s. + 25s.) \div 2 = 24s.$$

In the fourth issue:

Cumulative Receipts 2460; Cumulative Issues 1560

1560 exceeds Cumulative Receipts to January 10 (1260) but is still less than Cumulative Receipts to February 4 (1660), so price is

$$(23s. + 25s. + 22s.) \div 3 = 23s.\ 4d.$$

It was mentioned above that a profit or loss may be incurred by using this method. If we compare the value of closing stock (£519) with, for example, the value of closing stock under F.I.F.O., which was £575, we find that we have charged more to production than was necessary, so have made a profit on issue of £56.

STORES LEDGER ACCOUNT

Material: .... Code: .... Folio: ....
Maximum Quantity: .... Location: ....
Minimum Quantity: ....

Date	Receipts					Issues						Stock		
	G.R. No.	Quantity Actual	Cum.	Price	Amount £	S.R. No.	Quantity Actual	Cum.	Price	Amount £		Quantity	Price	Amount £
Jan. 1		1000	1000	20s.	1000							1000	20s.	1000
10		260	1260	21s.	273							1260		1273
20							700	700	20s. 6d.	718		560		555
Feb. 4		400	1660	23s.	460							960		1015
21		300	1960	25s.	375							1260		1390
Mar. 16							620	1320	22s. 3d.	690		640		700
Apr. 12							240	1560	24s.	288		400		412
May 10							380	1940	23s. 4d.	443		900		962
25		500	2460	22s.	550							520		519

Fig. 19.—*Stores Ledger Account* (6)

In this Simple Average method, the issue price is obtained by averaging the prices which have been paid on purchases. When prices are stable the average price will be fair and reasonable.

NOTE.—Under the average methods the identity of materials in store disappears, so that the closing stock figure cannot be verified as under the previous system.

5. WEIGHTED AVERAGE (Fig. 20)

This method is similar to the Simple Average Price in that a profit or loss on issue may be incurred due to the approximation of figures; but it is more complicated to operate than the Simple Average Price, due to the fact that total quantities and total costs are considered. It is essential to calculate issue prices to a considerable degree of accuracy if the benefit of the system is to be obtained; usually calculations are to four decimal places. However, this greater accuracy is an advantage of this method, particularly where the prices paid for materials fluctuate considerably.

It should be noted that this method differs from all the other methods described in this chapter, in that issue prices are calculated on *receipt* of materials, not on issue of materials.

In the Stock section above, as each delivery of material is received the total cost in the Stock column is divided by the total quantity in the Stock column. Thus:

$$\frac{£1273}{1260} = 20 \cdot 2063 \text{ shillings.}$$

On issue the quantity issued is multiplied by the last stock calculation of price, thus:

$$700 @ 20 \cdot 2063 = £707$$

6. PERIODIC SIMPLE AVERAGE PRICE (Fig. 21)

This method is similar to the two previous methods in that a profit or loss on issue may be incurred due to the approximation of figures, here caused by dividing the *total* prices of the materials obtained during that period by the number of prices used in the calculation.

The Periodic Simple Average Price is extremely simple to operate; the only calculation of issue price occurs at the end of the period concerned. It is very similar to the Simple Average Price, with the exception that it is calculated periodically, not on the occasion of each issue of material. The purchases during the period and the closing stock are included in the calculation, but it must be noted that the opening stock does not enter into the calculation because it was not purchased during the current period, and would have been included in last year's calculation.

A disadvantage of this method is that, although the calculation of the issue price is relatively easy, the fact that the issue prices of all materials in store will have to be calculated at the end of each period leads to a considerable amount of work at one time.

This system can be utilised in process industries where each individual order is absorbed into the general cost of producing a large quantity of articles, but where each individual order must be priced at each stage up to completion the method would be unsatisfactory.

STORES LEDGER ACCOUNT

Material: .... Code: .... Maximum Quantity: .... Folio: ....
Minimum Quantity: .... Location: ....

Date	Receipts				Issues				Stock		
	G.R. No.	Quantity	Price	Amount £	S.R. No.	Quantity	Price shillings	Amount £	Quantity	Price shillings	Amount £
Jan. 1		1000	20s.	1000					1000	20·0000	1000
10		260	21s.	273					1260	20·2063	1273
20						700	20·2063	707	560		566
Feb. 4		400	23s.	460					960	21·3750	1026
21		300	25s.	375					1260	22·2381	1401
Mar. 16						620	22·2381	689	640		712
Apr. 12						240	22·2381	267	400		445
May 10		500	22s.	550					900	22·1111	995
25						380	22·1111	420	520		575

FIG. 20.—*Stores Ledger Account* (7)

The Weighted Average is calculated afresh each time a purchase is made. The quantity bought is added to the stock in hand, and the revised balance is then divided into the new cash value of the stock. The effect of early prices is thus eliminated.

STORES LEDGER ACCOUNT

Material: ....   Code: ....   Maximum Quantity: ....   Folio: ....

Minimum Quantity: ....   Location: ....

Date	Receipts				Issues				Stock		
	G.R. No.	Quantity	Price	Amount £	S.R. No.	Quantity	Price	Amount £	Quantity	Price	Amount £
Jan. 1		1000	20s.	1000					1000	20s.	1000
10		260	21s.	273					1260		1273
20						700			560		
Feb. 4		400	23s.	460					960		
21		300	25s.	375					1260		
Mar. 16						620			640		
Apr. 12						240			400		
May 10		500	22s.	550					900		
25						380			520		505
		2460	111s.	£2658		1940	22/2·4	£2153			

Fig. 21.—*Stores Ledger Account* (8)

This method follows the principle of the Simple Average price (Figure 19) but a period is set over which the average will be calculated. The calculation made at the end of the period is then used as the issue price for the period in question.

NOTES

The Periodic Simple Average Price is:

$$\frac{\text{Total Prices of the Materials}}{\text{Number of Prices}} = \frac{111s.}{5} = 22/2\cdot4d. \text{ per unit.}$$

Receipts — Issues = Closing Stock.
£2658 — £2153 = £505.

However, if Closing Stock is valued at 22*s*. 2·4*d*. per unit, this would give 520 × 22*s*. 2·4*d*. = £577. This shows the discrepancy of the system.

7. PERIODIC WEIGHTED AVERAGE PRICE (Fig. 22)

As in all the average-price methods mentioned above, a profit or loss on issue of materials is incurred due to approximations; in this case it is caused by dividing the *total* cost of the materials obtained during that period by the quantity purchased. However, any differences will be very small owing to greater accuracy. Unlike the Weighted Average Price, this method is easy to operate, the only calculation of issue price occurring at the end of the period concerned. Due to the fact that quantities and costs are considered, this method is much more accurate than the Periodic Simple Average Price, otherwise comments mentioned in (6) above apply equally well to this system.

8. STANDARD PRICE (Fig. 23)

The Standard Price method also incurs a profit or loss on issue, but this is not due to approximation of calculations as noted in the average price methods; it is due to variances from a pre-determined price for each material in store.

A pre-determined price is ascertained which takes into consideration a number of factors which may influence the prices of materials in a future period; such factors include:

1. The quantity of materials to be purchased, which will affect quantity discounts.
2. The possibility of a rise in prices due to expected wage increases.
3. The likelihood of a rise or fall in prices due to market conditions.
4. The charging of freight and warehousing expenses to the material.
5. The charging of containers to the material.

The standard price will be set for each material, which can then be compared with the actual price paid. If the actual price paid exceeds standard, then a loss will be realised; if the actual price is less than standard a profit will be obtained.

This method is relatively easy to operate, because all issues of the material are calculated at the same price. A great advantage is the opportunity to check the efficiency of the purchase of materials, by seeing whether or not the actual price exceeds standard.

It should be noted that this method can be utilised in most industries, even though a system of standard costing is not in operation, although of course the greatest benefit will be obtained under a standard costing system.

STORES LEDGER ACCOUNT

Material: ....   Code: ....   Maximum Quantity: ....   Folio: ....

Minimum Quantity: ....   Location: ....

Date	Receipts				Issues				Stock		
	G.R. No.	Quantity	Price	Amount £	S.R. No.	Quantity	Price	Amount £	Quantity	Price	Amount £
Jan. 1		1000	20s.	1000					1000		1000
10		260	21s.	273					1260		1273
20						700			560		
Feb. 4		400	23s.	460					960		
21		300	25s.	375					1260		
Mar. 16						620			640		
Apr. 12						240			400		
May 10		500	22s.	550					900		
25						380			520		562
		2460		£2658		1940	21/7·3	£2096			

FIG. 22.—*Stores Ledger Account* (9)

The Periodic Weighted Average price is also calculated at the end of a given period, and is obtained by dividing the total cost of purchases by the total quantity received.

NOTES

The Periodic Weighted Average Price is:

$$\frac{\text{Total Cost of Materials}}{\text{Quantity Purchased}} = \frac{£2658}{2460} = 21s.\ 7\cdot3d.\ \text{per unit.}$$

Receipts — Issues = Closing Stock.
£2658 — £2096 = £562.

If closing stock is valued at 21s. 7·3d. per unit, this would give:

520 × 21s. 7·3d. = £562 (approx.). This shows that the figures are approximately correct.

STORES LEDGER ACCOUNT

Material: .... Code: .... Maximum Quantity: .... Folio: ....

Minimum Quantity: .... Location: ....

Date	G.R. No.	Receipts			S.R. No.	Issues			Stock		
		Quantity	Price	Amount £		Quantity	Price	Amount £	Quantity	Price	Amount £
Jan. 1		1000	20s.	1000					1000		1000
10		260	21s.	273					1260		1273
20						700	23s.	805	560		468
Feb. 4		400	23s.	460					960		928
21		300	25s.	375					1260		1303
Mar. 16						620	23s.	713	640		590
Apr. 12						240	23s.	276	400		314
May 10		500	22s.	550					900		864
25						380	23s.	437	520		427
		2460		£2658		1940		£2231			

FIG. 23.—*Stores Ledger Account* (10)

The Standard price method ensures that production is charged always at the Standard price for the commodity, variances from the actual price paid being transferred to Price Variance Account.

Assume that the standard price for this material is 23*s*. per unit.

It will be noticed that the closing value of stock is under-valued, due to the fact that production has been charged at a higher price (the standard price) than the actual price. If the actual price of the material had exceeded the standard price, the stock would have been over-valued.

To ascertain whether or not the buying of materials has been efficiently performed:

$$(\text{Actual Receipts} \times \text{Standard Price}) - \text{Actual Amount}$$
$$= (2460 \times 23s.) - £2658$$
$$= £2829 - £2658$$
$$= £171$$

It was expected that the cost of materials purchased would be £2829, so £171 represents the efficiency in purchasing.

If the closing stock is valued at standard price, the value would be:

$$520 \times 23s. = £598$$

Compare this figure with the amount shown in the above account (£427), and the resulting difference is £171, which has been shown to be the efficiency in purchasing.

H.I.F.O. AND N.I.F.O.

Two other systems are mentioned for reference purposes only. They are: highest in, first out (H.I.F.O.) and next in, first out (N.I.F.O.). These systems have not been widely adopted and operate in rather a similar way to F.I.F.O. and L.I.F.O.

The method adopted for pricing materials issued largely depends upon the nature of the materials, the undertaking concerned, and the circumstances which require to be taken into consideration.

The purpose of Cost Accounts is to arrive at the actual cost of each job, or of each process or operation of manufacture, and to this end it is desirable to charge out stores material at cost.

Some businessmen prefer that material issued should be charged to Cost Accounts at market prices ruling at the time the materials are used, because these are the prices which would have to be paid if the material were purchased at that time. This procedure introduces considerable confusion into the accounts, and at once involves departure from the principle of showing actual costs in the Cost Accounts.

There are a few kinds of business, however, where the particular nature of the transactions leads the management to desire that the Cost Accounts should represent the current position, and correspond with estimates, as well as that the efficiency of buying should be revealed.

This information is secured by charging stores at current market prices, regardless whether these are higher or lower than the actual figures paid. When this method is used a careful adjustment in a "Stores Adjustment Account" is necessary. The result of this procedure is that, in a period of falling prices, the costs of such manufacturers will show as lower than those of manufacturers who charge materials at actual prices paid at an earlier date. This does not mean that the first-named manufacturers are in a more competitive position, for the reason that when submitting estimates, or fixing prices, allowance must be made for the trend of market prices. Herein lies one of the chief points of difference between costs and estimates.

Mention must be made here also of materials which it is necessary to retain for purposes of maturing, of which perhaps the best example is timber. Logs are often sawn longitudinally and left in this rough state for seasoning, as also is timber cut into suitable sizes. In such cases the stock appreciates in value, and it is customary to increase the cost by at least the interest on the capital value the stock represents, and other special storage expenses may also be added. It is not considered that such an addition for interest to cost is valid; it is probably better to cover the value in the price.

There are many kinds of stock held for long periods for reasons other than maturing factors. Consider whisky and wines, which are held for many years. The storage, insurance, labour, etc., certainly add to the cost; but, better than charging interest in costs is to recognise that it must be included in the Selling Price. Profit for each year's tied-up capital must be included in the price, which therefore involves a calculation at Compound Interest.

STOCK VALUATION

The method of valuing stores for the Annual Balance Sheet, it is important to observe, is quite independent of the system of pricing for costing purposes. The recognised methods of pricing stores for the Balance Sheet compiled from the Financial Accounts is at cost, or market value, whichever is the lower. The cost price referred to in this connection is the average cost price of the stores on hand which, it may be assumed, will consist of the most recent purchases.

The problem which arises from valuing stock in the Cost Accounts at one price and the stock in the Financial Accounts at another price is discussed fully in Chapter 15.

SMALL PARTS USED IN LARGE QUANTITIES

Such parts, when of little individual value, are not generally requisitioned and charged separately for each production order. The average quantity used may be pre-determined and charged on that basis to each job. A quantity of each of such materials may be issued by the Stores to a Shop and a Shop Stores Account debited at an average cost price. This account will be credited, say weekly, with the estimated quantity for the number of orders dealt with, thereby eliminating much unnecessary detail.

An alternative procedure is for the cost of small items, for example glue used for sealing labels on cans, to be treated as indirect materials and charged to production through factory overhead recovery rates. These *indirect materials*, sometimes called Consumable Stores, include such items as lubricants and cleaning materials, and should be requisitioned in the same way as materials issued for manufacturing operations. The requisitions are summarised and charged to suitable expense accounts.

CHAPTER 7

LABOUR: ENGAGEMENT, TIME-KEEPING, AND TIME-BOOKING

NEW PERSONNEL

ESTABLISHMENT

IT is nowadays customary to fix an Establishment of workers for each department of a business, and this will show the numbers of each grading permitted, the salary scale or wages rate, with space for any changes made and a reference to the Minute authorising the change.

By this means it is possible for management to guard against any unauthorised growth in the numbers on the payroll, and ensures that a convincing case is made out for each addition.

ENGAGEMENT OF LABOUR

The engagement of labour is delegated by management to the Personnel Officer, or whoever in the particular business exercises that function. The Personnel Officer carries out this work in response to properly authorised requests for employees received from departmental managers, and always subject to the proviso that the vacancy exists within the allowed establishment.

A worker is not taken on, however, by the Personnel Officer alone, but likely candidates are sent by him to the departmental manager or foreman concerned, who may perhaps give them a practical test, and then report back as to the one he recommends for the vacancy.

A personnel record (Fig. 24) is kept for every employee, and this is designed to act as a history of all that takes place during the course of the employment. It will be seen from the illustration that on the front of the sheet are spaces for a number of personal particulars relating to the employee and his employment. On the reverse side of the form space is given for sickness records, lateness records, absenteeism, holiday periods, and any comments as to the employee's special interests, training, and abilities which may be a guide to promotion possibilities.

Upon engagement the following procedure is followed:

1. *Notice is given to the department concerned.*—A first notification is made at once that the employee is expected on a certain date. When the employee reports for duty he sees the Personnel Officer again, is

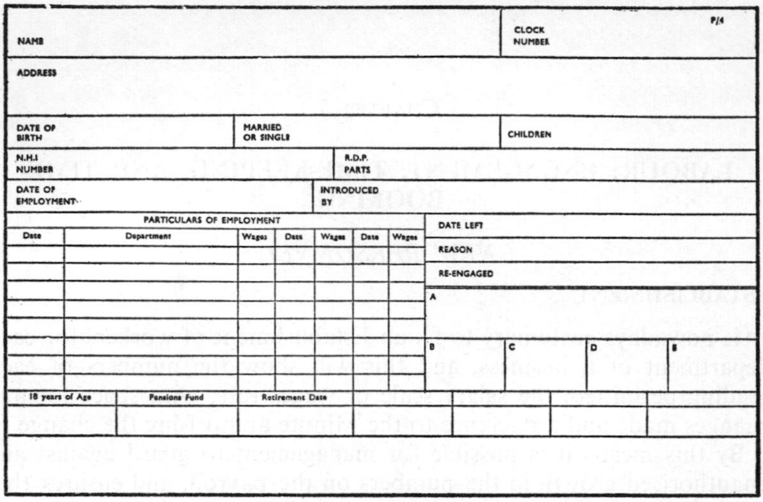

P/4
NAME
CLOCK NUMBER
ADDRESS
DATE OF BIRTH
MARRIED OR SINGLE
CHILDREN
N.H.I NUMBER
R.D.P. PARTS
DATE OF EMPLOYMENT
INTRODUCED BY
PARTICULARS OF EMPLOYMENT
Date | Department | Wages | Date | Wages | Date | Wages
DATE LEFT
REASON
RE-ENGAGED
A
B
C
D
E
18 years of Age
Pensions Fund
Retirement Date

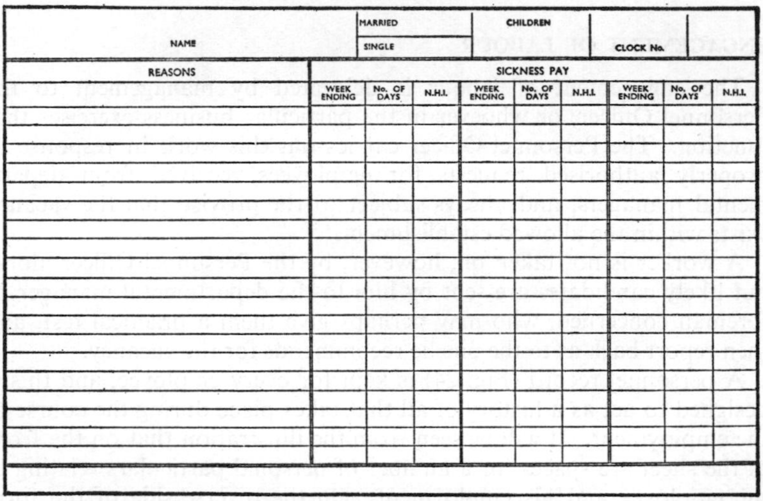

NAME
MARRIED
SINGLE
CHILDREN
CLOCK No.
REASONS
SICKNESS PAY
WEEK ENDING | No. OF DAYS | N.H.I. | WEEK ENDING | No. OF DAYS | N.H.I. | WEEK ENDING | No. OF DAYS | N.H.I.

FIG. 24.—*Personnel Record*

Each employee's record is kept by the Personnel Department, and contains details of the history of his employment. If it is prepared in the form of a stiff envelope printed back and front, the relative papers may be conveniently filed inside. Adequate space should be provided for changes of address, and records of promotions and transfers from one department to another. It is also useful to include the employee's private telephone number, or that of someone living close by who will take a message in case of emergency. The names of those from whom references were obtained should also be stated, as well as those to whom they may be subsequently given. On the reverse side of the record, details of holidays taken are often listed. Sickness is also noted down, the date of the first sickness becoming the "anniversary date" from which all subsequent sickness entitlement at full pay and half pay is calculated.

given a copy of the Works Rules, and a duplicate of the notification to take to his new foreman.

2. *Notice is given to the Wages Office.*—This notifies them of the new employee's name, the name of the former employee whom he replaces, the date of commencement, department, rate of pay, and clock number. Subsequently, the employee's National Insurance card and P.A.Y.E. record will also be passed on to this department.

TERMINATION OF EMPLOYMENT

When an employee leaves his employment for any reason, the Personnel Officer should seek to find out that reason. The truth is not always told on these occasions, but repeated labour changes in one particular department may point to a "difficult" foreman or to unsatisfactory working conditions.

A foreman should not have power to dismiss employees under him. That "hire and fire" mentality is quite out of keeping with modern ideas of employer–employee relationship. The foreman should therefore limit himself to making a recommendation to the Personnel Officer, who will then investigate all the facts before taking a decision. If the fault is not all on one side it may be possible to transfer the employee to another department. In such a case, however, the full co-operation of all concerned is necessary to secure a happy and permanent solution, and it is one of the fundamental tasks of personnel work to cultivate better "human relations" throughout the organisation.

LABOUR TURNOVER RATE

Any changing of employees occasions loss to a manufacturer. The cost of the Personnel Department itself, the loss of production while the new employees learn the routine of the works and the details of their duties, unabsorbed overhead, are all examples of these costs. For this reason, a check is kept on the rate at which employees who leave have to be replaced, and this is expressed as a Labour Turnover percentage:

$$\frac{\text{Number of leavers replaced}}{\text{Average total number of employees}} \times 100.$$

This figure may be compared with previous periods and, even more valuably, with the rate for the industry as a whole. In some trades, especially those which employ a high proportion of married women as part-time workers, the normal rate may be as high as 70–80%, whereas in others the rate may be as low as 10% or less. It does not always follow, however, that it is a good thing to have a very low Labour Turnover Rate in the more senior grades of workshop employment, because it may mean that there are few possibilities of promotion within the concern, and all the best of the younger workers are forced to look elsewhere for future advancement.

TIMEKEEPING METHODS

The methods of recording the gate, or factory, time of workers vary considerably, and although in most modern works time-recording clocks are used, older methods are still occasionally to be found.

THE CHECK OR DISC METHOD

Metal discs bearing the workers' numbers are placed on hooks on a board kept at the entrance of the works. The worker, on entering, removes his disc and places it in a box provided. This box is removed at starting time, and another "late" box is substituted. A variation of this procedure requires the worker to take his disc to the department in which he works, where there are a series of drawers under the supervision of the departmental foreman. The worker puts his disc in the next available drawer, which may be locked successively by the foreman as time elapses. This acts as a deterrent to latecomers, and provides a tighter check on any attempt to book on for a friend who has not yet arrived.

The timekeeper uses the discs to record attendances, and if required the individual times of latecomers may be recorded by making latecomers present their discs at the Timekeeper's window.

TIME-RECORDING CLOCKS

The substitution of mechanical for manual methods of timekeeping allows for greater accuracy and avoids much loss of time. However, the presence of a timekeeper is still necessary to prevent fraud and irregularities. The clocks in use fall into two main categories:

1. *Dial time recorders*

This type of time recorder consists of a large clock face, around the edge of which are about 150 holes, each of which bears a number which corresponds to the clock number of the worker concerned (*see* Fig. 25). All the worker has to do is to swing a radial arm mounted on the clock face and press it into the hole allotted to him. This automatically records the time on a roll of paper within the machine, and against his clock number. The numbering of these recorders can be arranged by departments, provided that more than sufficient are allocated in the first place, so that numbers do not have to be re-used immediately by a new employee when another leaves. Arrangements can also be made for the record of times to be an integral part of the payroll, thus avoiding the necessity of recopying the times.

2. *Card time recorders*

These give a weekly and, indeed, daily printed and tabulated record of the times of arrival and departure of employees, but use a separate card for each person. Some models give the incomings and outgoings in one-colour printing only, but others automatically print all lateness, overtime, or similar data in red, thus bringing it prominently to notice.

Fig. 25.—*Dial Time Recorder*

Where large numbers of men have to clock on, this method helps to prevent the formation of queues. The metal arm is swung round the face of the dial and punched into the appropriate hole. This gives an automatic time record in number order on a paper roll.

Fig. 26.—*Card Time Recorder*

In this latest type of Card Recorder it is only necessary for the worker to insert his clock card into the machine. The time is then automatically stamped in the correct position, and in red ink if he is late.

This is of great help to the wages clerks, and also helps to reduce the numbers of latecomers.

Fig. 26 shows one of the latest models, which merely requires the worker to insert his card in the machine. Racks are installed near each recorder, and cards bearing the workers' numbers are each week placed in numbered pockets in these racks. On entering, the card is taken by the worker from the "Out" rack, inserted in the recorder to have the time stamped, and placed in the "In" rack. The machines print the day of the week, and the hour and minute a.m. and p.m. Some concerns have adopted 6 minutes as being equivalent to 0·1 of an hour, and therefore the clock changes from say 8·5 to 8·6 only after an elapsed time of 6 minutes. This decimal system is of much assistance to the wages clerks in calculating the weekly time of workers.

CALCULATION OF ATTENDANCE TIME

This can be done: (*a*) daily, by extending the hours, and totalling at the end of the week; (*b*) weekly, by fixing a standard week. The total standard hours, plus overtime, less lost time, may be speedily determined, especially when used with the two-colour printing system. No calculation is needed at all for cards showing time wholly in blue, *i.e.* normal standard hours.

The totalled hours are shown at the foot of the clock card as shown in Fig. 27, and space is provided for overtime, which may be counted as time and a quarter, time and a half, or double time, as the case may be. It is suggested, however, that although it is important to know the hours of overtime worked, and the reasons therefor, a separation should be made between the actual hours and the premium hours (*see* Fig. 28). This would be of value for the reason that the standard weekly hours plus the actual overtime hours will, in the case of production departments, be chargeable as direct labour while the overtime premium hours will, generally speaking, be chargeable as overhead. Thus, assuming that overtime is paid at time and a half:

			£ s. d.
Direct Labour			
Standard weekly hours 44			
Overtime hours	3		
	—		
	47	5s.	11 15 0
Overhead			
Overtime premium hours 3		2s. 6d.	7 6
Gross wages payable			£12 2 6

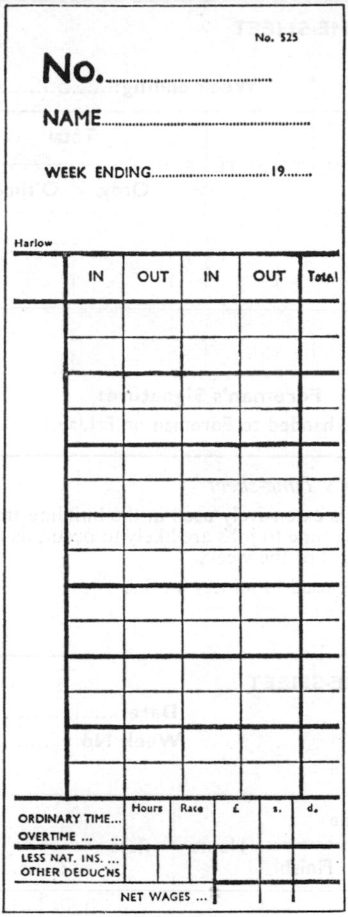
No. 525
No. ....
NAME ....
WEEK ENDING .... 19.......
Harlow

	IN	OUT	IN	OUT	Total

	Hours	Rate	£	s.	d.
ORDINARY TIME...					
OVERTIME					
LESS NAT. INS. ... OTHER DEDUC'NS					
NET WAGES ...					

FIG. 27.—*Clock Card—usual type*

This shows the normal type of clock card for use with a card time recorder. It provides sufficient space for the calculation of the wages due, prior to entry on the Wages Sheets.

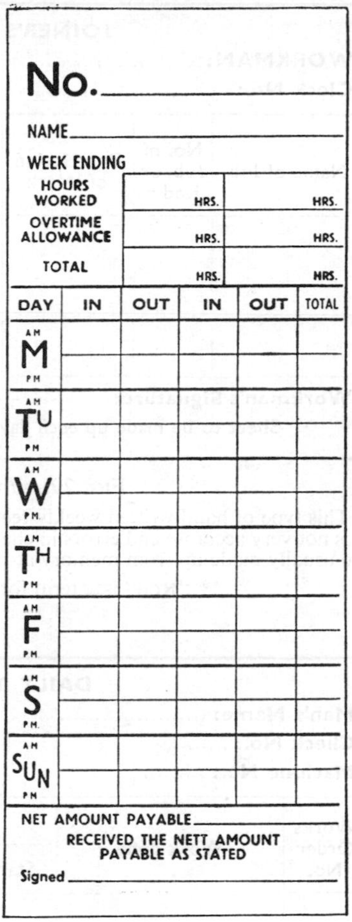
No. ______________
NAME ______________
WEEK ENDING

HOURS WORKED	HRS.	HRS.
OVERTIME ALLOWANCE	HRS.	HRS.
TOTAL	HRS.	HRS.

DAY	IN	OUT	IN	OUT	TOTAL
AM M PM					
AM TU PM					
AM W PM					
AM TH PM					
AM F PM					
AM S PM					
AM SUN PM					

NET AMOUNT PAYABLE ______________
RECEIVED THE NETT AMOUNT PAYABLE AS STATED
Signed ______________

FIG. 28.—*Clock Card—alternative type*

This type of card provides a means of differentiating between "straight time" and overtime premium. This is most valuable in the proper apportionment of wages.

TIME-BOOKING

In addition to registering workers' times of arrival and departure, it is necessary, in most instances, to record also particulars of work done, and the time spent on each order or operation.

In most cases, too, it is important that the information thus obtained should be capable of being reconciled with the gate times; which means,

JOINER'S TIME-SHEET

WORKMAN: ....

Clock No.: ....   Week ending:..................

Name of Job	No. of Job, or Rod *	Description of Work	S.	M.	T.	W.	Th.	F.	Total	
									Ordy.	O'time.

Workman's Signature: Foreman's Signature:

Sheet to be made up *each* day and handed to Foreman on Friday.

FIG. 29.—*Joiner's Time-sheet*

This type of hand-written weekly record is extensively used in the building trade. It is not very accurate and errors in charging time to jobs are likely to occur, as they are usually made up from memory at the end of the week.

* "Rod" is a term for job, used in joinery works.

DAILY TIME-SHEET

Man's Name: ....   Date:....................

Check No.: ....   Week No.: ....

Machine No.: ....

Works Order No.	Work done	Time		Hours	Rate	£ s. d.
		Start	Finish			

Signed (worker):   Certified (foreman):   Office Ref.:

FIG. 30.—*Daily Time-sheet*

These records are used in small works which have not gone to the expense of a card time recorder. There is a check on their correctness, since the foreman gives a daily signature as well as the worker. One of the chief disadvantages is that as records they tend to arrive in the Cost Office in a dishevelled state, and are unpleasant to handle.

in effect, that it must be possible to account for the whole of each worker's day, including idle time. This degree of precision is essential in factories, but not necessarily in every industry, and this is reflected in the methods of time-booking employed.

WEEKLY TIME SHEETS

A typical weekly time sheet is shown in Fig. 29, and it will be seen that the workers are required to fill in particulars of the time spent on each separate job each day; a different-coloured sheet would be used for each trade, *e.g.* machinists, joiners, etc. This method is rather rough and ready, but it is extensively used by builders and decorators, and by civil-engineering contractors, and is apparently found satisfactory in such cases.

DAILY TIME SHEETS

These have nearly the same disadvantages as the weekly time sheets. From the example given in Fig. 30 it will be observed that provision is made for recording the time spent on each job during the day, and there may be some advantage over the weekly sheet in that the worker must complete the sheet every day and hand it to the foreman for signature. Even so, there is a tendency for times to be approximate only, and periods of idle or wasted time are conveniently forgotten. If a conscientious foreman is in charge, greater accuracy may perhaps be obtained by having the job times entered on the forms in the foreman's office.

JOB TICKETS

The use of these for registering the time worked on each order is extensive. There is correspondingly a very large variety of forms, as nearly every manufacturer draws up his job tickets to suit the particular needs of his business. A typical form is shown in Fig. 31, but the student will be well advised not to endeavour to commit it to memory. He should rather note the salient points contained in it.

Only one ticket is issued to a worker at a time, usually by the foreman's office, and it serves the dual purpose of providing instructions as to the operation to be performed, and of recording the time spent in performing it. As the operator finishes the operation he is doing he submits his work with his job ticket, has the finishing time recorded (usually by clock), and is then issued with another job ticket with the starting time recorded, *i.e.* the same time.

If the operator cannot immediately carry on with a new job, as, for example, when he has to wait for work from a previous operation, an

JOB TICKET

Department: ....
Job No.:................
Works Order No.: ....
Date ....

Drawing No.: ....
Operation No.: ....
Machine No.: ....
Time allowance: ....

Time started: ....
   ,,   finished: ....
Hours on Job: ....

Description of Job	Hours	Rate	£	s.	d.

Worker's No.:   Certified   Office
Signature: (foreman or   ref.:
                inspection):

Fig. 31.—*Job Ticket*

The purpose of these tickets is to keep a close check on the time spent by an operator on each job which he does during the day. They may be used with a card time recorder if so designed.

UNALLOCATED TIME

Man No.: ....
Machine No.: ....
Type of Machine: ....

REASONS FOR WAITING

1. Machine break down .... ☐
2. Material .... ☐
3. Inspection .... ☐
4. Orders .... ☐
5. Tools .... ☐
6. Foreman's attention .... ☐
7. Previous operation .... ☐
8. Other reasons:

      ....
      ....
      ....
      ....

Fig. 32.—*Section of card showing reasons for* IDLE TIME: (*Time Registrations are on other side of card*)

It is important to know how much time in a factory is unproductive, and for what reason. If an operator's time is not covered by a job ticket, he must make use of an idle-time card in order to account for a full day's employment.

JOB COST CARD   I.T.R. LSF 1228

ORDER No. 422   DRAWING No. 90   PATTERN No. 437

Special Instructions: ....

Date   STARTED 29/8
       FINISHED 30/8

Workman No.	OPERATION		Cost S d	Rate S d	Time Taken Hrs. Min.		Date
17	Dressing	Off / On	1 3	2 3	-	34	AUG 29 8 34 / AUG 29 8 00
15	Marking Off	Off / On	4 8	3 1	1	30	AUG 29 10 06 / AUG 29 8 36
9	Rough Planing	Off / On	2 7	2 6½	1	01	AUG 29 11 09 / AUG 29 10 08
4	Rough Turning	Off / On	7 8	2 6½	3	02	AUG 29 5 02 / AUG 29 2 00
3	Turning	Off / On	11 5	2 6½	3	58	AUG 30 11 58 / AUG 30 8 00
21	Planing	Off / On	1 4	2 6½	-	28	AUG 30 12 28 / AUG 30 12 00
8	Grinding	Off / On	5 2	3 5½	1	29	AUG 30 3 01 / AUG 30 1 32
7	Drilling	Off / On	2 1	2 6½	·	50	AUG 30 3 54 / AUG 30 3 04
19	Cleaning Off	Off / On	1 3	2 ·	·	37	AUG 30 4 34 / AUG 30 3 57
38	Finishing	Off / On	3 4	3 1	1	05	AUG 30 5 40 / AUG 30 4 35
		Off / On					
		Off / On					

Total Labour Cost ... £ 2 : = s. 9 d.
ENTER MATERIAL USED ON REVERSE SIDE

FIG. 33.—*Labour Cost Card*

Instead of, or in addition to, a separate job ticket, a cost card sometimes travels with each job as it goes from operation to operation. In this way the times can be worked out and the total labour cost found. It will be noted that the illustration is headed "Job Cost Card" because it provides for materials to be entered on the reverse side. As this is somewhat unusual, the caption has been altered.

idle-time card should be started, so that the record of his day's activities may be complete, and yet not be unfairly charged against production and reflect adversely upon his competence as a worker. Similarly if, during the course of an operation, there is a machinery breakdown, the idle time thus caused must be recorded on an idle-time card, and not on the worker's job-time ticket. A specimen idle-time card is shown in Fig. 32.

LABOUR COST CARDS

This a variation of the job ticket method, for the tickets are combined on one card, which travels with the order. An illustration of this is given in Fig. 33. The total cost of the labour involved in completing the order may be calculated and totalled at the end of the card's circula-

I. T. R. Co. LTD.   FORM No. L.S. F.93Q.
DAILY COST CARD

No. _2/_ .... DATE _31/5/._._..

NAME ...... _James Kinten_ ....

JOB No.	Time		Time Record
_411_	OFF	_' //_	9 11
	ON		8 00
_328_	OFF	_1. 19._	10 34
	ON		9 15
_1098._	OFF	_1. 25._	12 01
	ON		10 36
_756°_	OFF	_2-23._	3 21
	ON		12 58
_438._	OFF	_. 25._	3 53
	ON		3 28
_521._	OFF	_1. 32._	5 31
	ON		3 59
	OFF		
	ON		
	OFF		
	ON		
	OFF		
	ON		

International System

FIG. 34.—*Daily Cost Card*

This type of card, instead of travelling with the work, is issued to each operator. On it he records the jobs on which he has worked during the day and the times are stamped by a card time recorder.

tion round the factory floor, and then if the coupons are made detachable, they may be sorted under the operators' clock numbers, and thus built up into a total to agree with their clock times.

Yet another variation of this idea is to be seen in Fig. 34, where a daily cost card is issued to each operator. He records the various jobs on which he has worked, with the starting and the stopping times of each and these, when extended and totalled, give an agreement with his gate times for the day as recorded at the top of the card. In this case if the coupons are detachable they are sorted under the various job numbers to build up the labour costs of each job, and one system allows for them to be inserted in slots, much as pictures may be mounted in a photographic album. The completed results may then be microfilmed to produce a permanent record.

PIECE-WORK TICKETS

Where a factory undertakes repetitive work, payment to the workers is often made on the basis of a rate per piece or number of pieces produced. In such cases the entitlement to wages is the possession of completed piece-work tickets, and a typical form is shown in Fig. 35.

It might be thought that under this system time records are unnecessary, and in some factories time is not, in fact, recorded for piece-

---

PIECE-WORK ORDER

Worker's Name: .... No.: ....
Clock No.: .... Date: .... Time Taken: ....

Part: .... Price: ....
Operation: .... Quantity: ....

No. Made	Passed	Rejected	Rate	£	s.	d.

Signed Worker: Signed Inspection:
Foreman:

FIG. 35.—*Piece-work Order*

These orders are the worker's entitlement to be paid for the quantity of pieces he has completed which satisfactorily pass inspection. The agreed piece-work price is stated as well as details of the work to be done.

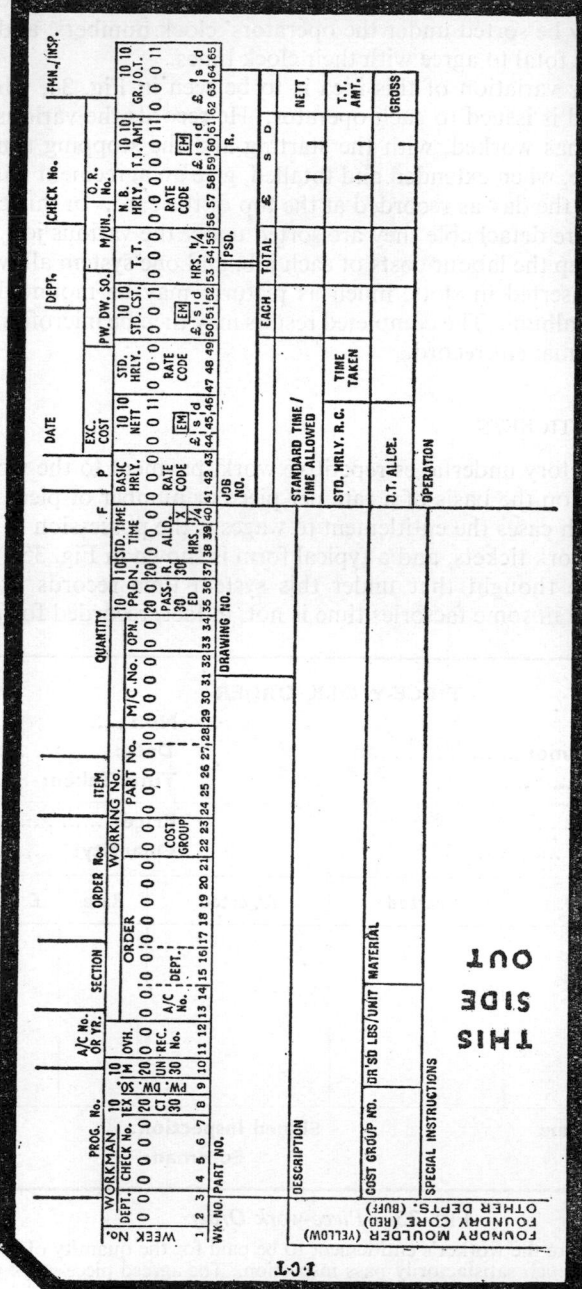

Fig. 36.—*Job Time Card*

The illustration is of a Job Time card suitable for punched-card accounting allied to Standard Costs.

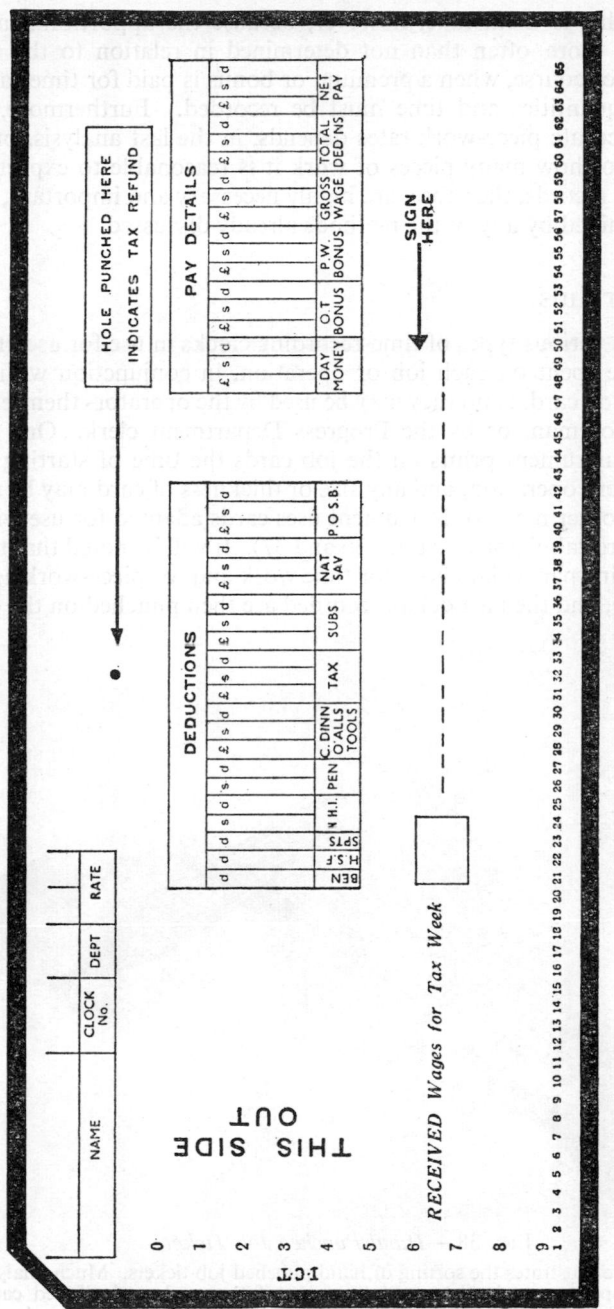

FIG. 37.—*Pay Slip*

This is a hand-written record, but the information is then punched into the card itself, which is sorted and tabulated. After signature by the employee it is retained by the Wages Office.

workers. This is a mistake, however, because the apportionment of overhead is more often than not determined in relation to the time factor and, of course, when a premium or bonus is paid for time saved, then both quantities and time must be recorded. Furthermore, the fixing of accurate piece-work rates depends, in the last analysis, on an assessment of how many pieces of work it is reasonable to expect per hour. Time records, therefore, are highly necessary and important, and may be obtained by any of the methods already discussed.

EQUIPMENT AIDS

There are various types of time-recording clocks in use for ascertaining the time spent on each job or operation, in conjunction with job tickets and job cards; and they may be used by the operators themselves, or by the foreman, or by the Progress Department clerk. One very adaptable instrument prints on the job cards the time of starting and stopping every operation, and any size or thickness of card may be used with it. Another make of instrument uses cards adapted for use with a punched-card tabulator (*see* Figs. 36 and 37). It will be noted that these cards combine particulars both for time work and for piece-work as the case may be, and the particulars recorded are then punched on the card itself.

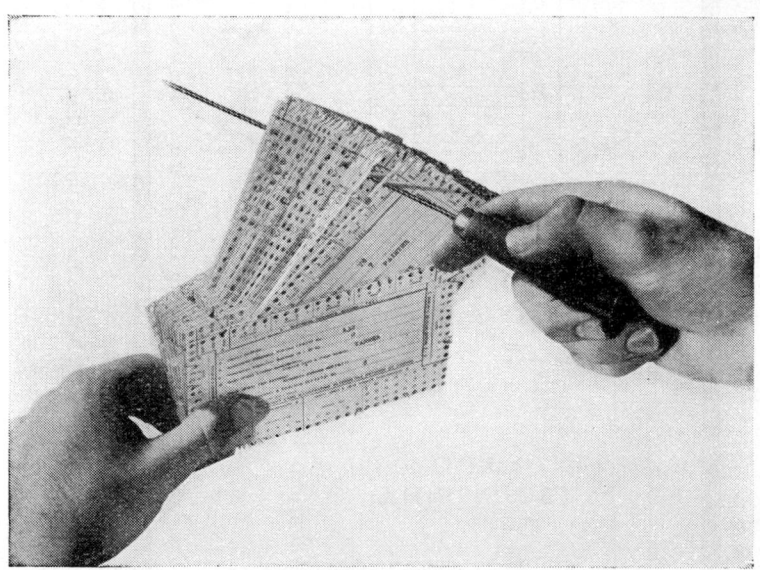

FIG. 38.—*Hand Punched Job Ticket*

This figure illustrates the sorting of hand punched job tickets. Much analysis may be clipped conveniently round the edge of the card, and clipped cards are not retained on the knitting needle.

Where the volume of work does not justify the installation of punched-card equipment of mechanised type, it should be remembered that hand-clipped records can be most useful for analysis purposes. Fig. 38 shows a job ticket of this kind, the operators instructions and order details having been previously prepared and run off on to the blank cards by means of a spirit duplicator. The times of the operations are then recorded by clock, and all the information on the card is then clipped on the edge of the card. The cards can then be sorted by means of knitting needles, one or two columns at a time, the clipped holes not being retained by the needle as it is pushed from front to back of the pack of cards.

TICKETOGRAPH COUPON SYSTEM FOR PIECE-WORK

The Ticketograph system is constructed for controlling costs and progress in a factory and is particularly, though not solely, suitable for

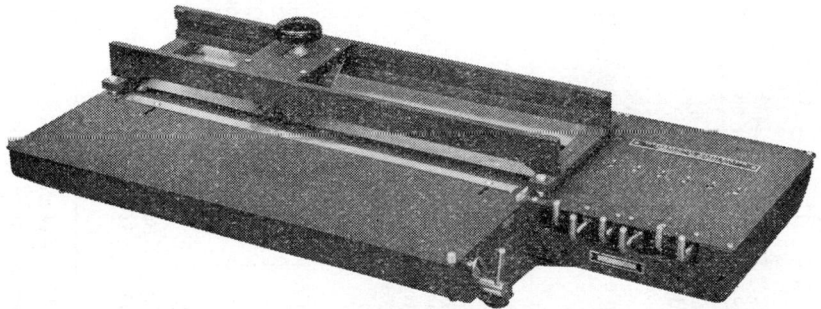

FIG. 39.—*Ticketograph Equipment*

piece-work. The equipment is shown in Fig. 39. It imprints a ticket, composed of coupons, one for each operation, and arranged in the same order as the work progresses through the factory. The coupon bears sufficient details to identify the work, and also gives the piece-work price to be paid. The card itself (Fig. 40) is usually about 10 in. × 5½ in. in size, although this may vary according to the number of operations.

The tickets are perforated between each coupon, and as the work passes from one operator to another, each worker detaches the coupon referring to his or her particular operation. He inserts his clock number, and then files it in a small pocket of a coupon-holder book, which thus becomes the worker's entitlement to pay. In the card illustrated, Ticket No. 12 shows that the Order No. is 432, the type of cloth is 56, and that the price is 2s. 6d. per dozen. Twelve tickets must therefore be collected to obtain that amount.

1 I	3 H	5 G	7 F	9 E	11 D	13 C	15 B	17 A	Despatch V	Warehouse or Cutting Room V
432 56 12 2/6	432 56 12 VOID	432 56 12 2/6	432 56 12 3½	432 56 12 2/6 *6d	432 56 12 1/11	432 56 12 6¾	432 56 12 4/-	432 56 12 3/3⅛	432 56 12	432 56 12
V Cutting	Back-making	Piecing Up	Shaping	Sew Round	Closing	Neck-making	Felling	Brushing and Pressing		
1	3	5	7	9	11	13	15	17		

PROGRESS

(The four coupons attached to this portion form progress reports and must be put in the collecting box immediately operation is finished.)

Workers, before detaching Coupons, must place their Clock No. in the square corresponding to their operation. REMEMBER—the Coupon is your voucher for pay.

INTERNATIONAL TICKETOGRAPH SYSTEM—FORM NO. T 376

1	2	3	4

2 V Fixing	4 Sleeve Making	6 Under Pressing	8 Linen to Edge	10 Baist Under	12 Baist Out	14 Stitching	16 Sleeving	18 Buttons and Button-holes	Cost Office V	Making Department V
432 56 12 1/7	432 56 12 DB	432 56 12 7½	432 56 12 3/-	432 56 12 9¾	432 56 12 2/6	432 56 12 1/9	432 56 12 3/-	432 56 12 4/11	432 56 12 DB	432 56 12
V Fixing	Sleeve Making	Under Pressing	Linen to Edge	Baist Under	Baist Out	Stitching	Sleeving	Buttons and Button-holes		
2	4	6	8	10	12	14	16	18		

FIG. 40.—*Ticketograph Piece-work Coupons*

NOTE.—The figures in bold type are printed a line at a time by the Ticketograph by one pressure of a lever.

* 6d. on coupon No. 9 is an "extra" added by a "plussing" device.

International Ticketograph
System–Form No. TDSC–2

STATEMENT CARD

Name: .... **No.:** .... **Operation:** ....

Dept.: .... **Week Ending:** ....

						Total	Doz. or Gross	Price	Amount £	s.	d.

TIME HAND Profit	Loss	Hours	Rate	£	s.	d.	Checked by				
								Total Wages + Time-work as at back			
Received amount stated							Examined by	% Added			
Signed								GROSS			

FIG. 41.—*Statement Card*

The worker uses this card to summarise the Ticketograph coupons in the coupon holder book. It is checked by the Wages Office and is the voucher for payment.

At the end of each day the worker enters up a statement card, illustrated in Fig. 41, which is then checked by the office, and returned to him in time for the next day's entries. At the end of each week the entries are cross cast, and easily worked out at the appropriate rate.

Progress coupons, sometimes known as "trumps," are used to keep track of the progress of the work, and as the work reaches certain inspection points, or other agreed progress control points, the operator who completes the operation at that point places the appropriate "trump" coupon in a box provided, which is cleared by the Progress Department at least once each day. These coupons are then placed on a control board, which thus shows at a glance the position of every order as it passes through the factory.

CHAPTER 8

LABOUR: METHODS OF REMUNERATION

GENERAL CONSIDERATIONS

The cost of labour is a factor which requires the most careful thought. It provides problems of major importance, and, on the solution of these, the success of any enterprise must largely depend.

Reduction in labour costs is one of the chief objectives of the Production Manager, and much guidance to this end can be secured from a suitably organised costing system. Low wages do not necessarily mean low costs—in fact, it is widely recognised now that efficiently organised factories may pay the highest wages, and yet have the lowest labour costs. A moment's reflection will be sufficient to grasp how this may come about. A firm, using rather old-fashioned methods, and with only moderately effective organisation, may pay its 100 machine shop employees at the rate of 5s. per hour, and in a week of 44 hours there may be 4000 pieces produced. The labour cost per piece in this case will be

$$100 \times 44 \times 5s. \text{ divided by } 4000, \text{ or } 5s. \text{ } 6d.$$

With better organisation and more up-to-date machinery the firm might be able to obtain this result:

$$90 \times 44 \times 8s. \text{ divided by } 6000, \text{ or } 5s. \text{ } 3d.$$

Many schemes for remunerating labour have been devised to secure more efficiency than is usually obtained from the method of paying at so much per hour or per week. Some of these have failed on account of their complexity, which resulted in strikes and agitations and compelled their withdrawal.

FACTORS TO BE CONSIDERED

Efficiency in production

When volume of production is the important factor, labour control and remuneration may be devised to this end; but when output is less important than great care and accuracy, wage payments based on production quantities are undesirable unless competent inspection is arranged at all stages.

Effect on workers

The attitude of workers is of great importance, and every wage system should be thoroughly explained to them, and be capable of being understood by those of average intelligence. Unless and until their co-operation is secured, the fullest advantage of the system will not be obtained.

Incidence of overhead

Some of the indirect expenses, or overhead, of an undertaking are, within limits, "fixed"—that is to say they do not fluctuate with changes in the volume of output. In consequence, any reduction of output results in an increased cost of production per unit of output. This is a factor of outstanding significance, and lies at the basis of all schemes of remuneration. The following will be seen to be involved:

(a) volume of output to be achieved,
(b) time which can be saved in producing it.

Fig. 42 will make the point clear.

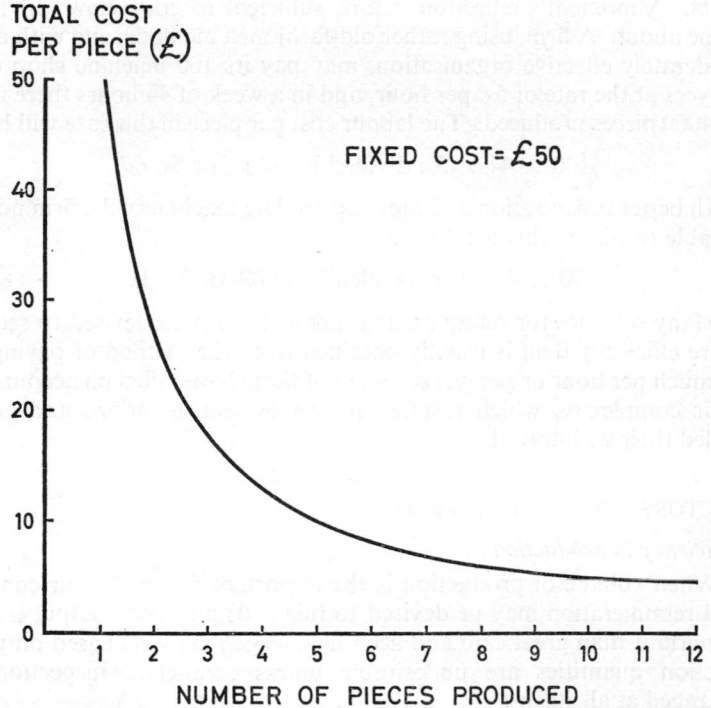

FIG. 42.—*Overhead Cost Curve*

This curve illustrates the fact that the presence of a fixed element in the Overhead has a marked effect on the cost per piece as the volume of output rises. Hence the importance of achieving greater productivity by well-chosen schemes of remuneration.

Labour turnover

As has already been pointed out, any excessive amount in the number of changes in employees involves the concern in a loss, and creates an atmosphere of uncertainty, so that when deciding upon the wages system, this aspect of the subject should be considered in order to see how far it is possible to create the right conditions for a contented body of employees.

METHODS OF REMUNERATION

1. TIME-WORK OR DAY-WORK METHOD

In this case the payment to the workers is based on the formula

Earnings = Clock hours worked × Rate per hour,

which may be conveniently shortened into

$$E = CHW . RH$$

(NOTE.—An extra premium is paid for overtime work.)

Let it be said at once that many large works operate successfully under this method of payment, but keen management and supervision are essential, because of the inherent tendency of employees

(*a*) to work no harder than necessary to "get by,"
(*b*) to refrain from seeking the next job to be done,
(*c*) to wait, rather than ask, for instructions from the foreman,
(*d*) to make the job last out until the next work break.

There are circumstances in which time wages are particularly advantageous, as, for example, in the Tool-room and Pattern Shop. Here the work demands a high degree of skill—the error in a jig being only one-tenth of that allowed in the finished work—and it is far more important that accuracy be maintained than speed. Indirect labourers, such as sweepers and cleaners, night watchmen, boiler-house stokers, and inspection staff, are all most suitably paid on a time basis.

Time work does, however, tend as a general rule to raise production costs, because it does not offer monetary reward for special effort, and thereby fails to secure anything like the maximum output.

Its chief merit is its simplicity: it is easy to understand, and it is easy to make the wage calculations required. Some manufacturers, indeed, are of the opinion that this simplicity outweighs other considerations, and they hold the opinion that, if the day rates are made high enough, the method is as effective as any other. The most notable adherent to this high-wages plan was Henry Ford, and he and other manufacturers have proved that high wages do not necessarily imply high costs, but that many costs are higher than they should be because of low wages, which command only the less-efficient workers. The *High-wages Plan* may be summarised as follows:

(a) A high rate of wages per hour is paid.

(b) Special interest and effort in the work is demanded.

(c) The high wages offered attract those who are confident of their own abilities, and are willing to pit their skill against a rather exacting standard.

(d) Standards of efficiency and output are set, which foremen are required to maintain. Work is set for each man to do, and he must do it. Often, as in Ford's or Vauxhall's, the work progresses on a conveyor, and each man must complete his operation within certain distance limits. Supervision is strict throughout the day.

(e) The work set is not more than can be accomplished by a competent worker, without undue fatigue, day after day. Overtime work, generally speaking, is not permitted.

Apart from the introduction of this High-wages Plan, the general characteristic of time wages is that the employee receives nothing beyond his CHW . RH, and the employer takes all the loss arising from his employees' inefficiency, and all the gain arising from their extra efficiency.

2. PIECE-WORK

This method is usually broken down into two major sub-divisions— straight piece-work and piece-work using differential rates.

(a) STRAIGHT PIECE-WORK

This method of payment lies, as it were, at the opposite pole to time wages, because here it is the employee who now stands to gain or lose as a result of the standard of efficiency which he attains.

The danger inherent in it is that production may be encouraged at the expense of the quality of production, so that a strict inspection of the work has to be provided. This additional cost offsets the fact that less supervision may be required.

There is another aspect of the matter, which is often not realised by piece-workers. They will, generally speaking, strive to increase their output, but at times they are satisfied with what they regard as a reasonable wage, and they then slacken off. They may even go home early, or absent themselves, being under the impression that it is only they who are the losers thereby; they overlook the fact that factory overhead is incurred and is part of the cost of production, so that any reduction in output is bound to result in some increase in the total cost per unit. For this reason piece-workers should be required to record their gate times in the same way as those on time wages, and also, normally, job times can also be required with advantage.

The information thus obtained will be useful in computing the cost of idleness.

The formula for the piece-work method of payment is

$$\text{Earnings} = \text{Number of units} \times \text{rate per unit,}$$

or, put more briefly

$$E = NU \cdot RU.$$

The basis for the piece-rate is usually the comparable time-rate for the same class of worker, but this basic rate is increased to constitute an inducement to greater output. At the same time the number of units which may be expected in a given time has to be established with great accuracy.

EXAMPLE

In a particular job of work the following factors apply:

> Basic hourly rate $= 5s.$
> Increase on rate to be 20%.
> Adjusted hourly rate is therefore $6s.$
> Output expected $= 12$ units per hour.

The piece-work rate is therefore

$$E = NU \cdot RU = 120\% \text{ CHW} \cdot \text{RH.}$$
$$12y = 1 \cdot 2 \times 1 \times 5$$
$$y = 6s. \text{ divided by 12, or } 6d.$$

That is, *the rate per unit is fixed at 6d.*

If therefore a worker produces 120 units in an 8-hour day he will be paid $120 \times 6d.$, or £3, which is a gain of £1 over the comparable time wages for the day's work. On the other hand, if he produces only 80 units he will be paid $80 \times 6d.$ or £2, which is the same as time wages for the day, viz., $8 \times 5s.$

It will be seen from the example that although the *labour* cost per unit remains the same, and the employer makes no payment for units not produced, yet the *total* cost per unit will vary considerably, owing to the incidence of overhead, as has already been shown.

It should be borne in mind that there is almost always one qualification to the above remarks, in that it is the rule that a time basis of payment is provided for piece-workers in cases where non-production is beyond their control, *e.g.* failure of machinery, waiting for work, etc.

(b) DIFFERENTIAL PIECE-WORK RATES

(i) The Taylor System

A scheme to increase the output of workers was introduced in the U.S.A. by Dr. F. W. Taylor, and it combines the time taken with the quantity of work produced, so that differential rates are paid. The rate rises abruptly as the output obtained in the allotted time increases beyond a stated quantity per hour. Rate-fixing for this scheme must be scientific if it is to be successfully applied, and the workers must be convinced that it has been done fairly and reasonably. A reference to rate-fixing is on p. 212.

The chief features of the scheme, as outlined by Taylor, are as follows:

1. Day wages are not guaranteed.
2. A standard time for a job is computed by the Ratefixer, so that what is demanded of the workers is entirely just, and such as can be reasonably accomplished.
3. Two piece-work rates are fixed, so that if the worker does the work in less than the standard time he receives the higher piece-rate, whereas, if he takes longer he receives the lower rate.
4. Thus, remunerate each workman well if he accomplishes his task, but make sure that when a worker fails to do so he will be the loser thereby.

EXAMPLE

The following particulars apply to a particular work process:

Standard time allowed = 100 units per hour.
Normal time rate per hour = 5s.
Differentials to be applied:
80% of piece-rate when below standard.
120% of piece-rate when at or above standard.

In an 8-hour day:

Worker A completes 700 units.
„ B „ 900 „

Now, as before,

$E = NU \cdot RU$, and $CHW \cdot RH = 8 \times 5s$.
RU therefore equals 40 divided by 800
or $0.6d$.

This means that Worker A would be paid

700 units at 80% of $0.6d$. per unit
or 28s.

And Worker B would be paid

900 units at 120% of $0.6d$. per unit
or 54s.

The sharp jump between $0.48d$. per unit in one case, to $0.72d$. per unit in the other will, perhaps, explain why the Taylor system has never been popular. Indeed, the lower rate has been regarded as "punitive" and "unfair."

(ii) The Merrick Differential or Multiple Piece-rate

This scheme is the same in essentials to the Taylor system, but with the following modifications:

1. The punitive lower piece-rate is not imposed.
2. Instead of one differential, there are several.

Thus,

> Up to standard—taken as 100% efficiency—100% of basic rate.
> 100–120% efficiency—108% of basic rate.
> Above 120% efficiency—120% of basic rate.

3. COMBINATIONS OF TIME AND PIECE-WORK

(i) Emerson's Efficiency System

This is another American scheme, which combines ordinary fixed day wages with a differential piece-rate. It is not, however, effective when efficiency is much above the 100% standard.

As reference is being made to "efficiency," it is, perhaps, opportune at this point to consider what is meant by it. By 100% efficiency is meant, not perfection, as might be supposed from thinking of 100% pass in an examination, but the normal rate of working of a good average worker, allowing for fatigue, personal time, etc. In other words, it is the rate of working which a worker can be expected to keep up from day to day without suffering any ill effects, either physical or mental. On one hand of this standard is 150%, which is regarded as corresponding to the un-hurried precision of a machine working without breakdown, and on the other hand is 60–62½% efficiency, which the workers paid by time wages, without time-and-motion study being applied, are likely to find just sufficient to "get by."

Under the Emerson scheme

1. Day wages are guaranteed.
2. A volume of output, decided upon from previous output records and test observations, is taken as standard (100% efficiency).
3. A bonus is paid to a worker whose output exceeds two-thirds (66⅔% efficiency) of the standard in any one week.
4. The bonus increases in a stated ratio to the increasing output up to and beyond the 100% efficiency level, and this bonus has to be calculated from special tables. Emerson used about thirty-two differential steps.

It will be seen that this scheme is far different from the Taylor system, and is founded on the philosophy of encouraging the slower worker to do a little better than before. Bonus begins at a low rate of efficiency, and therefore the scheme can be used as a means of transition from time wages to piece-work.

(ii) Gantt Task and Bonus Scheme

This is really a combination of day wages and a high piece-rate. It is regarded as being an extremely strong scheme. The main features are:

1. Day wages are guaranteed.
2. A definite task is set on which a bonus may be earned if completed within the standard time allowed.
3. The time allowed is computed on the same basis as for the Taylor system, *i.e.* a standard time.
4. The bonus is a fixed percentage on the time taken, if standard is reached.
5. If more than time allowed is taken day wages are paid without bonus, but if less, then a high piece rate takes the place of bonus.
6. The time and bonus are fixed for each job, and when a job is completed the man goes on with the next. The pay earned thus consists of day wages plus the sum of any bonuses for which the worker has qualified; or the high piece rate, which is better still.
7. The foreman may receive a bonus if the workers reach the standard of efficiency qualifying for a bonus.

The earnings may be gathered from the following assumed figures:

Job No.	Standard time	Time taken (hours)	Day rate 5s. p.h.	Bonus (say)	Total earnings
1	5	3	Not applicable		High piece rate
2	6	6	30s.	10s.	40s.
3	4	5	25s.	—	25s.
4	7	6	Not applicable		High piece rate

(iii) Bedaux Scheme, or schemes after this pattern

Very accurate time study is applied to every operation, and a standard minute of work is evolved, which represents a fraction of work plus a fraction of rest for fatigue, etc. Thus each standard minute of work is to be done in one minute, and each operation to be performed can be expressed as being so many standard minutes of work to be produced, or "B's." Payment is then made on the basis of the number of "B's" which have been credited to the worker.

Time wages are paid until the 100% efficiency rate is reached, so that this scheme is a real incentive to higher output above that level. Moreover, since it is possible to put up on a notice-board the "B's" earned by each worker in the department a competitive element is introduced which acts as an additional spur to production.

When the scheme was originally introduced the worker received only 75% of the bonus, the other 25% being diverted to "supervision." This made the scheme most unpopular, and it has since been amended to allow 100% of the bonus to be paid to the worker. Nowadays, similar schemes to the Bedaux are often adopted, and are referred to as "points schemes."

For its successful operation, a good system of production control is required to be in operation, and the "B's" allowed for each operation must be clearly indicated on the job tickets.

4. BARTH SCHEME

This scheme is unlike any of those which have so far been considered, and is especially applicable to apprentices or beginners, until they become proficient enough to go on to some other scheme. The formula for it is

$$\text{Earnings} = \text{The rate per hour} \times \sqrt{\frac{\text{Standard}}{\text{Hours}} \times \frac{\text{Clock Hours}}{\text{Worked}}}$$

or

$$E = RH \cdot \sqrt{SH \times CHW}$$

This would be applied in practice as follows:

> Rate per hour = 5s.
> Standard hours allowed = 3.
> Time taken = 5 hours.
> Earnings = $5\sqrt{3 \times 5}$ $5 \times \sqrt{15}$
> = 5 × 3·873s.
> = 19s. 4d.

For an additional note on this Scheme see p. 96.

5. PREMIUM BONUS METHODS OF PAYMENT

It has been seen that time wages are characterised by the fact that the employer gains or loses according to the degree of efficiency of the workers, whereas under the piece-work methods it is the employee who bears the brunt of inefficiency and secures the rewards of speed and skill.

The premium bonus schemes introduce a different principle, for they are a combination of time wages and a piece-rate, so that gains and losses in labour efficiency are shared by employer and employee. The premium bonus to be paid is calculated on the hours saved, that is the difference between time allowed and time taken. However, as the bonus is brought into operation at a low rate of efficiency, the incentive to greater production tends to be extremely ineffective. This is true however carefully the standard time is fixed; but, having regard to the loose way in which ratefixing is often done, it is not difficult to see why only limited use has been made of these schemes. Either the terms have been too liberal, and the business has suffered in consequence, or the terms have been too low to make any difference. Opposition to these schemes has also been encountered from the trade unions because of the principle of sharing between employer and employed.

The chief schemes to be noted under this heading are three in number as outlined below, the first two, being similar, are dealt with together.

(i) *The Halsey scheme and the Halsey–Weir scheme*

The essential feature of both these schemes is that the worker is given a bonus of a fixed percentage of the time saved. In the Halsey scheme the bonus is 50%, but in the Weir scheme it is 30%. Other percentages may be met with in practice, but the method is precisely the same in all cases.

The job is timed to establish the normal rate of working of the good average employee, and this is given the efficiency rating of 100%. To this is added a percentage which will give the worker a bonus of $33\frac{1}{3}\%$, so that he can earn time and one-third, *i.e.* 50% of the *time saved*, if the job is completed in the standard time.

EXAMPLE

The following times and rates apply to a job of work:

Standard time for job (100% efficiency)	3 hours.
Add $66\frac{2}{3}\%$	2 hours.
Job time allowed (60% efficiency)	5 hours.

Basic rate of pay 5s. per hour.

If the employee does the work in the 5 hours allowed he receives no bonus, as no time has been saved. He will therefore be paid 5 hours × 5s. or 25s.

If he does the work in 4 hours he saves an hour, and will therefore obtain a bonus of $\frac{1}{2}$ hour. He will therefore be paid 22s. 6d. for 4 hours work, which means that his rate per hour has increased from 5s. to 5s. $7\frac{1}{2}d$.

Full bonus will be earned if the worker does the work in the normal estimated time of 3 hours, for he will then be paid as though he had done 4 hours work, which is time and one-third: his hourly rate being equivalent to 6s. 8d.

Reducing this scheme to a formula, we have

Earnings =

$$\begin{pmatrix} \text{Clock} \\ \text{hours} \\ \text{worked} \end{pmatrix} \times \begin{pmatrix} \text{Rate} \\ \text{per} \\ \text{hour} \end{pmatrix} + \tfrac{1}{2} \begin{pmatrix} \text{Time} \\ \text{allowed} \end{pmatrix} - \begin{pmatrix} \text{Clock} \\ \text{hours} \\ \text{worked} \end{pmatrix} \times \begin{pmatrix} \text{Rate} \\ \text{per} \\ \text{hour} \end{pmatrix}$$

or, more briefly

$$E = CHW \cdot RH + \cdot5(TA - CHW)RH.$$

It should be noted that the worker has a guaranteed fixed hourly rate, even if he cannot do the work in less than the generous amount of time allotted.

(ii) The Rowan scheme

This scheme was introduced by David Rowan of Glasgow in 1901. As before, the premium to be paid as bonus is based on time saved, but instead of a fixed percentage being taken, as in the Halsey scheme, a *proportion* is taken. This proportion is that which the time saved bears to the time allowed, and this may be passed on to the worker either

(a) as an adjustment of the rate per hour, or
(b) as an addition to the normal time wages.

The application of each of these methods would be as follows:

Method (a)

$$E = CHW\left(RH + \frac{TA - CHW}{TA} \cdot RH\right).$$

Assume   Time allowed = 5 hours.
                       Clock hours worked = 4 hours.
                       Rate per hour = 5s.

Using the above formula

$$E = 4(5s. + \frac{5 - 4}{5} 5s.)$$
$$= 4 \times 6s.$$
$$= 24s.$$

Method (b)

$$E = CHW \cdot RH + \frac{TA . - CHW}{TA} (CHW . RH).$$
$$= 20s. + \frac{20s.}{5}$$
$$= 24s.$$

As in the Halsey scheme, the premium bonus is payable from about the 60% efficiency level—often it is made to begin from the $62\frac{1}{2}\%$ level—but in this case as soon as 50% saving of time has been reached the worker finds that his increase of wages is at a diminishing rate.

6. ACCELERATING PREMIUM BONUS

In this case the bonus to be paid is not a fixed percentage as in the Halsey, nor a decreasing proportion as in the Rowan, but is a bonus which increases at a faster and faster rate.

Obviously, it is a powerful incentive to higher output, but is perhaps unsuitable for the machine operator, who will tend to rush his work through. It is, however, valuable as a means of inducing supervisors and foreman to obtain the maximum production possible from the men under them.

Unfortunately, there is no simple formula for such a scheme, but the graph of $y = 0.8x^2$ gives a clue to the general picture.

$$
\begin{array}{lccccc}
\text{Let } x = & 1 & 1\cdot2 & 1\cdot4 & 1\cdot6 & 1\cdot8 \\
\text{Then } x^2 & 1 & 1\cdot44 & 1\cdot96 & 2\cdot56 & 3\cdot24 \\
0\cdot8x^2 = y & 0\cdot8 & 1\cdot15 & 1\cdot57 & 2\cdot05 & 2\cdot59
\end{array}
$$

Multiplying these results for x and y by 100 gives percentage wages earned (y) against percentage efficiency (x).

This seems to be a practical equation, as will be seen from Fig. 43, and at 150% efficiency gives earnings of 175% of basic wages.

It should be noted incidentally that the Barth Scheme to which reference was made on p. 93 would be unsuitable as an accelerating bonus method, as its rate of increase is much too slow, yielding as it does less than 120% of basic wages even at 140% efficiency.

TABLE I

$\dfrac{\%\ Efficiency}{\dfrac{\text{TA}}{\text{CHW}}}$ %	20	40	60	80	100	120	140	160
Number of units	9·6	19·2	28·8	38·4	48	57·6	67·2	76·8
Standard time, *i.e.* TA	1·6	3·2	4·8	6·4	8	9·6	11·2	12·8
TA for Halsey and Rowan	2·66	5·33	8	10·66	13·33	16·0	18·66	21·33
$\dfrac{\text{E}}{\text{CHW . RH}}$ %	Earnings in shillings (Basic/Percentage)							
Time	40/100	40/100	40/100	40/100	40/100	40/100	40/100	40/100
Piece-work	8/20	16/40	24/60	32/80	40/100	48/120	56/140	64/160
Taylor	6·4/16	12·8/32	19·2/48	25·6/64	48/120	57·6/144	67·2/168	76·8/192
Gantt	40/100	40/100	40/100	40/100	40/100	51·6/129	51·6/129	51·6/129
Barth	17·9/45	25·3/63	31/78	35·8/90	40/100	Use another scheme		
Halsey 50%	40/100	40/100	40/100	46·7/117	53·4/133	60/150	66·6/166	73·4/183
Rowan	40/100	40/100	40/100	50/125	56/140	60/150	62·8/157	65/163
Accelerating Premium	Use another scheme				32/80	46/115	62·8/157	82/205

1. The oblique strokes used in both Tables I and II are merely for separation purposes and are not meant to indicate fractional quantities.

2. The student will see that the number of units expected in an 8-hour day depends on the efficiency attained, *e.g.* 60% of 48 is 28·8.

3. In the same way, the standard times are calculated from the basic 8 standard hours of work to be produced in an 8-hour day.

4. The time allowed for the Halsey and Rowan schemes is calculated by adding two-thirds to the standard time.

5. The basic earnings for each scheme are given in shillings and decimals of a shilling, and have been worked out in accordance with the formulas already stated. In the case of piece-work, for the sake of comparison with other schemes, no addition has been given to the basic rate, so that

$$
\text{NU . RU} = \text{CHW . RH}
$$
$$
48 \times 10d. = 8 \times 5s.
$$

This would not accord with practice, for piece-work would not be effective unless some inducement was offered over and above mere time rates.

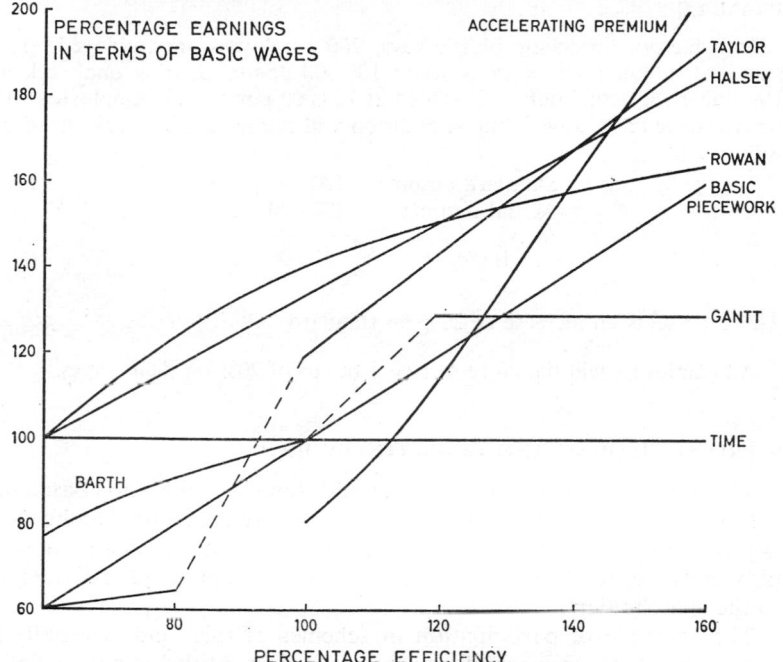

FIG. 43.—*Percentage Earnings and Efficiency*

From this graph can be seen the characteristic earnings curves of the schemes referred to in Table I. In particular, note that some of them begin to pay bonus from about $62\frac{1}{2}\%$ efficiency. The Gantt system is a powerful incentive to raise production from 100% to 120% efficiency.

7. COLLECTIVE BONUS SCHEMES

In many factories it is possible to arrange a group of employees to work together as a team, *e.g.* on assembly work, and then to pay them a bonus on the results of their production. This is shared out in agreed proportions between them.

The intention is to create a collective interest in the work, each group enforcing its own standards of efficiency; and by this means high output and economical production is achieved.

8. PRIESTMAN'S PRODUCTION BONUS

A standard is set for the output to be achieved weekly by a factory; this standard being measured in terms of units or points. The actual output, valued on the same basis, is compared with the standard, and if actual exceeds standard the employees are paid a bonus in proportion to the increase.

EXAMPLE

In a factory producing plastic toys, 200 employees are employed. The standard output for a week is set at 100,000 points. During one week in December the actual output is valued at 120,000 points. The employees will receive their basic wages, but in addition will receive a bonus calculated as follows:

Standard output:	100,000	points.
Actual output:	120,000	,,
Increase	20,000	,,

This represents an increase of 20% on standard.

All employees will therefore receive a bonus of 20% on their wages.

9. PROFIT SHARING AND CO-PARTNERSHIP

These methods of giving employees additional remuneration based on the prosperity of the concern are becoming more widespread and growing in importance. In one such scheme the amount shared among employees amounted to more than six times the sum paid in net dividends to the shareholders.

The principle of participation in schemes of this kind is usually a certain length of service, and employees are then entitled to a bonus of a percentage on their annual earnings. The shareholders have to receive a basic minimum first of all, but then the bonus to employees may increase as and when the shareholders receive more dividend.

A co-partnership scheme is often arranged in conjunction with a profit-sharing scheme, allowing the bonus to be left with the company as shares, or as a loan carrying generous interest. If at the same time a high wages plan is in operation the employees may well feel that they are being very fairly treated; morale will be high, and labour turnover will be low.

The student should note that details of profit-sharing and co-partnership schemes are given from time to time in Companies' Annual Reports, and will repay study. Each and every attempt to increase productivity must be carefully considered, and it would appear that many concerns are finding that the answer to their labour cost problems lies in this direction.

Advantage to Employers

1. Increased productivity.
2. Reduced labour turnover.
3. Greater care used in machine handling.
4. Higher employee morale.

TABLE II

% Efficiency	20	40	60	80	100	120	140	160
Number of units	9·6	19·2	28·8	38·4	48	57·6	67·2	76·8
Earnings/Rate per unit								
Time	40/50	40/25	40/16·6	40/12·5	40/10	40/8·3	40/7·1	40/6·3
Piece-work	8/10	16/10	24/10	32/10	40/10	48/10	56/10	64/10
Taylor	6·4/8	12·8/8	19·2/8	25·6/8	48/10	57·6/12	67·2/12	76·8/12
Gantt	40/50	40/25	40/16·6	40/12·5	40/10	51·6/10·70	51·6/9·20	51·6/8·00
Barth	17·9/22·4	25·3/15·80	31/12·9	35·8/11·1	40/10	Use another scheme		
Halsey	40/50	40/25	40/16·6	46·7/14·6	53·4/13·3	60/12·5	66·6/11·9	73·4/11·4
Rowan	40/50	40/25	40/16·6	50/15·6	56/14·0	60/12·5	62·8/11·2	65/10·2
A.P.	Use another scheme				32/8	46/11	62·8/13	82/14·6

NOTE.—The Labour cost per unit has been expressed in pence.

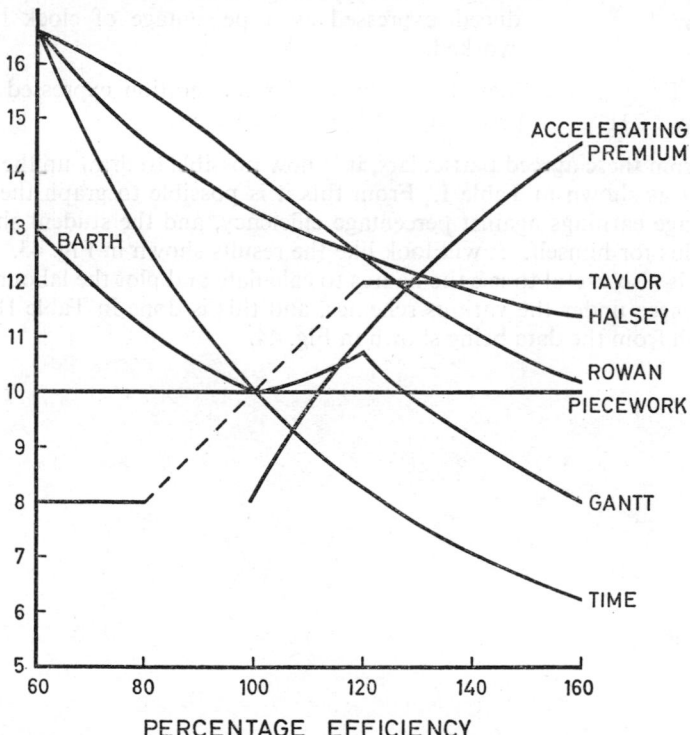

LABOUR COST PER PIECE (PENCE)

PERCENTAGE EFFICIENCY

FIG. 44.—*Labour Cost Curves*

In this graph, based on the details of Table II, is shown the way in which the labour cost per piece falls or rises as changes in efficiency take place. The Gantt scheme shows up favourably, for after the expected check at 120%, it begins to fall again steadily.

COMPARISON OF SCHEMES

It is a valuable exercise to compare the relative merits of the schemes which have been considered by showing the characteristic picture they make on a graph.

It is necessary to take certain basic data as agreed, and it is therefore being assumed as follows:

CHW, or clock hours worked = 8 hours.

RH, or rate per hour = 5s.

SH, or standard hours = varies.

TA, or time allowed, may be the same as SH, or, as in the case of the Halsey and Rowan schemes, may be increased from SH by $66\frac{2}{3}\%$.

NU, or number of units to be produced = 48 in an 8-hour day at 100% efficiency.

$\dfrac{TA}{CHW}\%$ Percentage efficiency, being standard hours of work produced expressed as a percentage of clock hours worked.

$\dfrac{E}{CHW \cdot RH}\%$ Earnings, being the total remuneration expressed as a percentage of basic time wages.

From these agreed particulars, it is now possible to draw up the data sheet as shown in Table I. From this it is possible to graph the percentage earnings against percentage efficiency, and the student should do this for himself. It will look like the results shown in Fig. 43.

It is also useful to use the figures to calculate and plot the labour cost per piece under the various schemes, and this is done in Table II, the graph from the data being shown in Fig. 44.

CHAPTER 9

WAGES

PREPARATION AND PAYMENT OF WAGES

WAGES SHEET

Whichever method of timekeeping is adopted, the wages due to the workers are entered up on the Payroll or Wages Sheets, a specimen of which is shown in Fig. 45.

Before making any entries, however, the calculation of the wages payable to each worker must have been checked, especially noting that all overtime has been properly authorised; and the gate times upon which payment is made must have been reconciled with the job-time records and idle-time cards for each worker.

All this work takes time, and often it is necessary to arrange for several days "lying time." This is the time which elapses before workers are paid for the week's work which they have completed. This temporary hardship at the end of their first week's employment is overcome by making them a temporary "sub" or loan. At the termination of their employment, however, they receive payment right up to the date of leaving, so that they lose nothing in the long run.

If the numbers employed are fairly large it may be considered desirable to preprint the Wages Sheets, and employees' pay slips, with certain standard information. Addressograph Ltd. make a metal plate on which can be recorded

Worker's name	Clock No.
Rate of pay	Standard deductions
Income Tax code no.	

and the metal of the plate is soft enough to allow for any alterations to be made should they become necessary.

It is convenient if a separate Wages Sheet is commenced for each department or cost centre, because in this way the actual wages incurred may be compared with the budgeted amount for that department, and a departmental labour rate may be easily calculated by dividing the total wages for the department by the direct labour hours incurred. It also materially assists in spreading the amount of work to be done.

As each clock card is entered, it is easy to check that it refers to the person whose particulars have been pre-printed on the Wages Sheet. The entries may be made either by hand or by accounting machine. In

PAYROLL

No.	Name	Total hours worked	Rate	Basic pay		Over-time premium		Gross pay		Free pay		Taxable pay to date		Tax due to date		Tax refunds		Deductions						Net pay		Em-ployer Nat. Ins.	
																		Tax		Nat. Ins.		Total					
				£	s. d.	£	s. d.	£	s. d.	£	s. d.	£	s. d.	£	s. d.	£	s. d.	£	s. d.	£	s. d.	£	s. d.	£	s. d.	s. d.

FIG. 45.—*Payroll*

This specimen of a payroll allows for an additional wages column to be used for a particular purpose such as Overtime premium. Most firms have them specially printed to suit their own requirements.

very large factories the wages are automatically tabulated from punched cards.

It is strongly recommended that in drawing up the Wages Sheet a distinction be made between

(*a*) normal time worked,
(*b*) overtime hours worked,
(*c*) overtime premium hours.

This is because (*a*) and (*b*) are both wanted for record purposes, and will be charged as Direct Labour in the case of Production Departments. The sum of (*a*) and (*b*) divided into the gross wages payable under these headings will also give the direct labour cost per hour for the department concerned, and this is important for comparative purposes; (*c*), on the other hand, will almost always be charged as overhead.

The Wages Sheets are now passed to another clerk for the Income Tax Record Cards and the tax columns on the Wages Sheets to be completed. This division of labour acts as a valuable internal check, for this second clerk would be specifically instructed to report any extraordinary increase in the earnings of any worker, and to list the names of those without tax records and to whom the emergency coding had been applied. Some firms, indeed, go so far as to withhold the pay of any worker who has not produced his Tax Record Card, and his National Insurance Card.

The remaining deduction columns, the net payable column, and the employer's contribution column, are now completed, and, if possible, by a third clerk. This clerk will also total the Wages Sheets, section by section, check the cross casts, and prepare the grand summary sheet.

CASH

As each section of the Wages Sheets is completed it is passed to the Cashier, who forthwith enters it on a Cash Summary Sheet. This shows the breakdown of the net payable column into £, 10s., silver, 3d., and copper required in order to make up the wage packets (*see* Fig. 46).

When the money is drawn from the Bank it is checked in the Cashier's department in total, and ranged in bundles of twenty notes, columns of £1 in silver, 1s. in 3d. pieces, 1s. in copper. The amounts required to make up the wages of the first section, as shown on the Cash Summary Sheet, are now counted out on to a "making-up" table. The pay envelopes for the section having been filled, there should be no cash remaining on that table. The amounts for the second and subsequent sections are similarly dealt with until all the wages have been put into the pay envelopes.

Department	Notes		Silver	3d.	Copper
	£	10s.			

FIG. 46.—*Cash Summary Sheet*

This is useful for summarising the cash required to make up the wages of each department. It could be provided with a total column if thought necessary, but it is not difficult to manage without it.

By following this routine carefully, any discrepancy is localised at once, and any checking over is confined to relatively few wage packets.

PAYING OUT WAGES

Payment of wages in a factory will be made, if possible, at one and the same time in all or several departments, to prevent any opportunity for a worker to be in two places. The clerk in the Cashier's Department should be a responsible person, and he should have the help of the departmental foreman, who will be present at the paying out, in order to identify the workers under him. In some cases workers are provided with brass discs bearing their clock number, and may be asked to call their names and show their discs. Alternatively, workers are often given their completed clock cards for prior examination. They initial these, and hand them in as a receipt for their wage packet.

The wage packets of absentees are entered in an "Unclaimed Wages Book" before being returned to the safe; and they should be signed for when subsequently claimed. No wages should be handed to anyone purporting to act on behalf of an absentee unless and until a written authority has been received from the employee. This authority should then be filed for reference.

A close check should always be kept on National Insurance Card and Tax Records, as they are an excellent guide to the correctness of the names and attendance of those on the Wages Sheets, but addresses should be checked with the personnel record sheet. In the case of men working on civil-engineering contracts, where a foreman can give a man his cards at a moment's notice, it used to be possible for the Wages Sheets to carry fictitious names of men supposed to have been engaged and sacked within a week. There is now no longer such a possibility, as it is usual for National Insurance Cards and Holidays with Pay Cards to be sent to Head Office, and wages are not paid until the cards are received. Any employee who has left in such circumstances as envisaged above must also make application in writing, and any pay due to him is sent by post direct.

ACCOUNTING ENTRIES FOR WAGES

In considering the entries to be made in the books to record wages, two matters have first to be decided:

(a) how is overtime to be treated?
(b) what is to be done with the employer's part of National Insurance?

Overtime

It has already been suggested that the ordinary hours of overtime be treated as direct labour hours, in the case of workers in Production Departments. Most overtime is called for because of general factory conditions, and, therefore, in considering the quantity of work produced we are not particularly concerned whether it was done at 11 a.m. or at 4 p.m. or 8 p.m. On the other hand, the overtime *premium* incurred is an additional indirect cost, and is not chargeable to the cost of the job or process, but should be treated as overhead. The only exception to this method of treatment would be when the overtime is specifically worked for a particular order or contract, and it can then be charged as part of the direct cost of the job (*see* p. 135).

National Insurance (Employers)

In financial book-keeping the custom is to charge the employers' part of National Insurance as an addition to the Wages and Salaries, and this is quite reasonable so long as detailed and analysed accounts are not required. When, however, as in Job Costing, each operative's time has to be divided between a number of jobs or operations, practical difficulties are raised, and these may be overcome in one of two ways:

(a) either an additional rate per hour may be charged to cover the employers' National Insurance

$$e.g.\ 48\tfrac{1}{2} \times 2d.\ \text{equals } 8s.\ 1d.$$

(b) or the National Insurance may be treated as an overhead.

As method (a) is usually time-wasting to apply, especially when the hours worked are different from the normal expected, it is recommended that method (b) be adopted.

WAGES ANALYSIS BOOK

With these assumptions, the accounting entries may now be prepared, and it will be found convenient in practice to make use of a Wages Analysis Book for the purpose.

The ruling for such a book is shown in Fig. 47, and it will be seen that provision is made for entering the wages by departments, and extending

Date	Total	Work in Progress	Factory Overhead Control	Administration Overhead Control	Selling and Distribution Overhead Control
Department					

Total	Net Cheque	Deduction Accounts			
		Tax	National Insurance	National Savings	Sick Club

FIG. 47.—*Wages Analysis Book*

An analysis of the wages to the main control accounts is essential for accounting purposes. The lower half of the figure is the credit side, for use in an integral system of accounts. If the cost accounts are separate from the financial accounts only one credit posting would be required—to the General Ledger Adjustment Account.

them to the various control accounts, viz., Work-in-progress, Factory Overhead Control Account, Administration Overhead Control Account, and Selling and Distribution Overhead Control Account.

The sources of information for compiling this series of extensions are as follows:

1. Wages Sheets.
2. Job-time cards for work-in-progress.
3. Idle-time cards.

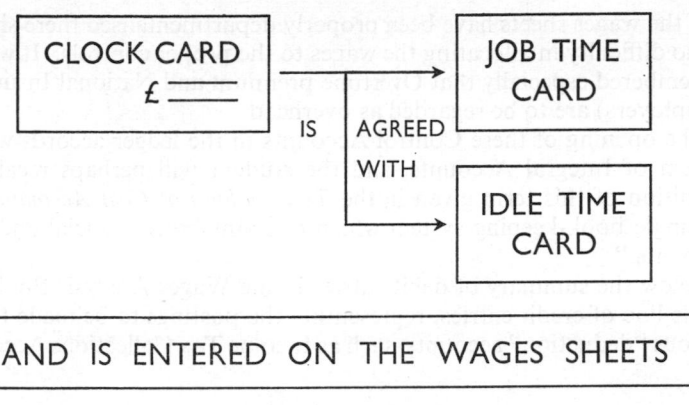

AND IS ENTERED ON THE WAGES SHEETS

WHICH ARE ANALYSED

DATE & DEPARTMENT	TOTAL	WORK IN PROGRESS	FACTORY O.CONTROL	ADMINISTN O.CONTROL	SELLING & DISTN O.CONTROL
		WAGES ANALYSIS BOOK			

FROM THIS WAGES ANALYSIS BOOK POSTINGS
ARE MADE TO WORK IN PROGRESS ACCOUNT
AND THE OTHER CONTROL ACCOUNTS

SUBSIDIARY RECORDS ARE IN LEDGERS OR

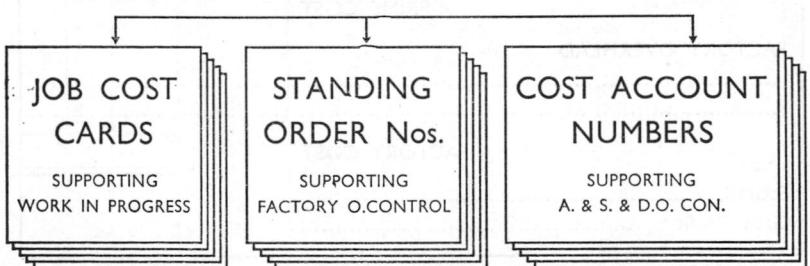

FIG. 48.—*Flow of Information for Labour Costs*

This chart summarises what has been stated in the text and in other figures. It shows how the information regarding Direct Labour Cost originates. Clock cards (but not Job Tickets) are used for Indirect Labour as well, and the information flows down in the same way.

If the wages sheets have been properly departmentalised there should be no difficulty in allocating the wages to the proper controls. It will be remembered especially that Overtime premium and National Insurance (Employers) are to be regarded as overhead.

The opening of these Control Accounts in the ledger accords with a system of Integral Accounts, and the student will perhaps recall the definition of this term given in the *Terminology of Cost Accountancy*: "a single book-keeping system which contains both financial and cost accounts."

Below the summary of debit entries in the Wages Analysis Book is a single line of credit entries, representing the postings to be made to the various "deduction" accounts, such as Income Tax Collections Account,

Date	**Order No.**	**Job No.** ....
Customer	**Estimate Ref.** ....
Job Description ....

MATERIALS

LABOUR

PRIME COST

FACTORY OVERHEAD

FACTORY COST

Estimate £...............
Gross Profit % ....

FIG. 49.—*Job Cost Card or Ledger Account*

The entries for materials will be picked up from stores requisitions, while those for labour will come from summaries of job tickets or from a Wages Abstract (Fig. 60). Factory Overhead will be added at pre-determined rates as described in Chapter 11. For another specimen of this type of record see Fig. 62.

National Insurance Collections Account—which contains both Employee's and Employer's contributions, Sick Club collections, and so on. The cross cast to agree the total is completed by the amount of the cheque for the net wages payable, and is posted from the Cash Book.

Putting the matter in diagrammatic form, the Ledger Accounts in the main books of account will be as shown in Fig. 48.

Furthermore, the job time cards of Wages Abstract (Fig. 60) which provided the total for work in progress will also provide the detailed entries on the job cost cards. Similarly, the Factory Overhead Control Account will be supported by the details contained in the Standing Order Numbers, which is the name often given to the subsidiary records relating to factory overhead. The details of the Administration Overhead Control Account and the Selling and Distribution Overhead Control Account will be contained in sets of Cost Account Numbers. A suggested ruling for a job cost card is given in Fig. 49, but rulings for Standing Order Numbers and Cost Account Numbers are given in the chapters dealing with overhead.

There are, of course, still many concerns which have separate financial and costing systems, and entries for wages on this basis are not difficult to arrange.

The Financial Accountant will no doubt keep a Wages Analysis Book himself, and allocate the wages to such headings as he may wish. He will also pick up the postings for the Deduction Accounts. Most important of all for the Cost Accountant, the Financial Accountant will post the total of the wages to a Cost Ledger Control Account. This is merely a memorandum account in his books, and forms no part of his double entry.

The Cost Accountant, for his part, will pick up the same figures as before in his Wages Analysis Book, and post the total to the *credit* of a General Ledger Adjustment Account. His cost books are now on a double-entry basis, and agreement between the Cost and Financial books is easily obtained through the Cost Ledger Control Account and the General Ledger Adjustment Account. The Cost books will not, of course, now include the Deduction Accounts, nor the posting from the Cash Book.

CHAPTER 10

OVERHEAD: CLASSIFICATION AND DISTRIBUTION

OVERHEAD is defined in the *Terminology of Cost Accountancy* as

"the aggregate of indirect material cost, indirect wages and indirect expense"

and by the word "indirect" in this connection is meant

"that which cannot be allocated, but which can be apportioned to, or absorbed by cost centres or cost units."

These sections of overhead may also be analysed into groups, viz.:

Production Overhead,
Administration Overhead,
Selling and Distribution Overhead.

Or again, for the purposes of Budgetary Control, they may be incorporated in departmental budgets.

And yet again, when marginal costing principles are to be applied, they may be subdivided into:

Fixed Overhead,
Semi-fixed Overhead,
Variable Overhead.

It is important, however, to grasp the fact that *it is the same overhead*, from whatever angle we are looking at it.

INDIRECT MATERIALS

In the course of manufacture of a product, various materials have to be purchased which do not themselves enter into the finished product. To take a simple example, a dustbin is made of galvanised metal, which is a *direct* cost. The side of the dustbin is either spot welded or seam welded, and the welding equipment requires the use of electrodes. These electrodes are an *indirect* material cost, and would be included within the "Production Overhead" group.

Again, some materials are used in such small quantities that it is often considered best to regard them as an indirect expense. In the manufacture of brooms and brushes, for example, pitch is sometimes used to assist in holding the tufts of fibres in place. This pitch is used in small, unmeasured quantities, and may satisfactorily be treated as being Production Overhead.

On the other hand, there are cases when materials which, at first sight, are "indirect" are regarded as "direct." In brick-making, for example, large amounts of coal or coke may be used in firing the kilns. This fuel does not enter into the finished product directly, but it may be said to do so in the form of applied heat to make a hard-baked brick, and therefore the fuel cost is treated as a "direct" cost.

As a general rule, it may be accepted that indirect materials are those which are used ancillary to manufacture and cannot be traced into the finished product.

INDIRECT WAGES

This comprises wages paid for all labour which does not help directly in changing the shape or composition of the raw materials from which a product is made. Obvious examples are the wages of factory foremen, the salaries of office executives, and the commission payable to representatives "on the road."

INDIRECT EXPENSES

Most expense items of expenditure are classified as "indirect," since they are incurred for the business as a whole rather than in regard to any particular order received or product made. Some items fall clearly under the head of production, administration, or selling and distribution, *e.g.* repairs of factory machinery; office stationery; advertising and catalogues. Other items, such as fire insurance, have to be suitably apportioned.

STANDING ORDER NUMBERS AND COST ACCOUNT NUMBERS

In order to systematise the analysis of overhead, and to ensure the grouping of like items with like in a convenient and expeditious manner, it is necessary to devise a syllabus of account headings, suitably coded. The guiding principle must be that the headings selected shall be clear and not to be confused one with another, and at the same time be sufficient in number to cover every contingency.

Standing Order Numbers are, by custom, applied to Factory expense headings; and Cost Account Numbers to Administration, and Selling and Distribution expense headings. The method of compilation is, however, the same in each case.

Some cost accountants like to use letter symbols as mnemonic aids, *e.g.* "R" for Repairs; "A" for Administration expenses; "S" for Selling expenses, and so on. Others prefer a decimal arrangement:

> 22 *Repairs to Buildings*
>
>> 2211 Repairs to foundry building
>> 2212 Repairs to power-house
>> 2213 Repairs to machine shop

or again:

> 27 *Maintenance of Plant*
>
>> 2711 Steam plant
>> 2712 Transmission
>> 2713 Electric-power plant

It should be noted that every business has its own particular scheme of nomenclature compiled to suit its own particular accounting organisation—the exception being that some industries have adopted a uniform system of accounting to which many of the firms engaged therein will conform.

The classification of Standing Order Numbers given below is a partial example only, and has been arranged on the decimal system because this is preferred for mechanical sorting and tabulating in conjunction with punched cards.

SECTION A—DEPARTMENTAL CODING

> 01 *Raw Material Store*
> 02 *Press Shop*
> 03 *Lathes*
>
>> 031 Capstans
>> 032 Turrets
>> 033 Centre
>
> 04 *Drilling machines*
>
>> 041 Horizontal
>> 042 Vertical
>> 043 Multiple
>
> 05 *Welding Shop*
>
>> 051 Multiple spot
>> 052 Single spot
>> 053 Seam
>> 054 Arc
>
> 06 *Grinding Shop*
>
>> 061 Surface
>> 062 Internal

SECTION B—CLASSIFICATION OF FACTORY OVERHEAD

11 *Supervision*

   111 Foremen

      111.01 Grade 1
      111.02 Grade 2

   112 Inspection

      112.01 Senior
      112.02 Assistants

12 *Internal transport*

   121 Drivers

      121.01 Fork lift truck
      121.02 Crane

13 *Sweepers and cleaners*

   131 Mechanical floor-scrubber
   132 Others

      132.01 Male
      132.02 Female

14 *Supplies*

   141 Machine tools

      141.01 Oils and grease
      141.02 Cotton waste

   142 Operators

      142.01 Overalls
      142.02 Goggles
      142.03 PVC gloves

   143 Factory-general

      143.01 Brooms
      143.02 Brushes
      143.03 Dustpans
      143.04 Dustbins
      143.05 Detergent powder
      143.06 Soap—green
      143.07   —liquid
      143.08   —toilet
        and so on

15 *Insurance—Factory*

   151 Fire
   152 Third Party

It follows from the above classification, that if a requisition was received from the press shop for a broom it would be referenced

143.01.02.

Again, if an overall was requisitioned for a capstan-lathe operator it would be coded

$$142.01.031.$$

the last number in each case giving the department concerned.

The classification would be continued to include the various headings required for service departments such as the Boiler-house, Plant Maintenance Department, Canteen, etc.

Entirely separate classifications would be prepared for the Cost Account Numbers required for Administration and Selling and Distribution analysis, but care must be taken to ensure that the reference numbers chosen do not in any way conflict with those used for Production Overhead.

Thus, suppose that the last main number used in the Factory overhead classification was 37, it would be advisable to leave a gap in the numbers and begin the Administration Classification with 51, and the Selling and Distribution Classification with say 81.

CLASSIFICATION OF ADMINISTRATION OVERHEAD

51 *Salaries*

 511 Executive and management

  511.01 Managing Director
  511.02 Secretary
  511.03 Cost Accountant

 512 Clerks

  512.01 Grade A
  512.02 Grade B

52 *Rent*
53 *Rates*

 531 General
 532 Water

54 *Printing and Stationery*
  and so on

CLASSIFICATION OF SELLING AND DISTRIBUTION OVERHEAD

81 *Salaries*

 811 Sales Manager
 812 Travellers
 813 Clerks

82 *Commissions*

 821 Sales Manager
 822 Travellers

83 *Catalogues*
>831 Catalogues
>832 Circulars and Price Lists

84 *Advertising*
>841 Newspapers
>842 Trade magazines
>843 Posters
>and so on

APPORTIONMENT OF OVERHEAD

The object of classifying overhead is to facilitate the correct apportionment to various departments, and thence to the cost units of production. The procedure follows the following general pattern:

1. All overhead is collected under the separate headings provided, *i.e.* the Standing Order Numbers and the Cost Account Numbers.
2. All the separate totals of expense in Standing Order Numbers are then apportioned to Production Departments and Service Departments.
3. The total overhead for each Service Department is then apportioned to the Departments which use those services, and this is repeated if necessary until all the overhead has been apportioned to Production Departments.
4. The final totals of overhead for the Production Departments are absorbed in such a way that each Works Order Number, or unit of production, is charged with its share of the overhead of the departments through which it passes.

Let us see how the plan operates.

1. COLLECTION OF OVERHEAD

There are four main sources of overhead:

(*a*) Invoices.
(*b*) Stores Requisitions.
(*c*) Wages Analysis Book.
(*d*) Journal entries.

(*a*) *Invoices*

In a hand-written accounting system the usual practice is for invoices to be entered in a Purchase Journal and extended into columns so that postings may be made to the nominal headings to be charged. In an integral costing system, however, these nominal headings may be conveniently grouped together under Control Accounts, and to make this

E

clear a specimen ruling of a Purchase Journal is given in Fig. 50. By this arrangement, all materials, of whatever kind, and for whatever purpose, find their way into the "Materials Control Account" and from thence the total of the Goods Received Notes will already have been posted to the Stores Ledger Control Account. Invoices for expense

Date	Suppliers	Total Creditors	Materials Control	Factory Overhead Control	Administration Overhead Control	Selling and Distribution Overhead Control	Payments in Advance	Accrued Charges

FIG. 50.—*Purchase Journal*

This is a specimen ruling of a Purchase Journal for costing purposes. The invoices are entered and allocated or apportioned to their respective Control Accounts. Note particularly the explanation of the two columns on the right as given in the text.

items are extended to one or more of the Overhead Control Accounts, as the case may be. The basis of this apportionment has to be the one most suitable to the type of expense. In some cases it might be relative areas of factory as compared with offices; in others there would be meter readings to act as a guide; and in yet others there would be technical estimates.

The accounting entries would therefore be:

Sundries   Dr.
  To Total Creditors Account
  Materials Control Account
  Factory Overhead Control Account
  Administration Overhead Control Account
  Selling and Distribution Overhead Account

It will be noted that in addition to the columns for the Control Accounts two others are provided, headed respectively as

Payments in Advance
Accrued charges.

The reason for these two headings is entirely one of practical convenience. In cases where invoices are received which cover a period, say January 1 to June 30, it is better to make use of these columns than to post the full amount at once to one of the Control Accounts, and thus throw out the agreement of the month's entries made to the Standing Order Numbers.

(b) Stores Requisitions

Stores Requisitions for "direct" materials are not now within our consideration, having already been dealt with in Chapter 5.

Those, however, which are for "indirect" materials will have been coded, and will therefore be posted to the debit of the respective Control Accounts, and credited to Stores Ledger Control Account.

(c) Wages Analysis Book

The accounting entries from the Wages Analysis Book have already been dealt with in Chapter 9, and it will be recalled that in addition to the Work-in-progress Account the various Overhead Control Accounts were also affected by items of indirect wages.

(d) Journal entries

The Journal entries referred to are the monthly apportionments from Payments in Advance and Accrued Charges.

The picture which the student should have in mind is therefore as shown in Fig. 51.

Subsidiary records

Standing Order Numbers—giving details of the Factory Overhead Control Account.

Cost Account Numbers—giving details of the Administration Overhead Control Account, and Selling and Distribution Overhead Control Account.

In the manner shown above the Control Accounts are built up from period to period, and indicate the cumulative amount of overhead incurred, while the subsidiary records give the information which would otherwise be given in Nominal Ledger Accounts.

2. ALLOCATION AND APPORTIONMENT

(a) Standing Order Numbers

The second stage of the general plan is to apportion the periodic total shown in the Factory Overhead Control Account to the Production and Service Departments.

This may be conveniently done as part of the ruling of the Standing Order Numbers. Whether these Order Numbers are composed of cards

INVOICES RECEIVED FOR MATERIALS
AND EXPENSES ETC
ARE ENTERED IN THE
PURCHASE JOURNAL

TOTAL	MATERIALS CONTROL	FACTORY O. CONTROL	ADMIN. O. CONTROL	S. & DIS. O. CONTROL	PAYMENTS IN ADVANCE	ACCRUED CHARGES

AND THE TOTALS ARE THEN POSTED

CREDITORS

CLEARED BY CHEQUES	TOTAL INVOICES

MATERIALS CONTROL

TOTAL GOODS RECEIVED NOTES	

STORES LEDGER CONTROL

	TOTAL STORES REQUISITIONS

FACTORY OVERHEAD CONTROL

(1) INVOICES

(2) STORES REQUISITIONS

NOTES—

ADMINISTRATION OVERHEAD CONTROL & SELLING AND DISTRIBUTION OVERHEAD CONTROL ARE BOTH SIMILAR IN FORM TO FACTORY OVERHEAD CONTROL,

MATERIALS CONTROL A/C CAN BE DISPENSED WITH IF GOODS RECEIVED NOTES ARE PRICED FROM INVOICES AND NOT FROM COPIES OF ORDERS.

FIG. 51.—*Flow Chart for Invoices*

The Materials Control Account proves the agreement of Invoices and Goods Received Notes. Only part of the Stores Requisitions credited to Stores Ledger Control Account are debited to Factory Overhead Control Account: the bulk going to Work in Progress Account (*see* Fig. 49).

or loose-leaf sheets depends on the number of departments concerned. A specimen ruling is suggested in Fig. 52.

The entry in the Factory Overhead Control Account which has been posted from the Purchase Journal is the first to be dealt with. For this purpose it is necessary to go back to the Journal and exhaust the items in the Control Account column, one by one, on to the appropriate Standing Order Numbers.

HEADING:					CODING:		
Basis of Apportionment:							
Ref.	Total	Departments					
		1	2	3	4	5	6

FIG. 52.—Standing Order Number

This is a suggested ruling for an account used for the collection of factory overhead. The Departments 1–6 might be extended as necessary: for example, as in Fig. 53.

Let it be supposed that one particular item in the Purchase Journal is a bill for the repair of a piece of equipment in the Power-house. It will appear in the total column and be extended to the Factory Overhead Control Account column. The coding on the invoice will be read, and the Standing Order Number for "Maintenance of Plant and Equipment" will be turned up. The necessary entry will then be made under the period concerned, both in the total column and also in this case in the Power-house column.

In the same way the Stores Requisitions are used as the basis for exhausting the entry in the Control Account for indirect materials; and the Wages Sheets for apportioning the indirect wages.

When all the required entries have been made on the Standing Order Numbers they are ruled off for the month, and summarised as shown in Fig. 53. The total of this summary must then be agreed with the total of the month's entries to the Control Account.

(b) Cost Account Numbers

An attempt used to be made to deal with Administration and Selling and Distribution Overhead on exactly the same lines as Production

DEPARTMENTAL DISTRIBUTION SUMMARY
Four Weeks to February 28, 19...

Items	Total as per Summary	General Factory Overhead	Services							Production		
			Buildings	Electricity Supply	Steam Supply	Motive Power	Stores Expenses	Heating Service	Lighting Service	Dept. A	Dept. B	Dept. C
	£	£	£	£	£	£	£	£	£	£	£	£
Indirect Labour:												
Foremen	199	—	20	25	20	25	16	10	10	33	20	20
Storemen	40	—	—	—	—	—	40	—	—	—	—	—
Shop clerks	32	32	—	—	—	—	—	—	—	—	—	—
Labourers	256	—	20	10	40	10	—	—	—	50	76	50
Works salaries	797	797	—	—	—							
National Insurance	269	—	2	1	1	1	2	1	1	92	84	84
Workmen's Compensation Insurance	32	—	1	1	1	1	1	1	1	9	8	8
Fire Insurance	30	—	20	—	—	—	10	—	—	—	—	—
Rent	257	—	257	—	—	—	—	—	—	—	—	—
Rates	298	—	272	—	26	—	—	—	—	—	—	—
Stationery, etc.	20	20	—	—	—	—	—	—	—	—	—	—
Indirect Material	179	—	—	5	5	15	4	3	2	45	52	48
Water	14	3	—	—	11	—	—	—	—	—	—	—
Electricity and Gas Pur.	120	—	—	—	—	100	—	—	20	—	—	—
Coal	582	—	—	240	220	—	—	122	—	—	—	—
Service Wages	250	—	70	50	80	32	—	10	8	—	—	—
Repairs	536	6	130	40	26	47	—	14	3	61	134	75
Maintenance	70	—	25	7	9	8	—	—	—	9	7	5
Stores adjustment	20	—	—	—	—	—	20	—	—	—	—	—
Dining-room	70	70	—	—	—	—	—	—	—	—	—	—
Welfare	40	40	—	—	—	—	—	—	—	—	—	—
Lighting Material	30	—	—	—	—	—	—	—	30	—	—	—
Fire Protection	8	8	—	—	—	—	—	—	—	—	—	—
Depreciation	365	—	85	45	80	30	—	25	3	35	30	32
Transport (internal)	100	—	—	—	—	—	—	—	—	36	24	40
Sundry Expenses	257	257	—	—	—	—	—	—	—	—	—	—
Experimental	32	32	—	—	—	—	—	—	—	—	—	—
	£4903	£1265	£902	£424	£519	£269	£93	£186	£78	£370	£435	£362

FIG. 53.—*Departmental Distribution Summary*

After the Standing Order Numbers have been completed each month, they are ruled off and summarised on a statement as shown.

Overhead. It has been realised, however, that this attempt must largely be based on guesswork, since the connection between these kinds of Overhead and the Production Departments is hard to discover. For this reason among others it has largely been abandoned, and a simple ruling for Cost Account Numbers can therefore be recommended, as shown in Fig. 54.

The procedure with regard to exhausting the items in the Control Accounts should be followed as before, and the periodic totals must be summarised and agreed with the Control Accounts.

HEADING:			CODING:					
Ref.	Details	Total	Months					
			J.	F.	M.	A.	M.	J.

FIG. 54.—*Cost Account Number*

This is a possible ruling for accounts used for the collection of Administration overhead. The columns for the months could be extended to cover the full year.

For management purposes, it is useful to prepare summaries of the Cost Account Numbers, period by period, and on a cumulative basis, so that expenditure incurred under each heading can be carefully watched. Apart from this, however, these sections of overhead dealing with Administration and Selling and Distribution Overhead drop out of our consideration for the time being.

c) *Basis of apportionment of overhead to departments*

This varies according to the type of overhead being considered, but similar factors will apply, as when apportioning between the Overhead Control Accounts. The main bases in use, and specimen examples of each, are:

(i) *Direct Allocation*

Overtime premium of men engaged in a particular department.
Power, when separate meters are available.
Jobbing repairs.

(ii) Capital values

Depreciation of plant and machinery.
Fire Insurance.

(iii) Relative areas of departments

Lighting and heating.
Fire-precaution service.
Building service.

(iv) Direct Labour Hours and/or Machine Hours

Majority of general overhead items.

(v) Number employed

Canteen expenses.
Recreation Room expense.
Timekeeping.

(vi) Technical estimate

Electric Light—Number of lights or watts used.
Electric Power—Operating time in conjunction with horse-power of machines.
Steam—Based on a consumption return, or on potential consumption.
Water—When for process use it is usually metered.

(d) Departments for costing purposes

These are not necessarily only production departments or shops. Sometimes a production "centre" is treated as a "department," instead of, or in addition to, the larger factory divisions. A centre may be an isolated work-bench, a machine, or a group of machines of one type, or an activity. By this arrangement closer distribution of expense and more detailed control are aimed at. This method of minute departmentalisation of cost involves a considerable amount of analysis and, in the majority of cases, the expense of the work would not be warranted. The value of the method lies in the more precise costs which are obtained, regardless of the variation in the product or the equipment. Unless great care is used in analysis, this elaboration may lead to erroneous results.

3. APPORTIONMENT OF SERVICE DEPARTMENTS TO PRODUCTION AND OTHER SERVICE DEPARTMENTS

The Departmental Distribution Summary having been prepared by summarising the Standing Order Numbers, it now becomes necessary to apportion the cost of the Service Departments to the Production Departments, and possibly to other Service Departments. Fig. 53 shows a specimen Departmental Distribution Summary, and from this it can be seen that there is a considerable problem in regard to the redistribution of the Service Department costs.

It is necessary to consider the use made of each of the Service Departments by every other Department, in terms of time and money values. The Service Departments will normally keep Time Sheets showing the hours spent on work done, and for whom it was done, and these records may well form the basis of calculation. In other cases estimates must suffice.

It is a good plan to tackle the work in two stages:

1. Make the inter-service departments transfers.
2. Apportion the totals so obtained to the Production Departments.

There are two methods available for dealing with inter-service departments transfers:

(a) simultaneous equations,
(b) repeated distribution.

In the first place let us take a simple case.

A company has three Production Departments and two Service Departments, and for a period the departmental distribution summary has the following totals:

	£
Production Department A	800
B	700
C	500
Service Department 1	234
2	300
	£2534

The expense of the Service Departments is charged out on a percentage basis as follows:

	A	B	C	1	2
1	20%	40%	30%	—	10%
2	40%	20%	20%	20%	—

You are required to show the apportionment of overhead.

(a) *Simultaneous-equation method*

Let x = total overhead of Department 1.
And y = total overhead of Department 2.
Then

$$x = 234 + 0 \cdot 2y$$
$$y = 300 + 0 \cdot 1x.$$

Rearranging, and multiplying to eliminate decimals,

$$10x - 2y = 2340 \quad . \quad . \quad . \quad . \quad . \quad . \quad \text{(1)}$$
$$- x + 10y = 3000 \quad . \quad . \quad . \quad . \quad . \quad \text{(2)}$$

Multiply equation (1) by 5, and add result to (2)

$$49x = 14,700$$
$$x = \underline{300.}$$

Substituting this value in equation (1),

$$y = \underline{330.}$$

All that now remains to be done is to take these values $x = 300$ and $y = 330$ and apportion them on the basis of the agreed percentages to the three production departments, thus

	Total	A	B	C
	£	£	£	£
Per distribution summary .	2000	800	700	500
1	270	60	120	90
2	264	132	66	66
	2534	992	886	656

Thus the amount of £60 apportioned for Service Department 1 to Production Department A is 20% of £300, and the £66 apportioned for Service Department 2 to Production Department C is 20% of £330.

(b) Repeated distribution method

In this case the totals as shown in the departmental distribution summary are put out in a line, and then the service department totals are exhausted in turn repeatedly according to the agreed percentages, until the figures become too small to matter. Thus,

	A	B	C	1	2
	£	£	£	£	£
Per distribution summary	800	700	500	234	300
1	47	94	70	(234)	23
2	129	65	65	64	(323)
1	14	25	19	(64)	6
2	2	2	2		(6)
	992	886	656		

NOTE.—The italicised figures are credits, necessary to exhaust the Service Department columns.

In many ways the repeated distribution method appears to be the easier method, but as a check it is useful to do the work by both methods.

Now let us tackle the example given in Fig. 53.

Let us assume that as a result of investigation it is agreed that the General Factory Overhead and other Services are charged out on the following percentage basis. (NOTE.—Any agreed proportion may be expressed for convenience in percentage terms.)

	Service Departments								Production Departments		
	a	*b*	*c*	*d*	*e*	*f*	*g*	*h*	*A*	*B*	*C*
	1	*2*	*3*	*4*	*5*	*6*	*7*	*8*			
1 *a* Fy. Gen. O	—	5	5	5	5	5	5	5	30	20	15
2 *b* Buildings	—	—	10	20	10	—	—	—	20	20	20
3 *c* Electricity	—	—	—	—	75	—	—	25	—	—	—
4 *d* Steam	—	—	—	—	—	—	40	—	30	15	15
5 *e* Motive Power	—	—	—	—	—	—	—	—	40	30	30
6 *f* Stores	—	—	—	—	—	—	—	—	30	35	35
7 *g* Heating	—	—	—	—	—	10	—	—	30	30	30
8 *h* Lighting	—	—	—	5	—	5	—	—	30	30	30

Simultaneous-equation method

Let a, b, c, d, e, f, g, h represent the total overhead of Service Departments 1–8 inclusive.

As there are several unknowns, a means of building up the equations by substituting one value for another is worth trying, thus

$$a = 1265 \qquad\qquad = 1265$$

$$b = 902 + 0{\cdot}05a \qquad\qquad = 965{\cdot}25$$
$$ = 902 + 63{\cdot}25$$

$$c = 424 + 0{\cdot}05a \; + 0{\cdot}1b$$
$$ = 424 + 63{\cdot}25 \; + 96{\cdot}53 \qquad = 583{\cdot}78$$

$$h = 78 + 0{\cdot}05a \; + 0{\cdot}25c$$
$$ = 78 + 63{\cdot}25 \; + 145{\cdot}94 \qquad = 287{\cdot}19$$

$$d = 519 + 0{\cdot}05a \; + 0{\cdot}20b \; + 0{\cdot}05h$$
$$ = 519 + 63{\cdot}25 \; + 193{\cdot}05 \; + 14{\cdot}36 \;\; = 789{\cdot}66$$

$$e = 269 + 0{\cdot}05a \; + 0{\cdot}10b \; + 0{\cdot}75c$$
$$ = 269 + 63{\cdot}25 \; + 96{\cdot}53 \; + 437{\cdot}84 \;\; = 866{\cdot}62$$

$$g = 186 + 0{\cdot}05a \; + 0{\cdot}40d$$
$$ = 186 + 63{\cdot}25 \; + 315{\cdot}86 \qquad = 565{\cdot}11$$

$$f = 93 + 0{\cdot}05a \; + 0{\cdot}10g \; + 0{\cdot}05h$$
$$ = 93 + 63{\cdot}25 \; + 56{\cdot}51 \; + 14{\cdot}36 \;\; = 227{\cdot}12$$

Apportioning the figures in the end column, and approximating, the result is as follows:

	A	B	C
	£	£	£
Per distribution summary	370	435	362
Factory General Overhead	379	253	190
Buildings	193	193	193
Electricity	—	—	—
Steam	236	118	118
Motive power	346	259	259
Stores expense	70	82	81
Heating service	170	169	169
Lighting service	86	86	86
	£1850	£1595	£1458

Repeated distribution method

	1	2	3	4	5	6	7	8	A	B	C
	£	£	£	£	£	£	£	£	£	£	£
Totals	1265	902	424	519	269	93	186	78	370	435	362
1	(1265)	63	63	63	63	63	63	64	380	253	190
2		(965)	97	193	96				193	193	193
3			(584)		438			146			
4				(775)			310		233	116	116
5					(866)				346	260	260
6						(156)			47	55	54
7						56	(559)		168	167	168
8				14		14		(288)	86	87	87
4				(14)			6		4	2	2
6						(70)			21	25	24
7							(6)		2	2	2
									£1850	£1595	£1458

Whether the period being dealt with is a calendar month or a four-weekly period, the Production Overhead Control Account has now been distributed to the various Production Departments or cost centres. It may be considered desirable to close off the Factory Overhead Control Account to separate accounts such as Production Department "A" Incurred Overhead Account, etc., but this is not really necessary, provided running totals are kept in some subsidiary record book: this might well be the file in which the Distribution Summaries are kept.

The fourth stage of the overhead plan is now ready for development, but as the subject of overhead application is such a large one, it is best to defer it until the following chapter.

CHAPTER 11

OVERHEAD: APPLICATION TO PRODUCTION

BY the phrase "application of overhead to production" is meant the charge to be made to each works order, process, or unit of production, over and above the Prime Cost, and which is intended to cover a proportion of the factory overhead incurred.

In the early days of cost accounting, just after the First World War, it was the era of the "cost-plus" contract. In order to avoid delays in estimating for urgent contracts, the Government had placed contracts for war work on the basis that they would reimburse the cost, plus a percentage to cover the administration and other overhead expense incurred.

Firms who took on several contracts were forced to account separately for each, and had to watch carefully lest their overhead should swallow up their percentage allowance. This might occur because they had taken a contract which provided relatively little by way of percentage addition. For example:

	Contract A	Contract B
	£	£
Wages	500,000	200,000
Materials	100,000	100,000
Prime Cost	600,000	300,000
Add 10%	60,000	30,000
	£660,000	£330,000

Contract A provided £60,000 to cover overhead: on the other hand, Contract B required the use of as much material, and perhaps a higher degree of managerial skill, and yet provided only £30,000.

Inevitably, questions discussed after the war revolved upon what was the "cost" of a contract, and particularly, what was the best method of recovering indirect expenses as part of the cost of a product.

At first the ease with which a percentage addition to wages, or to materials, or to Prime Cost, could be made, seemed to provide a solution. But it was soon observed that where two products were being made side by side, and were taking the same time to make, the application of overhead by any of these "rule-of-thumb" methods might be quite unsound.

It requires but a simple example to show this:

Cost of Metal Caps

	In brass	In steel
	£	£
Materials	4·00	2·00
Labour	0·90	0·90
Prime Cost	4·90	2·90
Works Overhead 75% on Material cost	3·00	1·50
Production cost	£7·90	£4·40

It must be concluded therefore that, except in the simplest cases, these methods are obsolete. The only circumstances in which they could be used would be when

(*a*) one product is being made,
(*b*) material prices are stable,
(*c*) labour rates are steady,
(*d*) equipment used remains unchanged.

As soon as it was realised that the cost of materials and labour had no direct relation to the amount of overhead incurred, cost accountants began to recognise the importance of the time factor. Overhead is incurred from year to year, from month to month, from day to day, and from hour to hour; and the overhead which is thus incurred "in time" may be satisfactorily related to the production hours worked in the factory.

Thus the following information may be available:

Dept.	Estimated Factory Overhead	Men	Weeks p.a.	Hours p.wk.	Total Direct Labour	Rate per D.L.H.
	£				Hours	£
A	12,000	30	50	50	75,000	0·16
B	17,000	40	50	50	100,000	0·17
C	14,000	70	50	50	175,000	0·08

The Prime Cost of the work done each week will be increased by the appropriate departmental rate or rates per direct labour hour worked, and thus the overhead will be absorbed. It will be recalled that in the previous chapter it was seen how Factory Overhead was departmentalised, and it is necessary to estimate in advance for each department separately, since perhaps some items produced do not pass through all departments. The method depends for its accuracy on two prior estimates, viz., what the Factory Overhead is likely to amount to, and how many direct labour hours are expected to be worked.

With these provisos, however, it is a satisfactory scheme of overhead application. It must, however, be stressed that the estimated direct labour hours have to take into account annual holidays, public holidays, and all anticipated normal idle time: only then can there be any hope that the application rate per hour will recover most of the overheads actually incurred.

A variation of the *direct-labour-hour method* is the *production-unit* method. Thus, if in the case just considered there were 2 units produced per direct labour hour, it would be expected that, on the assumption that the work of Departments A and B met at an assembly point, and then passed through Department C, there would be a total production of 175,000 × 2 complete units. The total estimated overhead is £43,000, so that Factory Overhead would be applied on the basis of £0·123 per unit of production.

This method is satisfactory when the Works are producing uniform units, as is often the case in process and single-output manufacturing. As soon as the units vary, however, conversions have to be made on a "points" basis into a common unit equivalent, and this introduces an element of arbitrary judgment which is not desirable. An illustration of this is seen in the somewhat doubtful practice by which hospitals equate a number of out-patients attendances with one in-patient day.

The departmental direct-labour-hour method of overhead absorption has certain drawbacks, which can sometimes be seen when a comparison is made between the classes of work carried on in a department, or between the work of one department and another.

In Department B shown above the Factory Overhead was estimated to be £17,000, which is high by comparison with the other Departments. Let it be supposed that the figure is made up as follows:

	£
Supervisory wages	2,500
Rent	1,200
Insurance	
Fire—Machinery	350
Building	150
Power	3,000
Depreciation of machinery	2,000
Lighting	800
Supplies	2,500
Service Department E	3,000
Service Department F	1,500
	£17,000

Clearly a large part of the overhead is incurred by the use of machinery, and for this reason, in such cases the use of *machine hour rates* is advocated.

The principle is that Production Overhead expenses of a machine cost centre are distributable in proportion to the operating hours of the machines. In factories where production is largely by machinery this method gives greater accuracy than any of those previously mentioned.

A machine rate can be set up for each machine, but as this would probably create too many different rates for convenience, and be too costly in administration, it is often the practice to fix a rate for each group of machines of similar type.

COMPUTATION OF A MACHINE HOUR RATE

METHOD 1

(a) All Factory Overhead is departmentalised as already shown, and the overhead of the Service Departments is apportioned to the Production Departments.

(b) More detailed analysis is carried out, however, because each cost centre is regarded as a separate production centre.

NOTE.—The *Terminology of Cost Accountancy* defines a cost centre as a location, person, or item of equipment (or group of these) in relation to which costs may be ascertained and used for the purpose of cost control.

(c) By this means every cost centre will be charged with its proportion of general Factory Overhead.

(d) The machine cost centres will, in addition, have been charged with their appropriate machine running expenses.

(e) Separate rates can now be calculated for machine cost centres

$$\frac{\text{estimated overhead}}{\text{machine hours anticipated}}$$

and for bench work cost centres

$$\frac{\text{estimated overhead}}{\text{direct labour hours anticipated}}$$

These calculations will follow the same pattern as the actual overhead incurred, and will probably be based to a large extent on the previous year's results.

METHOD 2

(a) All Factory overhead is departmentalised, but only to main accounts.

(*b*) The overhead of the Service Departments is apportioned to the main Production Departments, and the totals thus obtained are then subdivided for each department into:

(*i*) *Machine running costs.*
(*ii*) *Other overhead.*

(*c*) Two rates or more will therefore be applied in respect of each Production Department to cover these classes of overhead.

Fig. 55 gives a schedule showing the computation of a machine hour rate under Method 1, and it will be noted that the machine operator's time is not included. A machine hour rate does not cover this, because this item is already dealt with as direct labour.

MACHINE EXPENSE SCHEDULE
Machine No. B. 23; Shop "A"

Description: Grinder   **Date bought:** 5th June 19...
Maker: Samson   **Cost:** £600
Power: 4 h.p.   **Estimated life:** 10 years
Additions: ....   **Depreciation:** 9% p.a.

Item	Basis of Estimate	Cost per Annum £
Depreciation	9% to reduce to £60 in 10 years	54
Insurance	Actual	2
Repairs and maintenance	Estimated from records or otherwise	64
Indirect materials: oil, cotton-waste, etc.	Estimated on average issues	10
Rent of floor space allotted	300 sq. ft. at 1s. 4d.	20
Superintendence and shop expenses	$\frac{300}{3000} \times £1800$ (say)	180
Power	302 days of 8 hours less 20% idle time, estimated	190
Cost per annum		**£520**
Cost per operating hour (1933 hours) **Use, say, 5s. 5d. hour**		**5·38s.**

FIG. 55.—*Computation of a Machine Hour Rate*

Each piece of machinery is the subject of such a computation, and the overhead is recovered on production by means of an hourly rate for the time during which the machine operates.

While the machine hour rate gives a fairly reliable basis for absorption of overhead, the following reasons may be cited as possible causes of discrepancies:

(*a*) The inevitable irregularities of operating times.

(b) The necessity of using an estimated number of machine hours in advance.

(c) The amount of abnormal idle time, waiting time, and overtime. The qualifying word "abnormal" is used, because any normal, and therefore anticipated, idle time will have been taken into account when estimating. If there is a decided trend of increase in non-operating time a revision of rates might be called for, but generally speaking, this is not desirable, because comparisons are made difficult. (Students may, with advantage, refer at this point to p. 136, where the question of idle facilities and the cost of idleness is more fully discussed.)

Stand-by, or spare, machines, such as boilers, electric motors, etc., will be provided for in computing the rate, and their "idleness" is not included under (c) above.

ACCOUNTING ENTRIES

So far, in the main books there is a Factory Overhead Control Account, the details of which are to be found in the subsidiary records under Standing Order Numbers. When the Departmental Distribution Summary was completed there was the option of transferring the period's entries in the Factory Overhead Control Account to

(a) Factory Overhead Incurred—Department A
(b) Factory Overhead Incurred—Department B

and so on,

or, on the other hand, of keeping the details in some kind of running record.

What, then, happens when Factory Overhead is to be applied? In Fig. 49 was shown a specimen Job Cost card, and it will be seen that in addition to space being given for Materials and Direct Labour, room is provided for the inclusion of Factory Overhead. As each Job or Works Order is carried out, the Factory Overhead is applied at the end of each period on the Cost Card or Cost Sheet concerned, by one or more of the methods already outlined, and having regard to the departments through which the work has passed.

The Factory Overhead thus applied to each Cost Sheet is summarised, and forms the basis of the following Journal entry:

Work-in-progress Account   Dr.

To Factory Overhead Applied Accounts

Department A
Department B
and so on.

Alternatively, if the details are to be kept outside the Ledger, then the only entry would be:

Work-in-progress Account   Dr.

To Factory Overhead Applied Account

The entry to Work-in-progress Account adds to those already made for direct materials and expenses, and direct labour, so that the Work-in-progress Account now shows "in total" what the Cost Sheets reveal in detail.

It will be noted that the opening of Factory Overhead Applied Account(s) are suggested. In practice, it is useful to have these accounts separate so that the position may be seen at a glance at any time, but they are not strictly essential, and have not always been shown.

On completion of each Works Order the Cost Sheet is totalled and set aside. Then, at the end of the current period these completed Cost Sheets are summarised and the following Journal entry is put through:

Finished Goods Stock Account   Dr.

To Work-in-progress Account

In this way the Work-in-progress Account is reduced to show the balance of work now going through the factory, and is supported by the details on the file of uncompleted Cost Sheets.

ADJUSTMENT OF FACTORY OVERHEAD

It will be apparent that whatever basis is used for applying Factory Overhead there is little probability that the amount absorbed will exactly agree with the amount incurred. There will be a balance under- or over-recovered. Under-recovery will take place, for example, when

(a) the total expense incurred for a department exceeds the estimate,
(b) the output or hours worked are less than anticipated.

Alternatively, there would be over-recovery when

(a) the total overhead incurred is less than estimated,
(b) the output or hours worked exceed the estimate.

There are three methods of disposing of the balance:

1. Transfer the amount of the balance to Factory General Expenses, and absorb it by new rates to be fixed. This has nothing to commend it, as it vitiates comparisons between one period and another, and, indeed, gives untrue results.
2. Carry down the balance, on the assumption that it may be counterbalanced next time. This should be done only in intermediate

periods during the year, and when the balance is comparatively small.

3. Transfer the balance to Factory Overhead Under- and Over-absorbed Account, for eventual transfer to Costing Profit and Loss Account.

The entries should always be made in the Factory Overhead Applied Accounts, where these are kept, on the ground that no adjustment should be made in the Factory Overhead Incurred Accounts, as these represent actual expenditure incurred.

CLASSES OF FACTORY OVERHEAD

It is opportune to consider at this point certain kinds of Factory Overhead, and their method of treatment.

Estimating and Drawing Office Expenses

These are often apportionable as between Factory and Selling Overhead.

Royalties

Royalties payable are in the nature of a rent which is paid for the right to make use of a patent process or component in the course of manufacture, or possibly for the right to sell the finished product. In each case the payment is made to the owner of the rights in question. Whether or not the Royalties are to be regarded as a production cost or a selling cost depends on the facts of the case, and they may be apportionable between the two. If they are regarded as a production cost it may be possible to charge them as a direct expense, and consideration should be given to this, before putting them to Factory Overhead.

Depreciation and Interest

Students are asked to refer to Chapter 13 where this subject is more fully discussed.

Fixing new plant

The cost should be capitalised and written off with the asset as depreciation.

Moving and refixing existing plant

This cost adds nothing to the value of the asset: it must therefore be charged as Factory Overhead.

Rent charge for premises owned

No rent is actually payable in cash, but nevertheless it is considered reasonable to raise a charge in the overhead. Credit could be given to Accrued Charges Account, and from thence, at the end of the year, it would be transferred to the credit of Costing Profit and Loss Account.

Inspection

This is generally a Factory Overhead, and is apportioned to the Production Departments on the basis of the amount of work for each.

Tool setting

If the setting is for a specific order it may be conveniently made a direct charge to that order. When, however, a number of orders are dealt with on a machine with one setting only the expense is included in the overhead rate for the machine or department concerned.

Wages of engineers and millwrights

This is a Service Department cost, and will be apportioned to Production Departments and/or cost centres, and thus will be included in the machine hour rate. Work done of a capital nature will be charged to a Capital Order No. on suitable authority. To distinguish it from other work it is often found convenient to use different coloured stationery; the entry, on completion, will be

Capital Expenditure Account   Dr.

To Work-in-progress Account.

Overtime and special night-work wages

When overtime or night work is necessary, owing to the desire of a customer to have an order completed or rushed through within a specified time, the extra payment for overtime is legitimately charged to the job as direct labour.

When, however, the overtime is regular, or intermittent but recurring, and is for the purpose of generally increasing the output of the factory, *e.g.* to keep up with stock requirements, the cost of the overtime premium is charged to Factory Overhead, a Standing Order Number being provided for the purpose (*see* p. 105).

EXAMPLE

6 hours overtime
Rate per hour 5*s.*
Paid at time-and-a-half   £2   5*s.*

Charge

Direct Labour   £1 10*s.*
Standing Order No.   15*s.*

Distinction should be made between special intermittent overtime and night work, and that which is regular and budgeted. The latter can be recovered in overhead rates; the former, if not chargeable to a particular job, or if not suitable for inclusion in Factory Overhead, will be written off to Costing Profit and Loss Account.

Carriage inwards of stored materials

As is well known, this is usually treated in Manufacturing Accounts as an addition to the cost of raw materials purchased. In costing, however, it sets a problem in Stores accounting, for the carriage is not normally known at the time of purchase, and has to be estimated. This throws out the easy agreement of the Stores Accounts. For this reason it may be better to regard it as overhead.

Idle time

Broadly speaking, idle time falls into two main categories:

(*a*) Idle facilities,
(*b*) Idleness.

Idle facilities means that the machine is available for work but is not being used. It is not usual, in fact, to work a machine all the available time, because it has to be serviced, and is possibly of a kind which is only used intermittently during the process. The percentage of expected use has to be worked out for each machine, and, even if Standard Costing is not in force, it is convenient to refer to it as the Capacity Usage Ratio. This is defined in the *Terminology of Cost Accountancy* as

"the relationship between the budgeted number of working hours and the maximum number of working hours in a budget period."

Idleness, as distinct from idle facilities, is due to such causes as

(*i*) waiting for work,
(*ii*) waiting for foreman's instructions,
(*iii*) breakdown of machinery, etc.

In such cases it is generally regarded as correct to charge the unproductive labour element to a special Standing Order Number, or to a series of them, in order to analyse the cost by causes. However, there is far more to it than that: the unrecovered standing charges of a machine, and also a proportion of the fixed overhead of the concern as a whole, are legitimately to be regarded as the cost of idle time, and if management is to be fully aware of the true position the Cost Accounts must be designed to bring out the necessary information.

SPECIMEN QUESTION

The standing charges, maintenance cost, and depreciation for a machine are estimated to total £2400 per annum. The machine is capable of working 50 weeks × 46 hours, or 2300 hours, but it is anticipated that it will only work 80% of that time, or 1840 hours. The actual hours recorded for the machine were 1750 hours, and the operator's idle time is analysed by causes in Standing Order Numbers. These disclose that

> 30 hours were spent in waiting for work,
> 10   „   „   waiting for foreman,
> 30   „   „   breakdowns of machine.

The operator's rate of pay was 6s. per hour.   The fixed Administration overhead was £10,000, and the anticipated machine hours of the factory as a whole is 14,000 hours.

Prepare a Machine Utilisation Statement to bring to the notice of management the true cost of idle time.

ANSWER

Machine Utilisation Statement—Machine No. 84

Year ended ....

(*a*) Maximum possible hours	2300
Standard capacity expected	1840

Capacity Usage Ratio

$$\frac{1840}{2300} \text{ or } 0.8 \text{ or } 80\%.$$

(*b*) Standard capacity expected	1840
Actual hours recorded	1750

Capacity Utilisation Ratio

$$\frac{1750}{1840} \text{ or } 0.95 \text{ or } 95\%.$$

(*c*) Causes of idle time   Hours

    (i) Unavoidable

        Idle facilities 2300 − 1840   460

    (ii) Avoidable

        Idle facilities (above anticipated figure)   20
        Idleness of operator due to

Waiting for work	30	
Waiting for foreman	10	
Breakdown of machine	30	
	—	70
		550

(*d*) Cost involved   £

Labour of operator charged to Factory Overhead in Standing Order Numbers—70 hours at 6*s*.   21

    (NOTE.—Operator assumed to have been working with another machine during the 20 hours the machine was available for work.)

Fixed overhead   £

Machine standing charges   2400

Administration

Total £10,000

Proportion for machine No. 84:

$$\frac{\text{Standard capacity of this machine}}{\text{Standard capacity of whole factory}}$$

i.e. $\frac{1840}{14,000} \times 10,000$ 1314

                             £3714

This must be apportioned as follows:

$$\frac{\text{Hours lost}}{\text{Maximum hours}} \times 3714$$

$$\frac{550}{2300} \times 3714$$ 888

                             £909

(*e*) Breakdown of Cost

    Unavoidable causes

        Idle facilities

$$\frac{460}{550} \times 909$$ 760

    Avoidable causes

        Idle facilities

$$\frac{20}{550} \times 909$$ 33

    Waiting for work

$$\frac{30}{550} \times 909$$ 50

    Waiting for foreman

$$\frac{10}{550} \times 909$$ 16

    Breakdowns of machine

$$\frac{30}{550} \times 909$$ 50

                             149

                             £909

NOTE.—A transfer will be made from the Overhead Control Accounts to the Costing Profit and Loss Account of the total cost of idle time for all machines in the factory.

AUTOMATION

The growth of automatic processes will tend to merge direct wages with factory overhead. As a result the "added value" concept will doubtless be developed. By this is meant that Production overhead is collected by Cost centres, and the Cost centre costs, including labour, are recovered at predetermined rates for the time which the work spends within each centre. Thus the total factory cost becomes, *e.g.*

	£	£
Raw Materials		25
Cost centre 3—5 hours at 48s.	12	
Cost centre 4—3 hours at 40s.	6	
Cost centre 7—4 hours at 50s.	10	28
		£53

Where an automatic machine can perform either of several processes at the touch of the appropriate button, one of the problems is to apportion the operator's time. The single Cost centre has become, for all intents and purposes, several Cost centres: and in one case, at least, it has been thought necessary to assess "cam-cycle" hours as a basis of apportionment.

This whole subject will doubtless become increasingly important to the Cost Accountant.

CHAPTER 12

OVERHEAD: ADMINISTRATION, AND SELLING AND DISTRIBUTION

IN Chapter 10 it was seen that these types of overhead are collected in Cost Account Numbers, and that these in turn are agreed with the respective Overhead Control Accounts. It now remains to consider the nature of this overhead, and its proper treatment in the books of account.

ADMINISTRATION OVERHEAD

Generally speaking, the overhead incurred in administrative offices is incurred for the business as a whole. Production in a certain department may rise or fall, but the Administration Overhead goes on unchanged. Indeed, it is more likely to be geared to Sales than to manufacture. As, therefore, it has little or no connection with production in any direct kind of way, it is considered unrealistic to add little amounts of Administration Overhead as part of the cost of production of a unit.

Again, to charge any part of Administration Overhead to work-in-progress inflates the stock values at the end of the year, and carries forward to next year part of the overhead which should be borne in the current year.

In all normal financial accounting Administration Overhead is shown in the Profit and Loss Account, and has to be provided from year to year out of the gross profit for that year. There is no need it is suggested to depart from this time-honoured practice.

For these reasons it is recommended that students should "apply" Administration Overhead in the following manner

Finished Goods Stock Account   Dr.

To Administration Overhead Applied Account

If the year is divided up, for example, into 13 four-weekly periods, then each period will bear $\frac{1}{13}$ of the estimated annual expense.

At the same time a close watch will be kept on the details given in the Cost Account Numbers, as has already been suggested, to see that the incurred overhead is not far astray from the estimates.

With the entry above having been made, the Finished Goods Stock Account will look as follows:

Finished Goods Stock Account

To Balance b/d	By Transfer to Cost of Sales
Transfer from Work-in-progress Account, Factory Cost of goods completed	Account
	Balance c/d
Administration Overhead Applied Account	

In order to comply with normal accounting conventions the balances on the above account should be valued at factory cost, so that the whole allocation of Administration Overhead finds its way into the Cost of Sales Account.

It may well be argued that the Administration Overhead should have been put there in the first place, and there is little defence to this point of view. However, as cost accountants were originally, and to some extent still are, imbued with the idea that it should be charged to work-in-progress, the method advocated represents a compromise between the two positions: the student may make up his own mind.

The difference between Administration Overhead Control Account and Administration Overhead Applied Account will be written off from the latter account, at the end of the year, to Costing Profit and Loss Account.

Examples of Administration expenses are:

General Office expenses.
Managing Director's remuneration.
Stationery.
Postage and Telephones.
Rent of offices.
Professional fees.

None of them calls for special comment.

SELLING AND DISTRIBUTION OVERHEAD

For costing purposes these are generally considered together, although it is quite possible, and it may in some circumstance be desirable, to deal with them separately.

It is convenient to identify such expenses as those which are incurred subsequently to the manufactured goods being placed in the warehouse or finished goods store. The definitions given in the *Terminology of Cost Accountancy* are

Selling Cost
The cost incurred in promoting sales and retaining custom.

Distribution Cost

The cost of the process which begins with making the packed product available for despatch and ends with making the reconditioned returned empty package available for re-use.

As with Administration Overhead, the details of the expenditure incurred are given in a set of Cost Account Numbers, and if these are suitably ruled for the purpose it is possible to carry out a useful analysis from them. A suggested ruling is given in Fig. 56.

HEADING				CODING		
Basis of Apportionment:						
Details	Total	Sales Areas				
		N.W.	N.E.	S.W.	S.E.	London

FIG. 56.—*Cost Account Number*

This ruling is suggested for a series of accounts in which the Selling and Distribution overhead may be collected. The precise ruling is dictated by the needs of the business.

The monthly or periodical totals of these Cost Account Numbers will be analysed (as was done when dealing with Production Overhead) to a Distribution Summary, so that finally all the Selling and Distribution Overhead is apportioned to the sales areas. A satisfactory basis for making this distribution of departmental costs will be in proportion to Sales, *i.e.*:

Total Sales £15,000
Leeds Sales £5000
Advertising Department Overhead £1200

Apportionment to Leeds £1200 $\times \dfrac{5,000}{15,000} = \underline{£400}$

Having thus arrived at the Selling and Distribution Overhead for each Sales area, it is possible to break it down still further, viz. by salesmen. This might be done in one of three ways

(*a*) by equal division,

(*b*) in proportion to sales achieved by each salesman,
(*c*) by sales quotas.

The advantage of the sales quota method is that it takes account of the differing conditions of the areas, and of the abilities of the salesmen:

Overhead for Brighton area   £700
Sales quotas

| Salesman A | £3000 |
| Salesman B | £4000 |

Sales achieved £4000 in each case.
On a quota basis, Salesman A is "charged" with $\frac{3}{7}$ of £700, or £300.
On a sales basis, the figure would have been £350.

A further analysis can be made by classes of products sold, and the basis for distribution of the overhead would be "Sales," or "Gross profit on Sales."

Whether these subsidiary analyses are carried out by the Sales Department or the Costing Department is a matter of policy, but the Costing Department would certainly take the work as far as the accounting entry out of the Selling and Distribution Overhead Control Account.

This is as follows:

Area 1 Selling and Distribution Overhead Incurred Account   Dr.
Area 2 Selling and Distribution Overhead Incurred Account   Dr.
   etc.
   To Selling and Distribution Overhead Control Account

Of course, as in the case of Production Overhead, it may be considered sufficient to keep this information in the form of running totals outside the Ledger.

The application of Selling and Distribution Overhead is carried out very simply by the entry

Cost of Sales Account   Dr.
   To Selling and Distribution Overhead Applied Account

It is not necessary to detail the overhead for each area, but the amount is made up by taking, *e.g.* $\frac{1}{13}$ of the total estimate.

The accounting position is now as follows:

Costs of Sales Account

| To Transfer from Finished Goods Stock Account Selling and Distribution Overhead Applied Account | By Transfer to Costing Profit and Loss Account |

Costing Profit and Loss Account

To Transfer from Cost of Sales Account	By Sales
Overhead under-absorbed [details]	Overhead over-absorbed [details]
Abnormal Losses to be written off [details	Abnormal gains or income to be brought in details]
Net Profit per Cost Accounts	

Examples of Selling Overhead are:

Advertising, catalogues, samples, folders, etc.

Advertising by permanent signs would be regarded as capital outlay to be apportioned over the estimated effective life of the sign. The cost of shop displays, catalogues, and an extensive advertising campaign may similarly be spread over a period.

Rent and other expenses of Sales Department.

Royalties.

Sometimes these are more closely connected with Production than with Sales, and may be treated as a direct expense.

Travellers' Salaries and Commissions.

Market Research.

The amount to be spent in any year is usually a policy decision, to be modified by events.

Bad Debts.

When a fairly regular percentage of Bad Debts is incurred this item may be reasonably included in Selling Overhead. When a large bad debt is exceptional and abnormal it is better to exclude it from the Cost Accounts.

Examples of Distribution Overhead are:

Warehouse rent.

Warehouse labour and other expenses.

Depot expenses.

Finished Stock waste and loss.

Distinguish between

(*a*) unavoidable waste due to inherent qualities, *e.g.* shrinkage, evaporation, breaking bulk, etc.,

(*b*) deterioration due to lapse of time, obsolescence, and abnormal damage or abnormal loss,

(*c*) avoidable waste caused by faulty handling and storage.

Losses such as (*b*) should be written off direct to Costing Profit and Loss Account, but (*a*) and (*c*) should be included as part of the Distribution Overhead.

Carriage.

Carriage on goods despatched may be

(*a*) charged to customers direct,
(*b*) charged as a Distribution Overhead,
(*c*) charged as a Selling Overhead, being regarded as an inducement to potential customers.

Packages and containers for despatch purposes.
Finished Stock Insurances.

CHAPTER 13

OVERHEAD: DEPRECIATION AND INTEREST ON CAPITAL

HITHERTO it has been the practice to regard depreciation as representing the loss in value of the capital sunk in buildings, mines, quarries, leases, plant, machinery, and other equipment, due to the normal and inevitable process of making use of the asset over a number of years.

Nowadays, however, there is a school of thought which considers that "replacement cost" and not "original cost" is the important factor. In this view the term "depreciation" should no longer be used, and "replacement provision" should take its place. It is pointed out that in a period of rising prices merely to write down an asset over a period of years from its original cost to its scrap value provides no internal strength to meet replacement costs; and these may be considerably more than the original capital invested.

The factory cost of production, it is argued, should reflect not only rising wages costs and rising material prices, which it does automatically, but also rising costs of overhead, including capital replacement.

In periods of stable or falling prices the call for this additional provision would obviously not exist. It is entirely a matter of policy, but the student should note that no accounting difficulty would be caused by a decision to provide for replacement costs. The entry would merely be:

Manufacturing Account   Dr.
      To Depreciation Provision Account
      Asset Replacement Provision Account

and in the Cost Accounts the debit entry would be to Factory Overhead Control Account.

METHODS OF CALCULATING DEPRECIATION

The *Terminology of Cost Accountancy* sets out the following methods of calculating depreciation and, of course, any of them can be adapted for use to conform to the orthodox view of depreciation or to the replacement cost theory:

1. STRAIGHT-LINE METHOD

"The method of providing for depreciation by means of periodic charges, each of which is a constant proportion of the cost of the asset depreciated."

EXAMPLE

Cost of machine = £5000.
Estimated residual value after 10 years = £500.
Write off £4500 over 10 years, *i.e.* £450 per year.

This is a much used and recommended method, which is simple and effective and has the great advantage that the uniform annual charge affords better comparative costs. It requires little work for computing the amounts.

It has the recommendation of the Institute of Chartered Accountants (*Depreciation of Fixed Assets*, 1945).

2. REDUCING BALANCE METHOD

"The method of providing for depreciation by means of periodic charges, each of which is a constant proportion of the balance remaining after deducting from the cost of the asset depreciated, the aggregate of the amounts provided previously."

EXAMPLE

Cost of machine = £5000.
To be written down at the rate of 20% per annum.

Year	Cost and balance b/f	Depreciation	Balance c/f
	£	£	£
Year 1	5000	1000	4000
2	4000	800	3200
3	3200	640	2560
		and so on	

It is argued, in favour of this method, that a heavier depreciation charge is borne in the earlier years when repairs are lighter, and that the assumed increasing repair cost is counterbalanced, in later years, by the reduced annual charge for depreciation. Such a relationship between depreciation and repairs is obviously most haphazard.

It is found, in practice, that assets appear to hold their book values for an inordinate length of time, and it not infrequently happens that, when this method is used in the Financial Accounts heavier rates or other methods are employed in the Cost Accounts.

3. PRODUCTION UNIT METHOD

"The method of providing for depreciation by means of periodic charges, each of which is equivalent to the number of units of work

F

produced during the period by the asset depreciated, multiplied by a constant rate of depreciation per unit."

EXAMPLE

Machine to work 10 years × 50 weeks × 46 hours = 23,000 hours.
Estimated rate of production = 10 per hour.
Total estimated units = 230,000.
Cost, less residual value of machine = £5000.
Write off depreciation at the rate of

$$\frac{£5000}{230,000} \text{ or } £0.02174 \text{ per unit.}$$

This is a somewhat uncertain method, because it depends on the accuracy of the estimate of the number of units which a machine will produce in a given number of years.

4. PRODUCTION HOUR METHOD

"The method of providing for depreciation by means of periodic charges, each of which is equivalent to the number of hours during which the asset is operated, multiplied by a constant rate of depreciation per hour."

This method is so similar to (3) above, that it calls for no special comment.

5. REPAIR RESERVE METHOD

"The method of providing for the aggregate of depreciation and maintenance cost by means of periodic charges, each of which is a constant proportion of the cost of the asset depreciated and the maintenance cost."

EXAMPLE

Cost of Plant and equipment	£5000
Add cost of two major overhauls during life of asset, say 2 × £1000	£2000
	£7000

The straight-line method of depreciation is now applied to the £7000 less any residual value which is estimated, and the entry in the books each year is

Sundry Contracts and/or Works overhead   Dr.

    To Repairs Provision Account

Repairs Provision Account will be debited with the actual cost of repairs, and with a transfer to Aggregate Depreciation Account of the true amount of depreciation.

This method is often used by Public Works Contractors as a suitable method of charging the hire and use of their own plant to contracts.

6. ANNUITY METHOD

"The method of providing for depreciation by means of periodic charges, each of which is a constant proportion of the aggregate of the cost of the asset depreciated and interest at a given rate per period on the written-down values of the asset at the beginning of each period."

EXAMPLE

For the purposes of illustration, a short period is taken.
Cost of Asset = £3000.
Interest to be taken at the rate of 4% per year.
Period 4 years.
Annuity tables give the fact that £1 paid now will purchase an annuity of £0·27549 for 4 years at 4%.

$$\text{The formula is } PR^n = \frac{A(R^n - 1)}{R - 1}$$

where P = value of the asset, $R = 1 + \frac{r}{100}$,

n = term of years, and A = Annual sum.

The annual sum to be provided is, therefore,

$$£300 \times 0\cdot27549, \text{ } i.e. \text{ } £826\cdot47.$$

PROOF

Year	Cost and balance b/f	Interest at 4%	Annual provision	Balance c/f
	£	£	£	£
1	3000	120·00	826·47	2293·53
2	2293·53	91·74	826·47	1558·80
3	1558·80	62·35	826·47	794·68
4	794·68	31·79	826·47	—

This method is generally used for the redemption of leases over a fairly long period, since money invested for a lengthy period in a capital asset should be deemed to be earning interest.

7. SINKING FUND METHOD

"The method of providing for depreciation by means of periodic investments of the aggregate of a constant proportion of the cost of the asset depreciated and the interest received from the investment, the proceeds of the realisation of the investment at the end of the life of the asset being equal to the cost of the asset."

EXAMPLE

Cost of Asset £3000.

Interest at the rate of 4% (Compound).

Period = 3 years.

Sinking Fund Tables state that £0·320348 invested annually at 4% will amount
to £1 at the end of 3 years.

The formula is $P = A\dfrac{(R^n - 1)}{R - 1}$ the meanings to be attached to these letters
being the same as on page 149.

The annual sum to be provided is, therefore,

$$£3000 \times 0·320348, \text{ } i.e. \text{ } £961·044.$$

PROOF

Year	Balance b/f	Interest at 4%	Annual provision	Annual investment	Balance c/f
	£	£	£	£	£
1	—	—	961·044	961·044	961·044
2	961·044	38·443	961·044	999·487	1960·531
3	1960·531	78·425	961·044	Not invested	3000·000

This is the only method so far considered which provides cash for the
replacement of the asset at the end of the useful life forecast for it. It
may not provide sufficient cash, unless replacement costs are fully
covered.

At the end of the period, if the investments are sold and the proceeds
added to the cash retained, there will be £3000 available for the purchase of a new asset. The Depreciation Fund will also be £3000, which
will be written off to the Asset Account: the annual provision having
been credited to the Fund and debited to Factory Overhead Control
Account.

8. ENDOWMENT POLICY METHOD

"The method of providing for depreciation by means of periodic
payments of premiums under an endowment policy, the proceeds of
realisation of which at the end of the life of the asset are equal to the
cost of the asset depreciated."

This is similar in effect to the Sinking Fund method. Cash is taken
out of the business to pay the insurance premiums, and is made available again at the end of the period for the purchase of another asset.

9. REVALUATION METHOD

"The method of providing for depreciation by means of periodic
charges, each of which is equivalent to the difference between the
values assigned to the asset at the beginning and the end of the period."

This is the method commonly used for loose tools, laboratory glassware, horses, and, sometimes, patterns. The procedure often adopted

is to open a Loose Tools Account, etc., to which the cost is debited of all new tools (other than those purchased or made for a particular job, which are debited direct to the job) and of repairs to tools. At the end of each accounting period the amount of the revalued stock is credited and carried down, and the difference on the account is the depreciation (or appreciation) to be taken into the accounts.

10. REDUCING PROPORTION METHOD

In addition to the above methods of depreciation, all of which are used as thought appropriate, there is a method of quick depreciation for motor vehicles, which may be of interest.

The method is based on the idea of taking each year a reduced proportion of the sum of an arithmetical progression in respect of the years of life forecast, multiplied by the cost, less residual value, of the asset.

Cost of vehicle = £950
Residual value = £200
Period = 5 years
Years   1   2   3   4   5
Sum of years $n/2$ (a plus l) $\frac{5}{2}$ (1 plus 5)   15

Where n = no. of years; a = 1st term; and l = last term.

Write off

EXAMPLE

Year 1 $\frac{5}{15}$ of £750 = £250
2   $\frac{4}{15}$ £200
3   $\frac{3}{15}$ £150
4   $\frac{2}{15}$ £100
5   $\frac{1}{15}$ £50

The advantage claimed for this method is that it realistically takes account of the immediate drop in value of a new vehicle, however recently purchased. It also makes the decision to sell and repurchase before the estimated time an easier one, as after the first two years a loss on sale will not be apparent.

PLANT AND MACHINERY REGISTER

In order that the annual charge for depreciation may be easily ascertained, it is a good plan to record particulars of each piece of plant and major equipment in a Plant and Machinery Register. This register may be designed to show:

1. One machine on each page, with details of cost, purchase price, date of purchase, name and address of suppliers, particulars of any

guarantees given as to performance, estimated life, estimated residual value, rate of depreciation, method of depreciation to be used, and details and cost of repairs undertaken, with dates on which the work was carried out. Fig. 57 shows a suggested layout for this type of register, but it will be appreciated that a Deprecia-

J	F	M	A	M	J	Jy	A	S	O	N	D

Description: ....   Reference: ....
....

Makers: ....   Suppliers: ....
Date Purchased: ....   Estimated Life: ....
Purchase Price: .... Scrap Value: ....   Net to W/OFF: ....
Method of Depreciation to Be Used: ....
....

Folio of Deptn. Schedule: ....   Frequency of Maintenance: ....

Date	Men employed	Time taken	Maintenance carried out	Approx. cost

FIG. 57.—*Plant and Machinery Register*

A record of each piece of plant or machinery is kept with details of major expenditure on maintenance. Guides may be clipped in position along the top of the card to indicate when items are due for preventive maintenance.

Ref. No.	Date of purchase	Brief Description	Cost Price	Depreciation			Date of Sale	Sale Price	Profit or Loss on Sale
				19...	19...	19...			

FIG. 58.—*Depreciation Schedule*

Such a schedule is indispensable for arriving at the total annual depreciation. The headings shown are a minimum and might be extended to include Depreciation rate and Total Depreciation.

tion Schedule will also be necessary in order to summarise the annual figures. Such a schedule is shown in Fig. 58.

2. All machines of one type together, which probably means that one rate and method of depreciation is in force for them all. The Depreciation Schedule can be made integral with the Plant record.
3. All machines in one department together. This enables the charge for depreciation against each Production Department to be easily ascertained.

OBSOLESCENCE

As distinct from depreciation, though akin to it, obsolescence is generally used to indicate a sudden loss in value of an asset, not due to wear and tear. It arises because a machine has to be discarded in favour of one better adapted to its purpose and giving better results. It is difficult to provide for this in advance, since a machine of new and revolutionary design may be put on the market at any time. It therefore becomes a difficult and important management problem to decide whether the point has been reached when it would be more profitable to exchange one machine for another.

MACHINE REPLACEMENT CALCULATION

On the data shown in Table III, provided the increased production could be disposed of satisfactorily, the new machine shows a saving of £0·00145 per unit of cost, and the purchase would be recommended.

TABLE III

Particulars		Existing machine	Proposed machine
Rate of production per hour, units		500	800
		£	£
Present realisable value		1000	—
Replacement cost		—	2000
% on Capital investment	15		
% depreciation (straight line)	20		
	35	350	700
Maintenance, power, supplies, etc.		2100	2300
Operators wages		1500	1000
		£3950	£4000
Estimated production for 2000 hours in millions of units		1·0	1·6
Cost per unit		0·00395	0·0025

Although the *book value* of the existing machine will probably be higher than the realisable value, the difference between the two figures does not have to be brought into calculation. In the event of the sale and purchase taking place, then the difference would be regarded as a loss to be written off, which had arisen through insufficient depreciation having been written off in the past. It has no bearing on the profitability of the new plant in the future.

Other points to be noticed in the illustration are that straight-line depreciation has been assumed over a period of five years, and that interest on the capital invested has to take account of the reducing balance outstanding, the true rate of return has been estimated as being 25%. Use has been made of a commonly accepted formula

$$y = \tfrac{1}{2}x \left(\frac{n+1}{n} \right),$$

where n equals the terms of years, and x the true rate of return on capital invested in the business.

This gives

$$y = \tfrac{1}{2} \times 25 \left(\frac{5+1}{5} \right) = \underline{15\%},$$

which is the rate used in the calculation.

It is, however, considered that a better method is to use the formula for reducing interest, which is perhaps known to students

$$A = P(1 - r)^n$$

For then

$$A = 2000 \left(\frac{100 - 25}{100} \right)^5,$$

which works out to £475.

The interest during the five years is £2000 − £475, or £1525, which, spread evenly over the period, is £305 per annum.

INTEREST ON CAPITAL

Although interest on capital invested has often to be considered in making calculations as, for example, in the illustration given above regarding plant replacement, the consensus of opinion is against including it in the Cost Accounts.

The arguments for and against doing so may be summarised thus:

For	*Against*
1. Wages is the reward of labour. Interest is the reward of capital. It is as much a production cost as labour.	1. This argument is economics, not costing.

For	Against
2. Real profit is not made until interest on capital is paid or provided.	2. Interest is merely an anticipation of profit.
3. Stocks held for maturing, such as timber, whisky, beer, etc., cost more for rent and interest. The same is really true of the fixed assets.	3. If interest is included in manufactured stock it has to be written back for Balance Sheet purposes.
4. Comparative costs of differing methods and processes are untrue unless interest on plant used is taken into account.	4. Charging interest is unnecessarily complicated, and comparisons involving interest are best done on separate statements.
5. Interest has to be paid on capital borrowed. If the borrowing is to assist production, the interest paid is part of the production cost. A manufacturer who uses his own capital should similarly be credited with a sum representing interest.	5. Interest on capital borrowed is a matter of finance, not of costing.

CHAPTER 14

COST CONTROL ACCOUNTS

THE system of double-entry book-keeping has been widely adopted. At first, bound ledgers were used for the recording of transactions, but in many industries these have been replaced by loose-leaf ledgers, card ledgers, and tabulations produced by machines from punched cards. However, even in the modern systems, the theory of "every debit must have a corresponding credit" still applies.

There are three types of accounts, viz:

1. Personal accounts: accounts of persons, *e.g.* debtors.
2. Real accounts: accounts of tangible items, *e.g.* cash.
3. Nominal accounts: accounts of gains or losses, *e.g.* discount.

In most firms, except perhaps the very small ones, a Cost Department is operated in which detailed cost statements, reports, etc., are produced. This department is particularly interested in the nominal accounts, and to some extent, real accounts, which may be considered as impersonal accounts. The Accounting Department is interested in personal accounts, real accounts, and nominal accounts. Thus, in the main, the Cost Department is concerned with the income and expenditure of the business.

In Chapter 16 integrated accounts will be discussed, in which it will be shown how the accounting and costing departments operate together, using only one set of books. However, in a business using Cost Control Accounts each of the two departments operates separate ledgers. In this chapter the main consideration is cost book-keeping, but to understand thoroughly the system it is essential to discuss some of the financial transactions which complete the book-keeping entries.

LEDGERS REQUIRED

The most important ledgers required are as follows:

FINANCIAL LEDGERS

1. *General Ledger.*
2. *Debtors Ledger.*
3. *Creditors Ledger.*

COST LEDGERS

1. *Cost Ledger.*—This is the principal ledger of the Cost Department, in which is recorded the impersonal accounts.

2. *Stores Ledger.*—In this ledger all the Stores Accounts are maintained, a description of which was given in Chapter 6. An account will be opened for each item in store.

3. *Work-in-progress Ledger.*—This ledger records production during a period and the cost incurred. Each job, unit, batch, or process will be assigned a number—a job number—and an account will be maintained for each job. All expenditure incurred will be posted to the respective Job Accounts as is described in Chapter 18.

4. *Finished Goods Ledger.*—The completely finished products are recorded in this ledger. An account will be opened for each type of product.

These are the four important ledgers in the Cost Department, and it is suggested that each ledger should have a Control Account, one for each ledger; the Cost Ledger will consequently contain these four Control Accounts, plus perhaps others, such as the Materials Control Account.

1. General Ledger Adjustment Account

This account is often referred to as Cost Ledger Control Account. Into this account are posted all items of income or expenditure which have been extracted from the Financial Accounts. In effect, this account represents the personal accounts shown in the Financial Books. Any transfer from the Cost Books to the Financial Books, *e.g.* cost of capital work performed by the factory, will be entered in this account. The main object of this account is to complete the double entry in the Cost Ledger. It is important to note that no entry should be made direct from the Financial Books to the Cost Books; entries must pass through the General Ledger Adjustment Account. The balance on this account represents the total of all the balances of the impersonal accounts.

2. Materials Control Account

This account is sometimes dispensed with but shows the total transactions of materials, *e.g.* total receipts, per invoices; and total transfers to Stores Ledger Control per Goods Received Notes. These are brought into agreement.

3. Stores Ledger Control Account

This shows the receipts of materials per Goods Received Notes, and issues per Stores Requisitions. The balance represents in total the detailed balance of the Stores Accounts.

4. *Work-in-progress Ledger Control Account*

This account represents the total work in progress at any time. At the end of any period the total balances of the Job Accounts should equal the balance on this account.

5. *Finished Goods Ledger Control Account*

The total value of finished goods in stock is represented in this account.

In the Financial Books a Cost Ledger Control Account is opened in which is recorded all the items of income and expenditure which affect the Cost Accounts (it will be shown on p. 178 that there are a number of items which are regarded as purely financial items and are not shown in the Cost Accounts). This account contains the same items as in the corresponding account in the Cost Books, but of course they are on the opposite side of the account.

A simple illustration will show how the Cost Ledger Control Account is operated:

Materials priced at £1000 are bought during January.

In the Financial Books

The Financial Accountant will be requested to open a Cost Ledger Control Account in which will be recorded all items of expenditure and income which affect the Cost Accounts. This account is memorandum only, so in addition to the ordinary posting, there will be a memorandum entry as follows:

	£	£
Dr. Materials Account	1000	
Cost Ledger Control Account (memorandum)		
Cr. Creditors Account		1000

In the Cost Books

	£	£
Dr. Materials Control Account	1000	
Cr. General Ledger Adjustment Account		1000

Purchase of materials on credit for £1000.

COST ACCOUNTS

When the Elements of Cost were discussed in Chapter 2 it was suggested that the different types of expenditure can be grouped as follows:

Direct Material ⎫
Direct Labour ⎬ PRIME COST
Direct Expenses ⎭
Production Overhead
Administration Overhead
Selling and Distribution Overhead

It is now suggested that, when answering examination questions, it is useful to open accounts in the Cost Ledger in rather the same order as shown above. The accounts will then be as follows:

1. General Ledger Adjustment Account.
2. Materials Control Account.
3. Stores Ledger Control Account.
4. Wages Control Account.
5. Production Overhead Account.
6. Administration Overhead Account.
7. Selling and Distribution Overhead Account.

It will be observed that an account was not opened for Direct Expenses: this is because Direct Expenses are charged direct to production.

The main items of expenditure will be recorded in the above-mentioned accounts, so it is now possible to find the cost of production by opening:

8. Work-in-progress Ledger Control Account (or Work-in-progress A/c).
9. Finished Goods Ledger Control Account (or Finished Goods Stock A/c).

These two accounts were referred to on pp. 133 and 157.

The finished goods which are sold are transferred to:

10. Cost of Sales Account.

In this account is shown the total selling and distribution overheads recovered, which together with the cost of finished goods, represents the cost of sales.

It is now possible to produce:

11. Costing Profit and Loss Account.

Briefly the above accounts are the main accounts to be opened in the Cost Ledger, but it may often be necessary to open additional accounts, e.g. Overhead Adjustment Account or accounts for special repairs or capital work, but these accounts will be explained later in this chapter.

SPECIMEN BOOK-KEEPING ENTRIES

Materials

Financial Books

1. During a financial period materials amounting to £10,000 are purchased on credit.

	£	£
Dr. Purchases Account	10,000	
Cost Ledger Control Account (memorandum)		
Cr. Creditors Account		10,000

	£	£

2. Returns to suppliers amounted to £200.

Dr. Creditors	200	
Cr. Purchases Returns		200
Cost Ledger Control Account (memorandum)		

3. Cash purchases of £1000 are effected.

Dr. Purchases Account	1,000	
Cost Ledger Control Account (memorandum)		
Cr. Cash		1,000

Cost Books

1. Credit purchases £10,000 of which £500 was purchase for special job.

Dr. Materials Control Account	10,000	
Cr. General Ledger Adjustment Account		10,000
Dr. Stores Ledger Control Account	9,500	
Work-in-progress Ledger Control Account	500	
Cr. Materials Control Account		10,000

2. Returns £200.

Dr. General Ledger Adjustment Account	200	
Cr. Stores Ledger Control Account		200

3. Cash Purchases £1000.

Dr. Materials Control Account	1,000	
Cr. General Ledger Adjustment Account		1,000
Dr. Stores Ledger Control Account	1,000	
Cr. Materials Control Account		1,000

The following entries do not affect the Financial Accounts, they are merely transactions or transfers in the Cost Ledger, therefore will not appear in the General Ledger Adjustment Account.

4. Materials amounting to £9000 are issued to production.

Dr. Work-in-progress Ledger Control Account	9,000	
Cr. Stores Ledger Control Account		9,000

The individual job accounts in the Work-in-progress Ledger will be debited and individual Stores Accounts in Stores Ledger credited.

5. Issue of indirect materials amount to £500.

Dr. Production Overhead Account	500	
Cr. Stores Ledger Control Account		500

Individual Stores Accounts will be credited in the Stores Ledger, and the total of overhead analysis debited to Production Overhead Account.

	£	£

6. Materials returned from production to Stores at cost of £50.

    Dr. Stores Ledger Control Account — 50

    Cr. Work-in-progress Ledger Control Account — 50

Individual Stores Accounts in the Stores Ledger will be debited and Job Accounts in the Work-in-progress Ledger credited.

7. Materials amounting to £100 were transferred from Job No. 29 to Job No. 57.

    Dr. Job No. 57 Account — 100

    Cr. Job No. 29 Account — 100

In the Work-in-progress Ledger, only these two accounts are affected. No entry is required in Work-in-progress Ledger Control Account or Stores Ledger Control Account.

Labour

Financial Books

1. During the same period wages amounting to £5000 are earned; deductions, etc., amounting to £500 are effected, viz.:

National Insurance (Employers and Employees)	£60
P.A.Y.E. Income Tax	£400
Superannuation contributions	£40

    Dr. Wages Account (including N.I. Employers) — 5,000

    Cost Ledger Control Account (memorandum)

    Cr. National Insurance Suspense Account — 60

    P.A.Y.E. Income Tax Account — 400

    Superannuation Fund Account — 40

    Cash — 4,500

Cost Books

1. Dr. Wages Control Account — 5,000

    Cr. General Ledger Adjustment Account — 5,000

2. This amount is analysed in the Wages Analysis Book.

Direct Labour	£4000
Indirect Labour	£1000

The indirect labour is further analysed:

Production staff	£600
Administration staff	£300
Selling and distribution staff	£100

    Dr. Work-in-progress Account — 4,000

    Cr. Wages Control Account — 4,000

	£	£

The individual Job Accounts will be charged as per the Analysis of Job Time records

Dr. Production Overhead Account	600	
Administration Overhead Account	300	
Selling and Distribution Overhead Account	100	
Cr. Wages Control Account		1,000

Overhead

Financial Books

1. During the period services were supplied by creditors amounting to £2000.

Dr. Expense Accounts	2,000	
Cost Ledger Control Account (memorandum)		
Cr. Creditors		2,000

2. This amount owing to Creditors was paid.

| Dr. Creditors | 2,000 | |
| Cr. Cash | | 2,000 |

This transaction does not affect the Cost Accounts.

3. Petty cash expenditure £100.

Dr. Expense Accounts	100	
Cost Ledger Control Account (memorandum)		
Cr. Cash		100

Cost Books

1. Services £2000; analysed, *e.g.*

Production Overhead	£1200		
Administration Overhead	£600		
Selling and Distribution Overhead	£200		
Dr. Production Overhead Account		1,200	
Administration Overhead Account		600	
Selling and Distribution Overhead Account		200	
Cr. General Ledger Adjustment Account			2,000

2. Petty cash expenditure £100 analysed, *e.g.*

Administration Overhead	£60		
Selling and Distribution Overhead	£40		
Dr. Administration Overhead Account		60	
Selling and Distribution Overhead Account		40	
Cr. General Ledger Adjustment Account			100

The Cost Ledger now shows the total overhead incurred on behalf of Production, Administration, Selling, and Distribution. It is now necessary to record in the Cost Ledger the amount of overheads which have been absorbed by production. This information is obtained from the Work-in-progress Ledger; as each period is

£ £

completed the respective accounts will be debited with the appropriate charge for production overheads, thus by totalling these charges the total overheads recovered can be ascertained.

3. Production Overhead, £2,250 has been absorbed by production (Stores, Wages, and Services).

Dr. Work in Progress Ledger Control Account 2,250
Cr. Production Overhead Account 2,250

4. Invariably there will be a difference between overheads incurred and overheads absorbed. In this illustration £2,300 was incurred and £2,250 absorbed. The difference is due to such factors as increased or decreased production, actual expenditure being above or below estimated; this was discussed more fully in Chapter 11. The balance on the account, representing over or under recovered overhead, is transferred to Overhead Adjustment Account or direct to Costing Profit and Loss Account.

Dr. Overhead Adjustment Account 50
Cr. Production Overhead Account 50

5. *Administration Overhead*, £1,000 has been absorbed by production of finished goods.

Dr. Finished Goods Ledger Control Account 1,000
Cr. Administration Overhead Account 1,000

6. The balance of the Account is transferred:

Dr. Administration Overhead Account 40
Cr. Overhead Adjustment Account 40

7. *Selling and Distribution Overhead*, £325 has been recovered on goods sold.

Dr. Cost of Sales Account 325
Cr. Selling and Distribution Overhead Account 325
Selling and Distribution Overheads are not allocated to production, but form part of the Cost of Sales. It is therefore necessary to record the amount of selling and distribution overheads which have been recovered from sales.

8. The balance of the account is transferred:

Dr. Overhead Adjustment Account 15
Cr. Selling and Distribution Overhead Account 15

SPECIMEN QUESTION

The following balances appeared in the books of the Gosforth Engineering Co. Ltd. as at the beginning of the financial year:

	£	£
General Ledger Adjustment Account		15,237
Stores Ledger Control Account	8,751	
Work-in-progress Ledger Control Account	4,287	
Finished Goods Ledger Control Account	2,199	
	£15,237	£15,237

At the end of the year the following information is supplied:

Purchases for Stores		57,640
Purchases for Special Jobs		1,750
Direct Wages	38,627	
Indirect factory wages	9,543	
Administrative salaries	6,731	
Selling and Distribution salaries	4,252	
		59,153
Production Expenses		12,432
Administration Expenses		8,546
Selling and Distribution Expenses		5,437
Stores issued to Production		54,701
Stores issued to Maintenance Account		2,476
Returns to supplier		207
Production Overheads absorbed by production		24,500
Administration Overheads absorbed by finished goods		15,250
Selling Overhead recovered on sales		9,600
Products finished during year		117,717
Finished Goods sold—at cost		132,292
Sales		150,000

You are required to record the entries in the Cost Ledger for the year and prepare a Trial Balance.

ANSWER

COST LEDGER

General Ledger Adjustment Account

	£		£
Dec. 31 To Stores Ledg. Control A/c—		Jan. 1 By Balance b/d	15,237
returns	207	Dec. 31 ,, Stores Ledg. Control A/c—	
,, 31 ,, P. & L. A/c—sales	150.000	purchases	57,640
,, 31 ,, Balance c/d	18,029	,, 31 ,, W.I.P. A/c—special pur-	
		chases	1,750
		,, 31 ,, Wages A/c	59,153
		,, 31 ,, Production Overhead A/c	12,432
		,, 31 ,, Administration Overhead	
		A/c	8,546
		,, 31 ,, Selling Overhead A/c	5,437
		,, 31 ,, Costing P. & L. A/c—profit	8,041
	£168,236		£168,236
		Jan. 1 By Bal. b/d	18,029

Stores Ledger Control Account

	£		£
Jan. 1 To Balance b/d	8,751	Dec. 31 By W.I.P. Ledg. Control A/c	54,701
Dec. 31 ,, Gen. Ledg. Adj. A/c—purchases	57,640	,, 31 ,, Production Overhead A/c	2,476
		,, 31 ,, Gen. Ledg. Adj. A/c	207
		,, 31 ,, Balance c/d	9,007
	£66,391		£66,391
Jan. 1 To Balance b/d	9,007		

Wages Control Account

	£		£
Dec. 31 To Gen. Ledg. Adj. A/c	59,153	Dec. 31 By W.I.P. Ledg. Control A/c	38,627
		,, 31 ,, Production Overhead A/c	9,543
		,, 31 ,, Administration Overhead A/c	6,731
		,, 31 ,, Selling Overhead A/c	4,252
	£59,153		£59,153

Production Overhead Account

	£		£
Dec. 31 To Gen. Ledg. Adj. A/c	12,432	Dec. 31 By W.I.P. Ledg. Control A/c	24,500
,, 31 ,, Stores Ledg. Control A/c	2,476		
,, 31 ,, Wages A/c	9,543		
,, 31 ,, Overhead Adjustment A/c	49		
	£24,500		£24,500

Administration Overhead Account

	£		£
Dec. 31 To Gen. Ledg. Adj. A/c	8,546	Dec. 31 By F. Goods Ledg. Control A/c	15,250
,, 31 ,, Wages A/c	6,731	,, 31 ,, Overhead Adjustment A/c	27
	£15,277		£15,277

Selling and Distribution Overhead Account

	£		£
Dec. 31 To Gen. Ledg. Adj. A/c	5,437	Dec. 31 By Cost of Sales A/c	9,600
,, 31 ,, Wages A/c	4,252	,, 31 ,, Overhead Adjustment A/c	89
	£9,689		£9,689

Work in Progress Ledger Control Account

	£		£
Jan. 1 To Balance b/d	4,287	Dec. 31 By Fin. Goods Ledg. Control A/c	117,717
Dec. 31 ,, Gen. Ledg. Adj. A/c	1,750	,, 31 ,, Balance c/d	6,148
,, 31 ,, Stores Ledg. Control A/c	54,701		
,, 31 ,, Wages A/c	38,627		
,, 31 ,, Production Overhead A/c	24,500		
	£123,865		£123,865
Jan. 1 To Balance b/d	6,148		

Finished Goods Ledger Control Account

		£			£
Jan. 1	To Balance b/d	2,199	Dec. 31	By Cost of Sales A/c	132,292
Dec. 31	,, Administration Overhead A/c	15,250	,, 31	,, Balance c/d	2,874
,, 31	,, W.I.P. Ledg. Control A/c	117,717			
		£135,166			£135,166
Jan. 1	To Balance b/d	2,874			

Cost of Sales Account

		£			£
Dec. 31	To Selling Overhead A/c	9,600	Dec. 31	By P. & L. A/c	141,892
,, 31	,, Finished Goods Ledg. Control A/c	132,292			
		£141,892			£141,892

Overhead Adjustment Account

		£			£
Dec. 31	To Administration Overhead A/c	27	Dec. 31	By Production Overhead A/c	49
,, 31	,, Selling Overhead A/c	89	,, 31	,, Costing P. & L. A/c	67
		£116			£116

Costing Profit and Loss Account for year ending December 31

	£		£
To Cost of Sales	141,892	By Sales	150,000
,, Overhead Adjustment A/c	67		
,, General Ledger Adjustment A/c: profit for year	8,041		
	£150,000		£150,000

Trial Balance as at December 31

	£	£
Stores Ledger Control Account	9,007	
Work-in-progress Ledger Control Account	6,148	
Finished Goods Ledger Control Account	2,874	
General Ledger Adjustment Account		18,029
	£18,029	£18,029

OVERHEAD ADJUSTMENT ACCOUNT

Into this account is transferred all over- or under-recovered overhead; the balance being taken to Costing Profit and Loss Account. Often this account is not opened, any balances on overhead accounts being transferred direct to Costing Profit and Loss Account.

CAPITAL ORDERS

Improvements to plant, machinery, tools, buildings, etc., are frequently carried out by a manufacturing company's own workmen, and on many occasions tools and equipment are actually produced in the firm. It is absolutely essential that a record is kept of all expenditure incurred on these operations, so that successful work may be "capitalised." By this is meant the transfer of all expenditure incurred to an asset account, *e.g.* if materials amounting to £2000 and wages £1000 were incurred in producing a machine for use in the factory the accounting entries would be:

	£	£
Dr. Capital Order Account	3000	
Cr. Work-in-progress Ledger Control Account		3000

A Capital Order would be opened for each item of capital work to be performed, and on this order would be recorded all expenditure involved on each job. When the work was finished the above transfer would be effected. At the end of the period the asset would be transferred from the Cost Accounts to the Financial Accounts, as follows:

	£	£
Dr. General Ledger Adjustment Account	3000	
Cr. Capital Order Account		3000

It will be observed that no addition of Production Overhead has been made to the amount to be capitalised in the above illustration. Opinions differ on whether this ought to be done, but it is thought that provided such overhead is incurred in consequence of the capital work undertaken, it is legitimate to do so. It is obviously unsound practice, however, to load normal overhead on to capital projects to such an extent as to vitiate comparisons of product manufacture.

REPAIR ORDERS

Special repair and maintenance work is recorded in a rather similar way to capital equipment work. A repair order is issued, on which is recorded all expenditure incurred on that special job. When the repair is completed the repair order would be closed and the necessary adjustment effected in the Cost Ledger:

	£	£
Dr. Special Repair and Maintenance Account	3500	
Cr. Work in Progress Ledger Control Account		3500

Assuming that this expenditure had been incurred on behalf of departments as follows: Production Department £2000; Administration Department £1000; Selling and Distribution Department £500; the entries would be:

	£	£
Dr. Production Overhead Account	2000	
Administration Overhead Account	1000	
Selling and Distribution Overhead Account	500	
Cr. Special Repairs and Maintenance Account		3500

SPECIAL ORDERS

Sometimes orders are received for a special delivery of goods to a customer. A production order will be issued on which will be recorded all expenditure incurred on this special job. When the job is completed the goods can be despatched to the customer without being taken into Finished Stock. The entry will then be:

Dr. Special Order Account
Cr. Work-in-progress Ledger Control Account

CARRIAGE INWARDS

Where possible the cost of carriage inwards is often added to the purchase price of the materials. However, this is frequently found to be impracticable, so this expense is recovered on production through production overhead.

Dr. Production Overhead Account
Cr. General Ledger Adjustment Account

SPECIMEN QUESTION

The balances appearing in the Cost Ledger of the Ramsay Engineering Co. Ltd. at January 1 were as follows:

	£	s.	d.	£	s.	d.
General Ledger Adjustment Account				58,750	1	0
Stores Ledger Control Account	25,247	1	3			
Work-in-progress Ledger Control Account	12,560	11	7			
Finished Goods Ledger Control Account	20,942	8	2			
	£58,750	1	0	£58,750	1	0

At the end of the year the following information is supplied:

	£	s.	d.	£	s.	d.
Purchases for Stores				180,742	6	11
Purchases for Special Job No. 57				10,638	7	6
Materials issued to Production:						
Materials used on Special Repairs and Maintenance Order No. 29	3,526	10	8			
Material used on Capital Order No. 10	8,974	6	3			
Material used on Special Job No. 57	20,748	5	4			
Material used in products	140,915	11	2			
				174,164	13	5
Materials issued to repairs and maintenance				2,468	3	7
Materials returned to suppliers from Stores				1,253	6	1
Materials lost by theft				125	10	0
Carriage inwards on Stores				3,264	3	8
Total Wages paid to employees:	£	s.	d.			
Labour incurred on Special Repairs and Maintenance Order No. 29	2,431	9	4			
Labour incurred on Capital Order No. 10	6,327	12	8			
Labour incurred on Special Job No. 57	18,642	11	5			
Labour incurred on products	106,064	18	11			
				133,466	12	4
Indirect Wages	15,346	10	2			
Idle time due to power failure	575	6	8			
Normal idle time	992	16	5			
				16,914	13	3
Direct Expenses				596	17	3
Production Expenses				21,263	8	11
Administration Expenses				18,461	9	2
Selling Expenses				10,572	3	8
Distribution Expenses				5,432	11	6
Sales	330,000	0	0			
Selling Price of Special Job No. 57	70,000	0	0			
				400,000	0	0

At the end of the year the following balances were ascertained:

	£	s.	d.
Stores Ledger Control Account	27,844	12	4
Work-in-progress Ledger Control Account	14,106	3	8
Finished Goods Ledger Control Account	22,167	4	11

Production Overheads were recovered as follows: 15% on Prime Cost.
Administration Overheads were recovered on Finished Production, amounting to £20,000.

170   COST ACCOUNTING

Selling and Distribution Overheads were recovered on products sold, amounting to £17,500.

Capital Order No. 10 was completed during the year and is to be "capitalised."

Special Repair and Maintenance Order No. 29 was completed and is to be charged to Production, Administration, Selling and Distribution Departments in the ratio of 5 : 3 : 2.

Special Job No. 57 was also completed and was despatched to customer. Production Overhead is not to be charged to Capital Order No. 10. Administration Overhead and Selling and Distribution Overhead is not to be charged to Special Order No. 57.

You are required to enter the amounts in the Cost Ledger, prepare the Costing Profit and Loss Accounts, and show a Trial Balance at the end of the period.

ANSWER

General Ledger Adjustment Account

	£	s.	d.		£	s.	d.
To Stores Ledger Control A/c—				By Balance b/d	58,750	1	0
returns	1,253	6	1	,, Stores Ledger Control A/c:			
,, Capital Order No. 10	15,301	18	11	materials purchased	180,742	6	11
,, Profit & Loss A/c—sales	330,000	0	0	,, W.I.P. Ledger Control A/c:			
,, Special Job No. 57	70,000	0	0	materials for special orders	10,638	7	6
,, Balance c/d	64,118	0	11	,, Production Overhead A/c:			
				carriage inwards	3,264	3	8
				,, Wages Control A/c	150,381	5	7
				,, W.I.P. Ledger Control A/c:			
				direct expenses	596	17	3
				,, Production Overhead A/c	21,263	8	11
				,, Administration Overhead A/c	18,461	9	2
				,, Selling Overhead A/c	10,572	3	8
				,, ,,	5,432	11	6
				,, Costing P. & L. A/c: profit			
				for year	20,570	10	9
	£480,673	5	11		£480,673	5	11
				,, Balance b/d	64,118	0	11

Stores Ledger Control Account

	£	s.	d.		£	s.	d.
To Balance b/d	25,247	1	3	By W.I.P. Ledger Control A/c:			
,, Gen. Ledger Adj. A/c: purchases	180,742	6	11	materials issued to production	174,164	13	5
				,, Production Overhead A/c:			
				materials used for repairs	2,468	3	7
				,, Gen. Ledger Adj. A/c: materials returned	1,253	6	1
				,, Abnormal Loss A/c: materials lost by theft	125	10	
				,, Production Overhead A/c: normal loss of materials	133	2	9
				,, Balance c/d	27,844	12	4
	£205,989	8	2		£205,989	8	2
To Balance b/d	27,844	12	4				

Wages Control Account

	£	s.	d.		£	s.	d.
To Gen. Ledger Adj. A/c: Wages	150,381	5	7	By W.I.P. Ledger Control A/c: direct wages	133,466	12	4
				„ Production Overhead A/c: indirect wages	15,346	10	2
				„ Abnormal Loss A/c: idle time	575	6	8
				„ Production Overhead A/c: normal idle time	992	16	5
	£150,381	5	7		£150,381	5	7

Production Overhead Account

	£	s.	d.		£	s.	d.
To Stores Ledger Control A/c: materials for repairs	2,468	3	7	By W.I.P. Ledger Control A/c: overhead recovered	45,302	16	11
„ Gen. Ledger Adj. A/c: carriage inwards	3,264	3	8	„ Overhead Adj. A/c: (under recovered)	1,591	5	7
„ Wages Control A/c:							
Indirect wages	15,346	10	2				
Normal idle time	992	16	5				
„ Gen. Ledger Adj. A/c	21,263	8	11				
„ Stores Ledger Control A/c: normal loss	133	2	9				
„ Special Repairs & Maintenance O. 29	3,425	17	0				
	£46,894	2	6		£46,894	2	6

Administration Overhead Account

	£	s.	d.		£	s.	d.
To Gen. Ledger Adj. A/c	18,461	9	2	By Finished Goods Ledger Con. A/c: overhead recovered	20,000	0	0
„ Special Repairs & Maintenance O. 29: repairs	2,055	10	2	„ Overhead Adj. A/c: (under recovered)	516	19	4
	£20,516	19	4		£20,516	19	4

Selling and Distribution Overhead Account

	£	s.	d.		£	s.	d.
To Gen. Ledger Adj. A/c	10,572	3	8	By Cost of Sales A/c: overhead recovered	17,500	0	0
„ „ „	5,432	11	6				
„ Special Repairs & Maintenance O. 29: repairs	1,370	6	10				
„ Overhead Adj. A/c: (over-recovered)	124	18	0				
	£17,500	0	0		£17,500	0	0

Work-in-progress Ledger Control Account

	£	s.	d.					£	s.	d.
To Balance b/d	12,560	11	7	By Special Repair & Mainten-						
„ Gen. Ledger Adj. A/c: pur-				ance O. 29:	£	s.	d.			
chases	10,638	7	6	Materials	3,526	10	8			
„ Stores Ledger Control A/c:				Labour	2,431	9	4			
materials issued	174,164	13	5	Production						
„ Wages Control A/c: direct				overhead	893	14	0			
wages	133,466	12	4					6,851	14	0
„ Gen. Ledger Adj. A/c: direct				„ Capital Order No. 10:						
expenses	596	17	3	Materials	8,974	6	3			
„ Production Overhead A/c	45,302	16	11	Labour	6,327	12	8			
								15,301	18	11
				„ Special Job No. 57:						
				Materials	20,748	5	4			
				Labour	18,642	11	5			
				Production						
				overhead	7,504	7	8			
				Special pur-						
				chases	10,638	7	6			
								57,533	11	11
				„ Finished Goods Ledger Con-						
				trol A/c				282,936	10	6
				„ Balance c/d				14,106	3	8
	£376,729	19	0					£376,729	19	0
„ Balance b/d	14,106	3	8							

Finished Goods Ledger Control Account

	£	s.	d.		£	s.	d.
To Balance b/d	20,942	8	2	By Cost of Sales A/c: finished			
W.I.P. Ledger Control A/c	282,936	10	6	goods sold	301,711	13	9
„ Administration Overhead	20,000	0	0	„ Balance c/d	22,167	4	11
	£323,878	18	8		£323,878	18	8
„ Balance b/d	22,167	4	11				

Special Repair & Maintenance Order No. 29

		£	s.	d.		£	s.	d.
To W.I.P. Ledger Control A/c:					By Production Overhead A/c	3,425	17	0
	£	s.	d.		„ Administration Overhead A/c	2,055	10	2
Materials	3,526	10	8		„ Selling Overhead A/c	1,370	6	10
Labour	2,431	9	4					
Production								
overhead	893	14	0					
		6,851	14	0				
		£6,851	14	0		£6,851	14	0

Capital Order No. 10

		£	s.	d.		£	s.	d.
To W.I.P. Ledger Control A/c:					By Gen. Ledger Adj. A/c: cost of			
	£	s.	d.		capital work	15,301	18	11
Materials	8,974	6	3					
Labour	6,327	12	8					
		15,301	18	11				
		£15,301	18	11		£15,301	18	11

Special Job No. 57

	£ s. d.		£ s. d.
To W.I.P. Ledger Control A/c:		By Gen. Ledger Adj. A/c: sales	70,000 0 0
£ s. d.			
Materials 20,748 5 4			
Labour 18,642 11 5			
Overhead 7,504 7 8			
Special purchases 10,638 7 6			
	57,533 11 11		
P. & L. A/c: profit	12,466 8 1		
	£70,000 0 0		£70,000 0 0

Abnormal Loss on Materials Account

To Stores Ledger Control A/c	£125 10 0	By Costing P. & L. A/c	£125 10 0

Abnormal Idle Time Account

To Wages Control A/c	£575 6 8	By Costing P. & L. A/c	£575 6 8

Overhead Adjustment Account

	£ s. d.		£ s. d.
To Production Overhead A/c	1,591 5 7	By Selling Overhead A/c	124 18 0
„ Administration Overhead A/c	516 19 4	„ Costing P. & L. A/c	1,983 6 11
	2,108 4 11		2,108 4 11

Cost of Sales Account

	£ s. d.		£ s. d.
To Finished Goods Ledger	301,711 13 9	By Costing P. & L. A/c	319,211 13 9
„ Selling & Distribution Overhead A/c	17,500 0 0		
	£319,211 13 9		£319,211 13 9

Costing Profit and Loss Account for Period Ending December 31

	£ s. d.		£ s. d.
To Cost of Sales	319,211 13 9	By Sales	330,000 0 0
„ Abnormal loss: £ s. d.		„ Profit on Special Job No. 57	12,466 8 1
Materials 125 10 0			
Labour 575 6 8			
	700 16 8		
„ Overhead Adj. A/c: overhead under-recovered	1,983 6 11		
Gen. Ledger Adj. A/c: profit for year	20,570 10 9		
	£342,466 8 1		£342,466 8 1

Trial Balance as at December 31

	£ s. d.	£ s. d.
General Ledger Adjustment Account		64,118 0 11
Stores Ledger Control Account	27,844 12 4	
Work-in-progress Ledger Control Account	14,106 3 8	
Finished Goods Ledger Control Account	22,167 4 11	
	£64,118 0 11	£64,118 0 11

NOTES

Production Overhead Recovered

Production Overheads are to be recovered at 15% on Prime Cost. This is calculated:

	£ s. d.	£ s. d.
Balance of Work-in-progress	12,560 11 7	
Special Purchases	10,638 7 6	
Materials	174,164 13 5	
Wages	133,466 12 4	
Direct Expenses	596 17 3	
	331,427 2 1	
Less Balance c/d	14,106 3 8	
		£317,320 18 5

$$£317,320 \ 18s. \ 5d. \times \frac{15}{100} = £47,598 \ 2s. \ 9d.$$

This is analysed:

Special Repair and Maintenance Order No. 29

	£ s. d.	£ s. d.	£ s. d.
Prime Cost	5,958 0 0		
15%		893 14 0	

Capital Order No. 10

	£ s. d.	£ s. d.	
Prime Cost	15,301 18 11		
15%		2,295 5 10	

Special Job No. 57

	£ s. d.	£ s. d.	
Prime Cost	50,029 4 3		
15%		7,504 7 8	

Finished Production

	£ s. d.	£ s. d.	£ s. d.
Prime Cost	246,031 15 3		
15%		36,904 15 3	
			£47,598 2 9

However in this illustration, it is suggested that Production Overhead should not be charged to Capital Orders, so that the actual overheads recovered will be

	£ s. d.
	47,598 2 9
Less Capital Order No. 10	2,295 5 10
	£45,302 16 11

The profit for the year is debited to Costing Profit and Loss Account and credited to General Ledger Adjustment Account. If a loss had been realised the entries would have been reversed.

It has been shown in the above exercise how the Cost Accountant has ascertained the profit for the year. The Financial Accountant would also have prepared Final Accounts and ascertained the profit for the year. If management is to have any confidence in the information provided it is obvious that the profit for the year as ascertained by the Financial Accountant and Cost Accountant must be reconcilable. This will be discussed in the next chapter.

OVER- OR UNDER-ABSORBED OVERHEAD

In the above illustration over- or under-absorbed overhead was transferred to an Overhead Adjustment Account and the balance taken to Profit and Loss Account. This was because many accountants consider that overhead incurred in a financial period should be recovered during the same period. However, some accountants prefer to carry forward the balances on the various Overhead Accounts to the next year, so they show the balances in the Trial Balance. Where the latter method is used there will be a difference in profit shown in the Cost Accounts compared with that in the Financial Accounts.

WORK IN PROGRESS LEDGER

It will be observed that all work performed, whether routine, special, maintenance, or capital, has been recorded in the Work-in-progress Ledger. Job Accounts will be maintained for each job, and possibly different colours will be used to denote the various types of job, such as capital, maintenance orders. When, for example, a Capital Order is completed, the total material and labour cost can be transferred from the Work-in-progress Ledger to the Capital Order Account in the Cost Ledger, which will thus reveal the cost of the project to be capitalised.

CHAPTER 15

THE RECONCILIATION OF COST AND FINANCIAL ACCOUNTS

WHERE accounts are maintained on the Integral Accounts System there are no separate Cost Accounts and Financial Accounts, consequently the problem of reconciliation does not occur. However, where there is a financial-accounting system and a separate cost-accounting system it is imperative that the accounts be reconciled. A Memorandum Reconciliation Account is prepared, as will be illustrated later in the chapter.

At this stage it might be expedient to consider in more detail the General Ledger Adjustment Account which was prepared in the previous chapter. The account appeared thus:

General Ledger Adjustment Account

	£	s.	d.		£	s.	d.
To Stores Ledger Control A/c— returns	1,253	6	1	By Balance b/d	58,750	1	0
„ Capital Order No. 10	15,301	18	11	„ Stores Ledger Control A/c: materials purchased	180,742	6	11
„ Profit & Loss A/c—sales	330,000	0	0	„ W.I.P. Ledger Control A/c: materials for special orders	10,638	7	6
„ Special Job No. 57	70,000	0	0	„ Production Overhead A/c: carriage inwards	3,264	3	8
„ Balance c/d	64,118	0	11	„ Wages Control A/c	150,381	5	7
				„ W.I.P. Ledger Control A/c: direct expenses	596	17	3
				„ Production Overhead A/c	21,263	8	11
				„ Administration Overhead A/c	18,461	9	2
				„ Selling Overhead A/c	10,572	3	8
				„ „ „	5,432	11	6
				„ Costing P. & L. A/c: profit for year	20,570	10	9
	£480,673	5	11		£480,673	5	11
				„ Balance b/d	64,118	0	11

The items appearing in the above account may be analysed as follows:

DEBIT ITEMS

1. *Returns*

This figure should be the same as that appearing in the Financial Books where the entry would have been:

	£	s.	d.	£	s.	d.
Dr. Creditors	1253	6	1			
Cr. Purchase Returns Account				1253	6	1
Cr. Cost Ledger Control Account (memorandum)						

176

2. Capital work

It is a policy decision of management as to whether or not the value of capital improvements completed will be shown in the Asset Account in the Financial books at the cost price as recorded in the Cost Ledger. If the value is the same, then this item will not affect the reconciliation of the cost and financial accounts. However, if the value is lower, then the profit shown by the Cost Accounts will be greater than that shown by the Financial Accounts, so must be reconciled in the Reconciliation Account.

In the Financial Books:

	£	s.	d.	£	s.	d.
Dr. Asset Account	15,301	18	11			
Cr. Purchases Account				8974	6	3
Wages Account				6327	12	8
Cost Ledger Control Account (memorandum)						

3 and 4. Sales

This figure is obtained from the Financial Accounts.

	£	s.	d.	£	s.	d.
Dr. Sundry Debtors Account	400,000	0	0			
Cr. Sales Account				400,000	0	0
Cr. Cost Ledger Control Account (memorandum)						

5. Balance

This represents the various asset accounts, *e.g.* Stock, Work-in-progress, Finished Goods at end of period.

CREDIT ITEMS

1. Balance

This represents the various asset accounts, *e.g.* Stock, Work-in-progress, Finished Goods at beginning of period.

2. *Materials*
3. *Special materials*
4. *Carriage inwards*
5. *Wages*
6. *Direct expense*
7. *Production overhead*
8. *Administration overhead*
9. *Selling overhead*
10. *Distribution overhead*

As illustrated in the previous chapter, these charges were obtained from the Financial Accounts through the memorandum Cost Ledger Control Account.

11. *Profit*

The Financial Accountant will have ascertained the year's profit in the Profit and Loss Account, so will not wish to record the costing profit also in his Ledger. Consequently this item will be shown only in the Memorandum Cost Control Account as a debit, thus corresponding with the Credit in the General Ledger Adjustment Account.

It can be seen from the General Ledger Adjustment Account that most of the figures have been posted from the Financial Accounts, so in respect of these items no reconciliation is necessary. The only exceptions were:

(*a*) Opening and closing balances.
(*b*) Capital Order.
(*c*) Profit for year.

Thus, when preparing a Memorandum Reconciliation Account these three items are the only ones to be considered in relation to the Cost Accounts. If, however, over-or-under absorbed overheads are carried forward to the next period (as was mentioned in the previous chapter as an alternative to the method illustrated there), then this item will also affect reconciliation.

ITEMS SHOWN ONLY IN THE FINANCIAL ACCOUNTS

There will invariably be a number of items which appear in the Financial Accounts and not in the Cost Accounts. All such items of expenditure will have reduced the financial profit for the year, while any items of income will have increased the financial profit. When reconciling the Cost and Financial Accounts, any items under this category must be considered. The main items are:

1. *Purely financial charges*

(*a*) Losses of Capital Assets, arising from sale, exchange, or uninsured destruction. Fees of assessors and advisers on such destruction losses (fire, etc.) come under this heading, being unrelated to operating cost.
(*b*) Stamp duty and expenses on issues and transfers of capital stock, shares and bonds, etc.
(*c*) Losses on investments.
(*d*) Discounts on bonds, debentures, etc.
(*e*) Fines and penalties.
(*f*) Interest on bank loans, mortgages, etc.

2. *Purely financial income*

(a) Rent receivable; if, however, the rent is received from sub-letting part of the business premises, then allowance will probably have been made in the Cost Accounts.

(b) Profits arising from sale of Fixed Assets.

(c) Fees received on issues and transfers of shares, etc.

(d) Interest received on bank deposits, loans, etc.

(e) Dividends received.

3. *Appropriation of profit*

(a) Donations to charities.

(b) Items which appear in the Profit and Loss Appropriation Account, *e.g.*

    (i) Income Tax.

    (ii) Dividends paid.

    (iii) Amounts transferred to Sinking Funds for repayment of liabilities.

    (iv) Transfers to Reserves.

    (v) Amounts written off goodwill.

The items included in (b) above will not, of course, affect the net profit shown in the financial Profit and Loss Account.

ITEMS SHOWN ONLY IN THE COST ACCOUNTS

There are very few items which appear in the Cost Accounts and not in the Financial Accounts. All expenditure incurred, whether for cash or credit, passes through the financial accounting system, so the type of entry which can appear in the cost accounts only is a nominal charge, *e.g.*

1. *Interest on capital*

Sometimes management policy is to charge interest on capital employed in production in order to show the nominal cost of employing the capital rather than investing it outside the business.

2. *Charge in lieu of rent*

Again it is sometimes policy to charge a nominal amount for rent of premises owned, so as to be able to compare costs of production in a factory owned by a company with similar costs in a leasehold or rented factory.

G

However, these two items will not affect the Financial Profit or Loss because they are merely a transfer in the Cost Accounts:

Dr. Work in Progress Ledger Control Account.
Cr. Costing Profit and Loss Account.

A brief example of a Memorandum Reconciliation Account will illustrate the points mentioned above.

SPECIMEN QUESTION

Profit and Loss Account for Year Ending December 31

	£		£
To Office Salaries	5,641	By Gross Profit b/d	27,324
„ „ Expenses	3,257	„ Dividend Received	200
„ Salesmen's Salaries	2,461	„ Interest on Bank deposit	75
„ Sales Expenses	4,652		
„ Distribution Expenses	1,495		
„ Loss on sale of machinery	975		
„ Fines	100		
„ Discount on debentures	50		
„ Net Profit for year c/d	8,968		
	£27,599		£27,599
To Income Tax	4,000	By Net Profit b/d	8,968
„ Reserve	500		
„ Dividend	2,000		
„ Balance c/d	2,468		
	£8,968		£8,968

The above accounts have been prepared by the accountant of W.R. Ltd. The Cost Accountant has prepared his accounts for the year, from which he ascertains a profit of £9,818. Reconcile the two sets of accounts.

ANSWER

Memorandum Reconciliation Account

		£			£
To Items not charged in Cost Accounts:			By Profit as per Cost Accounts		9,818
Loss on machinery	975		„ Items not credited in Cost Account:		
Fines	100		Dividend Received	200	
Discount on debentures	50		Interest on Bank Deposit	75	
		1,125			275
„ Profit as per Financial Account		8,968			
		£10,093			£10,093

OVERHEAD

The recovery of overhead is always based on an estimate, *e.g.* percentage on Prime Cost, percentage on sales, etc., so that the amount recovered and the amount actually incurred will invariably disagree.

As was illustrated in the previous chapter, differences may be written off to an Overhead Adjustment Account or direct to Costing Profit and Loss Account, with the result that the actual amount shown in the Financial Accounts will now agree with that finally charged in the Cost Accounts. Consequently, when reconciling Cost and Financial Accounts no further adjustment in respect of overheads is necessary.

In some costing systems selling and distribution overheads are ignored, as a result of which the Costing Profit and Loss Account will show a greater profit or smaller loss than that shown by the Financial Accounts, in which obviously selling and distribution expenses would be included. When preparing a Memorandum Reconciliation Account an adjustment must be made in respect of any such expenses.

SPECIMEN QUESTION

The Profit and Loss Account of B.B. Ltd. is as follows:

Profit and Loss Account for the Year Ending December 31

	£		£
To Office Salaries	4,834	By Gross Profit b/d	25,000
,, Office Expenses	3,214		
,, Sales Manager's Salary	1,000		
,, Salemen's Salaries	4,256		
,, Sales Expenses	3,419		
,, Packing Costs	875		
,, Distribution Expenses	1,246		
,, Net Profit c/d	6,156		
	£25,000		£25,000

The Cost Accounts revealed a profit for the year of £16,952; selling and distribution overheads had been ignored. Reconcile the cost and financial accounts.

ANSWER

Memorandum Reconciliation Account

	£	£		£
To Items not charged in Cost A/c:	£	£	By Profit as per Cost Accounts	16,952
,, Sales Manager's Salary	1,000			
,, Salesmen's Salaries	4,256			
,, Sales Expenses	3,419			
,, Packing Costs	875			
,, Distribution Expenses	1,246			
		10,796		
,, Profit as per Financial A/cs		6,156		
		£16,952		£16,952

DIFFERENT BASES OF STOCK VALUATION

Frequently stocks will appear in the Cost Accounts at one figure, and in the Financial Accounts at a different figure, due to the use of different bases of stock valuation. The financial accountant invariably bases the valuation of his stock on the principle of cost or market value, whichever is the lower, as a matter of financial prudence. However, the cost accountant will value his stock according to the system adopted in the stock accounts, *e.g.* F.I.F.O. or L.I.F.O., whichever system he thinks best portrays the cost of the material. As will be appreciated, differences in stock valuations will affect the profits or losses shown by the two sets of books. In preparing a Reconciliation Account, consideration must be given to this important point.

Valuation of work in progress often proves to be very difficult. There are three main bases:

1. Prime Cost.
2. Prime Cost + Production Overhead.
3. Prime Cost + Production Overhead + Administration Overhead.

It is suggested that the second base is perhaps the most suitable because Production Overhead is usually incurred all the time production is proceeding, but Administration Overhead is incurred whether production is nil or 100%. It may be remembered that in the previous chapter, Production Overhead was charged to work in progress while Administration Overhead was charged to finished goods.

SPECIMEN QUESTION

The Manufacturing Account of G.B. Ltd., is as follows:

Manufacturing Account for Year Ended December 31

	£	£		£
To Raw Materials:			By Trading Account:	
Opening Stock	25,246		Cost of goods manufactured transferred	263,092
Purchases	112,648			
	137,894			
Less Closing Stock	29,461			
,, Materials consumed		108,433		
,, Wages—direct		87,461		
PRIME COST		195,894		
,, *Factory Overheads:*				
Power	21,468			
Wages—indirect	27,428			
Rent and Rates	10,641			
Heating and Lighting	2,467			
Depreciation	5,835			
Expenses	975			
		68,814		
GROSS WORKS COST		264,708		
Deduct Work in Progress:				
Closing Stock	17,468			
Less Opening Stock	15,852			
		1,616		
		£263,092		£263,092

The Profit and Loss Account reveals a profit of £57,634 for the year. In the Cost Accounts the valuations placed on Stocks were:

Raw Materials—   Opening Stock £25,348
                  Closing Stock £29,371

Work in Progress—Opening Stock £15,763
                 Closing Stock £17,409

Profit shown in the Costing Profit and Loss Account was £57,472. Prepare a Reconciliation Account.

ANSWER

Memorandum Reconciliation Account

	£			£
To Difference in Stock: Work in Progress—Opening Stock	89	By Profit as per Cost Accounts		57,472
„ Profit as per Financial Accounts	57,634	„ Difference in Stocks:		
		Raw Materials—	£	
		Opening	102	
		Closing	90	
		Work in Progress—		
		Closing	59	
				251
	£57,723			£57,723

NOTES

Raw Material—Opening Stock

The figure used in the Cost Accounts is £25,348, compared with £25,246 in the Financial Accounts; thus £102 more was charged in the Cost Accounts, so financial profit must be reduced.

Raw Material—Closing Stock

Cost Accounts £29,371; Financial Accounts £29,461.
£90 more credit was taken in the Financial Accounts, so financial profit must be reduced.

Work in Progress—Opening Stock

Cost Accounts £15,763; Financial Accounts £15,852.
£89 more was charged in the Financial Accounts, so financial profit must be increased.

Work in Progress—Closing Stock

Cost Accounts £17,409; Financial Accounts £17,468.
£59 more credit was taken in the Financial Accounts, so financial profit must be reduced.

SPECIMEN QUESTION

The Manufacturing, Trading, Profit and Loss and Profit and Loss Appropriation Accounts of E.B. Ltd. for the year ending December 31 are as follows:

	£	£		£
To Raw Materials:			By Trading Account:	
Opening Stock	27,458		Cost of Goods manufactured trans-	
Purchases	134,762		ferred	318,466
	162,220			
Less Closing Stock	29,326			
		132,894		
,, Wages—direct		112,378		
PRIME COST		245,272		
,, Factory Overhead:				
Power	23,246			
Wages—indirect	31,351			
Rent and Rates	10,724			
Heating and Lighting	2,841			
Depreciation	6,015			
Expenses	1,020			
		75,197		
GROSS WORKS COST		320,469		
Deduct Work in Progress:				
Closing Stock	21,382			
Less Opening Stock	19,379			
		2,003		
		£318,466		£318,466
To Finished Goods:			By Sales	500,000
Opening Stock	20,642			
Goods manufactured	318,466			
	339,108			
Less Closing Stock	22,435			
		316,673		
,, Gross Profit c/d		183,327		
		£500,000		£500,000
To Office Salaries		35,642	By Gross Profit b/d	183,327
,, ,, Expenses		20,326	,, Dividend Received	300
,, Salesmen's Salaries		18,421	,, Interest on Bank Deposit	50
,, Selling Expenses		15,263		
,, Distribution Expenses		13,248		
,, Loss on Sale of Plant		1,250		
,, Fines		200		
,, Interest on Mortgage		150		
,, Net Profit for Year		79,177		
		£183,677		£183,677
To Income Tax		25,000	By Balance b/d	35,246
,, General Reserve		10,000	Net Profit for year	79,177
,, Ordinary Share Dividend		20,000		
,, Preference Share Dividend		10,000		
,, Goodwill written off		4,000		
,, Balance c/d		45,423		
		£114,423		£114,423

The Cost Accounts revealed a profit of £127,411. In preparing this figure, Stocks had been valued as follows:

    Raw Materials—   Opening stock £27,342
                            Closing stock £29,457

    Work in Progress—Opening stock £19,488
                            Closing stock £21,296

Selling and Distribution Expenses had been ignored in the Cost Accounts. Prepare a Reconciliation Account.

ANSWER

Memorandum Reconciliation Accoun

	£	£		£	£	£
To Items not Charged in Cost Accounts:			By Profit as per Cost Accounts			127,411
	£	£	„ Items not credited in Cost Accounts:			
Loss on Sale of					£	
Plant	1,250		Dividend Received		300	
Fines	200		Interest		50	
Interest	150				—	350
	—	1,600	„ Difference in Stocks:			
Salesmen's			Work in Progress—			
Salaries	18,421		Opening		109	
Selling Expenses	15,263		Closing		86	
Distribution Ex-					—	195
penses	13,248					
	—	46,932				
		48,532				
Difference in Stocks:						
Raw Materials—						
Opening	116					
Closing	131					
	—	247				
Profit as per Financial Accounts		79,177				
		£127,956				£127,956

Sometimes in examination questions the profit as per the Cost Accounts is not revealed, and one is required to ascertain the profit and also prepare a Reconciliation Account. The account should be prepared in the usual way shown above, a blank being left for the profit figure; the account is then balanced and the balancing amount inserted in the blank space provided.

It is possible to prepare a Memorandum Reconciliation in the form of a Statement as an alternative method of presentation. The Statement would appear as follows:

Memorandum Reconciliation Statement

	£	£
Profit as per Cost Accounts		127,411
Less Items not charged in Cost Accounts:		
Loss on Sale of Plant	1,250	
Fines	200	
Interest	150	
	—	1,600
		125,811
Add Items not credited in Cost Accounts:		
Dividend Received	300	
Interest	50	
	—	350
	Carried forward	126,161

	Brought forward	126,161
Less Selling and Distribution Expenses:		
Salesmen's Salaries	18,421	
Selling Expenses	15,263	
Distribution Expenses	13,248	
		46,932
		79,229
Add Difference in Stocks:		
Work in Progress—Opening	109	
Closing	86	
		195
		79,424
Less Difference in Stocks:		
Raw Materials—Opening	116	
Closing	131	
		247
Profit as per Financial Accounts		£79,177

CHAPTER 16

INTEGRAL ACCOUNTS

IN many large firms the system of integral or integrated accounts has been adopted. Under this system one set of accounts only is operated, as distinct from the costing section keeping their records and the financial section maintaining their accounts. This eliminates the necessity of operating Cost Ledger Control Accounts and of reconciling the Cost and Financial Accounts. In some of the earlier chapters in this book a brief introduction to integral accounting was given, especially in connection with wages accounting. It is proposed in this chapter to give two comprehensive illustrations taken from recent examinations of the Institute of Cost and Works Accountants.

Basically, the integral accounts system is similar to the separate accounting and costing systems, except that of course it eliminates duplicate entries, and the maintaining of unnecessary accounts.

EXAMPLE I

Purchases of £10,000 of raw materials on credit.
This would be recorded in an accounting system:

	£	£
Dr. Purchases Account	10,000	
Cr. Creditors Account		10,000
(Dr. Cost Ledger Control Account—memorandum only)		

In the cost-accounting system, omitting Materials Control Account.

	£	£
Dr. Stores Ledger Control Account	10,000	
Cr. General Ledger Adjustment Account		10,000

However in an integral accounting system the entries would be:

	£	£
Dr. Stores Account	10,000	
Cr. Creditors Account		10,000

It will be observed that the essential points are recorded in both systems, viz., stores and creditors.

EXAMPLE II

Paid wages in cash £5,000.
In Financial Books:

	£	£
Dr. Wages Account	5,000	
Cr. Cash Account		5,000
(Dr. Cost Ledger Control Account—Memorandum only)		

In Cost Books:

	£	£
Dr. Wages Control Account	5,000	
Cr. General Ledger Adjustment Account		5,000

However, in an Integral Accounting System:

	£	£
Dr. Wages Control Account	5,000	
Cr. Cash Account		5,000

It will again be observed that the essential points are recorded in both systems, viz., wages and cash.

Readers may care to refer to the accounting entries in Chapter 14 on Cost Control Accounts and try to visualise how the entries would appear in an integrated accounting system.

THE THIRD-ENTRY METHOD

There is a method of integral accounting known as the Third-entry Method. This system is very similar to the one described above, except that a third entry is made in respect of elements of cost. All items of cost, *e.g.* purchases, are debited in total in a Cost Ledger Control Account, and credited to a Creditor's Account. The cost is then analysed into Third-entry Accounts (which are not part of a double-entry system) in respect of materials, factory overheads, administration overheads, etc. The totals of these accounts are then transferred to Finished Goods Account, Profit and Loss Account, etc., the double entry being in the Cost Control Account. However, it is felt that ordinary double entry principles are sufficient, because the analysis work described in the Third-entry Method would be obtainable from the Job cards, Standing Order cards, etc.

Two further illustrations of Integral Accounting are now included which should show clearly how the principles of double entry accounting are observed. Both examples are taken from recent examinations of the Institute of Cost and Works Accountants.

SPECIMEN QUESTION

As at November 30, 1958, the following balances existed in a company's integrated Standard Costs and Financial Accounts:

Balance Sheet Accounts

	£'000
Capital and reserves	300
Creditors and accruals	88
Fixed assets	140
Raw materials in store and process	80 ⎤
Direct wages in process	20 ⎪ (at standard)
Factory Overheads in process	10 ⎬
Finished stock	90 ⎦
Debtors	100
Cash at bank	10

Trading Accounts

Budgeted sales	585
Sales Variances	12 (Debit)
Standard factory cost of sales	493
Material Variance	5 (Credit)
Direct Wages Variance	7 (Debit)
Factory Overhead Variance	2 (Debit)
Administration and selling expenses	14

During December 1958 *the following transactions took place:*

Budgeted sales	105
Actual sales	98
Cash received—from debtors	95
Cash paid— to creditors	63
Cash paid— direct wages	23
Raw materials purchased	40 (actual cost)
Excess materials issued	1 (at standard)
Factory expenses incurred	17
Administration and selling expenses incurred	3

Output finished (at standard cost):

Materials	50
Direct wages	26
Factory Overhead	13
Standard factory cost of actual sales	82

The standard cost of materials purchased is £42,000
The closing valuations of Work-in-progress Accounts (which are debited at actual and credited at standard) are:

Direct wages (at standard)	£15,000
Factory Overhead (at standard)	£13,000

You are required to:

(a) write up and close off the ledger accounts and
(b) prepare a Trial Balance of the closing balances.

ANSWER

NOTE.—For illustration purposes a Profit and Loss Account and Balance Sheet have been prepared, but the Trial Balance called for by the question has not been shown.

Capital and Reserves Account

		By Balance b/d	£300,000

Creditors and Accruals Account

	£		£
To Bank	63,000	By Balance b/d	88,000
,, Balance c/d	85,000	,, Purchases	40,000
		,, Expenses:	
		Factory	17,000
		Administration	3,000
	£148,000		£148,000
		By Balance b/d	85,000

Fixed Assets Accounts

To Balance b/d	£140,000		

Raw Materials in Store and in Process Account

	£		£
To Balance b/d	80,000	By Finished Goods	51,000
,, Creditors	42,000	,, Balance c/d	71,000
	£122,000		£122,000
To Balance b/d	71,000		

Direct Wages in Process Account

	£		£
To Balance b/d	20,000	By Finished Goods	26,000
,, Bank	23,000	,, Wages Variance Account	2,000
		,, Balance c/d	15,000
	£43,000		£43,000
To Balance b/d	15,000		

Factory Overhead in Process Account

	£		£
To Balance b/d	10,000	By Finished Goods	13,000
,, Creditors	17,000	,, Overhead Variance	1,000
		,, Balance c/d	13,000
	£27,000		£27,000
To Balance b/d	13,000		

Finished Stock Account

	£		£
To Balance b/d	90,000	By Sales	82,000
,, Raw Materials	50,000	,, Balance c/d	97,000
,, Labour	26,000		
,, Factory Overheads	13,000		
	£179,000		£179,000
To Balance b/d	97,000		

Debtor's Account

	£		£
To Balance b/d	100,000	By Bank	95,000
,, Sales	98,000	,, Balance c/d	103,000
	£198,000		£198,000
To Balance b/d	103,000		

Cash at Bank Account

	£		£
To Balance b/d	10,000	By Creditors	63,000
,, Debtors	95,000	,, Wages	23,000
		,, Balance c/d	19,000
	£105,000		£105,000
To Balance b/d	19,000		

Budgeted Sales Account

	£		£
To Profit and Loss	690,000	By Balance b/d	585,000
		,, Debtors	105,000
	£690,000		£690,000

Sales Variance Account

	£		£
To Balance b/d	12,000	By Profit and Loss	19,000
,, Debtors	7,000		
	£19,000		£19,000

Cost of Sales Account

	£		£
To Balance b/d	493,000	By Profit and Loss	575,000
,, Finished Goods	82,000		
	£575,000		£575,000

Materials Variance Account

	£		£
To Raw Materials	1,000	By Balance b/d	5,000
,, Profit and Loss	6,000	,, Purchases	2,000
	£7,000		£7,000

Direct Wages Variance Account

	£		£
To Balance b/d	7,000	By Profit and Loss	9,000
,, Wages	2,000		
	£9,000		£9,000

Factory Overhead Variance Account

	£		£
To Balance b/d	2,000	By Profit and Loss	3,000
,, Overhead	1,000		
	£3,000		£3,000

Administration and Selling Expenses Account

	£		£
To Balance b/d	14,000	By Profit and Loss	17,000
,, Creditors	3,000		
	£17,000		£17,000

Profit and Loss Account for Period ending December 31

	£		£
To Cost of Sales	575,000	By Budgeted Sales	690,000
,, Sales Variance	19,000	,, Material Variance	6,000
,, Wages Variance	9,000		
,, Factory Overhead Variance	3,000		
,, Administration and Selling	17,000		
,, Net Profit	73,000		
	£696,000		£696,000

Balance Sheet as at December 31

	£	£		£	£
Capital	300,000		Fixed assets		140,000
Net Profit	73,000		Stock	97,000	
		373,000	Materials	71,000	
Creditors		85,000	Labour	15,000	
			Overhead	13,000	
					196,000
			Debtors	103,000	
			Bank	19,000	
					122,000
		£458,000			£458,000

SPECIMEN QUESTION

Record in ledger accounts in integral account form the under-noted transactions, give effect to the additional information provided, and close off the accounts as at the end of the period.

Trial Balance at Beginning of Period

	£	£
Cash	3,000	
Debtors	26,000	
Stock—Raw materials	22,000	
Work in progress	14,000	
Finished goods	6,000	
Plant and machinery	60,000	
Buildings	10,000	
Share capital		100,000
General reserve		10,000
Profit and loss		2,000
Creditors		29,000
	£141,000	£141,000

Transactions During Period

	£
Purchases—credit—materials	15,000
"expenses"	500
cash— "expenses"	500
Materials used—product direct	12,000
Service Dept. A direct	1,000
Service Dept. B direct	500
Production Dept.	2,500
"Expense" allotted to products	200
to Service Dept. A	200
to Service Dept. B	400
to Production Dept.	200
to Administration and Selling	100
Wages and salaries—Service Dept. A	200
Service Dept. B	400
Production Dept.	3,500
Administration and Selling	900
Deductions from salaries—P.A.Y.E.	700
Funds	100
Sales—production cost plus $16\frac{2}{3}\%$	28,000

Additional Information

Rate of apportionment of cost of Service Dept. A	30% of cost of all materials
Rate of apportionment of cost of Service Dept. B	40% of Production Dept. wages and salaries
Rate of apportionment of cost of Production Dept.	£2 per unit of product
Number of units of product produced and completed at cost of at £5 each	4000
Depreciation	1% of value of plant and machinery and $\frac{1}{2}$% of value of buildings to be charged to Production Dept.

ANSWER

Cash Account

	£		£
To Balance b/d	3,000	By Expenses	500
„ Balance c/d	1,700	„ Wages	4,200
	£4,700		£4,700
		By Balance b/d	1,700

Debtors Account

	£		£
To Balance b/d	26,000	By Balance c/d	54,000
„ Sales	28,000		
	£54,000		£54,000
To Balance b/d	54,000		

Stock—Raw Materials Account

	£		£
To Balance b/d	22,000	By Work in Progress	12,000
„ Purchases	15,000	„ Service Dept. A	1,000
		„ Service Dept. B	500
		„ Production Dept.	2,500
		„ Balance c/d	21,000
	£37,000		£37,000
To Balance b/d	21,000		

Work-in-Progress Account

	£		£
To Balance b/d	14,000	By Finished Goods	20,000
„ Raw Materials	12,000	„ Balance c/d	15,450
„ Production Dept.	9,250		
„ Expenses	200		
	£35,450		£35,450
To Balance b/d	15,450		

Stock—Finished Goods Account

	£		£
To Balance b/d	6,000	By Profit and Loss	24,000
,, Work in Progress	20,000	,, Balance c/d	2,000
	£26,000		£26,000
To Balance b/d	2,000		

Plant and Machinery Account

To Balance b/d	£60,000		

Buildings Account

To Balance b/d	£10,000		

Share Capital Account

		By Balance b/d	£100,000

General Reserve Account

		By Balance b/d	£10,000

Profit and Loss Appropriation Account

	£		£
To Balance c/d	4,800	By Balance b/d	2,000
		,, Net Profit	2,800
	£4,800		£4,800
		By Balance b/d	4,800

Creditors' Account

	£		£
To Balance c/d	44,500	By Balance b/d	29,000
		,, Purchases	15,000
		,, Expenses	500
	£44,500		£44,500
		By Balance b/d	44,500

Expenses Account

	£		£
To Creditors	500	By Work in Progress	200
,, Cash	500	,, Service Dept. A	200
,, Profit and Loss	100	,, Service Dept. B	400
		,, Production Dept.	200
		,, Administration and Selling	100
	£1,100		£1,100

Wages and Salaries Control Account

	£		£
To Wages Payable	5,000	By Service Dept. A	200
		,, Service Dept. B	400
		,, Production Dept.	3,500
		,, Administration and Selling	900
	£5,000		£5,000

Wages Payable Account

	£		£
To P.A.Y.E.	700	By Wages Control	5,000
,, Funds	100		
,, Cash	4,200		
	£5,000		£5,000

P.A.Y.E.

	By Wages payable	£700

Funds Account

	By Wages payable	£100

Service Dept. A Account

	£		£
To Stores	1,000	By Service Dept. B	200
,, Expenses	200	,, Production Dept.	1,000
,, Wages	200	,, Profit and Loss	200
	£1,400		£1,400

Service Dept. B Account

	£		£
To Stores	500	By Production Dept.	1,400
,, Expenses	400	,, Profit and Loss	100
,, Wages	400		
,, Service Dept. A	200		
	£1,500		£1,500

Production Dept. Account

	£		£
To Stores	2,500	By Work in Progress—	
„ Expenses	200	Units completed	8,000
„ Wages	3,500	Units not completed	1,250
„ Service Dept. A	1,000		
„ Service Dept. B	1,400		
„ Depreciation on Plant	600		
„ Depreciation on Buildings	50		
	£9,250		£9,250

Administration and Selling Expenses Account

	£		£
To Expenses	100	By Profit and Loss	1,000
„ Wages	900		
	£1,000		£1,000

Depreciation Provision on Plant and Machinery Account .

		By Production Dept.	£600

Depreciation Provision on Building Account

		By Production Dept.	£50

Profit and Loss Account for Period

	£		£
To Finished Goods	24,000	To Expenses—Over-recovered	100
„ Administration and Selling Expenses	1,000	„ Sales	28,000
„ Service Dept. A } Under-recovered	200		
„ Service Dept. B	100		
„ Net Profit	2,800		
	£28,100		£28,100

Trial Balance at End of Period

	£	£
Cash		1,700
Debtors	54,000	
Stock:		
Raw Material	21,000	
Work in Progress	15,450	
Finished Goods	2,000	
Plant and Machinery	60,000	
Buildings	10,000	
Share Capital		100,000
General Reserve		10,000
Profit and Loss Appropriation		4,800
Creditors		44,500
P.A.Y.E.		700
Funds		100
Depreciation Provision on Plant and Machinery		600
Depreciation Provision on Buildings		50
	£162,450	£162,450

1. Cost of goods sold is calculated:

Sales = Production Cost + $16\frac{2}{3}\%$ = £28,000
Therefore Cost   = £24,000

2. Service Dept. A apportionment:

Materials used by depts.   A   1,000
                          B   500
                Production 2,500

                        £4,000

$$4{,}000 \times \frac{30}{100} = 1{,}200$$

This cost is allocated between:

Dept. B $\frac{500}{3000} \times 1200 =$ £200

Production Dept. $\frac{2500}{3000} \times 1200 = £1{,}000$

3. Service Dept. B is apportioned:

$$\frac{40}{100} \times 3500 = £1{,}400$$

4. Production Dept. is absorbed:

4000 units at £2 = £8,000

The total cost of the dept. was £9250, and since only £8000 has been absorbed, the balance of £1250 has been regarded as being the Production Dept.'s contribution to work in progress.

This can be checked:

	£	£
Work-in-progress Balance at beginning		£14,000
,, ,, ,, end		£15,450
Increase of		£1,450

Represented by:

Direct Expenses	200	
Production Dept.	1,250	
		£1,450

5. It will be observed that there is a credit balance on the Cash Account. In practice, this should not happen, but in this question full information has not been given, *e.g.* there has been no cash received from debtors.

CHAPTER 17

CONTRACT COSTS

IN Contract Costing the principles of Job Costing are applied, and a separate Cost Account is kept for each individual contract or job undertaken. Builders, Civil Engineering Contractors, Constructional and Mechanical Engineering firms, and similar concerns make use of this type of cost accountancy. Factory Job Costing is more detailed, and is dealt with in the next chapter.

THE PROCEDURE

It is usual to give each contract a distinguishing number, to facilitate reference in the books and on the various forms which are used. This number identifies the Cost Account to which are charged the labour, materials, and expenses.

THE COST OF MATERIALS

Stores material

Materials from the Store are issued against a Material Requisition (Fig. 8) which is the authority of the Storekeeper to issue. Each requisition bears the number of the job for which it is required, and a weekly or monthly summary may be made, called a Material Issue Analysis, in which an analysis of materials chargeable to job numbers may be made (*see* Fig. 59). The total value of the material under each job number is then debited to the appropriate Cost Account bearing the same number.

In most cases no Analysis Sheet is now prepared, postings being made direct from the priced requisitions, or rather, from machine-added summaries for each job number.

Direct material

Sometimes material is purchased outside, or manufactured in the works, for a particular job or contract. The cost of this material will usually be debited direct to the Cost Account for the job concerned.

In the case of large constructional contracts, sub-contracts for specialised work or material—*e.g.* polished granite or heavy steel girders—are placed with specialist suppliers, and the cost is a direct debit to the contract.

199

MATERIAL ISSUE ANALYSIS SHEET

Week ending: February 7, 19... No. 12

	Job No. 90				Job No. 91				Job No. 98				Job No. 100				R. 13				N. 31				Summary				
	I.R. No.	£	s.	d.	I.R. No.	£	s.	d.	I.R. No.	£	s.	d.	I.R. No.	£	s.	d.	I.R. No.	£	s.	d.	I.R. No.	£	s.	d.	Job No.	£	s.	d.	Cost Led. fol.
	91	4	9	0	93	1	2	0	92	7	15	0	94	2	1	0	96	8	6	0	88	6	3	0	90	7	9	0	
	95	3	0	0	97	3	7	0					98		15	0	99	3	2	0	89	5	19	0	91	4	9	0	
																	90	1	5	6					98	7	15	0	
																									100	2	16	0	
																									R. 13	12	13	6	
																									N. 31	12	2	0	
		7	9	0		4	9	0		7	15	0		2	16	0		12	13	6		12	2	0			47	4	6	

FIG. 59.—*Material Issue Analysis Sheet*

A form like this is admirable for summarising Stores requisitions when the Office has no equipment to provide machine-added summaries.

Materials returned to Store

It is sometimes necessary to issue certain kinds of material in excess of requirements, as, for instance, cement, bricks, pipes, man-hole covers, etc. The surplus is later returned to the Store, accompanied by a Material Return Note, which gives details of the material returned, and states the job to be credited.

Materials on site

At the end of each accounting period the value of materials on site is carried forward as a charge against the next period. It should be noted that, although this is the usual practice, in a few special cases the terms and conditions of the contract may allow for payment on account to be made in respect of materials on site.

THE COST OF LABOUR

Method of remuneration

Generally speaking, the method employed on contracts is by means of an hourly rate, with a bonus addition if work is completed to time.

Calculation of wages

On large engineering contracts it is customary to have a resident Timekeeper—one for about every 300 men—who is responsible for noting down the attendance of the men, working out their pay on the Time Sheets, and sending the Pay Sheets complete to Head Office by a specified time each week.

Payment of wages

The pay packets are made up by the Head Office cashier, after the Pay Sheets have been checked, and the packets and a copy of the sheets are taken out to the contract by a responsible member of the staff—possibly an engineer who is visiting the site. In more distant sites arrangements have to be made with a Bank to cash the weekly wages cheque for the contract cashier, subject to an agreed maximum. The foreman, or ganger, will be present when wages are paid out, and only those present to receive their wages will be paid. Any packets left over will be taken or sent back to Head Office, and not left on the contract. On written request, Head Office will post off a Money Order to the address given, if it agrees with that on the National Insurance card, or is vouched for by the contract foreman. Payment of wages by cheque, if it becomes common, will save a great deal of trouble for all concerned; however, it is doubtful whether such a method of payment could ever be applied to the changing population on civil-engineering contracts.

WAGES ANALYSIS SHEET

																					No. 32

Week ending, February 7, 19...

Job No. 90			Job No. 91			Job No. 98			Job No. 100			R. 13			N. 31			Summary			
Clock No.	Hrs.	Amount	No.	Hrs.	Amount	No.	Hrs.	Amount	No.	Hrs.	Amount	No.	Hrs.	Amount	No.	Hrs.	Amount	Job No.	Hrs.	Amount	Cost Led. fol.
		£ s. d.			£ s. d.			£ s. d.			£ s. d.			£ s. d.			£ s. d.			£ s. d.	
12	4	8 0	22	5	7 6	23	4	8 0	12	4	8 0	22	3	4 6	14	8	16 0	90	15	1 11 11	
13	8	16 8	23	4	8 0	17	40	4 0 0	18	2	5 0	18	14	1 15 0	17	8	16 0	91	9	15 6	
18	2	5 0							21	2	4 6	21	2	4 6	21	3	6 9	98	44	4 8 0	
21	1	2 3										12	20	2 0 0	22	40	3 0 0	100	8	17 6	
												19	6	15 0				R. 13	45	4 19 0	
																		N. 31	59	4 18 9	
15	1 11 11		9	15 6		44	4 8 0		8	17 6		45	4 19 0		59	4 18 9		180	17 10 8		

FIG. 60.—*Wages Analysis Sheet*

This is useful for the analysis of Job tickets and idle-time cards of workers whose wages are charged as direct labour. The total will be posted partly to Work-in-progress Account and partly to Factory Overhead Control Account, probably via the Wages Analysis Book (Fig. 47).

The total shown in the summary column must agree with the direct wages on the payroll.

Wages Analysis Sheet

A Wages Analysis Sheet is not required on contracts for which separate pay sheets are prepared, but smaller firms, such as builders and decorators, need them so that the men's time can be apportioned to the various jobs on which they have been working during the week. The information is compiled from the Time Sheets, and the sheet is usually in sections, according to trades, so that separate totals for each job for each class of work are obtained—*e.g.* bricklayers, plumbers, joiners, etc. The total against each job is posted to the appropriate Cost Account (*see* Fig. 60), and the grand total is agreed with the total of the Pay Sheets to ensure that the wages charged in the detailed Cost Accounts agrees with the summary figure posted to Work-in-progress Account.

THE COST OF OVERHEAD

In some cases indirect expense may be easily allocated to the contract concerned, but where this cannot be done it is posted to appropriate Standing Order Numbers. A Distribution Summary is then prepared, and an apportionment of overhead is made on the basis, for example, of a rate per direct labour hour.

FORM OF CONTRACT COST LEDGER ACCOUNTS

The exact form of each Contract Cost Account will depend on individual requirements, but in Fig. 61 is shown a specimen ruling for a firm of builders.

Use of plant on contracts

In some cases the book value of plant and tools sent to the site of a contract is debited to the contract and the Plant Account is credited. In due course, when the plant is returned to the yard, the depreciated value is credited to the contract.

However, it is not considered that this is the best way to deal with plant sent to contracts. An "upkeep" account should be opened for each major piece of plant, to which is debited the cost of maintenance, depreciation, obsolescence provision, fuel oil, etc. A hire rate is then fixed and charged weekly to the contract. This rate, although it may be lower than the charge from an outside plant-hiring firm, is sufficient to cover the upkeep of the plant. By receiving this charge against his contract the contract agent or foreman will take steps to see that the plant is returned or made the responsibility of Head Office when no longer wanted. From a book-keeping point of view, this method has the advantage that the contract accounts are not swamped with the capital cost of plant which is eventually to be returned for credit.

CONTRACT COST LEDGER ACCOUNT

Name: ....

The Southern Bank Ltd.
New Premises, 296 High Street,
London.

Contract No.: ......

Week Ending	Ref.	Debits						Credits			Prime Cost	Overhead Charges	Total Cost to date
		Stores Materials	Direct Materials	Use of Plant, etc.	Wages	Direct Expenses	Total	Stores returned	Other Income	Total			
		£ s. d.	£ s. d.	£ s. d.	£ s. d.	£ s. d.	£ s. d.	£ s. d.	£ s. d.	£ s. d.	£ s. d.	£ s. d.	£ s. d.

FIG. 61.—*Contract Cost Ledger Account*

A ruling of this kind would be suitable for a firm of builders and contractors. The plant sent to the contract might be recorded on the reverse side, and the charge raised for the use of it would be calculated there each month before entry on the front side of the account form.

Sub-contracts

When a sub-contractor is engaged for a special piece of work the accounts received are dealt with as direct materials, even though the cost may largely consist of labour.

Jobbing work

During the course of completion of major contracts the contractor is often approached to do jobbing work of a minor nature, *e.g.* the use of an excavator to clear a site for some garages; the use of a roller on a footpath; the use of a concrete mixer and the supply of sand and cement, for putting roughcast on the walls of a house. The charges made are treated as income to the contract.

CERTIFICATION OF WORK DONE

As the work proceeds, the architect or surveyor appointed by the contractees issues Certificates to the effect that so much money is now due to the contractors in accordance with the terms of the contract. These payments on account are credited either to the contract account or to the account of the contractees, depending on the precise book-keeping method being used. The contract will usually stipulate that a retention of say 10% is held back for twelve months after the contract is completed. At that time the surveyor will go round with the contractor and indicate any faults in the work which have been disclosed within the year, and which have to be remedied before release of the retention money.

PROFIT ON UNCOMPLETED CONTRACTS

In view of the hazards involved in contract work, such as the discovery of a spring of water in the middle of a contract site or of a bed of running sand in the course of digging the foundations, and in view of the liability to make good any defects in the work which develop within the retention period, it is an accepted principle that no profit should be taken on uncompleted contracts, except in the case of very long contracts when a conservative sum may be credited. This is usually based on the formula

$$\tfrac{2}{3} \times \text{Notional profit} \times \frac{\text{Cash received}}{\text{Work certified}}.$$

When a large contract is nearing successful completion use is sometimes made of the formula

$$\text{Notional profit} \times \frac{\text{Work certified}}{\text{Contract price}}$$

and, of course, individual firms may have their own particular basis of calculation.

SPECIMEN CONTRACT ACCOUNTS

In order to illustrate the way in which contract cost accounts may be kept, the following examples are given of:

1. A builder's business.
2. A civil engineering contract.

SPECIMEN QUESTION

Short & Co. are in business as builders and decorators, and they undertake small contracts and also jobs for local residents, most of which are below £100 in value. They employ bricklayers, joiners, painters, and paperhangers. In the three months ending March 31 the results of their business is as follows:

Materials

	£
In store January 1	860
Purchases:	
January	710
February	760
March	970
Issues to contracts:	
January	410
February	270
March	350
Issues to Jobbing account:	
January	300
February	520
March	460
Issues to Joiners' Shop:	
March	300

Wages

Gross wages paid:	
January	1590
February	1630
March	1720
Allocated direct to contracts	2460

Apportioned to:

Joiners' Shop	1070
Jobbing Account (joiners)	790
Overhead Control Account	620

Overhead

Rent and Rates	900
Haulage	300
Office Expenses	600
Lighting and Heating	125
Repairs	170
Depreciation	235

Overhead *applied* as follows:

To Contracts	2049
To Joiners' Shop	375
To Jobbing Account	520

Work Done on Contracts completed

To March 31	8160

NOTE.—A loss of £130 was sustained on one contract.

Work in Progress

£

On Contracts:

January 1	1200
March 31	1400

On Jobbing Accounts:

January 1	200
March 31	300

In Joiners' Shop:

January 1	—
March 31	145

Jobbing Sales for quarter 4140

The work done in the Joiners' Shop

Charged to:

Contracts	600
Jobbing Account	1000

It is required to show the main Control Accounts in the Ledger, the assumption being made that individual contract accounts are kept only on a card index, subsidiary to the book-keeping system.

ANSWER

Stores Ledger Control Account

	£		£
To Balance b/f	860	By Issues	410
,, Purchases	710		300
	760		270
	970		520
			350
			460
			300
		,, Balance c/d	690
	£3300		£3300
To Balance b/d	690		

Wages Control Account

	£		£
To Gross Wages	1590	By Contracts	2460
	1630	,, Joiners	1070
	1720	,, Jobbing	790
		,, Overhead Control	620
	£4940		£4940

Work in Progress—Contracts

	£		£
To Balance b/f	1200	By Completed work	8160
,, Stores	410	,, Loss on contract	130
	270	Balance c/d	1400
	350		
,, Wages	2460		
,, Overhead	2049		
,, Joiners	600		
,, Profit to date	2351		
	£9690		£9690
To Balance b/d	1400		

Joiners' Shop Account

	£		£
To Wages	1070	By Contracts	600
,, Stores	300	,, Jobbing	1000
,, Overhead	375	Balance c/d	145
	£1745		£1745
To Balance b/d	145		

Jobbing Account

	£		£
To Balance b/f	200	By Sales	4140
,, Stores	300	Balance c/d	300
	520		
	460		
,, Wages—Joiners	790		
,, Work done in Joiners' Shop	1000		
,, Overhead	520		
,, Profit	650		
	£4440		£4440
To Balance b/d	300		

Overhead Control Account

	£		£
To Wages	620	By Applied Overhead A/c	2950
,, Rent and Rates	900		
,, Haulage	300		
,, Expenses	600		
,, Heating	125		
,, Repairs	170		
,, Depreciation	235		
	£2950		£2950

Applied Overhead Account

	£		£
To Transfer to Overhead Control A/c	2950	By Contracts	2049
		,, Joiners' Shop	375
		,, Jobbing A/c	520
		,, Balance, Overhead under-absorbed to	
		P. & L. A/c	6
	£2950		£2950

Contracts Summary Account

	£		£
To Loss on contract (detail)	130	By Profits on contracts (set out in detail)	2351
,, Balance to Profit & Loss A/c	2221		
	£2351		£2351

Profit and Loss Account

	£		£
To Under-absorbed overhead	6	By Contracts	2221
,, Net Profit	2865	,, Jobbing	650
	£2871		£2871

SPECIMEN QUESTION

The South Park Construction Co. Ltd. have undertaken the construction of a bridge over the River Till for the Champton Council. The value of the Contract is £125,000, subject to a retention of 20% until one year after the certified completion of the contract, and final approval of the Council's surveyor. The contractors have given the contract number 86 for reference, and the following are the details as shown in the books:

	£
Labour on site	40,500
Materials direct to site, less returns	42,000
Materials from store and workshops	8,120
Plant Upkeep Account—Hire and use of plant	1,210
Direct Expenses	2,300
General Overhead apportioned to this contract	3,710
Materials on hand June 30	630

	£
Wages accrued at June 30	780
Direct expenses accrued	160
Work not yet certified, at cost	1,650
Amount certified by the Council's Surveyor	110,000
Cash received on account	88,000

Prepare the Contract Accounts to show the position at June 30, retaining an adequate provision against possible losses before final acceptance of the contract.

ANSWER

Contract No. 86—Expenditure Account

	£		£
To Materials Direct	42,000	By Materials on hand c/d	630
,, Other materials	8,120	,, Cost of contract to date c/d	98,150
,, Wages	40,500		
,, Direct expenses	2,300		
,, Plant upkeep A/c	1,210		
,, General Overhead	3,710		
,, Wages accrued c/d	780		
,, Direct expenses accrued c/d	160		
	£98,780		£98,780
To Cost to date b/d	98,150	By Wages b/d	780
,, Materials on site b/d	630	,, Direct expenses b/d	160

Contract No. 86—Certificates Account

	£		£
To Balance c/d	111,650	By Certificates 1–17	110,000
		,, Work done, not yet certified, at cost c/d*	1,650
	£111,650		£111,650
To Balance b/d	1,650	By Balance b/d	111,650

* This amount could be carried down on the expenditure account, instead of this account, if preferred.

Contract No. 86—Retentions Account

To Certificates Account	£22,000	

Champton Council's Account—Contract No. 86

To Certificates Account	£88,000	By Cash on A/c	£88,000

Contract No. 86—Profit Provision Account

	£		£
To Transfer to P. & L. A/c	7,200	By Provision c/d	7,200
To Balance b/d	7,200		

NOTE.—The calculation of the profit provision is done by taking two-thirds of the notional profit (£111,650 — £98,150) and still further reducing the result by the proportion which the cash received bears to the work certified.

$$£$$

Thus $\qquad$ £111,650 — £98,150 = 13,500
$$Less\ 33\tfrac{1}{3}\% \qquad = 4,500$$
$$\overline{9{,}000}$$

$$£9000 \times \frac{88}{110} = 900 \times 8$$
$$= £7200$$

It will be noted that by this method, the Expenditure Account is maintained at cost, as work in progress.

If this contract represented the whole of the work in hand the figures could be shown on the Balance Sheet as follows:

Assets side of the Balance Sheet

	£	£
Work in progress, including profit taken to date	105,350	
Less Cash on account	88,000	
		17,350
Materials on site		630

Liabilities side of the Balance Sheet

Accrued Charges:		
Wages	780	
Direct Expenses	160	
		940

The chief merit of this method is that it is simple, does not give a false impression of the amount of the assets, and especially does not disclose the amount of Retentions Account, which is not immediately realisable.

SECTIONALISATION OF CONTRACTS

On large civil-engineering contracts it is often possible for the accountant, in conjunction with the engineering staff, to divide the Bill of Quantities into sections, especially when the work is to begin simultaneously at several places. By suitably coding these sections the contract costs can be made to correspond more closely to the monthly certificates, and then, if the estimates are seen to have been low in certain directions, the engineer is able to give special attention to those sections of the work.

H

CHAPTER 18

FACTORY JOB COSTING

THE PRODUCTION ORDER NUMBER

FACTORY Job Costing is concerned with those undertakings, mostly of a general engineering kind, which may undertake jobs of the "one-off" type, or orders for a batch of similar components. Costs are therefore generally recorded against each individual job or order, and this requires careful routing and scheduling, since there is no pre-determined flow line for the work to follow. In consequence, this type of costing is characterised by a great deal of paper work.

The costs are collected and recorded under the production order number, a separate Cost Account such as shown in Fig. 62 being set up for each number. By using a well-arranged numbering scheme, work of different categories, and work done in different departments, can be readily identified.

The method of numbering and some of the procedure varies according to whether the order is for:

(a) repetition work;
(b) work involving sectional operations, or the making of components for assembly;
(c) a simple straight job.

When an order is received, Production Control allots a number to it. If necessary, the work will be divided into sections, and in this case a master order number would be given to the order as a whole, and sub-section order numbers to the parts composing it, e.g. sub-numbers for components.

In some works this is an elaborate process, often involving the setting up of many operations, for each of which the Planning Department and the Rate-fixing Department decide the extent of each operation, and the time allowed for performing each.

EXAMPLE

The Ratefixer has observed an operation being done by a worker for twenty or thirty times. The average time taken (or maybe, the mode) is 0·8 minutes. He rates performance as 65/60. 15% relaxation factor is to be allowed for the class of work being done.

212

$$\text{Normal time} = \frac{65}{60} \times 0.8 \ = 0.87$$

Add relaxation factor $15\% = 0.13$

Standard time allowed $\qquad 1.00$

NOTE.—If the Halsey, Halsey–Weir, or Rowan schemes of remuneration are used it will be remembered that the time allowed would be $166\frac{2}{3}\%$ of this standard time, viz., 1.67 minutes.

			Cost	
COST CARD				
Description: .... **Quantity:** .... **Job No.:**				
Date	Ref.	Particulars	Detail	Total
		MATERIAL:		
		LABOUR:		
		FACTORY OVERHEAD:		
		ADMINISTRATION AND SELLING OVERHEAD:		
Make-up of Estimate				
Ref.	Material	Labour	Factory Overhead	A.D. & S.O.	Total

FIG. 62.—*Factory Job Cost Account*

This, as in Fig. 49, shows a ruling for a Job Cost card or Account. These cards constitute the details of the Work-in-progress Account, and when the job is finished the card which applies is removed; the total of such removed cards is used as the basis of a transfer from Work in Progress to Finished Work.

Clipper Card Sheath.

Illustration	Index Letter	Description
	R.C.A.	Milling Card Sheath Castings.
	R.C.B.	Drilling to Jig.
	R.C.C.	Mouthpieces, Drill & Oxidise
	R.C.D'	Cutter Holder, Boring & Turning.
	R.C.D²	Cutter Holder, Machining
	R.C.D³	" " Drilling to Jig & Tapping.
	R.C.E'	Cutter Plates, Punching
	R.C.E²	" " Flatten Drill & Tap.
	R.C.F'	Cutters, Machining.
	R.C.F²	" File to Jig.
	R.C.F³	" Grinding after Hardening.
	R.C.G'	Cutter Shanks, Cut off Straighten & Drill
	R.C.G²	" " Machining.
Casting.	R.C.H'	Brass Top Plate Making.
Casting.	R.C.H²	" Bottom Plate "
	R.C.I.	Aligning Stud, Make in Captan.
	R.C.J.	Springs for Card Cutters.
	R.C.K.	Assembling Clipper Card Sheath Complete.

FIG. 63.—*Schedule of Operations*

For repetition work, the Planning Department decides how the work is to be split up, draws up a schedule of jobs, and identifies each job or operation by a distinguishing number or index letter. An index letter or symbol, combined with an operation number, is often used with great advantage. The example in Fig. 63 shows how a schedule of operation can be indexed; in this case the operations for making a Clipper Card Sheath for a Gledhill-Brook time recorder are shown.

THE PRODUCTION ORDER

After the Production Planning Department has made out the Production Orders for the various parts to be made the requisite information given on them is run off by spirit duplicator or other means on to a number of other forms arranged in sets. Fig. 64 illustrates such a Production Order and Fig. 65 the flow of information for Part 2, under

PRODUCTION ORDER			
			Progress Copy to Circulate with Work
Date to commence	Number required	Machine Yes/No	Production Order Number
Part Name	Part No.	Material Required	
		Per Part	This Order

Operation Nos.						
Machine Nos.						

Clock Times	Op. No.	Dept. No.	Operation		Quantity		
			No.	Details	Made	Rej.	c.f.

FIG. 64.—*Production Order*

These are made out by the Planning Department in respect of each type of part required either for a particular job or for finished parts stock.

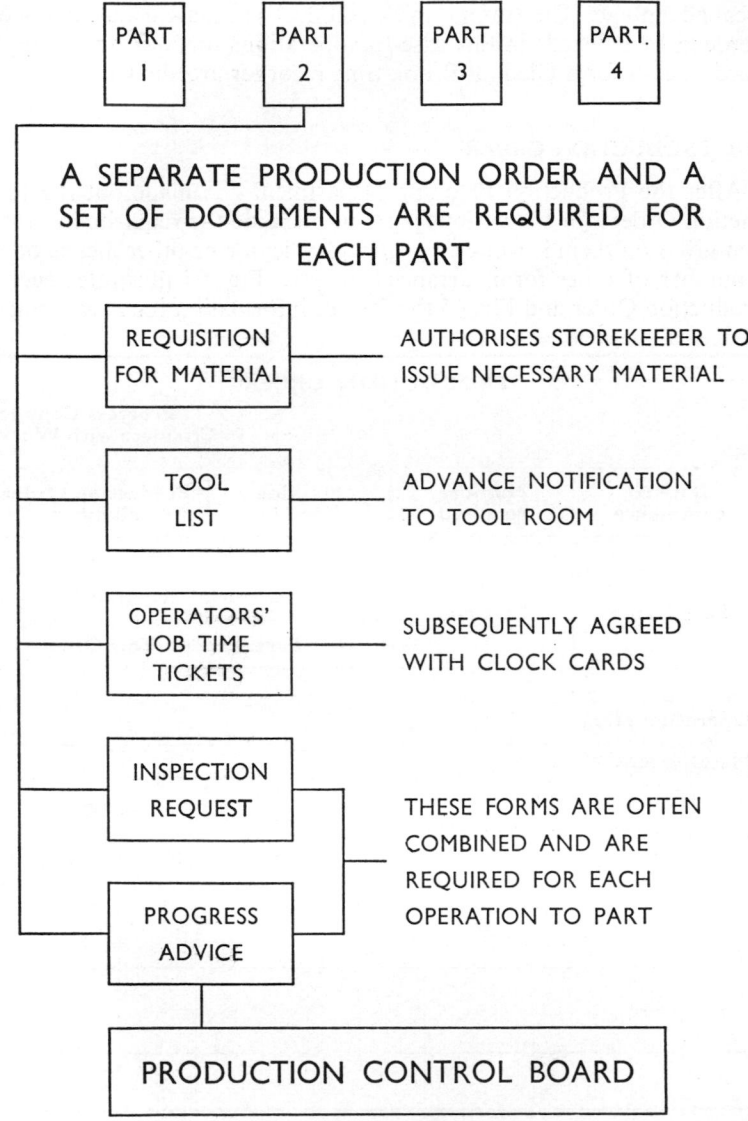

PRODUCTION OR WORKS
ORDER

| PART 1 | PART 2 | PART 3 | PART 4 |

A SEPARATE PRODUCTION ORDER AND A SET OF DOCUMENTS ARE REQUIRED FOR EACH PART

| REQUISITION FOR MATERIAL | AUTHORISES STOREKEEPER TO ISSUE NECESSARY MATERIAL |

| TOOL LIST | ADVANCE NOTIFICATION TO TOOL ROOM |

| OPERATORS' JOB TIME TICKETS | SUBSEQUENTLY AGREED WITH CLOCK CARDS |

| INSPECTION REQUEST | |
| PROGRESS ADVICE | THESE FORMS ARE OFTEN COMBINED AND ARE REQUIRED FOR EACH OPERATION TO PART |

PRODUCTION CONTROL BOARD

FIG. 65.—*Production Department Documents*

The flow of information required in Jobbing and Batch production: much paper work is involved in ensuring that the production is completed by the date required.

Production Order No. 2456. It will be seen that the actual issue of the forms to the factory is made by the Control Section of Production Control, for the Planning Department's responsibility ended with the decision as to the route and operations necessary.

The material required for Part 2 was doubtless scheduled by the Drawing Office in the first place, and picked up by the Planning Department from that information. It now appears on a Materials Requisition, and it will be sent by Production Control to the Storekeeper a little before work is to commence on this Order 2456. It may entail cutting material to length, and this can be done before the material is collected from Stores.

In the same way the Tool-room is advised in advance, so that the necessary tools and jigs may be looked out; longer notice would, of course, have to be given if any of these have to be specially made.

The Production Order itself refers to all the work to be done to complete Part 2, and accompanies the work as it passes from operation to operation. The time of commencement and finishing work on each operation is stamped on the card, together with the operator's name, and from this information the total labour cost of producing the part can be calculated.

At the same time each operator has a time ticket for his operation, and the total of his tickets for the week—different operations for different Works Orders—together with his idle-time cards, are agreed with his gate times on the clock cards.

The Inspection Department also receives advice at the appropriate moment that work has to be inspected, and Internal Transport are requested from time to time to move the material being worked on from one point to another.

These advices to Inspection and Internal Transport may be combined with a Progress Advice, which, of course, is required after every operation to the part is completed. Each set of documents therefore contains

One Material Requisition—unless material is issued at a later stage as well.
One Tool Issue list for the part to be made.
As many operators' job time tickets as there are operations.
As many Progress Advices as there are operations.

To complete the picture in the student's mind, Fig. 66 shows a specimen Progress Advice.

Orders for Service Departments

In addition to the Production Orders carried out as part of the planned production, there are many jobs which are done in a factory

PROGRESS ADVICE			
For the Attention of Production Control			
Date commenced	Number required	Machine Yes/No	Production Order Number
Date finished	Part Name	Part No.	Operators No.

From Dept. No.		To Dept. No.		
Quantity produced	Quantity inspected	Quantity passed	Quantity rejected	Inspector

FIG. 66.—*Progress Advice*

One of the documents referred to in Fig. 65 was of this type. After the operator has completed his operation the work goes by internal transport to the Inspector. This form notifies Production Control of the stage reached by the work.

for Service Departments, and which are therefore in the nature of overhead. Often it is the practice to open a special Standing Order Number for such jobs, but it is suggested that there is no need to vary the procedure outlined above. The same routine can be followed, using perhaps stationery of a distinctive colour, or a reference number which will clearly identify it as being an internal works order.

Orders carried out by Service Departments

In some cases certain parts can be made for stock by a Service Department—such as the Tool-room or the Plant Maintenance Department—whenever they have time and opportunity to spare. Such orders remain in force until countermanded, and are therefore sometimes referred to as "Standing Orders." This is bound to cause confusion, since the term "Standing Order Numbers" is by custom applied to overhead. It would be best therefore to refer to them as "Stock Orders."

On the other hand, such Service Departments will, for the most part, use their time in maintaining the workshop tools, carrying out maintenance, etc., so that the labour cost of each has to be carefully recorded and accounted for. No new problems arise, however, and the student is referred to one of the methods outlined in Chapter 7.

TIME AND MATERIALS SPENT IN REPLACING REJECTED WORK

There is no need to vary the normal procedures, except to use stationery of a distinctive colour. This will make the compilation of a scrap report easier.

It is suggested that the additional charges incurred under these headings become a direct charge to the job concerned. Of course, if Standard Costing is in force they would constitute Material Usage and Labour Efficiency variances.

OVERTIME

A distinction must be drawn between overtime, that is the time worked over and above the normal working hours, and overtime premium, which is the additional payment made over the normal rate for those additional hours.

When the overtime is worked on a special job, say outside the works, or when it is due to the insistence of a customer that a job be completed within the time specified, the extra payment for overtime premium is legitimately charged to the job as direct labour. On the other hand, if the overtime is for the purpose of generally increasing the output of the factory, *e.g.* to keep up with stock requirements or to take on additional jobs, the cost of the overtime premium is treated as overhead and charged to a Standing Order Number.

PAYROLL AND WAGES ANALYSIS

The payroll is made up from the clock cards, and/or piece-work tickets. When a premium bonus, or other output or efficiency bonus, is paid an extra column will be provided for the inclusion of these amounts.

In the Cost Office the wages, having been agreed with the time tickets, are dissected so that the correct allocation of direct wages to the Job Cost Cards and of indirect wages to the appropriate Standing Order Numbers can be made. Statistical data regarding labour cost rates per department may also be prepared.

The student is referred to p. 187 for the relative accounting entries on the basis of integral accounts, and to p. 161 for those where separate cost and financial systems are in operation.

STORES MATERIALS

There is a good deal to be said for arranging that all materials received in the factory, even for special jobs, pass through exactly the same routine as for Stores materials proper. In the first place they are covered by Goods Received Notes, and then when issued to the factory, they, like the usual stores items, are all covered by requisitions. These requisitions, when priced, are charged out to the various Job Cost Cards, and the total will then support the entry from Stores Ledger Control Account to work in progress.

TOOL-ROOM AND TOOL-STORE PROCEDURE

The careful selection, and the making and maintenance, of tools for manufacturing purposes are of great importance. In connection with the organisation dealing with tools, there are three divisions:

1. Manufacturing.
2. Maintenance and Inspection.
3. Storage and Issue.

Tool manufacture

The making of tools for production will be costed by the job-costing methods already described in this chapter.

Tool maintenance and inspection

As tools are returned from the factory floor to the tool store they are inspected before being placed on the racks ready for reissue. No doubt the tool inspector is highly skilled and experienced, and is able, by training and adherence to agreed tolerances, to decide on what maintenance treatment is required. Such work becomes part of the cost of running the Tool-room, and will be apportioned with other items of expense as Service Department Overhead.

Tool storage and issue

The tool stock can be conveniently recorded by the use of the bin-card procedure outlined in Chapter 5. If, as has been suggested, written requisitions are used for the issue of tools they should be made out in triplicate. One copy is kept by the workman, one in a file at the bin in numerical order of the recipients, and one in a file on the Tool-stores clerk's desk arranged numerically according to tool nomenclature. When a tool is returned the requisitions are withdrawn from the files, and completed as to time and date of return.

An alternative method is to issue brass checks to the workmen, numbered according to their clock numbers. A check is given in, in exchange for a tool, and is hung on a peg on the bin. Each tool bin has checks also, bearing the symbol and number of the tools. When the workman's check is placed by the bin a tool check is removed to correspond, and is hung on a control board under the workman's number. Track of the tools is therefore easily kept. This method provides none of the useful data obtainable from the requisition-note procedure, and therefore a combination of both methods is sometimes used.

Tools returned

These are examined and reconditioned before being replaced, and the cost is charged to a Standing Order Number for Upkeep of Tools.

Apportionment of tool expense

All the expense of running the Tool-room and Tool Store are collated and apportioned as overhead to the machine departments, except for the value of tools capitalised. Regard must also be paid to the fact that tools are made for

(a) Tool-room use,
(b) other centres,
(c) sale.

The basis on which apportionment may be made is the machine hours worked in the Tool-room.

FACTORY OVERHEAD

The procedure to be adopted in the collection, apportionment, and absorption of Factory Overhead has already been described in Chapters 10 and 11, and Factory Job costing does not call for any variation.

BATCH COSTING

This is used when the production consists of limited repetition work and a definite number of articles are manufactured in one batch. Where a number of different parts enter into the article, sufficient for each batch are passed through the works for the quantity required. The cost of the operations is ascertained as described for job costing, the batches being given a Production Order Number.

In determining the optimum quantity to constitute an economical batch there are five main considerations:

1. The cost and time taken in setting up the tools on the machines.
2. The cost and time taken in manufacturing the parts.
3. The rate of interest on the capital invested in the parts.
4. The cost of storage.
5. The rate at which the parts are demanded.

In addition, it is necessary to postulate an agreed period, say one month. We have then,

1. *Setting up cost per piece* $= \dfrac{\text{Total setting up cost}}{\text{Quantity in batch}} = \dfrac{S}{X}$.

2. Manufacturing cost per piece =
Cost of material, labour, and Factory Overhead per piece = C.

3. Interest charge on capital invested. This raises some preliminary considerations:

(a) The average stock of units. This ranges from the minimum quantity which is in stock when a new batch is put in hand, to this figure plus the quantity in the batch. If M be used to denote the minimum, then the *average* is

$$\frac{M + (M + X)}{2} \text{ or } M + \frac{X}{2}.$$

(b) The average investment in stock is therefore

$$\left(\frac{S}{X} + C\right)\left(M + \frac{X}{2}\right).$$

(c) Assuming I represents the annual rate of interest, then the interest charge per month is

$$\frac{I}{12}\left(\frac{S}{X} + C\right)\left(M + \frac{X}{2}\right).$$

4. The monthly storage charge. This is arrived at as follows:

(a) The total annual storage charges, including wages of store-keepers, rent, provision for obsolescence, etc., are calculated.
(b) A proportion of this figure is taken to represent that part of the storage space allotted for the type of components under consideration.
(c) This result is divided by 12 to obtain the monthly storage charge to be borne by the average quantity.

As in the present context, this is a constant, we may denote the final answer by the mnemonic for "Bin"

$$\frac{B}{12}.$$

5. The rate of demand per month, which may be denoted by D.

Now, let the total cost of a month's supply $= Y$.
Then

$$Y = \frac{\text{Cost of units}}{\text{demanded}} + \frac{\text{Monthly interest on}}{\text{cost of average}} + \frac{\text{Monthly storage cost}}{\text{of average quantity}}$$
$$\text{quantity}$$

Using the symbols suggested

$$Y = D\left(\frac{S}{X} + C\right) + \frac{I}{12}\left(\frac{S}{X} + C\right)\left(M + \frac{X}{2}\right) + \frac{B}{12}.$$

Multiplying out

$$Y = \frac{DS}{X} + \frac{DC}{1} + \frac{ISM}{12X} + \frac{ISX}{24X} + \frac{ICM}{12} + \frac{ICX}{24} + \frac{B}{12}.$$

Using the calculus, if Y is a minimum, then $\frac{dy}{dx} = 0$,

And $\frac{dy}{dx} = \frac{-DS}{X^2} - \frac{ISM}{12X^2} + \frac{IC}{24} = 0.$

Rearranging

$$\frac{12DS + ISM}{12X^2} = \frac{IC}{24}.$$

Multiply both sides by $24X^2$

$$24DS + 2ISM = X^2(IC).$$

Hence $X^2 = \frac{24DS + 2ISM}{IC}.$

And $X = \sqrt{\frac{24DS + 2ISM}{IC}}.$

In order to shorten this formula, it is often arranged that M, the minimum quantity, is to be regarded as too small to affect the calculation, so that

$$X = \sqrt{\frac{24DS}{IC}}.$$

EXAMPLE

Let the monthly demand for a certain part be   200
Let the set up cost (pence) be   120
Let the annual rate of interest be   6%
Let the cost of manufacture per unit be (pence)   6

Then, X, the economic batch quantity is

$$\sqrt{\frac{24 \times 200 \times 120}{0 \cdot 06 \times 6}} = \underline{1265.}$$

NOTE.—In the above illustration, had the rate of interest been taken as 25%, it would have offset the diminishing total cost per piece for larger batches to such an extent that the economic batch would be only $\underline{620.}$

SIMPLIFICATION OF COSTING WORK IN JOB COSTING

Owing to the vast amount of paper work involved in obtaining the separate cost of each job undertaken, it is often found that the expense incurred is out of all proportion to the value of the result. Measures may therefore be taken to simplify the work, as follows:

1. Estimates for each job are carefully prepared when submitting the quotation to the customer. These estimates are based on data sheets giving information on similar time-studied operations.
2. The factory or works is split up into cost centres.
3. Costs are collected as to—

    (a) direct materials used,
    (b) labour costs per cost centre,
    (c) cost centre Factory Overhead incurred.

4. No attempt is made to allocate these costs to particular jobs, the original estimates being assumed to be approximately correct.
5. The material content of the estimates is compared in total with the direct materials issued and used.
6. The labour content of the estimates is analysed to cost centres and compared with the total direct labour hours recorded for the cost centre. At the same time the average direct labour hour rate for the cost centre is found and compared with those recorded for previous periods.
7. The Factory Overhead content of the estimates is summarised and compared with the Factory Overhead applied to the cost centre.

Adjustments have to be made on the analysis of the estimates to take care of beginning and ending work in progress, but this is not too difficult, since the progress advices give the necessary information as to the stage of completion reached. By arranging the work in this way

1. Material requisitions are dealt with in total and not one by one.
2. Operators' individual job-time tickets are not required.
3. Payment to the operators is made on the basis of the clock card alone, split as to

    (a) productive time,
    (b) idle time.

SPECIMEN QUESTION *

A joinery factory commences business on January 1, and institutes a job-costing system in which the costs of each order are recorded on a separate cost card. A summary of these cards at the end of six months gives the following figures:

	Completed orders £	Work in Progress £
Materials used	4610	916
Labour	2130	581
Works expenses	710	194
Works cost	7450	1691

* This Question is based on one given in the Intermediate Examination of the Corporation of Secretaries.

The following figures for the same period are taken from the financial books:

	£
Materials Purchased	7,430
Wages	2,711
Works Expenses	1,142
Selling and Administration Expenses	1,793
Sales	10,547

Selling and administration expenses are applied in the Cost Department on the basis of £300 per month.

1. Write up Cost Ledger Total Accounts on a double-entry basis so as to form a reconciliation between the financial books and the costing system. All work is invoiced to customers immediately on completion and there have been no losses of materials.
2. Write up the accounts using an integral system.

ANSWER

In the answer given, figures only are used, the entries being numbered where necessary to show the double entry. A Materials Control Account is used so that the agreement of Invoices and Goods Received Notes can be demonstrated.

1. USING COST ACCOUNTS SEPARATE FROM FINANCIAL ACCOUNTS

Financial Books

Materials Account
7,430 |

Wages Account
2,711 |

Works Expenses Account
1,142 |

Selling and Administration Expenses Account
1,793 |

Sales Account
| 10,547

Cost Ledger Control Account—Memorandum

7,430		10,547
2,711	c/d	2,529
1,142		
1,793		
13,076		13,076

Costing Books

General Ledger Adjustment Account

10,547 (10)	7,430 (1)
c/d 2,529	2,711 (4)
	1,142 (5)
	1,793 (7)
13,076	13,076

Materials Control		*Work in Progress*	
7,430 (1)	7,430 (2)	5,526 (3)	7,450 (8)
		2,711 (4)	c/d 1,691
		904 (6)	
Stores Ledger Control			
7,430 (2)	5,526 (3)	9,141	9,141

Works Expenses Incurred	
1,142 (5)	

Works Expenses Applied		*Cost of Sales*	
	904 (6)	7,450 (8)	
		1,800 (9)	

Selling and Administration Expenses Incurred		*Sales*	
1,793 (7)			10,547 (10)

Selling and Administration Expenses Applied	
	1,800 (9)

2. USING AN INTEGRAL SYSTEM

Materials Control		*Creditors*		*Debtors*	
7,430 (1)	7,430 (2)	Paid in due course	7,430 (1)	10,547 (11)	Collected in due course
			1,142 (6)		
			1,793 (8)		

Stores Ledger Control		*Sales*	
7,430 (2)	5,526 (3)		10,547 (11)

Wages Control		Wages Payable	
2,711 (4)	2,711 (5)	Net wages and transfers to deduction accounts	2,711 (4)

Works Expenses Incurred
1,142 (6)

Works Expenses Applied		Work in Progress	
	904 (7)	5,526 (3)	7,450 (10)
		2,711 (5)	c/d 1,691
Selling and Administration		904 (7)	
Expenses Incurred		9,141	9,141
1,793 (8)			

Selling and Administration Expenses Applied		Cost of Sales	
	1,800 (9)	7,450 (10)	
		1,800 (9)	

In both systems of accounting shown above there will be certain subsidiary costing records:

(a) Stores Ledger in agreement with the Stores Ledger Control.

(b) Job Cost Cards giving details of Work in Progress: Cards for completed work will be transferred to another cabinet, so that the "live" cards agree with the balance of work in progress carried forward.

(c) Standing Order Numbers in agreement with, and giving details of Works Expenses incurred.

(d) Cost Account Numbers giving details of Selling and Administration Expenses incurred.

It will be seen that when separate systems of accounting are used, some work is duplicated, but agreement between the records is made through the Cost Ledger Control Account in the Financial books, and the General Ledger Adjustment Account in the Costing books.

For a fuller treatment of the subject the student is referred to Chapter 15.

CHAPTER 19

OPERATING COSTS

OPERATING COST is defined in the *Terminology of Cost Accountancy* as "The cost of providing a service"

Such a service might consist of transport; steam and hot water; catering; and so on, as departments of a firm, or it might be applied to large public-utility undertakings, such as Gas and Electricity Boards.

This method of costing is different from that used in connection with production manufacturing, and the difference lies chiefly in the manner of assembling the cost data, and in its allocation to cost units.

1. TRANSPORT COSTING

(a) PURPOSE

The records are designed to show the total cost of operating each vehicle, and then to apply this cost to particular units, *e.g.* per ton, per mile run, per ton-mile, or per hour worked. These units have to be chosen with care, because when materials are being carried which vary in bulk, weight, and type, to cost per ton, per mile run, or per ton-mile is somewhat unsuitable. The costs ascertained are useful for:

(i) Comparison between the cost of using motor vehicles owned and that of using alternative forms of transport.

(ii) Determining what should be charged against departments, or others, using the service.

(iii) Deciding at what price the use of a vehicle can be charged, profitably, to anyone hiring a vehicle.

(iv) Comparing the cost of maintaining one vehicle with another, or one group of vehicles with another group.

(b) COLLECTION OF DATA

Most of the details required by the Transport Manager for controlling the vehicles under his authority is obtained from the Daily Log Sheet, a specimen of which is to be seen in Fig. 67. In addition, he will doubtless inaugurate a system of requisitions for transport, so that he may allocate them to the most suitable vehicles available. His aim will be to avoid idleness of vehicles, to prevent waste of capacity by too much light running, and to guard against unnecessary duplication of journeys.

LOG SHEET

Vehicle No.: ....   Date: ....19...
Driver: ....   Time left Garage: ....
Route No.: ....   Time returned: ....

Trip Record.

Trip No.	From	To	Tons or Packages		Miles	Time	
			Out	Collected en route		Out	In
1							
2							
3							
4							
5							
6							
etc.							
		Totals					

Supplies	Workers' Time	Exceptional Delays
Petrol:	Driver:	Loading delays: ....
Oil:	Assistant:	Traffic delays: ....
Grease:	Cleaners:	Accidents: ....
etc.	Mechanics:	

FIG. 67.—*Log Sheet*

Each driver hands in daily a log sheet of this kind, from which the Transport Manager can extract details by which he maintains control.

(c) EXPENDITURE ON REPAIRS

If the driver has to arrange for any repairs or adjustments when away from his own garage he may be required to note the fact on the back of the Log Sheet, so that the account, when received, may be linked up and checked from his record. Work done by the firm's own garage staff is usually recorded on repair tickets, and is then costed. The cost of repairs may be collected for each individual vehicle, or for groups of similar vehicles, and should be stated as so much "per mile run."

Special statistics on tyre performances are often kept, and this is not so difficult as it might seem, since reference numbers are marked on the wall of the tyre.

If the repair tickets are filed for reference a handy repair history for each vehicle can be accumulated, and will be most useful when a decision has to be taken on whether to incur further repair expenditure or not. It is considered advisable to prepare an estimate for each proposed major repair: if these estimates are done conscientiously experience will lead to greater and greater accuracy, and finally it may then be found unnecessary to find the actual cost of each job done.

(d) EXPENDITURE ON FUEL

Each night or morning the tanks of all vehicles are filled, and the gallons supplied are noted at once on the Log Sheet. Any fuel obtained *en route* has to be accounted for by garage tickets, and also noted on the Log Sheet.

The basis of control in this case will be "miles per gallon."

(e) COST SUMMARY AND PERFORMANCE STATEMENT

This is shown in Fig. 68. It will be seen that there are three main subdivisions of cost:

  (i) *Operating and running costs.*—These vary from day to day, and are incurred by the actual operation of the vehicle; expenses which would not be incurred if the vehicle were "laid up" come under this heading, *e.g.* petrol, oil, grease, and part of the driver's wages.

  (ii) *Maintenance charges.*—These include wear on tyres, repairs and overhauls, painting, hire of spare vehicles when the firm's own are under repair, garaging, etc.

  (iii) *Fixed charges.*—These are incurred whether a vehicle is operating or not. They include insurance, tax, depreciation, and part of the driver's wages. Interest on capital might also be included.

(f) RECOVERY OF TRANSPORT COSTS

It is customary to charge a rate per hour or a rate per mile, based on the cost summary figures, to the various departments making use of the transport.

2. BOILER-HOUSE COSTING

The necessary statistics for arriving at the cost of steam produced and used are based on accounts prepared by the Cost Office and technical data provided by the Engineering Department as to steam pressures, evaporations, meter readings, and distribution to processes, factory heating, turbines, losses, etc.

The costs may be considered under the following headings:

  (a) *Supervision.*—Wages of foreman, and a proportion of the works engineer's salary.

  (b) *Labour.*—Coal handlers, stokers, and ash removers.

COST SUMMARY AND PERFORMANCE STATEMENT

No. of Car: 19   **Month ended** April 19...
Chassis No.: 14966A   **Capacity in lbs** ....

MONTHLY CHARGES

A. Operating Charges				B. Maintenance Charges			
	£	s.	d.		£	s.	d.
Petrol				Tyres			
Oil				Repairs			
Grease				Overhaul			
etc.				Spare Car			
Driver				Garage Charge			
Assistant				etc.			
Mechanics							
Total	102	12	5	Total	26	15	3

C. Fixed Charges				Proportion for Month		
				£	s.	d.
Insurance	at £...... per year					
Interest	at .... % ,,					
Depreciation	at .... % ,,					
Tax, licence	at £...... ,,					
Other items	at £...... ,,					
	Total			68	12	4

MONTHLY COST SHEET

1. Total Capital Cost, complete	£1123·95
Performance Record.	
2. Days operated	26
3. Days idle	4
4. Days maintained (Item 2 + Item 3)	30
5. Total hours operated	232
6. Total miles covered	803
7. Total trips made	28
Performance Averages.	
8. Average miles per day maintained (Item 6 ÷ Item 4)	26·76
9. Average miles per day operated (Item 6 ÷ Item 2)	30·88
10. Average miles per trip (Item 6 ÷ Item 7)	28·67
Costs for the Month.	
11. Total expenses for month (Sum of Items A, B and C above)	£198
12. Cost per day operated (Item 11 ÷ Item 2)	£7·61
13. Cost per day maintained (Item 11 ÷ Item 4)	£6·6
14. Cost per mile operated (Item 11 ÷ Item 6)	4s. 11d.
15. Cost per hour (Item 11 ÷ Item 5)	17s. 0d.

FIG. 68.—*Cost Summary and Performance Statement*

This provides summarised details in regard to the running of each vehicle or group of similar vehicles. Comparison of period with period and of one vehicle with another should yield useful information for control purposes.

(c) *Maintenance.*—Furnace repairs, renewal of fire bars, replacement of fire irons, etc.

(d) *Indirect materials.*—Service materials and small tools.

(e) *Fuel.*—This may be coal, or fuel oil. The cost will include cartage, handling, and storage.

(f) *Water.*—The cost of purification and softening is included, as well as the cost of supply.

(g) *Fixed overhead.*—Rent, rates, depreciation, insurance, and possibly interest on capital. It should be noted that the capital value of the boiler-house plant is included in the rating assessment, whereas that in manufacturing machinery is not. This must be borne in mind when apportioning rates as between shops, departments, and boiler-house.

A specimen Boiler-house Cost Sheet is shown in Fig. 69. The costs are apportioned to departments on the basis of technical data of consumption supplied by the engineer. Separate consumption returns are required for processes, heating, and domestic hot water.

A simple system is to ascertain by technical calculation the rate of consumption of steam in pounds per hour for each appliance connected with the mains and service pipes. Then, by estimating or recording the times during which each unit is consuming steam, a reasonably reliable record for steam allocation is obtained.

3. *CANTEEN COSTING*

The main headings of expense will be:

(a) *Provisions.*—Meat; fish and poultry; vegetables; fruit (fresh) and (dried); flour; cakes; milk and cream; tea; coffee; sugar; soft drinks; and often cigarettes are included too under this heading.

(b) *Labour.*—Supervision; cooks; waitresses; kitchen assistants; porters.

(c) *Services.*—Steam; gas; electricity: power and light; water.

(d) *Consumable Stores.*—Table linen; cutlery; crockery; glassware; mops and washing-up cloths; drying-up cloths; cleaning materials; dustpans and brushes, etc.

(e) *Miscellaneous Overhead.*—Rent and rates; depreciation; insurances, etc.

(f) *Credit.*—Charges for meals, teas, and other sales. Sale of swill.

The Canteen Manageress will have the duty of estimating the quantities of food required each day. Adequate cold-store facilities will greatly help her in the avoidance of waste and in economical buying.

She will probably have a general responsibility to the Personnel

| BOILER-HOUSE COST SHEET | | | | | | |
| For the month of June 19... | | | | | | |

S.O. Nos.	Expense Items	Total Cost		Cost per 1000 lbs. of Steam		Incr. or decr. %
		This Year	Last Year	This Year	Last Year	
	Fuel	£	£	s. d.	s. d.	
	Fuel Handling					
	Ash Removal and Disposal					
	Electric Power					
	Stokers and Coal Wheelers					
	Water Purchased					
	„ Softening					
	Boiler Cleansing					
	Sundry Indirect Materials					
	Gas and Electric Light					
	Maintenance Services:					
	Fixed Plant					
	Meters					
	Boilers					
	Economisers					
	Softening Plant					
	Mechanical Stokers					
	Steam Service Pipes					
	Barrows					
	Weighing Machine, Tools, etc.					
	Coal Bunkers					
	Furnace					
	Miscellaneous Expenses:					
	Supervision					
	Sweepers, Cleaners, and General Labour					
	Rent, Rates, etc.					
	Depreciation Plant					
	„ Buildings					
	Renewals					
	Steam Mains					
	Allocation of General Charges					
	Total					

Steam Produced in 1000 lbs.: ......   Less Boiler House Use: ......   Less Mains Losses: ......   Total Consumption: ......

Remarks:

FIG. 69.—*Boiler-house Cost Sheet*

The main points to notice here will be the fuel costs, the labour costs, and the maintenance costs as against the steam raised. Other information, of a more technical kind, as for example the CO_2 recording, will be watched by the Engineer.

The expense headings would be modified should the fuel used be oil and not coal.

Manager, or to the Works Manager, and from time to time, with her co-operation, he should initiate an examination of the swill bins, which more than anything will reveal whether food is being wasted unnecessarily.

Whether it is possible to introduce a choice of dishes each day depends largely on the numbers being catered for. An experienced Canteen Manageress will, however, aim at a weekly cycle, without repetition, of main joints and entrees, and about a ten-day cycle in respect of sweets. Generally speaking the average worker likes plain food, well cooked and attractively served.

Costing with a view to fixing a price for main meals and subsidiary meals is difficult to arrange, as it necessitates equating one type of meal with another. However, by recording the numbers of persons served, using different coloured dockets according to the type of meal provided, experience will be gained from which the cost involved may be approximated. Canteen-management training also helps by providing knowledge as to the quantities which can be expected from various joints of meat and kinds of fish; the numbers of cups of tea from 1 pound of tea and 1 pint of milk; the number of slices of bread and butter from a quartern loaf and a pound of butter; and so on.

Most factory canteens have to be subsidised to some extent, since to charge prices sufficient to cover not only the direct costs but full overhead as well would result in the canteen being neglected—and on production grounds this may be undesirable.

It is therefore suggested that the best kind of operating-cost statement to prepare will be on the lines of the expense headings already given, with comparative figures for the last period and the corresponding period last year.

By the use of moving-average charts for the main headings of expense, the income received, and the numbers of each type of meal provided, a close watch can be obtained on the trends which are significant.

CHAPTER 20

PROCESS COSTING

Introduction and General Principles

PROCESS COSTING is a method of costing used to ascertain the cost of the product at each process, operation, or stage of manufacture, where processes are carried on having one or more of the following features:

1. Where the product of one process becomes the material of another process or operation.
2. Where there is simultaneous production, at one or more processes, of different products, with or without by-products.
3. Where, during one or more processes or operations of a series, the products, or materials, are not distinguishable from one another, as, for instance, when finished products differ finally only in shape or form.

The system provides for showing the cost of the main products and of any by-products, and thus is very different from Job Order Costing, where each job is separately costed. Orders may be combined for common process production to a certain state, and then be costed for subsequent operations by Job Cost methods.

In most cases Process Costing requires fewer forms, and less details, than are needed for Job Costs, but a closer analysis of operations is needed. For example, there is not the need for the allocation of labour to so many order numbers, and material is issued in bulk to departments, rather than to many specific jobs. In continuous processes, as in a coal distillation plant, the men are occupied continuously on each process.

In Process Costing the terms by-product, joint product, scrap, and wastage frequently occur, so it might be expedient to define these terms before proceeding.

BY-PRODUCTS

The *Cost Accountant's Handbook*,* from which this and the other definitions given below are taken, defines these as

"any saleable or usable value incidentally produced in addition to the main product."

* *The Cost Accountants' Handbook*, edited by Theodore Lang (The Ronald Press Company, 1944. New York).

235

In the process of producing the main product it frequently occurs that materials or other products emerge which are of lesser value. These are the by-products, and even if subsequent processing enhances their value, the resulting profit will be less than that from the main product, otherwise of course the by-product would become the main product, and vice versa. A typical example of the creation of by-products is in the oil refinery industry, where the crude oil is processed and refined oil might be the main product, with sulphur, bitumen, and chemical fertilisers among the many by-products.

It is possible for a main product of one industry to be the by-product of another. An example of this occurs in the production of coke and gas. In coke ovens production is concentrated on the main product—coke—and gas is incidentally produced, and thus becomes a by-product. However, in a gas-works gas is the main product, while coke is a by-product. This situation may raise a difficult problem when the by-product of one firm is being sold at a cheaper rate than the same commodity which is a main product of another firm.

JOINT PRODUCTS

These

"represent two or more products separated in the course of the same processing operations, usually requiring further processing, each product being in such proportion that no single product can be designated as a major product."

In a process where two or more products are inevitably produced, and each one earns approximately the same profit as another, the products would be considered joint products. The term is also used to describe various qualities of the same product, as for example, the many grades of coal which may be used.

SCRAP

This is defined as

"the incidental residue from certain types of manufacture, usually of small amount and low value, recoverable without further processing."

Products which are found to be defective or raw materials which prove to be not up to standard may be used in other departments of the firm or sold at a much lower price than the cost. In many firms off-cuts are unavoidably produced, as for example, when can lids are pressed out of a sheet of tin-plate; the remaining tin-plate may be collected and returned to the supplier, who can re-process the tin and credit the firm returning the material with the scrap value.

It is essential to keep the quantity of scrap produced to a minimum and, if possible, make it more profitable by further processing, *e.g.* metal turnings could be made into pan scrapers.

WASTE

The same publication defines this as

"that portion of a basic raw material lost in processing, having no recovery value."

Anything which has no value is considered to be waste. An example of waste is a tank of soup into which broken glass has fallen, with the result that the soup is unfit for consumption and must be destroyed.

THE APPLICATION OF THE METHOD

The industries in which Process Costs may be used are very many, in fact, except where Job, Batch, or Unit Operation Costing is necessary, a Process Costing system can usually be devised. In particular, the following may be mentioned as a few examples:

Chemical works	Textiles, weaving, spinning, etc.
Soap-making	Food products
Box-making	Canning factories
Distillation processes	Coking works
Paper mills	Paint, ink, and varnishing, etc.
Biscuit works	Meat products factory
Oil refining	Milk Dairy

Process Costing is used by firms having a continuous flow of identical products, where it is not possible to distinguish one unit from another. The amount of production is determined to a large extent by supply and demand for the product, rather than by a specific order. The cost per unit is averaged over a period, *e.g.* a week or a month.

To illustrate the above statement, let us assume the following details:

Production for the month of January was 60,000 units.
Direct materials consumed amounted to £6,000.
Direct labour costs were £4,000.
Production overhead incurred was £2,000.

The cost per unit is determined by dividing the total cost by the total number of units produced.

$$\frac{£12,000}{60,000} = 4s. \text{ per unit.}$$

This cost of 4s. per unit will relate to each one of the 60,000 units produced, irrespective of the fact that on one day the units produced cost 4s. 2d. while on another day the cost was 3s. 11d. The important fact is that 4s. per unit is the average cost for the period.

THE GENERAL FEATURES OF THE PROCESS COST SYSTEM

The factory is divided into departments or processes, which are limited to a certain operation, e.g. in a canning factory one department may bake the beans, another department may prepare the sauce for the beans. The process may perform a certain operation or operations, each of which completes a special stage in the production routine. Each process is usually the responsibility of one person, who may be a foreman or a supervisor.

An account is kept for each process or operation. Materials, labour, and overhead are debited, by-products and scrap are credited, while the material as modified at the first operation is passed on to the next process. If by-products require further treatment the same procedure is followed.

Put in another way, the "finished product" of the first process becomes the "raw material" of the next one, and so on, until the final products are completed. Each Process Cost Account, in fact, represents a subdivision of a Manufacturing Account, so that the works cost of each process is separately ascertained, and from which the unit cost at each operation may be calculated.

Single or Output Costing resembles Process Costing, in which there is but one process where every unit is identical. Sometimes Unit Costing is combined with Process Costing, the method being to cost by the unit of production, where manufacture is continuous and the units are identical, or can be made equivalent by means of ratios.

Departmental Costing differs in that separate products are generally dealt with in each department, whereas in Process Costing the same material passes from one operation or process to another in altered form. When two or more distinct varieties of goods are manufactured separate departmental costs are desirable, so that the profit made by each department may be revealed. Any normal loss suffered in a process is borne by the good production, thus increasing the average cost per unit. Any abnormal loss is valued at the ordinary rate and the amount transferred to an Abnormal Loss Account, which reveals to management any losses due to inefficiency, accidents, etc.

STANDARD COSTS IN PROCESS COSTING

In industries where Process Costing is suitable Standard Costs may be used with great advantage. Standard Costs provide a measure against which actual costs may be compared. Standard Costing, in connection with Process Costs, gives the management an excellent measure of the efficiency of production, and it may be mentioned that accounting systems on these lines are being more widely used every year. This method is dealt with fully in another chapter.

THE USE OF NUMERICAL NOMENCLATURE

In an earlier chapter the use of Works Order Numbers and Standing Order Numbers was described. The identification of cost to processes by means of Process Order Numbers facilitates the collection of the necessary details, ensures a proper allocation of expenditure to each process, and simplifies overhead analysis.

The adoption of departmental or process numbers is necessary when mechanical sorting and tabulating machines are used, as is the case in many large firms today. Numbers are also essential where electronic computing machines are in operation. Mechanical or electronic machines are indispensable in large factories if prompt cost and production figures are required.

THE ELEMENTS OF PRODUCTION COST

Materials

Frequently in Process Costing all the material required for production is issued to the first process, where after processing it is passed to the next process, and so on: each process merely performs some operation on the material which has been passed from the first process. In other systems material may pass from the first process to the second process, where extra or new materials are added, then more material added in the next process; this may continue until completion.

Whichever method is used, sufficient supplies of raw materials must be available to meet production needs. Materials may be requisitioned in the way described in Chapter 5 or bulk requisitions may be issued. When bulk requisitions are used, materials are issued from the Stores to the department in bulk quantities, where they are held in departmental stock until such time as they are needed.

Labour

Generally, the cost of direct labour is a very small part of the cost of production in industries adopting Process Costing; for example, in one large firm in the chemical industry the cost of direct labour represents 4% of the total cost. With the introduction of more and more automatic machinery the direct-labour element becomes smaller and smaller, while the overhead element increases.

Compared with, for example, Job Costing, the recording and allocating of time spent on production is relatively easy. Where employees are engaged continuously on one process, as is frequently the case, the time spent by the employees is analysed and posted to the debit of the Process Account concerned. However, if employees are engaged on more than one process it will be necessary to record the time spent on each one, or an approximate apportionment of the total time will be allocated to each process concerned.

Direct Expenses

Each item of expenditure which can be directly attributed to a process will be debited to the relative Process Account. An example of direct expense is the design cost of a can used in canning vegetables.

Production Overhead

In Process Costing the overhead element of total cost is normally very high. Great care will be needed to ensure that each process is charged with a reasonable share of the production overhead. The actual overhead to be debited to each Process Account will be calculated as suggested in Chapter 11.

EXAMPLE

The manufacture of Product "Exe" requires four distinct processes, numbered 1–4. On completion, the product is passed from Process Number 4 to Finished Stock. During Period 10, the following information was obtained in relation to Product "Exe."

Element of Cost	Total	Process 1	Process 2	Process 3	Process 4
	£	£	£	£	£
Direct material	2600	1500	400	—	700
Direct labour	2650	250	300	900	1200
Direct expense	800	100	—	200	500
Production Overhead	7950				

Production Overhead is allocated to processes on the basis of 300% of direct wages.

Production during the period was 1000 tons.

There was no stock of raw material or work in progress either at the beginning or end of the period.

Process 1

Description:

Period No. 10
Output 1000 tons

	Amount	Cost per ton		Amount	Cost per ton
	£	£		£	£
Direct material	1,500	1·50	Output transferred to Process 2	2,600	2·60
Direct labour	250	0·25			
Direct expense	100	0·10			
Production overhead	750	0·75			
	£2,600	£2·60		£2,600	£2·60

Process 2

Description:

Period No. 10
Output 1000 tons

	Amount	Cost per ton		Amount	Cost per ton
	£	£		£	£
Output transferred from Process 1	2,600	2·60	Output transferred to Process 3	4,200	4·20
Direct material	400	0·40			
Direct labour	300	0·30			
Production overhead	900	0·90			
	£4,200	£4·20		£4,200	£4·20

Process 3

Description:

Period No. 10
Output 1000 tons

	Amount	Cost per ton		Amount	Cost per ton
	£	£		£	£
Output transferred from Process 2	4,200	4·20	Output transferred to Process 4	8,000	8·00
Direct labour	900	0·90			
Direct expense	200	0·20			
Production overhead	2,700	2·70			
	£8,000	£8·00		£8,000	£8·00

Process 4

Description:

Period No. 10
Output 1000 tons

	Amount	Cost per ton		Amount	Cost per ton
	£	£		£	£
Output transferred from Process 3	8,000	8·00	Output transferred to Finished Stock	14,000	14·00
Direct material	700	0·70			
Direct labour	1,200	1·20			
Direct expense	500	0·50			
Production overhead	3,600	3·60			
	£14,000	£14·00		£14,000	£14·00

It will be observed that the "finished" product of Process 1 is the "raw material" of Process 2 and so on, each transferred at cost. Sometimes these transfers are made to show the transferring process a profit; the reason and stock valuation problems arising, are dealt with later in Chapter 22. The finished output of Process No. 4 is transferred to Finished Stock Account.

Finished Stock Account—Product "Exe"

	Tons	Cost per ton	Amount		Tons	Cost per ton	Amount
		£	£			£	£
Output of 1000 tons transferred from Process 4 at Cost	1,000	14·00	14,000				

PROCESS LOSS, SCRAP, AND WASTAGE

Some loss, scrap, and/or wastage is inevitable in process industries, so it is essential that accurate records are maintained to enable control of these items to be effected. The Cost Department must be kept well informed through the medium of scrap tickets, material credit notes, and loss reports.

It should be pointed out to foremen and supervisors that scrap, etc., should be measured and recorded, otherwise production costs will be adversely affected. Materials which have been processed and are then found to be defective and scrapped, have incurred their share of labour and variable overhead up to the point of rejection, so obviously the financial loss to the firm increases with each stage of production. Where possible, scrap should be baled as it is incurred, because baled scrap is usually valued higher than loose scrap, and needs less storage space.

In most process industries the loss of material which is inherent in the processing operation can be worked out in advance. Usually this is calculated by formula or by experience, and it reveals the loss which would be expected in normal conditions. Process loss is often caused by such factors as evaporation and that loss inherent in large-scale production, but may often include scrap and waste already defined. This is considered to be the Normal Process Loss.

Abnormal Process Loss is that loss caused by unexpected or abnormal conditions, such as sub-standard materials, carelessness, and accidents. All losses under this category must be thoroughly investigated, and where necessary, steps taken to try to prevent any recurrence.

The accounting treatment of normal and abnormal losses differ. In the first case the cost of any normal loss is absorbed in the cost of production of good products, while a separate account is opened for abnormal losses, to which is debited the cost of material, labour, and appropriate overhead incurred by the wastage. Abnormal losses should be written off to the Costing Profit and Loss Account.

WASTE

Waste has no value. If waste is part of the normal process loss the cost will be absorbed by the good production. On the other hand, if it is part of the abnormal process loss the cost will be transferred from the Process Account to Abnormal Loss Account.

SCRAP

The problem of scrap is more complex than that of waste, and may be treated as follows:

1. Scrap resulting from one process which is to be utilised in another process should be credited to the first process at the value at which it was originally debited, and debited to the relative Stores Account. This value is thus related to the market price of the good material. On issue to the next process it is valued at the same price as that which it would have been charged if bought specifically for the purpose. This method is advantageous in that if a comparison of the cost of production of a firm is to be made with the cost of having the product produced elsewhere, accurate costs will be obtainable.
2. Scrap which cannot be utilised for subsequent production should be credited to the Process Account and debited to the appropriate Stores Account at a value which is not greater than the market price of such scrap material.
3. Scrap which is of small value may be sold periodically, and the amount realised credited to Works Overhead Account. This method saves the expense of allocating credit to each process which has incurred the scrap.

To illustrate the different treatment of normal loss and abnormal loss in Process Costing, the following illustration is given:

In the manufacture of product "Wye," 1000 lb of material at 4s. per lb were supplied to the first process. Labour costs amounted to £50 and Production Overheads of £25 were incurred. The normal process loss has been estimated at 10%, of which half can be sold as scrap at 2s. per lb. The actual production realised was 850 lb.

Process 1

Description:

Period No. 1
Output 850 lb

	lb.	Cost per lb.	Amount		lb.	Cost per lb.	Amount
Direct material	1000	4s.	200	Normal loss	100	1s.	5
Direct labour			50	Abnormal loss	50	6s.	15
Production over-head			25	Process 2 output	850	6s.	255
	1000		£275		1000		£275

I

Normal loss is calculated as follows:

Estimated loss 10% of production (1000 lb) = 100 lb.
Half can be sold as scrap = 50 lb

$$50 \text{ lb at } 2s. \text{ per lb} = \underline{\underline{£5.}}$$

Abnormal loss is calculated as follows:

Estimated production	900 lb
Actual production	850 lb
Abnormal loss	50 lb.

Cost of normal production = £275 − £5 = £270.

$$\text{Cost of normal production per lb} = \frac{£270}{900}.$$

$$\text{Cost of abnormal loss } \frac{£270}{900} \times 50 = \underline{\underline{£15.}}$$

However, some of the abnormal loss will probably possess scrap value, so if we assume for purposes of illustration that half can be sold, then 25 lb at 2s. per lb will be realised.

In the Abnormal Loss Account will appear the debit of £15 transferred from Process No. 1, while on the credit side will be shown the £2 10s. realised on sale of the scrap. The net cost of the abnormal loss is thus £12 10s.

ABNORMAL GAIN

Mention was previously made of allowances being made for losses which would be expected in process industries in normal conditions. Then it was shown how abnormal losses occur when the allowances were exceeded. Sometimes, however, the actual loss in a process is smaller than was expected, in which case an abnormal gain results. The value of the gain will be calculated in a similar manner to an abnormal loss previously described, then posted to an Abnormal Gain Account.

EXAMPLE

In the manufacture of Product "Wye," 1200 lb of material at 4s. per lb were supplied to the first Process in Period 2. Labour costs amounted to £60 and Production Overheads of £30 were incurred. The normal process loss has been estimated at 10%, of which half can be sold as scrap at 2s. per lb. The actual production realised was 1120 lb.

Process 1

Description: Period No. 2
                                                                     Output 1120 lb

	lb.	Cost per lb.	Amount		lb.	Cost per lb.	Amount
			£				£
Direct material	1200	4s.	240	Normal loss	120	1s.	6
Direct labour			60	Process 2 output			
Production over-head			30	transferred	1120	6s.	336
Abnormal gain	40	6s.	12				
	1240		£342		1240		£342

Normal loss is calculated as follows:

Estimated loss 10% of Production (1200 lb) = 120 lb.
Half can be sold as scrap = 60 lb.

$$60 \text{ lb. at } 2s. \text{ per lb} = \underline{\underline{£6.}}$$

Abnormal gain is calculated as follows:

Estimated production	1080 lb
Actual production	1120 lb
Abnormal gain	40 lb.

Cost of normal production £330 − £6 = £324.

$$\text{Cost of normal production per lb: } \frac{£324}{1080}.$$

$$\text{Cost of abnormal gain } \frac{324}{1080} \times 40 = \underline{\underline{£12.}}$$

In the Abnormal Gain Account will appear the credit of £12 transferred from Process No. 1, while on the debit side will be shown an item of £2 calculated as follows:

Normal loss estimated at 120 lb.
Half is sold as scrap at 2s. per lb.

$$60 \text{ lb at } 2s. = £6.$$

However, the actual loss realised was only 80 lb. Assuming for the purpose of illustration that half is sold as scrap, then the value realised will be

$$40 \text{ lb at } 2s. = £4.$$

This means that there is a reduced income of £2 from scrap, so the loss of income will partly offset the gain of £12 arising from the abnormal gain in production.

Abnormal Gain Account

Process 1	2	Process 1	12
Profit and Loss	10		
	£12		£12

It will be observed that in the two illustrations above the cost per lb of output transferred to the next process has not changed: 6s. per lb in each case. The introduction of Abnormal Loss and Abnormal Gain Accounts should ensure that minor variations in production do not cause the cost of production to fluctuate. In addition, the attention of management is drawn to these accounts, which may reveal efficiencies or inefficiencies, or possible need for revision of allowances.

A complete illustration of process costing involving normal loss, abnormal loss, and abnormal gain is now shown.

Product "Zed" passes through three processes to completion. In Period 3 the costs of production were as follows:

Element of Cost	Total	Process		
		1	2	3
	£	£	£	£
Direct material	8,482	2,000	3,020	3,462
Direct labour	12,000	3,000	4,000	5,000
Direct expense	726	500	226	—
Production overhead	6,000			

1000 units at £5 each were issued to Process 1.
Output of each process was:

Process 1	920 units
„ 2	870 „
„ 3	800 „

Normal loss per process was estimated as:

Process 1	10%
„ 2	5%
„ 3	10%

The loss in each process represented scrap which could be sold to a merchant at a value as follows:

Process 1	£3 per unit
„ 2	£5 „
„ 3	£6 „

There was no stock of materials or work in progress in any department at the beginning or end of the period. The output of each process passes direct to the next process and finally to Finished Stock. Production Overhead is allocated to each process on a basis of 50% of the cost of direct labour.

Process 1

Description:

Period No. 3
Output 920 units

	Units	Cost per unit	Amount		Units	Cost per unit	Amount
			£				£
Units introduced	1000	£5	5,000	Normal loss	100	£3	300
Direct material			2,000	Process 2 output			
Direct labour			3,000	transferred	920	£13	11,960
Direct expense			500				
Production overhead			1,500				
Abnormal gain	20	£13	260				
	1020		£12,260		1020		£12,260

Process 2

Description:

Period No. 3
Output 870 units

	Units	Cost per unit	Amount		Units	Cost per unit	Amount
			£				£
Process 1	920	£13	11,960	Normal loss	46	£5	230
Direct material			3,020	Abnormal Loss	4	£24	96
Direct labour			4,000	Process 3 output			
Direct expense			226	transferred	870	£24	20,880
Production overhead			2,000				
	920		£21,206		920		£21,206

Process 3

Description:

Period No. 3
Output 800 units

	Units	Cost per unit	Amount		Units	Cost per unit	Amount
			£				£
Process 2	870	£24	20,880	Normal loss	87	£6	522
Direct material			3,462	Finished stock out-			
Direct labour			5,000	put transferred	800	£40	32,000
Production overhead			2,500				
Abnormal gain	17	£40	680				
	887		£32,522		887		£32,522

Abnormal Loss Account

	Units	Cost per unit	Amount		Units	Cost per unit	Amount
			£				£
Process 2	4	£24	96	Debtor	4	£5	20
				Profit and Loss			76
	4		£96		4		£96

Abnormal Gain Account

			£				£
Process 1	20	£3	60	Process 1	20	£13	260
Process 3	17	£6	102	Process 3	17	£40	680
Profit and Loss			778				
	37		£940		37		£940

Finished Stock Account

To Process 3	800	40	£32,000

NOTES

PROCESS 1

Normal loss

$$10\% = \frac{10}{100} \times 1000 = 100 \text{ units.}$$

Scrap value £3 per unit. $100 \times £3 = £300$.

Abnormal gain

Normal cost £12,000 − £300 = £11,700.
Normal production 1000 units − 100 = 900.

$$\frac{£11,700}{900} \times 20 = £260.$$

PROCESS 2

Normal loss

$$5\% = \frac{5}{100} \times 920 = 46.$$

Scrap value £5 per unit. $46 \times £5 = £230$.

Abnormal loss

Normal cost £21,206 − £230 = £20,976.
Normal production 920 units − 46 = 874.

$$\frac{20,976}{874} \times 4 = £96.$$

PROCESS 3

Normal loss

$$10\% = \frac{10}{100} \times 870 = 87 \text{ units.}$$

Scrap value £6 per unit. $87 \times £6 = £522$.

Abnormal gain

Normal cost £31,842 − £522 = £31,320.
Normal production 870 units − 87 = 783.

$$\frac{31,320}{783} \times 17 = £680.$$

ABNORMAL GAIN ACCOUNT

This account is debited with £60 and Process 1 Account credited with £60. This figure is calculated as follows:

Normal Loss 10% of 1000 units = 100 units
Actual Loss   80   „

Abnormal Gain   20   „

Process Normal Loss of 100 Units would realise £300, but as only 80 units were scrapped, only £240 would be received as scrap value. Consequently the difference (300 − 240) = £60 must reduce the gain on Abnormal Gain Account. Thus the item normal loss in Process 1 is built up as follows:

Scrap Value   80 Units at £3   240
Transfer to Abnormal Gain Account   20   „   „   60

                                              100   „   „   £300

A similar calculation would be effected in respect of Process 3.

CHAPTER 21

PROCESS COSTING

Work in Progress, Joint Products, and By-products

THE problem of work in progress in process industries has not yet been discussed; it is, however, a very important problem and frequently a difficult one. In most firms manufacture is on a continuous basis, as a result of which a process may frequently be uncompleted at the end of an accounting period. How is the cost to be related to the uncompleted work? One way of solving this problem is by calculating what is known as the Equivalent or Effective Production, to which is allocated the cost incurred.

EQUIVALENT PRODUCTION

This represents the production of a process in terms of completed units. Thus, it is considered that an opening stock of 10 units which is 50% completed is equivalent to a stock of 5 units which is 100% completed. In each process an estimate is made of the percentage completion of any work in progress. A production schedule and a cost schedule will then be prepared.

The work in progress is inspected and an estimate is made of the degree of completion, usually on a percentage basis. It is most important that this estimate is as accurate as possible, because a mistake at this stage would affect the stock valuations used in the Final Accounts and Balance Sheet.

EXAMPLE

During January 2000 units were introduced into Process 1. The normal loss was estimated at 5% on input. At the end of the month 1400 units had been produced and transferred to the next process; 460 units were uncompleted and 140 units had been scrapped. It was estimated that the uncompleted units had reached a stage in production as follows:

Material	75% completed	
Labour	50%	„
Overhead	50%	„

The cost of the 2000 units was £5,800.
Direct materials introduced during the process amounted to £1440.
Direct wages amounted to £3340.
Production Overheads incurred were £1670.

Units scrapped realised £1 each.
The units scrapped had passed through the process, so were 100% completed as regards material, labour, and overhead.

Statement of Production

Process 1   January

| Input | Units | Output | Units | Equivalent production (Units) | | | | | |
| | | | | Material | | Labour | | Overhead | |
				Quantity	%	Quantity	%	Quantity	%
Units	2000	Normal loss	100	—	—	—	—	—	—
		Abnormal loss	40	40	100	40	100	40	100
		Finished production	1400	1400	100	1400	100	1400	100
		Work in progress	460	345	75	230	50	230	50
	2000	TOTAL	2000						
		EQUIVALENT PRODUCTION		1785		1670		1670	

Statement of Cost

Process 1   January

Element of Cost	Cost	Equivalent production (units)	Cost per unit
	£		£
Materials:			
Units introduced	5,800		
Direct	1,440		
	7,240		
Less Scrap value of normal Loss	100		
	7,140	1785	4
Labour: direct	3,340	1670	2
Overhead: Production	1,670	1670	1
TOTAL	£12,150		£7

Statement of Evaluation

Process 1   January

Production	Element of cost	Equivalent production (units)	Cost per unit	Cost	Total cost
			£	£	£
Abnormal loss	Material	40	4	160	
	Labour	40	2	80	
	Overhead	40	1	40	
					280
Finished production	Material	1400	4	5,600	
	Labour	1400	2	2,800	
	Overhead	1400	1	1,400	
					9,800
Work in progress	Material	345	4	1,380	
	Labour	230	2	460	
	Overhead	230	1	230	
					2,070
					£12,150

Process 1 Account

	Units	£		Units	£
Units introduced	2000	5,800	Normal loss	100	100
Material		1,440	Abnormal loss A/c	40	280
Labour		3,340	Process 2 A/c	1400	9,800
Overhead		1,670	Balance c/d	460	2,070
	2000	£12,250		2000	£12,250
Balance b/d	460	2,070			

Process 2 Account

	Units	£		Units	£
Process 1	1400	£9800			

Abnormal Loss Account

	Units	£		Units	£
Process 1	40	280	Debtors	40	40
			Profit and Loss		240
	40	£280		40	£280

NOTES

Normal loss

Normal loss is absorbed by the good production, as was illustrated in the previous chapter.

This procedure has been followed throughout the Examples given because it is normal practice to do so. However, in strict theory care should always be taken to establish

(a) the degree of completion of the scrap;
(b) the cost of it;
(c) upon whom the cost should fall.

In this particular example the scrap is not discovered until fully processed. There is, therefore, none in the closing work in progress, and it is suggested that the cost of the scrap (less scrap value) *ought* to be borne only by the completed units transferred to the next process. This, in some instances, would make a substantial difference to the valuation of the closing work in progress.

Finished production

These units have been completed, so obviously will have incurred total cost per unit of material, labour, and overhead.

Abnormal loss

These units have been completed, then found defective, but must still bear the total cost per unit of material, labour, and overhead.

Work in progress

These units are not yet completed, but according to the estimate will be charged with 75% of material cost, and 50% of labour and overhead charges.

Credit of £1 per unit has been effected in the Cost Statement in relation to units scrapped due to normal loss.

Material, labour, and overhead costs have been divided by the equivalent production units, to obtain a cost per unit.

Finished production, abnormal loss, and work in progress have been evaluated at the equivalent production unit rate.

1. £9800, the cost of finished production, will be transferred to the next process.
2. £280, the cost of abnormal loss, will be credited to Process 1 Account and debited to Abnormal Loss Account. The scrap value of these units (40 at £1), £40, will be credited to Abnormal Loss Account and debited to the Scrap Merchant's Account on sale of the scrap.
3. £2070 is the estimated value of Work in Progress and will be carried forward to the next accounting period.

Where there is an opening stock in a Process which is only partially completed this requires careful consideration, particularly in a process which is not the first stage of a production routine. Thus Process 2 will receive the finished output of Process 1; if in Process 2 direct materials are added to the units transferred from the previous process, then any opening stock in Process 2 will be fully completed as far as the material transferred is concerned, but not necessarily completed as regards the material added in process. It is therefore necessary to calculate two material rates of equivalent production:

1. Rate for material transferred from previous process.
2. Rate for material added in process.

EXAMPLE

The following information is obtained in respect of Process 2 for the month of June:

Opening stock: 600 Units £105
Degree of completion: Materials 80%
                               Labour   60%
                          Overhead 60%
Transfer from Process 1: 11,000 Units at £550
Transfer to Process 3:   8800 Units
Direct material added in Process 2: £241
Direct labour amounted to £715 10s.
Production Overhead incurred £954
Units scrapped: 1200
Degree of completion: Material 100%
                              Labour   70%
                              Overhead 70%

Closing stock: 1600 Units

Degree of completion: Material 70%
Labour 60%
Overhead 60%

There was a normal loss in the process of 10% of production. Units scrapped realised 1s. per unit.

Statement of Production

Process 2   June

| | | | | Equivalent production (units) | | | | | | | |
| | | | | Material (1) | | Material (2) | | Labour | | Overhead | |
Input	Units	Output	Units	Quantity	%	Quantity	%	Quantity	%	Quantity	%
Opening stock	600	Opening stock	600	—	—	120	20	240	40	240	40
Process 1	11,000	Normal loss	1,000	—	—	—	—	—	—	—	—
		Abnormal loss	200	200	100	200	100	140	70	140	70
		Completely processed during period	8,200	8,200	100	8,200	100	8,200	100	8,200	100
		Closing stock	1,600	1,600	100	1,120	70	960	60	960	60
	11,600	TOTAL	11,600								
		EQUIVALENT PRODUCTION		10,000		9,640		9,540		9,540	

NOTES

Material (1) refers to transfer from previous Process.
Material (2) refers to materials added in Process.
Materials (1) will always be 100% completed, because it is the *finished* product of the previous process

Statement of Cost

Element of cost	Cost			Equivalent production (units)	Cost per unit	
	£	s.	d.		s.	d.
Material:						
1. Transferred from previous Process	550					
Less Scrap value of normal loss 1000 units at 1s. per unit	50					
	500	0	0	10,000	1	0
2. Added in Process	241	0	0	9,640		6
Labour: direct	715	10	0	9,540	1	6
Overhead: production	954	0	0	9,540	2	0
TOTAL	£2410	10	0		5	0

Statement of Evaluation

Production	Element of cost	Equivalent production (units)	Cost per unit	Cost	Total cost
			s. d.	£ s. d.	£ s. d.
Opening stock	Material (1)	—	1 0	—	
	Material (2)	120	6	3 0 0	
	Labour	240	1 6	18 0 0	
	Overhead	240	2 0	24 0 0	
					45 0 0
Abnormal loss	Material (1)	200	1 0	10 0 0	
	Material (2)	200	6	5 0 0	
	Labour	140	1 6	10 10 0	
	Overhead	140	2 0	14 0 0	
					39 10 0
Completely processed during the period	Material (1)	8200	1 0	410 0 0	
	Material (2)	8200	6	205 0 0	
	Labour	8200	1 6	615 0 0	
	Overhead	8200	2 0	820 0 0	
					2050 0 0
Closing stock	Material (1)	1600	1 0	80 0 0	
	Material (2)	1120	6	28 0 0	
	Labour	960	1 6	72 0 0	
	Overhead	960	2 0	96 0 0	
					276 0 0
	TOTAL				£2410 10 0

NOTES

Statement of Production

Opening stock.—20% material (2) and 40% labour and overhead required for completion.

Normal loss.—Absorbed in good production.

Closing stock.—Not yet completed.

Completely processed during period.—8800 units were transferred to Process 3, comprising opening stock of 600 and 8200 completely processed during period.

Statement of Cost

1. *Material.*—11,000 units valued at £550 were transferred.

    600 units were opening stock and 1600 units closing stock. Therefore 10,000 units were processed. (11,000 + 600 − 1600 Units.) 10% normal process loss = 1000 Units.

    The Equivalent Production is as follows:

Goods completed during period	8,200
Abnormal loss	200
Work in progress at close	1,600
	10,000 Units

2. *Opening stock.*—No material from Process 1 required; the material would have been calculated last period. The only requirements are material (2), labour, and overhead in Process 2.

3. *Closing stock.*—There are 1600 units in stock, so there will be 1600 units worth of the output of Process 1 included in this valuation. There is also 70% of material (2) and 60% of labour and overhead added in Process 2.

The accounts in respect of the above transactions would appear as follows:

Process 2 Account

	Units	£ s. d.		Units	£ s. d.
Balance b/d	600	105 0 0	Normal loss	1,000	50 0 0
Process 1 A/c	11,000	550 0 0	Abnormal Loss A/c	200	39 10 0
Material		241 0 0	Process 3 A/c *	8,800	2200 0 0
Labour		715 10 0	Balance c/d	1,600	276 0 0
Overhead		954 0 0			
	11,600	£2565 10 0		11,600	£2565 10 0
Balance b/d	1,600	276 0 0			

Process 3 Account

	Units	£ s. d.		Units	£ s. d.
Process 2 A/c	8,800	2200 0 0			

Abnormal Loss Account

	Units	£ s. d.		Units	£ s. d.
Process 2 A/c	200	39 10 0	Debtors	200	10 0 0
			Profit and Loss A/c		29 10 0
	200	£39 10 0		200	£39 10 0

£
* Units completely processed during period 8200 at 5s. per unit 2050
  Opening stock completed during period   600 ,, ,,   150

£2200

In the previous illustration the question of evaluating equivalent production of a process in which there was an opening and closing stock of work in progress was considered; a process in which an abnormal loss was incurred. What would have been the effect of an abnormal gain? Briefly the position would be as follows:

1. The transfer to the next process would be greater than expected.
2. If faulty units are normally scrapped before they are completed, then any production in excess of normal will necessitate an increased cost of the factors of production. Thus in the previous illustration, units scrapped had reached this stage of completion:

Material 100%, labour 70%, and overhead 70%

Any above-normal production will therefore incur 30% labour costs and 30% overhead costs to bring these units up to completion.

EXAMPLE

The following information is obtained in respect of Process 2 for the month of July:

Opening stock: 1600 units £276
Degree of completion: Material 70%
       Labour 60%
       Overhead 60%

Transfer from Process 1: 10,200 units at £510
Transfer to Process 3:   9200 units
Direct material added in Process 2 = £224
Direct labour amounted to £657
Production Overhead incurred: £876
Units scrapped: 800

Degree of completion: Material 100%
       Labour 70%
       Overhead 70%

Closing stock = 1800 units

Degree of Completion: Material 60%
       Labour 40%
       Overhead 40%

There was a normal loss in the process of 10% of production. Units scrapped realised 1*s*. per unit.

Statement of Production

Process 2   *July*

				Equivalent production (units)							
Input	*Units*	*Output*	*Units*	*Material* (1)		*Material* (2)		*Labour*		*Overhead*	
				Quantity	*%*	*Quantity*	*%*	*Quantity*	*%*	*Quantity*	*%*
Opening stock	1,600	Opening stock	1,600	—	—	480	30	640	40	640	40
Process 1	10,200	Normal loss	1,000	—	—	—	—	—	—	—	—
		Completely processed during the period	7,600	7,600	100	7,600	100	7,600	100	7,600	100
		Closing stock	1,800	1,800	100	1,080	60	720	40	720	40
			12,000	9,400		9,160		8,960		8,960	
		Abnormal gain	200	200	100	200	100	200	100	200	100
	11,800		11,800								
		EQUIVALENT PRODUCTION	9,200		8,960		8,760		8,760			

Statement of Cost

Process 2 . July

Element of cost	Cost			Equivalent production (units)	Cost per unit	
	£	s.	d.		s.	d.
Material:						
1. Transferred from Process 1	510					
Less Scrap value of normal loss 1000 units at 1s. each	50					
	—					
	460	0	0	9200	1	0
2. Added in process	224	0	0	8960		6
Labour: direct	657	0	0	8760	1	6
Overhead: production	876	0	0	8760	2	0
TOTAL	£2217	0	0		5	0

Statement of Evaluation

Process 2 July

Production	Element of cost	Equivalent production (units)	Cost per unit		Cost			Total cost		
			s.	d.	£	s.	d.	£	s.	d.
Opening stock	Material (1)	—	1	0	—					
	Material (2)	480		6	12	0	0			
	Labour	640	1	6	48	0	0			
	Overhead	640	2	0	64	0	0			
								124	0	0
Completely processed during period	Material (1)	7600	1	0	380	0	0			
	Material (2)	7600		6	190	0	0			
	Labour	7600	1	6	570	0	0			
	Overhead	7600	2	0	760	0	0			
								1900	0	0
Closing stock	Material (1)	1800	1	0	90	0	0			
	Material (2)	1080		6	27	0	0			
	Labour	720	1	6	54	0	0			
	Overhead	720	2	0	72	0	0			
								243	0	0
								2267	0	0
Abnormal gain	Material (1)	200	1	0	10	0	0			
	Material (2)	200		6	5	0	0			
	Labour	200	1	6	15	0	0			
	Overhead	200	2	0	20	0	0			
								50	0	0
								£2217	0	0

Process 2 Account

	Units	£	s.	d.		Units	£	s.	d.
Balance b/d	1,600	276	0	0	Normal loss	1,000	50	0	0
Process 1	10,200	510	0	0	Process 3 A/c	9,200	2300	0	0
Material		224	0	0	Balance c/d	1,800	243	0	0
Labour		657	0	0					
Overhead		876	0	0					
Abnormal gain A/c	200	50	0	0					
	12,000	£2593	0	0		12,000	£2593	0	0
Balance b/d	1,800	243	0	0					

Abnormal Gain Account

	Units	£ s. d.			Units	£ s. d.
Process 2	200	10 0 0	Process 2		200	50 0 0
Profit and Loss		40 0 0				
	200	£50 0 0			200	£50 0 0

NOTES

Statement of Production

Opening stock.—100% material (1), 70% material (2), 60% labour, and 60% overhead costs would have been charged to opening stock last period.

Normal loss.—Absorbed by good production.

Abnormal gain.—These units have been completely processed, so will be transferred to Process 3. However, as illustrated earlier in this chapter, abnormal gains or abnormal losses must be shown in separate accounts so as to show clearly any losses or gains which were not expected.

Statement of Cost

Material.—For convenience, the value of scrap realised has been deducted from material (1). This is an arbitrary decision: the scrap value is fairly small, so it is felt that it is not necessary to allocate the value in any greater detail.

Process 2 Account

Process 3.—The amount transferred from Process 2 to Process 3 is 9200 units valued at £2300.

This is composed of Opening stock 1600 units at 5s.   400
Completed process 7600   „   5s. 1900
                                                              ————   ————
                                                                9200   £2300
                                                              ════   ════

Abnormal Gain Account

It was expected that 1000 units would be scrapped and would realise £50. However, only 800 were actually scrapped, so the credit would only be £40. It is therefore necessary to debit Abnormal Gain Account with £10 so as to offset the balance of £10. In Process 2 Account the corresponding entry of £10, together with the £40 received for scrap, makes up a total of £50.

Stocks

It is very important to realise that opening stock of work in progress is partially completed, and therefore requires only a given percentage of cost to complete the process. The Statement of Production shows the production for the current period only. Closing stock will be valued at cost price, and so will include the cost incurred to that date. In this illustration it was assumed for convenience that costs did not fluctuate from one period to another. Thus opening stock was valued as follows:

Element of cost	Units	Cost per unit	Amount	Percentage completed	Cost
		s. d.	£ s. d.		£ s. d.
Material (1)	1600	1 0	80 0 0	100	80 0 0
Material (2)	1600	6	40 0 0	70	28 0 0
Labour	1600	1 6	120 0 0	60	72 0 0
Overhead	1600	2 0	160 0 0	60	96 0 0
TOTAL		5 0	£400 0 0		£276 0 0

£

Check Work done in June 276

   ,,   ,,   July 124

£400

1600 units at 5s. = £400

JOINT PRODUCTS

Joint products were discussed on p. 236, but it is now necessary to mention some of the methods which may be employed in costing joint products. The difficulties inherent in valuing the various products passing through the same process will be appreciated in this simple example:

In a meat-products factory, pork may be the raw material. The carcase is carved, boned, etc., cut into pieces, then divided and allocated to various production lines. Some meat may be used for making sausages, some for pies, some for luncheon meat, etc. The problem is how to evaluate the meat which is to be used in each of the various lines. Once the meat is separated into the various requirements, the normal process-costing procedure will apply, but it is the apportioning of costs up to the point of separation which creates the problem. Much will, of course, depend upon the special conditions and circumstances prevailing in the factory or type of industry, but some of the methods which may be used in apportioning these costs up to the point of separation are as follows.

1. MARKET VALUE AT POINT OF SEPARATION

The market value of the joint products at the separation point is ascertained, and the total cost is allocated in the ratio of these values.

Products "Exe" and "Wye" are jointly produced in a factory. The values at separation point are known to be £5 and £6 respectively. The cost will then be allocated $\frac{5}{11}$ to "Exe" and $\frac{6}{11}$ to "Wye." This is subject to giving weight to the quantities produced.

This method is useful where further processing of the products incurs disproportionate costs.

2. MARKET VALUE AFTER FURTHER PROCESSING

This method is easy to operate because the selling prices of the various joint products will be readily available. These prices are used as the basis for allocating costs up to the point of separation, in that the pre-separation costs are apportioned in proportion to the selling prices of the finished products.

The selling price of "Exe" and "Wye" is £10 and £8 respectively. The pre-separation costs will be allocated $\frac{10}{18}$ to "Exe" and $\frac{8}{18}$ to "Wye."

This system is, however, unfair where further processing costs of products are disproportionate: these further costs may therefore be deducted from the Selling Prices to arrive at adjusted figures which are fair and reasonable.

3. PHYSICAL MEASUREMENT

A physical base, $e.g.$ raw material, is the proportion used to allocate pre-separation-point costs to joint products.

There is 40% beef in Product "Exe" and 60% beef in Product "Wye." $\frac{4}{10}$ of the costs up to separation point will be charged to "Exe" and $\frac{6}{10}$ to "Wye."

This system is not suitable where, $e.g.$ one product is a gas and another a liquid.

BY-PRODUCTS

By-products were discussed on p. 235, but it is now necessary to detail some of the systems utilised in costing by-products. In some industries there are many by-products produced, and it is frequently very difficult to ascertain the cost of production of any one by-product. The special conditions pertaining to any factory or industry will affect the choice of system. However, some methods which may be used are as illustrated below.

1. MARKET VALUE

The market value of the by-product is obtained, and this figure is used as a base for calculating the amount to be credited to the Process Account. If any further processing costs are required to make the by-product saleable, or any selling and distribution overheads are incurred, these amounts must be subtracted from the market value, and the resulting figure is regarded as being the value of the by-product at separation point.

In the manufacture of 1000 units of Product A, 100 units of Product B, a by-product, are produced. The market value of Product B is 5s. per unit.

After Product B is separated from the Process in which Product A is produced, further processing costs amounting to £5 are necessary, and selling and distribution overheads amounting to £2 10s. are incurred. The amount to be credited to the Process Account in respect of Product B will be:

	£	s.	d.	s.	d.	£	s.	d.	s.	d.
Sales Price						25	0	0	5	0
Less Processing costs	5	0	0	1	0					
Selling and Distribution Overheads	2	10	0		6	7	10	0	1	6
						£17	10	0	3	6

The header columns "Total" appear above the first £ s. d. group and "Per unit" above the second.

This method suffers from the disadvantage that if the market value of Product B fluctuates, the credit to the Process Account of Product A will fluctuate accordingly. Due to the fact that credits to the main Process Account fluctuate, inefficiencies in that Process may be concealed.

2. STANDARD COST

A standard cost is set for each by-product produced. The standard may be determined by averaging costs recorded in the past, or adopting arbitrary figures.

During the past five years records have been kept of the production costs of Product C and Product D, which is a by-product of Product C. These records show the following data in respect of Product D:

1st Year	Produced	100	Tons	Estimated Cost	£500
2nd Year	,,	150	,,	,,	£800
3rd Year	,,	120	,,	,,	£620
4th Year	,,	160	,,	,,	£840
5th Year	,,	140	,,	,,	£735
TOTAL	,,	670	,,	,,	£3495

The average cost per ton is $\frac{£3495}{670} = £5\ 4s.$ (approx.).

The standard cost of Product D would be £5 4s. If in future periods costs fluctuated, then the standard would probably be revised.

3. COMPARATIVE PRICE

Under this method, the value of the by-product which will be credited to the main product is ascertained by reference to the price of a similar or an alternative material. Thus, e.g. in a large motor-car factory a blast furnace not only provides the steel required for the car bodies but also produces gas which is utilised in the factory. This gas is a by-product, which can be valued at the price which would have to be paid to the gas industry for the supply of gas which would be required if the factory was unable to produce its own supply. On the other hand, the price of an alternative material, *e.g.* in this case electricity, could be used as the base for ascertaining a price for the by-product.

In the production of Product E a by-product F is obtained. In one month 100 units of Product F are produced, which are transferred to another department where they are consumed. If Product F was purchased from outside suppliers, the price would be 5s. each. The amount to be credited to Product E in respect of by-product F would be 100 × 5s. = £25.

WHERE BY-PRODUCTS ARE OF LITTLE VALUE

It will be appreciated from the above examples of pricing of by-products that ascertaining a reasonable price is not an easy task; in fact, in many cases it can be an extremely difficult one. Consequently, if the by-product is of little value it may be considered uneconomic to incur the expense of calculating the price of each unit produced. Where this is so, the amount realised on the sale of by-products may be treated as a profit and shown in the Profit and Loss Account. Alternatively, the amount realised may be credited to the main product, thus reducing the cost of the product.

CHAPTER 22

PROCESS COSTING

Internal Process Profits

SOMETIMES the output from one process is transferred to a subsequent process, not at cost as shown in the preceding examples, but at a price showing a profit to the transferor process. Transfer may be made, for instance, at a price corresponding to current wholesale market prices or at cost plus an agreed percentage. The object is:

(a) to show whether the cost of production competes with market prices;

(b) to make each process stand on its own efficiency and economies, *i.e.* the transferee processes are not given the benefit, when comparing the cost at that stage with external prices, of economies effected in the earlier process.

The system involves a rather unnecessary complication of the accounts, as the desired comparisons could be prepared on separate cost reports for each process or by adopting a Standard Costing system, when standards could be set for each process. The complexity brought into the accounts arises from the fact that the inter-process profits so introduced remain included in the price of process stocks, finished stocks, and work in progress. For Balance Sheet purposes, inter-process profits cannot be included in stocks, because a firm cannot make a profit by trading with itself, so a provision must be created to reduce the stocks to actual cost price. This problem arises only in respect of stocks on hand at the end of the period, because goods sold will have realised the internal profits. The procedure is illustrated in the examples shown below.

EXAMPLE

Product A passes through three processes before it is completed and transferred to finished stock. There were no stocks in hand at June 1, and no work in progress at June 1. The following data were available in respect of Processes 1, 2, and 3 for the month of June:

Details	Process		
	1	2	3
	£	£	£
Direct material	20,000	5,000	4,000
Direct wages	15,000	10,000	20,000
Stock of material	5,000	6,500	9,500

Sales of finished goods amounted to £110,000; stock was valued at £5000. The output of each process is transferred to the next process at an amount which will yield 20% profit on the transfer price; the transfer from Process 3 to finished stock is to be similarly treated.

For this illustration, overheads have been excluded. It will be noted that in the accounts illustrated below, three columns have been used in preference to the usual one-column ledger. This method is adopted to facilitate the calculation of the provision for profit in closing stocks. It was mentioned previously that the calculation of this provision is difficult, which will be appreciated when one considers that, for example, the stock of finished goods includes a proportion of profit added by Processes 1, 2, and 3.

The Process Accounts would appear as follows:

Process 1 Account

	Total	Cost	Profit		Total	Cost	Profit
	£	£	£		£	£	£
Materials	20,000	20,000	—	Stock c/d	5,000	5,000	—
Labour	15,000	15,000	—	Transfer to Process 2	37,500	30,000	7,500
	35,000	35,000	—				
Profit (20% on transfer, 25% on cost)	7,500	—	7,500				
	£42,500	£35,000	£7,500		£42,500	£35,000	£7,500
Stock b/d	5,000	5,000	—				

Process 2 Account

	Total	Cost	Profit		Total	Cost	Profit
	£	£	£		£	£	£
Transfer from Process 1	37,500	30,000	7,500	Stock c/d	6,500	5,571	929
Material	5,000	5,000	—	Transfer to Process 3	57,500	39,429	18,071
Labour	10,000	10,000	—				
	£52,500	£45,000	£7,500				
Profit (20% on transfer, 25% on cost)	11,500	—	11,500				
	£64,000	£45,000	£19,000		£64,000	£45,000	£19,000
Stock b/d	6,500	5,571	929				

Process 3 Account

	Total	Cost	Profit		Total	Cost	Profit
	£	£	£		£	£	£
Transfer from Process 2	57,500	39,429	18,071	Stock c/d	9,500	7,394	2,106
Materials	4,000	4,000	—	Transfer to Finished Stock	90,000	56,035	33,965
Labour	20,000	20,000	—				
	£81,500	£63,429	£18,071				
Profit (20% on transfer, 25% on cost)	18,000	—	18,000				
	£99,500	£63,429	£36,071		£99,500	£63,429	£36,071
Stock b/d	9,500	7,394	2,106				

Finished Stock

	Total	Cost	Profit		Total	Cost	Profit
	£	£	£		£	£	£
Transfer from Process 3	90,000	56,035	33,965	Stock c/d	5,000	3,113	1,887
Profit	25,000	—	25,000	Sales	110,000	52,922	57,078
	£115,000	£56,035	£58,965		£115,000	£56,035	£58,965
Stock b/d	5,000	3,113	1,887				

NOTES

Stocks

Stocks are calculated as follows:

Process 2.—This includes a proportion of the transfer from Process 1 and part of the Prime Cost of Process 2

$$\frac{\text{Cost}}{\text{Total}} \times \text{Stock} = \frac{45,000}{52,500} \times 6500 = £5571.$$

Total £6500 − Cost £5571 = Profit £929.

Process 3.—This includes a proportion of the transfer from Process 2 and part of the Prime Cost of Process 3

$$\frac{\text{Cost}^{\text{i}}}{\text{Total}} \times \text{Stock} = \frac{63,429}{81,500} \times 9500 = £7394$$

Total £9500 − Cost £7394 = Profit £2106.

Finished Stock.—This includes a proportion of the transfer from Process 3

$$\frac{56,035}{90,000} \times 5000 = £3113$$

Total £5000 − Cost £3113 = Profit £1887.

Profit

Provision for internal process profits not yet realised will be:

Process 2		929
,, 3		2106
Finished Stock		1887
		£4922

Gross Profit for the year will be:

	£	£
Process 1		7,500
Process 2	11,500	
Less Provision	929	
		10,571
Process 3	18,000	
Less Provision	2,106	
		15,894
Finished Stock	25,000	
Less Provision	1,887	
		23,113
TOTAL		£57,078

Balance Sheet

Stocks will appear in the Balance Sheet at cost as revealed in the cost column above:

	£
Stock in Process 1	5,000
„ „ 2	5,571
„ „ 3	7,394
Finished Stock	3,113
TOTAL	£21,078

In the above illustration the question of Production Overhead, opening stocks in process, and previous provisions for unrealised profit were ignored. These items can now be considered.

EXAMPLE

Product B passes through three processes before it is completed and transferred to Finished Stock. The following data were available for the month of June.

Details	Process			Finished stock
	1	2	3	
	£	£	£	£
Opening stock	5,000	8,000	10,000	20,000
Direct material	40,000	12,000	15,000	—
Direct labour	35,000	40,000	35,000	—
Production overhead	20,000	24,000	20,000	—
Closing stock	10,000	4,000	15,000	30,000

Output of Process 1 is transferred to Process 2 at 25% on the transfer price.

     ,,   2   ,,   ,,   ,,   3 ,, 20% ,,   ,,

     ,,   ,,   3   ,,   ,,   Finished Stock at 10% on the transfer price.

Stocks in Process have been valued at Prime Cost.

Finished stock has been valued at the price at which it was received from Process 3.

Sales amounted to £400,000.

Provisions for internal process profits as at June 1 were:

		£
Included in Process 2		1,395
,,	,, 3	2,690
,,	Finished stock	6,534
		£10,619

These provisions would be created in the previous month in respect of closing stock. Consequently, they are brought into the accounts for June as provisions in respect of internal process profits in opening stock.

A three-column ledger is again used for the Process Accounts, but, in order to conform to the usual method of setting out accounts to obtain the Prime Cost, the closing stock has been deducted on the debit side. Students must remember, however, not to forget its existence, and be careful to bring it down after ruling off the account.

Process 1 Account

	Total	Cost	Profit		Total	Cost	Profit
	£	£	£		£	£	£
Stock b/d	5,000	5,000	—	Transfer to Pro-			
Direct materials	40,000	40,000	—	cess 2	120,000	90,000	30,000
Direct labour	35,000	35,000	—				
	80,000	80,000	—				
Less stock c/d	10,000	10,000	—				
PRIME COST	70,000	70,000	—				
Production over-head	20,000	20,000	—				
PROCESS COST	90,000	90,000	—				
Gross profit (25% on transfer, 33⅓% on cost)	30,000	—	30,000				
	£120,000	£90,000	£30,000		£120,000	£90,000	£30,000
Stock b/d	10,000	10,000	—				

Process 2 Account

	Total	Cost	Profit		Total	Cost	Profit
	£	£	£		£	£	£
Stock b/d	8,000	6,605	1,395	Transfer to Process 3	250,000	169,303	80,697
Transfer from Process 1	120,000	90,000	30,000				
Direct material	12,000	12,000	—				
Direct labour	40,000	40,000	—				
	180,000	148,605	31,395				
Less Stock c/d	4,000	3,302	698				
PRIME COST	176,000	145,303	30,697				
Production overhead	24,000	24,000	—				
PROCESS COST	200,000	169,303	30,697				
Gross profit (20% on transfer, 25% on cost)	50,000	—	50,000				
	£250,000	£169,303	£80,697		£250,000	£169,303	£80,697
Stock b/d	4,000	3,302	698				

Process 3 Account

	Total	Cost	Profit		Total	Cost	Profit
	£	£	£		£	£	£
Stock b/d	10,000	7,310	2,690	Transfer to Finished Goods Stock	350,000	235,648	114,352
Transfer from Process 2	250,000	169,303	80,697				
Direct material	15,000	15,000	—				
Direct labour	35,000	35,000	—				
	310,000	226,613	83,387				
Less Stock c/d	15,000	10,965	4,035				
PRIME COST	295,000	215,648	79,352				
Production Overhead	20,000	20,000	—				
PROCESS COST	315,000	235,648	79,352				
Gross profit (10% on transfer, ⅑ on cost)	35,000	—	35,000				
	£350,000	£235,648	£114,352		£350,000	£235,648	£114,352
Stock b/d	15,000	10,965	4,035				

Finished Stock

	Total	Cost	Profit		Total	Cost	Profit
	£	£	£		£	£	£
Stock b/d	20,000	13,466	6,534	Sales	400,000	228,916	171,084
Transfer from Process 3	350,000	235,648	114,352				
	370,000	249,114	120,886				
Less Stock c/d	30,000	20,198	9,802				
	340,000	228,916	111,084				
Gross profit	60,000	—	60,000				
	£400,000	£228,916	£171,084		£400,000	£228,916	£171,084
Stock b/d	30,000	20,198	9,802				

Stocks

Stocks are calculated as follows:

Process 2:

$$\frac{148,605}{180,000} \times 4000 = £3302.$$

Total £4000 − Cost £3302 = Profit £698.

Process 3:

$$\frac{226,613}{310,000} \times 15,000 = £10,965.$$

Total £15,000 − Cost £10,965 = Profit £4035.

Finished Stock:

$$\frac{249,114}{370,000} \times 30,000 = £20,198.$$

Total £30,000 − Cost £20,198 = Profit £9802.

Profit

Provision for Profit Account

	£	£		£	£
Profit and Loss A/c:			Balance b/d:		
Proportion of provision in respect of Process 2 not required		697	Process 2	1,395	
			,, 3	2,690	
Balance c/d:			Finished stock	6,534	
Process 2	698				10,619
,, 3	4,035		Profit and Loss A/c:		
Finished stock	9,802		Additional provision required:		
		14,535	Process 3	1,345	
			Finished stock	3,268	
					4,613
		£15,232			£15,232
			Balance b/d:		
			Process 2	698	
			,, 3	4,035	
			Finished stock	9,802	
					14,535

Gross Profit for the month will be:

	£	£
Process 1		30,000
Process 2	50,000	
Plus Provision w/o	697	
		50,697
Process 3	35,000	
Less Provision	1,345	
		33,655
Finished stock	60,000	
Less Provision	3,268	
		56,732
		£171,084

Balance Sheet

Stocks will appear in the Balance Sheet as

		£
Process 1		10,000
„ 2		3,302
„ 3		10,965
Finished stock		20,198
	TOTAL	£44,465

NOTE.—The Gross Profit for the month of £171,084 should be checked with the Profit column on the Sales side of the Finished Stock Account on p. 269.

CHAPTER 23

UNIFORM COSTING

UNIFORM OR STANDARDISED COSTING SYSTEMS

THE DEVELOPMENT OF UNIFORM COSTING

Amalgamations and close working arrangements between groups of manufacturers in particular industries, and organisation for rationalisation, have necessitated, to a certain extent, the establishment of some degree of uniform costing by industries. In the case of particular manufacturers who control a number of factories situated in different districts, co-ordinated uniform costing has been introduced in order that the costs at each factory may be properly comparable. Uniformity of application of principles; of allocation and recovery of overhead expenses; and of determining cost and selling prices are found to be advantageous for comparing efficiencies and as a means of controlling unit costs.

In a different class may be considered those uniform systems which have been devised and introduced into particular industries by various federations or associations of manufacturers, as, for example, in such industries as paper-bag making, printing, tin-box making, etc. One of the purposes of these particular schemes is to render competition less destructive, by ensuring that all the members know what is included in cost, and how to arrive at it, but this does not include any provision for disclosure of members' costs. Other purposes of this type of uniform costing are connected with a standardised method of collecting figures in order to fix selling prices on a basis acceptable to those engaged in the industry.

Various associations and federations have issued a uniform costing system for their respective industries. The adoption by individual firms is voluntary, and many of them do not put the approved uniform system into operation, although in some cases some of its features may be introduced into their existing system.

Of the systems organised by trade associations, that of the British Master Printers' Federation was the first serious attempt at devising a uniform system of costing, and is probably the most complete. An official outline of the system is given in this chapter.

REQUIREMENTS FOR UNIFORM COSTING

Apart from any decision whether single, process, or job costing is desirable, the following details require to be determined:

272

1. The bases for the apportionment and allocation of overhead.
2. The departments, sections, or production centres to be used for analysis and comparison of costs.
3. What items shall be regarded as factory as distinct from administration expense.
4. How expenses of administration, distribution, and selling shall be applied to Prime Cost, *i.e.* the basis of recovery rates.
5. How expenses in connection with the buying, storing, handling, and issuing of stores materials shall be treated.
6. What rates of depreciation shall be applied to plant and machines.
7. Whether interest on capital is to be included, and, if so, how, and on what basis.
8. What rent charge is to be made for building if freehold or leasehold.
9. How service departmental costs shall be arrived at.
10. The demarcation between direct and indirect wages.
11. In the case of time- and piece-work, whether the time or wage basis, or both, shall be used for determining expense rates.
12. What organisation can be set up to prepare comparative statistics for the use of those adopting the uniform system. Privacy of individual data and confidence in the co-ordinating office are essential factors.

THE PURPOSES AND VALUE OF UNIFORM COSTING

In a group of amalgamated manufacturers, or in the case of a firm controlling a number of factories, actual detailed costs can be compared, standard costs may be set up, and controls by comparisons secured. The most economical and suitable distribution of orders received can be made. Actual and relative efficiencies of production can be compared. By suitable organisation costs may be reduced.

Where manufacturers are only associated, or where the system is organised by a manufacturers' federation, less precise cost comparisons may be provided, as, for instance:

1. The cost value of production on some common basis, *e.g.* per £ of direct wages or other factor.
2. The cost of rent, light, heat, etc., on the basis of say per 1000 sq. ft.
3. The ratio of indirect labour to direct labour, say by units, by operations, or by processes.
4. The number of plant-hours worked, and the output per hour for similar operations.
5. The ratio of each kind of expense to Prime Cost, or to direct wages.
6. An index-number as a guide to the degree of utilisation of capacity.
7. The quantity of output to which the above information relates.

By these means comparison (*a*) of efficiencies, (*b*) of costs by selected units, (*c*) of periodical averages of costs of different firms, etc., can be made.

It will be obvious that greater advantage is obtained by those actually controlling a group of factories than by individual manufacturers operating a common system organised for their particular industry owing to the dangers of disclosure of facts to competitors.

The British Institute of Management has for some time operated a department for carrying out inter-firm comparisons, and information of great value to the participants has come to light. Much more of this kind of intercharge of information is done in the United States than in Great Britain, and has not been found to harm the business interests of those taking part. On the contrary, "spreading the light" has benefited the industry.

THE BRITISH MASTER PRINTERS' COSTING SYSTEM

OUTLINE OF THE SYSTEM

In 1911 the Federation of Master Printers set up a special committee charged with the responsibility of compiling a system of costing that could be uniformly applied to printing businesses of all sizes. Today the cost of probably more than 80% of the work produced by printers in this country is found by means of this system as modified, by official agreement, to make it more up to date.

Budget of expenses.—Operational costs are established by means of a budget, based on the expenses incurred over a year or, where deemed necessary, a shorter period. Direct allocation of expenses to departments and, later, to operations (both hand and machine) is one of the main principles of the system.

Use of hourly cost rates.—Inclusive hourly cost rates are set up for all operations. These rates comprise wages, direct expenses as departmentalised, and overhead expenses that are not possible of departmentalisation.

Expenses of Stores, etc.—The cost of buying, receiving, storing, issuing, and delivering direct material is ascertained and recovered as "handling charges" by adding to the cost of material a fixed percentage of the invoice price.

Interest on capital employed in the business is taken in as an item of cost, due, partly, to the fact that hand and machine operations are essential to the production of every order, and, sometimes, a choice of these operations may be deemed desirable; machines vary enormously in price, and one type of machine may serve equally as well for certain classes of work as another type of a higher value. Depreciation is taken in on the basis of diminishing value.

Testing the rates used

In order to prove the correctness, or otherwise, of the set-up hourly rates, and also to ascertain whether the full costs are being recovered on the volume of the work produced, two *weekly* statements are prepared:

1. On a form, Federation Form No. 4, called the "Value of Production," is tabulated the whole of the hours of "chargeable" (*i.e.* productive) time for all operations, gathered from daily time-dockets. This time is shown against the name of each hand-worker and each machine. In addition, the non-chargeable time is collated. Thus, not only is the total of each worker shown, but the ratio of chargeable to non-chargeable time of each individual is apparent. Columns are provided for progressive totals of both sets of figures, and it is thus possible to make comparisons over chosen periods.
2. On another form (Federation Form No. 3) are tabulated weekly the departmental wages and expenses, the latter being fixed on a basis of a fiftieth part of the annual budget figures. To the sum of these two items is added the ascertained percentage to recover the overhead expenses, and the total represents the cost of production for the department concerned.

Effect of the overhead rates used.—The application of overhead expenses by a percentage of the departmental cost has the effect of increasing the cost of production when pressure of work increases the departmental wages, and correspondingly decreases the cost of production when lack of work reduces the departmental wages bill. This applies to the normal fluctuations, and not to abnormal conditions, which would necessitate a recasting of the budget.

The departmental totals of value of production from Form 4 can be compared with the cost of production, and the difference shown as a surplus, or a deficit, as the case may be.

These two forms provide the management with information of great value as to whether the capacity of the factory to produce is being maintained.

The Federation publishes a text-book containing full details of the system, and illustrations of a great variety of forms for use in connection with the system, but these are too numerous to reproduce in this book.

THE BASIS OF ALLOCATION USED

The Departments into which costs are divided are dependent upon the size and nature of the business. For a large firm they might be as follows: composing, foundry, machining, ruling, binding, lithography,

K

materials. The composing may be further divided into hand composing, Monotype, and Linotype.

Rent, Rates, Heat, Light, and Water are in most cases apportioned to departments on the basis of square feet of area.

Fire insurance.—That on buildings by area; on plant and contents according to value in each department; on standing formes and work on litho stones and plates, separate accounts with a view to recovery by a

---

PRINTERS COST SHEET

Customer's Name: F. Smith & Co.   **Work Ticket No.** 391

Address: High Street, London

Details: 20,000 Annual Reports as per Work Ticket, La. Post 4to fly, printed black and red.

Composing Room *						Materials					
19...	State Hand or Mono.	Hrs.	£	s.	d.	19... Aug. 2			£	s.	d.
July 30	W. Jones, Hand Comp.	3½				10,080 Sheets Cr. Ld. L. Post			9	10	0
„ 31	W. Jones, Hand Comp.	6½				Ink No. 8				5	0
Aug. 3	W. Jones, Author's corrections	2				„ No. 4				2	6
						20 M. Envelopes	16s.	16	0	0
						Add handling charges	20%	5	3	6
	At 6s. 6d.	12	£3	18	0			£31	1	0

Machine Room							Outwork				
19... Aug. 2	Man 15	Machine E 3	Time 8	Rate	£	s.	d.	19... Aug. 7		£	s.	d.
„ 3	„	„	8					Addressing Envelopes		2	0	0
„ 4	„	„	8					*Add* charges	12½%		5	0
„ 5	„	„	6									
			30	5/6	£8	5	0			£2	5	0

Binding Room							Summary				
19... Aug. 5	Folding	Hrs. 10	At. 3/-	£ 1	s. 10	d. 0			£	s.	d.
	Cutting	—			4	6	Composing		3	18	0
	Piecework	—			16	0	Machining		8	5	0
	225% on 16s.			1	16	0	Binding		4	6	6
							Materials		31	1	0
							Sundries		2	5	0
		£4	6	6				£49	15	6

FIG. 70.—*Printers Cost Sheet*

It will be seen that this follows the general pattern of Cost Cards as shown in Figs. 49 and 62, but makes no provision for showing the amount of the estimate given to the customer: this might be added with advantage.

* Where Mono- or Linotype composing is used a separate section may be introduced, as this will be charged at a different hourly rate from hand composing.

The form is kept in the office and entered up daily from the daily dockets, and on completion is filed with the Work Ticket.

The hourly rates are used only for the purpose of an example.

definite charge. Insurance for consequential loss (profits and standing charges) is treated as general overhead.

Interest on capital.—A charge of at least 5% is debited to each department on the value of the plant and stock therein. Interest on the balance of the capital in the business is included in general overhead.

Depreciation.—Usually, type 10%, plant $7\frac{1}{2}\%$ on the diminishing value. Replacement values of pre-war plant should be used. Loss in melt of metal used by Monotype and Linotype plant depends on the frequency of melting; 2% per melt (of which there are two) is usually taken, and by multiplying 4% by the total value of metal melted, the depreciation per annum is arrived at.

Holiday payments.—The cost of fixed holidays, and annual holidays given to employees, is included in the annual expense budget for each department; thus the cost is evenly distributed over the year.

General expenses on materials.—Handling charges, *e.g.* buying, receiving, storing, issuing, delivering, are added to the cost of materials; also a proportion for management and office expenses.

The remaining general expenses, *i.e.* travellers' salaries, commission, expenses, spoilage, and the sundry expenses, are also applied as a percentage on materials. In the case of customers' own paper, an addition is made for handling and storage cost.

Cost Sheets.—A convenient form of Cost Sheet is shown in Fig. 70.

CHAPTER 24

MARGINAL COSTING

MARGINAL Costing is not a system of costing, such as Job Costs, Process Costs, Operating Costs, etc., but is a special technique concerned particularly with the effect which Fixed Overhead has on the running of a business.

As was pointed out at the beginning of Chapter 10, overhead can be analysed in various ways. Instead of dividing it up into Production Overhead, Administration Overhead, and Selling and Distribution Overhead, the division is now into

Variable Overhead,
Semi-variable Overhead,
Fixed Overhead.

Nevertheless, it is the *same* Overhead.

A costing system may be so arranged as to give information under the former headings, and there is no reason to make any change. All the introduction of marginal cost principles does is to give the management a fresh, and perhaps a refreshing, insight into the progress of their business; if this leads eventually to a weakening of those ties which bind overhead so closely to unit product cost, then the revolution can be peacefully achieved. It has already been suggested that Administration Overhead should be excluded from manufacturing cost. That is the first step: Marginal Costing goes further in the same direction.

First of all, it is necessary to begin with the realisation that certain items of overhead vary "up" or "down" with changes in the volume of production, while others do not. Those which do not vary constitute the Fixed Overhead.

EXAMPLE

Fixed Overhead = £5000
Variable Overhead cost per unit = £0·25
Production—Period 1 = 5,000 units
Period 2 = 10,000 units.

From the above figures it can be seen that in Period 1 the Fixed Overhead works out at £1 per unit, and in Period 2 it is only 10s. per unit. The Variable Overhead, on the other hand, remains at the rate of 5s. per unit throughout both periods.

The above example is, of course, over-simplified, but it is possible to deduce a general principle of the first importance, viz.:

Other things being equal, the Fixed Overhead will, in total, remain "fixed" during changes in production achieved, and the rate per unit will consequently vary; whereas the Variable Overhead will remain constant per unit of production, and vary in total.

Consider now the figures given in Table IV. A chart, as shown in Fig. 71, can be made from these figures to show the cost per unit for any number of units within the range of readings available.

Thus, as the Fixed Overhead is spread over more units, its influence on the cost per unit becomes less and less marked, and if 300 units were produced, the total cost per unit would only be 6s.

Again, consider the following results, as presented by two methods of accounting:

OLD METHOD

	£	£
Direct materials		3,000
Direct wages:		
Department A	1200	
Department B	800	
	——	2,000
Prime Cost		5,000
Factory Overhead:		
Department A	1000	
,, B	600	
	——	1,600
Factory Cost		6,600
Administration, Selling, and Distribution Overhead:		
20% on Factory Cost		1,320
Total Cost		7,920
Profit		2,080
Sales		£10,000

TABLE IV

Number of units	Average variable cost per unit	Total variable cost	Fixed cost	Total cost	Total cost per unit
	shillings	shillings	shillings	shillings	shillings
5	5	25	300	325	65
10	5	50	300	350	35
15	5	75	300	375	25
20	5	100	300	400	20
25	5	125	300	425	17
30	5	150	300	450	15

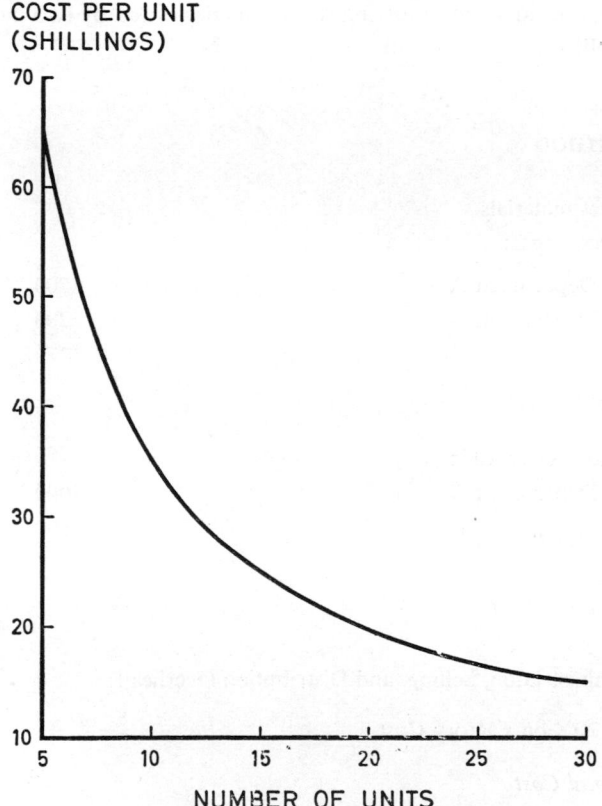

FIG. 71.—*Unit Cost Chart*

This chart depicts the fall in the cost per unit achieved as production rises. This is due to the lessening incidence of fixed overhead.

MARGINAL METHOD

Direct materials		3,000
Direct wages:		
Department A	1200	
„ B	800	
		2,000
Variable Factory Overhead:		
Department A	600	
„ B	400	
		1,000
Factory Marginal Cost		6,000
Variable Administration, Selling, and Distribution Overhead		370
Total Marginal Cost		6,370
Contribution towards Profit and Fixed Overhead		3,630
Sales		£10,000
Contribution as above		3,630
Less Fixed Costs:		
Factory	600	
Administration, Selling, and Distribution	950	
		1,550
Net Profit		£2,080

By the old method the position is clearly seen *as it is*, but it would not be easy to say what the profit would be if sales increased or decreased. On the other hand, the marginal method does help management to do precisely this.

It has been noted that variable costs per unit do not change over the short run: it is a matter of proportion

$$\text{Present Marginal Cost} : \text{Anticipated Marginal Cost} :: \text{Present Sales} : \text{Proposed Sales}$$

$$\pounds 6370 \quad : \quad x \quad :: \pounds 10,000 : \pounds 12,000$$

$$x = \frac{12,000 \times 6370}{10,000} = \underline{\pounds 7644}$$

That is to say, the *marginal cost per unit* remains the same as before, *i.e.* £0·637 per unit, although sales have risen. Similarly, the contribution available towards profit is 36·3% of sales, and this tends to be a stable percentage which management may and should watch.

If, then, it is desired to know what profit will be made when sales go up from £10,000 to £12,000—

$$36 \cdot 3\% \text{ of £12,000 is } \underline{£4356}$$

The fixed costs, by definition, will remain the same (though this is true only within limits) and so the profit will be

$$£4356 - £1550 \text{ or } \underline{£2806}$$

MARGINAL COST EQUATION

For the sake of convenience, it is possible to make an equation in general terms as follows

Sales—Direct and Variable costs = Fixed Costs + Profit,

(*i.e.* the contribution)

and this is shortened to

$$S - V = F + P.$$

In any given problem, therefore, if we know three of the above factors, it is always possible to find the fourth. The equation is of the greatest importance to all students.

SPECIMEN QUESTION

If a business finds its profits fall to nil it is at break-even point. The contribution is only just sufficient to cover the Fixed Overhead. What would be the sales at break-even point?

ANSWER

Let $S - V = F + P$.

When P equals "0," $S - V$ equals F.

Multiply both sides by S.

Then $S(S - V)$ equals FS.

And S equals $\dfrac{FS}{S - V}$.

Going back to the illustration given:

$$\text{Sales at BEP} = \frac{F \times S}{S - V}.$$

$$\frac{1550 \times 10,000}{10,000 - 6370} = £4270.$$

Check

	£
When S =	4270
V for 4270 units × £0·637 =	2720
Leaving F =	£1550

BREAK-EVEN CHARTS

As an aid to management, and in order to obtain a clearer view of the position of a business, it is often desirable to construct what is known as a "break-even chart." There are two ways of doing this, shown in Figs. 72 and 73. In either case make the y axis (vertical) correspond to sales and costs, and the x axis (horizontal) to output or capacity.

EXAMPLE

Output in thousands	5	10	15	20	25
Fixed Costs	£2000	£2000	£2000	£2000	£2,000
Variable Cost per unit 4s.	£1000	£2000	£3000	£4000	£5,000
Sales at 8s. per unit	£2000	£4000	£6000	£8000	£10,000

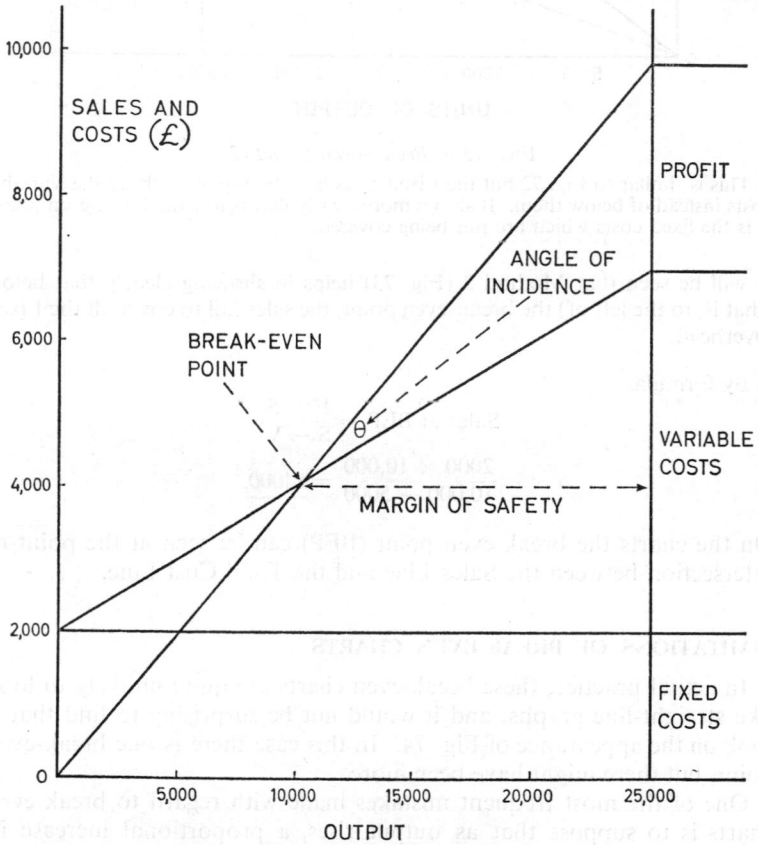

FIG. 72.—*Break-even Chart (1)*

The usual form of break-even chart, showing in this case a break-even point at £4000 Sales, and what appears to be a healthy position for the firm.

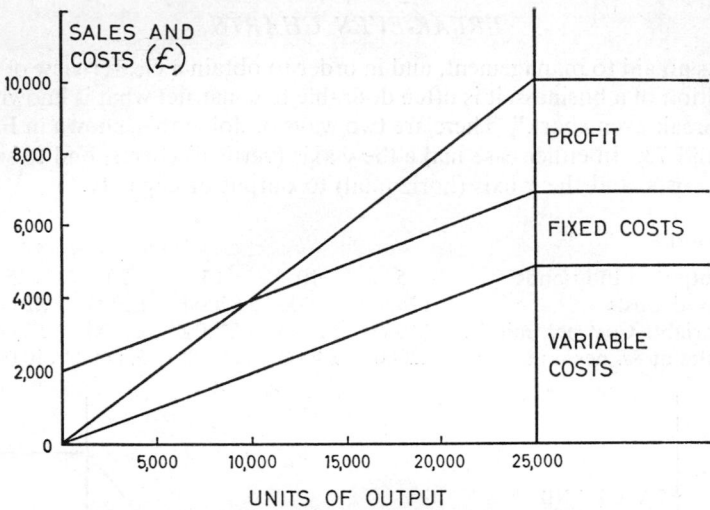

FIG. 73.—*Break-even Chart (2)*

This is similar to Fig. 72 but the Fixed costs have been placed above the Variable costs instead of below them. It shows more clearly that below the break-even point, it is the fixed costs which are not being covered.

It will be seen that Method 2 (Fig. 73) helps in showing clearly that below (that is, to the left of) the break-even point, the sales fail to cover all the Fixed Overhead.

By formula

$$\text{Sales at BEP} = \frac{F \times S}{S - V}.$$

$$\frac{2000 \times 10,000}{10,000 - 5000} = £4000.$$

On the charts the break-even point (BEP) can be seen at the point of intersection between the Sales Line and the Total Cost Line.

LIMITATIONS OF BREAK-EVEN CHARTS

In actual practice, these break-even charts are quite unlikely to look like straight-line graphs, and it would not be surprising to find that it took on the appearance of Fig. 74. In this case there is one break-even point, but there might have been more.

One of the most frequent mistakes made with regard to break-even charts is to suppose that as output rises, a proportional increase in sales revenue can be achieved; and, moreover, that this can be done with no changes per unit in variable costs or in total fixed costs. Policy decisions often cause such changes.

It is wise, therefore, not to place too much reliance on a break-even chart alone as a means of judging the profits to be obtained at higher levels. Nevertheless, if the limitations are accepted, and the chart is

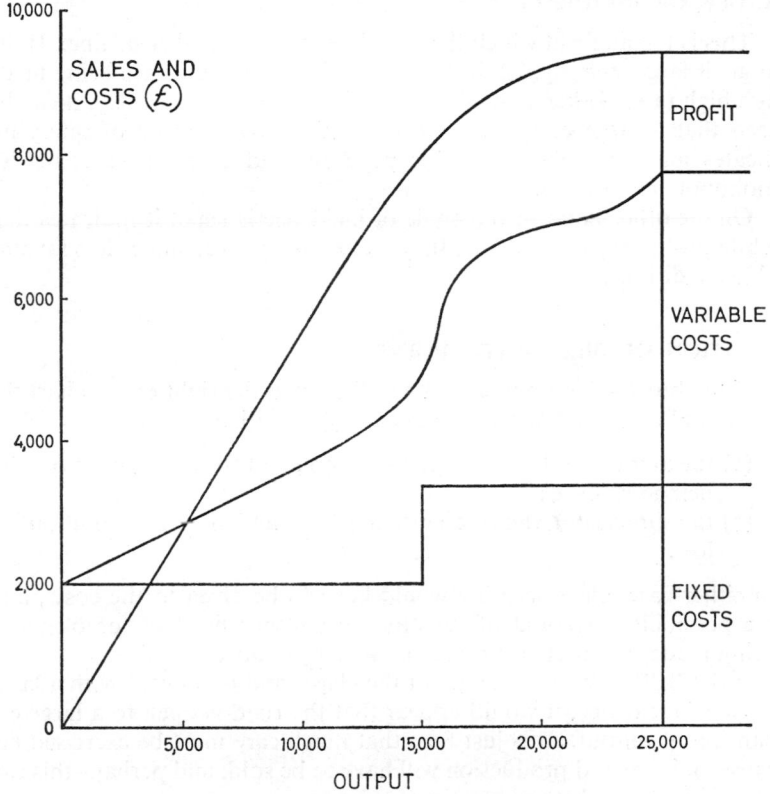

FIG. 74.—*Break-even Chart* (3)

From this chart it can be seen that when fact rather than theory is considered, a break-even chart is unlikely to be a series of straight lines. There might be several break-even points at different levels of output and sales.

considered as being an instantaneous photograph of the present position and possible trends, there are some very important conclusions to be drawn from such a chart.

MARGIN OF SAFETY

This is represented on the chart as the distance between the BEP and the output being produced. If the distance is relatively short it indicates that a small drop in productive capacity or sales will reduce profits considerably. If the distance is long it means that the business could still be making profits after a serious drop in production.

ANGLE OF INCIDENCE

This is the angle at which the sales line cuts the total costs line. If the angle is large (*see* Fig. 72) it is an indication that profits are being made at a high rate. Taken in conjunction with the margin of safety, it can be seen that a large angle of incidence with a high margin of safety indicates an extremely favourable position, and even the existence of monopoly conditions.

On the other hand, if the angle of incidence is small it indicates that while profits are being made, they are being achieved under less favourable conditions.

POSITION OF BREAK-EVEN POINT

If the break-even point appears well over to the right of the chart the margin of safety is low and the cause may be either

(*a*) the amount of Fixed Overhead is too great for the amount of sales being achieved;

(*b*) the direct and variable costs are high and the "contribution" is low.

In either case, close scrutiny would have to be given to the costs, and the possibility explored of substituting another product for one now being made, in order to provide a greater "contribution."

If the BEP is over to the left of the chart, and is coupled with a large angle of incidence, it would appear that the road is open to a large expansion of output. It is just here that much care must be exercised because an increased production will have to be sold, and perhaps this can be achieved only by a reduction of price.

PROFIT/VOLUME RATIO

This is one of the most important ratios to watch in business, and is given by the formula

$$\frac{S - V}{S}.$$

If the result arrived at by the use of the formula is multiplied by 100 the product will be a percentage, and this may be desired. The profit/volume (p/v) ratio expresses the relation between "contribution" and sales, and marks the change in the percentage of contribution in relation to changes in the volume of sales. In making investigations into the records of businesses, it is instructive to take the past five or six years' results and analyse all expenditure so that the variable costs are segregated. If the business is going along steadily it will be found, in all probability, that its P/V ratio has also remained steady.

PROFIT VOLUME GRAPH

This is a simplified form of break-even chart, and will help the student to grasp what the P/V ratio really is. For any given data relating to a business from which a normal break-even chart can be drawn, it is possible to construct a P/V graph.

EXAMPLE

Present volume of output = 10,000 units
Present volume of sales = £25,000
Variable cost for this output = £15,000
Fixed costs = £5,000

The required P/V graph is shown in Fig. 75, and it will be observed that along the x axis is shown the volume of sales. On this axis is marked the BEP of

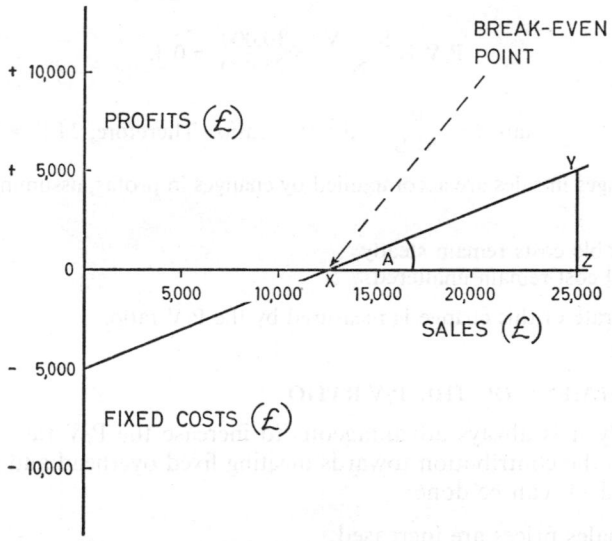

FIG. 75.—*Profit Graph (1)*

This is a simplified form of break-even chart. It can be drawn if any two points on the Contribution Line are known, *i.e.* Fixed Costs, break-even point, or profits at a given level. From the graph can be read the probable profits at any other level within the range.

sales, which can be obtained either by first drawing a normal break-even chart or by calculation, using the formula as before:

$$\text{Sales at BEP} = \frac{F \times S}{S - V} \text{ or } F \div P/V$$

$$\frac{5000 \times 25,000}{25,000 - 15,000} = \underline{£12,500.}$$

The y axis is drawn vertically through the point of origin; above the x axis it represents profits, while below it represents fixed costs. The amount of fixed costs is therefore marked on the y axis as though it were a loss, and this point is joined by a straight line to the BEP of sales, being extended to a position a little beyond the present volume of sales. Looking at this graph, it will be seen that the tangent of angle A is the $\dfrac{\text{side opposite}}{\text{side adjacent}}$, so that when, in triangle XYZ, sales are £25,000, the length of YZ is 5000, representing profit, and the length of XZ is 25,000 − 12,500, or 12,500, representing the margin of safety.

Then

$$\tan A \text{ is } \frac{P}{M/S} \text{ and is } \frac{5000}{12,500} \text{ or } \underline{0.4.}$$

Now, since

$$S - V = F + P$$
$$V = S - F - P$$
$$25,000 - 5000 - 5000 = \underline{£15,000.}$$

And

$$P/V \text{ is } \frac{S - V}{S} = \frac{10,000}{25,000} = \underline{0.4.}$$

So then

$$\tan A = \frac{P}{M/S} = \text{the P/V ratio.} \quad \text{Therefore, } M/S = P \div P/V$$

and changes in sales are accompanied by changes in profits, assuming always that

> variable costs remain steady,
> fixed cost remain unaltered,

and the rate of this change is measured by the P/V ratio.

IMPROVEMENT OF THE P/V RATIO

Clearly it is always advantageous to increase the P/V ratio, for by doing so the contribution towards meeting fixed overhead and profit is increased. It can be done:

(a) if sales prices are increased,
(b) if direct and variable costs can be reduced by improved methods of manufacture,
(c) if production can be switched to those products showing a higher P/V ratio.

It should be noted that a reduction in the Fixed Overhead does not affect the P/V ratio, although it increases the amount of profit available.

P/V RATIOS FOR INDIVIDUAL PRODUCTS

The slope of the profit line in the P/V graph indicates the degree of contribution made, so that a 60% contribution would be steeper than the 40% shown. Instead of drawing one profit graph for the concern as a whole, it is possible, and indeed desirable, to show the cumulative effect of various products.

EXAMPLE

Product	Sales Volume	Contribution	P/V ratio
	£	£	%
A	10,000	8,000	80
B	10,000	3,000	30
C	5,000	−1,000	−20
	25,000	10,000	
Fixed Overhead		5,000	
Profit		5,000	

Plotted on a P/V graph, these results would appear as in Fig. 76. It would be concluded that Product C should no longer be made and that the manufacture of Product A should be developed, provided the plant available was flexible enough to cope with more of the same product.

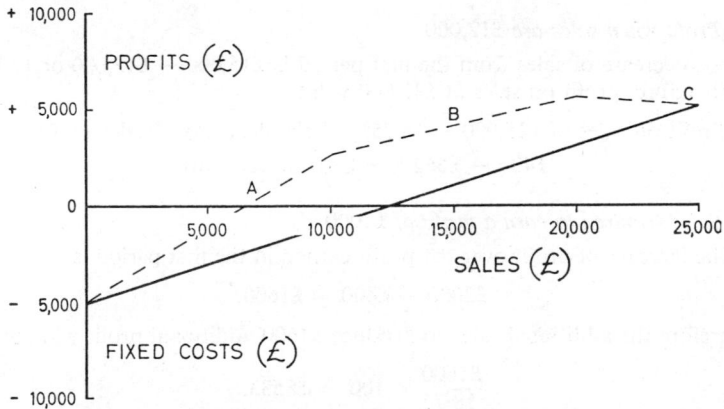

FIG. 76.—*Profit Graph* (2)

This shows a profit graph similar to that in Fig. 75, but in addition to the single contribution line for the business as a whole, those for the individual products are shown as well, revealing which gives the greatest contribution.

USES OF THE P/V RATIO

When the P/V ratio has been found, it is often possible to make good use of it in answering management enquiries.

SPECIMEN QUESTION

Given

	Period 1	Sales £15,000	Profit £400
	2	Sales £19,000	Profit £1150

Calculate

(a) the P/V ratio,
(b) the profit when sales are £12,000,
(c) the sales required to earn a profit of £2,000.

ANSWER

(a) *The P/V ratio*

Form a pair of simultaneous equations:

$$19,000 - V_1 = F + 1150$$
$$15,000 - V_2 = F + 400$$

Subtracting

$$4000 - V = 750.$$

Hence

$$\frac{S - V}{S} \text{ or } P/V = \frac{4000 - 3250}{4000}$$

$$= 0.1875 \text{ or } 18.75\%.$$

(b) *Profit when sales are £12,000*

The decrease of sales from the first period is £15,000 − £12,000 or £3000 Therefore, profit on sales at £12,000 will be

Profit on sales of £15,000 − 18.75% of the decrease of sales of £3000

£400 − £562.5 = Loss of £162 10s.

(c) *Sales required to earn a profit of* £2000

The increase of profit over the profit earned in the first period is

$$£2000 - £400 = £1600.$$

Therefore the additional sales to produce £1600 additional profit will be

$$\frac{£1600}{18.75} \times 100 = £8533.$$

The total sales required to earn a profit of £2000 under these conditions will therefore be

$$£15,000 + £8533 = £23,533.$$

EFFECT OF REDUCTION OF PRICES

There is sometimes a temptation to reduce prices in order to encourage sales, but the effects of doing so have always to be considered most carefully.

EXAMPLE

The sales of a product are at the rate of 100 per month at £5 per unit. The total sales revenue per month is therefore £500. The Fixed Overhead is £100 per month, and the variable costs amount to £3 per unit.

The proposal is to reduce prices by 10%.

Note first of all that a 10% reduction in prices will result in an immediate loss of profit of £50, and this will have to be counterbalanced

(a) by additional sales, and/or
(b) by reduced costs.

For the purposes of the illustration it is assumed that (b) is considered unlikely.

Then, because

$$S - V = F + P$$
$$\frac{S(S - V)}{S} = F + P$$

and

$$S = \frac{F + P}{P/V}.$$

The profit in the above illustration is

$$P = S - V - F$$
$$500 - 300 - 100 = £100,$$

and it is assumed that this has to be maintained.

Now, the P/V ratio falls thus (using unit figures) from

$$\frac{5 - 3}{5} \text{ to } \frac{4 \cdot 5 - 3}{4 \cdot 5}$$
$$40\% \text{ to } 33\tfrac{1}{3}\%.$$

The new figure of sales will therefore have to be

$$\frac{F + P}{33\tfrac{1}{3}\%} = \frac{100 + 100}{33\tfrac{1}{3}\%} = £600.$$

That is to say, 133⅓ units will have to be sold at £4 10s. per unit to maintain a profit of £100.

$$S - V = F + P$$
$$600 - 3(133\tfrac{1}{3}) = 100 + 100.$$

From this it can be seen that if management carry out their proposals to reduce prices by 10% sales must go up by a third to achieve exactly the same result as before. The effect of a price reduction is always to reduce the P/V ratio, to raise the BEP, and to shorten the margin of safety. It is therefore a serious decision to make.

SELLING AT OR BELOW MARGINAL COST

There are occasions when to reduce prices to Marginal Cost, or even below it, may be justified for a short while. Some of the reasons for doing so would be as follows:

1. To maintain production and to keep employees occupied.
2. To keep plant in use in readiness to go "full steam ahead." Plant may also depreciate more quickly when standing than when being used. This is said to be true of the hosiery industry.
3. To prevent loss of future orders. If a firm's product is in short supply other firms, or other products, take its place: and later on it may be difficult to recover the trade.
4. If a loss has already occurred because prices have fallen throughout the market it may be advisable to follow suit.
5. To dispose of perishable goods.
6. To eliminate the competition of weaker rivals.
7. To popularise a new product.
8. To help in the sales of a conjoined product which is making a considerable profit.

There are dangers in price cutting, however, as it may start a landslide in prices which becomes permanent and does damage to the whole industry.

DIFFERENTIAL SELLING

Sometimes there is a limited market for a certain brand of goods. This is made to bear all the Fixed Overhead. The remainder of the production is then sold unbranded or under another brand name, at a lower price, and in a different market.

APPLICATION OF MARGINAL COSTING

OPTIMUM LEVEL OF PRODUCTION

The assumption often made that direct and variable unit costs will not vary is based on the following two underlying assumptions:

(a) that the present methods of production are to remain unchanged,

(b) that the skill and output of additional workers will not diminish.

However, it ought to be borne in mind that large-scale production would probably induce a change in methods of manufacture, and this would in turn cause a variation in the variable cost rate. Similarly, the fixed costs vary in total because additional supervision, office staff, and plant depreciation are incurred.

It will be seen, therefore, that there is an optimum level of production for the capacity of any plant, and this is the point at which the plant is fully occupied in producing goods which can be sold to give the maximum profit without disproportionate increase in the Fixed Overheads.

SALES VALUE AT WHICH A PROFIT IS EARNED

Sufficient has already been said to warn the student against applying the Marginal Cost formula indiscriminately: that is to say, given certain trading results, it is not possible to think of *any* figure of profit, and then apply the formula with certainty to find what the sales would be. Within limits this can be done, and these limits are:

(*a*) the unit sales prices are to remain unaltered,
(*b*) the unit variable costs are to remain unaltered,
(*c*) the total Fixed Overhead is to remain unaltered.

With this proviso, the formula used in the illustration given above will hold.

EXAMPLE

With sales at £5 per unit, a P/V ratio of 40%, and Fixed Overhead of £200, what would be the sales value for a profit of £500?

It will be noticed that the first statement regarding the sales price per unit is not required, unless the quantity of Sales is to be found in number as well as value.

$$\frac{200 + 500}{40\%} = \frac{700 \times 100}{40} = \underline{£1750.}$$

KEY FACTORS IN PRODUCTION

Sometimes a decision has to be made on whether to produce one product or another instead. It has already been seen that a profit graph can be drawn, and the products giving the greatest "contribution" are seen to be those with the steepest slope. However, this is not necessarily the only criterion by which a decision may be reached. For example, if a factory is established in one of the new satellite towns there is often a difficulty in obtaining a sufficient labour force for certain kinds of machine work; if the proposal was to increase production requiring labour which could not be found, the limiting factor or key factor in the situation might not be sales, but labour. In other cases it might be the time involved in producing product A as against product B.

EXAMPLE

Suppose that a unit of product A takes 2 hours to produce, and that a unit of product B takes 3 hours.
The following data apply:

	A	*B*
	shillings	
Direct material	25	15
Direct labour at 5s. per hour	10	15
Variable Overhead at 3s. per hour	6	9
Marginal Cost	41	39
Contribution	59	81
Selling price	100	120
P/V ratio	0·59	0·67

It would seem from this that as product B has the better P/V ratio, the manufacture of this product should be encouraged. The key factor, however, is the time involved. The contribution *per hour* is

$$A \quad \frac{59}{2} \text{ or } 30s. \text{ approx.}$$

$$B \quad \frac{81}{3} \text{ or } 27s.$$

so that product A becomes more important, especially if the labour force is limited as well.

COMPARISONS OF METHODS OF MANUFACTURE

Marginal Costing principles are often used to disclose whether there is an advantage in using one machine instead of another; one machine with one operator or two machines with one operator; hand work or machine work; and so on.

EXAMPLE

	Machines	
	1	2
Production per hour	3 doz.	6 doz.
Unit costs disclosed by normal costing (pence):		
Material	36	36
Labour	60	70
Overhead	84	79
	180	185
Selling price	200	200
Apparent net profit	20	15
Unit costs disclosed by Marginal Costing (pence):		
Material	36	36
Labour	60	70
Marginal Overhead	46	41
	142	147
Selling price	200	200
Contribution	58	53
Contribution per minute	34·8	63·6

This illustration is given to bring home to the student that, in examination work, weight *must always* be given to the time factor whenever it is stated. It is, of course, quite unsound to say that with machine 2 there is an apparent net profit of 1s. 3d. per unit, without thinking of how many are to be made; and, when Marginal principles are applied, the key factor is again time—the contribution per unit is 4s. 5d. for machine 2, but the contribution per minute is 5s. 4d. approx. against 2s. 11d. approx. for the other machine.

At this stage the attention of students is drawn to Chapter 29, and the discussion on the subject of profitability.

However, the following link-up of ratios should be noted at once

$$P/V \times \frac{M/S}{S} = \frac{P}{S}$$

and

$$\frac{P}{S} \times \frac{S}{CE} = \frac{P}{CE}$$

P = profit, and CE = Capital employed, and the other letters carry the meanings already explained.

SEPARATION OF SEMI-VARIABLE OVERHEAD INTO FIXED AND VARIABLE ELEMENTS

In the theoretical discussion of Marginal Costing, no attempt has yet been made to indicate the practical difficulties there may be in deciding which items of overhead are to be classed as "Fixed" and which as "Variable."

In fact, those which are entirely fixed can usually be agreed without much difficulty. For example, the Managing Director's salary, Rent, Rates, Fire Insurance, etc., may be regarded as fixed within the limits of a particular situation.

The majority of items of overhead, however, fall at first into the classification of "Semi-variable," since they are partially variable and yet have a hard core within them of fixed expense. In most cases it is best to regard *all* overhead, other than that which can be definitely labelled as fixed, as being semi-variable.

The problem now becomes one of apportioning these items between fixed and variable, so that eventually all overhead is in one camp or the other. A great deal of work is involved in doing this for each overhead expense heading separately, but as each may vary in different ways it is not really sufficient to deal with the total of all Semi-variable Overhead in one set of calculations.

There are two usual ways of making the apportionment:

1. Comparison of periods.
2. Regression line.

METHOD 1

In this case the levels of expense reached in two periods are compared with one another, and related to output achieved in those periods. This output may be measured in any convenient unit, such as number of units, direct labour hours, machine hours, or even sales.

EXAMPLE

| Period 1 | 1300 Direct Labour Hours | £2000 |
| 2 | 1500 „ „ „ | £2200 |

Since it is to be assumed that Fixed Overhead is "fixed" for the two periods, and for the levels of overhead observed, it becomes clear that the "change" in the levels must be due to Variable Overhead. From this it is easy to deduce the variable cost per direct labour hour—

$$\frac{\text{Change in level of expense}}{\text{Change in level of hours}} = \frac{£200}{200} = \underline{20s.}$$

Therefore,

Period 1	1300 hours at 20s.	£1300 variable and £700 fixed
2	1500 „ „	£1500 variable and £700 fixed

This must be regarded as "rough and ready."

METHOD 2

This is based on finding a "line of best fit" for a number of observations. This is perhaps rather advanced for most first-year students.

It is necessary to go back to first principles. The students will recall from school algebra:

(a) the graph of a straight line in the form of

$$y = mx + c,$$

(b) the graph of a quadratic in the form of

$$y = ax^2 + bx + c.$$

A line of best fit may perhaps be closer to one than to the other, and for any set of observations, both should be considered.

SPECIMEN QUESTION

The following data have been collected over a period of six weeks, relating to the expense heading of a factory:

Week No.	Output	Level of Expense
		£
1	5	48
2	8	76
3	7	72
4	4	38
5	8	74
6	7	50

It is required to draw a line of best fit, and to state the estimate of the fixed expense contained in the figures.

ANSWER

If we regard the various expense levels in the illustration as so many examples of y values, and the output levels as so many examples of x values it will be seen that in investigating whether it is truer to say, in this connection,

$$y = mx + c$$
$$\text{or } y = ax^2 + bx + c$$

we are considering whether there is a relationship between output and expense at every level, and the nature of it. Let us consider the linear equation first of all.

In general terms we have a series of such linear equations, one for each week:

$$y = mx + c$$
$$y' = mx' + c$$
$$y'' = mx'' + c$$

and these, if added together, will amount to

$$\Sigma y = m . \Sigma x + N . c,$$

where the sign Σ means "the sum of things like ..." and N means "the number of examples taken."

Now, our aim is to determine the values of m and c respectively, but as these constitute *two* unknowns, it is necessary to have another equation, in order to solve the problem by means of simultaneous equations. It has been found that this may be done merely by taking each of the linear equations in turn and multiplying both sides by x.

They then become

$$xy = mx^2 + xc$$
$$x'y' = mx'^2 + x'c$$
$$x''y'' = mx''^2 + x''c$$

and so on, which, when added together, become

$$\Sigma xy = m . \Sigma x^2 + c . \Sigma x.$$

Putting the two equations together, we now have a pair of simultaneous equations

$$\Sigma y = m . \Sigma x + N . c \qquad \ldots \ldots \quad (1)$$
$$\Sigma xy = m . \Sigma x^2 + c . \Sigma x \qquad \ldots \ldots \quad (2)$$

However, it will be seen that using these equations will involve squaring the values of x and calculating the values of xy. It could be most unwieldy to do this, and if a means of cutting down the work was available it would be most welcome. Fortunately there is such a device.

To explain this, go back to the figures of the illustration. Let us put $X =$ output and $Y =$ level of expense; and put $x = (X - 4)$ and $y = \dfrac{Y - 48}{2}$.

These variates, x and y, are chosen at will as being likely to yield the smallest possible values for x and y.

Let us now construct a table of values (Table V). For convenience later on it contains values which are not wanted for our present purpose, but to which we shall refer in due course.

If substitution is made of the figures required, from Table V, in equations (1) and (2) we have

$$35 = 15m + 6c \qquad \ldots \ldots \quad (3)$$
$$147 = 51m + 15c \qquad \ldots \ldots \quad (4)$$

Multiplying (3) by 5 and (4) by 2 leads to

$$m = 4\cdot4.$$

Substituting this value in equation (3) leads to

$$c = -5\cdot16.$$

TABLE V

X	Y	$x =$ $(X - 4)$	$y =$ $\left(\dfrac{Y - 48}{2}\right)$	x^2	x^3	x^4	xy	x^2y
5	48	1	0	1	1	1	0	0
8	76	4	14	16	64	256	56	224
7	72	3	12	9	27	81	36	108
4	38	0	−5	0	0	0	0	0
8	74	4	13	16	64	256	52	208
7	50	3	1	9	27	81	3	9
39	358	15	35	51	183	675	147	549
		Σx	Σy	Σx^2	Σx^3	Σx^4	Σxy	Σx^2y

Finally, we must now translate our derived values back into the original terms, and in the form of $y = mx + c$

$$\frac{Y - 48}{2} = 4 \cdot 4(X - 4) - 5 \cdot 16.$$

Multiplying by 2,

$$Y - 48 = 8 \cdot 8(X - 4) - 10 \cdot 3.$$

Hence

$$Y = 8 \cdot 8X + 2 \cdot 5$$

and this is the linear equation we require, which would more usually be expressed as

$$y = \underline{8 \cdot 8x + 2 \cdot 5.}$$

Now let us look at the quadratic in the form of

$$y = ax^2 + bx + c.$$

In this case there are *three* unknowns, and we require three simultaneous equations. They are obtained on similar principles to those previously found, viz., by multiplication by x. Thus,

$$\Sigma y = a\Sigma x^2 + b\Sigma x + Nc$$
$$\Sigma xy = a\Sigma x^3 + b\Sigma x^2 + c\Sigma x$$
$$\Sigma x^2y = a\Sigma x^4 + b\Sigma x^3 + c\Sigma x^2$$

Again substituting the figures required from the table, we have

$$35 = 51a + 15b + 6c \quad \cdots \cdots \quad (1)$$
$$147 = 183a + 51b + 15c \quad \cdots \cdots \quad (2)$$
$$549 = 675a + 183b + 51c \quad \cdots \cdots \quad (3)$$

When solved in the usual way, these yield

$$a = 0 \cdot 516$$
$$b = 2 \cdot 26$$
$$c = -4 \cdot 2.$$

Translating these derived values back again we have

$$\frac{Y-48}{2} = 0.516(X-4)^2 + 2.26(X-4) - 4.2$$

$$Y - 48 = 1.032(X^2 - 8X + 16) + 4.52(X-4) - 8.4$$
$$Y = 1.032X^2 - 3.736X + 38$$

That is

$$y = x^2 - 3.8x + 38 \text{ approx.}$$

The graphs of both the linear equation and the quadratic equation are shown in Figs. 77 and 78, in which the levels of expenditure given in the illustration

---

Graph of $y = 8.8x + 2.5$

Table of Values

Let $x =$	0	2	4	6	8
$8.8x =$	0	17.6	35.2	52.8	70.4
Constant $=$	2.5	2.5	2.5	2.5	2.5
$y =$	2.5	20.1	37.7	55.3	72.9

Graph of $y = x^2 - 3.8x + 38$

Table of Values

Let $x =$	0	2	4	6	8
$x^2 =$	0	4	16	36	64
$-3.8x =$	0	-7.6	-15.2	-22.8	-30.4
	0	-3.6	0.8	13.2	33.6
Constant $=$	38	38	38	38	38
$y =$	38	34.4	38.8	51.2	71.6

FIG. 77.—*Table of Values*

This is a table of values for the linear and quadratic equations found as possible lines of best fit for certain data relating output and levels of expense.

have been plotted against the output. The correlation test necessary to determine which of these lines is the line of best fit for the observations goes beyond the scope of this book, and the student who wishes to pursue the matter is referred to text-books on statistics.

Although, therefore, for Marginal Costing purposes it is customary to work on the linear-equation basis, it has to be remembered that such a straight line is *assumed* to fit the results, when in fact it may not do so. On this basis, and with considerable reserve, the fixed costs on the illustration may be taken as £2.5.

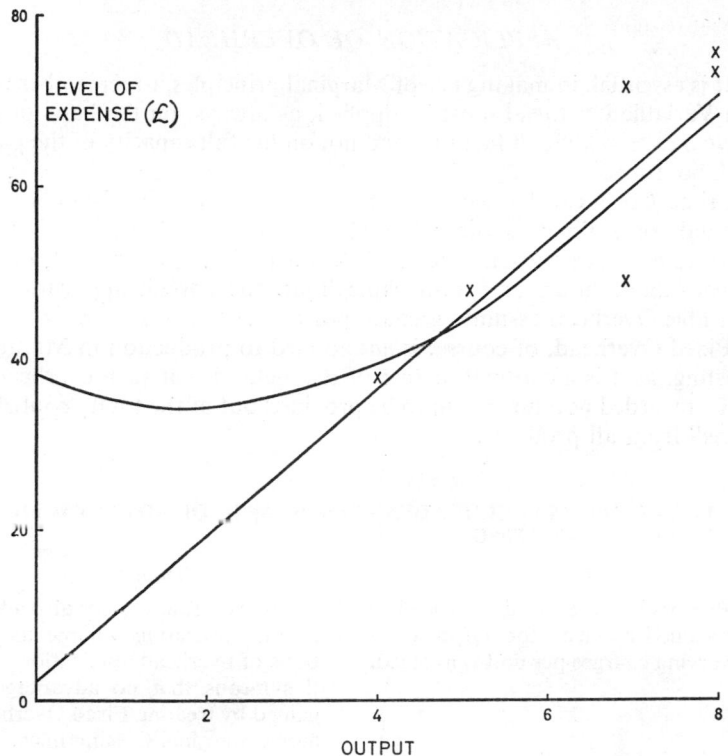

FIG. 78.—*Graphs of Linear and Quadratic Equations*

These graphs are of the values contained in Fig. 77. Which is the line of best fit for the observations marked is not readily seen. It is assumed that the linear graph is sufficiently correct and that where the line cuts the 'y' axis is the fixed cost element in the expense.

ACCOUNTING ENTRIES IN MARGINAL COSTING

When all overhead has been duly apportioned between "Variable" and "Fixed," whether or not any accounting entries are put through the books will depend to the extent to which Marginal Costing has been adopted as a thoroughgoing philosophy. In many cases it is only used for *ad-hoc* investigations such as have been discussed, but if entries are to be made, it is quite a simple matter to make the following Journal transfers

Variable Overhead Incurred Account Dr.
Fixed Overhead Incurred Account Dr.
    To Factory Overhead Incurred Account
        Administration Overhead Incurred Account
        Selling and Distribution Overhead Incurred Account

APPLICATION OF OVERHEAD

It is essential, in making use of Marginal principles, to remember that the Variable Overhead must be applied, as always, on the basis of the *normal expected use* of facilities and not on the full capacity of the plant or labour force.

Prime Costs can be accurately measured, but overhead application depends on estimates. Since the whole concept of Marginal Costing hinges on accurately stated rates of "contribution" per product, or per direct labour hour, or per machine hour, the correct application of Variable Overhead assumes great importance.

Fixed Overhead, of course, is *not* applied to production in Marginal Costing, as it is a cardinal feature of the method that such overhead is to be regarded as a lump sum to be provided out of the total "contributions" from all products.

SUMMARY OF ALLEGED ADVANTAGES AND DISADVANTAGES OF MARGINAL COSTING

For	*Against*
1. By not charging Fixed Overhead to production cost, the effect of a varying charges per unit is avoided.	1. Normal costing systems also adopt normal operating volume as the basis of overhead application, and this means that no advantage is gained by treating Fixed Overhead along Marginal Costing lines.
2. Stock valuations do not include some of the current year's Fixed Overhead.	2. Application of Marginal Costing is difficult in Job Costs.
3. Simple to understand, and can be combined with Standard Costing.	3. Difficult to analyse overhead into "Fixed" and "Variable."
4. Eliminates large balances being left in Overhead Control Accounts.	4. The application of Variable Overhead still depends on estimates, so that there is bound to be some over- or under-recovery.
5. Attention is concentrated on controllable features of the business.	5. A selling price cannot reasonably be determined simply by looking at "contribution." Some reference must be made as to how much Fixed Overhead is justified in the price.
6. Effects of alternative sales and production policies are more easily grasped and appreciated.	6. Standard Costing provides the answers just as well. Volume variance figures disclose the effect of fluctuating output on Fixed Overhead.

CHAPTER 25

BUDGETARY CONTROL

DEFINITIONS OF BUDGETARY CONTROL AND BUDGETS

The Institute of Cost and Works Accountants gives the following definitions:

A Budget

"A financial or quantitative interpretation prior to a defined period of time, of a policy to be pursued for that period to attain a given objective."

Budgetary Control

"The establishment of departmental Budgets relating the responsibilities of executives to the requirements of a policy, and the continuous comparison of actual with budgeted results, either to secure by individual action the objectives of that policy or to provide a firm basis for its revision."

A budget is thus a standard with which to measure the actual achievements of people, departments, firms, etc. Budgetary Control is the planning in advance of the various functions of a business so that the business as a whole can be controlled.

In many large firms in this country, and particularly in the U.S.A., a system of Budgetary Control is used. Usually Budgetary Control is operated with a system of Standard Costing because both systems are interrelated, but it must be emphasised that they are not interdependent. Budgetary Control can be operated without Standard Costing, as often occurs in industries in which it may be difficult to operate a system of Standard Costing, but Budgetary Control is certainly facilitated where Standard Costing is in operation. On the other hand, it would be difficult to operate a system of Standard Costing if budgets were not in use.

Budgetary Control relates expenditure to the person who incurs the expenditure, so that actual expenses can be compared with budgeted expenses, thus affording a convenient method of control. This is in contrast to Standard Costing, which relates expenditure to a product.

THE OBJECTIVES OF BUDGETARY CONTROL

The general objectives of a system of Budgetary Control are:

1. To plan the policy of a business.
2. To co-ordinate the activities of a business so that each is part of an integral total.
3. To control each function so that the best possible results may be obtained.

PREPARATION OF THE BUDGET

In large companies the preparation of the budget is usually the responsibility of a Budget Committee. Normally the Chief Executive is Chairman of the Committee, but the responsibility for operating the system is undertaken by a Budget Officer. The Budget Officer is generally a senior member of the accounting staff. Other members of the committee may be representatives of various departments, *e.g.* Sales, Purchases, Production, and Works Engineering. In small companies the preparation of the budget is usually the responsibility of the Cost Accountant or the Accountant.

The Budget Committee will formulate a general programme for the preparation of the budget, and then the Budget Officer will be responsible for such functions as:

1. Issuing instructions to various departments.
2. Receiving and checking budget estimates.
3. Providing historical information to departmental managers to help them in their forecasting.
4. Suggesting possible revisions.
5. Discussing difficulties with managers.
6. Ensuring that managers prepare their budgets in time.
7. Preparing budget summaries.
8. Submitting budgets to the committee and furnishing explanations on particular points.
9. Co-ordinating all budget work.

THE BUDGET PERIOD

No specific period of time can be formulated as being the best budget period, although it can be said that many firms regard the period of a year as being a natural period for budgeting. The determining of the budget period is usually related to two factors:

1. The type of business

In industries in which capital expenditure is high and long-time planning is necessary, budget periods of up to twenty years may be required. Examples of this occur in the shipping trade and the electrical supply industry, where future requirements must be planned in advance.

On the other hand, many firms experience seasonal fluctuations in demand for their products, so must adopt a shorter budget period, of perhaps six months. Examples of this occur in the clothing and food industries, where fashions and weather exert a great influence on demand.

2. The control aspect

Budgetary Control implies control, and it is obvious that long budget periods cannot be effective means of controlling a business. Particularly is this so in respect of expenditure, which must be rigidly scrutinised at short intervals, usually in practice monthly. It is therefore usually arranged that the budget period should be divided into months so that actual results can be compared with those budgeted; this ensures that if any adverse variances have resulted immediate action can be undertaken.

The effect of the above two factors is that a long-term budget is prepared showing future expectations, while monthly budget periods assure speedy control of the business. In this respect the Institute of Cost and Works Accountants *Terminology* gives the following definitions:

Basic Budget

"A budget which is established for use unaltered over a long period of time."

Current Budget

"A budget which is established for use over a short period of time and is related to current conditions."

THE KEY FACTOR

In the preparation of budgets it is essential to consider the Key Factor, or as it is sometimes termed in budgeting the Principal Budget Factor. This is the factor, the extent of whose influence must first be assessed in order to ensure that the functional budgets are reasonably capable of fulfilment. For example the time taken to obtain delivery of motor vehicles will influence the budget of a road-transport firm. Key Factors are discussed further in Chapters 24 and 29.

FUNCTIONAL BUDGET

A functional budget is one which relates to any of the functions of an undertaking. Functional budgets are subsidiary to the *Master Budget*, which is the summary budget, incorporating its component functional budgets, which is finally approved, adopted, and employed.

There are many types of functional budgets, of which the following are frequently used:

1. Sales budget.
2. Production budget.
3. Production cost budget.
4. Plant utilisation budget.
5. Capital expenditure budget.
6. Selling and distribution cost budget.
7. Purchasing budget.
8. Cash budget.

SALES BUDGET

This is probably the most difficult functional budget to prepare. It is not easy to estimate consumers' future demands, especially when a new product is being introduced. It is possibly the most important subsidiary budget, because if the sales figure is wrong, then practically all the other budgets will be affected, especially the Master Budget.

The sales budget is usually prepared in terms of quantities, then evaluated at budgeted unit prices. It is classified under a number of headings, of which the following are in common use:

Products

Not many businesses sell only one product, so estimates must be prepared of sales for each product.

Territories

Sales of each product, expressed in quantities and values to be sold in each territory.

Type of Customer

This may be important if different customers receive special discounts, special rates, etc.

Salesmen

The sales to each salesmen or agent in a territory. This may be useful also for comparative purposes.

Month

Comparison of actual results with those budgeted for each period is important. In addition, it is necessary when calculating budgeted stock positions to know monthly sales.

The Sales Manager will be responsible for the preparation of the sales budget, particularly as regards to the quantities part of the budget. He may have many aids in estimating sales, of which the following may be important.

Historical analysis of sales

Statistical measurements, *e.g.* cyclical movement, trends, and seasonal fluctuations, may provide valuable information.

Business conditions

International and political influences on markets.

Reports by salesmen

Salesmen are in frequent contact with customers and can report on customers' habits, demands, etc., as well as possible competitors' activities.

Market analysis

In large firms market analysts may be employed, while smaller firms may engage specialist agents to investigate potential market demands.

Special conditions

There may be events planned outside the business which will have an effect on the sales of the business, *e.g.* the introduction of electricity to a village will lead to a demand for heaters, radios, etc.

If the Principal Budget Factor or Key Factor is production capacity, then the sales budget will be determined by output, and preparation of the budget will be relatively easy. However, if sales is the Key Factor, then the production budget will be determined by estimated sales.

SPECIMEN QUESTION

In the Stansales Co. Ltd. there are four sales divisions, each consisting of four areas, N., S., E., and W. The company sells two products, "Exe" and "Wye." Budgeted sales for the six months ended June 30, 1959, in each area of Division 1 were as follows:

L

N. "Exe" 10,000 units at £10 each
"Wye" 6,000 units at £5 each
S. "Wye" 12,000 units at £5 each
E. "Exe" 15,000 units at £10 each
W. "Exe" 8,000 units at £10 each
"Wye" 5,000 units at £5 each

Actual sales for the same period of Division 1 were as follows:

N. "Exe" 11,500 units at £10 each
"Wye" 7,000 units at £5 each
S. "Wye" 12,500 units at £5 each
E. "Exe" 16,500 units at £10 each
W. "Exe" 9,500 units at £10 each
"Wye" 5,250 units at £5 each

From the Salesmen's Reports and observations of the Area Sales Managers, it is thought that sales could be budgeted for the six months ended June 30, 1960, as follows:

N. "Exe" Budgeted increase of 2000 units on June 1959 Budget
"Wye" ,, ,, 500 ,, ,, ,,
S. "Wye" ,, ,, 1000 ,, ,, ,,
E. "Exe" ,, ,, 2000 ,, ,, ,,
W. "Exe" ,, ,, 1000 ,, ,, ,,
"Wye" ,, ,, 500 ,, ,, ,,

At a meeting of Area Sales Managers with the Divisional Sales Manager it is decided that sales campaigns will be undertaken in Areas S. and E. It is anticipated that these campaigns will result in additional sales of 3000 units of "Exe" in the S. Area and 5000 units of "Wye" in the E. Area.

Prepare for presentation to top management the sales budget for the six months ended June 30, 1960, showing also the budgeted and actual sales for June 30, 1959, which are to be provided as a guide in fixing the sales budget.

ANSWER

The required sales budget, when completed, will appear as shown in Fig. 79. Similar budgets will be prepared for each Division, then a sales budget prepared for the Company as a whole showing sales by Divisions rather than areas. Sales in each Division will be further analysed to show sales by salesmen and by customer.

PRODUCTION BUDGET

This shows the quantity of products to be manufactured. It is prepared by the Production Manager and is based upon:

1. The sales budget.
2. The factory capacity.
3. The budgeted stock requirements.

SALES BUDGET

Division No. 1   **Six months to:** June 30, 1960

Area	Product	Budget			Budget June 30, 1959			Actual June 30, 1959		
		Q.	P.	V.	Q.	P	V.	Q.	P.	V.
NORTH	Exe	12,000	10	120,000	10,000	10	100,000	11,500	10	115,000
	Wye	6,500	5	32,500	6,000	5	30,000	7,000	5	35,000
	Total	18,500		£152,500	16,000	—	£130,000	18,500		£150,000
SOUTH	Exe	3,000	10	30,000	—	—	—	—		—
	Wye	13,000	5	65,000	12,000	5	60,000	12,500	5	62,500
	Total	16,000		£95,000	12,000		£60,000	12,500		£62,500
EAST	Exe	17,000	10	170,000	15,000	10	150,000	16,500	10	165,000
	Wye	5,000	5	25,000	—	—	—	—	—	—
	Total	22,000		£195,000	15,000		£150,000	16,500		£165,000
WEST	Exe	9,000	10	90,000	8,000	10	80,000	9,500	10	95,000
	Wye	5,500	5	27,500	5,000	5	25,000	5,250	5	26,250
	Total	14,500		£117,500	13,000		£105,000	14,750		£121,250
TOTAL	Exe	41,000	10	410,000	33,000	10	330,000	37,500	10	375,000
	Wye	30,000	5	150,000	23,000	5	115,000	24,750	5	123,750
	Total	71,000		£560,000	56,000		£445,000	62,250		£498,750

FIG. 79.—*Sales Budget*

This shows the Sales Budget as compiled from details given in a specimen question in the text. The budget is compiled in the light of the budget for the corresponding period last year, and the actual achievement attained.

The production budget is classified under various headings:

(*a*) Products.
(*b*) Manufacturing departments.
(*c*) Months.

When the production budget is completed it forms the basis of the production cost budget.

PRODUCTION COST BUDGET

This is the quantity of products to be manufactured, expressed in terms of cost. It is classified under various headings, *e.g.*

(*a*) Products.
(*b*) Manufacturing Departments.
(*c*) Months.
(*d*) Element of Cost.

Many companies prepare a raw material budget, labour budget, and overheads budget, which give analysed figures of the element-of-cost section of the production cost budget.

PLANT UTILISATION BUDGET

This represents the plant requirements to meet the production budget. This budget may be very important because:

1. It details the machine load in every manufacturing department.
2. It draws attention to any overloading in time for any corrective action to be taken, *e.g.* shift working; purchasing of new machinery; overtime working; sub-contracting.
3. It draws attention to any underloading so that the Sales Manager can be requested to investigate possible increased sales.

CAPITAL EXPENDITURE BUDGET

This represents the estimated expenditure on fixed assets during the budget period. It is based on such information as:

1. Overloading shown in the plant utilisation budget.
2. Reports of the Production Manager requesting new production machinery.
3. Reports of the Works Engineer requesting new service machinery.
4. Reports of the Distribution Manager requesting new transport.
5. Reports of the Sales Manager requesting new cars.
6. Reports of the Accountant requesting new office machinery.
7. Decisions of the Board to extend buildings, etc.

SELLING AND DISTRIBUTION COST BUDGET

This represents the cost of selling and distributing the quantities shown in the sales budget. The Sales Manager, Advertising Manager, and Sales Office Manager will co-operate with the Budget Officer in the preparation of this budget.

SPECIMEN QUESTION

Selling expenses in Division No. 1 were budgeted for the six months ended June 30, 1959, as shown in Table VI.

The sales budget illustrated previously is used as a basis for the preparation of this budget.

TABLE VI

Element of cost	Area				Total
	North	South	East	West	
Direct Selling Expenses					
Salesmen's Salaries	4,500	2,250	4,680	3,120	14,550
Salesmen's Commission	2,600	1,200	3,000	2,100	8,900
Salesmen's Expenses	440	220	538	352	1,550
Car Expenses	3,000	1,500	3,600	2,400	10,500
	10,540	5,170	11,818	7,972	35,500
Distribution Expenses					
Warehouse Wages	2,000	1,500	2,500	1,500	7,500
Warehouse Rent, Rates, Electricity	300	300	400	250	1,250
Lorry Expenses	2,500	1,800	2,800	1,900	9,000
General Expenses	400	400	500	450	1,750
	5,200	4,000	6,200	4,100	19,500
Sales Office					
Salaries	2,600	1,900	3,000	2,500	10,000
Rent, Rates, Electricity	600	300	700	400	2,000
Depreciation	300	100	400	200	1,000
Postage, Stationery, Telephone	1,300	500	1,500	700	4,000
General Expenses	600	400	500	500	2,000
	5,400	3,200	6,100	4,300	19,000
Advertising					
Press	1,000	1,000	1,000	1,000	4,000
Television	2,000	2,000	2,000	2,000	8,000
Coupon Offers	1,500	—	—	1,200	2,700
Shop Window Displays	500	200	200	400	1,300
	5,000	3,200	3,200	4,600	16,000
TOTAL	£26,140	£15,570	£27,318	£20,972	£90,000

For the Budget for the six months ending June 30, 1960:

1. Sales commission is based on 2% of the sales.
2. Salesmen's salaries to be increased by 5%.
3. Salesmen's expenses to be increased by 10%.
4. Car expenses to be increased by 10%.
5. Warehouse wages to be increased by 5%.
6. Lorry expenses to be increased by 10%.
7. Sales Office salaries to be increased by 10%.
8. One extra clerk to be engaged by E. Area at £10 per week.
9. Postage, stationery, and telephone to be increased by 5%.
10. Press and T.V. advertising to be increased in all areas by 10%.
11. Coupon offers in Areas S. and E. to be £2000 and £3000 each, respectively.
12. Shop-window schemes in Areas S. and E. to be £1000 and £1500 each, respectively.

An additional commission of 5% will be paid to salesmen in Areas S. and E. for sales of the introductory offer of "Exe" and "Wye."

Prepare the selling cost budget for the six months ended June 30, 1960.

ANSWER

Fig. 80 shows the type of budget that would be prepared. Similar budgets would be made out for each Division, then a Summarised Budget prepared for the Company as a whole, showing sales by Divisions rather than areas.

PURCHASING BUDGET

This represents the total purchases to be made in the budget period. It is composed of direct materials, indirect materials, fixed assets, and research and development requirements.

Purchases will normally be in line with budgeted requirements, with the exception of orders already placed with suppliers and any adjustments to budgeted stock positions.

CASH BUDGET

This represents the cash receipts and payments, and the estimated cash balances each month of the budget period. Its main functions are:

1. To ensure that sufficient cash is available when required.
2. To reveal any expected shortage of cash, so that action may be taken, e.g. a bank overdraft or loan arranged.
3. To reveal any expected surplus of cash, so that if management desire, cash may be invested or loaned.

SELLING AND DISTRIBUTION COST BUDGET

Division No. 1   **Period Six months to:** June 30, 1960

Element of Cost	Budget					Budget for six months to June 30, 1959				
	Area					Area				
	North	South	East	West	Total	North	South	East	West	Total
DIRECT SELLING EXPENSES										
Salesmen's salaries	4,725	2,363	4,914	3,276	15,278	4,500	2,250	4,680	3,120	14,550
Salesmen's commission	3,050	3,400	5,150	2,350	13,950	2,600	1,200	3,000	2,100	8,900
Salesmen's expenses	484	242	592	387	1,705	440	220	538	352	1,550
Car expenses	3,300	1,650	3,960	2,640	11,550	3,000	1,500	3,600	2,400	10,500
	11,559	7,655	14,616	8,653	42,483	10,540	5,170	11,818	7,972	35,500
DISTRIBUTION EXPENSES										
Warehouse Wages	2,100	1,575	2,625	1,575	7,875	2,000	1,500	2,500	1,500	7,500
Warehouse rent and rates, electricity	300	300	400	250	1,250	300	300	400	250	1,250
Lorry expenses	2,750	1,980	3,080	2,090	9,900	2,500	1,800	2,800	1,900	9,000
General expenses	400	400	500	450	1,750	400	400	500	450	1,750
	5,550	4,255	6,605	4,365	20,775	5,200	4,000	6,200	4,100	19,500
SALES OFFICE										
Salaries	2,860	2,090	3,560	2,750	11,260	2,600	1,900	3,000	2,500	10,000
Rent, rates, and electricity	600	300	700	400	2,000	600	300	700	400	2,000
Depreciation	300	100	400	200	1,000	300	100	400	200	1,000
Postage, stationery, and telephone	1,365	525	1,575	735	4,200	1,300	500	1,500	700	4,000
General expenses	600	400	500	500	2,000	600	400	500	500	2,000
	5,725	3,415	6,735	4,585	20,460	5,400	3,200	6,100	4,300	19,000
ADVERTISING										
Press	1,100	1,100	1,100	1,100	4,400	1,000	1,000	1,000	1,000	4,000
Television	2,200	2,200	2,200	2,200	8,800	2,000	2,000	2,000	2,000	8,000
Coupon offers	1,500	2,000	3,000	1,200	7,700	1,500	—	—	1,200	2,700
Shop Window Displays	500	1,000	1,500	400	3,400	500	200	200	400	1,300
	5,300	6,300	7,800	4,900	24,300	5,000	3,200	3,200	4,600	16,000
	£28,134	£21,625	£35,756	£22,503	£108,018	£26,140	£15,570	£27,318	£20,972	£90,000

FIG. 80.—*Selling and Distribution Cost Budget*

This budget has been compiled after taking into account all the relative facts and trends known to the budget officer: these are referred to in the text.

SPECIMEN QUESTION

Prepare a cash budget in respect of the six months to December 31 from the information given in Table VII.

TABLE VII

Month	Sales	Materials	Wages	Overheads				
				Pro-duction	Adminis-tration	Selling	Distri-bution	Research and develop-ment
April	50,000	20,000	5,000	2,200	1,500	800	400	500
May	60,000	30,000	5,600	2,400	1,450	850	450	500
June	40,000	20,000	4,000	2,500	1,520	750	350	600
July	50,000	30,000	4,200	2,300	1,480	850	450	600
August	60,000	35,000	4,600	2,600	1,510	950	550	700
September	70,000	40,000	5,000	2,700	1,540	1,000	600	700
October	80,000	45,000	5,200	2,900	1,560	1,025	625	800
November	90,000	50,000	5,400	3,000	1,570	1,075	675	800
December	100,000	55,000	5,800	3,200	1,600	1,150	750	800

Cash Balance on July 1, was expected to be £75,000.
Expected capital expenditure:

Plant and machinery to be installed in August at a cost of £20,000 will be payable on September 1.
Extension to Research and Development Department amounting to £5000 will be completed on August 1. Payable £1000 per month as from completion date.

Under a hire purchase agreement £2000 is to be paid each month.
A sales commission of 5% on sales is to be paid within the month following actual sales.

Period of credit allowed by suppliers	3 months
„ „ „ to customers	2 months
Delay in payment of overheads	1 month
„ „ wages	$\frac{1}{8}$ month

Income tax of £50,000 is due to be paid on October 1.
Preference shares dividend of 10% on capital of £1,000,000 is to be paid on November 1.
10% calls on ordinary share capital of £200,000 is due on July 1 and September 1.
Dividend from investments amounting to £15,000 expected on November 1.
Cash sales of £1000 per month are expected; no commission payable.

ANSWER

The cash budget prepared from the above information is shown in Fig. 81.

CASH BUDGET

Period Ending: December 31, 19...

Details	Month					
	July	August	September	October	November	December
RECEIPTS						
Balance b/d	75,000	122,105	117,375	131,115	93,900	25,615
Debtors	60,000	40,000	50,000	60,000	70,000	80,000
Cash Sales	1,000	1,000	1,000	1,000	1,000	1,000
Capital	20,000	—	20,000	—	—	—
Dividend	—	—	—	—	15,000	—
Total	£156,000	£163,105	£188,375	£192,115	£179,900	£106,615
PAYMENTS						
Materials	20,000	30,000	20,000	30,000	35,000	40,000
Wages	4,175	4,550	4,950	5,175	5,375	5,750
Production Overhead	2,500	2,300	2,600	2,700	2,900	3,000
Administration Overhead	1,520	1,480	1,510	1,540	1,560	1,570
Selling Overhead	750	850	950	1,000	1,025	1,075
Distribution Overhead	350	450	550	600	625	675
Research Overhead	600	600	700	700	800	800
Commission	2,000	2,500	3,000	3,500	4,000	4,500
Capital	2,000	3,000	23,000	3,000	3,000	3,000
Income Tax	—	—	—	50,000	—	—
Dividend	—	—	—	—	100,000	—
Total	£33,895	£45,730	£57,260	£98,215	£154,285	£60,370
Balance c/d	£122,105	£117,375	£131,115	£93,900	£25,615	£46,245

FIG. 81.—*Cash Budget*

A cash budget is an essential requirement of budgetary control: it enables a business to plan in advance to meet heavy commitments and to avoid being caught unawares.

NOTES

Wages are calculated thus:

July—⅛ June (£4000)	500	
⅞ July (£4200)	3675	
		£4175.
August—⅛ July (£4200)	525	
⅞ August (£4600)	4025	
		£4550.

It will be noted that cash resources have been built up to meet the large amount of payments budgeted for October and November. At the end of November the cash balance is down to £25,615, which, if the budget is reasonably accurate, should be sufficient. In any case where it is not it may be necessary to arrange for a bank overdraft.

It can be observed how invaluable is a cash budget, as one can see at a glance if there will be sufficient cash, or too much cash at any time in the budget period.

TABLE VIII

Budgeted Profit and Loss Account

Details	Current year		Previous year	
	Amount	*%*	*Amount*	*%*
Net Sales	1,800,000	100·0	1,700,000	100·0
Production Cost	960,000	53·3	910,000	53·5
GROSS PROFIT	840,000	46·7	790,000	46·5
Less Operating expenses:				
Administration	77,000	4·3	71,000	4·2
Selling	106,000	5·9	98,000	5·8
Advertising	330,000	18·3	300,000	17·6
Distribution	112,000	6·2	106,000	6·2
Research and Development	14,000	0·8	12,000	0·7
Financial	21,000	1·2	20,000	1·2
TOTAL	660,000	36·7	607,000	35·7
OPERATING PROFIT	180,000	10·0	183,000	10·8
Add Other income	2,000	0·1	2,000	0·1
NET PROFIT before Taxation	182,000	10·1	185,000	10·9
Less Provision for Taxation	85,000	4·7	86,000	5·1
NET PROFIT	£97,000	5·4	£99,000	5·8

ADDITIONAL BUDGETS

In addition to the budgets detailed above, there may be many more budgets prepared, but it is not necessary to detail them here. For example, budgets will be prepared for the Administration and Research and Development Departments, but these are rather similar to the Selling and Distribution cost budget already detailed.

THE MASTER BUDGET

When the functional budgets have been completed the Budget Officer will prepare a Master Budget (see Table VIII), in which he will incorporate the Production, Sales, and Costs estimated for the budget period. The Board of Directors will then consider the budget, and if they are not satisfied will call for amendments. However, when the budget is finally approved it represents a standard which should be achieved by each department in the business.

Notes would be given to management explaining why the budgeted net profit for the current budget period was lower than for the corresponding budget period in the previous year. Information would be readily available in the subsidiary budgets which make up this Master Budget.

THE OPERATION OF BUDGETARY CONTROL

The Head of each department or section will receive a copy of the budget appropriate to his activity. Each month he will receive a copy of the departmental budget report, a simple illustration of which is given in Fig. 82.

The Head of the department receiving the report (in this illustration the Cost Accountant) can see immediately where he has over- or underspent his budgeted allowance. From the performance percentage he can see that he has been efficient this month (102%), and cumulatively he has also been efficient (101%).

On investigating the variances it is apparent that the most important item was Code 11, Clerical Salaries. It would appear that the Department has been operating below strength, which has resulted in increased overtime costs and reduced National Insurance charges. Code 28, Personnel Service Costs, are over-spent, presumably caused by advertising and interviewing candidates to fill the vacancy.

It must be emphasised that speed of presentation, and corrective action if necessary, is essential in Budgetary Control. Unless monthly budget reports are issued soon after the monthly period in question, adverse costs may go undetected for a considerable time, and will be much more difficult to locate.

BUDGET REPORT ON CONTROLLABLE EXPENSES

Budget Centre: 57	Date Issued: 6th July
Department: Cost Accounting	Prepared by: C.G.B.
	Checked by: P.J.B.

Performance %	Month: JUNE	
	Month	Cumulative
	102	101

		Month			Cumulative		
		Expense			Expense		
Code	Description	Budget	Actual	Variance	Budget	Actual	Variance
	INDIRECT MATERIAL						
01	Printing and stationery	75	70	5	450	460	(10)
02	Photographic supplies	30	32	(2)	180	185	(5)
03	Cleaning materials	10	8	2	60	50	10
04	General	5	5	—	30	28	2
	INDIRECT LABOUR						
11	Clerical salaries	1,020	987	33	5,800	5,680	120
12	Executive salaries	400	400	—	2,200	2,200	—
13	Overtime	30	36	(6)	90	120	(30)
14	Absence	28	24	4	150	154	6
15	National insurance	40	39	1	220	210	10
	MISCELLANEOUS						
21	Repairs: Buildings	10	12	(2)	40	45	(5)
22	Transport	—	—	—	—	—	—
23	Equipment	4	3	1	60	75	(15)
24	Depreciation: Buildings	20	20	—	120	120	—
25	Transport	—	—	—	—	—	—
26	Equipment	10	10	—	60	60	—
27	Heat, Light, and Power	15	12	3	120	110	10
28	Personnel Service	8	12	(4)	60	80	(20)
29	Postage	5	6	(1)	30	34	(4)
30	Telephone	30	28	2	180	166	14
31	Staff expenses	8	10	(2)	50	55	(5)
32	General expenses	2	1	1	10	8	2
		£1,750	£1,715	£35	£9,920	£9,840	£80

Fig. 82.—*Budget Report*

Every month the head of each budget centre receives a report like this. It enables him to pay particular attention to those items of expense which call for it because of their "exception" to the rule.

Budget reports will be issued for each department or Budget Centre, then summarised reports issued for Divisions of the business. A report to Management concerning all significant variances will be presented, explaining how the variances occurred, and any corrective action which may have been taken.

FLEXIBLE BUDGETARY CONTROL

In order to avoid the wide discrepancies which may emerge when comparisons of actual results are made with a fixed budget, the use of flexible budgets are to be recommended.

Such a budget is defined in the *Terminology of Cost Accountancy* as

"A budget which is designed to change in accordance with the level of activity attained."

In order to explain how such a budget operates, consider a simple hypothetical case. This must be done under two conditions:

1. Flexible budget without Standard Costing.
2. Flexible budget with Standard Costing.

CASE (1)—WITHOUT STANDARD COSTING

Department A, for which a flexible budget is to be set up, consists of five similar machines. At normal practical rates of working these machines are estimated to work in a 13-week period.

Machines	Weeks	Hours per week	Estimated Utilisation	
5	× 13	× 44	× 75%	= 2145 machine hours.

NOTE.—In other departments, it should be noted, the capacity might well be measured in direct labour hours.

This normal practical capacity is taken as 100% capacity, and it will be necessary to take capacities on either side of this, in case the actual capacity achieved is less or more than the norm.

The next matter to be considered is the expenditure budgeted to be incurred at these various levels of activity. It is desirable to separate all expenditure into "fixed" and "variable," as the behaviour of them differs in circumstances which are themselves subject to fluctuation. Thus as production increases, economies of large-scale buying may reduce the direct material costs, but an increase in the fixed costs may take place. The semi-fixed costs must first be subdivided as shown in the chapter on Marginal Costing.

As a result, the flexible budget, simplified into main headings, might be as follows:

Budgeted machine hours	1287		1716		2145		2574		3003	
Capacity %	60		80		100		120		140	
	Unit Cost	£	Unit Cost	£	Unit Cost	£	Unit Cost	£	Unit Cost	£
Direct and variable costs	3	3861	3	5148	3	6,435	2·7	6,950	2·7	8,108
Fixed costs		4000		4000		4,000		4,500		4,500
		7861		9148		10,435		11,450		12,608

Now if in the actual period 2000 machine hours were recorded, comparison of actual costs would be made with the flexible budget at this level, thus:

Direct and variable costs	2000 × 3	= £6,000
Fixed costs		= £4,000
		£10,000

The difference between the actual expense incurred and the allowance would reflect in the Budget Comparison Statement as a Variance requiring explanation.

CASE (2)—WITH STANDARD COSTING

The same details as for Case (1) apply, but standards have been set up.

It has been found that in Department A the five operators who look after the machines are a little more skilled than the average, and have been given a rating of 62/60. The relaxation factor has been fixed at 5% and 10% is also allowed to cover set up time, gauge time, etc.

Time study establishes that the average time required by these operators to finish a unit of production is 70 minutes. The standard time per unit is therefore

$$70 \times \frac{62}{60} \times 1\cdot15 = \underline{83\cdot2 \text{ minutes.}}$$

It follows that the budgeted standard hours will be

$$2145 \text{ machine operating hrs.} \times \frac{60}{70} \times \frac{83\cdot2}{60} = \underline{2550 \text{ standard hours.}} \text{ (approx)}$$

(to be performed in the same number of clock hours).

If the level of activity of the operators, as measured in standard hours of work produced, rises or falls, it will mean either

(*a*) they have worked faster or slower than they were rated; or
(*b*) the relaxation and other factors have been fixed incorrectly; or
(*c*) the machine hours available have been varied.

There are, therefore, two measures of achievement now open for consideration:

1. *The standard capacity ratio*

$$\text{Either} \quad \text{(i)} \ \frac{\text{Machine hours recorded}}{\text{Budgeted machine hours}} \times 100.$$

$$\text{or} \quad \text{(ii)} \ \frac{\text{Direct labour hours recorded}}{\text{Budgeted direct labour hours}} \times 100.$$

2. *The level of activity ratio*

$$\frac{\text{Standard hours actually produced}}{\text{Budgeted standard hours}} \times 100.$$

The flexible budget in Case (2) is likely to be drawn up on the basis of budgeted standard hours, so that it might be:

Budgeted standard hours	1530		2040		2550		3060		3570	
Activity level, %	60		80		100		120		140	
	Unit Cost	£	Unit Cost	£	Unit Cost	£	Unit Cost	£	Unit Cost	£
Direct and variable costs	2·52	3861	2·52	5148	2·52	6,435	2·27	6,950	2·27	8,108
Fixed costs		4000		4000		4,000		4,500		4,500
		7861		9148		10,435		11,450		12,608

If 2400 standard hours of work are produced the level of activity achieved, in terms of standard hours is

$$\frac{2400}{2550} \times 100 = \underline{94 \cdot 1\% \text{ approx.}}$$

Comparison of actual costs would therefore be made with the flexible budget at this level.

As far as the direct and variable expense is concerned, the matter is straightforward:

$$2400 \times 2 \cdot 52 = \underline{£6050.}$$

(or to a greater degree of accuracy £6058).

But what is to be done regarding the fixed expense? What is the "allowance" to be?

In considering the level of activity achieved, it is seen that it is inter-related with standard capacity attained; and the Institute of Cost and Works Accountants, in its publication on *Budgetary Control and Standard Costing*, considers that both ratios should be made use of.

Suppose, therefore, at the same time as 94·1% activity level was reached, the standard capacity ratio was 98%.

The "allowance" in this case is

$$\pounds 4000 - \pounds 4000 \ (98\% - 94 \cdot 1\%)$$
$$= 4000 - (4000 \times 3 \cdot 9\%)$$
$$= 4000 - 157$$
$$= \underline{\pounds 3843}$$

Had the standard capacity ratio been used alone, the result would have been

$$\pounds 4000 \times 98\% = \underline{\pounds 3820}.$$

On the other hand, the activity level percentage alone would give

$$\pounds 4000 \times 94 \cdot 1\% = \underline{\pounds 3764}.$$

The allowance of £3843 allows for the fact that both capacity and activity have had a share in producing the result.

The total allowed expense will therefore be £6058 Variable, plus £3843 Fixed, *i.e.* £9901.

For the benefit of the advanced student it is as well to follow this through to its conclusion. It should not, however, be attempted on the first reading of the book.

Let us suppose the actual overhead incurred was £4100 Fixed and £6500 Variable. We have already seen that:

Budgeted Machine hours 2145 convert to budgeted standard hours 2550
Actual hours worked are, say 2500
The standard hours of work produced, say 2400
The budgeted overhead is £4000 Fixed and £6435 Variable
The hourly budgeted rates of recovery are therefore £1·57 Fixed and £2·52 Variable
The allowance for Fixed overhead is £3883
The allowance for Variable overhead is £6058

As far as the Variable overhead is concerned, there is a Controllable or Expenditure variance:

Allowed overhead — Actual overhead

$$\pounds 6058 - \pounds 6500 = \underline{\pounds 442 \text{ Adverse}}$$

As far as the Fixed overhead is concerned, compare the allowance with

(a) Actual to obtain a controllable variance;

(b) Standard to obtain a Capacity (Volume) Variance.

Thus—

Standard Fixed overhead for production achieved

2400 hours × 1·57 = £3768

Controllable variance

£4100 − £3843 = £257 (Adverse)

Capacity variance

£3768 − £3843 = £75 (Adverse)

Actual overhead incurred £4100

Now, working on the normal basis of obtaining the variances, we should

(a) Apply the 2500 hours actually worked at predetermined rates, *i.e.*

| Fixed 2500 hours at 1·57 | £3925 |
| Variable 2500 hours at 2·52 | £6310 |

(b) Transfer to Efficiency variance 100 hours in respect of the difference between 2400 standard of hours of work produced and the 2500 hours taken to produce them. But as this variance affects only Fixed overhead, we should put the variable portion back to Expenditure variance, where it really belongs.

| Fixed 100 hours at 1·57 | £157 |
| Variable 100 hours at 2·52 | £252 |

(c) Adjust the Factory overhead applied in respect of the Capacity or Volume variance. This represents the hours which the machines did not work, and again variable overhead is not incurred for these hours.

2550 − 2500 = 50 hours, and 50 at 1·57 = £78

(d) Transfer the difference between the incurred overhead and the adjusted applied overhead to Expenditure variance.
All this can be readily seen in account form:

Factory Overhead

Incurred		Applied		Work in Progress			
F	V	F	V	F	V	F	V
4100	6500	3925	6310	3925	6310	157	252
		78	—				
		97	190				
£4100	£6500	£4100	£6500				

	Efficiency Variance			*Capacity Variance*	
F	V		F	V
157	—		78	—

Expenditure Variance

F	V
—	252
97	190

Summary of Variances

	F	V
Expenditure variance	97 (A)	442 (A)
Capacity variance	78 (A)	—
Efficiency variance	157 (A)	—
	£332 (A)	£442 (A)

It will be observed that the two-variance technique gave the following results:

	F	V
Controllable variance	257 (A)	442 (A)
Capacity variance	75 (A)	—
	£332 (A)	£442 (A)

Which is the better method to use is a matter of opinion, and both have their supporters.

CHAPTER 26

STANDARD COSTING

Introduction; Simple Variances

STANDARD COSTS are pre-determined, or budgeted estimates of cost to manufacture a single unit, or a number of units of a product, during a specified immediate future period. They are used as a measure with which the Actual cost, as ascertained, may be compared. Standard costs are usually the planned costs of the product under current and anticipated conditions, but sometimes they are the costs under normal or ideal conditions of efficiency, based upon an assumed given output, and having regard to current conditions. They are revised to conform to supernormal or subnormal conditions, but more practically to allow for persisting alterations in the prices of material and labour.

Standard Costing is a method of ascertaining the costs whereby statistics are prepared to show:

(a) the Standard cost,
(b) the Actual cost,
(c) the difference between these costs, which is termed the *variance*.

The utility of Standard Costs has been widely recognised in recent years, particularly in the U.S.A., and to a considerable extent in Great Britain. In the principal factories in Britain producing on a large scale, as, for example, in the textile industry, electrical and other engineering, biscuit-making, and chemical industries, Standard Costs are in use, and there is every indication that Standard Costing will be used to a very large extent in future.

Much depends upon the arrangement of the records as to whether a Standard Costing system entails additional clerical work. In some instances it has resulted in less work. In a certain American factory making a standard product, cost variances only are recorded. It may be said that, even if the procedure does involve additional clerical work, the close control effected enables considerable saving to be made in production costs.

ADVANTAGES

The chief advantages secured may be summarised as follows:

1. Actual performance is readily comparable with the pre-determined standards, showing separately favourable or adverse variances.

2. The variances can be analysed in detail, enabling the management to investigate the cause. Any inefficiencies of labour, of the use of materials, and of the operation of machines, for example, will be discovered.

3. The principle of "management by exception" can be applied. Managements do not spend time and effort searching through unnecessary information, but can concentrate their attention on important matters.

4. Gains or losses due to market fluctuations in prices of raw materials, as distinct from variations due to manufacturing conversion, are revealed.

5. The effects on costs of variations in the price and use of materials, the ratio of labour wages, the volume of production, and altered expenses are demonstrated at short intervals.

This information enables the management to see whether shops or processes are being worked economically, and are producing a satisfactory output. It further serves as a guide as to whether prices can be adjusted to meet competition. In periods of trade depression the records show at what price work may be undertaken to secure trade sufficient to cover overheads; this is discussed in more detail in the chapter on Marginal Costing.

LEVEL OF ATTAINMENT

When setting Standard costs it is obviously necessary to determine at which level of attainment the firm should aim. There are three levels normally considered:

1. That which past performances suggest is capable of attainment

This level may be considered satisfactory in that the standard achievement should be easily attained, but may lead management into complacency.

2. That which would necessitate maximum possible efficiency

This level is rather unrealistic and will almost invariably reflect adverse variances due to the high standard demanded. These variances may stimulate management to greater effort, but frequently may have the effect of discouraging staff.

3. That which is possible by efficient working and management

This level is usually the most satisfactory as it is realistic. Any adverse variances reflected will point the way to possible economies. Management will feel that with a reasonable amount of effort the standards should be achieved.

These levels of attainment may be better understood by means of an illustration:

EXAMPLE

In Process Department No. 1 of the G.B. Manufacturing Co. Ltd., the output for last year was 50,000 units. This year it is considered that if the department is operated at maximum possible efficiency the output could be 60,000 units; this estimate does not allow for such possible occurrences as plant breakdowns, power failures, shortage of material, etc. It is considered that under existing conditions an output of 52,000 units might be achieved, but if better planning was introduced an output of 55,000 units could be produced. Which level of attainment should be adopted as the Standard?

(1) Above was said to suffer for the disadvantage of leading management into complacency, while (2) above suffered from being unrealistic. However, (3) was said to be usually the most satisfactory. Thus in this illustration it would be considered that an output of 55,000 units should be the Standard output.

The Budgetary Control of sales, production, and finance is almost a necessity for the most advantageous and successful use of a Standard Costing System. For Budgetary Control all factors affecting production and cost are pre-determined as closely as possible. Sales quotas are determined in consultation with the Sales Manager and the selling staff. The cost of financing is carefully considered. The volume of production and its planning are fixed. From the budget so prepared, the Standard cost of each product is calculated.

In the setting up of these Standards, consideration is given to statistics of production costs in the preceding periods, but total reliance on these is inadvisable, it being more satisfactory to have regard to the tendency of prices of materials and labour and to the prospects of the immediate future. It will be apparent that marketing conditions, financing methods, selling methods, purchasing power, mechanical equipment, production possibilities, and labour conditions all have an influence on Standards and for determining Standard costs, they must be taken into consideration.

The determination of Standards is a long and difficult task, and, consequently, it is not usual to vary the Standards unduly. By the use of cost ratios, or efficiency percentages, such a course may be rendered unnecessary. It is convenient, however, to alter the standards if labour costs or prices of materials are definitely changed for the future.

REVISION VARIANCE

The Terminology of Cost Accountancy defines revision variance as

"The amount by which a budget is revised, which, as a matter of policy is not incorporated in the standard cost rate."

After Standards are set, circumstances may change which could not have been envisaged. If the changes are of a temporary or a minor nature, then rather than revise Standards, it is possible to create a Revision Variance. Any changes in cost will be posted to a Revision Variance Account, so that management can be informed of the extent of the change in cost.

In the next chapter Mix Variances will be illustrated; these are a form of Revision Variance. It is sometimes necessary to change the mix of a product for a short period, in which case the standard may be "revised" by means of a Revision Variance—which is regarded as a Mix Variance.

THE STANDARD HOUR

Production is frequently expressed in terms of units, pounds, gallons, etc. This may be satisfactory in many cases, but as will be appreciated, it may be inconvenient when considering different types of products, especially when the products are measured in different units, for example, gases and liquids.

In Standard costing systems production can be expressed in terms of a measure common to all products—this measure is termed the "Standard hour."

The "Standard hour" is the quantity of output or amount of work which should be performed in one hour. For example, if 100 units of Product X can be produced in 10 hours, and 60 units of Product Y produced in 12 hours, a Standard hour represents 10 units of X and 5 units of Y. Thus an output of 600X and 300Y would represent 120 Standard hours.

By using the Standard hour it is not difficult to calculate the production for a period. Thus if there are 1050 hours in a budget period, and it is desired to produce an equal number of Product X and Product Y, the production expected would be:

Product X—1 Standard hour represents 10 units.
Product Y—1 Standard hour represents 5 units.
Therefore Y takes twice as much time to manufacture as X.
Therefore $\frac{2}{3}$ of the period will be devoted to Y and
$\frac{1}{3}$ of the period will be devoted to X
700 hours represents 3500 units of Y.
350 hours represents 3500 units of X.
The output is thus 3500 units of both products.

EXAMPLE

A company manufacturing food products markets three brands: "Exe" jam, "Wye" marmalade, and "Zed" lemon curd. It is estimated that 2000 jars of jam, 6000 jars of marmalade, and 4000 jars of curd could be filled in 1

hour. The output for the month of February was 300,000 units of "Exe," 1,000,000 units "Wye," and 600,000 units "Zed."
Production could be measured in terms of Standard hours as follows:

Actual Production

February

Product	Production	Standard units per hour	Production in standard hours
"Exe" jam	300,000	2,000	150
"Wye" marmalade	1,000,000	6,000	$166\frac{2}{3}$
"Zed" curd	600,000	4,000	150
			$466\frac{2}{3}$

EFFICIENCY RATIO

The I.C.W.A. *Terminology of Cost Accountancy* defines efficiency ratio as:

"The Standard hours equivalent to the work produced, expressed as a percentage of the actual hours spent in producing that work."

This can be expressed:

$$\frac{\text{Actual production in terms of Standard hours}}{\text{Actual hours worked}} \times 100.$$

This ratio measures the efficiency with which the firm is operating.

EXAMPLE

A company manufactures office chairs and desks. It is estimated that 1 chair can be made in 2 hours and 1 desk in 10 hours. In March the Actual production is 100 chairs and 24 desks. Actual hours worked were 320. Actual production in terms of Standard hours is therefore:

> *Chairs:* 100 units at 2 hours per unit   200
> *Desks:*   24 units at 10 hours per unit   240
>
>   440

The efficiency ratio is: $\dfrac{440}{320} \times 100 = 137 \cdot 5\%$.

ACTIVITY RATIO

The *Terminology of Cost Accountancy* gives the activity ratio as:

"The number of Standard hours equivalent to the work produced, expressed as a percentage of the budget Standard hours."

This can be expressed:

$$\frac{\text{Actual production in terms of Standard hours}}{\text{Budgeted production in terms of Standard hours}} \times 100.$$

This ratio measures the level of activity at which the firm is operating.

EXAMPLE

Continuing the illustration above and assuming the budgeted production for the month to be 125 chairs and 20 desks, one can now calculate the activity ratio.

Budgeted production in terms of Standard hours is:

Chairs: 125 units at 2 hours per unit	250
Desks: 20 units at 10 hours per unit	200
	450

The activity ratio is: $\frac{440}{450} \times 100 = 97\cdot8\%$.

THE ESTABLISHMENT OF STANDARD COSTS

Standards of performance, usage of material, quantity of production, and cost rates must be established. Usually the Cost Accountant will be responsible for setting the Standard, but he must work in very close co-operation with time-and-motion-study engineers, production engineers, buyers, and other personnel.

Standard costs must be ascertained for each of the following elements of cost:

1. Direct material.
2. Direct labour.
3. Variable overhead.
4. Fixed overhead.

1. DIRECT MATERIAL

(*a*) Standard quantities of material should be set for each product. It is thus necessary to establish a Standard drawing, formula, or specification, which should be adhered to except in special circumstances, when a revision may be necessary.

(*b*) If there is a normal loss in process, a Standard loss should be set based on past experience or by scientific analysis.

(*c*) Standard prices of all materials consumed should be set for each product. Prices should be fixed in co-operation with the buyer, and allowing for

(i) Stocks in hand.
(ii) The possibility of price fluctuations.
(iii) The extent of contracts already placed for materials.

2. DIRECT LABOUR

(a) The different grades of labour required in the production of various products should be ascertained. It should be then possible to establish the labour cost by evaluating the grades of labour at the Standard rates per hour set by the personnel department.

(b) Standards of performance should be set in conjunction with the work-study engineers. Thus the number of units produced per hour at the number of hours required per unit can be established.

3. VARIABLE OVERHEAD

It is assumed that variable overheads move in sympathy with production; therefore it is necessary to consider only the cost per unit or cost per hour. Irrespective of production, the variable overhead will remain the same. Thus if packing costs are 6d. per unit of production, then the variable overhead cost of 1000 units will be £25 and of 10,000 units, £250.

4. FIXED OVERHEAD

Fixed overhead relates to all items of expenditure which are more or less constant irrespective of fluctuations in the level of output, within reasonable limits. The following points must be considered:

(a) The total cost of fixed overheads for the period.
(b) The budgeted production for the period.
(c) The number of hours expected to be worked during the period.

It should now be possible to estimate the Standard fixed overhead cost for each product manufactured. A Standard cost per unit can now be prepared, an example of which is as follows:

Standard cost of Product A

1 Unit		£	s.	d.	£	s.	d.
Direct material:	60 lb of "Exe" at 5s. per lb	15	0	0			
	40 lb of "Wye" at 6s. per lb	12	0	0			
	100				27	0	0
	10 Normal loss 10%						
	90 lb				27	0	0
	Scrap value				1	0	0
	Carried forward				26	0	0

Standard cost of Product A (contd.)

		£	s.	d.	£	s.	d.
	Brought Forward				26	0	0
Direct labour:	Process 1—2 hours at 10s. per hour	1	0	0			
	Process 2—5 hours at 8s. per hour	2	0	0			
	Process 3—2 hours at 10s. per hour	1	0	0			
					4	0	0
Variable Overhead:	Process 1—£2 per unit	2	0	0			
	Process 2—£2 10s. per unit	2	10	0			
	Process 3—£1 10s. per unit	1	10	0			
					6	0	0
Fixed Overhead:	Production 50% of labour cost	2	0	0			
	Administration 25% of labour cost	1	0	0			
	Selling and Distribution 25% of labour cost	1	0	0			
					4	0	0
	TOTAL				40	0	0
Profit					10	0	0
	Selling price				£50	0	0

If during a period 10,000 units of Product A are manufactured and sold, and the Actual costs are ascertained as below, the Standard costs and Actual costs could be compared as follows:

Total Variances

Product A   Period

Element of cost	Standard	Actual	Variances Favourable	Variances Adverse
	£	£	£	£
Direct material	260,000	280,000		20,000
Direct labour	40,000	36,000	4,000	
PRIME COST	300,000	316,000	4,000	20,000
Variable overhead	60,000	55,000	5,000	
Fixed overhead	40,000	41,000		1,000
TOTAL COST	400,000	412,000	9,000	21,000
Profit	100,000	108,000	(8,000)	
Sales Variance			20,000	
SALES	£500,000	£520,000	£21,000	£21,000

The above illustration demonstrates the main advantage of a Standard Costing system: management are given clear information to enable them to decide on future policy. It can be clearly seen that the total cost of Product A during the period was £12,000 more than the Standard set. The adverse variance of £20,000 on direct material should be closely investigated. Despite adverse costs, profit is £8000 higher than anticipated, due to selling prices exceeding those budgeted.

VARIANCES

The variances illustrated above show only the main variances. However, there are many other variances which can be calculated and which show why costs differed from the standards set. Thus, for instance, a Material Price Variance would denote that a variance was caused as a result of differences in prices rather than as a result of inefficient use of material; similarly a Labour Efficiency Variance would reveal a difference due to the efficiency or inefficiency of labour, not due to rates of pay being above or below the standard set. It is therefore easy to ascertain who is responsible for any cost variances from standard, so that the necessary action can be taken.

There are many variances used in practice, some of them particular to a certain industry, e.g. flight-time variance in the air-transport trade, but there are a number of variances common to many industries, and these are explained and illustrated below:

1. MATERIALS

(a) *Price Variance.*—This represents the difference between the Standard price and the Actual price of materials used.

(b) *Usage Variance.*—The difference between the Standard quantity and the actual quantity of materials.

(c) *Mix Variance.*—The variance caused by the ratio of materials being changed from the Standard ratio set.

(d) *Yield Variance.*—This represents the difference between the Standard output of a process and the Actual output obtained.

2. LABOUR

(a) *Rate Variance.*—The difference between the Standard rate and the Actual rate of pay.

(b) *Efficiency Variance.*—The difference between the Standard time set and the Actual time taken in doing a job.

(c) *Idle-time Variance.*—The Standard cost of the Actual hours any employees were idle due to abnormal circumstances.

(d) *Mix Variance.*—The variance caused by the actual grades of labour being different from Standard.

3. VARIABLE OVERHEAD

Expenditure Variance.—The Actual expense being different from the Standard allowed.

4. FIXED OVERHEAD

(*a*) *Volume Variance.*—The difference in overhead recovery due to the budgeted quantity of products being greater or less than the actual production.

(*b*) *Efficiency Variance.*—This variance is related to the Labour Efficiency Variance (2 (*b*)). If the workers have been efficient, then the production will be above Standard, so overheads will be over-recovered. The difference between Standard quantity and Actual quantity produced.

(*c*) *Capacity Variance.*—Over- and under-utilisation of plant and equipment.

(*d*) *Calendar Variance.*—Due to the hours which could possibly be worked being more or less than the hours budgeted, *e.g.* the difference could be caused by the incidence of a public holiday.

(*e*) *Expenditure Variance.*—The difference between the Budgeted expenditure and the Actual expenditure.

5. SALES

There are two main methods of calculating sales variances: one shows the effect of variances in terms of profits and the other shows the effect in terms of turnover.

(*a*) *Effect on profits*

(*i*) *Price Variance.*—The difference between the Standard price and the Actual price of sales.

(*ii*) *Volume Variance.*—The budgeted quantity of sales compared with the actual quantity. This variance is due to two factors:

1. *Quantity Variance.*—Sales effected being more or less than budgeted and
2. *Mix Variance.*—The ratio of actual sales being different from the budgeted ratio.

(*b*) *Effect on turnover*

(*i*) *Value Variance.*—This represents the difference between the Budgeted sales and the Actual sales.

(*ii*) *Price Variance.*—This variance is the same as 5 (*a*) (*i*) above.

(*iii*) *Volume Variance.*—The difference between the Budgeted sales and the Standard value of the Actual mix of sales.

(*iv*) *Quantity Variance.*—The Budgeted sales compared with the Standard value of the revised Standard mix of sales.

(*v*) *Mix Variance.*—The difference between the Standard value of the Standard mix of sales and the revised Standard value of Actual mix.

These definitions will be more fully explained in the next chapter.

THE COST ACCOUNTS

There are a number of ways of recording Standard Costs in the accounts, but it is proposed to mention only one method in this chapter, viz., all expenses incurred are charged at Actual to the accounts concerned, but are recovered in the Work-in-progress Account at Standard; work completed is then transferred to Finished Goods Account at Standard cost. This has the effect of maintaining the Work-in-progress Account at Standard cost, so that any balance of the Account at the end of a period will inevitably be valued at Standard cost. Finished goods at the end of a period will be similarly valued. Consequently if market prices fall so the Standard cost is greater than the Actual cost it will be necessary to revalue the stocks so as to conform to the "cost or market price valuation whichever is the lower."

DEFINITIONS

At this point it is important to define six of the terms to be used in this chapter.

1. *Actual production* (*APn*).—The Actual quantity produced during the Actual hours worked.
2. *Budgeted production* (*BPn*).—The Budgeted quantity to be produced during the Budgeted hours to be worked.
3. *Standard production* (*SPn*).—The Budgeted quantity to be produced during the actual hours worked.
4. *Actual cost* (*AC*).—The Actual quantity produced at the Actual cost per unit.
5. *Budgeted cost* (*BC*).—The Budgeted quantity to be produced at the Budgeted cost per unit.
6. *Standard cost* (*SC*).—The Actual quantity produced at the Budgeted cost per unit.

For the convenience of the student the above abbreviations are repeated in tabular form, together with others used in this and the following two chapters.

AC	= Actual cost	BC	= Budgeted cost	SC	= Standard cost
AFO	= Actual fixed over-head	BFO	= Budgeted fixed overhead		
AH	= Actual hours			SH	= Standard hours
AL	= Actual loss	BH	= Budgeted hours	SL	= Standard loss
AM	= Actual mix			SM	= Standard mix
AP	= Actual price	BP	= Budgeted price	SP	= Standard price
APn	= Actual production	BPn	= Budgeted production	SPn	= Standard production
APt	= Actual profit	BPt	= Budgeted profit	SPt	= Standard profit
AQ	= Actual quantity	BQ	= Budgeted quantity	SQ	= Standard quantity
AR	= Actual rate			SR	= Standard rate
AS	= Actual sales	BS	= Budgeted sales	SS	= Standard sales
AT	= Actual time	PH	= Possible hours	ST	= Standard time
AV	= Actual value			SV	= Standard value
AVO	= Actual variable overhead	RBQ	= Revised budgeted quantity	SVO	= Standard variable overhead

EXAMPLE—1. MATERIAL VARIANCES

In an engineering factory one product, P, is manufactured. From every ton of raw material consumed it is estimated that 200 articles will be produced. £20 per ton is to be taken as the Standard price of the material. 50 tons of material were issued to production during February. The Actual price of the material was £19 15s. per ton. Production during the month was 10,100 articles.

(a) Price Variance

	£	s.	d.
Standard price of materials used: 50 tons at £20	1000	0	0
Actual price of materials used: 50 tons at £19 15s.	987	10	0
Variance	£12	10	0 (F)

Formula = Actual Quantity (Actual Price − Standard Price)
= AQ (AP − SP)
= 50 (£19 15s. − £20)   = £12 10 0 (F)

NOTES.—Quantity relates to quantity of materials used.
F means a favourable variance. A means an adverse variance.

Accounting entries

	£	s.	d.	£	s.	d.
Dr. Work in progress	1000	0	0			
Cr. Material Price Variance				12	10	0
Stores Ledger control				987	10	0

It should be observed that work in progress is shown at Standard cost.

(b) Usage Variance

In (a) above the variance due to changes in price was eliminated so that in calculating the usage variance only the Standard price of materials need be considered.

From every ton of material consumed it is estimated that 200 articles will be produced, therefore as 50 tons of materials were used, 10,000 articles should have been produced.

	£	s.	d.
Standard price of Standard quantity: 10,000 at 2s.	1000	0	0
Standard price of Actual quantity: 10,100 at 2s.	1010	0	0

£10 0 0 (F)

Formula = Standard Price (Actual Quantity − Standard
           Quantity)

$$= SP (AQ − SQ)$$
$$= 20(50 − 50\tfrac{1}{2}) \qquad\qquad = £10 \ \ 0 \ \ 0 \,(F)$$

NOTES.—$SQ = \dfrac{\text{Actual output}}{\text{Standard output per ton}} = \dfrac{10,100}{200}$

Actual quantity used was less than standard, so a favourable variance results.

Accounting entries

	£	s.	d.	£	s.	d.
Dr. Work in progress	10	0	0			
Cr. Material Usage Variance				10	0	0
Dr. Finished Goods Ledger	1010	0	0			
Cr. Work-in-progress Ledger				1010	0	0

It should be observed that as usage variance is favourable it is credited to the Variance Accounts while Work-in-progress Account is debited so as to bring the amount up to Standard cost of Actual production.

Check I

(i) Finished goods = Standard cost of Actual production
                   = 10,100 at 2s.   = £1010
(ii) Entries in Finished Goods Ledger (above)   = £1010

Check II

(i) Material Variance = SC − AC
                     = £1010 − £987 10s.   = £22 10s. (F)
(ii) Material Variance = Price Variance + Usage Variance
                      = £12 10s. F + £10 F   = £22 10s. (F)

EXAMPLE—2. LABOUR VARIANCES

In the manufacture of the product, 200 employees are engaged at a rate of 4s. per hour. A 42-hour working week is in operation and there are 4 weeks in February. The Standard performance is set at 60 articles per hour. During February 182 employees were paid at the Standard rate of 4s. per hour, but 10 employees were paid at 4s. 3d. per hour, while 8 employees were paid at 3s. 6d. per hour. The factory stopped production for 2 hours due to a power failure.

(a) **Rate Variance**

Standard cost of hours worked:

	£ s. d.	£ s. d.
200 employees × 42 hours × 4 weeks × 4s. per hour		6720 0 0
Actual cost of hours worked:		
182 employees × 42 hours × 4 weeks × 4s. per hour	6115 4 0	
10 employees × 42 hours × 4 weeks × 4s. 3d. per hour	357 0 0	
8 employees × 42 hours × 4 weeks × 3s. 6d. per hour	235 4 0	6707 8 0

£12 12 0 (F)

Formula = Actual Time (Actual Rate — Standard
Rate)

= AT (AR — SR)

$$= \begin{cases} 1680 \ (4s. \ 3d. - 4s.) \\ 1344 \ (3s. \ 6d. - 4s.) \end{cases} \quad \begin{matrix} £ & s. & d. \\ 21 & 0 & 0 \ (A) \\ 33 & 12 & 0 \ (F) \end{matrix} \Big\} = \underline{£12 \quad 12 \quad 0} \ (F)$$

NOTE.—A rate variance can only occur where Actual rate differs from Standard, so only those hours worked at non-Standard rates are considered, *e.g.* 10 employees × 42 hours × 4 weeks = 1680 hours at 4s. 3d.

(b) **Efficiency Variance**

Standard labour cost of 1 article:

$$\frac{\text{Employees}}{\text{Articles per hour}} \times \text{Rate per hour}$$

$$= \frac{200}{60} \times 4s. = 13s. \ 4d.$$

		£ s. d.
Standard cost of production = Actual quantity × Standard cost per unit		
= 10,100 × 13s. 4d.		6733 6 8
Actual hours worked at Standard Rate = hours worked at Standard rate		
= 200 employees × 166 hours × 4s.		6640 0 0

£93 6 8 (F)

NOTE.—The Standard rate per hour must be used because the Actual rate was eliminated in the Rate Variance. Idle time amounting to 2 hours is considered in the next variance.

Formula = Standard Rate (Actual Time — Standard Time)

= SR (AT — ST)

= 4s. (33,200 — 33,666⅔) = £93 6 8 (F)

NOTES.—Actual time = 200 employees × 166 hours worked

Standard time = Number of men × $\dfrac{\text{Quantity produced}}{\text{Standard quantity per hour}}$

$$= 200 \times \frac{10,100}{60}$$

(c) Idle Time Variance

Cost = Hours idle × Standard hourly rate
= 200 employees × 2 hours × 4s. per hour = £80 (A)

Accounting Entries

	£	s.	d.	£	s.	d.
Dr. Work in progress	6720	0	0			
Cr. Rate Variance				12	12	0
Wages				6707	8	0
Dr. Idle-time Variance	80	0	0			
Finished Goods	6733	6	8			
Cr. Efficiency Variance				93	6	8
Work in progress				6720	0	0

Check I

(i) Finished goods = Standard cost of Actual production   £   s.   d.
= 10,100 articles × 13s. 4d. per unit = 6733   6   8

(ii) Entries in Finished Goods Ledger (above)   £6733   6   8

Check II

(i) Labour Variance = SC − AC
= £6733 6s. 8d. − £6707 8s. 0d. = £25 18 8 (F)

(ii) Labour Variance =
$\dfrac{\text{Rate}}{\text{Variance}} + \dfrac{\text{Efficiency}}{\text{Variance}} + \dfrac{\text{Idle Time}}{\text{Variance}}$
= £12 12s. F + £93 6s. 8d. F + £80 A = £25 18 8 (F)

EXAMPLE—3. VARIABLE OVERHEAD VARIANCE

The term variable overhead implies that this element of cost varies directly with production. It is therefore relatively easy to calculate the standard variable overhead per article produced. Thus, *e.g.* if Budgeted output is 2000 articles and the Budgeted variable overheads are £1000, the rate per article will be 10s. If 3000 articles are actually produced the variable overheads incurred will be 3000 × 10s. = £1500. Irrespective of the number of articles produced or the time taken to produce them, the variable overhead cost per unit will not change. If the Actual variable overhead is different from the Standard rate per unit this will be due to an Expenditure Variance.

M

The Budgeted variable overhead for the month was £5000. Budgeted production for the month was 10,000 articles. Actual variable overheads incurred were £5000. Actual production was 10,100 articles.

Expenditure Variance

Standard variable overhead (SVO) per unit is $\dfrac{£5000}{10,000} = 10s.$

Standard variable overhead 10,100 × 10s.   = 5050

Actual variable overhead (AVO)   = 5000

                                               £50 (F)

Formula = SVO − AVO

        = £5050 − £5000   = £50 (F)

Accounting entries

	£	£	£
Dr. Work in progress	5050		
Cr. Variable Overhead Expenditure Variance		50	
Variable Overhead		5000	
Dr. Finished Goods Ledger	5050		
Cr. Work in progress		5050	

Check

(i) Finished goods = SC of APn

            = 10,100 articles at 10s.   = £5050

(ii) Entries in Finished Goods Account (above)   = £5050

EXAMPLE—4. FIXED OVERHEAD VARIANCES

Of all the variances considered in this illustration, the Fixed Overhead Variances are the most difficult. The term fixed overhead implies that this element of cost does not vary directly with production. In Chapter 11 the recovery of overheads was discussed, from a study of which the student should realise that recovery depends on two factors, viz., production of articles and expenses incurred. It therefore follows that Fixed Overhead Variances occur due to these two factors which are now classified as Volume Variance and Expenditure Variance, Volume Variance being itself composed of Efficiency Variance and Capacity Variance.

There are a number of reasons why the volume of production in a factory may be above or below that budgeted, *e.g.* fewer hours worked than expected; inefficient utilisation of machinery. All the variances mentioned above will be calculated in this illustration.

The Production Budget is 126,000 articles per year. £12,600 was budgeted for fixed overheads for the year. During February the amount of overheads actually incurred was £1050.

There are 50 working weeks in the year, of which 4 are in February. The production Standard was 60 articles per hour. Actual production during February was 10,100 articles. 2 hours were lost due to idle time.

The budgeted fixed overheads (BFO) for the month of February amount to £1008. This is calculated:

$$\frac{\text{BFO} \times \text{Weeks in month}}{\text{Weeks in year}} = \frac{12,600}{50} \times 4.$$

OR

$$\frac{\text{BFO} \times \text{Budgeted production for month}}{\text{Budgeted production for year}} = \frac{12,600 \times 10,080}{126,000}$$

$$\text{Budgeted cost per unit} = \frac{\text{Budgeted cost}}{\text{Budgeted production}} = \frac{£1008}{10,080} = 2s.$$

The Standard fixed overheads for the month:

Actual production at Budgeted cost per unit = 10,100 at 2s. = £1010.

(a) Expenditure Variance

This variance is in effect a price variance, rather similar to the Material Price Variance, Labour Rate Variance, and Variable Overhead Expenditure Variance.

	£
Budgeted fixed overhead	= 1008
Actual fixed overhead	= 1050
	= £42 (A)

Formula = BFO − AFO
£1000   £1050   = £42 (A)

Accounting entries

	£	£
Dr. Expenditure Variance	42	
Dr. Work in progress	1008	
Cr. Fixed Overhead Account		1050

(b) Volume Variance

Formula = Standard Cost (Actual Quantity − Budgeted Quantity)
= SC (AQ − BQ)
= 2s. (10,100 − 10,080)   = £2 (F)

More output was achieved than budgeted, therefore £2 would be over-recovered.

(c) Efficiency Variance

Formula = Standard Cost (Actual Quantity − Standard Quantity)
= SC (AQ − SQ)
= 2s. (10,100 − 9,960)   = £14 (F)

NOTE.—The Standard quantity produced is calculated:

Hours worked × Articles produced per hour (standard)
= 166 × 60 = 9960

9960 articles should have been produced in the time available, but as 10,100 were actually produced, a favourable variance results.

(d) Capacity Variance

Formula = Standard Cost (Budgeted Quantity − Standard Quantity)
= SC (BQ − SQ)
= 2s. (10,080 − 9960) = £12 (A)

The quantity expected during February was 10,080 units, but in the time available only 9960 units could be produced; due to idle time, machine capacity was reduced.

Accounting entries

	£	£
Dr. Capacity Variance	12	
Finished goods	1010	
Cr. Efficiency Variance		14
Work in progress		1008

NOTE.—Volume Variance is not shown in the accounting entries because it is composed of Efficiency Variance and Capacity Variance, both of which are shown above.

Check I

(i) Finished goods = Standard cost of Actual production
= 10,100 units at 2s. = £1010

(ii) Entries in Finished Goods Account (above) = £1010

Check II

(i) Overhead Variance = SC − AC
= £1010 − £1050 = £40 (A)

(ii) Overhead Variance = Efficiency Variance + Capacity Variance + Expenditure Variance
= £14 (F) + £12 (A) + £42 (A) = £40 (A)

Standard Cost of Production
(Output = 10,100 articles)

Element of cost	Per unit	Total production
	£ s. d.	£ s. d.
Direct material	2 0	1,010 0 0
Direct labour	13 4	6,733 6 8
Variable overhead	10 0	5,050 0 0
Fixed overhead	2 0	1,010 0 0
TOTAL	£1 7 4	£13,803 6 8

All production for the month was sold for £15,000. The accounts would appears as follows:

Stores Ledger Control Account

	£ s. d.		£ s. d.
Purchases	987 10 0	Work in progress	1,000 0 0
Material Price Variance	12 10 0		
	£1,000 0 0		£1,000 0 0

Wages Control Account

	£ s. d.		£ s. d.
Wages paid	6,707 8 0	Work in progress	6,720 0 0
Rate Variance	12 12 0		
	£6,720 0 0		£6,720 0 0

Variable Overhead Control Account

	£ s. d.		£ s. d.
Expenses paid	5,000 0 0	Work in progress	5,050 0 0
Expenditure Variance	50 0 0		
	£5,050 0 0		£5,050 0 0

Fixed Overhead Control Account

	£ s. d.		£ s. d.
Expenses paid	1,050 0 0	Expenditure Variance	42 0 0
		Work in progress	1,008 0 0
	£1,050 0 0		£1,050 0 0

Work-in-progress Ledger Control

	£	s.	d.		£	s.	d.
Stores Ledger Control A/c	1,000	0	0	Labour Idle-time Variance	80	0	0
Wages Control A/c	6,720	0	0	Fixed Overhead Capacity Vari-			
Variable Overhead Control A/c	5,050	0	0	ance	12	0	0
Fixed Overhead Control A/c	1,008	0	0	Finished Stock	13,803	6	8
Labour Efficiency Variance	93	6	8				
Material Usage Variance	10	0	0				
Fixed Overhead Efficiency Vari-							
ance	14	0	0				
	£13,895	6	8		£13,895	6	8

Finished Stock Control Account

Work in progress	£13,803	6	8	Cost of Sales	£13,803	6	8

Cost of Sales

Finished Stock	£13,803	6	8	Profit and Loss A/c	£13,803	6	8

Material Price Variance Account

Profit and Loss A/c	£12	10	0	Stores Ledger Control A/c	£12	10	0

Material Usage Variance Account

Profit and Loss A/c	£10	0	0	Work in progress	£10	0	0

Labour Rate Variance Account

Profit and Loss A/c	£12	12	0	Wages Control A/c	£12	12	0

Labour Efficiency Variance Account

Profit and Loss A/c	£93	6	8	Work in progress	£93	6	8

Labour Idle-time Variance Account

Work in progress	£80	0	0	Profit and Loss A/c	£80	0	0

Variable Overhead Expenditure Variance Account

Profit and Loss A/c	£50	0	0	Variable Overhead Control A/c	£50	0	0

Fixed Overhead Efficiency Variance Account

Profit and Loss A/c	£14 0 0	Work-in-progress Control A/c	£14 0 0

Fixed Overhead Capacity Variance Account

Work-in-progress Control A/c	£12 0 0	Profit and Loss A/c	£12 0 0

Fixed Overhead Expenditure Variance Account

Fixed Overhead Control A/c	£42 0 0	Profit and Loss A/c	£42 0 0

It will be observed that the "price" variances, *i.e.* Material Price, Labour Rate, Variable Overhead, Expenditure, and Fixed Overhead Expenditure Variances, are calculated in the respective expense accounts, while the "quantity" variances, *i.e.* Material Usage, Labour Efficiency, Labour Idle Time, Fixed Overhead Efficiency, Fixed Overhead Capacity Variances are calculated in the Work-in-progress Ledger Control Account.

PRESENTATION

It is essential that management is presented with details of Standard and Actual costs of each product manufactured, together with the appropriate variance. This information must be made available quickly if full benefit is to be obtained from the Standard Costing System. Quick action is vital if adverse variances are to be investigated and possibly rectified.

If a Standard Costing system was not in operation, management would be presented with a simple Financial Account such as the following:

Trading and Profit and Loss Account
for Period ending February 19...

	£	s.	d.		£	s.	d.
Direct Materials Consumed	987	10	0	Sales	15,000	0	0
Direct Wages	6,707	8	0				
Variable Expenses	5,000	0	0				
Fixed Expenses	1,050	0	0				
Net Profit	1,255	2	0				
	£15,000	0	0		£15,000	0	0

This account reveals that a profit of £1255 2*s.* was made for the month, which represents a profit of 8·4% on turnover. Management may consider this figure satisfactory, but they are unable to know whether this figure could be improved upon; efficiencies or inefficiencies are not revealed.

In a Standard Costing system, however, the information to be presented to management may be shown in such form as below:

Profit and Loss Statement
for Period ending February 19...

	£	s.	d.	£	s.	d.
Sales:				15,000	0	0
Less Standard cost of sales:						
Materials	1,010	0	0			
Labour	6,733	6	8			
Variable overhead	5,050	0	0			
Fixed overhead	1,010	0	0			
				13,803	6	8
STANDARD NET PROFIT				£1,196	13	4

Variances	F £	s.	d.	A £	s.	d.	F £	s.	d.	A £	s.	d.			
Material: Price	12	10	0												
Usage	10	0	0												
							22	10	0						
Labour: Rate	12	12	0												
Efficiency	93	6	8												
Idle Time				80	0	0									
							25	18	8						
Variable Overhead: Expenditure	50	0	0												
										50	0	0			
Fixed Overhead: Efficiency	14	0	0												
Capacity				12	0	0									
Expenditure				42	0	0									
										40	0	0			
													58	8	8
ACTUAL NET PROFIT													£1,255	2	0

From this statement, management can see quite easily that the net profit expected was £1196 13s. 4d., compared with the Actual net profit obtained of £1255 2s., a favourable difference of £58 8s. 8d. It can be ascertained that this increase in profit is mainly due to labour efficiency and expenditure on variable expenses being less than expected; partly offset by abnormal idle time and increased costs of fixed expenses. Management is thus able to take quick action in respect of any inefficiencies thus revealed.

CHAPTER 27

STANDARD COSTING

Calculation of Advanced Variances

THE previous illustration showed the normal type of variance which can be easily illustrated in a composite example. There are, however, a number of variances which most students find difficult; it is therefore proposed to illustrate these variances individually.

1. MATERIAL MIX VARIANCE

The establishment of Standard Costs was discussed earlier in the previous chapter, and an example was given in which the Standard material cost of Product A was

60 lb of "Exe" at 5s. per lb £15   and
40 lb of "Wye" at 6s. per lb £12

This is known as the *standard mix* of the Product. If during any period different quantities of "Exe" and "Wye" were used in the production of Product A, then a variance would arise. This situation frequently arises in a process industry, *e.g.* in the manufacture of sausages more pork and less beef may be introduced, owing to a temporary shortage of beef. Two situations may arise:

(a) The Weight of Standard Mix (SM) and Actual Mix (AM) is the same

Formula = Standard cost of Standard mix − Standard cost of Actual mix
= SC of SM − SC of AM

EXAMPLE

	Standard mix		£		Actual mix	£
X	60 tons at £3	=	180	55 tons at £3		= 165
Y	40 tons at £6	=	240	45 tons at £6		= 270
	100 tons		£420	100 tons		£435

£420 − £435 = £15 (A)

(b) The Weight of Standard Mix Differs from Actual Mix

$$Formula = \left(\frac{\text{Weight of AM}}{\text{Weight of SM}} \times \text{SC of SM}\right) - \text{SC of AM}$$

EXAMPLE

Standard mix			Actual mix		
		£			£
X	60 tons at £3	= 180	50 tons at £3		= 150
Y	40 tons at £6	= 240	35 tons at £6		= 210
	100	£420	85		£360

$$\left(\frac{85}{100} \times 420\right) - 360 = \underline{\underline{£3 \text{ (A)}}}$$

It is only fair to warn the student that the above generally accepted explanation of Mixture Variance does not lack challengers. There are those who consider that the term refers to a deliberate rather than to a fortuitous change of formula. Thus in example (a) on page 347, suppose the standard mix in the ratio of 3 : 2 was deliberately altered to 5 : 3·5. Then the revised standard mix for 100 tons would be

X   58·8 tons
Y   41·2 tons

According to this view the Mixture Variance would then be

X   SP (SM − RSM) = 3(60 − 58·8) = £3·6 (F)
Y   6(40 − 41·2) = £7·2 (A)
                                       £3·6 (A)

and the balance of the Usage Variance would be

X   SP (RSM − AM) = 3(58·8 − 55) = £11·4 (F)
Y   6(41·2 − 45) = £22·8 (A)
                                   £11·4 (A)

                                     £15 (A)

2. YIELD VARIANCE

In the chapter on Process costing the problem of normal loss is discussed in detail. In most processes a normal loss in process is expected, so it is possible to set a Standard for the normal yield expected. The Standard yield is the output expected from the Standard input. Quite frequently the Actual yield may differ from the Standard yield; this difference is termed the Yield Variance. Three situations may arise:

(a) The Weight of Standard Mix and Actual Mix is the same, but Actual Yield differs from Standard Yield

$$Formula = \frac{\text{Standard cost}}{\text{(per ton)}} \left(\frac{\text{Standard loss}}{\text{on Actual mix}} - \frac{\text{Actual loss}}{\text{on Actual mix}} \right)$$

$$= \text{SC (SL on AM} - \text{AL on AM)}$$

EXAMPLE

Standard mix			Actual mix		
		£			£
X	60 tons at £3	= 180		55 tons at £3	= 165
Y	40 tons at £6	= 240		45 tons at £6	= 270
	100	420		100	435
	10 (10%)			8	
	90	£420		92	£435

$$\frac{420}{90} (10 - 8) = \underline{\underline{\text{£9 } 6s. \text{ } 8d. \text{ (F)}}}$$

Accounting entries

Standard cost of 90 tons $= £420$

$\therefore$ Standard cost of 92 tons $= \dfrac{420}{90} \times 92$

$$= \underline{\underline{\text{£429 } 6s. \text{ } 8d.}}$$

The Mix Variance calculated in 1 (*a*) above can be shown with the Yield Variance.

Work-in-progress Account

	£	s.	d.		£	s.	d.
Actual	435	0	0	Mix Variance	15	0	0
Yield Variance	9	6	8	Standard	429	6	8
	£444	6	8		£444	6	8

To simplify the calculation of the Mix and Yield Variance, the Price Variance has been ignored. As was shown in the previous chapter, the Price Variance is calculated first so as to restore Actual prices to Standard prices. Thus if, for example, the Actual prices paid for X and Y were £2 10s. and £6 5s. respectively, the Price Variance would be calculated as follows:

AQ (AP − SP)

$$= \begin{cases} 55 \text{ (£2 } 10s. - \text{£3)} = \text{£27 } 10s. \text{ (F)} \\ 45 \text{ (£6 } 5s. - \text{£6)} = \text{£11 } 5s. \text{ (A)} \end{cases} = \underline{\underline{\text{£16 } 5s. \text{ (F)}}}$$

The Mix Variance and Yield Variance would then be calculated in the way shown above. The Actual figure of £435 therefore refers to Actual input at Standard price.

(b) The Weight of Standard Mix and Actual Mix differs, and Actual Yield differs from Standard Yield

Formula = SC (SL on AM − AL on AM)

EXAMPLE

	Standard mix			Actual mix	
		£			£
X	60 tons at £3	= 180	50 at £3		= 150
Y	40 tons at £6	= 240	35 at £6		= 210
	100 tons	420	85		360
	10 tons		7		
	90	£420	78		£360

$$\frac{420}{90}\,(8\cdot5 - 7\cdot0) = \underline{£7\ (F)}$$

NOTE—Standard loss on Actual mix is 10% of 85 tons = 8·5 tons.

Accounting entries

Standard cost of 90 tons   = £420

$$\therefore \text{ Standard cost of 78 tons} = \frac{420}{90} \times 78$$

$$= \underline{£364}$$

The Mix Variance calculated in 1 (*b*) above can be shown with the Yield Variance.

Work-in-progress Account

	£	s.	d.		£	s.	d.
Actual	360	0	0	Mix Variance	3	0	0
Yield Variance	7	0	0	Standard	364	0	0
	£367	0	0		£367	0	0

The Actual figure of £360 refers to Actual input at Standard price.

(c) The Weight of Standard Mix differs from Actual Mix, but Actual Yield is the same as Standard Yield

Formula = SC (SL on AM − AL on AM)

EXAMPLE

Standard mix			Actual mix		
		£			£
X	60 tons at £3	= 180	50 tons at £3		= 150
Y	40 tons at £6	= 240	45 tons at £6		= 270
	100 tons at £6	420	95 tons		420
	10 tons		5 tons		
	90 tons	£420	90 tons		£420

$$\frac{420}{90} \ (9{\cdot}5 - 5{\cdot}0) = \underline{\underline{£21 \ (F)}}$$

NOTE—Standard loss on Actual mix is 10% of 95 tons = 9·5 tons.

Accounting entries

The Mix Variance must be calculated in this example because the actual mix differs from that used in 1 (*a*) or 1 (*b*) above. It will be as follows:

$$\left(\frac{\text{Weight of AM}}{\text{Weight of SM}} \times \text{SC of SM} \right) - \text{SC of AM}$$

$$= \left(\frac{95}{100} \times 420 \right) - 420$$

$$= \underline{\underline{£21 \ (A)}}$$

Work-in-progress Account

	£	s.	d.		£	s.	d.
Actual	420	0	0	Mix Variance	21	0	0
Yield Variance	21	0	0	Standard	420	0	0
	£441	0	0		£441	0	0

The Actual figure of £420 refers to Actual input at Standard price.

In Brief

$$Mix \ Variance = \left(\frac{\text{Weight of AM}}{\text{Weight of SM}} \times \text{SC of SM} \right) - \text{SC of AM}$$

$$Yield \ Variance = \text{SC (SL on AM} - \text{AL on AM)}$$

3. LABOUR MIX VARIANCE

In theory this variance is rather similar to the Material Mix Variance; if during a period different grades of labour are used in production from those budgeted, a variance will arise.

EXAMPLE

The Budgeted labour force for producing article Z in one week is:

	£	s.	d.
40 men at 6s. per hour for 40 hours =	480	0	0
20 women at 4s. per hour for 40 hours =	160	0	0
10 boys at 3s. per hour for 40 hours =	60	0	0
	£700	0	0

The Actual labour force employed during a week was:

	£	s.	d.
35 men at 6s. per hour for 40 hours =	420	0	0
20 women at 4s. per hour for 40 hours =	160	0	0
10 women at 5s. per hour for 40 hours =	100	0	0
5 boys at 3s. per hour for 40 hours =	30	0	0
	£710	0	0

Labour Rate Variance

Formula = AT (AR − SR)

= 400 (5s. − 4s.)

= £20 (A)

NOTE.—10 women only have been paid a rate which differs from Standard rate, and as a 40-hour week is in operation, 400 hours is the Actual time which has been thus paid.

Labour Mix Variance

Formula = Standard cost of Standard mix − Standard cost of Actual mix

= SC of SM − SC of AM

Standard cost of Standard mix is given as £700.

Standard cost of Actual mix is:

	£	s.	d.
35 men at 6s. per hour for 40 hrs. =	420	0	0
30 women at 4s. per hour for 40 hrs. =	240	0	0
5 boys at 3s. per hour for 40 hrs. =	30	0	0
	£690	0	0

∴ Labour Mix Variance is £700 − £690 = £10 (F)

Accounting entries

	£	£
Dr. Work in progress	690	
Rate Variance	20	
Cr. Wages		710
Dr. Finished goods	700	
Cr. Labour Mix Variance		10
Work in progress		690

4. OVERHEAD CALENDAR VARIANCE

Many companies which operate a yearly budget divide the year into 13 budget periods of 4 weeks. However, some firms divide the yearly budget into 12 budget periods according to the calendar months. Where a firm adopts the latter system, it is necessary to operate a Calendar Variance.

Fixed overheads do not vary with production, and they are usually recovered at an hourly rate. The Budgeted total fixed overheads for the year will be divided by the 12 budget periods in the year thus giving a fixed rate per budget period. The Actual recovery of fixed overheads will depend on how many hours are worked during a budget period, and because the number of hours worked in each period will frequently differ, a variance from budget will occur.

EXAMPLE

Fixed overheads for the year are budgeted at £17,640. The factory operates an 8-hour day and a 5-day week. The number of days which could be worked in the year are given in Table IX:

$$\text{Overhead recovery} = \frac{£17,640}{1960 \text{ hours}} = £9 \text{ per hour.}$$

$$\text{Accrued} = \frac{£17,640}{12 \text{ months}} = £1470 \text{ per month.}$$

It should be noted that the Calendar Variance over a period of 1 year is self-eliminating.

To find the Calendar Variance for a month, the following formula can be used:

Formula = Budgeted Rate for Fixed Overhead (Budgeted Hours − Possible Hours)

= BFO (BH − PH)

e.g. Consider the Month of *July:*

Possible hours = 104
Budgeted hours = 163⅓ (*i.e.* 1960 hours ÷ 12 months)
9 (163⅓ − 104)
9 (59⅓) = £534 (A)

e.g. Consider the Month of *October*:

Possible hours = 184
Budgeted hours = 163⅓ (*i.e.* 1960 hours ÷ 12 months)
9 (163⅓ − 184)
9 (20⅔)   = £186 (F)

TABLE IX

Month	Days worked	Hours worked	Over-head rate per hour	Over-head re-covered	Over-head accrued	Variance Adverse	Variance Favour-able
			£	£	£	£	£
January	23	184	9	1,656	1,470	—	186
February	20	160	9	1,440	1,470	30	—
March	21	168	9	1,512	1,470	—	42
April	20 (Easter)	160	9	1,440	1,470	30	—
May	21 (Whit.)	168	9	1,512	1,470	—	42
June	21	168	9	1,512	1,470	—	42
July	13 (Annual Hol.)	104	9	936	1,470	534	—
August	20 (Bank Hol.)	160	9	1,440	1,470	30	—
September	22	176	9	1,584	1,470	—	114
October	23	184	9	1,656	1,470	—	186
November	20	160	9	1,440	1,470	30	—
December	21 (Christmas)	168	9	1,512	1,470	—	42
		1,960	—	£17,640	£17,640	—	—

Hours worked = Number of days × Hours per day.

SALES VARIANCES

All the variances previously discussed have been concerned with costs: the effects on profits due to adverse or favourable variances on materials, labour, or overheads. Some companies calculate cost variances only, but to obtain the full advantages of Standard Costing, many companies also calculate Sales Variances. Sales Variances show the effect on the business of changes in quantities of sales or prices obtained for sales.

There are two distinct ways of calculating Sales Variances; two systems which show the effect of a change in sales as regards:

1. Turnover.
2. Profit.

It is proposed to discuss only the first method here; the second method will be dealt with in Chapter 28.

The definitions of the various Sales Variances were given earlier in the previous chapter.

SPECIMEN QUESTION

A sales budget has been prepared in respect of four Standard products. The budgeted sales for 1 month and the Actual results achieved are as follows:

Product	Budget			Actual		
	Quantity	Price	Value	Quantity	Price	Value
		£	£		£	£
W	1000	5	5,000	1200	6	7,200
X	750	10	7,500	700	9	6,300
Y	500	15	7,500	600	14	8,400
Z	250	20	5,000	200	21	4,200
	2500		£25,000	2700		£26,100

Calculate the Sales variances.

ANSWER

Before computing the variances, two calculations are required, viz.:

1. The Standard value of the Actual mix. This is the Actual quantity sold at the Standard price; and
2. The Standard value of the revised Standard mix. This is the Standard ratio of the Actual sales at Standard prices, e.g. if 6 units of A and 12 units of B are Budgeted sales, then the ratio of A is $\frac{1}{3}$ and B $\frac{2}{3}$. If 24 units of A and B are sold, then the Standard ratio of Actual sales would be $A\frac{1}{3} = 8$, $B\frac{2}{3} = 16$. If the Standard price of A is £1 and B is £2, then the Standard value of the revised Standard mix would be: A 8 at £1: B 16 at £2.

Product	1. Standard value of Actual mix			2. Standard value of revised Standard mix		
	Quantity	Price	Value	Quantity	Price	Value
		£	£		£	£
W	1200	5	6,000	1080	5	5,400
X	700	10	7,000	810	10	8,100
Y	600	15	9,000	540	15	8,100
Z	200	20	4,000	270	20	5,400
TOTAL	2700		£26,000	2700		£27,000

NOTE.—Standard value of revised Standard mix is calculated:

$$
\begin{array}{llllll}
 & & & & & £ \\
W & \dfrac{1000}{2500} \times 2700 & = & 1080 \text{ at } £5 & = & 5,400 \\[2mm]
X & \dfrac{750}{2500} \times 2700 & = & 810 \text{ at } £10 & = & 8,100 \\[2mm]
Y & \dfrac{500}{2500} \times 2700 & = & 540 \text{ at } £15 & = & 8,100 \\[2mm]
Z & \dfrac{250}{2500} \times 2700 & = & 270 \text{ at } £20 & = & 5,400 \\[2mm]
 & & & & & \overline{£27,000}
\end{array}
$$

(a) Value Variance

Formula = Budgeted Sales — Actual Sales
$$= BS - AS$$

					£	
W	£5,000	—	£7,200	=	2,200	(F)
X	£7,500	—	£6,300	=	1,200	(A)
Y	£7,500	—	£8,400	=	900	(F)
Z	£5,000	—	£4,200	=	800	(A)
	£25,000	—	£26,100	=	£1,100	(F)

This variance represents the difference between the value of sales expected and that actually achieved.

(b) Price Variance

Formula = Actual Quantity (Actual price — Standard price)
$$= AQ\,(AP - SP)$$

			£	
W	1200 (6 — 5)	=	1200	(F)
X	700 (9 — 10)	=	700	(A)
Y	600 (14 — 15)	=	600	(A)
Z	200 (21 — 20)	=	200	(F)
			£100	(F)

Check

Actual Sales — Standard value of Actual mix

$$= AS - SV \text{ of } AM$$
$$= £26,100 - £26,000 = \underline{£100 \ (F)}$$

The effects of changes in prices on value of sales can be determined by this variance.

(c) **Volume Variance**

Formula = Standard Price (Actual Quantity — Budgeted Quantity)
= SP (AQ — BQ)

£

W	5 (1200 — 1000)	=	1000 (F)
X	10 (700 — 750)	=	500 (A)
Y	15 (600 — 500)	=	1500 (F)
Z	20 (200 — 250)	=	1000 (A)

£1000 (F)

Check

Budgeted Sales — Standard value of Actual mix

= BS — SV of AM
= £25,000 — £26,000 = £1000 (F)

This variance shows the effect on sales of Actual quantities of sales differing from those budgeted.

(d) **Mix Variance**

Formula = Standard value of revised Standard mix — Standard value of Actual mix
= SV of SM — SV of AM

£

W	£5,400	—	£6,000	=	600 (F)
X	£8,100	—	£7,000	=	1100 (A)
Y	£8,100	—	£9,000	=	900 (F)
Z	£5,400	—	£4,000	=	1400 (A)
	£27,000		£26,000		£1000 (A)

The Mix Variance forms part of the Volume Variance and relates to the change in ratio of quantities of sales. Thus if sales of 100 units were budgeted, composed of 80% X and 20% Y, it is highly improbable that exactly these sales will be achieved; for example, there might be 75% X and 25% Y. This represents the Mix Variance.

(e) **Quantity Variance**

Formula = Budgeted sales — Standard value of Standard mix
= BS — SV of SM

£

W	£5,000	—	£5,400	=	400 (F)
X	£7,500	—	£8,100	=	600 (F)
Y	£7,500	—	£8,100	=	600 (F)
Z	£5,000	—	£5,400	=	400 (F)
	£25,000		£27,000		£2000 (F)

The Quantity Variance also forms part of the Volume Variance and relates to actual sales being greater or less than those budgeted. Thus, if sales of 100 units were budgeted, composed of 80% X and 20% Y, and actual sales were achieved of 160 X and 40 Y, there would be no Mix Variance as the ratio of X to Y has not changed, but the quantity sold has changed.

Check I

$$\frac{\text{Volume}}{\text{Variance}} = \frac{\text{Mix}}{\text{Variance}} + \frac{\text{Quantity}}{\text{Variance}}$$

£1000 (F) = £1000 (A) + £2000 (F)

Check II

$$\frac{\text{Value}}{\text{Variance}} = \frac{\text{Volume}}{\text{Variance}} + \frac{\text{Price}}{\text{Variance}}$$

£1100 (F) = £1000 (F) + £100 (F)

Accounting entries

Sales Account

	£		£
Price Variance	100	Actual Sales	26,100
Quantity Variance	2,000	Mix Variance	1,000
Budgeted Sales	25,000		
	£27,100		£27,100

CHAPTER 28

STANDARD COSTING

Comprehensive Illustration of Variance Analysis

IN this chapter an advanced illustration is given which includes practically all of the variances mentioned in the previous chapters. This illustration shows how variances could be calculated in a process factory which had adopted a Standard Costing technique.

Variances have been calculated in respect of two products, "Exe" and "Wye." It is suggested that the reader should follow through the variances shown for "Exe," then should try to calculate those for "Wye," using exactly the same principles as were used for "Exe." Reference could then be made to the illustration to check whether or not the reader had understood the calculation of variances.

At the end of the chapter Overhead and Sales Variances are calculated by methods differing from those used in Chapters 26 and 27.

EXAMPLE

The Standard Engineering Co. Ltd. manufactures two products "Exe" and "Wye." Details of the direct material cost of these products are as follows:

"Exe"	"Wye"
Material C: 60% at £20 per ton	Material E: 30% at £15 per ton
Material D: 40% at £15 per ton	Material F: 70% at £5 per ton

Normal loss in production of "Exe" is 10% and that of "Wye" is 20%. Due to a shortage of materials D and E, it was not possible to use the Standard mix in February. However, normal loss in production is expected to be the same as formerly. Actual results for the month were:

"Exe"	£	"Wye"	£
Material C: 280 tons at £19 =	5320	Material E: 100 tons at £17 =	1700
Material D: 120 tons at £18 =	2160	Material F: 300 tons at £4 =	1200
	400	7480		400	2900
Loss	36		Loss	84	
	364	£7480		316	£2900

1. MATERIAL

Show in respect of Products "Exe" and "Wye":
(a) Price Variance.
(b) Mix Variance.
(c) Yield Variance.

I. "EXE"

Material input	Standard Cost			Actual Cost			Standard Cost of A. Mix		
	Tons	Price	Amount	Tons	Price	Amount	Tons	Price	Amount
			£			£			£
C	240	20	4800	280	19	5320	280	20	5600
D	160	15	2400	120	18	2160	120	15	1800
	400		7200	400		7480	400		7400
Loss	40		—	36		—	36		—
TOTAL	360		£7200	364		£7480	364		£7400

(a) Price Variance

Formula = AQ (AP − SP)

$$= \begin{cases} \text{C: } 280\,(19-20) = 280\,(F) \\ \text{D: } 120\,(18-15) = 360\,(A) \end{cases} = \underline{\underline{£80\,(A)}}$$

(b) Mix Variance

Formula = SC of SM − SC of AM

$$= \begin{cases} \text{C: } 4800 - 5600 = 800\,(A) \\ \text{D: } 2400 - 1800 = 600\,(F) \end{cases} = \underline{\underline{£200\,(A)}}$$

(c) Yield Variance

Formula = SC (SL on AM − AL on AM)

$$= \frac{7200}{360}\,(40 - 36) = \underline{\underline{£80\,(F)}}$$

Check

(i) SC − AC = Material Cost Variance
  £7280 − £7480 = £200 (A)

(ii) $\dfrac{\text{Price}}{\text{Variance}} + \dfrac{\text{Mix}}{\text{Variance}} + \dfrac{\text{Yield}}{\text{Variance}} = \dfrac{\text{Material Cost}}{\text{Variance}}$

  £80 (A) + £200 (A) + £80 (F) = £200 (A)

Accounting entries

Stores Ledger Control Account

	£		£
Actual Cost	7480	Price Variance	80
		Work in progress	7400
	£7480		£7480

Work-in-progress Ledger Control Account

	£		£
Stores	7400	Mix Variance	200
Yield Variance	80	Standard Cost	7280
	£7480		£7480

NOTE.—Standard cost = Actual production at Standard cost per unit
= 364 tons at £20 per ton
= £7280

II. "WYE"

Material input	Standard Cost			Actual Cost			Standard Cost of A. Mix		
	Tons	Price	Amount	Tons	Price	Amount	Tons	Price	Amount
			£			£			£
E	120	15	1800	100	17	1700	100	15	1500
F	280	5	1400	300	4	1200	300	5	1500
	400		3200	400		2900	400		3000
Loss	80		—	84		—	84		—
TOTAL	320		£3200	316		£2900	316		£3000

(a) Price Variance

$Formula = AQ\ (AP - SP)$

$$= \begin{cases} E: 100\ (17 - 15) = 200\ (A) \\ F: 300\ (4 - 5) \quad = 300\ (F) \end{cases} = \underline{£100\ (F)}$$

(b) Mix Variance

$Formula = SC\ of\ SM - SC\ of\ AM$

$$= \begin{cases} E: 1800 - 1500 = 300\ (F) \\ F: 1400 - 1500 = 100\ (A) \end{cases} = £200\ (F)$$

(c) Yield Variance

$Formula = SC\ (SL\ on\ AM - AL\ on\ AM)$

$$= \frac{3200}{320}\ (80 - 84) = \underline{£40\ (A)}$$

Check

(i) $SC - AC$ = Material Cost Variance

$$£3160 - £2900 = \underline{£260\ (F)}$$

(ii) $\dfrac{Price}{Variance} + \dfrac{Mix}{Variance} + \dfrac{Yield}{Variance} = \dfrac{Material\ Cost}{Variance}$

$$£100\ (F) + £200\ (F) + £40\ (A) = \underline{£260\ (F)}$$

Accounting entries

Stores Ledger Control Account

	£		£
Actual Cost	2900	Work in progress	3000
Price Variance	100		
	£3000		£3000

Work-in-progress Ledger Control Account

	£		£
Stores	3000	Yield Variance	40
Mix Variance	200	Standard Cost	3160
	£3200		£3200

NOTE.—Standard cost = Actual production at Standard cost per unit
= 316 tons at £10 per ton
= £3160

2. LABOUR

In the factory of the Standard Engineering Co. Ltd. 100 men and 35 women were employed. A 5-day week of 40 hours is worked. There were 4 weeks in the month, so the Budgeted number of working hours was 160 hours. 21 days were actually worked.

Standard wages costs were:

"*Exe*": 60 men at 5s. ⎫
        15 women at 4s. ⎬ per hour for 160 hours
"*Wye*": 40 men at 5s. ⎪
        20 women at 4s. ⎭

There was a temporary shortage of men operatives, which necessitated an increase in the number of women operatives employed.

Actual wages paid during the month were:

"*Exe*": 50 men at 5s. 6d. ⎫
        25 women at 4s. ⎬ per hour for 168 hours
"*Wye*": 30 men at 5s. 6d. ⎪
        30 women at 4s. ⎭

Show the Labour Variances in respect of products "Exe" and "Wye."

I. "EXE"

Operatives	Standard Cost			Actual Cost			Revised Standard Cost		
	Hours	Rate	Amount	Hours	Rate	Amount	Hours	Rate	Amount
Men	9,600	5s.	£ 2,400	8,400	5s. 6d.	£ 2,310	8,000	5s.	£ 2,000
Women	2,400	4s.	480	4,200	4s.	840	4,000	4s.	800
TOTAL	12,000		£2,880	12,600		£3,150	12,000		£2,800

(a) Rate Variance

Formula = AT (AR − SR)

= Men: 8400 (5s. 6d. − 5s.) = £210 (A)

(b) Mix Variance

Formula = SC of SM − revised SC

$$= \begin{cases} \text{Men:} & 2400 - 2000 = 400 \text{ (F)} \\ \text{Women:} & 480 - 800 = 320 \text{ (A)} \end{cases} = £80 \text{ (F)}$$

NOTE.—Where there is a specific change in mix of labour, the revised Standard cost is compared with the original Standard cost to show the Mix Variance.

(c) Efficiency Variance

Formula = SR (AT − ST)

$$= \begin{cases} \text{Men:} & 5s. \ (8400 - 8000) = £100 \text{ (A)} \\ \text{Women:} & 4s. \ (4200 - 4000) = £40 \text{ (A)} \end{cases} = £140 \text{ (A)}$$

NOTE.—Due to the introduction of a Mix Variance, the revised Standard time must be used.

It was pointed out earlier that the many variances described were items generally used in many industries. Of course, there are a number of other variances peculiar to some industries, and one such variance occurs in this illustration.

It will have been noted that this illustration is applicable to a process industry, two products "Exe" and "Wye" being manufactured in a continuous process in which normal losses in production occur; in addition, in the current month there was an abnormal gain of 4 tons of "Exe" and an abnormal loss of 4 tons of "Wye." In many firms losses in production are not related to inefficiency of labour: they may be caused by poor-quality materials, adverse weather conditions, etc. Thus, abnormal gains or abnormal losses may not necessarily be due to efficiency or inefficiency, therefore a separate variance may be shown, viz.: Yield Variance.

(d) Yield Variance

The Labour Yield Variance is analogous to the Material Yield Variance, and reflects the gain or loss to the firm in terms of labour, of an increase or decrease in yield.

Formula = SC (SL on AM − AL on AM)

= 8 (40 − 36) = £32 (F)

NOTE.—£2880 ÷ 360 tons = £8 per ton.

Check

(i) SC − AC = Labour cost variance

£2912 − £3150 = £238 (A)

(ii) $\dfrac{\text{Rate}}{\text{Variance}} + \dfrac{\text{Mix}}{\text{Variance}} + \dfrac{\text{Efficiency}}{\text{Variance}} + \dfrac{\text{Yield}}{\text{Variance}} = \dfrac{\text{Labour Cost}}{\text{Variance}}$

£210 (A) + £80 (F) + £140 (A) + £32(A) = £238 (A)

Accounting entries

Wages Control Account

	£		£
Actual wages	3150	Rate Variance	210
		Work in progress	2940
	£3150		£3150

Work-in-progress Ledger Control Account

	£		£
Wages	2940	Efficiency Variance	140
Mix Variance	80	Standard Cost	2912
Yield Variance	32		
	£3052		£3052

NOTE.—Standard cost = Actual production at Standard cost per unit
= 364 tons at £8 per ton
= £2912

II. "WYE"

Operatives	Standard Cost			Actual Cost			Revised Standard Cost		
	Hours	*Rate*	*Amount*	*Hours*	*Rate*	*Amount*	*Hours*	*Rate*	*Amount*
			£			£			£
Men	6400	5s.	1600	5,040	5s. 6d.	1386	4800	5s.	1200
Women	3200	4s.	640	5,040	4s.	1008	4800	4s.	960
TOTAL	9600		£2240	10,080		£2394	9600		£2160

(a) Rate Variance

Formula = AT (AR − SR)
= Men: 5040 (5s. 6d. − 5s.) = £126 (A)

(b) Mix Variance

Formula = SC of SM − revised SC
= $\begin{Bmatrix}\text{Men:} & £1600 − £1200 & = £400\ (F) \\ \text{Women:} & £640 − £960 & = £320\ (A)\end{Bmatrix}$ = £80 (F)

(c) Efficiency Variance

Formula = SR (AT − ST)
= $\begin{Bmatrix}\text{Men:} & 5s.\ (5040 − 4800) & = £60\ (A) \\ \text{Women:} & 4s.\ (5040 − 4800) & = £48\ (A)\end{Bmatrix}$ = £108 (A)

(d) **Yield Variance**

Formula = SC (SL on AM — AL on AM)
= 7 (80 — 84) = £28 (A)

NOTE.—£2240 ÷ 320 tons = £7 per ton.

Check

(i) SC — AC = Labour Cost Variance
£2212 — £2394 = £182 (A)

(ii) $\dfrac{\text{Rate}}{\text{Variance}}$ + $\dfrac{\text{Mix}}{\text{Variance}}$ + $\dfrac{\text{Efficiency}}{\text{Variance}}$ + $\dfrac{\text{Yield}}{\text{Variance}}$ = $\dfrac{\text{Labour Cost}}{\text{Variance}}$

£126 (A) + £80 (F) + £108 (A) + £28(A) = £182 (A)

Accounting entries

Wages Control Account

	£		£
Actual Wages	2394	Rate Variance	126
		Work in progress	2268
	£2394		£2394

Work-in-progress Ledger Control Account

	£		£
Direct wages	2268	Efficiency Variance	108
Mix Variance	80	Yield Variance	28
		Standard Cost	2212
	£2348		£2348

NOTE.—Standard cost = Actual production at Standard cost per unit
= 316 tons at £7 per ton
£2212

3. VARIABLE OVERHEAD

The Standard variable overhead has been set at £5 per ton in respect of "Exe" and £4 per ton in respect of "Wye." The Actual variable overhead incurred during the month was £1880 and £1300 in respect of "Exe" and "Wye" respectively.

I. "EXE"

Expenditure Variance

Formula = Actual Variable Overhead — Standard Variable Overhead
= AVO — SVO
= £1880 — £1820 = £60 (A)

Accounting entries

Variable Overhead Control Account

	£		£
Actual Overhead	1880	Expenditure Variance	60
		Work in progress	1820
	£1880		£1880

NOTE.—Standard cost = Actual production at Standard cost per unit
                   = 364 tons at £5 per ton
                   = £1820

II. "WYE"

Expenditure Variance

Formula $= AVO - SVO$

$= £1300 - £1264 = £36 \text{ (A)}$

Accounting entries

Variable Overhead Control Account

	£		£
Actual overhead	1300	Expenditure Variance	36
		Work in progress	1264
	£1300		£1300

NOTE.—Standard cost = Actual production at Standard cost per unit
                   = 316 tons at £4 per ton
                   = £1264

4. FIXED OVERHEAD

The Budgeted production for the year is:

"Exe" 4500 tons, "Wye" 4000 tons

The Budgeted fixed overheads for the year are:

"Exe" £90,000, "Wye" £60,000

There are 50 working weeks in the year; 4 weeks in February. One extra day was actually worked during the month.

The Actual fixed overheads for February amounted to £7100 and £4750 in respect of "Exe" and "Wye" respectively.

Show the Overhead Variances.

I. "EXE"

Actual production for the month = 364 tons
Budgeted   „   „   „   = 360 „
Standard   „   „   „   = 378 „

(Budgeted production is 18 tons per day, therefore the Standard production for 21 days is 378 tons.)

Budgeted fixed overhead $= \dfrac{4}{50} \times £90,000 = £7200$

Check: Budgeted Production at B.F.O. per ton $\left(= \dfrac{£90,000}{4,500} = £20 \right)$

$$= 360 \text{ tons at } £20 = £7200$$

Standard fixed overhead $=$ Actual Production at Standard Cost per ton

$$= 364 \text{ tons at } £20 = £7280$$

(a) Expenditure Variance

Formula $=$ AFO $-$ BFO
$= £7100 - £7200 = £100 \text{ (F)}$

(b) Volume Variance

Formula $=$ SC (AQ $-$ BQ)
$= 20 \, (364 - 360) = £80 \text{ (F)}$

(c) Efficiency Variance

Formula $=$ SC (AQ $-$ SQ)
$= 20 \, (364 - 378) = £280 \text{ (A)}$

NOTE.—This variance does not reflect the true Efficiency Variance, because, as in the case of materials and labour, one must consider the effect of the increase in yield, which was an abnormal gain. In effect, the work performed was on 400 tons processed, out of which 360 tons finished production was expected. It is incidental that 364 tons was actually produced; it was not necessarily caused by efficient use of machinery. Therefore this variance can be split to show the effect of increased yield. This would have the effect of showing the Actual quantity produced, as being the work commensurate with the actual effort involved.

The position would then be:

(c) Efficiency Variance

Formula $=$ SC (AQ $-$ SQ)
$= 20 \, (360 - 378) = £360 \text{ (A)}$

(d) Yield Variance

Formula $=$ SC (SL on AM $-$ AL on AM)
$= 20 \, (40 - 36) = £80 \text{ (F)}$

As can be observed the net total of the last two variances is the same as the previous Efficiency Variance.

(e) Capacity Variance

Formula $=$ SC (RBQ $-$ SQ)
$= 20 \, (378 - 378) = \text{NIL}$

(f) Calendar Variance

Formula = BFO (BH − PH)

This formula was illustrated on p. 353 and is convenient when calculating variances on a standard hour basis which is discussed on p. 377. However in this illustration we are using the standard cost per unit method, so students might find the following formula more convenient:

$$SC (RBQ − BQ)$$
$$20(378 − 360) = \underline{£360 \text{ (F)}}$$

When a Calendar Variance occurs it is necessary to revise the formula for the Capacity Variance, because if more hours are available the capacity of the plant is obviously increased; alternatively, less hours available would reduce the capacity of the plant. Thus the Budget is revised to allow for the increased/decreased capacity. The revised Budgeted quantity is

21 days worked at 18 tons per day = <u>378 tons</u>

Check I

(i) SC − AC = Overhead Variance

£7280 − £7100 = <u>£180 (F)</u>

(ii) Expenditure Variance + Volume Variance = Overhead Variance

£100 (F) + £80 (F) = <u>£180 (F)</u>

Check II

$$\frac{\text{Volume}}{\text{Variance}} = \frac{\text{Efficiency}}{\text{Variance}} + \frac{\text{Yield}}{\text{Variance}} + \frac{\text{Capacity}}{\text{Variance}} + \frac{\text{Calendar}}{\text{Variance}}$$

£80 (F) = £360 (A) + £80 (F) + NIL + £360 (F)

Accounting entries

Fixed Overhead Control Account

	£		£
Actual Overhead	7100	Work in progress	7200
Expenditure Variance	100		
	£7200		£7200

Work-in-progress Ledger Control Account

	£		£
Fixed Overhead	7200	Efficiency Variance	360
Calendar Variance	360	Standard Cost	7280
Yield Variance	80		
	£7640		£7640

NOTE.—Standard cost = Actual production at Standard cost per unit
= 364 tons at £20 per ton
= <u>£7280</u>

II. "WYE"

Actual production for the month = 316 tons
Budgeted „ „ „ = 320 „
Standard „ „ „ = 336 „

Budgeted fixed overheads $= \dfrac{4}{50} \times £60,000 = \underline{\underline{£4800}}$

Check: Budgeted production at B.F.O. per ton $\left(= \dfrac{£60,000}{4,000} = £15 \right)$

$$= 320 \text{ tons at } £15 = \underline{\underline{£4800}}$$

Standard fixed overhead = Actual production at Standard cost per ton
$$= 316 \text{ tons at } £15 = \underline{\underline{£4740}}$$

(a) Expenditure Variance

Formula = AFO − BFO
$$= £4750 - £4800 = \underline{\underline{£50 \text{ (F)}}}$$

(b) Volume Variance

Formula = SC (AQ − BQ)
$$= 15 (316 - 320) = \underline{\underline{£60 \text{ (A)}}}$$

(c) Efficiency Variance

Formula = SC (AQ − SQ)
$$= 15 (320 - 336) = \underline{\underline{£240 \text{ (A)}}}$$

(d) Yield Variance

Formula = SC (SL on AM − AL on AM)
$$= 15 (80 - 84) = \underline{\underline{£60 \text{ (A)}}}$$

(e) Capacity Variance

Formula = SC (RBQ − SQ)
$$= 15 (336 - 336) = \underline{\underline{\text{NIL}}}$$

(f) Calendar Variance

Formula = SC (RBQ − BQ)
$$= 15 (336 - 320) = \underline{\underline{£240 \text{ (F)}}}$$

Check I

(i) SC − AC = Overhead Variance
$$£4740 - £4750 = \underline{\underline{£10 \text{ (A)}}}$$

(ii) Expenditure Variance + Volume Variance = Overhead Variance

$$£50 \text{ (F)} + £60 \text{ (A)} = \underline{£10 \text{ (A)}}$$

Check II

$$\frac{\text{Volume}}{\text{Variance}} = \frac{\text{Efficiency}}{\text{Variance}} + \frac{\text{Yield}}{\text{Variance}} + \frac{\text{Capacity}}{\text{Variance}} + \frac{\text{Calendar}}{\text{Variance}}$$

$$£60 \text{ (A)} = £240 \text{ (A)} + £60 \text{ (A)} + \text{NIL} + £240 \text{ (F)}$$

Accounting entries

Fixed Overhead Control Account

	£		£
Actual overhead	4750	Work in progress	4800
Expenditure Variance	50		
	£4800		£4800

Work-in-progress Ledger Control Account

	£		£
Fixed overheads	4800	Efficiency Variance	240
Calendar Variance	240	Yield Variance	60
		Standard Cost	4740
	£5040		£5040

NOTE.—Standard cost = Actual quantity at Standard cost per unit
= 316 tons at £15 per ton
= £4740

SALES

The Sales Budget and the Actual sales achieved for the month of February are as follows:

Product	Budget			Actual		
	Quantity	Price	Value	Quantity	Price	Value
		£	£		£	£
"Exe"	360	60	21,600	364	59	21,476
"Wye"	320	40	12,800	316	41	12,956
TOTAL	680		£34,400	680		£34,432

Show the Sales Variance in respect of products "Exe" and "Wye."

The Standard value of the Actual mix of sales and the Standard value of the Standard mix of sales must be calculated.

Product	SV of AM			SV of SM		
	Quantity	Price	Value	Quantity	Price	Value
		£	£		£	£
"Exe"	364	60	21,840	360	60	21,600
"Wye"	316	40	12,640	320	40	12,800
TOTAL	680		£34,480	680		£34,400

I. "EXE"

(a) Value Variance

$Formula = BS - AS$
$= £21,600 - £21,476 = \underline{£124 \text{ (A)}}$

(b) Price Variance

$Formula = AQ (AP - SP)$
$= 364 (59 - 60) = \underline{£364 \text{ (A)}}$

(c) Volume Variance

$Formula = SP (AQ - BQ)$
$= 60 (364 - 360) = \underline{£240 \text{ (F)}}$

(d) Mix Variance

$Formula = SV \text{ of } SM - SV \text{ of } AM$
$= £21,600 - £21,840 = \underline{£240 \text{ (F)}}$

(e) Quantity Variance

$Formula = BS - SV \text{ of } SM$
$= £21,600 - £21,600 = \underline{\text{NIL}}$

Check

(i) BS − AS = Value Variance
$$£21,600 - £21,476 = \underline{£124 \text{ (A)}}$$

(ii) Price Variance + Volume Variance = Value Variance
$$£364 \text{ (A)} + £240 \text{ (F)} = \underline{£124 \text{ (A)}}$$

Check II

Volume Variance = Mix Variance + Quantity Variance
$$£240 \text{ (F)} = £240 \text{ (F)} + \text{NIL}$$

N

Accounting entries

Sales Account

	£		£
Mix Variance	240	Actual sales	21,476
Budgeted sales	21,600	Price Variance	364
	£21,840		£21,840

II. "WYE"

(a) **Value Variance**

$Formula = BS - AS$
$= £12,800 - £12,956 = £156 (F)$

(b) **Price Variance**

$Formula = AQ (AP - SP)$
$= 316 (41 - 40) = £316 (F)$

(c) **Volume Variance**

$Formula = SP (AQ - BQ)$
$= 40 (316 - 320) = £160 (A)$

(d) **Mix Variance**

$Formula = SV \text{ of } SM - SV \text{ of } AM$
$= £12,800 - £12,640 = £160 (A)$

(e) **Quantity Variance**

$Formula = BS - SV \text{ of } SM$
$= £12,800 - £12,800 = NIL$

Check I

(i) $BS - AS = $ Value Variance
$£12,800 - £12,956 = £156 (F)$

(ii) Price Variance + Volume Variance = Value Variance
$£316 (F) + £160 (A) = £156 (F)$

Check II

Volume Variance = Mix Variance + Quantity Variance
$£160 (A) = £160 (A) + NIL$

Accounting entries

Sales Account

	£		£
Price Variance	316	Actual sales	12,956
Budgeted sales	12,800	Mix Variance	160
	£13,116		£13,116

Standard cost of "Exe"
(Output = 364 tons)

Item	Per unit	Total production
	£	£
Direct material	20	7,280
Direct labour	8	2,912
Variable overhead	5	1,820
Fixed overhead	20	7,280
TOTAL	53	19,292
Profit	7	2,548
SALES	£60	£21,840

Standard cost of "Wye"
(Output = 316 tons)

Item	Per unit	Total production
	£	£
Direct material	10	3,160
Direct labour	7	2,212
Variable overhead	4	1,264
Fixed overhead	15	4,740
TOTAL	36	11,376
Profit	4	1,264
SALES	£40	£12,640

PRESENTATION TO MANAGEMENT

Simplified Trading and Profit and Loss Account for the Month of February

	"Exe"	"Wye"	Total		"Exe"	"Wye"	Total
	£	£	£		£	£	£
Direct material	7,480	2,900	10,380	Sales	21,476	12,956	34,432
Direct labour	3,150	2,394	5,544				
Variable overhead	1,880	1,300	3,180				
Fixed overhead	7,100	4,750	11,850				
Net profit	1,866	1,612	3,478				
	£21,476	£12,956	£34,432		£21,476	£12,956	£34,432

The above account reveals to management that a net profit of £3478 has been achieved, of which product "Exe" contributed £1866 and product "Wye" £1612, but it does not give much more guidance. It does not reveal what profit could have been expected, or whether the Actual profit realised was due to efficient or inefficient utilisation of the firm's resources.

Under a Standard Costing system, information could be presented to management which would reveal the expected profit and clearly illustrate where any efficiency or inefficiency had been experienced. The information could be presented in a form such as the following:

Profit and Loss Statement for the Month of February

	"Exe"	"Wye"	Total	"Exe"	"Wye"	Total
Budgeted sales				21,600	12,800	34,400
Sales Variances:						
Price	364 (A)	316 (F)	48 (A)			
Quantity	Nil	Nil	Nil			
Mix	240 (F)	160 (A)	80 (F)			
				124 (A)	156 (F)	32 (F)
Actual sales				21,476	12,956	34,432
Less Standard cost of						
sales:						
Material	7,280	3,160	10,440			
Labour	2,912	2,212	5,124			
Variable overhead	1,820	1,264	3,084			
Fixed overhead	7,280	4,740	12,020			
				19,292	11,376	30,668
STANDARD NET PROFIT				2,184	1,580	3,764
Production Variances:						
Material—						
Price	80 (A)	100 (F)	20 (F)			
Mix	200 (A)	200 (F)	—			
Yield	80 (F)	40 (A)	40 (F)			
				200 (A)	260 (F)	60 (F)
Labour—						
Rate	210 (A)	126 (A)	336 (A)			
Mix	80 (F)	80 (F)	160 (F)			
Efficiency	140 (A)	108 (A)	248 (A)			
Yield	32 (F)	28 (A)	4 (F)			
				238 (A)	182 (A)	420 (A)
Variable overhead:						
Expenditure	60 (A)	36 (A)	96 (A)	60 (A)	36 (A)	96 (A)
Fixed overhead:						
Expenditure	100 (F)	50 (F)	150 (F)			
Efficiency	360 (A)	240 (A)	600 (A)			
Yield	80 (F)	60 (A)	20 (F)			
Capacity	Nil	Nil	Nil			
Calendar	360 (F)	240 (F)	600 (F)			
				180 (F)	10 (A)	170 (F)
TOTAL				318 (A)	32 (F)	286 (A)
ACTUAL NET PROFIT				£1,866	£1,612	£3,478

The above statement reveals that sales of £34,400 were expected, which would yield a profit of £3732 (£34,400 − £30,668). Due to an increase in sales value, achieved by a better mix of sales, the profit should have been increased to £3764. However, this figure was not achieved, due to the following main factors:

1. MATERIAL

A favourable Mix Variance on "Wye" was offset by an adverse variance on "Exe." A favourable Yield Variance on "Exe" was only partly offset by an adverse variance on "Wye."

2. LABOUR

Due to a shortage of men operatives, there was a high adverse Rate Variance. This probably affected the efficiency of the labour force, resulting in an adverse Efficiency Variance. The fact that women operatives were paid less than men operatives resulted in a favourable Mix Variance, but this was not enough to offset the high adverse Rate and Efficiency Variances.

3. VARIABLE OVERHEAD

There was a small adverse variance owing to increased expenditure due to higher prices.

4. FIXED OVERHEAD

The inefficiency already referred to under (2) above resulted in inefficient utilisation of plant and equipment, resulting in a high adverse variance. This variance cancelled out the benefit which should have been obtained by the working of one extra day during the month. There was an adverse Expenditure Variance due to increased prices.

The Actual profit realised was £3478, which was £254 less than that which should have been achieved. Investigation into the main variances shown should be made immediately.

This investigation of variances, part of "management by exception," concentrates attention on things which have gone wrong, thus saving time and effort of management and staff. It must be emphasised that if a Standard Costing system is to be efficiently operated, action is essential. Variances must be investigated, explained and the necessary action taken.

ALTERNATIVE PROCEDURES

SALES VARIANCES

In Chapter 27 it was mentioned that Sales Variances based on profits could be calculated, as an alternative to those based on turnover. These variances will be briefly illustrated now.

EXAMPLE

The sales Budget and the Actual sales for the month of January, of two products "Jay" and "Kay" are as follows:

Product	Budgeted cost			Budgeted sales			Actual sales		
	Quantity	Price	Value	Quantity	Price	Value	Quantity	Price	Value
		£ s.	£		£ s.	£		£ s.	£
"Jay"	5,000	4 0	20,000	5,000	5 0	25,000	4,000	5 0	20,000
							1,500	4 15	7,125
"Kay"	10,000	1 10	15,000	10,000	2 0	20,000	8,000	2 0	16,000
							1,600	1 18	3,040
TOTAL	15,000		£35,000	15,000		£45,000	15,100		£46,165

Show in respect of "Jay" and "Kay":

(a) Sales Price Variance,
(b) Sales Volume Variance,
(c) Sales Mix Variance,
(d) Sales Quantity Variance.

Product	Standard Sales			Standard Cost of Actual Sales			Revised Budgeted Sales
	Quantity	Price	Value	Quantity	Price	Value	
		£ s.	£		£ s.	£	£
"Jay"	5,500	5 0	27,500	5,500	4 0	22,000	25,944
"Kay"	9,600	2 0	19,200	9,600	1 10	14,400	20,756
TOTAL	15,100		£46,700	15,100		£36,400	£46,700

NOTES.—Standard Sales = Actual sales at budgeted prices.
    Revised budgeted sales = Total standard sales allocated to products in the same proportions as budgeted sales.
It is now necessary to calculate the budgeted profit per £1 of sales. This is calculated as follows:
    "Jay" £1 profit on £5 sales = 4/- per £1
    "Kay" 10/-   „   £2   „ = 5/-   „

(a) Price Variance

Formula = AQ (AP − SP)
$$= \begin{array}{l} \text{"Jay" } 1500 \ (\pounds 4 \ 15s. - \pounds 5) = 375 \ (A) \\ \text{"Kay" } 1600 \ (\pounds 1 \ 18s. - \pounds 2) = 160 \ (A) \end{array} \Big\} = \underline{\pounds 535 \ (A)}$$

(b) Volume Variance

Formula = BPt (AQ − BQ)
$$= \begin{array}{l} \text{"Jay" } \pounds 1 \ (5500 - 5000) \ \ \ \ = 500 \ (F) \\ \text{"Kay" } 10/- \ (9600 - 10{,}000) = 200 \ (A) \end{array} \Big\} = \underline{\pounds 300 \ (F)}$$

(c) Mix Variance

Formula = Profit per £ of sales (S Sales − RB Sales)
$$= \begin{array}{l} \text{"Jay" } 4/- \ (27{,}500 - 25{,}944) \ \ = 311 \ (F) \\ \text{"Kay" } 5/- \ (19{,}200 - 20{,}756) = 389 \ (A) \end{array} \Big\} = \underline{\pounds 78 \ (A)}$$

(d) Quantity Variance

Formula = Profit per £ of sales (RB Sales − B Sales)
$$= \begin{array}{l} \text{"Jay" } 4/- \ (25{,}944) - 25{,}000) = 189 \ (F) \\ \text{"Kay" } 5/- \ (19{,}200 - 20{,}000) = 189 \ (F) \end{array} \Big\} = \underline{\pounds 378 \ (F)}$$

Check I
Volume V = Mix V + Quantity V
£300 (F) = £78 (A) + £378 (F)

Check II (a) Total Sales Variance = BPt − APt
          £10,000 − £9765 = £235 (A)
    (b) „   „   „   = Price V + Quantity V
          £535 (A) + £300 (F) = £235 (A)

Profit and Loss Statement

	£	£
Budgeted profit on Sales		10,000
Variances: Sales Mix	78 (A)	
Sales Quantity	378 (F)	
		300
Standard profit on Sales		10,300
Variances: Sales Price		535 (A)
Actual profit on Sales		£9,765

Check

AS − SC = APt

£46,165 − £36,400 = £9,765

It will be noted that under this system of calculating Sales Variances, the Profit and Loss Statement begins with Budgeted profit on Sales, followed by variances in terms of profit, while on p. 374 the Profit and Loss Statement began with Budgeted sales, followed by variances in terms of turnover. This demonstrates the main difference in the two systems.

OVERHEAD VARIANCES CALCULATED BY THE STANDARD HOUR

In this chapter Overhead Variances have been calculated with reference to the Standard cost per article. However, it is sometimes desired to calculate the variances by the Standard-hour method. It is proposed to illustrate this system very briefly, because it is basically the same as the former method, except of course that production is expressed in terms of Standard hours rather than units.

The Overhead Variances which were discussed on pp. 340 and 342 would be calculated in Standard hours as follows:

(a) Expenditure Variance

(As before) = £42 (A)

(b) Volume Variance

Formula = Standard cost (Budgeted hours − Standard hours)

= SC (BH − SH)

= 6 (168 − 168⅓) = £2 (F)

NOTE.—Standard cost per hour = $\dfrac{\text{Budgeted costs for month}}{\text{Budgeted hours per month}}$

$$= \frac{£1008}{168} = £6$$

$$\text{Standard hours} = \frac{\text{Actual production}}{\text{Standard quantity per hour}}$$
$$= \frac{10,100}{60} = 168\tfrac{1}{3}$$

(c) Efficiency Variance

Formula = Standard cost (Actual hours − Standard hours)
    = SC (AH − SH)
    = 6 (166 − 168⅓) = £14 (F)

Although 166 hours only were worked, 168⅓ hours worth of work were produced.

(d) Capacity Variance

Formula = SC (AH − PH)
    = 6 (166 − 168) = £12 (A)

Actual hours worked were 166, but possible hours which could have been worked were 168.

These calculations result in the same variances as were found previously. It is suggested that readers should calculate the variances which were discussed on p. 366, using the Standard-hour method to check the accuracy of the Standard cost per article system, and so become conversant with both methods.

MATERIAL PRICE VARIANCE

There are two popular ways of showing Material Price Variance; the variance may be calculated when:

1. The material is taken into stock.
2. The material is issued to production.

If Method 1 is adopted, stocks will be kept at standard cost so that stores accounting is relatively easy: purchases and issues appearing at the same price.

EXAMPLE

Purchase of 1000 units at Standard price of 5s. each; actual price 5s. 6d. each. Of the units bought, 600 were issued to production. Under an integral accounting system, show the entries relating to the above transactions.

	£	£
Dr. Stock A/c	250	
Dr. Material Price Variance A/c	25	
Cr. S. Creditors A/c		275
Dr. Work in Progress A/c	150	
Cr. Stock A/c		150

Readers may care to visualise the entries under a separate Cost Accounting and Financial Accounting system.

If Method 2 is adopted, purchases will be recorded at Actual price, issues at Standard price, and the resulting variance shown. The above illustration would appear thus:

	£	£
Dr. Stock A/c	275	
Cr. S. Creditors A/c		275
Dr. Work in Progress A/c	150	
Cr. Stock A/c		150
Dr. Material Price Variance A/c	15	
Cr. Stock A/c		15

In practice, entries of Material Price Variances would not be made in the accounts on the occasion of every issue. Periodically, totals would be posted to the accounts, in a similar manner to those shown above.

CHAPTER 29

PROFITABILITY

THE concept of profitability is very important in considering many problems in management and cost accounting. It is frequently considered when, for example, policy decisions are to be made on:

(a) a change in product design,
(b) the introduction of a new pack,
(c) the increasing or decreasing volume of production,
(d) the introduction of a new product,
(e) the quantity of various products to be manufactured,
(f) a change in selling price,
(g) the introduction of new machinery to replace old machinery,
(h) the replacement of labour by machinery.

The cost accountant will frequently be expected to produce statements of anticipated costs and profits relating to such problems as those listed above. Profitability measurement is thus a guide to effective management.

Profitability can be measured in a number of ways; five measurements being as follows:

1. Comparison of total or unit-profits.
2. Percentage profit related to sales.
3. Percentage profit related to capital employed.
4. Profit related to the time factor.
5. Contribution related to the Key Factor.

These measurements will be discussed in this chapter.

THE KEY FACTOR

In budgeting for production or sales it is very important to consider the Key Factor, sometimes termed the Limiting or Principal Budget Factor. This factor limits the production and/or sales potential, and is to be found in most industries.

Typical examples of Key Factors are:

1. *Materials*   (a) Availability of supply.
                (b) Restrictions imposed by licences, quotas, etc.

2. *Labour*   (a) General shortage.
                (b) Shortage in certain grades.

380

3. *Plant* (*a*) Insufficient capacity due to shortage in supply.
     (*b*) ,, ,, ,, lack of capital.
     (*c*) ,, ,, ,, ,, space.

4. *Management* (*a*) Insufficient capital, restricting policy.
     (*b*) Policy decisions, *e.g.* maintaining sales prices by limiting production.
     (*c*) Shortage of efficient executives.

5. *Sales* (*a*) Consumer demand.
     (*b*) Inefficient or insufficient advertising.
     (*c*) Shortage of good salesmen.

Any of these factors may influence budgets.

It is common practice to measure net profit of commodities produced in terms of percentage net profit to turnover, or the rate of profit per article. Two products, X and Y, may be sold at the same price and produce the same percentage profit, but due to a Key Factor, may yield a different periodic contribution to profit. The Key Factor may be a shortage of materials needed in the manufacture of product Y, as a result of which it may be possible to produce twice as many of product X as compared with product Y. Assuming that all production can be sold, then product X will yield profits twice as large as those from product Y.

EXAMPLE

XYZ Ltd. is a manufacturing company engaged in the production of three products: X, Y, and Z. The budgeted output per day of the three products is 140, 100, and 50 respectively. The cost of production is as follows:

Element of cost	Cost per product		
	X	Y	Z
	£	£	£
Direct material	11	8	11
Direct labour	4	8	10
PRIME COST	15	16	21
Production overhead	2	4	5
PRODUCTION COST	17	20	26
Administration overhead	1	2	3
Selling and Distribution overhead	1	1	2
TOTAL COST	£19	£23	£31

The selling prices are: X £21; Y £26; Z £36.
The production limiting factor is a shortage of machine capacity.

Profitability statements of X, Y, and Z are:

Details	Product		
	X	Y	Z
Selling price	£ 21	£ 26	£ 36
Total cost	19	23	31
Net profit per product	2	3	5
Net profit % to sales	9·5	11·5	13·9
Net profit per day	£280	£300	£250

The following points emerge:

1. Maximum net profit per product is obtained by product Z.
2. Maximum net profit to sales is obtained by product Z.
3. Maximum net profit per day is obtained by product Y.

Assuming that the demand for Y is enough to absorb the total potential production of the product, XYZ Ltd. should concentrate their production resources on product Y. If eventually the market cannot absorb all of product Y at £26 each, it may be necessary to reduce the selling price so as to stimulate fresh sales by appealing to a wider group of consumers.

Let us assume that the selling price of Y would be reduced to £25 per article. The position may be:

Details	Product		
	X	Y	Z
Selling price	£ 21	£ 25	£ 36
Total cost	19	23	31
Net profit per product	2	2	5
Net profit % to sales	9·5	8·0	13·9
Net profit per day	£280	£200	£250

It can now be seen that product X reflects the greatest relative profitability per product, so the production budget should allow for additional production of product X. In brief, XYZ Ltd. will produce and sell as many of product Y at £26 as possible; however, when the market demand at that price is absorbed the price will not be lowered to £25, but instead product X will be produced and sold at £21 each. This process of evaluating the relative profitability per product will continue until maximum plant capacity is utilised.

LEVEL OF ACTIVITY PLANNING

Profitability is important when budgeting the level of activity at which the manufacturing unit is to be operated. The ratio of profit to the amount of capital employed should be ascertained.

EXAMPLE

The E.R. Co. Ltd. is a company which specialises in the manufacture of product X. The present production capacity of the company is 10,000 units per year. There is a potential sales market for 8000 units at £16 each or 10,000 units at £15 each. The marginal cost of manufacturing product X is:

	£
Direct material	5
Direct labour	3
PRIME COST	8
Variable production overhead	2
TOTAL	£10

The fixed overheads amount to £25,000 per year. It is estimated that if the production capacity of the factory were increased to 15,000 units, sales could be achieved of 12,000 units at £14 10s. each, or 15,000 units at £14 each.

The cost of installing the additional plant and machinery required to achieve the extra production capacity was estimated at £50,000. Due to this additional capital expenditure, the fixed overheads would be increased by £5000 per year (additional depreciation of plant, etc.).

In addition to the overheads already mentioned, selling overheads are estimated as follows:

Capacity	£
8,000 units	4000
10,000 „	5000
12,000 „	6000
15,000 „	8000

The present capital of the company is £300,000. The additional capital required to finance the new plant and machinery required will be obtained by a new issue of shares.

The budgeted position of the company at the four levels of activity specified will be:

Details	Level of activity			
Units produced	8,000	10,000	12,000	15,000
Capital employed	£300,000	£300,000	£350,000	£350,000
Element of cost	£	£	£	£
Direct material	40,000	50,000	60,000	75,000
Direct labour	24,000	30,000	36,000	45,000
PRIME COST	64,000	80,000	96,000	120,000
Variable production overhead	16,000	20,000	24,000	30,000
Variable selling overhead	4,000	5,000	6,000	8,000
MARGINAL COST	84,000	105,000	126,000	158,000
Fixed overhead	25,000	25,000	30,000	30,000
TOTAL COST	109,000	130,000	156,000	188,000
PROFIT	19,000	20,000	18,000	22,000
SALES	£128,000	£150,000	£174,000	£210,000
Net profit per product	£2·375	£2·000	£1·500	£1·466
% net profit to sales	14·8	13·3	10·3	10·5
% net profit to capital	6·3	6·7	5·1	6·3

The following points emerge:

1. At 8000 units the maximum percentage profit to sales is achieved, and also the maximum amount of net profit per product.
2. At 10,000 units the maximum percentage profit to capital is obtained.
3. At 12,000 units the lowest percentage profit to both sales and capital is realised.
4. At 15,000 units the maximum amount of net profit is earned.

It is obvious that to increase the capital of the business, instal new plant and machinery, and to increase production to 12,000 units is not profitable: the increase in sales revenue is not enough to absorb the sharp rise in fixed overhead expenditure. If production is increased to 15,000 units, then the resulting profit is high, but owing to the increased selling overheads incurred to attract the greater amount of sales, the burden of fixed overheads, and the effects of reduced selling prices, the percentage profit to capital is less than would be achieved if no additional production capacity had been installed.

At 8000 units the maximum percentage to sales is achieved, but at this level of activity the full potential of plant and machinery utilisation is not achieved, with the resulting higher cost per article than that which results at 10,000 units (£13 12s. 6d. as compared with £13). The decreased selling price obtained at 10,000 units level has affected the profit to some extent, but the amount of £20,000 profit obtained from an investment of £300,000 gives a yield of 6·7% which is the maximum percentage profit to capital.

The management of E.R. Co. Ltd. would be recommended to utilise their present plant and machinery at a level of activity of 10,000 units per year.

CAPITAL AND THE SHAREHOLDER

A shareholder in a company or the owner of a business can reasonably expect a return on his capital invested for two basic reasons:

1. Payment for the use of his capital.
2. Payment for the risk he takes in investing his resources.

It follows that an investor is primarily concerned with his return on capital. If this is so, then it would seem reasonable that the success of a business may be measured in terms of profitability: the percentage profit realised related to capital employed. This concept and measurement of profitability is very important. The board of a company may consider that their products are providing a satisfactory rate of profit, but to achieve this position the value of investment may be so high that the return on investment is much too low.

EXAMPLE

Typit Ltd. is a manufacturing company specialising in the manufacture of typewriters. The investment in operating assets is £500,000. The budgeted production for the year is 4000 units. The standard cost of production is as follows:

Element of cost	Per unit
	£
Direct material	8
Direct labour	5
Variable overhead	3
MARGINAL COST	£16

Fixed overheads for the year are budgeted at £16,000. It is company policy to add 25% to the total cost of the product; this is considered to be a satisfactory figure.

The budgeted position of Typit Ltd. is analysed:

Budget	Total production
Output in units	4,000
Investment	£500,000

Element of cost	£
Direct material	32,000
Direct labour	20,000
Variable overhead	12,000
MARGINAL COST	64,000
Fixed overhead	16,000
TOTAL COST	80,000
Profit—25% on cost	20,000
SALES	£100,000

The following points emerge:

1. Profit for the year is £20,000.
2. Percentage profit to sales is 20%.
3. Percentage profit to capital employed is 4%.

It will be appreciated that even though there is a profit expected for the year, and the percentage profit to sales appears quite satisfactory, the return on investment is ludicrous. It is obvious that the shareholders of the business are not obtaining a return on investment which is sufficient to cover both use of capital and risk of losing it. If all the profits of the company were distributed to shareholders the return could be a maximum of only 4%. The situation is even worse than this if one considers that:

1. Only operating assets were considered; the actual capital of the company may be greater than £500,000.
2. There has been no reference to taxation, which in practice could not be ignored.
3. There was no provision for "ploughing-back" profits into the firm, which is often a very necessary step.

The position is far from satisfactory, especially when one compares this dividend with a 4% tax-free dividend paid by a Building Society.

There are many channels of investigation which management may pursue, some or all of which may prove profitable; possible improvements are discussed later in this chapter. If the company does not consider the profitability of its production or ignores the warning signals given by this device it may leave the company open to the possibility of take-over bids. Other people may realise that the company has some useful assets which they think could be used advantageously. Investors will probably take over the company and initiate improvements which the old management failed to do.

CONTRIBUTION AND THE KEY FACTOR

Marginal Costing has been discussed in a previous chapter, in which the aspect of contribution was illustrated; Key Factors were discussed earlier in this chapter. It is possible to measure profitability in terms of the Key Factor, the formula for which, is as follows:

$$\% \text{ Profitability} = \frac{\text{Contribution}}{\text{Key Factor}} \times 100.$$

EXAMPLE

Keyfact Ltd. is a manufacturing company which specialises in the manufacture of electrical equipment. Three products are manufactured: X, Y, and Z. The production budget for the year reveals the following information:

Details	Product		
	X	Y	Z
Output in units	5560	2000	4000
Machine hours per unit	2	3	1
Element of cost	£	£	£
Direct materials	20	30	15
Direct labour	15	17	12
Direct expense	3	3	1
PRIME COST	38	50	28
Variable overhead	7	9	3
MARGINAL COST	£45	£59	£31

Fixed overhead is budgeted at £105,600 for the year, and for illustration purposes only are allocated to total production of the three products on a basis of machine-hour rates. The Key Factor is a temporary shortage of raw materials required in this industry; delivery of increased supplies is not possible for at least three years. Due to the shortage of materials, the factory is operating at 80% activity level. Selling prices of the products are as follows: X £60; Y £80; Z £40.

The profitability statement would appear:

Profitability Statement

Details	Product		
	X	Y	Z
Output (units)	5,560	2,000	4,000
Machine hours per unit	2	3	1
Element of cost	£	£	£
Direct materials	111,200	60,000	60,000
Direct labour	83,400	34,000	48,000
Direct expense	16,680	6,000	4,000
PRIME COST	211,280	100,000	112,000
Variable overhead	38,920	18,000	12,000
MARGINAL COST	250,200	118,000	124,000
Fixed overhead	55,600	30,000	20,000
TOTAL COST	305,800	148,000	144,000
PROFIT	27,800	12,000	16,000
SALES	£333,600	£160,000	£160,000
Profit per article	£5	£6	£4
% Profit to sales	8·3	7·5	10·0
% Profitability	75	70	60

The following points emerge:

1. Maximum profit per article is obtained by Y.
2. Maximum % profit to sales is obtained by Z.
3. Maximum % profitability is obtained by X.
4. Minimum amount of Key Factor per unit is required by Z.

NOTES

1. Fixed overheads are calculated:

Budgeted fixed overhead for year = £105,600
Budgeted machine hours = X: 5560 at 2 = 11,120
Y: 2000 at 3 = 6,000
Z: 4000 at 1 = 4,000
———— = 21,120

Therefore machine hour rate:

$$\frac{£105,600}{21,120} = £5$$

Budgeted fixed overhead $=$ X: 11,120 at £5 $=$ 55,600
Y: 6000 at £5 $=$ 30,000
Z: 4000 at £5 $=$ 20,000 $=$ £105,600

2. Maximum percentage Profitability is calculated:

$$\frac{\text{X: Fixed overhead} + \text{Profit}}{\text{Key Factor}} \times 100$$

$$\frac{55,600 + 27,800}{111,200} \times 100 = 75\%$$

similarly for Y and Z.

Maximum profitability is realised by product X, so management would be advised to concentrate production resources on this product. This can be explained as follows:

It was mentioned earlier in the illustration that production of all three products cannot be expanded. One or two products could be produced in greater quantity, but only at the expense of another product. If the market can absorb more units of X, then if possible the company should discourage sales of one or both of the remaining products, preferably of Z, which realises the lowest relative profitability. If production is carried out as budgeted, then the following should be the contribution of the products to fixed overhead and profit:

Budgeted Contribution

Details	Product			
	X	Y	Z	Total
	£	£	£	£
Fixed overhead	55,600	30,000	20,000	105,600
Profit	27,800	12,000	16,000	55,800
TOTAL CONTRIBUTION	£83,400	£42,000	£36,000	£161,400

It is now possible to consider the effect on contribution if management decided to adopt the recommendation outlined above, viz., to concentrate production on one product only.

Under the current budget, the cost of materials to be purchased is:

	£
Material cost—X:	111,200
Y:	60,000
Z:	60,000
TOTAL	£231,200

If production resources are to be concentrated on one product only, the position would be:

Details	Product		
	X	or Y	or Z
Direct materials	231,200	231,200	231,200
% Profitability	75	70	60
	£173,400	£161,840	£138,720

The position can be summarised:

	£
Total contribution at present	161,400
Total contribution if only X produced	173,400
	£12,000

Thus if only product X is produced, the contribution will be £12,000 greater than that originally expected. This can be checked as follows:

If total purchases of £231,200 were used in the production of X only, then 11,560 units could be produced (£231,200 ÷ £20). The position would then be:

	£
Sales 11,560 at £60	693,600
Marginal cost 11,560 at £45	520,200
Contribution of X	173,400
Original budgeted contribution	161,400
Increased contribution	£12,000

It is a policy decision of management whether to produce as originally budgeted or to manufacture only product X.

THE INTRODUCTION OF NEW MACHINERY

Management are often confronted with the problem of whether or not they should introduce new machinery either to replace old machinery, to replace labour, or to increase machine capacity. Good decisions are vital when one considers:

1. Future company operations may be determined by these decisions.
2. Large amounts of capital may be locked up.

It is therefore essential that capital projects should be undertaken which will utilise resources to the best possible advantage. Normally the projects are measured in terms of profitability; in other words, which project is the most profitable? There may, occasionally, be projects which cannot be measured in this way, *e.g.*

(*a*) where there is no alternative machinery,
(*b*) the introduction of new or better safety devices,
(*c*) urgent replacement of a damaged section of a production line.

However, in this chapter only the profitability aspect will be considered. Profitability of new projects is usually measured in at least one of three ways:

1. The Pay-off Period.
2. The Percentage Return on Investment.
3. Discounted Cash Flow.

1. THE PAY-OFF PERIOD

This is the period required for the savings in marginal costs to recover the investment. The real profitability of an investment depends on the number of years it will continue to operate after the pay-off period.

Formula

$$\text{Pay-off period in years} = \frac{\text{Cost of asset}}{\text{Savings per year}}.$$

EXAMPLE

It is proposed to introduce a new machine to increase the production capacity of Department X. Two machines are available, Type A and Type B. The following information is available in respect of A and B respectively:

Details	A	B
Cost of machine	£18,000	£35,000
Estimated life (years)	5	10
Number of operatives not required if project introduced	9	11
Average earnings of operatives per year	£500	£500
Additional cost of maintenance men, supervisors, etc., required if project introduced	£1000	£1500
Expected savings in indirect materials	£500	£200
Expected savings in scrap losses due to better efficiency	£500	£800

Profitability Statement

Details	Machine A	Machine B
Estimated working life (years)	5	10
Cost	£18,000	£35,000
Savings in marginal costs per year:	£	£
Direct labour	4,500	5,500
Indirect labour	(1,000)	(1,500)
Indirect material	500	200
Scrap	500	800
	£4,500	£5,000
Pay-off period in years: Cost / Savings per year	4	7
PROFITABILITY	£4,500	£15,000

Profitability is calculated as follows:

Savings per year (Working life — Pay-off period)

Thus   A £4500 (5 — 4)   £4,500
               B £5000 (10 — 7)   £15,000

It will be observed that under this method of calculating profitability, machine B is the more profitable investment.

2. THE PERCENTAGE RETURN ON INVESTMENT

This measures the relationship between the amount invested and the amount of expected additional profits which will be earned yearly arising from the use of the machine.

Formula

$$\frac{\text{Average yearly additional profit}}{\text{Average amount invested}} \times 100.$$

EXAMPLE

It is proposed to introduce a new machine, D, to replace an old machine, C. The following information is available in respect of C and D respectively:

Details	C	D
Cost of machine	£10,000	£100,000
Estimated life of machine (years)	10	10
Number of operatives required @ £500 p.a.	40	30
Cost of maintenance men, supervisors, etc., required if project adopted	£2,000	£4,500
Disposal value now	£2,000	
Disposal value next year	£1,000	
Direct material cost per article £2 at present level of output, but if new project is introduced a discount of 1s. 0d. per article will be obtained		
Indirect material cost	£1,000	£2,000
Output (units)	20,000	30,000
Sales value per unit	£5	£5
Scrap value is estimated at	Nil	Nil

Profitability Statement

Details	Machine	
	C	D
Output (units)	20,000	30,000
Selling price per unit	£5	£5
Investment	£10,000	£100,000
Disposal value now	£2,000	—
Disposal value next year	£1,000	—
	£	£
Sales	100,000	150,000
Less Marginal costs:		
Direct material	40,000	58,500
Direct labour	20,000	15,000
Indirect material	1,000	2,000
Indirect labour	2,000	4,500
	63,000	80,000
MARGINAL INCOME	37,000	70,000
Depreciation	1,000	10,000
	£36,000	£60,000
PROFITABILITY		48%

Profitability is calculated as follows:

$$\frac{£24,000}{£50,000} \times 100 = \underline{\underline{48\%.}}$$

NOTE.—Administration expenses, etc., have been ignored.

There has been considerable controversy concerning the calculation of average amount invested. There are two main schools of thought:

1. The purchase price of the new asset less the disposal value of the old asset should be regarded as the amount invested. The profitability calculation would then be:

$$£100,000 - £2000 = \underline{\underline{£98,000.}}$$

£98,000 to be written off over the economic life of the asset results in an average amount of capital locked up per year of £49,000.

Depreciation costs would be £9800, thus increasing the profit to £60,200.

$$\frac{£24,200}{£49,000} \times 100 = \underline{\underline{49\%.}}$$

2. The purchase price of the new asset should be regarded as the amount invested. The profitability calculation would be as shown in the illustration.

3. DISCOUNTED CASH FLOW

This method deduces the present cash value of future earnings, and thus enables an estimate to be made of how much should be invested *now*. Thus, £3333 invested now at 20% interest will amount to £4000 at the end of one year.

EXAMPLE

A piece of plant is offered for £8000. Its estimated life (shortened for the sake of simplicity) is three years. During that period it is estimated that the net incremental earnings of the plant will be at the rate of £4000 per annum, and the rate of interest to be taken is 20%.

Note that the net incremental earnings exclude depreciation, because it is not a cash flow, but only a book entry.

We have, using the Compound Interest formula

$$A = PR^n$$

where A = net incremental earnings

$R = 1 + r/100$; r = rate %; P = present value

(a) Year	(b) Net Incremental Earnings or Cash Flow	(c) R^n	(d) $1/R^n$	(e) $= \dfrac{(b) \times (d)}{P}$
1	£4000	$1 \cdot 2$	0·8333	£3333
2	£4000	$1 \cdot 2^2$	0·6944	£2778
3	£4000	$1 \cdot 2^3$	0·5787	£2315
				£8426

We should be justified in paying up to £8426 for the piece of plant, to produce £4000 earnings per annum over its life of three years assuming that 20% on capital invested is the acceptable rate of return.

HOW PROFITABILITY CAN BE IMPROVED

In this chapter a number of measurements of profitability have been illustrated, all of which may be useful to management. However, in addition to calculating profitability the Cost Accountant should be able to suggest ways of improving profitability where necessary.

Possible suggestions are as follows:

1. *Increased rate of profit*

This could be effected by

(a) Reduced costs. Perhaps a system of Budgetary Control and/or Standard Costing could be introduced. If such a system is in existence perhaps Standard Costs could be reduced and quick action initiated to correct adverse variances where possible.

(b) Increased selling prices. Research could be undertaken into possible market reaction to higher prices.

(c) Reduced selling prices. The possibility of greater sales due to a lower selling price should be investigated. Greater sales mean greater production which may lead to reduced costs.

(d) Improved planning of production and sales. Review of techniques should be undertaken.

2. *Reduced investment*

(a) Reduced stocks. Capital is often locked up unnecessarily in stocks.

(b) Reduced amounts owing by debtors. Better credit control may be instituted.

(c) Better utilisation of plant and equipment. Capacities could be investigated; over- and under-loading could be corrected; idle plant disposed of.

The subject of profitability is an interesting and fascinating one, and there is wide scope for research. It is expected that there will be many developments in techniques, uses, and measurements in the future.

CHAPTER 30

AUDITING OF COST ACCOUNTS

INTERNAL auditing is a recognised feature of modern business life, and there is every reason for applying it to the activities of the Cost Office, just as much as in the other departments.

The intention behind the appointment of an internal auditor is to protect management against errors of principle and against neglect of duty, and it is therefore essential that he should be responsible direct to management as a whole and not be dependent on any one department or sectional interest.

In the broad scope of his activities the internal auditor is in a position to sit back and survey the accounting, financial, costing, and other operations, subjecting them to a critical appraisal as to their effectiveness, and giving constructive advice to management on any changes in system which seem to be called for.

No doubt each departmental head has methods of checking postings, records, and so on for his own purposes, but the internal auditor is not concerned with them, and pursues his task in his own way and in his own time.

In the first place, an audit programme is drawn up for the year ahead, but it is made flexible enough to admit of a change of sequence, if thought desirable. It is therefore arranged in sections, and for each section there will be specified:

(*a*) which books, accounts, and records are to be checked;
(*b*) against which original sources the check is to be made.

Space is left at the end of each section of the audit programme to allow for notes to be made during the course of the audit, and for the initials of those clerks who have completed it.

The checking referred to is usually termed *vouching*, and this is more than merely ticking one figure to another in order to check the arithmetical accuracy: it is rather the careful scrutiny of the vouchers constituting the basis of the original entries, and ensuring that errors of principle have not crept in. In fact, carried out intelligently and purposefully, vouching lies at the heart of every well-conducted audit.

TYPICAL COST AUDIT PROGRAMME

In a typical cost audit programme the following action would be taken.

1. Comparison of actual production and sales with budget estimates.
2. An analysis of Standard Variances to confirm that they are being correctly interpreted to management.

For example, in the illustration given on p. 363 it will be seen that a Yield Variance occurs for the labour element due to the fact that an additional 4 tons of product "Exe" was obtained over and above the Standard rate of production. This, however, may not be attributable to any greater efficiency of labour. Indeed the Efficiency Variance is adverse.

3. An examination with a critical eye of all statements put forward for management attention.
4. A discussion of queries with the officers concerned, and a follow-up to ensure that action agreed upon is actually taken.

Questionaire forms.—These are useful to "break down" the information required, and to find out if satisfactory procedures are in operation. A specimen of such a form is shown in Fig. 83.

INTERNAL AUDIT 19.../19...

QUESTIONNAIRE—STORES DEPARTMENT

Question	Reply	Initial
1. Are Goods Received Notes obtained for all incoming goods?		
2. Are Bin Cards entered daily from Goods Received Notes?		
3. Are Stores Requisitions checked as to authorisation?		
4. Are stores taken from bin recorded daily on Bin Cards?		
5. Have Stores Debit Notes been received for all materials returned to store?		
6. Have they been recorded at once on Bin Cards?		
7. Have the Works' rules been observed at all times as to admission to the Stores?		
8. Have all known losses, from whatever cause, been reported at once?		
9. Have fire appliances been checked regularly?		
10. Have weighing machines been regularly maintained?		
11. Has the Inspector's attention been called to all cases of damage to goods?		
12. Have you any suggestions to put forward to management re the work of your department?		
For use by internal auditor **Form sent** **Reply received** **Initialled**		

FIG. 83.—*Internal Audit Questionnaire*

These forms are used to obtain confirmation that acceptable procedures are in force in the various departments, and they have some moral effect in ensuring that they are not neglected.

INTERNAL CHECK

As has been pointed out, this proceeds side by side with, but independently of, the work of the internal auditor. It is initiated by the head of the department concerned, and the aim is to make the procedure followed by the department as self-checking as possible. It is not done blatantly, however, thus calling attention to the security aspect: one clerk is not set the specific task of checking the work of another colleague. Instead, the work is so organised that while one clerk automatically and inevitably checks the work of another, this arises quite naturally and in the ordinary course of routine, and no ill feeling or atmosphere of tension is created. As an example of this, consider the case of Stores Control. The Production Control Department manages the balances of Stores; the Stores Ledger is kept by the Stores Ledger clerk; and the Stores and Bin Cards are in the charge of the Storekeeper. In addition, there are frequent physical checks carried out as part of the perpetual-inventory system, and the various records have to agree or be reconciled. Discrepancies must be dealt with according to a specified procedure.

This internal checking helps to make the work of the Internal Auditor easier, but he does not entirely rely on it, for he has to be personally satisfied on behalf of management on all matters which he deems necessary to investigate.

Although security measures are kept in the background, they cannot be totally ignored. Thus, every clerk must take at least one holiday per annum, the reason being that any cash or stocks for which he is responsible have then to be handed over to someone else. Again, it is usually possible to arrange a daily check on the entries made in the books, by means of Total Accounts. It is important, too, that clerks should not be given responsibility which exceeds the status which is accorded to them. Employers are not free from fault when they expect large sums of money to be handled by those who are not paid adequately, and in such circumstances the temptation to misappropriate may become too strong.

INTERNAL AUDITING IN RELATION TO MECHANISED ACCOUNTING

In accountancy systems which have been mechanised, either by use of keyboard machines or by the use of punched cards, a change of emphasis is required in regard to internal audit:

1. Greater reliance can be placed on the arithmetical accuracy of the figures.
2. Greater care is necessary in checking the original sources from which the entries and calculations have been made.

3. Greater care is required in the control of the issue of new ledger sheets and the transfer of completed sheets.

VERIFICATION OF ASSETS

This is an important duty laid on the shoulders of the external auditor, but nevertheless the internal auditor, too, is vitally interested.

Stocks.—Are the stocks of raw materials, stores, and finished goods as stated? On what basis have they been valued for costing purposes? Has this basis been consistently followed? Is it different from that used for Balance Sheet purposes? If so, a check must be made on the reconciliation between the two.

Work in progress.—On what basis is work in progress valued? What methods are used to determine the state of completion? Are they adequate?

Incomplete contracts.—Have measurements of work been regularly obtained? Are there any particular hazards to be provided for? Is a conservative policy being followed in regard to profit to be taken? Are materials on site excessive, or left there too long before being incorporated into the work?

Plant and machinery.—Is the method of depreciation used suitable and sufficient for the type of plant? Is the basis used for costing purposes different from that used in the Financial Accounts? If so, which has the greater merit? What provision has been made for replacement costs? What are the risks of obsolescence?

Capital Expenditure.—Has the distinction between capital and revenue expenditure been scrupulously observed?

These questions indicate some of the points on which the internal auditor will want to be satisfied, and on which he will frame his report to Management.

EFFICIENCY AUDIT

In taking a broad view of the business as a whole, the internal auditor will consider the Organization Chart (see, for example, Fig. 84), and assess the functional efficiency of its detailed parts.

Job evaluation.—Although this would be done in the first place by time-and-motion-study personnel, or by an Organization-and-Methods Department, the internal auditor would be expected to cast a critical eye on the results, and to note any anomalies which had arisen.

Merit rating.—In the same way the internal auditor would make sure that the general pattern of the agreed wages and salaries structure was being adhered to, and that adequate reasons were being advanced for abnormal pay increases.

It will be seen that the internal auditor's task is to act as the watchdog for the Directors, just as the external auditor acts on behalf of the Shareholders and Creditors. To some extent their duties are similar, but

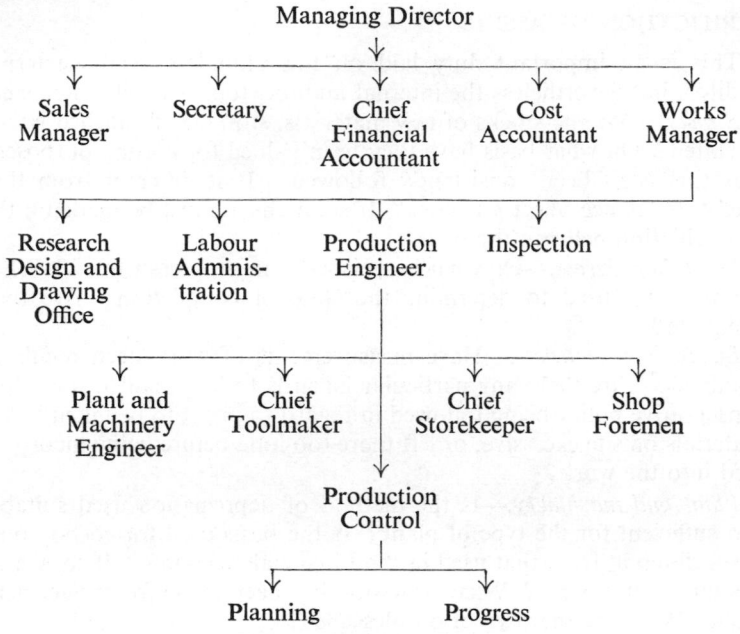

FIG. 84.—*Organisation Chart*

This shows the usual type of management organisation of a business. The internal auditor would consider the chart for his own concern, and advise on whether it was in conformity with what was really needed.

that is purely coincidental, and the internal auditor goes into his investigations much more closely and continuously, and with a different motive. He is less concerned with adherence to law than with adherence to policy; less concerned with giving sufficient information than with giving maximum information in the most assimilable form.

CHAPTER 31

MECHANISED COST ACCOUNTING

INTRODUCTION

IF the meaning of the original Greek word from which "mechanism" is derived is accepted as being "a contrivance," there is a wide variety of accounting aids which could be included under the heading.

There is not scope in a book of this kind for more than a cursory glance at such types of equipment, and those who wish to pursue the matter in greater detail are advised to consult *Office Management*, by J. C. Denyer.*

Items of particular interest to the cost accountant are:

The slide rule

The use of a slide rule is sometimes permitted in examination work, and results in a valuable saving of time in calculations. It is not essential for the student to purchase an expensive type, and as they are usually sold with simple instructions as to their use in the fundamental operations of multiplying and dividing, there is no need to give any further explanation.

Hand-operated payroll equipment

A number of firms supply equipment by which all the relative information for payroll, employees' tax cards, pay slips, etc., can be recorded in one hand-written operation.

Tape recorders

Dictation of stock balances can now be made by the person taking stock on to a tape recorder, and the result can be typed back on to the stock sheets. This reduces the personnel involved in taking stock, and enables the finished result to be ready immediately stock-taking has been completed.

Direct-entry accounting machines

The posting of entries direct from original documents to the ledgers can be speedily done on front-feed keyboard machines, and at the same time the storage and recording of totals and sub-totals is provided quite automatically. One particular machine can deal with very detailed

* Macdonald & Evans, 1958.

analysis, and many others have features which make them suitable for specific applications.

Duplicators

There are two main types:

1. Stencil.
2. Spirit.

Both of these have their special and appropriate uses. Reports and accounts for which the highest degree of clarity and permanence are required would be satisfactorily dealt with by a stencil machine. Spirit duplicators are extensively used nowadays in the reproduction of Production Control information on a series of documents.

Besides these two main types of duplicator other machines are also in use. *Photocopying machines* produce dry duplicates in a matter of seconds; this is invaluable to the Cost Accountant faced with a management meeting and required to submit statements which have only just been completed. *Microfilming* stores records photographically in miniature form. Filing space is kept to a minimum, and records can be presented at any time either in a special viewer or reproduced as a photographic facsimile of the original document. *Letterpress* and *lithographic* printing machines are really scaled-down versions of commercial printing apparatus and are beyond the scope of this book.

Card sorting by the use of hand-clipped cards

In cases where the volume of work is not such as to justify the heavy capital expenditure involved in a power-operated system of punched cards, a well-tried compromise can be achieved by the use of:

(a) a pre-punched card which is used as the document to record the original information,
(b) a pair of clippers such as a railway ticket collector uses, and
(c) a knitting needle.

The use of this method was referred to on p. 80, and a Job Time Ticket of this type was illustrated in Fig. 38.

A similar method involves the use of centrally punched cards, where two adjacent holes are clipped into an oval according to the information it is desired to record. Sorting is effected by stacking the cards, passing needles through the pack in positions that will select the required cards, then inverting the pack. The required cards will drop down and may be removed for analysis.

Wall charts

Information which can be conveyed visually in the form of graphs, charts, coloured patterns, strip indices, and signals makes a decisive impact on the mind which is not obtained by more conventional methods.

These wall charts may be used for such purposes as personnel records, sales performance, Production Control, machine loading, etc.

Counting devices

In many factories either mechanical or electronic counting devices may be used to advantage, and will aid in the accurate recording of quantities processed.

Change-giving machines

Automatic cashiers, such as are used on London's Underground and in cafés, help the wages clerks of many factories to add the silver and copper to wage packets quickly and accurately.

These, together with the time recorders referred to elsewhere, are merely a few of the many types of equipment which are available to the Cost Accountant, but as punched-card accounting using power-operated sorters and tabulators is coming more and more into prominence, it has been considered advisable to deal with this subject in somewhat greater detail, and this is done below and in the chapter which follows.

PUNCHED-CARD SYSTEMS USING SORTERS AND TABULATORS

The principle of controlling machines through the medium of punched cards is over 150 years old (the invention of the Jacquard loom in 1801 is the earliest known instance), while the use of cards in conjunction with accounting or statistical machines has continued since about 1900. Punched-card accounting machines are now well established, and because of the facility they afford for the rapid analysis of figures, so essential in costing, they are widely used in all fields of industry and commerce.

The introduction of electronic devices for accounting work at one time gave rise to the opinion that punched cards might be superseded, but practice has proved that these simple media are likely to remain in use for many years to come. In fact, many electronic computers use cards as recording media.

The main advantage of the punched-card system is that only one original recording is usually necessary. One accounting fact or happening is perforated into one card, and that card can then be manipulated mechanically at high speeds so that the data it contains, in conjunction with that in other cards, can be represented in almost limitless **combinations** and styles.

o

PUNCH–SORT–TABULATE

The punch–sort–tabulate technique starts with the transcription of data concerning a transaction into holes in a card which represent a language code that other machines can understand, the coding sometimes being done automatically.

Sorting is a simple mechanical process which groups together many cards related to one type of transaction; for example, all the cards representing movements in one Stores Account, and all the groups into the sequence, maybe numerical, in which the final results must appear.

The tabulating operation translates the coded perforated data into readable form, and at the same time it may carry out such processing as adding or subtracting. In the case of the Stores Accounts this tabulation would include striking a balance from cards representing opening balance, receipts, and issues.

Although there are many ancillary machines which facilitate the processing of the data, all punched-card systems are based on this punch–sort–tabulate technique.

THE CARD

The card, the unit which forms the medium for these systems, is available in several different sizes, the choice of which depends upon the amount of data it is required to record in connection with any one happening and the expenditure which the work will justify. It may in some instances suit the budget better to employ two small cards for one transaction rather than one large one.

Cards, and machines to suit them, are made in three basic sizes. The smallest has a capacity of 21 columns of punched information and is used for simple analysis work (Fig. 85). Where more reference or qualitative data, account number, employee's number, etc., are necessary a larger card with 40 columns can be used (Fig. 86). Process or quantitive data, such as gross pay, quantity issued, etc., do not vary so much, and the columns necessary to accommodate them will be found to be similar in many businesses.

For those cases where there is an even larger amount of data there is a physically larger card with 80 columns (Fig. 87), and, by a process known as interstage working, which permits the use of the vertical spaces between the normal punching positions, this card can accommodate 160 columns of information. The 21-column card has 11 punching positions in each column and the others have 12, so 1 to 12 months, for example, can be punched in one column.

When a card is designed for a specific purpose it is divided into fields, the sizes of which are regulated by the maximum magnitude of the fact to go into each field. Thus a month can be accommodated in a single-

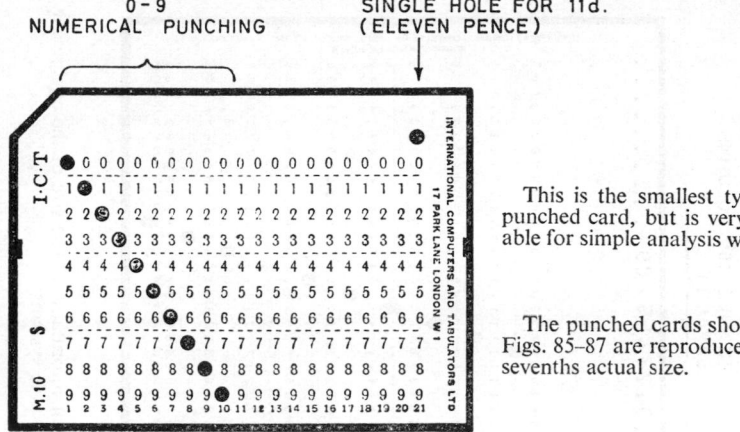

0 - 9
NUMERICAL PUNCHING

SINGLE HOLE FOR 11d.
(ELEVEN PENCE)

This is the smallest type of punched card, but is very suitable for simple analysis work.

The punched cards shown in Figs. 85–87 are reproduced six-sevenths actual size.

21 COLUMN CARD

FIG. 85.—*Punched Card—21 Columns*

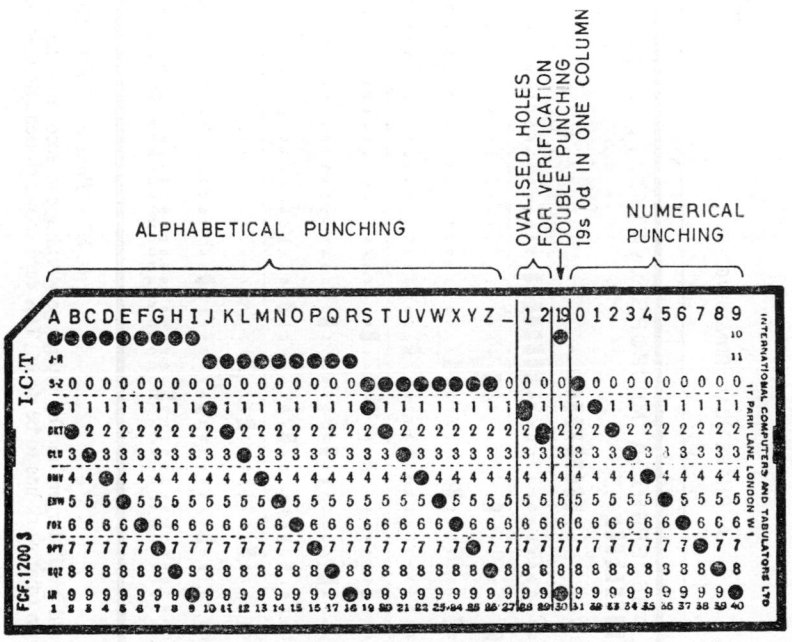

ALPHABETICAL PUNCHING

OVALISED HOLES FOR VERIFICATION DOUBLE PUNCHING 19s 0d IN ONE COLUMN

NUMERICAL PUNCHING

40 COLUMN CARD
WITH INTERPRETATION OF PUNCHING

FIG. 86.—*Punched Card—40 Columns*

This card contains more columns and therefore a greater number of facts can be recorded.

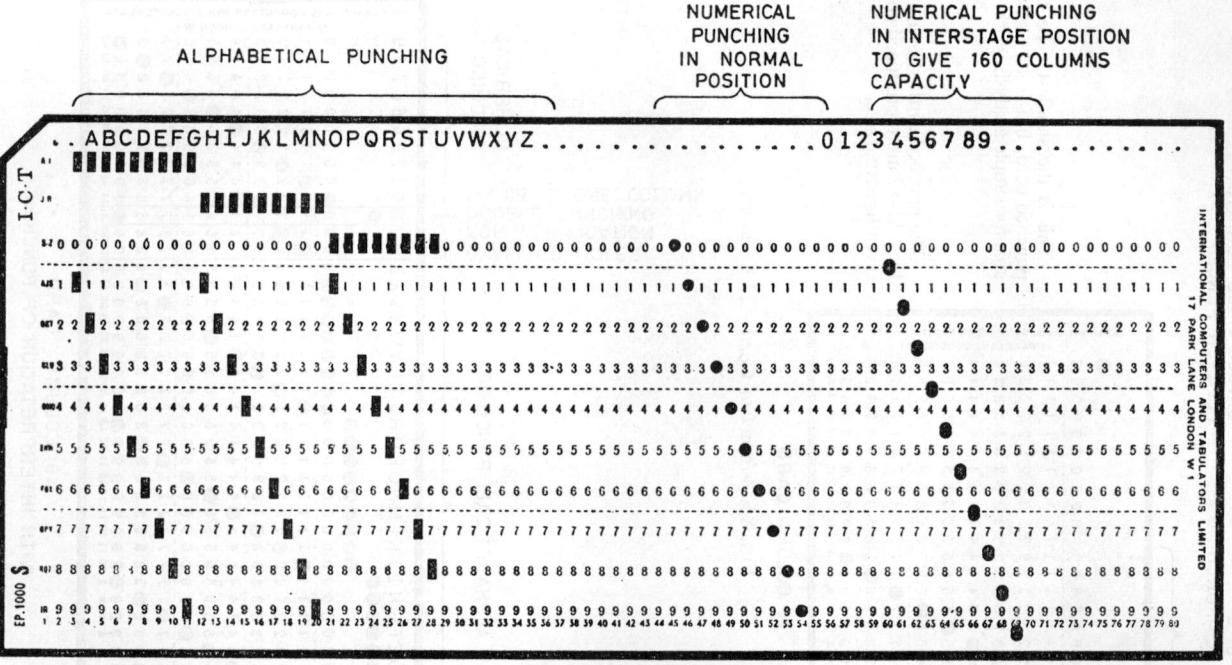

FIG. 87.—*Punched Card—80 Columns*

This card is still larger, and by interstage working can accommodate 160 columns of information. The size of the equipment depends on what work has to be done. This card shows slotted, circular, and ovalised hole systems.

column field (except in the 21-column card), and if quantities are issued in thousands the field must have four columns.

The layout of the fields is most important, and it should, as far as possible, follow the same sequence as the information on the document from which the card is being punched. In some instances the layout of the original record may with advantage be changed to facilitate and clarify the punch operator's task.

Many applications use cards as original documents, and they may be bound with duplicates, and used, for example, as Stores Requisitions or Piece-work Tickets. Such cards are known as "dual-purpose", as they are subsequently perforated with the same information as they contain in written form.

CODING

The machines can accept information only in their own language, which necessitates coding some data to suit. This is not necessarily a separate operation, as it may be done automatically or by the operator of the punching machine. Many of the customary codes are already in normal use—for example, employees for accounting purposes are usually known by numbers. Similarly, materials held in the Stores have account numbers rather than names.

Where such codes do not exist they must be designed to suit the work and system in mind, and the use of "block-coding" will make the machine operations simpler and faster. For instance, instead of numbering Stores Accounts consecutively separate sub-codes can be made thus:

Material group	say	1– 99
Material type	say	1– 99
Material size	say	1–999

Half-inch round mild-steel bar might thus be 17,04,012.

17 representing mild-steel
04 representing round bar
012 representing $\frac{1}{2}$ in.

With this type of coding it would, for example, be necessary only to sort on the first two columns if it were desired to bring together all cards by material group.

Although coding is advisable to facilitate machining, it does not mean that the accountant must be able to read the coded results. Automatic de-coding can be introduced, so that the name of accounts or departments, etc., can be printed alongside the relevant data.

PUNCHING

In the most straightforward systems the punching process consists of transcribing written data into perforated cards, and this is done with key punches which may either be entirely manually operated or be power assisted. Hand punches are fed with cards one at a time and the holes are made serially by depressing numbered keys (Fig. 88). In the

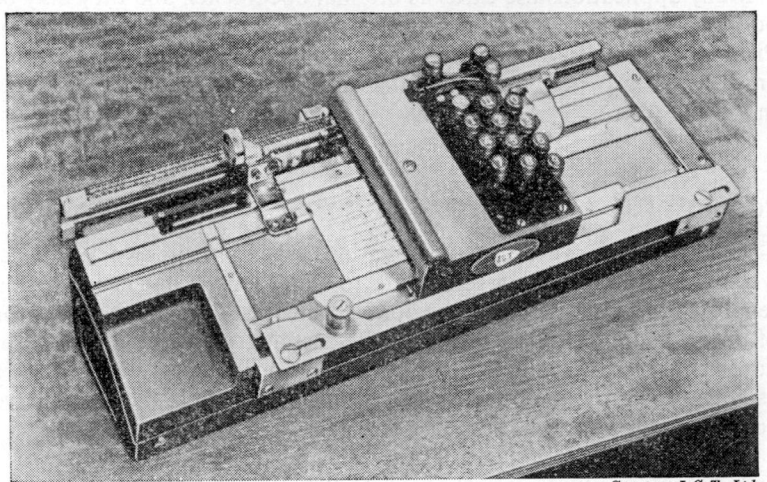

Courtesy I.C.T. Ltd.

FIG. 88.—*Manually Operated Punch*

The cards are fed into the machine one at a time and the holes are made by hand operation of the numbered keys.

automatic machines (Fig. 89) the machine feeds its own cards and the punching is done in parallel: that is, pressing the keys pre-sets the punch, but all the holes to be perforated in a particular card are punched in one stroke by electric power.

This is not only quicker and easier for the operator, but it permits known errors to be corrected before the card is actually punched. It also makes possible the repeated punching of common data without repeated keying: for example, if a batch of requisitions came from one department on a given date, that date and the department number can be repeated automatically without making key depressions for every card.

Numerical information is punched by pressing the corresponding numbered keys, while alphabetical matter is represented in code. Two holes are punched in one column for each letter, and this is usually done by an operator who has memorised the code.

Various practices are adopted to reduce the amount of original punching. One of them utilises another machine, known as a repro-

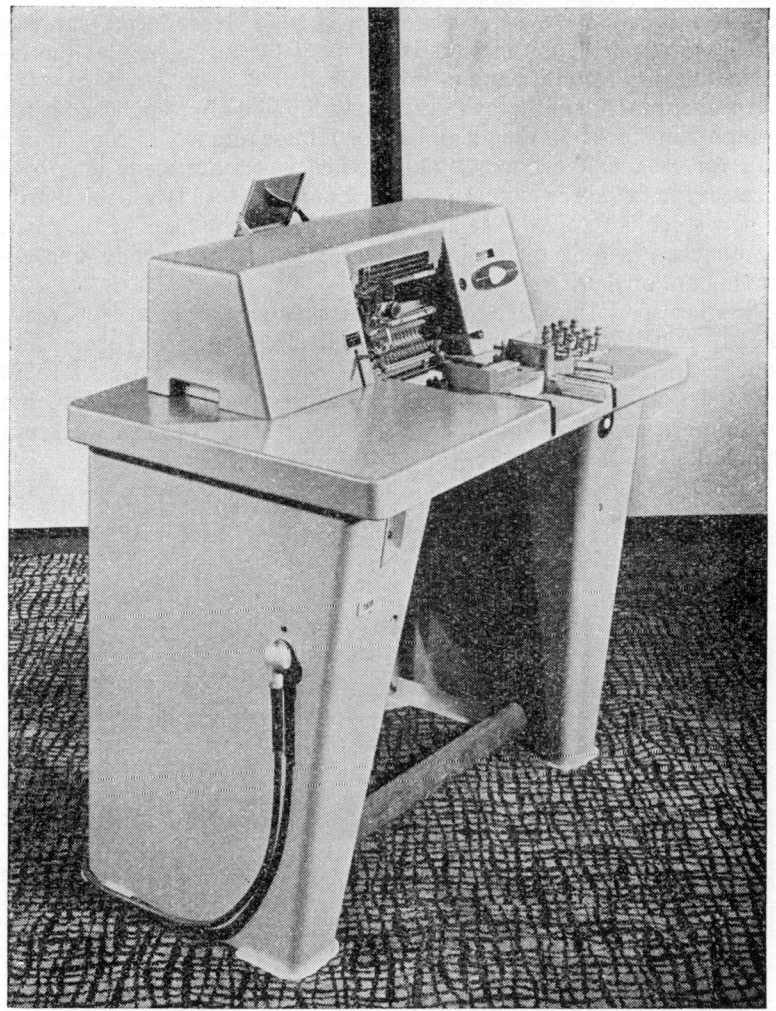

Fig. 89.—*Automatic Punch*

This machine feeds its own cards; the punch keys are depressed; and then the machine perforates all the holes at one stroke with the aid of electric power.

ducing punch, which can copy perforations from an existing card into one or more new cards. Thus, if a set of cards exists with, say, pay details for one week, and they include the employee's name and number, a further set containing only this reference data can be reproduced automatically.

Files of "master" cards which may contain names and numbers of accounts or employees are also used for making "reproduced" cards as and when required, the masters being available for as long as the information they contain remains unchanged.

Another practice in Stores work is to set up files of pre-punched cards to represent stock. In their simplest form these files would contain one card for each unit of stock. Then, when issues are made it is only necessary to extract as many cards as the units of stock issued; similarly, as new stock is received new cards are added to the file. As the cards are punched in bulk quantities, individual punching, pricing, and extending are obviated.

Another special punching machine, usually electronic, accepts cards already punched with, say, quantity and price, multiplies them, and punches the result into the same card. Such machines can work in all four functions of arithmetic—addition, subtraction, multiplication, and division—at speeds of up to 120 cards per minute and can work out calculations such as $A \times B \pm C \pm D \pm E = X$ (Fig. 90).

Courtesy I.C.T. Ltd.

Fig. 90.—*Electronic Punch*

A machine like this is able to accept cards punched with certain information, use it to make calculations, punch the result into cards; and perform this at a rate of up to 120 cards per minute.

Another type of punching machine can be coupled to a tabulator (see Tabulating), so that as the latter prints totals or balances and the relevant reference data, memory cards are automatically punched. These cards are then carried forward to the next period as an opening balance. Another machine combines summary-card punching with reproducing.

INTERPRETING

Where it is possible to use files of partly or completely pre-punched cards, their selection, or "pulling," as it is called, is difficult if the clerk has to read the perforations. Another machine is therefore frequently used to transcribe the punched information into words printed or typed along the top of the card.

VERIFICATION

The verification of the accuracy of punching is essential, and it can be carried out in several ways with different machines. In the simplest

FIG. 91.—*Automatic Verifier*

This machine detects any incorrectly punched cards
and inserts a signal card where they occur.

machines the perforated card is inserted and the operator repeats the same key-depressing actions as in punching; but if a key is pressed for which there is no corresponding hole in the card the machine locks to signal the difference (Fig. 91).

In a more automatic process the cards are re-punched—slightly "off-centre"—by a second operator, and as long as the same keys are depressed the superimposition of the two round holes simply creates one oval one. But if the two operators have not pressed similar keys one or two round holes will remain in the column where the discrepancy has arisen. The cards are then passed through a high-speed automatic verifier which detects the round holes and inserts a different-coloured card next to the incorrect card. The detection of errors is not, consequently, dependent upon the human element, as the incorrectly-punched cards are signalled automatically.

SORTING AND INTERPOLATING

The most important advantage of punched-card systems is that only one accounting fact is usually punched into each card. Groups of facts can therefore be re-arranged in any desired order without manual manipulation.

The grouping and sequencing is achieved in a sorting machine (Fig. 92) which senses the cards at a very high speed (up to 60,000 an hour) and puts them into numerical or alphabetical order. At the same time it groups together all cards with similar perforations within the sequence. Thus, when sorting piece-work cards by employee's number, all cards relating to each employee will be grouped together and the cards for all employees grouped in numerical sequence.

Sorting is carried out one column at a time, and if a field ran to, say, five figures (up to 99,999), this would necessitate five passages, the usual order being to sort on units, tens, hundreds, etc. When sorting, cards or perforations can be counted if necessary.

Where large quantities of cards have to be processed another machine known as the collator or interpolator is used to reduce the number of sorting passages. These machines take two batches of cards already in numerical sequence and merge them, in one passage, to form one pack in numerical order.

Collators or interpolators are used frequently to merge opening-balance cards, which can be kept permanently in account-number order, with the current month's movement cards (in any event, the latter have, of course, to be sorted numerically). When merging, if the machine detects an unmatched card, such as a balance card with no corresponding movement cards, it can be ejected into a separate receiver. The same machines can also extract cards without disturbing the order of the main pack.

Courtesy I.C.T. Ltd.

FIG. 92.—*Sorting Machine*

This senses the cards at speeds of up to 60,000 per hour, and puts them into numerical or alphabetical order one column at a time.

TABULATING

After the cards have been arranged in the correct order the information therein has to be transcribed into legible form and processed, for example, added or subtracted, where necessary. This is done by a tabulator (Fig. 93). But because of the variety of work, invoicing, payroll, costing, etc., which may have to be carried out in one installation, tabulators are not usually standard machines; they are made up of standard components, and the final specification is arranged by the investigator to suit the types of work envisaged.

The tabulator reads perforations and will print or process any desired figure or letter from any one perforation or a combination of perforations. The layout of the printing depends on the type of work; for example, on an invoice it may be required to print the number of the items sold in the second field from the left, but on a sales analysis the first field on the left may be preferred.

This disposition is arranged by inserting a "connection box" or plug-board between the card-sensing and printing mechanisms, and this permits considerable latitude in the layout of the final documents. Alphabetical or numerical data can be distributed and processed with equal facility.

Cards are automatically fed into the tabulator at speeds of up to 150 a minute, and the information on each card can be printed out in one cycle. At the same time, quantitive information can be added or subtracted, and the machine will automatically print totals—sub, progressive, or grand—or strike balances where debits and credits have been fed in. Since it is not always required to print every item, details

FIG. 93.—*Tabulator with Summary Card Punch*

The purpose of this machine is to transcribe the information already punched into the cards automatically on to payrolls, invoices, stores records, etc. The left-hand unit (shown disconnected) punches cards with the totalled data printed by the right-hand unit.

can be suppressed and the machine set to print totals or balances only.

Various types of paper-feeding mechanism are available which allow of normal line spacing for straightforward tabulation such as paysheets. The feed can also be controlled automatically, sometimes from holes in the cards, to give variable long spaces such as might be required for invoicing. In such a case the invoice form would be located automatically at the correct place to start printing the name and address, after which it would space several inches to reach the correct point to print the details and total. After the total has been printed the form is ejected from the carriage and the next form brought into position.

Tabulators are made to suit the size of card used, and the standard components available make it possible to process data and print forms for practically any branch of accounting work.

COMPUTING

The application of electronic digital computers to cost accountancy is a specialised study, but as certain types of these machines are suitable for integration into conventional punched-card installations a brief description of their functions is included.

The main difference between the punch–sort–tabulate technique and computing techniques is that the few responsibilities left to operators in the former are automatically carried out in the latter. Instead of a series of machines controlled by separate operators, the computer has its various units coupled electrically so data can be automatically passed between them at very high speed.

The master unit is that which does the calculating, and as it may be capable of thousands of calculations per second, far beyond human capacity, it is regulated by an automatic device known as a programme controller.

The controller is fed with a programme of instructions which is worked out in advance and which tells the machine what to do with the data to be processed. It is retained in the machine for as long as is required to complete the processing.

The media on which both programme and data are recorded may be punched cards, perforated paper tape, or magnetic tape, some of the largest machines using combinations of all three.

There is also a storage or memory unit which can store the programme and which is also used for holding partial products which may be necessary to a calculation but not required for records. For example, in a wages calculation the payment for overtime might be computed by multiplying the hours worked by the standard rate, the product being stored. Then the hours might be multiplied by the uplift rate, say, 25% and that product stored. On the next instruction the two products are added together and the sum recorded. Actually the store plays a very important part, as the machine is capable of only the very simplest of arithmetic in any one step, and a calculation which would be simple mentally may necessitate storing many partial results before the final one can be recorded.

The store is also used for holding constants which are fed in before processing and which may be applied repeatedly, without having to be fed in afresh for every calculation. Again, in wages work, the taxable income having been calculated, constants are applied to calculate the income tax payable.

A useful function of the computer is its ability to chose between alternative courses of action; this is used in the tax-calculation example.

but to even greater advantage in Stores control work. Here it is possible for the machine, having struck a balance in stock, to compare it with the desirable minimum or maximum and print out a special record if there is a discrepancy. The Stores controller is thus relieved of the work of visually examining possibly thousands of balances, the majority of which are normal.

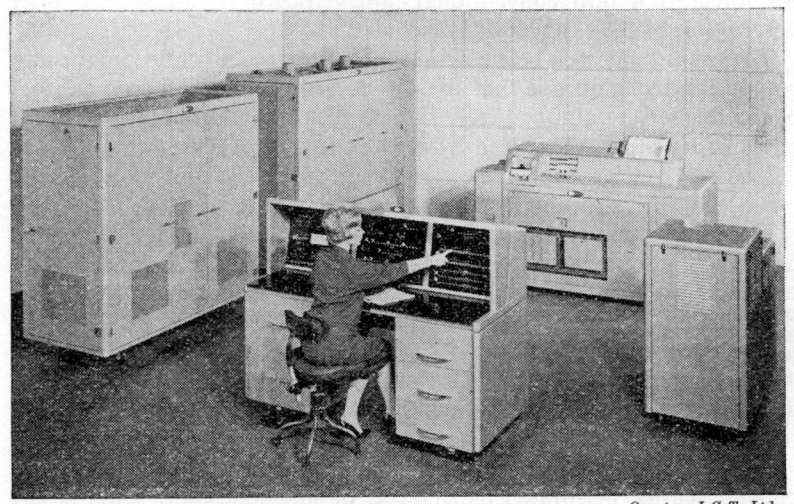

Courtesy I.C.T. Ltd.

FIG. 94.—*Computer Installation*

This installation is not only able to process data fed to it at incredibly high speeds, but has a coupled printing device attached to it which directly records the results in printed form.

The computers which function solely with punched cards fall into two main groups. One type records results in punched cards, which are in turn tabulated to produce the printed records, and the other in addition has a coupled printing device which directly records results in printed form (*see* Fig. 94). Both may be integrated with other punched-card machines, but the latter needs only punching and sorting machines to make a complete data-processing installation.

CHAPTER 32

THE APPLICATION OF PUNCHED-CARD MACHINES TO COSTING

CHOICE OF EQUIPMENT

THERE are few industries where punched-card techniques cannot be applied with advantage to costing and allied work, and since the introduction of smaller cards and machines, the size of a business is no longer a criterion.

The applications which are described in this chapter are not, therefore, restricted to one type of industry nor to large organisations, and although some generalisation has been necessary, the applications are based on actual installations.

Strictly speaking, the size of a manufacturing business alone has no bearing on its suitability for using punched cards, and it is necessary to consider the complexity of the product as well as the quantities in which it is made. Obviously there are big products, such as ocean-going liners, which are built only by large firms, but there are also simple products made by large or small organisations which can be satisfactorily costed on even 21-column machines. The choice of machine and card size cannot, therefore, be based on one factor alone.

Complications do arise when a firm makes a variety of products, and some sacrifice of economy or speed in some stages of the system may be necessary to arrive at the best overall efficiency. In smaller concerns it may also be desirable to include work other than costing, such as payroll, invoicing, etc., and consequently the final choice of machine may depend upon many factors. Punched-card machines are very flexible in operation, and consequently can be successfully applied in most industries and to a wide range of sizes of manufacturing unit.

In costing services, such as those found in local government, hospitals, etc., where there is little or no manufacturing, it is the magnitude of the factors and the volume of movement which mainly influence the choice of equipment; here again no particular size of machine can be said to be universally the best for one particular field.

USES OF SOME MACHINES

As an example of the use of the smallest machines, a simple job-costing application, for which a flow chart is illustrated (Fig. 95), has been chosen. This is based on a concern whose products are mainly

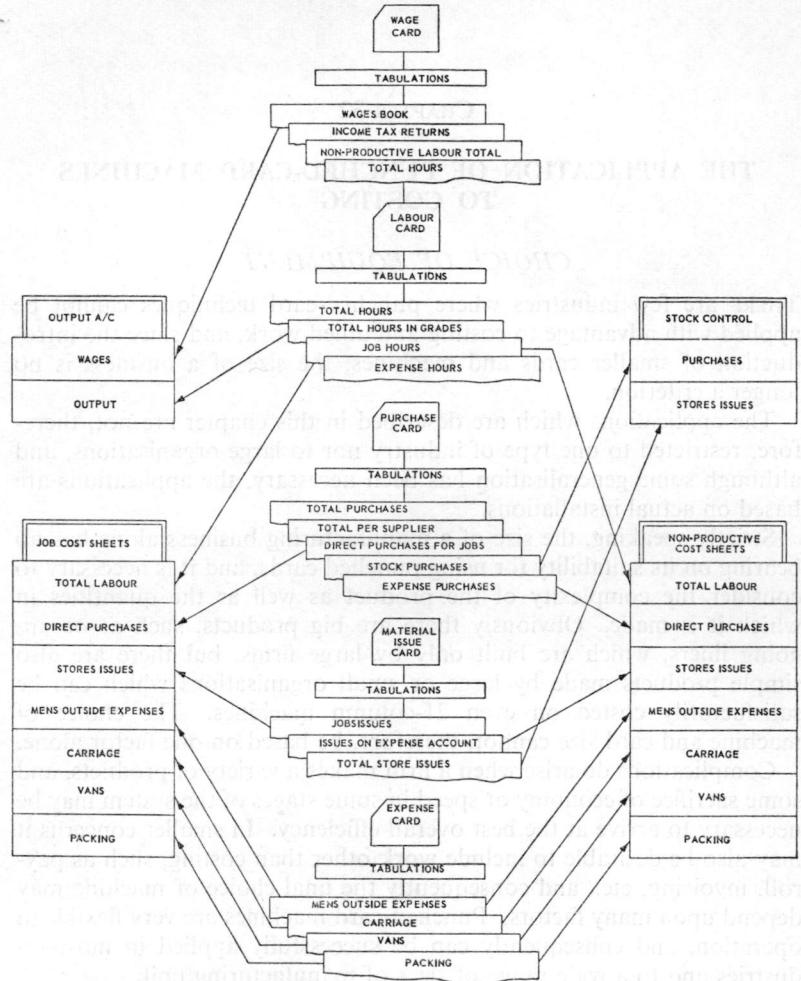

FIG. 95.—*Flow Chart—Job Costing*

This shows an application of punched card accounting which could be tackled by one of the smallest machines.

made to individual requirements and which are the subject of maintenance contracts after the goods have been delivered. So the problem resolves itself into:

1. Ascertaining the cost of manufacture of each product.
2. Ascertaining the cost of maintenance under each service agreement.

CODING

The codes for this work are simple, but follow principles which can be used in more complex applications.

Job or maintenance code

A six-figure number indicating class of job (1 digit), district (1 digit), and job number (4 digits).

Materials code

A five-figure code indicating store and class of materials.

Employee's code

A four-figure number indicating class of employee (1 digit) branch or department where working (1 digit), and individual's number (2 digits).

Accounts code

A three-figure code indicating financial accounts and standing order numbers.

As far as possible, the codes are correlated so as to use the same numbers for similar information in different codes. For example, Job No. 621293 and Employee No. 6293 indicate:

Job. No. 621293	Employee No. 6293
6—Maintenance job	6—Maintenance electrician
2—Glasgow	2—Glasgow staff
1293—Maintenance contract no.	93—Employee's no. in branch

To accommodate the various charges which have to be handled, five different card forms are used:

1. Purchase Card.
2. Materials (or Stores) Card.
3. Wages Card.
4. Labour Card.
5. Expense Card.

In practice, the cards are in different colours for each class of charge, but red cards of the same designs are used for all credits.

Purchase Cards

Incoming invoices provide the basic data for punching, and these are coded manually. An automatic key punch is used and one card (Fig. 96) punched for every item chargeable to job, contract, Financial Account, or Stores Account. After verification, these cards are accumulated to

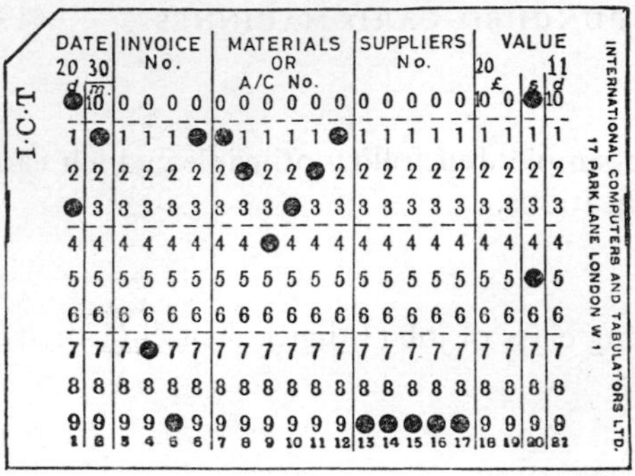

FIG. 96.—*Purchase Card* *(left)*

These cards are punched from incoming invoices to provide information as to Purchases and Creditors.

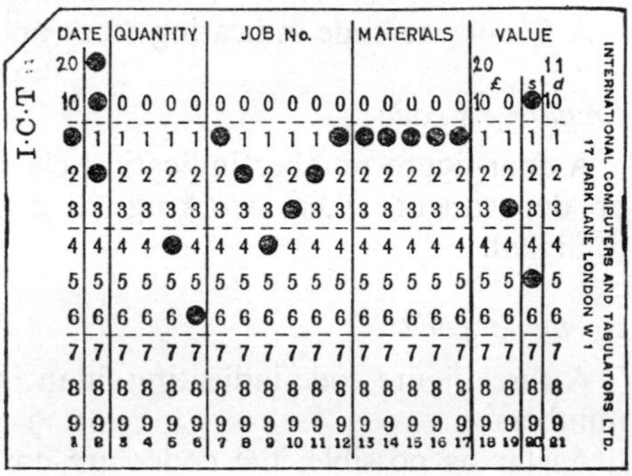

FIG. 97.—*Material Requisition Card* *(right)*

Hand-written Material Requisitions are converted into punched cards for sorting and tabulating.

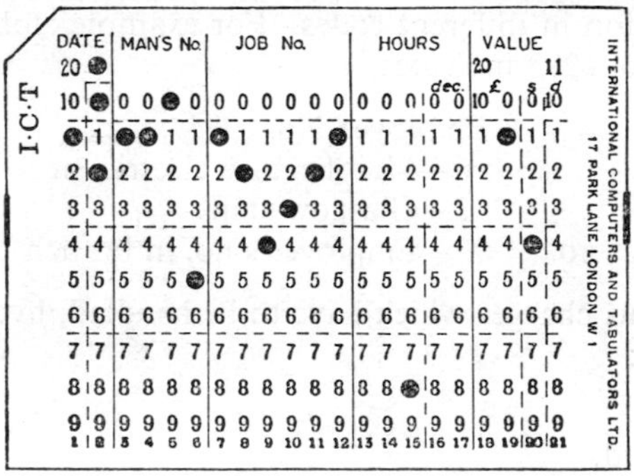

FIG. 98.—*Labour Card* *(left)*

This card is based on the worker's job tickets. The hours worked on a job is however multiplied by a rate calculated to recover labour and overhead together.

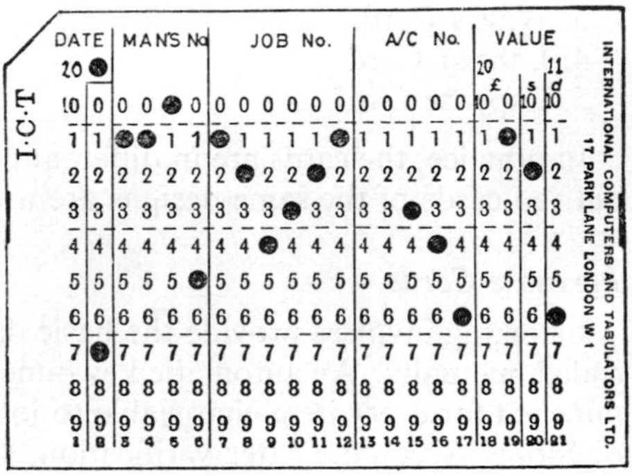

FIG. 99.—*Expense Card* *(right)*

This card is punched for all expenses chargeable to jobs.

the end of the month, when they are sorted and tabulated to produce the following statements:

1. In invoice number order to arrive at total purchases and for proving other totals;
2. In suppliers order to give totals for posting to the Bought Ledger.
3. In Financial and Stores Account number order for Budgetary Control purposes.

Materials Cards

Hand-written requisitions are used to control the issue of all materials from Stores, and these are similarly coded. Cards (Fig. 97) are punched from them, sorted to department number, and then tabulated to arrive at the total credits to each of the various stores. They are then resorted to job-number order and placed in the work-in-progress file.

When the purchase Cards (referred to above) are being punched a materials Card is also punched for those items which are directly chargeable to a job number. These cards, after verification, are immediately sorted to job-number order and filed in the work-in-progress files.

Wages Cards

These cards are not directly associated with the job costing, but provide statistics for management which may affect overhead costs.

The wages are prepared each week from clock cards, and punched cards are made therefrom. They provide tabulations which form the Wages Book and show the total hours worked and wages paid in each department, the figures also being used for proving subsequent analyses.

Labour Cards

The information punched into these cards (Fig. 98) is obtained from worker's daily dockets. In computing the "value" item (*i.e.* hours × rate) on these dockets the normal pay rate is not used as the multiplicand but a special "output" rate; this includes an element for the particular departmental overhead rate.

The cards are checked by tabulating and comparing the total hours with similar totals from the wage cards and then analysed by department. The latter tabulation reveals if the weekly scheme of work is truly carrying the overhead expense.

Other tabulations provide totals of hours worked by each grade of employee, by job, and by expense allocation, after which the cards go to the work-in-progress file.

Expense Cards

These cards (Fig. 99) are punched for all expenses chargeable to jobs or standing maintenance orders and include such items as packing, delivery, travelling, etc. After proving, these cards also go to the work-in-progress file.

JOB COST STATEMENTS

On the completion of each job the cards are extracted from the file and tabulated to show the detailed and total expenditure on the job (*see* Fig. 100).

The general overhead charge is then applied as a percentage and the total immediately compared with the charge to the customer. Actually, this total is entered on a copy of the invoice so that the profit or loss is immediately discernible and ready for investigation, if necessary. The Cost Sheet illustrated shows the breakdown of the charges prior to the application of the overheads.

The application described above is a typical example of the use of the smallest punched-card machines. It also illustrates how a small amount of inconvenience is tolerated, through having to punch two cards (Purchase and Materials) from incoming invoices, in the interest of economy.

If there had been a considerable number of direct-material items it would probably have been advisable to use larger equipment, say 40-column, which would permit the amalgamation of Purchase and Material card designs, and so reduce the punching and processing time.

COSTING FOR LOCAL AUTHORITIES WITH MEDIUM-SIZED MACHINES

In the earlier editions of this book it was foreseen that ever-increasing attention would be paid to costing in local authorities, and reference was also made to the desirability of some measures of centralisation and standardisation in the methods of financial control.

In recent years much progress had been made along these lines, and the student is referred to the Institute of Municipal Treasurers and Accountants' publication *The Form of Published Accounts of Local Authorities*. These developments, added to the closer liaison with central government departments which has resulted in increased standardisation, have led to wide use of mechanical procedures.

While all sizes of punched-card equipment are used by local authorities, the 40-column machines have proved adequate in quite a large number of cases; and because of the moderate price, they are within the reach of many authorities who could not, economically, justify larger machines. In order to give this section the widest appeal, the functions of county or borough authorities have not been segregated under such groupings, but treated as individual accounting problems.

Much of the costing work in local authorities is for services such as

DATE		MAN'S No.	JOB No.	HOURS		VALUE
Day	Mth.			Hrs.	Dec.	
LABOUR						
6	1	1 1 0 5	1 2 4 3 2 1	8	0 0	1. 4. 0
6	1	1 1 0 4	1 2 4 3 2 1	8	0 0	1. 4. 0
6	1	1 1 1 1	1 2 4 3 2 1	3	0 0	5. 0
6	1	1 1 1 3	1 2 4 3 2 1	3	0 0	5. 0
1 3	1	1 1 0 5	1 2 4 3 2 1	6	0 0	18. 0
1 3	1	1 1 0 4	1 2 4 3 2 1	6	0 0	18. 0
		TINSMITHS TOTAL		3 4	0 0	4.14. 0 *
6	1	1 2 0 2	1 2 4 3 2 1	3	0 0	6. 6
6	1	1 2 0 7	1 2 4 3 2 1	1	0 0	2. 2
6	1	1 2 0 3	1 2 4 3 2 1	1	5 0	1. 11
		BLACKSMITHS TOTAL		5	5 0	10. 7 *
2 0	1	2 3 0 7	1 2 4 3 2 1	8	0 0	8. 0
		PAINT TOTAL		8	0 0	8. 0 *
2 4	1	4 2 0 5	1 2 4 3 2 1	7	0 0	16. 4
2 4	1	4 2 1 7	1 2 4 3 2 1	7	0 0	16. 4
2 7	1	4 2 0 5	1 2 4 3 2 1	8	5 0	19. 10
2 7	1	4 2 1 7	1 3 4 3 2 1	8	5 0	19. 10
		OUTSIDE ELECTRICIANS TOTAL		3 1	0 0	3.12. 4 *
			TOTAL LABOUR			1 5.15. 9 **
MATERIAL						
6	1		1 2 4 3 2 1	1 1 1	1 1	3. 15. 0
			TINSMITHS			3. 15. 0 *
6	1		1 2 4 3 2 1	1 2 1	1 1	8. 10
			BLACKSMITHS			8. 10 *
2 4	1		1 2 4 3 2 1	6 2 1	1 1	1.15. 0
			CABLE			1.15. 0 *
			TOTAL MATERIAL			1 5. 6. 3 **
EXPENSES						
2 3	1		1 2 4 3 2 1	1	6 7	17. 6
			PACKING			17. 6 *
2 4	1		1 2 4 3 2 1	1	2 3	6. 6
			TRAVELLING			6. 6 *
			TOTAL EXPENSES			4. 1. 6 **
MATERIAL BOUGHT OUT		QUANTITY	MATERIALS			
1 3	1	9 1	1 2 4 3 2 1	9 9 9 9 9		15. 0 *
1 7	1	6 4	1 2 4 3 2 1	9 9 9 9 9		8. 9 *
8	1	1 1	1 2 4 3 2 1	9 9 9 9 9		12. 0 *
			TOTAL MATERIAL BOUGHT OUT			1.15. 9 **
			TOTAL COST			3 6.19. 3

FIG. 100.—*Job Cost Statement*

This tabulation is made from the filed cards as soon as a job is finished.

cleansing, highways, education, etc., and although unit costing does arise, in house construction, for example, the work in connection with highways costing has been selected for the main description because of the diversity of factors which have to be taken into account. In some authorities, of course, the costing work is a small percentage of the total, and is part of a fully integrated expenditure-control scheme; in others, some county councils particularly, its volume is great enough to justify an exclusive installation.

CODING

The codes used for highways costing are special to the work, but, of course, linked with the main expenditure codes which cover all services. The special headings are:

Division (2 digits)—1st digit—Territorial division
2nd digit—Sub-location (Repair Depot, Garage, etc.).

Main number (3 digits)—Road classification (Class 1-100
Class 2-200, etc.
330 unclassified
400 major improvements
900-999 sundry charges).

Sub number (4 digits)—Job No.
Work (2 digits)—Class of work (surfacing, footpaths, etc.).

Repairs to highways involve the use of plant, labour, and materials; and for these further codes are used. Plant is identified by a simple three-digit code: the first indicates the class (lorry, road-roller, etc.) and the second two the actual vehicle number.

Labour is coded by using the employee's number, one digit of which gives the grade (driver, labourer, etc.), and materials by a sectional code. Two digits indicate the class of material and three the item and size where applicable.

PLANT ACCOUNTING

The maintenance and construction of roads involves the use of expensive plant and vehicles, and the cost of running and maintaining such equipment contributes substantially to the total cost of each job. Two problems are associated: (*a*) building up the cost of supplying and running the plant; and (*b*) the extraction of statistics to guide economic usage and in conjunction with (*a*) to arrive at charging rates. The factors to be covered include driver's wages, fuel, lubricants, repairs, tyres, sundries, licences and insurance, depreciation, and garaging.

Time is first recorded by the driver or operator on Daily Time Sheets, and is then summarised on to weekly records which are maintained in the office. The form (Fig. 101) when completed includes a

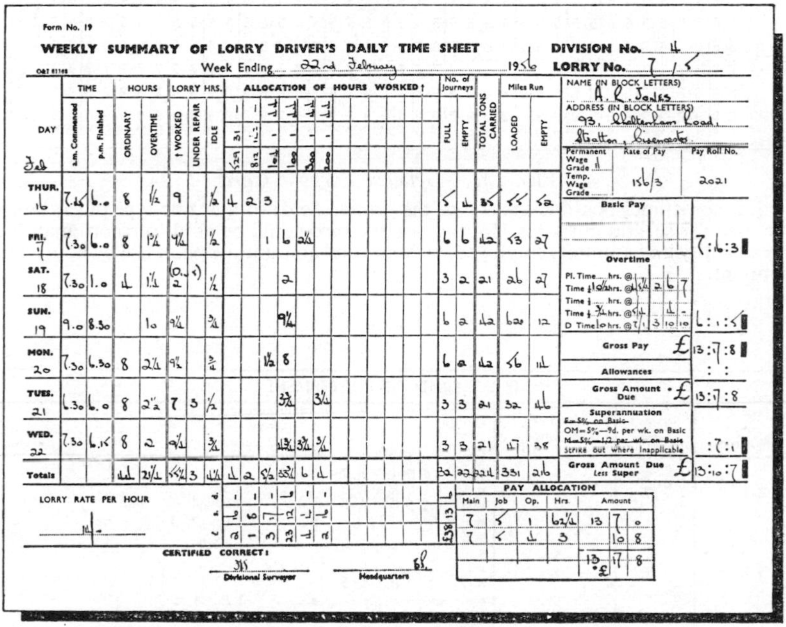

FIG. 101.—*Lorry Driver's Weekly Summary*

This is a hand-written record but is arranged in coding order: subsequent punching is easily carried out.

comprehensive record of the work done each week by the employee concerned and carries all the necessary coding ready for punching.

The card design (Fig. 102) has been standardised for several tasks and can be used for other services as well as highways. Several cards are punched from the information on the Summary Record and are used in the preparation of payroll (gross wages), wages costs, allocation of vehicle costs, and statistics.

The cards for wages costs only are used for Plant Accounting, and these may be augmented by similar cards punched from Job Tickets which are made out for repairs to plant or tyres.

If materials have been used on repairs, for example, they are covered by a Stores Issue Note, and a card is punched for each item. For spare parts pre-punched cards may be used, the cards being punched from the

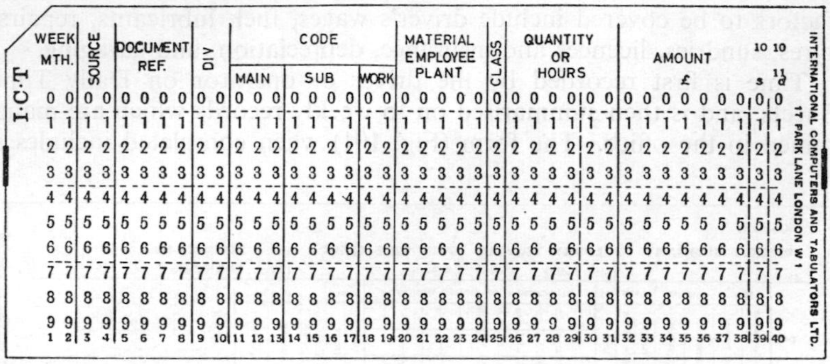

FIG. 102.—*General Purpose Card*

It is sometimes possible to arrange the printed fields so that one type of card may be used for several purposes. In this case the card could be used to record material by quantity and amount; employees by hours and amount; or plant use by hours and amount.

PLANT GROUP COST STATEMENT

SOURCE OF EXPENDITURE	VEHICLE GROUP	CLASS OF EXPENDITURE			EXPENDITURE TO			
1	7	1	**	274. 5. 7				
21	7	1	*	76. 1. 8				
			**	350. 7. 3				
			*		*	350. 7. 3		
			**					
2	7	3	*	13. 12. 7				
52	7	3	*	4. 11. 10				
			**	18. 4. 5				
			*		*	18. 4. 5		
			**					
1	7	4	*	38. 18. 3				
2	7	4	*	5. 19. 1				
7	7	4	*	4. 3				
21	7	4	*	11. 14. 0				
22	7	4	*	32. 0. 8				
			**	88. 16. 3				
			*		*	88. 16. 3		
			**					
2	7	5	*	114. 19. 7				
			**	114. 19. 7				
			*		*	114. 19. 7		
			**					
7	7	7	*	5. 0				
			**	5. 0				
			*		*	5. 0		
			**					
1	7	8	*	2. 2. 1				
21	7	8	*	11. 4				
			**	2. 13. 5				
			*		*	2. 13. 5	*	575. 5. 11

FIG. 103.—*Plant Group Cost Statement*

This is a tabulation of expenses incurred by a Local Authority in respect of certain groups of plant. It will be seen that the automatic sorter has not only grouped the cards by vehicle classification but also under expenditure headings. The tabulator throws out sub-totals for each section of expenditure, and a grand total at the end.

incoming invoices, when the goods are received, and kept in a file. When a part is issued it is then only necessary to extract the corresponding card, already priced, and punch in the vehicle number, etc.

Similar cards are punched for every item of expense and accumulated until the end of the month, when they are sorted together under the plant group number and type of expense and a tabulation of a Plant Group Cost Statement (Fig. 103) made. Should any of the group figures appear anomalous, it is re-tabulated with full details of each item of plant in the group.

Detailed statements are correlated with the vehicle statistics and the average running costs calculated. The cost is usually worked out on the basis of a rate per hour, and is used for comparison with previous figures and for charging out the use of plant.

Although the cost is computed at more frequent intervals, the charging-out rate is usually based on several years' (three is quite usual) running to avoid abnormal uplifts which might be caused if a major overhaul were charged into a short period.

PLANT STATISTICS

The plant and vehicle statistics are extracted from cards which are punched from the Summary Record and include ton/miles run and fuel consumption, etc.; these are used by the engineers as well as for arriving at the charging rate mentioned above.

HIGHWAYS COSTS

The main items which make up the total cost of repairs or construction are employees' wages, materials, and plant usage cost. The amounts for wages, other than for employees working with plant, are computed on Time Sheets from which cards are punched.

The extraction of material costs is linked with the Stores accounting procedure, which covers issues, receipt, returns, manufactured, and so on. Cards are punched from Requisition Notes and returns, and are used both for tabulating the Stores Ledgers, in conjunction with cards for the other entries, and for calculating the cost figures. The charges for plant usage are punched into cards from the data on the Record Summary and include the wages of the driver.

At the end of each month all the cards are sorted together on the code and a tabulation (Fig. 104) made which shows the total cost of each job subdivided by the class of work and source (labour, materials, etc.). In some authorities this tabulation has to be broken down to make returns, according to the class of road, to the county authority or to the Ministry of Transport.

PROGRESSIVE COST STATEMENT							
SOURCE OF EXP.	DIVISION	MAIN CODE	JOB CODE	OPERATION CODE	VALUE	ACCUMULATIVE TOTALS	CHARTING TOTALS
1	6	1 0 3	1		* 8 4. 7. 9		
2	6	1 0 3	1		* 1 7. 4. 3		
3	6	1 0 3	1		* 1 5 5 19.10		
4	6	1 0 3	1		* 1 1. 8. 0		
5	6	1 0 3	1		* 3. 0 0		
6	6	1 0 3	1		* 1 2. 3. 9		
7	6	1 0 3	1		* 1. 2. 9		
8	6	1 0 3	1		* 59.10 4		
					* ※ 3 4 4. 16. 8		
1	6	1 0 3	1	1	* 1 2. 18 4		
2	6	1 0 3	1	1	* 9 7. 6		
3	6	1 0 3	1	1	* 2 0.10 6		
					* ※ 4 2. 16. 4		
1	6	1 0 3	1	1 1	* 2. 1 3.10		
					* ※ 2. 1 3.10		
1	6	1 0 3	1	1 2	* 6. 5. 9		
6	6	1 0 3	1	1 2	* 5. 0		
					* ※ 6.10 9	* 3 9 6.17 7	* 3 9 6.1 7. 7

FIG. 104.—*Accumulated Costs: Highways*

This figure shows how cards recording such diverse costs as Wages, Materials, and Plant usage, may be sorted under jobs and types of expense, and then tabulated to give the total cost of each job.

OTHER SERVICES

As the main code is designed to include all the main heads of expenditure and the card designed to accommodate it, the same form can be used for punching all types of expenses regardless of the service or department, the periodical tabulations (Fig. 105) made from these being similar to that made for the highways costing. It does not necessarily have to be in such fine detail, and in many cases it mainly provides a progress check against the annual estimates and the public accounts.

STANDARD COSTING IN THE STEEL INDUSTRY

Iron ore is the basic ingredient of all forms of steel, but it is submitted to many processes before emerging as a finished product. These processes are rarely all found in one location, some works being devoted to the earlier smelting stages and others to the intermediate or finishing operations. For this section a works has been selected which receives the steel in large billets or slabs and via a number of operations converts them into finished bars or sheet.

When the system was introduced at this plant the first task was to set up the Standard Cost rates for each operation, and these are subject to modification only when experience reveals the need or when new products are introduced.

The rates are punched into cards for each and every operation, the cards being kept in a standing file and used repeatedly each week or month. The cards (Fig. 106, at back) contain the Product and Operation codes, the Charged Value, Scrap Value, Standard Material Value, and Standard Production Value (these values are rates chargeable per ton or $\frac{1}{100}$ ton for smaller quantities). Although only one card design is used, separate cards are made for each of the rates to facilitate subsequent machine operations.

CUMULATIVE EXPENDITURE TABULATION

MONTH OR WEEK	SOURCE OF EXPENDITURE	DOCUMENT REFERENCE	MAIN EXPENDITURE CODE	SUBDIVISION FOR SPECIAL JOBS	EMPLOYEE No. OR COMMODITY CODE OR PLANT No.	AMOUNT
8	O		350200			1 8 0. 2. 6
3 6	1		350200		W 2 2 9	8.11
3 6	1		350200		W 2 5 1	7. 6
3 6	1		350200		W 4 2 2	1. 6. 6
3 6	2	2 5 3 0	350200		P O 7 7	1. 4
3 6	2	2 5 3 0	350200		S O 8 9	11
3 6	2	2 5 3 0	350200		T 2 8 3	2. 5
3 6	2	2 5 3 0	350200		B 1 3 3	5. 6
3 7	2	2 5 4 6	350200		S O 2 7	1
3 7	2	2 5 4 8	350200		G O O 4	6. 8
3 9	2	2 5 6 8	350200		B O 5 5	1 4. 4
3 9	3		3 5 0 2 0 0		T 2 1 2	4. 8
9	4		350200		S 1 7 6	1 0. 6
9	4		350200		S 1 7 5	1 1. 9
9	4		350200		S 1 8 5	5. 6
9	5	M O O 8	350200		B R K E T S	2. 6
9	5	S O 1 9	350200		D P U L L S	4. 6
9	5	S O 2 5	350200		R E P S	1 4. 1 3. 11
9	5	T O 1 8	350200		M A T S 1 N	5. 4
9	5	G O 4 9	350200		B U L B S	1. 5. 0
					*	2 0 2. 0. 4
8	O		350245	O 1		8 7 2. 1 3.11
3 6	1		350245	O 1	W 6 9	1 0. 3
3 6	1		350245	O 1	W 7 7	1 0. 3
3 6	1		350245	O 1	W 3 2 8	1 0. 6
9	5	B O 5 7	350245	O 1 S	L E A D	1. 1 5. 0
9	5	B O 5 7	350245	O 1 S	L E A D	1. 4. 0
9	5	S O 2 5	350245	O 1 L	1 G H T S	5 6. 9. 2
9	5	T O 1 2	350245	O 1 L	1 F T S	1 0. 1
9	5	G O 5 1	350245	O 1	1 N S C L	3 2. 3. 7
					*	9 6 6. 6. 9
8	O		350245	O 2		1 0. 1 9. 5
3 6	1		350245	O 2	W 3 5 1	9. 3
3 6	1		350245	O 2	W 3 6 3	1 4. 7
3 6	1		350245	O 2	W 4 5 9	1 1. 7
3 6	3		350245	O 2	T 2 1 2	9. 4
9	5		350245	O 2	H T R A N S	2. 4. 0
					*	1 5. 8. 2

FIG. 105.—*Accumulated Costs: Other Services*

Other services as well as Highways can be catered for. This shows another tabulation of cumulative expenditure for a department in a Local Authority.

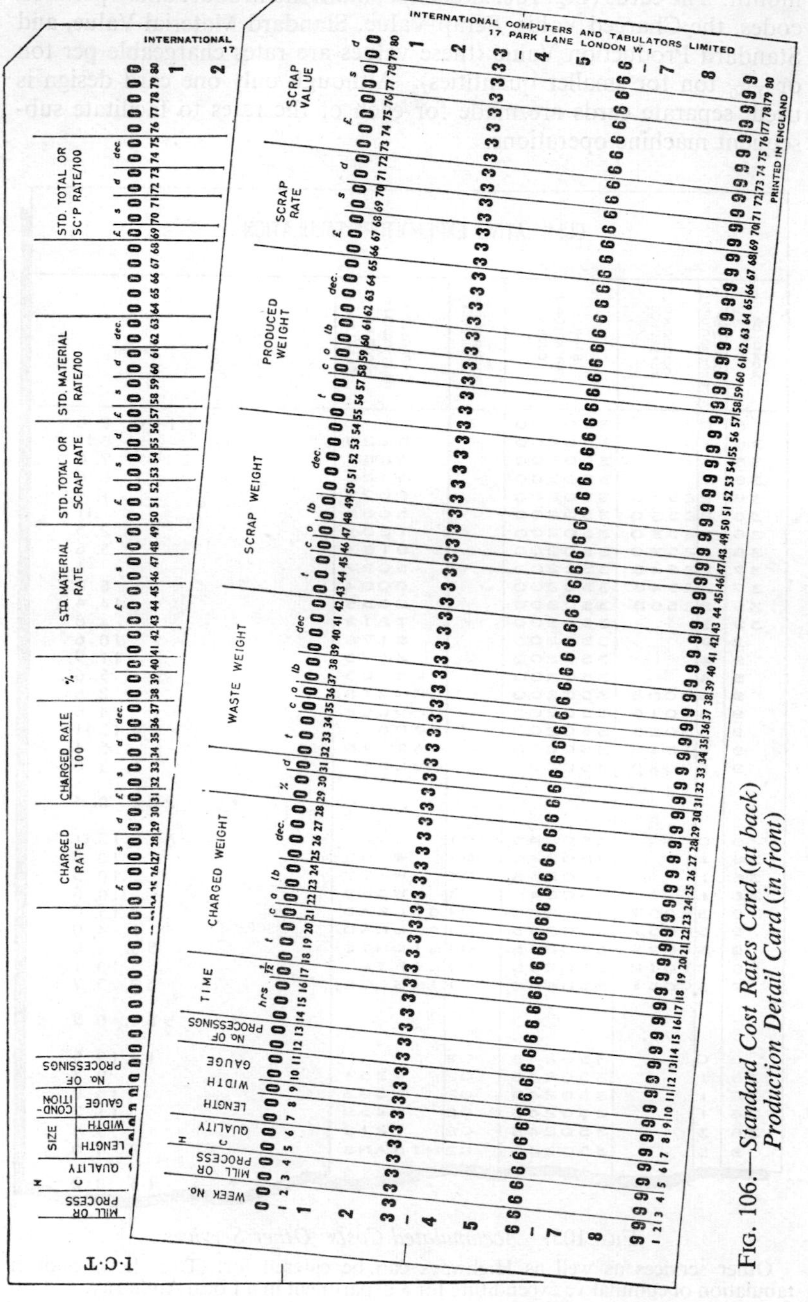

FIG. 106.—*Standard Cost Rates Card (at back)*
Production Detail Card (in front)

PRODUCTION COST

Production is in "batches," and weekly Production Records from each process point show the details of the batches passing through. The record includes the following information:

Week Number
Department or Process Number
Product Code Number
Time Taken
Charged Weight: (The actual weight received at the start of the process.)
Waste Weight: (An allowance for natural weight reductions when processing, and is applied as a percentage.)
Scrap Weight: (The weight of metal scrapped in the process. This may be recoverable later.)
Produced Weight: (The weight of good production in the particular operation.)

A Production Detail Card (Fig. 106, in front) is punched with the above information for each batch or each report and verified in the usual way. The cards are then processed through an electronic calculator which converts all the avoirdupois fractional weights into decimals and punches the equivalents into the same card. For example, 2 tons 5 cwt becomes 2·25 tons. This considerably simplifies and speeds up subsequent operations.

To check the conversions, the cards are tabulated and totals of groups taken. The decimal totals are converted back to avoirdupois and compared with the tabulated avoirdupois. If these figures agree it is not necessary to check each card.

In the next operation the scrap value is computed; this is done by taking the Scrap Rate Cards and first sorting them together with the Production Details Cards into Product number order. The cards are then passed through the electronic calculator, which senses and stores the scrap rate from the first (Rate) card of each group and applies it as a multiplier to the quantities sensed from each following Detail Card, the extensions being punched into the same Detail Card. When another Rate Card is sensed the rate in store in the machine is automatically changed.

The cards are next separated and the Rate Cards filed away for future use. The Detail Cards are used to make tabulations with totals for each product to provide progress figures for each product at each stage of production. This is done weekly.

At the month end all the Detail Cards are sorted on the product code and tabulated. The results show the monthly total production and scrap figures for each product. While this tabulation is being made a summary card punch coupled to the tabulator automatically punches a

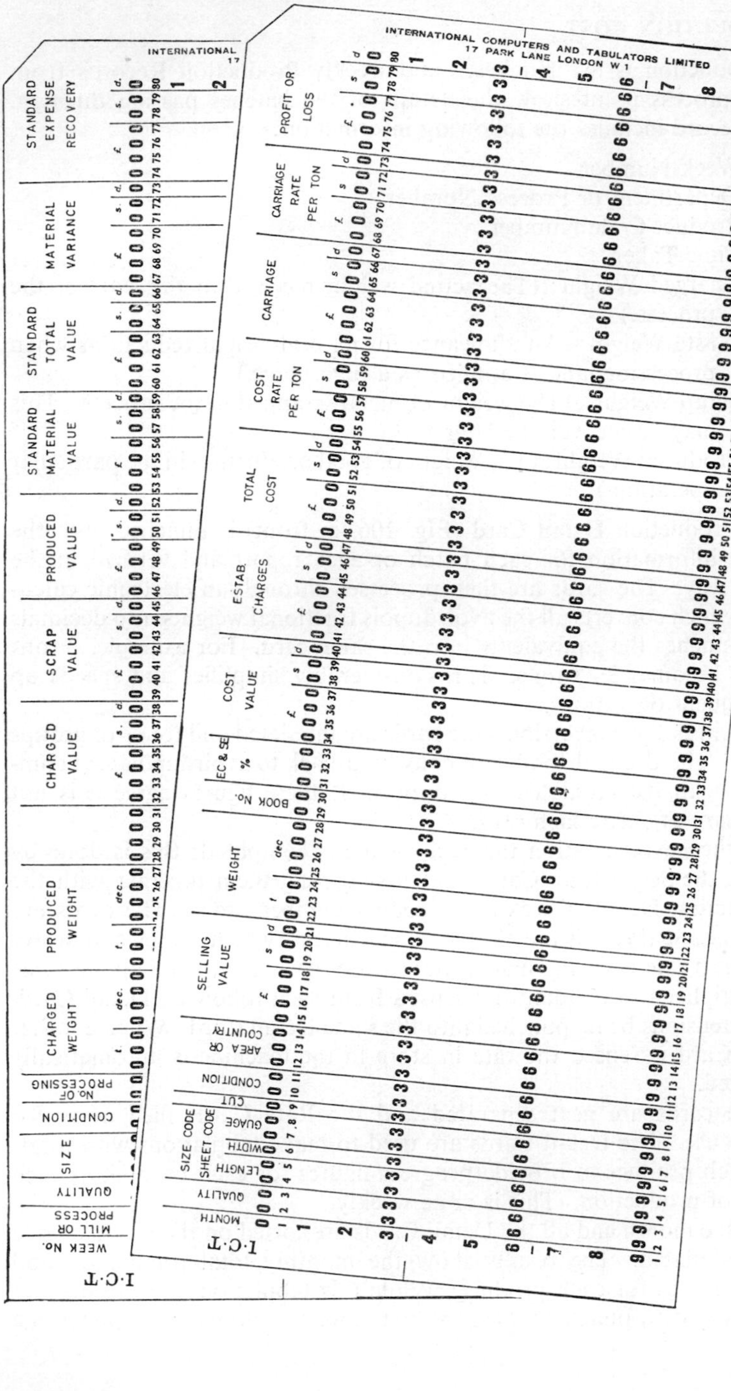

FIG. 107.—*Material Variance Card (at back)*
Sales Cost Summary Card (in front)

summary card for each product with: (A) Period; (B) Department or Process No.; (C) Product Code; (D) Charged Weight; (E) Produced Weight (with decimal fraction); and (F) Scrap Value. This summary card (Fig. 107, at back) has a different form and is called the Material Variance Card, and there is one for every product passing through each operation.

The appropriate Rate Cards are next "married in" with the Variance Cards on an interpolator and the combined groups passed through the electronic calculator to arrive at the following figures:

Charged Weight (D) $\times$ Rate (Z) = Charged Value (G)

Produced Weight (E) $\times$ Standard Material Rate (Y) = Standard Value (I)

Produced Weight (E) $\times$ Standard Total Rate (X) = Standard Total Value (J)

Charged Value (G) $-$ Scrap Value (F) = Produced Value (H)

Produced Value (H) $-$ Standard Material Value (I) = Material Variance

Standard Total Value (J) $-$ Standard Material Value (I) = Standard Expense Recovery

The results are automatically punched by the electronic calculator into the same Variance Card as carries the relevant factors, excepting the X, Y, and Z factors, which are sensed from the Rate Cards.

The Variance Cards are next tabulated and the schedule (Fig. 108) which is produced provides a comprehensive report on the month's working on each product.

NON-PRODUCTION COSTS

The procedure for bringing in non-production items and building up to total costs commences on the sales side, where in the first instance cards are punched from copy invoices, the relevant data for this work being the product details and the weight and value of steel sold.

These cards are subjected to processing similar to that on the production cards, and this includes conversion of the weights to decimals, sorting to product code, and tabulating to produce Sales Cost Summary Cards (Fig. 107, at front).

Rate Cards are maintained which carry the following factors:

Establishment Charges and Selling Expense; percentage to be applied to the Sales Value.

Production Cost

Carriage Cost

The last two factors are punched as a rate per ton and per $\frac{1}{100}$ ton for applying to large or small quantity sales respectively.

PRODUCT CODE	PRODUCED WEIGHT TONS	CHARGED VALUE	SCRAP VALUE	PRODUCED VALUE	STANDARD MATERIAL VALUE	STANDARD TOTAL VALUE	MATERIAL VARIANCE	STANDARD EXPENSE RECOVERY
1000 31	19937	480.14.7	15. 0.8-	465.13.11	426.19.6	441.18. 5	38.14.5 +	14.18.11 +
1000 41	297992	6644. 1.3	196. 6.0-	6447.15.3	6381.17.5	6505. 4.10	65.17.10+	223. 7.5 +
1600 41	41924	1004.12.8	62.12.8-	942. 0.0	904.19.3	936.17.11	37. 0.9 +	31.18.8 +
2000 31	875	12.11.2		19.11.2	16.13.5	19. 5. 7	17.9 +	12. 2 +
2000 41	125545	2712.13 0	43.13.8-	2668.19.4	2678.14.3	2766. 3. 6	9.14.11-	87. 9.3 +
2000 51	11000	233 3.1	2. 1.10-	231. 1.3	234.14.1	242. 7. 4	3.12.10-	7.13.3 +
3000 41	95999	1865. 7.1	32. 0.9-	1833. 6.4	1813. 6.6	1852. 8.4	19.19.10+	39. 1.10+
3000 51	2317	61. 2.11	5.19.7-	55. 3.4	48.171	49.18. 2	6. 6.3 +	1. 1.1 +
4000 51	12884	267.15 8		267.15.8	228. 2.10	244.16.11	39.12.10+	16.14.1 +
4000 61	19987	418. 8.0		418. 8.0	353.16.5	379.16.7	64. 9.7 +	25.16.2 +
4029 41	68673	1498. 5.4	29.11.9-	1468.13.7	1435.11.0	1492. 0. 2	33. 2.7 +	56. 9.2 +
	687133	15205.14 9	387. 6.11-	14818. 7.10	14525.13.9	15030.17. 9	292.14.1 +	505. 4.0 +

FIG. 108.—*Variance Schedule*

This tabulation gives a comprehensive report on the month's working on each product.

SUMMARY OF DELIVERIES and COSTS

WEEKS ENDED _____ 195 ____

SECTION AND DESCRIPTION			DELIVERY		INVOICE VALUE c s d	MANUFACTURING COST c s d	CARRIAGE, FREIGHT AND INSURANCE c s d	ESTABLISHMENT AND SELLING EXPENSES c s d	TOTAL COST c s d	PROFIT — LOSS + c s d
			WEIGHT TONS	RATE						
8 1 0 8 4	1	4 1	4 9 0 1 8		1 0 2 5 6. 7⁻	8 7 5 9 8	1 4. 1 6 7	4 4. 1. 9	9 3 4. 8 0+	9 0. 1 8. 7⁻
8 1 0 8 4	3	4 1	1 5 3 4 8		1 0 0 0 3⁻	1 0 0 1 9 1 1	1. 1 2. 4	4. 6. 0	1 0 6. 1 8. 3+	6 1 8. 0+
	—		5 4 3 6 6.		1 1 2 5. 6 1 0⁻	9 7 6. 9. 7	1 6. 8. 1 1	4 8. 7. 9	* 1 0 4 1. 6. 3+	* 8 4. 0. 7⁻
1 3 1 0 9 S	3	5 1	2 0 2 2 7.		5 5 7. 5. 5⁻	5 3 3. 4. 6	6. 2. 4	2 3. 1 9. 3	5 6 3. 6. 1+	6. 0. 8+
1 3 1 0 9 1	4	5 1	1 8 6 7 9		5 4 2 1 2 3⁻	5 3 2. 1. 7	5. 1 3. 0	2 3. 6. 8	5 6 1. 1. 3+	1 8. 9. 0+
1 3 1 0 9 2	3	5 1	7 0 5 4		1 8 3 1 4. 1 1⁻	1 8 0. 1 3. 0	2. 2. 8	7. 1 8. 0	1 9 0. 1 3. 8+	6 1 8. 9+
			4 5 9 6 0.		1 2 8 3. 1 2 7⁻	1 2 4 5 1 9. 1	1 3. 1 8. 0	5 5. 3 1 1	*· 1 3 1 5. 1. 0+	* 3 1. 8. 5+

Fig. 109.—*Summary of Deliveries and Costs*
This is a final tabulation showing Sales Value, total Costs, and Profit or Loss.

The Sales Cost Cards and the Rate Cards are interpolated and then passed through the electronic computer to calculate and punch the following data:

Cost × Weight Rate/Ton = Cost Value

Establishment Charge % × Selling Value = Establishment Charge

Carriage Rate (£ s. d.) × Weight = Carriage Charge

Cost Value + Establishment Charge + Carriage = Total Cost

Total Cost − Selling Value = Profit or Loss

A final tabulation, the Summary of Deliveries and Cost (Fig. 109), is made from the completed Sales Cost Card.

DEPARTMENTAL COST ACCOUNTS

The cost records are fully integrated with the Financial Accounts, and other analyses are necessary to effect this integration. All other work is, however, processed by the simple punch–sort–tabulate technique described earlier; it is derived from cards punched from vouchers which show the department number and expense head together with the value chargeable.

TERMINOLOGY OF COST ACCOUNTANCY

(Reprinted, by permission, from the official terminology issued by the Institute of Cost and Works Accountants).

Costing Terminology, issued by the authority of the Council of the Institute, was first published in the March 1937 issue of *The Cost Accountant.* Since then it has been used extensively at home and abroad, textbooks have included the terminology in whole or in part, and Government Departments, trade or other associations when establishing systems of accounting or terminologies in which costing terms appear have found it of benefit. This terminology had resulted from work first begun by the founders of the Institute in 1919 and steadily continued throughout the early years of its life.

It was stressed in the introduction to the original terminology that such a list could be neither comprehensive nor final, for like all other forms of living language, the terminology of cost accountancy must evolve and develop in response to the needs of the profession and in accordance with business requirements.

The various committees responsible for subsequent research in this field faced the problem of all lexicographers, for if common English words have changed and are changing their meaning during the course of time, this revised terminology for a technique of relatively recent growth must be subject to like limitations. It is for this reason that no attempt has been made in *Terminology of Cost Accountancy* to include equivalent terms, as was done previously, as it has not been found practicable to relate the shades of meaning of the many terms in common use in an industry, trade, or district to the terms now officially defined.

As in the case of other professions, certain words in everyday use have acquired a particular significance—for example, "land" in the economic sense; thus in this *Terminology of Cost Accountancy,* "expense"—one of the three elements of cost—is given a special meaning, but in common parlance the word could be used also to denote the other two—cost of materials and wages.

If comparison is made with *Costing Terminology,* now superseded, it will be seen that *Terminology of Cost Accountancy* excludes those terms contained in the previous list which do not specifically relate to cost accountancy. The remaining terms concerning cost accountancy have been reviewed, and with few exceptions are included in this new edition, either in their original or in a modified form. On the other hand, a considerable number of new terms have been included which were not in the previous terminology, their appearance resulting mainly from the development of the techniques of Standard Costing and Budgetary Control. When considering the revision of existing definitions and defining new terms, special attention has been paid to the wording so that the definitions can be applied over the whole field of cost accountancy, and every effort has been made to avoid defining terms in such a way that they might have only a limited meaning applicable to a particular type of industry.

This is the first stage in the preparation of a wider terminology incorporating terms covering the whole field of what has become known as Management Accounting. Research work is continuing on this project and the wider terminology will become available at a later date.

As far as students are concerned, *Terminology of Cost Accountancy* came into operation after the June 1952 examinations, after which date all examination questions set by the Board of Examiners were worded in accordance therewith. Candidates therefore will need to acquire a thorough knowledge of these terms of definitions, to enable them not only to understand the questions they have to answer but also to express their answers in orthodox language.

COST ACCOUNTANCY

Cost Accountancy.—The science, art, and practice of a cost accountant.

COSTING

Costing.—The technique and process of ascertaining costs.

TYPES OF COSTING

Historical Costing.—The ascertainment of costs after they have been incurred.

Standard Costing.—The ascertainment and use of standard costs and the measurement and analysis of variances.

Marginal Costing.—The ascertainment, by differentiating between fixed costs and variable costs, of marginal costs, and of the effect on profit of changes in volume or type of output.

Uniform Costing.—The use by several undertakings of the same costing principles and/or practices.

COSTS

Cost.—(*a*) The amount of expenditure incurred on a given thing.

(*b*) To ascertain the cost of a given thing.

Fixed Cost.—A cost which tends to be unaffected by variations in volume of output.

Semi-fixed Cost.—A cost which is partly fixed and partly variable.

Semi-variable Cost.—Semi-fixed cost.

Variable Cost.—A cost which tends to vary directly with variations in volume of output.

Controllable Cost.—A cost which is influenced by the action of a given member of an undertaking.

Uncontrollable Cost.—A cost which is not influenced by the action of a given member of an undertaking.

Normal Cost.—A cost which is normally incurred at a given level of output in the conditions in which that level of output is normally attained.

Abnormal Cost.—A cost which is not normally incurred at a given level of output in the conditions in which that level of output is normally attained.

Primary Costs (Elements of Cost).—Costs which are classified according to the factors upon which expenditure is primarily incurred, viz., cost of materials, wages, and expense.

Material Cost.—The cost of commodities supplied to an undertaking.

Wages.—The cost of remunerating (by wages, salaries, commissions, bonuses, etc.) the employees of an undertaking.

Expense.—The cost of services provided to an undertaking and the notional cost of the use of owned assets.

Depreciation.—The diminution in the intrinsic value of an asset due to use and/or the lapse of time.

Obsolescence.—The loss in the intrinsic value of an asset due to its supersession.

Direct Material Cost.—Material cost which can be allocated to cost centres or cost units.

Direct Wages.—Wages which can be allocated to cost centres or cost units.

Direct Expense.—Expense which can be allocated to cost centres or cost units.

Indirect Material Cost.—Material cost which cannot be allocated, but which can be apportioned to or absorbed by cost centres or cost units.

Indirect Wages.—Wages which cannot be allocated but which can be apportioned to or absorbed by cost centres or cost units.

Indirect Expense.—Expense which cannot be allocated but which can be apportioned to or absorbed by cost centres or cost units.

Overhead.—The aggregate of indirect material cost, indirect wages, and indirect expense.

Absorbed Overhead.—The overhead which, by means of rates of overhead absorption, is allotted to a cost unit.

Over- or Under-absorbed Overhead.—The difference between the amount of absorbed overhead and the amount of overhead incurred.

Prime Cost.—The aggregate of direct material cost, direct wages, and direct expense.

Production Cost.—The cost of the process which begins with supplying materials, labour, and services, and ends with primary packing of the product.

Conversion Cost.—The production cost (excluding the cost of direct material, but including the cost resulting from variations in direct material weight or volume), of producing partly- or fully-finished products.

Selling Cost.—The cost incurred in promoting sales and retaining custom.

Distribution Cost.—The cost of the process which begins with making the packed product available for dispatch and ends with making the reconditioned returned empty package available for re-use.

Administration Cost.—The cost of formulating the policy, directing the organisation, and controlling the operations, of an undertaking, which is not related directly to a research, development, production, distribution, or selling activity or function.

Total Cost.—The sum of all the costs incurred.

Cost of Sales.—The total cost which is attributable to the sales made.

Policy Cost.—Cost which is additional to current requirements, incurred in accordance with the policy of an undertaking.

Idle Facilities Cost.—The cost of abnormal idleness of fixed assets or available services.

Deferred Maintenance Cost.—The cost of repairs, renewals, or upkeep of fixed assets which should be undertaken and charged in an accounting period, but which are deferred to a subsequent period.

Cost of Defectives.—The cost of defective products produced.

Rectification Cost.—The cost of restoring faulty materials or products to a usable condition.

Research Cost.—The cost of searching for new or improved products or new or improved methods.

Development Cost.—The cost of the process which begins with the implementation of the decision to produce a new or improved product or employ a new or improved method and ends with the commencement of formal production of that product or by that method.

Pre-production Cost.—That part of development cost which consists of making a trial run of producing a product preliminary to its formal production.

Material Handling Cost.—The cost of storing and moving materials within an undertaking.

Maintenance Cost.—The cost of maintaining fixed assets in running order.

Setting-up Cost.—The cost of the process which begins after the production of one product is completed and ends when the production of another product which requires a change of materials, jigs, dies, etc., is begun.

Predetermined Cost.—A cost which is computed in advance of production on the basis of a specification of all the factors affecting cost.

Standard Cost.—A predetermined cost which is used in standard costing.

Marginal Cost.—Prime cost plus variable overhead.

Operating Cost.—The cost of providing a service.

Current Cost.—A cost calculated in relation to current conditions.

Cost Provision.—An amount included in costs at the date of a cost statement which represents a cost incurred but not entered in the cost accounts at that date.

PROCEDURES

Cost Classification.—(*a*) The process of grouping costs according to their common characteristics.

(*b*) A series of specified groups according to which costs are classified.

Cost Allocation.—The allotment of whole items of cost to cost centres or cost units.

Cost Apportionment.—The allotment of proportions of items of cost to cost centres or cost units.

Overhead Absorption.—The allotment of overhead to cost units.

PRICES

Price.—(*a*) A money rate used to calculate a cost.
(*b*) To record a money rate in order to calculate a cost.
Specific Price.—The price actually paid.
Standard Price.—A predetermined price fixed on the basis of a specification of all the factors affecting price.
First in First out Price (FIFO).—The price paid for the material first taken into the stock from which the material to be priced could have been drawn.
Last in First out Price (LIFO).—The price paid for the material last taken into the stock from which the material to be priced could have been drawn.
Replacement Price.—The price at which, at the date of consumption of an asset, there could be purchased an asset identical to that whose consumption is being priced.
Re-use Price.—The price which is used to value a material in its re-use.
Simple Average Price.—A price which is calculated by dividing the total of the prices of the materials in the stock from which the material to be priced could have been drawn, by the number of prices used to calculate the average price.
Weighted Average Price.—A price which is calculated by dividing the total cost of material in the stock from which the material to be priced could have been drawn, by the total quantity of material in that stock.
Periodic Simple Average Price.—A price which is calculated by dividing the total of the prices of the materials purchased during the accounting period in which the material to be priced is used, by the number of prices used to calculate the average price.
Moving Simple Average Price.—A price which is calculated by dividing the total of the periodic simple average prices of a given number of periods (including and preceding the period in whioh tho matcrial to bc piiced ls used), by the number of periods.
Inflated Price.—A price which includes a charge designed to cover the cost of contingencies or related costs.

METHODS OF CALCULATING DEPRECIATION

Straight Line Method.—The method of providing for depreciation by means of periodic charges, each of which is a constant proportion of the cost of the asset depreciated.
Reducing Balance Method.—The method of providing for depreciation by means of periodic charges, each of which is a constant proportion of the balance remaining after deducting from the cost of the asset depreciated, the aggregate of the amounts provided previously.
Production Unit Method.—The method of providing for depreciation by means of periodic charges, each of which is equivalent to the number of units of work produced during the period by the asset depreciated, multiplied by a constant rate of depreciation per unit.
Production Hour Method.—The method of providing for depreciation by means of periodic charges, each of which is equivalent to the number of hours during the period for which the asset depreciated is operated, multiplied by a constant rate of depreciation per hour.

Repair Reserve Method.—The method of providing for the aggregate of depreciation and maintenance cost by means of periodic charges, each of which is a constant proportion of the aggregate of the cost of the asset depreciated and the maintenance cost.

Annuity Method.—The method of providing for depreciation by means of periodic charges, each of which is a constant proportion of the aggregate of the cost of the asset depreciated and interest at a given rate per period on the written down values of the asset at the beginning of each period.

Sinking Fund Method.—The method of providing for depreciation by means of periodic investments of the aggregate of a constant proportion of the cost of the asset depreciated and the interest received from the investment, the proceeds of realisation of the investment at the end of the life of the asset being equal to the cost of the asset.

Endowment Policy Method.—The method of providing for depreciation by means of periodic payments of premiums under an endowment policy, the proceeds of realisation of which at the end of the life of the asset are equal to the cost of the asset depreciated.

Revaluation Method.—The method of providing for depreciation by means of periodic charges, each of which is equivalent to the difference between the values assigned to the asset at the beginning and the end of the period.

RATES OF DEPRECIATION

Single Rate of Depreciation.—A depreciation rate which is calculated by reference to the estimated life of a single asset.

Composite Rate of Depreciation.—A depreciation rate which is calculated by dividing by the aggregate of the costs of a number of assets of various individual lives, the aggregate of the depreciation charges for one period of each of the assets depreciated, each aggregated depreciation charge being calculated by reference to the life of the appropriate asset.

Group Rate of Depreciation.—A composite rate of depreciation which is calculated by reference to a group of assets.

Accelerated Rate of Depreciation.—A depreciation rate which consists of a normal depreciation rate, augmented to provide for additional depreciation sustained by the asset depreciated because of abnormally increased usage of that asset.

COST RATES

Specific Cost Rate.—A rate of cost apportionment which is the specific price of a service.

Market Cost Rate.—A rate of cost apportionment which is the current market rate payable for a comparable service.

Standard Cost Rate.—A predetermined rate of cost apportionment or overhead absorption calculated by dividing the predetermined cost to be apportioned or absorbed, by the predetermined quantity of the base to which the rate is to be applied.

Material Cost Percentage Rate.—An actual or predetermined rate of cost apportionment or overhead absorption, which is calculated by dividing the cost to be apportioned or absorbed, by the material cost incurred or expected to be incurred, and expressing the result as a percentage.

Wages Percentage Rate.—An actual or predetermined rate of cost apportionment or overhead absorption, which is calculated by dividing the cost to be apportioned or absorbed, by the wages expended or expected to be expended, and expressing the result as a percentage.

Prime Cost Percentage Rate.—An actual or predetermined rate of cost apportionment or overhead absorption, which is calculated by dividing the cost to be apportioned or absorbed, by the Prime Cost incurred or expected to be incurred, and expressing the result as a percentage.

Labour Hour Rate.—An actual or predetermined rate of cost apportionment or overhead absorption, which is calculated by dividing the cost to be apportioned or absorbed, by the labour hours expended or expected to be expended.

Machine Hour Rate.—An actual or predetermined rate of cost apportionment or overhead absorption, which is calculated by dividing the cost to be apportioned or absorbed by the number of hours for which a machine or machines are operated or expected to be operated.

Cost Unit Rate.—An actual or predetermined rate of cost apportionment or overhead absorption, which is calculated by dividing the cost to be apportioned or absorbed by the number of cost units produced or expected to be produced.

COST CENTRES

Cost Centre.—A location, person, or item of equipment (or group of these) in or connected with an undertaking, in relation to which costs may be ascertained and used for the purpose of cost control.

Impersonal Cost Centre.—A cost centre which consists of a location or item of equipment (or group of these).

Personal Cost Centre.—A cost centre which consists of a person or group of persons.

Operation Cost Centre.—A cost centre which consists of those machines and/or persons which carry out the same operation.

Process Cost Centre.—A cost centre which consists of a continuous sequence of operations.

COST UNITS

Cost Unit.—A unit of quantity of product, service, or time, in relation to which costs may be ascertained or expressed.

Job (Cost Unit).—A cost unit which consists of a single order (or contract).

Batch (Cost Unit).—A cost unit which consists of a group of identical products which maintains its identity throughout one or more stages of production.

Product Group (Cost Unit).—A cost unit which consists of a group of similar products.

Unit of Output.—A cost unit which consists of the unit in which output is expressed.

STANDARD COSTING

Standard Costing.—The ascertainment and use of standard costs and the measurement and analysis of variances.

STANDARDS

Basic Standard.—A standard which is established for use unaltered over a long period of time.

Current Standard.—A standard which is established for use over a short period of time, and is related to current conditions.

Expected Standard.—The standard which it is anticipated can be attained during a future specified budget period.

Normal Standard.—The average standard which it is anticipated can be attained over a future period of time, preferably long enough to cover one trade cycle.

Ideal Standard.—The standard which can be attained under the most favourable conditions possible.

Standard Hour.—A hypothetical hour which measures the amount of work which should be performed in one hour.

RATIOS

Efficiency Ratio.—The standard hours equivalent to the work produced, expressed as a percentage of the actual hours spent in producing that work.

Activity Ratio.—The number of standard hours equivalent to the work produced, expressed as a percentage of the budgeted standard hours.

Calendar Ratio.—The relationship between the number of working days in a period and the number of working days in the relative budget period.

Capacity Usage Ratio.—The relationship between the budgeted number of working hours and the maximum possible number of working hours in a budget period.

VARIANCE ANALYSIS

Variance Analysis.—The resolution into component parts, and the explanation of variances.

COST VARIANCES

Cost Variance.—The difference between a budgeted cost or a standard cost and comparable actual cost incurred during a period.

Revision Variance.—The amount by which a budget is revised, which, as a matter of policy, is not incorporated in the standard cost rate.

Controllable Cost Variance.—A cost variance which can be identified as the primary responsibility of a specified person.

Material Cost Variance.—The difference between the standard cost of material specified and the actual cost of material used.

Material Price Variance.—The portion of the Material Cost Variance which is due to the difference between the standard price specified and the actual price paid.

Material Usage Variance.—The portion of the Material Cost Variance which is due to the difference between the standard quantity specified and the actual quantity used.

Material Mixture Variance.—The portion of the Material Usage Variance which is due to the difference between the standard and the actual composition of a mixture.

Wages Variance.—The difference between the standard wages specified and the actual wages paid.

Wages Rate Variance.—The portion of the Wages Variance which is due to the difference between the standard rate specified and the actual rate paid.

Labour Efficiency Variance.—The portion of the Wages Variance which is due to the difference between the standard labour hours specified and the actual labour hours expended.

Expense Variance.—The difference between the standard expense specified and the actual expense incurred.

Expense Price Variance.—The portion of the Expense Variance which is due to the difference between the standard price of the service specified and the actual price paid.

Expense Utilisation Variance.—The portion of the Expense Variance which is due to the difference between the standard quantity of the service specified and the actual quantity of the service used.

Yield Variance.—The difference between the standard yield specified and the actual yield obtained.

Overhead Variance.—The difference between the standard overhead specified and the actual overhead incurred.

Calendar Variance.—The portion of the Overhead Variance which is due to the difference between the number of working days in the budget period and the number of working days in the period to which the budget is applied.

Volume Variance.—The portion of the Overhead Variance which is due to the difference between the budgeted level of output and the actual level of output attained.

Overhead Efficiency Variance.—The portion of the Overhead Variance which is due to the difference between the budgeted efficiency of production and the actual efficiency attained.

Total Cost Variance.—The difference between the total standard cost and the total cost.

Methods Variance.—The portion of the Total Cost Variance which is due to the use of methods other than those specified.

SALES VARIANCES

Sales Value Variance.—The difference between the standard value and the actual value of sales effected during a period.

Sales Price Variance.—The portion of the Sales Value Variance which is due to the difference between the standard price specified and the specific price charged.

Sales Allowance Variance.—The portion of the Sales Value Variance which is due to the difference between the standard rebates, discounts, etc., specified and the actual rebates, discounts, etc., allowed.

Sales Mixture Variance.—The portion of the Sales Value Variance which is due to the difference between the standard and the actual inter-relationship of the quantities of each product or product group of which the sales are composed.

PROFIT VARIANCES

Profit (or Loss) Variance.—The difference between the standard profit (or loss) and the actual profit (or loss).

MARGINAL COSTING

Marginal Costing.—The ascertainment, by differentiating between fixed costs and variable costs, of marginal costs and of the effect on profit of changes in volume or type of output.

Contribution.—The difference between sales and the marginal cost of sales.

COST ACCOUNTING

Cost Accounting.—The process of accounting for cost, which begins with the recording of expenditure and income or the bases upon which they are calculated and ends with the preparation of statistical data.

BASIC DOCUMENTS

Material Requisition.—A document which authorises and records the issue of material for use.

Material Return Note.—A document which records the return of unused material.

Material Transfer Note.—A document which records the transfer of material from one store to another, from one cost centre to another, or from one cost unit to another.

Material Issue Analysis Sheet.—A document which, for cost accounting purposes, is a classified record of material issues, returns, and transfers.

Labour Time Record.—A document which records the amount of time spent by an employee of an undertaking and the manner of its spending and which may record the wages cost of the time spent.

Wages Analysis Sheet.—A document which, for cost-accounting purposes, is a classified record of time and/or wages compiled from time records.

Expense Analysis Sheet.—A document which, for cost-accounting purposes, is a classified record of expense.

Cost Journal Voucher.—A document which provides the details necessary to support an entry in the Cost Journal.

Machine Time Record.—A document which records, *inter alia*, the amount of time an item of equipment is operated or remains idle, and the work done by the machine, and which may record the cost of the time so recorded.

BOOKS AND ACCOUNTS

Integral Accounts.—A single book-keeping system which contains both financial and cost accounts.

Cost Journal.—A journal which records those transactions which affect solely the cost ledger, and which it is customary to journalise.

Cost Ledger.—A subsidiary ledger whose accounts record those transactions which are included in costs.

Cost Control Account.—An account which is maintained in the principal ledger (and sometimes in the Cost Ledger) which records the totals of the transactions recorded in detail in the Cost Ledger.

Cost Account.—An account in the Cost Ledger.

STATEMENTS

Cost Estimate Sheet.—A document which gives an approximation of the cost of a cost centre or a cost unit.

Cost Sheet.—A document on which is assembled the detailed cost of a cost centre or of a cost unit.

Cost Statement.—A document which shows in summarised form the operating results of the whole or part of an undertaking and which may be interim, periodic, or final.

Operating Statement.—A Cost Statement which is prepared in Budgetary Control and/or Standard Costing and which may provide, *inter alia*, quantitative, budget and standard data, and variances.

"Break-even" Chart.—A chart which shows the profitability or otherwise of an undertaking at various levels of activity, and as a result indicates the point at which neither profit nor loss is made.

MISCELLANEOUS

Cost Manual.—A document which sets out, *inter alia*, the responsibilities of the persons engaged in, the routine of, and the forms and records required for, costing and cost accounting.

Cost Code.—A series of alphabetical and/or numerical symbols, each of which represents a descriptive title in a cost classification.

COST AUDIT

Cost Audit.—The verification of the correctness of cost accounts and of the adherence to the cost-accounting plan.

COST CONTROL

Cost Control.—The guidance and regulation by executive action of the costs of operating an undertaking.

BUDGETARY CONTROL

Budgetary Control.—The establishment of budgets relating the responsibilities of executives to the requirements of a policy, and the continuous comparison of actual with budgeted results either to secure by individual action the objective of that policy or to provide a basis for its revision.

BUDGETS

Budget.—A financial and/or quantitative statement, prepared prior to a defined period of time, of the policy to be pursued during that period for the purpose of attaining a given objective.

Fixed Budget.—A budget which is designed to remain unchanged irrespective of the level of activity actually attained.

Flexible Budget.—A budget which is designed to change in accordance with the level of activity actually attained.

Basic Budget.—A budget which is established for use unaltered over a long period of time.

Current Budget.—A budget which is established for use over a short period of time and is related to current conditions.

Functional Budget.—A budget which relates to any of the functions of an undertaking.

Summary Budget.—A budget which is prepared from and summarises all of the functional budgets.

Master Budget.—The Summary Budget, incorporating its component functional budgets, which is finally approved, adopted, and employed.

MISCELLANEOUS

Principal Budget Factor.—The factor the extent of whose influence must first be assessed in order to ensure that the functional budgets are reasonably capable of fulfilment.

Budget Period.—The period for which a budget is prepared and employed.

Budget Manual.—A document which sets out, *inter alia*, the responsibilities of the persons engaged in, the routine of, and the forms and records required for, Budgetary Control.

Budget Centre.—A section of the organisation of an undertaking defined for the purposes of budgetary control.

Budget Cost Allowance.—The cost (exclusive of the direct materials cost) which a budget centre is expected to incur during a given period of time, in relation to the level of activity attained by the budget centre.

Budget Overhead Allowance.—The overhead which a budget centre is expected to incur during a given period of time, in relation to the level of activity attained by the budget centre.

Budget Control Basis.—The variability of a cost, *i.e.* fixed, semi-fixed, or variable, which determines the manner in which the budget cost allowance is calculated.

EXAMINATION QUESTIONS

Purchasing Procedure (Chapters 1-4)

1. What do you understand by maximum and minimum stocks and ordering level?

(R.S.A. Advanced)

2. Describe in detail a method of controlling the replenishment of stocks of manufactured component parts.

(I.C.W.A. Inter.)

3. Do you consider that the Storekeeper should see and pass invoices for material received? What alternative method is suggested for checking the quantities and prices?

(I.C.W.A. Inter.)

4. In connection with a stock record the term "ordering level" is sometimes used. In what way does this differ from the terms "minimum" and "maximum" stocks?

(I.C.W.A. Inter.)

5. What are the factors which determine the maximum and minimum figures for stock control? Illustrate your answer with examples.

(I.C.W.A. Inter.)

6. Describe a system that would definitely link up the Purchasing Department, Goods Receiving Department, and Cost Department; giving all information for passing invoices, checking goods received and posting to costs.

(I.C.W.A. Inter.)

7. A company has a finished goods warehouse at its factory in Bristol and a sales depot in Glasgow. List each stage in the routine procedure for quantity control, from the time when Glasgow realises the need for a quantity of an article until the quantity is received.

(I.C.W.A. Inter.)

8. Describe what you consider to be an adequate system of checking the receipt of goods and payment for them.

(I.C.W.A. Inter.)

9. The management of Cutcost Ltd. is seriously concerned over the size of its stocks of materials which, it considers, is regularly greater than should be necessary to maintain efficient production. Orders for materials are placed by the Company's buyer against purchase requisitions submitted by departmental managers to cover production schedules drawn up by the production planning department. It has been found, among other things, that managers tend to requisition too much and too early with a view to avoiding, as far as

possible, all risk of any shortage occurring and production being thereby held up.

Consideration is being given to various alternative systems of procedure regarded as likely successfully to co-ordinate and control purchasing and to have full regard for stock presently held and for stock on order.

One suggestion is that the managers should notify the buyer immediately of any requisition materials no longer required owing to deletions from the production schedule. This would enable the buyer to cancel the corresponding purchasing order or reduce orders for similar materials.

You are required to submit four other suggestions likely to assist in the preparation of a satisfying scheme for requisitioning and ordering materials and controlling the volume of material stock of Cutcost Ltd.

(C.A. Final, May 1956)

10. Describe fully the routine for control of the purchase and receipt of material from outside suppliers.

(I.C.W.A. Inter.)

11. Discuss the considerations that influence the setting of maximum and minimum stock levels and re-ordering levels.

(I.C.W.A. Inter.)

12. Describe fully a system by which orders for materials are initiated and placed on outside suppliers, and list the essential information to be included in such orders. What sections of the organisation should be kept informed and why?

(I.C.W.A. Inter.)

13. Name the essential documents for Stores Stock Control, and briefly define the function of each document.

(Com. A. Inter.)

14. What factors should be taken into account in determining whether or not to buy increased quantities of materials for stock with discounts given for large quantities?

(Com. A. Inter.)

15. Describe the main function of a Works Stores organisation. Up to five functions may be briefly described.

(Com. A. Inter.)

Stores Routine (Chapter 5)

1. Draft a form of Bin or Locker Card with three specimen entries thereon and explain the purpose and utility of such cards.

(I.A. Inter.)

2. Draw up a specimen bin card for use in a general store and give your reasoned advice as to whether it should be kept in the store office or alongside the goods to which it relates.

(R.S.A. Advanced)

3. Departmental Stores situated in a works frequently interchange various materials. Describe an accounting system showing how these transactions should be recorded.

(*I.C.W.A. Inter.*)

4. What steps would you take to ascertain and to eliminate over-investment of capital in stocks?

(*I.C.W.A. Inter.*)

5. Give a specimen ruling of a stores requisition and describe fully its routine throughout the workshops and cost department.

(*I.C.W.A. Inter.*)

6. Assume all records of stock are kept in the Cost Office—devise a scheme for checking at irregular periods the actual stock in the store-room.

(*I.C.W.A. Inter.*)

7. Discuss the respective merits and demerits of keeping store records of quantities:

(*a*) Alongside the stocks to which they relate;
(*b*) In cabinets in an office conveniently placed in the storehouse;
(*c*) In the cost office.

(*I.C.W.A. Inter.*)

8. Describe the arrangements you would make for stocktaking throughout a large works in order that completion may be reached as quickly as possible.

(*I.C.W.A. Inter.*)

9. Describe with sample card and a few specimen entries, the working of the maximum and minimum method of stock-keeping.

(*I.C.W.A. Inter.*)

10. Describe briefly how you would conduct the audit of a system of continuous stocktaking and what procedure you would adopt to deal with differences.

(*I.C.W.A. Inter.*)

11. The moving of material from stores to, and in, departments involves both labour and overhead expenses. Do you consider these should all be recovered by a direct charge against material or as a departmental overhead? Briefly explain your reasons for the method you suggest.

(*I.C.W.A. Final*)

12. In a factory where "continuous stocktaking" is carried out periodically discrepancies are discovered. Suggest possible causes of these discrepancies.

(*A.C.C.A. Final*)

13. Briefly describe a system of recording the receipt and issue of goods from store to departments in any manufacturing business with which you are familiar.

(*C.I.S. Inter.*)

14. The following comparisons have been taken from the Material Control records of a company:

	Material A		Material B		Material C	
	Quan-tity	Value	Quan-tity	Value	Quan-tity	Value
		£ s. d.		£ s. d.		£ s. d.
Bin Card	20	—	4	—	20	—
Stores Ledger	40	20 0 0	—	10 12 6	25	—
Perpetual Inventory (Physical Count)	15	—	5	—	20	—

Surmise as to the causes of these discrepancies and state how you would investigate them.

(I.C.W.A. Inter.)

15. In the costing records relating to the receipt and issue of stores certain differences may arise from time to time between the values shown by the actual physical stocktaking and the balances shown by the stores ledger.

You are required:

(*a*) to state various ways in which these differences may be caused, and
(*b*) to describe how they should be dealt with in the stores ledger.

(C.A. Inter., November 1955)

16. Paperwork Ltd. maintain a separate building to store materials used in the maintenance of plant and premises. A Stores Ledger is kept in which details of the materials are recorded in both quantity and value. Issues are made only against a maintenance requisition form.

You are required to draft suitable forms:

(*a*) of stores ledger for use in the maintenance materials store of Paperwork Ltd., and
(*b*) for the requisition of maintenance materials.

(C.A. Final, November 1955)

17. How would you deal with the following in stores records and what procedure would you adopt:

(*a*) Breakages in stores.
(*b*) Scrap returned to stores.
(*c*) Gain or loss in weight through climatic conditions.
(*d*) Excess materials requisitioned and returned to stores without advice?

(C.A.A. Part 2)

18. In the cost accounts of a chemical manufacturing company, how would you deal with:

(*a*) losses of raw materials in manufacture;
(*b*) storage losses of raw materials?

(C.A.A. Part 2)

19. What are the advantages of keeping stores by the Perpetual Inventory System?

(C.A.A. Part 2)

20. State the comparative advantages to a manufacturing company of maintaining its stocks in: (*a*) central stores; (*b*) sub-stores.

(I.C.W.A. Inter.)

21. During the year, your company has purchased and received 1500 tons of bulky raw material which is stored in the factory yard. Issues have been recorded amounting to 1200 tons. Physical stocktaking at the accounting year-end reveals only 200 tons in stock. How would you deal in your cost records with the deficit of 100 tons in physical stock? What procedure would you instal to ensure that deficits will not occur in the future?

(I.C.W.A. Inter.)

22. You are asked to consider the advisability of issuing stores of minor value in bulk to user departments in order to save expense in handling and accounting for individual stores requisitions of small value. List the factors you would take into account before giving your views.

(I.C.W.A. Inter.)

23. Design a Material Issue Requisition suitable for use in a general stores. Outline briefly the procedure for authorising these documents.

(I.C.W.A. Inter.)

24. Your managing director wishes to reduce the investment in stocks and stores as disclosed by a recent Balance Sheet and asks you to investigate and report. List the type of information you would submit and the factors to which you would draw attention.

(I.C.W.A. Inter.)

25. Outline briefly the points to be observed in the efficient stocking of materials.

(I.C.W.A. Inter.)

26. List the documents necessary for the physical and accounting control of stores, and briefly describe the purpose of each.

(I.C.W.A. Inter.)

27. As Cost Accountant to a manufacturing company, what information relating to materials and material costs would you supply to different levels of management?

(I.C.W.A. Inter.)

28. What is the difference in the form and functions of a Stores Ledger Card and a Bin Card? Illustrate your answer with specimen forms of each.

(I.C.W.A. Inter.)

29. Explain the imprest system of stores control and discuss its advantages and disadvantages.

(I.C.W.A. Inter.)

30. Describe and explain briefly the following documents relating to stores, in cost accounting:

(a) Bin Card;
(b) Stores Requisition;
(c) Materials Transfer Note;
(d) Purchase Requisition.

(*C.A. Inter., November 1957*)

Methods of Valuing Material Issues (*Chapter 6*)

1. State the various methods of pricing Stores Requisitions with which you are familiar, and discuss their respective merits.

(*R.S.A. Adv.*)

2. What are the various methods by which stores issues may be priced, and in what circumstances do you consider the practices can be varied with advantage? State reasons.

(*I.C.W.A. Inter.*)

3. Copper is purchased at £60 per ton in January for general stock and is used in the following June when the market price has risen to £70 per ton. What figure would you use in your costs? Give reasons for your answer.

(*R.S.A. Advanced*)

4. In Costing, materials may be charged out to jobs at cost price, or at market price. Explain which method is in your view preferable, giving your reasons, and state how, under the respective methods, fluctuations in the Costing Accounts will arise, and under what headings they will appear.

(*C.A. Final*)

5. A manufacturing concern purchases from time to time large quantities of a commodity used in the manufacture of one of its products. The following are the details of purchases during the six months ended June 30, 19..:

19..	Quantity	Cost Price per 100
		s. d.
February 2	10,000	10 0
March 15	25,000	10 6
April 20	20,000	9 6
May 3	15,000	9 0
June 1	12,000	9 0
June 20	3,000	8 6

There were 15,000 units in stock at January 1, 19.., which were valued at 9s. 6d. per 100.

Quantities issued from store during the six months were as under:

19..	
January 25	10,000
February 28	8,000
March 29	25,000
April 30	20,000
May 15	18,000
June 29	15,000

At what prices should the issues be charged and the closing stock valued? Prepare a Stores Ledger Account illustrating your views.

(*I.A. Final*)

6. During periods of rapid increase or decrease in prices of materials used in production, which of the following methods of pricing stores issues results in the most accurate costing of goods manufactured and sold:

(*a*) first-in, first-out method;
(*b*) Actual Cost method;
(*c*) Average Cost method;
(*d*) last-in, first-out method;
(*e*) Standard Cost method?

Give reasons in support of your answer.

(*I.C.W.A. Inter.*)

7. For Balance Sheet purposes it is customary to value stores at cost or market price, whichever is the lower. Would you adopt the same basis in charging out stores for costing purposes? Give reasons for, and explain the effect of, the method you advocate.

(*I.A. Inter.*)

8. The following transactions occur in the purchase and issue of a material:

January 29   Purchased 100 at £5   each
February 5   „   25 at £5 5*s.* „
   „   12   „   50 at £5 10*s.* „
   „   14 Issued   80
March 6   Purchased 50 at £5 10*s.* „
   „   20   Issued   80
   „   27   Purchased 50 at £5 15*s.* „

Complete the stock account showing the balance at March 31, the end of the accounting year. State clearly your method of pricing the issues, why this method has been adopted, and the price and value of the closing stock.

(*I.C.W.A. Inter.*)

9. Discuss four of the accepted methods of pricing stores issues. Indicate which method will result in the most accurate costing of goods manufactured and sold during periods of rapid increases in prices of raw materials used in production.

(*A.I.A. Final*)

10. State the advantages and disadvantages of using standard prices for issuing materials from store.

(*I.C.W.A. Inter.*)

11. Midwest Engineers Ltd. charges stores out to jobs on the F.I.F.O. basis. Among the stores stocked is "Component A.Z.," on which a provision for spoilage by rust is made of 1% on the balance on the Stores Account at the beginning of each month. Stock is taken physically at three-monthly intervals and the balances on the Stores Ledger Accounts are appropriately adjusted. On July 31, 1957, the stock of "Component A.Z." was 2500, on which the

cost was 9s. 6d. per 100. During the next three months the transactions were as follows:

	Purchases Quantities	Price per 100 s. d.	Issues
August	10,000	10 0	9,150
September	20,000	11 0	20,316
October	25,000	12 0	18,070

At October 31, 1957, stocktaking recorded a shortage of 150 components. You are required:

(a) to write up the Stores Ledger Account for "Component A.Z." for the three months to October 31, 1957; and
(b) to state how you would deal with the components spoiled by rust and the shortage in stock.

(C.A.A. Part 2)

12. The following are the purchases and issues of a component part for the six months to March 31, 1956:

1955	Purchases	Cost s. d.	Issues
October	1000	12 3	1500
November	3000	12 0	2200
December	2000	12 6	1600
1956			
January	3000	11 3	3200
February	2500	10 6	3000
March	1600	10 0	1300

At October 1, 1955, there were 2000 of these component parts in stock valued at 13s. each and at March 31, 1956, 2300 were in stock valued at 10s. 2d. each. Discuss the method adopted for the pricing of stores issued and stock values and suggest any alternative method you favour in the given circumstances.

(C.A.A. Part 2)

13. What principles should be used in determining the price at which items from stock should be charged to cost accounts at a time when prices are rising? Is it correct practice to use the same rule as for Balance Sheet valuations— "cost or market price, whichever is the lower"? Give reasons for your answer.

(C.A.A. Part 2)

14. Discuss three of the following methods of pricing stores issues:

(a) first in, first out (F.I.F.O.);
(b) last in, first out (L.I.F.O.);
(c) highest in, first out (H.I.F.O.);
(d) next in, first out (N.I.F.O.).

Indicate which method will result in the most accurate costing of goods manufactured and sold during periods of rapid increases and decreases in prices of raw materials used in production.

(C.A.A. Part 2)

15. Define: (a) simple average price;
(b) weighted average price.

What circumstances are best suited to the use of each method for pricing issues from stores?

(I.C.W.A. Inter.)

16. Due to shortage of supplies in this country, raw materials (*e.g.* steel) are being imported into the country at a price considerably higher than that of the home product. How would you treat this extra cost? For example, would you charge it only to the products and orders using imported materials, would you absorb the cost as a spread charge to all production, or would you charge it direct to Profit and Loss?

(Com. A. Final)

17. The following transactions occur in respect of purchased components forming part of an assembly:

January 15	100 purchased at 1s. 1d. each	
„ 22	200 issued	
February 7	100 purchased at 1s. 2d.	„
„ 21	200 issued	
March 5	100 purchased at 1s. 3d.	„
„ 12	100 „ at 1s. 2d.	„
„ 20	300 issued	

The stock at January 1 was 500 valued at 1s. each. At what price(s) would you price the issues to production? State the basis of your method of pricing, giving reasons. What value would you place on stocks at March 31, the financial year end, and how would you deal with the balance (if any) on the stock account at that time?

(I.C.W.A. Inter.)

Labour Administration and Remuneration (Chapters 7–9)

1. What do you understand by labour turnover? Discuss its significance in industry today, and its effect on the production costs of a company manufacturing a specialised product.

(I.C.W.A. Final)

2. You are required to submit a report on labour turnover in a factory. Indicate in the form of a skeleton report (without figures) the general contents of such a report.

(C.A.A.)

3. As Cost Accountant of a factory in a very busy industrial area, you find that there is a high rate of labour turnover in certain departments. Write a report to management drawing attention to this fact, and suggesting practical methods of retaining your labour.

(I.C.W.A. Final)

4. Where workers are paid by results, describe the method you would adopt to ensure that piece-rates and/or bonus payments are entered correctly on job cards.

State the system you would install in the factory to ensure maintenance of accurate Labour Cost Records.

(I.C.W.A. Inter.)

5. Is it necessary to keep time records for piece-workers? Give full reasons for your answer.

(C.A.A.)

6. Outline a practical method of keeping records of labour cost in an industry where the average number of jobs on which each man is engaged is three per day.

(C.A.A.)

7. As Cost Accountant of a large company, you are charged by the Financial Controller with the task of ensuring that the system of computing earnings, the payroll routine, and the payment of wages is adequate. List the internal checks you would perform. What types of deliberate fraud would you need to guard against?

(I.C.W.A. Inter.)

8. Draft a suitable payroll with columns for typical deductions, and insert four specimen entries therein. It may be assumed that the business employs 300 operatives, some of whom are engaged on time-work and the remainder on piece-work. Indicate the accounts to which the various totals should be posted.

(C.A.A.)

9. Design a return of analysis of the payroll for the use of the Shop Superintendents. The form used should be for presentation weekly, and should be designed so that changes from week to week can be interpreted as trends which may call for action.

(I.C.W.A. Inter.)

10. A small company manufacturing a single complex product has three separate production departments, but the nature of the organisation and work does not lend itself readily to piece-work wage-rates.

It is proposed to introduce a group bonus scheme to include all the workers, by fixing a monthly added value standard, and distributing a proportion of any monthly excess achieved as a percentage increase to wages. What criticisms would you make of such a scheme, and what difficulties would you expect to arise? (Added value is the sales price of a product, less the cost of direct materials in it.)

(I.C.W.A. Final)

11. Write a short essay on the underlying principles of employee remuneration and incentives as they affect the employer, the employee, and the national economy.

(I.C.W.A. Final)

12. What do you understand by accelerating premium plans? State their purpose, effects, advantages, and disadvantages.

By means of a diagram show the shape of the earnings and labour cost curves related to output for such plans.

(I.C.W.A. Inter.)

13. In a factory where workers under 20 years of age are paid weekly rates varying according to age, similar work is done by workers earning different rates. What method of charging out wages costs can be used to ensure uniformity for different jobs?

(C.A.A.)

14. Give a tabular illustration of the working of any premium bonus system of remuneration and discuss the merits and demerits of such a system.

(C.A.A.)

15. Describe, briefly, three methods of payment by results, indicating in each case the formula by which the payment to the employee is computed. State what, in your opinion, are the respective advantages and disadvantages of each method.

(C.A.A.)

16. It is proposed to institute a system of payment of wages by results in a general engineering factory, and you are required to consider the safeguards that should be provided for both employer and employee in order to ensure that the proposed system will operate on an equitable basis.

Submit your Report to the Board of Directors, assuming any data that may be relevant.

(C.A.A.)

17. Explain the fundamental differences between:

(a) Straight piece-work;
(b) differential piece-work;
(c) the "Rowan" system of premium bonus.

In what circumstances would you recommend the use of each of the three systems?

(I.C.W.A. Inter.)

18. Following the introduction of a piece-work bonus system in a small engineering works, it has been found that, although the output per worker has increased substantially, the benefits to the employer resulting from such increased output have been largely offset by losses arising on the greatly increased proportion of faulty parts produced.

You are requested to suggest the various steps which might be taken by the employer to obtain a reduction in the loss caused by the production of faulty parts, without departing from the principle of paying the workers an incentive bonus related to output.

(C.A. Final, November, 1954)

19. One of the principal factory departments of Redlite Ltd., known as the No. 1 Machine Shop, undertakes a variety of machining work falling into six classes, of which "cutting" and "forming" are two.

Some 200 work-people are employed in the department, of whom 160 are remunerated on an individual piece-work basis with a guaranteed minimum weekly wage, and the others are remunerated at fixed hourly rates. Additional payments are made in respect of overtime working and, in the calculation of piece-work earnings, additional allowances (treated by Redlite Ltd. as overhead expenses) are made for such matters as short runs, learning time, etc. The 40 employees remunerated at fixed hourly rates are wholly engaged on duties such as supervision, machine setting, shop cleaning, etc., the cost of which is regarded by the company as overhead expense.

The Accounts Department, which is responsible, among other matters for payment of wages and for costing, is adequately mechanised and is able to meet any reasonable request for accounting or costing information.

It is desired to introduce a form of report or reports (restricted to labour cost only) for submission weekly by the accountant to the manager of the No. 1 Machine Shop, and incorporating such information as is likely to assist the manager in running the department efficiently.

Redlite does not employ Standard Costing, and budgeted figures are not available.

The manager of the department is paid monthly. His salary should not be included in the information to be supplied.

You are required to submit a draft for labour cost report or reports suitable for submission to the manager of the No. 1 Machine Shop.

Detailed figures are not required, but may be included if desired for the purpose of making clear the use of the report or reports.

(*C.A. Final, May, 1956*)

20. (*a*) State briefly two fundamental rules, in the classification of accounts, governing the division into classes.

(*b*) In classifying and coding accounts relating to wages paid, illustrate with a simple tabulation how you would subdivide and code the following two of the main divisions:

(i) payments for lost time;
(ii) extra payments.

(*I.C.W.A. Final*)

21. In what circumstances is the institution of a direct wage-incentive system inadvisable and when impracticable?

What effective indirect incentives may be usefully introduced in such circumstances?

(*I.C.W.A. Inter.*)

22. (*a*) State briefly the advantages

(i) to employers, and
(ii) to operatives

of a premium bonus system or remuneration.

(*b*) In an engineering works the standard time for a job is 16 hours and the basic wage is 4*s*. per hour. A bonus scheme is instituted so that the operative is to receive his normal rate for hours actually worked and for half the hours saved. Material for the job cost £2 and the factory overhead is charged out on the basis of 6*s*. per labour hour.

Calculate the wages and the effective rate of earnings per hour if the job is completed:

(i) in 12 hours;
(ii) in 14 hours.

Tabulate the total factory cost of the job on the same basis.

(*Incorp. Accts. Inter.*)

23. Describe five methods of remunerating workmen. State the merits and demerits of each.

(I.C.W.A. Inter.)

24. The analysis of wages is an essential part of cost accounting and assists in cost control. In what differing ways can such an analysis be made? State the purpose of each form of analysis.

(I.C.W.A. Inter.)

25. Ten men work as a group. When the weekly production of the group exceeds standard (200 pieces per hour) each man of the group is paid a bonus for the excess production in addition to his wages at hourly rates. The bonus is computed thus:

The percentage of production in excess of the standard amount is found and one-half of this percentage is considered as the men's share. Each man in the group is paid as a bonus this percentage of a wage-rate of 6s. 8d. per hour. There is no relationship between the individual workman's hourly rate and the bonus rate. The following is one week's record:

	Hours worked	Production
Monday	90	22,100
Tuesday	88	20,600
Wednesday	90	24,200
Thursday	84	20,100
Friday	88	20,400
Saturday	40	10,200
	480	117,600

(a) compute the rate and amount of bonus for the week, and

(b) compute the total pay of Jones who worked $41\frac{1}{2}$ hours and was paid 4s. 9d. per hour basic, and of Smith who worked $44\frac{1}{2}$ hours and was paid 5s. 3d. per hour basic.

(I.C.W.A. Inter.)

26. List the general principles which should apply to all wage incentive schemes.

(I.C.W.A. Inter.)

27. Detail fully, in logical sequence, the flow of information regarding labour costs, through a business from the time that attendance is recorded to its final inclusion in product costs. Show by journal entries the accounting treatment.

(I.C.W.A. Inter.)

28. Prepare a Labour Cost Sheet for a machined component, using your own figures, assuming three operations and the following additional information:

Commenced with 300 units;
10 units scrapped in Operation 1;
12 units scrapped in Operation 2 and 14 units rejected for adjustment;
8 units scrapped in Operation 3.

(A.I.A. Final)

29. Testgear Ltd. manufactures non-standard specialised test gear and measuring equipment to the individual specifications required by its customers. Cost records are maintained on an historical job cost basis. The system provides that the workmen, of whom there are 100, submit at the end of each week time-sheets showing the employee's name, the date, the code numbers of the jobs concerned, and the length of time spent on each job. Numerous inaccuracies have been found in the times and job numbers so recorded, and the management feel that, as a consequence, the job costs produced cannot be relied upon.

You are required to submit, in the form of a report addressed to the Managing Director, your suggestions:

(a) for securing a satisfactory standard to time recording by Testgear Ltd.; and

(b) for the making of such checks and counterchecks on the accuracy of the time records as you consider desirable.

Your own name and address must *not* be given.

(*C.A. Final, November 1957*)

30. Prepare in tabulated form an accounts classification for employee remuneration with each item suitably coded.

(*I.C.W.A. Final*)

31. What factors must be borne in mind where, by reason of increased demand for a product, a decision has to be made between:

(a) introducing a second shift;

(b) sub-contracting the work.

Embody in your answer a report to your Managing Director covering the cost of these alternatives.

(*I.C.W.A. Final*)

32. A manufacturer introduces new machinery into his factory, with the result that production per worker is increased. The workers are paid by results, and it is agreed that for every 2% increase in average individual output, an increase of 1% on the rate of wages will be paid. At the time the machinery is installed the selling price of the product falls by $8\frac{1}{3}\%$.

Show the net saving in production costs which would be required to offset the losses expected from reduced turnover and bonus paid to workers.

	1st Period	2nd Period
Number of workers	175	125
Number of articles produced	168,000	140,000
Wages paid	£33,600	—
Total sales	£75,600	—

(*I.C.W.A. Final*)

33. How would you deal in your cost accounts with:

(a) wages paid for idle time during a shortage of work owing to seasonal fluctuation in demand;

(b) compensatory payment on account of redundancy, the payment depending on the length of service of the employee;

(c) payments made in lieu of bonus to operators unable to work owing to a major machine breakdown?

Give your reasoning in each case.

(I.C.W.A. Inter.)

34. A company finds that costs of a certain product leave insufficient margin to meet competition in the open market. An examination of the records shows that the main reason for this is the excessive labour cost, which has arisen from the difficulty of recruiting suitably trained labour in the area. Times occupied in certain operations are consistently greater than estimated, and an abnormal amount of spoiled work and reprocessing has resulted. Overheads are absorbed by a percentage addition to direct wages of 200%.

Using suitable figures draft a report to management.

(I.C.W.A. Final)

35. Distinguish between direct and indirect labour. What difficulties are experienced in practice in making this distinction? Illustrate each type of labour with *two* clear examples taken from a particular industry.

(I.C.W.A. Inter.)

36. In what circumstances would you propose that the bonus paid for overtime or for night shift work should be charged to:

(a) the particular jobs worked upon during the overtime or night shift periods;

(b) the shop overheads; or

(c) general overheads?

(A.I.A. Final)

37. In a manufacturing company there are occasions when whole departments have to be changed over from one type of product to another requiring quite different production operations. Wages are paid during the idle time of machine change-over, and it is found that operators require a three-week period of re-training on the new type. The proportion of faulty work is higher than normal during the re-training period. How would you propose to charge into cost the operators' wages during this change-over period? Give your reasons.

(I.C.W.A. Inter.)

38. How would you deal in the cost accounts with wages paid for the following:

(a) the excavation of foundations for the installation of a large press, abandoned after several weeks' work, the site being discovered geologically unsuitable;

(b) transfer of direct labour from a slack department, the employees retaining their existing wage-rates, which exceed the rate normally paid in their new department;

(c) work on a project to manufacture an existing product more cheaply;

(d) wages, including overtime premiums, paid to inspectors employed on direct productive operations during overtime only.

Give reasons.

(I.C.W.A. Inter.)

39. For some selected industry, describe the cost accounting treatment you would give to wages cost relating to defective work of all kinds, and to its correction where correction is possible.

(*I.C.W.A. Inter.*)

40. In a large factory certain departments are working at higher than normal capacity, while other departments are on short time. As a result, although the total hours worked in the factory approximate to a normal total, the total costs are not normal. Explain the nature of the cost abnormalities.

(*I.C.W.A. Final*)

41. How would you deal in the Cost Accounts with the wages of a foreman in a small engineering shop, and what variations would you suggest in the case of a "working" foreman?

(*C.A.A.*)

42. The following figures show the relation of the direct wages to indirect wages (exclusive of supervisory wages) in certain manufacturing departments for the year to December 31, 19..:

Departments

	A £	B £	C £
Weeks	*Direct Wages*		
1–13	4275	6892	8219
14–26	3829	5420	5268
27–39	2926	4624	5476
40–52	2178	4379	6081
Weeks	*Indirect Wages*		
1–13	641	689	1027
14–26	670	813	1317
27–39	731	1156	1369
40–52	₊871	2190	1520

Prepare a table of percentages (approximated to the nearest whole number) of indirect wages to direct wages for each thirteen-weekly period.

Does such a table provide useful information to management? If you think so, state what conclusions you would draw from the results shown.

(*C.A.A.*)

43. Job Evaluation is to be used as the basis of the wages structure for a firm employing over 1000 production and ancillary workers. List six evaluation factors which might be used in such a scheme giving a brief definition of each.

(*I.C.W.A. Inter.*)

44. Explain the meaning of the following terms in relation to Time and Motion Study:

(*a*) element time;
(*b*) contingencies allowance;
(*c*) Standard Time.

Illustrate your answer by an example showing how the standard time is computed where an operation is done on a machine tool.

(*C.A.A.*)

45. A factory is running on operation cards which travel with the work, and all time is booked, when completed, on these cards. What means would you suggest to check these times with the employees' weekly time so as to ensure correct balancing?

(*I.C.W.A. Inter.*)

46. A factory producing parts in quantities uses Job Cards which follow the batches of work as they progress through the shops, each operative booking his time on the cards. Some of the batches are in hand for several weeks. How would you ensure that each operative's time in any wage week is satisfactorily balanced?

(*I.C.W.A. Inter.*)

47. Describe several methods of allocating wages to jobs when individual operators work on several jobs each day.

(*I.C.W.A. Inter.*)

48. A tool room is engaged on:

(*a*) new designs of jigs, gauges, and fixtures for future quantity production;

(*b*) repairs and renewals to current designs;

(*c*) maintenance cutting tools, etc., for general work.

On what basis would time be booked and subsequently analysed as wages costs?

(*I.C.W.A. Inter.*)

49. In a factory where a system of piece-work is in operation outline the necessary forms and records. How would you deal in the cost account records with "Make-up" wages—that is, those cases where the operators' piece-work earnings are less than the minimum weekly rate?

(*I.C.W.A. Inter.*)

50. Distinguish between profit-sharing and co-partnership. Estimate the value of such schemes as incentives to employees, and list their defects. Describe briefly two methods used in such schemes.

(*I.C.W.A. Inter.*)

51. What types of fraud have to be guarded against in the procedures for computing earnings, preparing the payroll, and paying out wages? State what safeguards should be used to counter any attempt to commit such fraud.

(*I.C.W.A. Inter.*)

52. In a certain plant the employees are often moved from one department to another several times a day as production demands. Suggest a means of recording time so that the correct wages are charged to each department, and draft a specimen form for this purpose.

(*I.C.W.A. Inter.*)

53. A business operates a large fleet of delivery vans to distribute a perishable product from depots to retailers on a nation-wide scale. What factors

do you consider should be taken into account in devising a monetary incentive scheme for the van drivers? Describe briefly how you would set about measuring the work of a driver.

(I.C.W.A. Inter.)

54. Analysis of labour turnover indicates a large proportion of leavers who have joined other firms in the locality for higher wages. As a consequence, the wages structure is to be reviewed. List and annotate the factors which would need examination for this purpose.

(I.C.W.A. Inter.)

Overhead (Chapters 10–13)

1. A Company is about to produce two articles whose Prime Cost is composed as follows:

	Cost per dozen A		Cost per dozen B	
	s.	d.	s.	d.
Direct material	10	0	15	0
Direct wages				
8 hours at 3s. including			4 hours at 4s. 6d. includ-	
5 machine hours	24	0	ing 2 machine hours	18	0
Prime Cost	34	0		33	0

For the three months ending September 30, 19.., the budget shows the following information:

Budgeted Output of A ...... 1000 dozen
      ,,   ,,   B ...... 2000 dozen
Overhead £6000.

You are requested:

(*a*) to name three cost rates by which overhead to be absorbed by each product could be calculated;
(*b*) to calculate the overhead to be absorbed by each product under each of the cost rates that you name.

Show your workings.

(I.C.W.A. Inter.)

2. "The Modern Company" is divided into four departments; A, B, and C are producing departments, and D is a service department. The actual costs for a period are as follows:

	£		£
Rent	1000	Supervision	1500
Repairs to plant	600	Fire Insurance	500
Depreciation of plant	450	Power	900
Light	100	Employers' Liability In-	
		surance	150

The following information is available in respect of the four departments:

	Dept. A	Dept. B	Dept. C	Dept. D
Area, sq. ft.	1500	1100	900	500
Number of employees	20	15	10	5
Total wages	£6,000	£4,000	£3,000	£2000
Value of plant	£24,000	£18,000	£12,000	£6000
Value of stock	£15,000	£9,000	£6,000	—

Apportion the costs to the various departments on the most equitable method.

(I.C.W.A. Inter.)

3. The allotment of overheads and their absorption by individual products often presents difficulties to the Cost Accountant. Discuss this point in relation to a manufacturing concern which produces a variety of products with different classes of labour, and where each class of overhead (factory, administration, and selling) includes elements of fixed, variable, and semi-variable expenses.

(I.C.W.A. Final)

4. What are the advantages and disadvantages of the following two methods of cost assembly:

(a) all component parts to be brought into the summary bearing their full share of overheads and administration charges; and

(b) all materials, wages, and overheads for component parts to be summarised separately to show the full cost under each head on the final summary.

(C.A.A.)

5. Discuss overheads as a factor in the determination of managerial policy of a concern manufacturing a variety of products which are not subject to any price control.

(I.C.W.A. Final)

6. "Management's interest in overheads is not in the method of their absorption, but in their behaviour under various conditions of production." As a Cost Accountant, what are your reactions to this statement?

(I.C.W.A. Final)

7. A company manufactures a product in three qualities of material. The value of the material used in these products is 40s., 50s., and 60s. per unit. The direct labour cost remains constant at 10s. per unit. The company absorbs overhead expenditure by:

(a) a percentage addition to the material content calculated to recover the fixed overheads on the budgeted output;

(b) a percentage addition to direct wages calculated to recover the variable overheads on the budgeted output.

Describe the effect of this method of absorption on the cost of the products, and state with reasons whether you consider it to be an equitable method in the circumstances.

(I.C.W.A. Final)

Q

8. Criticise the statement "the more machinery employed, the more the manufacturer is at the mercy of the market."

(*I.C.W.A. Final*)

9. Your Company operates an engineering works which acts as a service department to its several factories. The management decide to use the idle capacity of the works by accepting work for outside customers in order to reduce overheads and thus cheapen the cost of the work done for the Company. As Cost Accountant you are asked to advise regarding:

(*a*) the make-up of the minimum price at which work for third parties can be executed; and

(*b*) the method of crediting any profit earned on outside work.

Give your reasons for the advice tendered.

(*I.C.W.A. Final*)

10. In many industries the making of expensive patterns or dies is necessary before production of an article can take place. How would you deal with this factor of cost:

(*a*) in preparing estimates of the cost of one particular article;

(*b*) in determining the overhead of the department making use of these patterns or dies;

(*c*) at the year end?

(*I.C.W.A. Final*)

11. Describe briefly the routine for dealing with the collection, allocation, apportionment, and absorption of overheads in an industry with which you are familiar.

(*I.C.W.A. Inter.*)

12. What are the two basic causes of under-absorption of works overhead? Mention two examples, which may be met in practice, of each cause.

Where such under-absorption at the end of a month applies to production delivered, work in progress, and finished products awaiting despatch, show a composite journal entry indicating the general ledger accounts affected.

(*I.C.W.A. Final*)

13. (*a*) Explain briefly the circumstances in which a machine hour rate may suitably be used in cost accounting.

(*b*) Calculate from the following data the machine hour rate for Machine A:

Cost of the machine	£1050
Estimated scrap value	£50
Effective working life	20,000 hours
Running time per 4-weekly period	150 hours
Weekly amount payable under a maintenance agreement covering all repairs	£2 10*s*.
Standing charges allocated to machine per 4-weekly period	£5
Power used by machine	5 units per hour at 2*d*. per unit

(*C.A. Inter., November 1956*)

14. Department 19 of a works consists of two sections occupying equal floor area, known respectively as Section "A" and Section "B".

Section "A" comprises twelve identical machines operated intermittently by eight operators. Each machine in this section requires the full attention of an operator while in production.

Section "B" comprises a single large machine controlled by two operators who are continuously engaged thereon.

The following budgeted figures relative to Department 19 have been agreed for the 26 weeks commencing December 1. During this period the department will be entirely closed for the equivalent of one week on account of Christmas and other holidays.

Normal working time, 42 hours per operator per week.

Allowance for normal working time not paid for, *i.e.* sickness, etc., 2 hours per operator per week.

Overtime—Nil

	£
Operators' basic wages (2s. 6d. per hour)	1250
Operators' piecework bonus (20% of basic pay) for Section "A" and Section "B"	250
Foreman's wages	300
Rent and Rates	80
Space heating and lighting	60

Consumable Stores:	£	
Section "A"	70	
Section "B"	80	
	—	150

Repairs and Maintenance (undertaken outside normal working hours)		
Section "A"	40	
Section "B"	100	
	—	140
Electric power		200
Proportion of works general expenses		500
Proportion of office general expenses		300

Provision is to be made for depreciation of plant and equipment:

Section "A"—10% on £2400 being the cost of the machines.
Section "B"— 8% on £6250 being the cost of the machine.

In addition, the following facts and estimates have been accepted as correct:

(1) All materials and tooling costs are charged direct to the products.
(2) Non-productive time, *i.e.* setting-up time, etc. (which is paid for and regarded as an overhead) is

Section "A"—4 hours per operator per week.
Section "B"—8 hours per operator per week.

(3) The electrical power ratings are

Section "A"—each machine, $\frac{1}{3}$ h.p.
Section "B"—the machine, 3 h.p.

(4) The same percentage piece-work bonus is expected to be paid in both sections.

(5) Works general expenses (which include the appropriate allowance for holiday pay for the period) are to be allocated in proportion to the number of operators.

(6) Office general expenses are to be allocated in proportion to the total of all other costs of operating the machines.

(7) The foreman estimates that he will spend two-thirds of his time in Section "A" and one-third in Section "B," and that no part of his time will be spent directly on production.

You are required to prepare, in respect of the six months commencing December 1, a statement showing:

(a) the cost of operating for one hour a machine of the type used in Section "A," *i.e.* the machine hour rate for Section "A";
(b) the cost of operating for one hour the machine used in Section "B," *i.e.* the machine hour rate for Section "B"; and
(c) how such costs have been built up.

(*C.A. Final, November 1952*)

15. The following particulars refer to a process used in the treatment of material subsequently incorporated in a component forming part of an electrical appliance:

(1) The original cost of the machine used (purchased in June 1955) was £1000, its estimated life is 10 years, the estimated scrap value at the end of its life is £100, and the estimated working time per year (50 weeks of 40 hours) is 2200 hours, of which machine maintenance, etc., is estimated to take up 200 hours. No other loss of working time is expected; setting-up time, estimated at 5% of total productive time, is regarded as productive time. (Bank holidays are to be ignored.)

(2) Electricity used by the machine during production is 16 units per hour at a cost of $1\frac{1}{2}d.$ per unit. No current is taken during maintenance or setting up.

(3) The machine requires a chemical solution which is replaced at the end of each week at a cost each time of £2.

(4) The estimated cost of maintenance per year is £120.

(5) Two attendants control the operation of the machine together with five other identical machines. Their combined weekly wages, insurance, and the employer's contributions to holiday pay amount to £12.

(6) Departmental and general works overheads allocated to this machine for the year 1955/56 amount to £200.

You are required to calculate the machine hour rate necessary to provide for recoupment of the cost of operating the machine.

(*C.A. Final, November 1955*)

16. In Department 10 a group of 6 machines produce an article, the factory cost of the output of which has been calculated as follows:

13 weeks to April 27, 1956

Group output	13,500 units
	£
Raw material used	450
Wages, machine operators	360
	810
Factory Overhead, say 60% of wages	216
	£1026

Each machine is of equal size and capacity, and fully occupies the attention of one operator. In the above period Department 10 was closed for the equivalent of one week in respect of holidays and roof repairs. A 40-hour week is worked, which includes $1\frac{1}{2}$ hours and 1 hour per machine for setting and cleaning time respectively.

The standard wage rate is 2s. 6d. per hour.

The management wants to know what is the factory cost per unit of output in the light of the above, recovering the overhead by a machine hour rate instead of by a percentage on wages.

The following further particulars become available:

Department 10	*Per annum*
	£
Foreman, salary	500
Rent and rates	80
Heat and Light	60
Machine stores	44
„ repairs	72
„ setting and cleaning	?

Each machine cost £300, and depreciation is provided at 10% p.a. on cost. Submit your report in good style.

(*C.C.A. Final*)

17. A productive department of a manufacturing company has five different groups of machines, for each of which it is desired to establish machine hour rates.

A budget for this department for the year ending June 30, 1959, shows the following overhead:

	£	£
Consumable supplies—		
Machine group 1	150	
2	300	
3	500	
4	600	
5	950	
	—	2,500
Maintenance—		
Machine group 1	350	
2	400	
3	600	
4	850	
5	500	
	—	2,700
Power		700
Rent and rates		2,400
Heat and light		400
Insurance of buildings		200
Insurance of machinery		500
Depreciation of machinery		8,000
Supervision		4,800
General expenses		600
		£22,800

Additional operating information is available as follows:

Group	Effective h.p.	Area occupied (sq. ft.)	Book value of machinery £	Working hours
1	5	250	2,500	12,000
2	20	750	12,500	20,000
3	10	100	5,000	8,000
4	25	500	20,000	10,000
5	40	400	10,000	30,000

You are required to:

(a) Calculate a machine hour rate for each of the five groups of machines. Show clearly the basis of apportionment that you use.

(b) Calculate the overhead that will be absorbed by one unit of Product X and one unit of Product Y on the manufacture of which the following times (in hours) are spent in the machine groups of this department:

	Machine groups				
	1	2	3	4	5
Product X (each unit)	2	–	7	1	2
Product Y	4	1	–	6	1

(I.C.W.A. Inter.)

18. List *five* documents that you would expect to find in connection with the collection and apportionment of overhead. In respect of each of the documents listed, specify briefly *two* types of significant error that might occur.

(*I.C.W.A. Inter.*)

19. A jobbing manufacturer assesses the overhead to be absorbed by each job by adding to the prime cost a fixed percentage of direct material cost and direct wages. This percentage is calculated on his previous year's accounts.

Although each individual job appears to show a reasonable profit, his Profit and Loss Account for the year shows a loss. His total overhead, however, has not varied to any appreciable extent from that of the previous year.

(*a*) How can you explain this position?

(*b*) In view of the adverse position revealed by the annual accounts, what alteration to the system would you recommend?

(*I.C.W.A. Inter.*)

20. The following figures have been extracted from the books of a manufacturing company. All jobs pass through the company's two departments:

	Working Dept.	Finishing Dept.
Material used	£6,000	£500
Direct labour	£3,000	£1500
Factory overheads	£1,800	£1200
Direct labour hours	12,000	5000
Machine hours	10,000	2000

The following information relates to Job A. 100:

	Working Dept.	Finishing Dept.
Material used	£120	£10
Direct labour	£65	£25
Direct labour hours	265	70
Machine hours	255	25

You are required:

(*a*) to enumerate four methods of absorbing factory overheads by jobs, showing the rates for each department under the methods quoted;

(*b*) to prepare a statement showing the different cost results for Job A. 100 under any two of the methods referred to.

(*I.C.W.A. Final*)

21. As Cost Accountant you are asked to advise a company on the best method of absorbing overheads and to compute the rate or rates to be applied. No cost accounts have been kept, but estimates have been prepared for jobs undertaken on the following basis:

Estimated materials and direct wages, plus 150% on direct wages for factory overheads, plus 15% on factory cost for all other overheads. To this figure a further 15% is added for profit.

The accounts for the year show the following figures:

	£
Direct material	21,000
Factory overheads	27,500
Selling overheads	3,000
Sales	75,000
Direct wages	18,500
Administration overheads	5,000
Distribution overheads	1,500
Net loss	1,500

There are two production departments, and the overhead rates for the departments vary considerably.

(a) Summarise your computation and observations.
(b) State what advice you would give to the management.
(c) Suggest lines on which further investigation should proceed.

(*I.C.W.A. Final*)

22. The Blank Manufacturing Company Ltd. consists of four production departments and two service departments. For the month of September the direct departmental expenses were as follows:

Production departments—A, £4800; B, £5600; C, £6800; D, £2400.
Service departments—X, £1800; Y, 2400.

The cost of service departments X and Y are allocated to the other departments on a percentage basis, viz.:

	A	B	C	D	X	Y
X	30	20	25	15	—	10
Y	20	30	10	25	15	—

Prepare a statement showing the distribution of the service department expenses.

(*C.A.A.*)

23. Owing to the exclusive nature of his product, a manufacturer is forced to undertake the manufacture of his own machinery. Discuss the problem of the application of overheads to this part of his activities and the valuation of such machinery for capital and depreciation purposes.

(*I.C.W.A. Final*)

24. The overheads incurred in a certain department are estimated to amount to 250% of direct wages, but at the end of a year's working you find that they have risen to 350% of direct wages. Explain what factors must be considered, and how they would be evaluated in assessing the significance of the variation.

(*I.C.W.A. Final*)

25. As Cost Accountant in a large factory, draw up a memorandum on stock valuation of raw materials, work-in-progress, and finished goods.
Assume:

(a) that market prices of some materials have changed since purchases were made;

(b) that departmental rates of overhead absorption include—

    (i) percentage on labour;
    (ii) labour hour rate;
    (iii) machine hour rate;

(c) that administration, selling, and distribution expenses are usually absorbed as a percentage of production cost.

(I.C.W.A. Final)

26. In computing rates of overhead absorption, what consideration would you give to cost classification, allocation, and apportionment? Explain how the three procedures mentioned must be used in order to make the computation, and give illustrations of bases used for cost apportionment and overhead absorption.

(I.C.W.A. Final)

27. Discuss the statement: "You make progress only when you raise your overhead rates."

(I.C.W.A. Final)

28. A company which has surplus production capacity has acquired the whole of the share capital of a smaller company in the same industry which also has spare capacity. As Cost Accountant to the larger company, make a report to management indicating how *production* economies may be made.

(I.C.W.A. Final)

29. Discuss the economic importance of plant utilisation in a highly mechanised factory. Draft a suitable form for reporting periodically to management upon plant utilisation.

(I.C.W.A. Final)

30. In every manufacturing business there is usually a considerable amount of idle time for which payment is made but for which no return is received in productive effort. Thus, there may be considerable loss of time by stopping of machinery for cleaning purposes, lack of materials, etc. Enumerate other similar examples of idle time and explain how you would deal with this loss in the costing records.

(C.A.A.)

31. In considering generally the subject of product cost improvement how should plant maintenance arrangements be surveyed and controlled?

(I.C.W.A. Final)

32. Show how overhead costs are affected by each of the following:

    (a) idle capacity;
    (b) variety of products;
    (c) contraction and expansion of size of the production facilities.

(I.C.W.A. Inter.)

33. Prepare an idle machine report for use in an engineering factory. Provision should be made for all the details you consider necessary, including causes, and such percentages as may be usefully informative.

(I.C.W.A. Inter.)

34. Explain concisely what is meant by:

(a) idle capacity;
(b) excess capacity.

Mention *three* possible ways in which production capacity may be expressed, and outline the circumstances in which each of the three may be used in practice, naming an industry to which each may apply.

(*I.C.W.A. Final*)

35. What information would you present to management with regard to machine utilisation? How would you do this?

(*I.C.W.A. Final*)

36. Draft a form of machine utilisation statement for a department in which twenty machines of varying types are located. Indicate the sources from which the information on the statement is derived.

(*I.C.W.A. Final*)

37. As Cost Accountant in a business you observe that although the volume of business in a certain department is increasing, productivity is decreasing.

Using suitable figures, present a report to the Works Manager drawing attention to the facts which have given rise to this situation.

(*I.C.W.A. Final*)

38. Your Directors have decided to manufacture an entirely new product to utilise spare capacity within the works. Describe in detail how you would compute the approximate selling price of this new product.

(*I.C.W.A. Final*)

39. How would you charge into cost of production the expenditure relating to movable machinery set to work in one cost centre for a short period, withdrawn to a central reconditioning shop, and sent back to work in another cost centre? Assume these conditions to be recurrent.

(*I.C.W.A. Final*)

40. A tool room in a general engineering factory:

(a) makes tools for sale;
(b) makes new tools for use in the factory;
(c) repairs tools for use in the factory.

What problems of cost ascertainment, allocation, and apportionment arise, and how are these problems dealt with?

(*I.C.W.A. Final*)

41. In a certain business it has been the custom to absorb administration costs as a percentage of production costs. A customer buys otherwise identical products in different materials, one cheap, one expensive, and complains about the difference in the prices quoted. which he contends should amount to the difference in material price only. Give fully your views on the problem.

(*I.C.W.A. Final*)

42. In a certain business administration costs are absorbed as a percentage of production costs. It is found that tenders for work made of expensive materials are regularly being lost on account of price, whereas tenders for work using cheap materials are accepted. What explanations and/or recommendations would you make to management regarding the matter?

(I.C.W.A. Final)

43. Administration costs have been defined as the cost of formulating policy which is not directly related to other functions of the business.

Prepare a schedule of administration costs for a company with many departments, employing a large sales force. State on what bases you would make any appropriate apportionments.

(I.C.W.A. Final)

44. What method would you recommend for the absorption of administration costs in product costs? Point out the virtues and defects (if any) of the method suggested.

(I.C.W.A. Inter.)

45. How may the levels of expenditure be governed, short of fixing amounts arbitrarily, in respect of the cost of administration? Your answer should embody ideas likely to assist the various officials in controlling those costs for which they are responsible.

(I.C.W.A. Final)

46. Your company manufactures five varieties of product, distributed nation-wide at fixed retail prices. Selling and distribution costs form a substantial part of total cost. Design a summarised statement to inform your Board of the monthly results of their operations.

(I.C.W.A. Final)

47. In a business producing consumer goods subject to seasonal demand, list the items of information which should be given by:

(a) the Cost Accountant to the Sales Manager;
(b) the Sales Manager to the Cost Accountant.

Indicate against each item the suggested frequency of presentation.

(I.C.W.A. Final)

48. Do you consider that amounts charged to cost for depreciation should vary with changes in productive activity? Give your reasons, and state also the opposite arguments.

(I.C.W.A. Final)

49. When considering the rate of depreciation of plant and machinery, what influence would expenditure on repairs have upon your recommendation? Give reasons for your answer.

(I.C.W.A. Final)

50. A very expensive machine has recently been purchased, for which the normal rate of depreciation is regarded as $12\frac{1}{2}\%$ per annum on diminishing value. Your management feels that due to the introduction of improved machinery there will be a serious risk of obsolescence in about five years'

time. Using suitable figures, write a report to your management, making appropriate recommendations.

(I.C.W.A. Final)

51. What are the advantages to be gained by maintaining separate accounts for "Fixed Assets at Cost" and "Accumulated Depreciation relating to the Fixed Assets."

What are your views on depreciation provided on a replacement-cost basis? What method of provision for depreciation do you prefer and want?

(A.I.A.)

52. (a) The following expenditure was incurred in installing new boilers:

	£
Removal of old boilers	90
Demolition of old foundations	60
Erection of new foundations	350
Demolition of wall	20
Extension of boiler-house to take additional boiler	1780
Installation of new boilers	5500
Architect's fees	120

State in respect of each of the above items of expenditure and each item of old plant replaced, what amounts would be charged to revenue and/or to capital.

(b) Where fixed assets are revalued and show a surplus over book values, how would you treat the excess in the accounts of the business? What effect will such increase have on future profits?

(c) What are the merits of the straight line method of calculating depreciation?

(I.C.W.A. Final)

53. List the advantages to the Cost Department which may be expected to result from an efficiently operated plant and equipment record.

(I.C.W.A. Inter.)

54. A machine was purchased by a manufacturing company for £2000. The estimated operating costs for each year of its maximum possible working life and its estimated scrap value (if sold) at the end of each year, are set out in the following table:

	Annual operating costs	Scrap value at end of year
	£	£
1st year	1000	1200
2nd „	1300	800
3rd „	1500	600
4th „	1800	400
5th „	2200	200

When and why will it pay to replace the machine by a new one of the same type assuming that a new machine can be purchased at any time for £2000.

(C.I.S. Final, Part question)

Cost Control Accounts (Chapter 14)

1. (a) Explain the purpose of the following accounts in a costing system and indicate the sources from which entries in such accounts might be expected to come:

(1) Cost of Sales Account;
(2) Finished Stock Account.

(b) What difference, if any, would you expect to find between the sources of entries in the Work-in-progress Account in the Financial Ledger of a manufacturing business and in the Work-in-progress Account in the Costing Ledger?

(C.A. Final, May 1956)

2. Define "Cost Control Accounts" and give examples.
Show their relation to the financial accounts and the details of cost summaries, presenting your answer in the form of a chart.

(I.C.W.A. Final)

3. The following balances are shown in a Cost Ledger as at October 1, 1954:

	Dr. £	Cr. £
Work-in-progress Account	7,840	
Finished Stock Account	5,860	
Works Overhead Suspense Account	400	
Office and Administration Overheads Suspense Account	200	
Stores Ledger Control Account	10,500	
Cost Ledger Control Account	——	24,800

Transactions for the year ended September 30, 1955, were:

	£
Wages—direct labour	61,200
Wages—indirect labour	2,800
Works overheads allocated to production	18,700
Office and Administration overheads allocated to production	6,200
Stores issued to production	39,300
Goods finished during year	120,000
Finished goods sold	132,000
Stores purchased	36,000
Stores issued to factory repair orders	1,500
Carriage inwards on stores issued for production	600
Works expenses	14,000
Office and administration expenses	6,000

Write up accounts in the Cost Ledger to record the above transactions, make the necessary transfers to Control Accounts, and prepare a Trial Balance as at September 30, 1955. Compute the profit or loss for the year.

(C.A.A. Part 2)

4. The Cost Accounts of the Round Manufacturing Co. Ltd. show the following information in respect of the year ended September 30, 1957:

	October 1, 1956	September 30, 1957
	£	£
Stores on hand	1600	2,253
Stock of finished goods	2435	2,562
Work in progress	3100	2,480
Purchases		7,500
Carriage inwards		113
Stores issued		6,900
Wages—direct labour		6,660
Wages—indirect labour		2,340
Works expenses—including rent, power, etc.		6,700
Repairs to materials in store		60
Cost of completed jobs		24,627
Cost of finished goods sold		24,500
Selling expenses		567
Office and administration expenses		1,325

The Cost Journal shows that £9133 and £1315 were allocated to work in progress in respect of Works Overheads and Office Overheads respectively. You are required to show how the above transactions would be recorded in the various Cost Ledger Accounts and to extract a Trial Balance as at September 30, 1957.

(C.A.A. Part 2)

5. The following balances were extracted from the Cost Ledger of Alluse Ltd., as on January 1, 1951:

	£
Work in progress	5,000
Finished goods	2,000
Stores	3,600

Transactions during the year were:

Stores purchased	21,000
Wages—productive	60,000
Wages—unproductive	18,000
Stores issued	22,000
Works expenses	12,000
Administration expenses	8,000
Works expenses recovered	19,500
Administration expenses recovered	15,200
Sales	130,000

On December 31, 1951, stocks were valued as follows:

Work in progress	7,350
Finished goods	4,200
Stores	2,900

Unproductive wages are allocated equally between works and administration expenses.

You are required to write up the appropriate accounts in the Cost Ledger of Alluse Ltd. and to prepare a Trial Balance as on December 31, 1951.

(C.A. Inter., November 1952)

6. Given the following information, you are required to write up the appropriate accounts, bring down the closing balances at June 1, and take out a Trial Balance, under account code numbers, at May 31, 1959. The following balances existed in the Company's Cost Ledger as at April 30, 1959:

Code		£	£
1	Control account		397,576
2	Cost of sales	315,631	
3	Material price variance		1,025
4	Material wastage	14,187	
5	Wages over/under-absorbed	346	
6	Overhead over/under-absorbed		763
7	Finished stock	29,864	
	Work in Progress:		
8	Process A—Materials	8,613	
	Wages	856	
	Overhead	1,712	
9	Process B—Materials	6,424	
	Wages	689	
	Overhead	689	
10	Process C—Materials	3,987	
	Wages	420	
	Overhead	630	
11	Raw materials	15,316	
		£399,364	£399,364

During May 1959 the following transactions took place:

	£	£
Actual cost of materials purchased		12,008
Actual wages incurred		1,266
Wages were allocated to: Process A	784	
„ B	232	
„ C	168	
		1,184
Actual overhead incurred		2,346
Raw materials issued from store to Process A		7,200
Work in progress, valued and transferred:		
From Process A to B:		
Material	9206	
Wages	986	
		10,192

	£	£
From Process B to C:		
Material	8614	
Wages	790	
		9,404
From Process C to Finished Stock:		
Material	6308	
Wages	510	
		6,818
Finished stock sold (at cost)		15,719

Overhead is absorbed by processes on the basis of wages.

Inter-process and finished stock transfers also carry overhead on the same basis.

Materials purchased are taken into stock at standard cost, which allows for a 0·5% price loss.

Standard material wastage allowances (based on cost of material input) are: Process A, 3%; Process B, 1%; Process C, 2%.

(I.C.W.A. Inter.)

7. From the following balances extracted from the Cost Ledger construct a Cost Control Account and show the Trial Balance of the Cost Ledger:

	£		£
Stores	1,366	Finished Stock	17,508
Direct material	25,346	Direct wages	48,682
Works overheads	46,548	Sales from stock	2,006
Job No. 794	1,142	Profit on completed Jobs	22,138
Job No. 852	1,964	Office Overhead Suspense	
Profit on sale from stock	460	A/c	416
Office Overheads	10,648	Completed Jobs	131,578
Direct Expenses	456	Works Overhead Suspense	
		A/c	1,030

(A.I.A. Final)

8. You wish to institute control accounts in respect of materials purchased and used in your factory. What purposes do control accounts serve? What accounts would you institute and from what sources would the entries be derived?

(I.C.W.A. Inter.)

9. The balances in the Cost Ledger of a manufacturing company on January 1, 1956, were:

	£
Stores Ledger Control Account	7,000
Work in Progress Account	12,800
Finished Stock Account	2,000
Cost Ledger Control Account	21,800

You are given the following information for year 1956:

	£
Purchases of materials	40,000
Direct factory wages	60,000
Manufacturing expenses	34,600
Selling and distribution expenses	5,400
Materials issued to production	37,200
Manufacturing expenses recovered	34,440
Selling and distribution expenses recovered	5,320
Sales	150,000
Stock of material at December 31, 1956	9,800
Stock of finished goods at December 31, 1956	4,700
Work in Progress at December 31, 1956	14,700

You are required to show the accounts in the Cost Ledger for year 1956, to prepare the Costing Profit and Loss Account for the year, and extract a Trial Balance.

(C.I.S. Final)

10. The following is an extract from the accounts of a contractor for the year to March 31, 1957:

Trading and Profit and Loss Account

	£		£
Stock of materials	3,400	Contracts completed	38,000
Work in progress	6,300	Stocks of materials	4,000
Purchases, materials	14,200	Work in progress	7,800
Wages	16,300		
Gross Profit	9,600		
	£49,800		£49,800
Establishment charges	3,900	Gross profit	9,600
Net profit	5 700		
	£9,600		£9,600

The costing system is separate from the financial books, and includes Stores and Contract Ledgers.

Work in progress is valued in the financial accounts at Prime Cost, and the figures are identical with those shown by the Contract Ledger at the relevant dates, the breakdown of the valuations being as follows:

	April 1, 1956	March 31, 1957
	£	£
Direct materials	2090	4500
Direct labour	4210	3300
	£6300	£7800

Materials used, as shown in the Trading Account after adjusting stocks, includes wastage in stores £420 and indirect material £760; wages in the Trading Account includes indirect labour £450; apart from these exceptions, all materials used and wages incurred as shown above are charged in detail to the contract accounts. Establishment charges (including indirect expenditure) are debited in the Contract Ledger by adding 27½% of the direct labour cost to each contract on completion of the work when the invoice is sent to the customer.

Prepare on a double-entry basis suitable accounts for the costing books, which will reveal the financial results, act as control accounts where necessary, and also serve to reconcile the cost records with the financial books after taking into account establishment charges under- or over-recovered.

(*C.C.S. Final*)

11. From the following figures (standard, except where otherwise stated) relating to a month's activities draw up the various control accounts required, showing the total variances from standard:

		£	£
Stock brought forward—			
Steel bars		7000	
Pressings		5000	
Tools		1000	
Consumable stores		2000	
			15,000
Work in progress brought forward			11,000
Direct wages—			
Machine Shop		3000	
Assembly Shop		7000	
Tool-room		2000	
			12,000
Overheads—			
Machine Shop		6000	
Assembly Shop		3500	
Tool-room		3000	
			12,500
Sales (actual)			42,000

	Actual	*Standard*	
Purchases—	£	£	
Steel bars	6,140	6000	
Pressings	6,090	6000	
Tools	1,050	1000	
Consumable stores	1,020	1000	
	14,300		14,000

Issues from stores—		
Steel bars to Machine Shop		6500
Pressings to Assembly Shop		5500
Tools		500

Consumable stores—	£	£	£
Machine Shop	750		
Tool-room	250		
		1000	
			13,500
Production—			
Machine Shop			20,500
Assembly Shop			16,750
Scrapped work in progress—			
Machine Shop		750	
Assembly Shop		250	
			1,000
Work in progress carried forward			12,000
Cost of sales			35,250
Allocation of Tool-room cost—			
Machine Shop		5000	
Assembly Shop		750	
			5,750

NOTE.—Total variance only is required, and no attempt should be made to analyse by causes.

(*I.C.W.A. Final*)

The Reconciliation of Cost and Financial Accounts (*Chapter 15*)

1. Indicate the reasons why it is usually necessary for the cost and financial records of a factory to be reconciled and explain the main sources of difference which might enter into such a reconciliation.

(*C.A.A. Part 2*)

2. The profit disclosed by the Manufacturing Account prepared from the Cost Books is in excess of that shown by the Trading Account prepared from the Financial Books. To what could such difference be attributable, and what steps would you take to obviate or minimise similar differences in future?

(*A.I.A. Final*)

3. A business expanding rapidly uses historical costing methods. Towards the end of a year the reconciliation of Cost and Financial Accounts reveals considerable difference between overheads incurred and overheads absorbed in production. It is suggested that the differences would not have occurred if a Standard Costing system had been used.

Give your views on this suggestion, indicate the type of difference likely to have arisen, and show how the difference would have been avoided and/or indicated in standard costing.

(*I.C.W.A. Final*)

4. (*a*) Why is it important that Cost and Financial Accounts should be capable of reconciliation one with the other?

(*b*) Give three examples of items which would not normally appear in the Cost Accounts, though they would quite properly be taken to account in the Financial Revenue Accounts.

(*C.A. Final*)

5. A private manufacturing company commenced business on January 1, 1955. One product of a standard type is produced.

The following information has been obtained from the Company's Books:

	1955	1956
	£	£
Materials used at cost	18,000	31,000
Manufacturing wages	22,000	39,000
Overhead expenses—		
Manufacturing	12,000	15,750
Selling and distribution	3,900	4,300
	Units	Units
Output	4,000	7,000
Sales (at a selling price of £17 per unit throughout the two years)	3,900	4,300
Stock at end of year	100	2,800

There was no stock of partly finished units at the end of either year.

The output of 1955 was produced at an even rate throughout that year and, similarly, production was at an even rate during 1956. Costs in both years were also evenly spread.

The Company's Accountant has prepared accounts which show that the Net Profit of 1956 is less than that of 1955, but a professional accountant has produced amended figures which show that the Net Profit of 1956 is higher than that of 1955.

You may take it that the difference between the two sets of figures is due not to any mistake but to a difference of opinion as to the method of valuing stocks, and that both methods can be regarded as legitimate.

You are required: (1) to set out Trading and Profit and Loss Accounts for each of the two years as they might have been prepared by the Company's Accountant; and (2) to show your calculation of the Net Profit for each year, on the basis which you think may have been adopted by the professional accountant. (C.I.S. Final)

6. The following is a summary of the Trading and Profit and Loss Account of A.B. Ltd., for year ending December 31, 1956:

	£			£
Materials consumed	68,500	Sales (60,000 units)		150,000
Wages	37,750	Finished stock		
Factory expenses	20,750	(2000 units)		4,000
Administration expenses	9,560	Work in progress—	£	
Selling and Distribution		Materials	1600	
expenses	11,250	Wages	900	
Preliminary expenses w/o	1,000	Factory expenses	500	
Goodwill w/o	500		——	3,000
Net Profit	8,140	Dividends		450
	£157,450			£157,450

The Company manufactures a standard unit.

In the Cost Accounts factory expenses have been allocated to production at 20% of Prime Cost, administration expenses at 3s. per unit, and selling and distribution expenses at 4s. per unit. The Net Profit shown by the Cost Accounts was £8200.

Prepare:

(a) control accounts for factory expenses, administration expenses, and selling and distribution expenses;

(b) a statement reconciling the profit disclosed by the cost records with that shown in the financial accounts.

(I.C.W.A. Inter.)

7. During the year a company's profits have been estimated from the costing system to be £23,063, whereas the final accounts prepared by the auditors disclose a profit of £16,624. Given the following information, you are required to:

(a) prepare a reconciliation statement showing clearly the reasons for the difference;

(b) describe an alternative accounting system which would obviate the need for reconciling the Financial and Cost Accounts.

Profit and Loss Account
Year ended March 31, 1959

	£	£		£
Opening stocks	247,179		Sales	346,500
Purchases	82,154			
	329,333			
Closing stocks	75,121			
		254,212		
Direct wages		23,133		
Factory overhead		20,826		
Gross Profit c/d		48,329		
		£346,500		£346,500
Administration		9,845	Gross Profit b/d	48,329
Selling expenses		22,176	Sundry Income	316
Net Profit		16,624		
		£48,645		£48,645

The costing records show:

(a) a Stock Ledger closing balance of £78,197;

(b) a direct wages absorption account with a closing credit balance of £24,867;

(c) a factory overhead absorption account with a closing credit balance of £19,714;

(*d*) administration expenses calculated as 3% of the selling price;
(*e*) selling prices include 5% for selling expenses;
(*f*) no mention of sundry income.

(I.C.W.A. Inter.)

8. You are required, as the Cost Accountant of a manufacturing organisation, to prepare a statement reconciling the financial records with the cost records. You are also required to write briefly on the possible causes of such differences between the two sets of records as disclosed by the comparison. The following information relating to the operations for a given month has been supplied to you:

(*a*) Extract from Profit and Loss Statement prepared from financial books:

	£	£	£
Sales			36,128
Less Cost of Goods Sold			
Stock at beginning of period—			
Raw material	3984		
Work in progress	2216		
Finished goods	7842		
		14,042	
Raw materials		10,224	
Direct wages		7,163	
Manufacturing expenses		5,289	
		36,718	
Less Stock at end of period—			
Raw material	4285		
Work in progress	3072		
Finished Goods	8177		
		15,534	
			21,184
Gross Profit			£14,944

(*b*) Data obtained from costing records:

	£	£
Work in process at beginning of period—		
Material	956	
Wages	700	
Expenses, 80% of wages	560	
		2,216
Work in process at end of period—		
Material	1,398	
Wages	930	
Expenses, 80% of wages	744	
		3,072
Material and wages charged to work in process during period—		
Material		9,528
Wages		6,634

(I.C.W.A. Final)

Integral Accounts (Chapter 16)

1. What do you understand by "Integrated" Accounts, and what are the principles involved?

(Com. A. Final)

2. Set out your views on the separation and integration of costing and financial accounting records.

(A.I.A. Final)

3. It is proposed to integrate the cost and financial accounts in a company in which they have previously been separate. State the advantages to be derived from this process and the main adjustments to procedure which will be needed.

Also show how the process might affect the organisation of the cost department and its relation to other departments.

(I.C.W.A. Final

4. (a) What do you understand by integral accounts?

(b) Design a code of accounts illustrating the principles of integral accounts in a limited-liability company selling a single standardised product which passes through one production department.

(I.C.W.A. Inter.)

5. From the following information relating to a year's operations, you are required to compile and close off the cost and financial accounts of a company whose accounts are integrated and prepare a Trial Balance:

Balances at Beginning of Period	*Actual* £	*Standard* £
Customers	185,000	
Suppliers	84,000	
Cash	39,000	
Materials		40,000
Fixed Assets	200,000	
Depreciation provision	94,000	
Work in progress		60,000
Investments	12,000	
Ordinary Share Capital	300,000	
Profit and Loss Account (credit)	58,000	
Transactions during Year		
Sales	404,000	385,000
Cost of sales		249,000
Wages (gross) (70% Direct)	112,000	
Materials issued (85% Direct)		106,000
Materials purchased	137,000	131,000
Materials returned	4,000	5,000
Cash paid—		
Wages	102,000	
Expenses	7,000	
Suppliers	125,000	
Interim dividend	23,000	

Transactions during Year		*Actual*	*Standard*
		£	£
Cash received—			
From customers		416,000	
Income from investments		4,000	
Overhead allowance			65,000

Variances—Adverse:

Direct wages—rate	3% of actual output
efficiency	4% ,, ,, ,,
methods	3% ,, ,, ,,
Indirect materials—price	4% ,, standard

Depreciation at 10% is to be charged to costs.

(I.C.W.A. Final)

6. You are required to record the undernoted transactions in the accounts in the financial and cost ledgers which are affected by them. The cost and financial books are integrated. You are required to prove the accuracy of your work by taking out a Trial Balance.

	£
Materials purchased during period—	
At cost	32,856
At standard	29,324
Salaries—	
Research and development	3,900
Production	5,400
Selling	3,800
Distribution	1,600
Administration	2,100
Wages—	
Research and development	950
Production	14,680
Selling	1,300
Distribution	4,920
Administration	1,150
Supplies—	
Research and development	940
Production	1,350
Selling	540
Distribution	2,920
Administration	750
Expenses—	
Research and development	1,800
Production	3,640
Selling	980
Distribution	430
Administration	1,340

	£
Cheques drawn in favour of trade creditors	46,500
Cheques drawn for salaries, wages, supplies, and expenses	41,000
Deductions made from wages and salaries	4,900
Stock of materials on hand at beginning of period at standard	10,640
Trade creditors at beginning of period	29,440
Cash at bank at beginning of period	56,820
Sales during period—	
At actual	97,500
At standard	72,100
Trade debtors at beginning of period	51,430
Cash received from trade debtors	48,600
Discount allowed—	
To customers	1,250
By suppliers	1,890
Depreciation—	
Financial provision	4,200
Charge against costs	4,950
Research expenditure capitalised	2,000
Cost of work carried out on new factory extension by building	
Maintenance Department	2,600
Notional rent of freehold factory	1,000

(*I.C.W.A. Final*)

7. Record in ledger accounts in integral form the following transactions, giving effect to the additional information provided, and closing off at the end of the month.

Trial Balance at Beginning of Month

	£	£
Share capital		100,000
General reserve		15,000
Profit and Loss Appropriation Account		8,000
Plant and machinery	87,000	
Plant and machinery depreciation		20,000
Stock (materials)	14,200	
Work in progress	12,000	
Stock (finished products)	20,600	
Sales Ledger Control	38,400	
Bought Ledger Control		40,000
Bank	10,800	
	£183,000	£183,000

	£	£
Transactions for month		
Purchases:		
Materials for stock	18,720	
Materials (direct to products)	1,480	
Works overheads (materials and services)	1,700	
Administration, Selling, and Distribution		
Overhead (materials and services)	2,320	
Plant and machinery	1,180	
		25,400
Wages:		
Cash drawn for wages	7,300	
Cash drawn for N.I. stamps	485	
P.A.Y.E. deductions not yet paid to the		
Inland Revenue	365	
		8,150
Wages direct to products	7,085	
Factory indirect labour	1,065	
	£8,150	

	£
Salaries (administration, selling, and distribution)	825
Other cash disbursements (administration, selling, and distribution)	255

Depreciation to be provided at 10% of original cost for one month (ignore additions)

Rent £1200 per annum. One month to be provided for and apportioned 75% Factory and 25% Offices

	£	£
Issues:		
Production	14,870	
Expense materials	1,250	
		16,120

Works overheads—recovery rate 65% of direct wages

	£
Factory cost of completed products	26,840
Factory cost of work in progress at end of month	13,200
Stock of finished products at end of month	22,450
Sales for month	29,700

(*I.C.W.A. Final*)

8. Give journal entries (narratives are not required) to give effect to the double-entry principles of integral accounting in respect of the following:

	£
(*a*) Payment of—	
Net wages cheque	800
National Insurance cheque	100
And the deduction from wages of P.A.Y.E. tax	100

£

(b) Allocation of gross wages and National Insurance—

Direct wages (in progress)	600
Departmental indirect wages	150
(Wages are paid a week in arrear)	

(c) Credit purchases of raw materials 2,000
and returnable packages 120

(d) Charging into departmental costs of a proportion of annually paid insurances 70

(e) Credit charging by outside engineers of departmental plant repairs 240

(f) Payment of supplier's accounts (after £60 taken for cash discounts) 1,130

(g) Factory cost of production of finished stocks 10,000
(Ratios: direct materials, 12; direct wages, 2; factory overheads, 6.)

(h) Factory cost of finished stocks sold 8,000

(i) Sale of finished stocks on credit (after allowing £370 sales rebates) 10,370

(j) Payment by customers of credit sales (after taking £120 in cash discounts) 13,380

(*I.C.W.A. Inter.*)

Contract Costs (*Chapter 17*)

1. J. Smelt & Co. Ltd. are public works contractors, and maintain a separate account for each contract. Contract No. 142 was commenced in February 19.., and the expenditure to December 31 of that year was as follows:

	£
Materials purchased direct	11,960
Materials issued from stores	590
Plant (purchased April 1, 1955)	6,500
Wages	7,890
Direct expenses	740

The stock of materials at December 31, was £1410.

The life of the plant is 5 years, and an addition for overheads has to be made equal to 50% of wages. On December 1 the architect certified the value of work done at £25,000. The total contract price is £100,000. The contract will take three years to complete, and at December 31 it is estimated that 30% of the total cost (£90,000) had been incurred.

From the above information prepare the Contract Account, and state the amount which, in your opinion, should be brought into work-in-progress at December 31.

(*A.I.A. Final*)

2. A public works contractor secured a contract at a price of £500,000. Work began on July 1, 19.., and the Contract Ledger account showed the following items debited up to March 31 in the following year:

	£
Materials	90,000
Wages	105,000
Direct charges	5,000
Plant	16,000

The measurement at March 31 read as follows:

Total work done certified to date	240,000
Total work done per last measurement	210,000
Total work done for month	30,000
Less Retention money 10%	3,000

	£	27,000
Materials on site	5000	
Less 20%	1000	
		4,000
Amount payable		£31,000

Prepare a *pro forma* account for the contract showing the profit earned to date, and indicate by means of a note the basis on which you arrive at the amount which might be carried to Profit and Loss Account. Allow for depreciation on the plant at 10% per annum.

(*I.C.W.A. Final*)

3. Hope Builders Ltd. makes up its accounts annually to December 31 Contract No. 123 commenced on April 1, 19... The costing records show the following information at December 31 that year:

	£
Materials charged to site	4,300
Labour	10,022
Overheads	1,262

A machine costing £3000 has been on the site for 73 days. Its working life is estimated at 5 years and its final scrap value at £200.

A supervisor, who is paid £1000 per annum, has spent approximately one-half of his time on this contract.

All other expenses and administration to December 31 amounted to £2522, and materials on site at that date cost £496.

The contract price is £40,000. At December 31, two-thirds of the contract was completed; architects' certificates had been issued for £20,000, and £16,000 had been paid on account.

Prepare a contract account and state how much profit or loss you would include in respect of Contract No. 123 in the cost accounts to December 31.

(*C.A.A.*)

4. A firm of speculative builders have in the past delegated the work of roofing and wall-tiling to sub-contractors. In future they propose to undertake the work themselves by direct labour. You are required to state what alterations will require to be made in the costing system.

(*C.A.A.*)

5. In contract cost accounts it may be necessary to make a charge for the use of plant and machinery. Explain briefly two methods of dealing with the charge, and state in what circumstances you would adopt each method.

(*C.A. Inter., November 1957*)

6. A contract account in the books of J. McHugh Ltd. appears as follows:

19..		£
June 30	Materials issued to site	5,000
	Plant issued to site	12,500
	Direct labour	4,600
	Indirect labour	640
	Overhead expenses	1,950

You are informed that it is the practice of the firm to take credit for two-thirds of the profit earned on the contracts in progress after taking into account the value of the work certified for payment by professional surveyors. You are required to complete this account to June 30 and show the transfer to Profit and Loss Account, for which purpose you are supplied with the following further information as at that date:

	£
Value of work certified for payment	10,000
Cost of work carried out, but not certified	3,800
Stock of materials not used	950
Value of plant on site, after depreciation	11,875

(*A.C.C.S. Final*)

7. Dominion Erectors Ltd. undertook three contracts in one year; one on January 1, one on July 1, and one on October 1. On December 31, when the Company's accounts were prepared, the position was as follows:

Contract No.	1	2	3
	£	£	£
Contract Price	150,000	101,250	37,500
Expenditure—			
Materials	27,000	21,750	2,500
Wages	41,250	42,150	1,750
General expenses	1,500	1,050	125
Plant installed	7,500	6,000	1,500
Materials on site	1,500	1,500	250
Wages accrued	1,275	1,350	200
General expenses accrued	225	150	25
Work certified	75,000	60,000	4,500
Cash received on work certified	56,250	45,000	3,375
Work completed, but uncertified	2,250	3,000	275

The plant was installed on the commencing dates of the contracts, and depreciation is calculated at 10% per annum.

Prepare the respective accounts in the Contracts Ledger and give suitable entries in the Company's Balance Sheet at December 31. A columnar layout may be adopted and calculations approximated to the nearest £.

(*A.I.A. Final*)

8. Brickworkers Ltd., building contractors, commenced work on a certain contract on January 1, 19... The agreed price for the contract was £200,000, and the work was to be finished by December 31 in the *following* year.

Expenditure charged to the contract account during the first year was:

	£
Materials purchased	38,000
Plant purchased	16,000
Wages	42,000
Administrative Expenses	6,500

The stock of unused materials on the site at December 31 amounted at cost to £2500. It was estimated that the residual value of the plant at the termination of the contract will be £4000. Depreciation is to be apportioned over the period of the contract by the straight-line method.

All work completed up to the end of November was certified by the Architect in December, and in that month the Company received a payment of £96,000, representing the contract price of the work certified less 20% retention money.

When the Company's accounts for the year to December 31 were prepared it was decided to take credit in the Profit and Loss Account for a proportion of the total estimated profit on the contract, the proportion being that which the contract price of the work certified in the first year bears to the total contract price. For the purposes of this calculation it was estimated that the expenditure from January 1 (second year) to completion, including a provision of £10,000 for contingencies, would amount to £56,000 in addition to the cost of materials on site brought forward, and to depreciation of plant.

You are required to set out the entries in the Contract Account for the year ended December 31 (first year), showing the transfer to Profit and Loss Account; and show how any balances resulting from the above matters would appear in the Balance Sheet.

(*C.I.S. Final*)

9. The following particulars are extracted from the books of Constructors Ltd. for the year to June 30, 19..:

Contract No.	Work in Progress brought forward from previous year £	Wages £	Materials £	Sales £
11	8640	7,030	6090	30,500
12	4050	4,810	4600	18,500
13		10,400	6240	23,250
14		6,080	4570	4,450
15		2,930	1800	2,100

In respect of work in progress (valued consistently at wages and material costs) it is the Company's practice to provide, for Balance Sheet purposes, 10% for contingencies.

On June 30:

(a) Contract 14 was 75% complete. In April the customer was invoiced with 25% of the contract price and has paid £2500 on account. This latter amount has been credited to Work-in-progress Account.

(b) Contract 15 was 50% complete. In May the customer paid an instalment of 20% of the contract price. This amount has been credited to Sales Account. Wages include a payment of £645 to sub-contractors, yielding a profit to them of $7\frac{1}{2}$%.

Submit

(1) corrective journal entries as you think necessary;
(2) summarised trading account;
(3) a reasoned comment on the profits for which you think credit might be taken.

(C.C.A. Final)

Factory Job Costing (Chapter 18)

1. From the following information, prepare a Job Cost Sheet for Order B. 1329 for the A.B. Company Ltd. for 120 identical castings.

Metal used   40 cwt at 13s. per cwt
Mould labour   20 hours at 4s. per hour
Core-making labour   10 hours at 3s. 10d. per hour
Finishing labour   86 hours at 3s. $1\frac{1}{2}d$. per hour

Overhead absorption rates:

Moulding   233% on direct process labour
Core-making 265%   ,,   ,,
Finishing   180%   ,,   ,,

Three pounds of scrap metal are fettled off each finished casting. One hundred and twenty-six castings were made, but six were found defective after pouring and scrapped. Scrap value is 4s. per cwt. Show the cost per casting and per cwt of finished casting.

(I.C.W.A. Inter.)

2. In an organisation making a wide variety of engineering products each order is the subject of a job cost. It is found that for a number of smaller jobs the cost of compiling these costs is up to 50% of the total production cost of the job.

Give your reactions to this situation, suggesting alternative procedures. Would the introduction of mechanical accounting equipment have any effect on the basic problem?

(I.C.W.A. Inter.)

3. A company manufacturing components for the motor-car industry consists of a light Machine Shop and an Assembly Department. In a normal year, when sales amounted to £120,683, its costs were made up as follows:

	£
Direct materials	24,832
Direct wages, Machine Shop	16,694
Direct wages, Assembly	8,090
Factory overhead, Machine Shop	31,742
Factory overhead, Assembly	7,264
Administration costs	8,767
Selling costs	4,445
Distribution costs	6,427

Direct labour hours amounted to 67,284 in the Machine Shop and 40,073 in the Assembly Department.

It is the custom of the company to absorb overheads as follows:

Factory Overhead:

Machine Shop at 9s. 6d. per direct labour hour.
Assembly Department at 3s. 8d. per direct labour hour.
Administration, selling, and distribution costs at $22\frac{1}{2}\%$ on production cost.

A certain component is made from 50 lb of steel strip costing £56 per ton and requires $3\frac{1}{2}$ hours of machine shop labour charged at 5s. per hour, and $1\frac{3}{4}$ hours of assembly labour charged at 4s. per hour. The customer is being charged a price of £6 each, and asks for quotations for exactly the same component: (a) made in "free issue" material, and (b) made from brass strip requiring 50 lb per article at a cost of 2s. 3d. per lb.

Management asks for information to enable quotations to be made as required, and also to see whether the present selling price is reasonable.

Present figures as required.

(*I.C.W.A. Final*)

4. (a) Explain how costing can be employed to provide management with information sufficient to enable it to compare and control costs without the necessity of preparing terminal or job costs.

(b) Explain how costing methods enable periodical estimated accounts to be prepared without the necessity of stocktaking.

(*C.A. Final, November 1957*)

5. In a manufacturing organisation short runs are almost invariably more costly than long runs.

Using appropriate figures, produce a report to management illustrating this fact, first indicating the nature of the industry and the size of the business.

(*I.C.W.A. Final*)

6. A Production Order is issued for the manufacture of 3000 Type "X" Machines, for which will be required, among other items, 9000 Components "Y." Trace by means of a diagram the progress of such components through

the cost and financial books from the time of purchase to their subsequent use in fulfilling the Production Order, assuming that under inspection 110 of the components are scrapped as being not up to standard.

(*C.A.A.*)

Operating Costs (*Chapter 19*)

1. A brewery maintains a motor service consisting of twelve lorries, delivering barrelled and bottled beer, and bringing back empties.

Outline a system of cost control, covering the cost of running, maintenance, and depreciation, recommending the unit of measurement to be applied.

(*I.C.W.A. Inter.*)

2. In a group organisation consisting of twelve individual companies it has been the practice for each company to maintain its own Transport Department. Top management has decided to pool all vehicles and staff into a central Transport Department which will in future give service to all companies within the group. Approximately thirty vehicles are involved, ranging in type from saloon cars to 5-ton lorries, and the vehicles are used for purposes ranging from inter-company communication to direct sales delivery service.

Discuss the effect of this change on costs. Outline the bases upon which you would propose to absorb the operating costs of this new service department.

(*I.C.W.A. Final*)

3. With a mixed fleet of a hundred goods-transport vehicles how would you calculate an hourly rate per vehicle for charging to jobs and services?

(*I.C.W.A. Final*)

4. A factory which uses a large amount of coal is situated between two collieries "A" and "B," the former being 5 miles and the latter 10 miles distant from the factory. A fleet of lorries of 5-ton carrying capacity is used for the collection of coal from the pit-heads. Records reveal that the lorries average a speed of 20 miles an hour when running and regularly take 10 minutes in the factory yard to unload. At colliery "A" loading time averages 30 minutes per load; at colliery "B" 20 minutes per load.

Drivers' wages, licences, depreciation, garage, and similar charges are found to cost 6s. per hour operated. Fuel, oil, tyres, repairs, and similar charges are found to cost 6d. per mile run.

Draw up a statement showing the cost per ton-mile of carrying coal from each colliery. If the coal is of equal quality and price at pit-head, from which colliery should the purchases be made?

(*I.C.W.A. Final*)

5. Describe a method to ensure recovery of all expenditure on repair work in a motor garage when immediate charges are made to customers.

(*C.A.A.*)

6. Draw up a *pro forma* cost statement for a canteen subsidised by the company, serving a firm of 1500 employees.

What measures of efficiency would you use in such a case, and on what basis would canteen prices be fixed?

(*I.C.W.A. Final*)

R

7. The works canteen of a large industrial organisation shows a considerable loss on the first year's trading, although it was intended that the amounts charged for meals, etc., should just cover the cost. You are instructed to investigate the matter and to suggest any improvements you consider necessary in the existing costing system. You may assume whatever facts you consider appropriate as having been discovered during your investigation. Submit the main headings of your report.

(C.A.A.)

8. What is a departmental operating statement?
Prepare such a statement to indicate the efficiency of the use of each element of cost.

(I.C.W.A. Final)

Process Costing (Chapters 20–22)

1. A certain product passes through five distinct processes at a factory before it becomes a finished article ready for sale. Each process is dealt with in a separate department, but in the fourth process some of the raw material is purchased and not obtained from the prior processes. State and explain your views as to the price at which the transfers from process to process should be made.

(I.A. Inter.)

2. Point out the difference between the "job" and "process" methods of costing. Name any industry with which you are familiar and state which of these methods you would employ and why. Sketch out a general scheme that you would ultimately set in motion for costing in that concern.

(I.A. Final)

3. The information given below is extracted from the Cost Accounts of a factory producing a commodity in the manufacture of which three processes are involved. Prepare Process Cost Accounts showing the cost of the output and cost per unit at each stage of manufacture:

(1) The operations in each separate process are completed daily.
(2) The value at which units are to be charged to processes "B" and "C" is the cost per unit of Processes "A" and "A" plus "B" respectively.

	Process		
	A	B	C
	£	£	£
Direct wages	640	1200	2,925
Machine expense	360	300	360
Factory overhead	200	225	240
Raw materials consumed	2,400	—	—
	Units	Units	Units
Production (gross)	37,000	—	—
Wastage	1,000	1500	500
Stock, July 1	—	4000	16,500
Stock, July 31	—	1000	5,500

(I.A. Final)

4. What do you understand by:

(1) normal, and

(2) abnormal

wastage of materials during the process of manufacture?
State briefly how each should be treated in cost accounts.

(*C.A. Inter., May 1955*)

5. 10 tons of material, valued at £85, pass through process A, yielding
8·5 tons of product, 0·8 tons of process scrap, and 0·5 tons of finished material
failing to pass inspection. The operating cost of the process is £15 and the
market value of scrap is 62*s*. 6*d*. per ton. Give the Journal entries to deal with
these transactions and show the cost of production of the processed material.

(*I.C.W.A. Inter.*)

6. The following details are extracted from the costing records of an oil
refinery for the week ended September 30:

	Crushing Plant	Refining Plant	Finishing
Purchase of 500 tons of Copra		£20,000	
	£	£	£
Cost of labour	250	100	150
Electric power	60	36	24
Sundry materials	10	200	—
Repairs to machinery and plant	28	33	14
Steam	60	45	45
Factory expenses	132	66	22
Cost of casks			750

300 tons of crude oil were produced.

250 tons of oil were produced by the refining process.

248 tons of refined oil were finished for delivery.

Copra sacks sold	£40
175 tons of Copra residue sold	£1100
Loss in weight in crushing	25 tons
45 tons of by-products obtained from refining process	£675

You are required to show the accounts in respect of each of the following
stages of manufacture for the purpose of arriving at the cost per ton of each
process, and the total cost per ton of the finished oil:

(*a*) copra crushing process;

(*b*) refining process;

(*c*) finishing process, including casking.

(*I.A. Final*)

7. The metal charged to a cupola in an iron foundry during a period was as
follows:

76 tons pig-iron "A" at £23 per ton
52 „ „ "B" at £21 „
17 „ steel scrap at £12 „
55 „ iron scrap at £20 „

During the period 100 tons good castings were produced and 85 tons of scrap work, runners, heads, etc., were returned to stock.

Draw up a statement for management showing the costs of metal charged, metal poured, and good castings produced in total and "per ton."

Show also the savings in cost which would have been effected if the loss in melt had amounted to 5% of metal charged, and the same weight of scrap work, runners, heads, etc., had been returned to stock. It is the practice of the business to credit scrap, etc., returned to stock at average cost of metal content.

(*I.C.W.A. Final*)

8. A company operates a processing plant to produce four products A, B. C, and D. There are three processes X, Y, and Z. Process hours per unit of product vary as follows:

Product	Process hours		
	X	Y	Z
A	3	2	6
B	2	4	4
C	2·5	1	5
D	1·25	1	2·5

The process costs for the period under review are as follows:

X   £15,000
Y   £5,000
Z   £6,000

No work in progress at beginning or end of the period figures in the results Output amounts to:

A   5000 units
B   2500   „
C   3000   „
D   2000   „

(*a*) Prepare a production statement, excluding costs, but including weighted figures for process hours, classified according to products and processes.

(*b*) Prepare a simple cost statement showing unit and total process costs for each of the four products.

(*I.C.W.A. Final*)

9. A brass alloy of 70% copper and 30% zinc is made into extruded brass section by the two consecutive processes of casting and extrusion. Copper costs £170 per ton and zinc £65 per ton.

In casting there is a loss in melt of 3%, and 10% of total input is returned to stock as scrap brass. Casting process costs in addition amount to £24 per ton of total input. In extrusion, 30% of the input of the process is returned to stock as scrap brass, and other extrusion process costs amount to £27 per ton of the input of this process.

Administration, selling, and distribution costs amount to £21 per ton sold. Scrap brass is credited to the process in which it arises and debited to scrap brass stock account at the cost of metal content.

Present figures showing the process and total costs per ton of output.

(*I.C.W.A. Final*)

10. What do you regard as the special feature of process costs? To what classes of manufacture are they generally applied?

(*R.S.A. Advanced*)

11. How would you deal with scrap material in process costs? Give a concrete example.

(*I.C.W.A. Inter.*)

12. How should by-products be dealt with in the cost records? What varying circumstances should decide the exact method employed?

(*I.C.W.A. Final*)

13. In crediting the proceeds from sale of by-products to the Cost Account for a primary product, would you include the profit realised on the by-product, or would you credit it at a value which excludes profit? Give reasons for your preference.

(*I.C.W.A. Final*)

14. A chemical undertaking manufactures a number of products. The early processes in the manufacturing chain are joint for all products.

The Cost Department allocates the corresponding joint costs of these processes to the various products on the basis of the final sales value of each product. A director argues that this procedure is a waste of time and money because it provides no information on which any useful action can be taken. You are asked to give your reasoned opinion.

(*C.C.A. Final*)

15. A factory having its own gas-making plant utilises in its manufacturing processes the whole of the residual coke. How would you determine the price at which to credit the gas factory for the coke so used?

(*I.C.W.A. Inter.*)

16. Discuss the problem involved in the costing of products made by processes which also produce a large number of by-products.

(*I.C.W.A. Final*)

17. How should a scheme of costing be designed to suit the conditions operating in a concern which has a number of by-products? Mention the factors which tend to govern the choice of any effective scheme.

(*I.C.W.A. Final*)

18. Differentiate between the problems arising out of the Accounting treatment of joint-products and by-products. Illustrate the main features of each treatment.

(*I.C.W.A. Final*)

19. Discuss the treatment of by-products in the cost accounts when:

(a) The by-product has a considerable market value.
(b) The by-product is subjected to further processes before utilisation as the raw material of a new product.
(c) The by-product is unsaleable and expense is incurred in its disposal.

(C.A.A. Part 2)

20. (a) X Ltd. manufactures a chemical product passing through two consecutive processes A and B. Waste material from A is used to form the basis of a by-product C and is charged to C at the ex-stores price (below).

Cost summaries for the 3 months to December 31, 1957 show:

	A		B		C	
	Tons	*£*	*Tons*	*£*	*Tons*	*£*
Materials ex-raw stores	72	2076	18	1272	5	192
Direct labour		3220		830		428
Indirect shop labour and variable overheads		1050		370		160

Fixed shop overheads for the three months amounted in total to £1400, and are to be charged on the basis of Conversion Cost: A, 20%; B, 40%; and C, 25%; any balance being carried temporarily in suspense. Interest is to be charged in the costing at 4% per annum on the process capital employed, which is A, £10,100; B, £8400; and C, £3300. During the three months to December 31, 1957, 6 tons of waste material were transferred to C and 66 tons to process B.

Compute the cost per ton of output from A, B, and C.

(b) Discuss concisely the method of overhead allocation adopted in (a) above in relation to the provision of information to management.

(C.C.A. Final)

21. X.Y. Ltd. manufactures product A, which yields two by-products B and C. The actual joint expenses of manufacture for a period were £8000.

It was estimated that the profit on each product as a percentage of sales would be 30%, 25%, and 15%, respectively. Subsequent expenses were as follows:

	A	B	C
	£	£	£
Materials	100	75	25
Direct wages	200	125	50
Overheads	150	125	75
	£450	£325	£150
Sales were	£6000	£4000	£2500

Prepare a statement showing the apportionment of the joint expenses of manufacture over the different products.

(I.C.W.A. Final)

22. A foundry produces castings in a number of different alloys, in each of which scrap metal from previous meltings is used. It is the practice to charge this scrap metal at the average price of metal content; but as the market price of scrap metal of an identical mixture is lower, a suggestion is made that this market price should be used in the cost accounts in respect of the foundry's own scrap.

As Cost Accountant, present a report to management on the subject, illustrating your recommendations by the use of figures in respect of your most important product, the material content of which is:

50% material A costing £200 per ton
20%   „   B   „   £580   „
10%   „   C   „   £120   „
20% scrap metal of identical mixture.

The market price of this scrap metal is £100 per ton, and in making the alloy, 5% of metal charged is lost in melting, and, from the production of the product in question 30% is returned to scrap metal stock to be used in future meltings.

In making the report, give consideration to the positions which arise when:

(a) all scrap cannot be used in future melting processes;
(b) the scrap returned to store after pouring is (1) lower than, (2) equal to, and (3) higher than, the input of scrap.

(*I.C.W.A. Final*)

23. The costs of a manufacturing company for a year are as follows:

	£
Direct material	120,000
Direct wages	80,000
Production overhead (variable)	60,000
„ „ (fixed)	40,000
Selling and distribution costs (variable)	20,000
„ „ (fixed)	40,000

During the period sales were as follows:

	£
Main product	340,000
By-product A (8000) units	40,000
„ B (5000) „	20,000

It is discovered that a further process combining by-product B with some of by-product A and adding further material will yield a saleable product C. Investigation shows that if the 5000 units of B are combined with 4000 units of A, together with additional material costing £60,000, and an additional direct wages cost of £30,000 the production of C will give a sales value of £180,000.

Plant, machinery, and facilities are available in the business to accommodate this extra work, but it is estimated that additional fixed expenses amounting to £12,000 will be incurred during a year if the additional process is carried out.

Present a report to management, making recommendations on the course of action you suggest.

(*I.C.W.A. Final*)

24. The following details relate to a process costing system:

	% degree of completion	No. of units	Cost £
Opening stock—		300	1,230
(*a*) Material	50%		
(*b*) Labour	80%		
(*c*) Overhead	80%		
Material			790
Wages			3,710
Overhead			1,484
Transferred from previous process	100%	3800	13,680
Transferred to next process	100%	3500	
Scrap—		100	
(*a*) Material	100%		
(*b*) Wages	50%		
(*c*) Overhead	50%		
Closing stock—		500	
(*a*) Material	100%		
(*b*) Wages	80%		
(*c*) Overhead	80%		

(*a*) Prepare Statement of Production, showing opening and closing stocks, output completed, and scrap, in terms of (1) material and (2) wages and overhead, converted from the percentages into equivalent completed "effective units."

(*b*) Prepare a statement of unit valuations, grouped as to quantity and value, into cost of scrap and cost of good production.

(*c*) Prepare a cost of production analysis, giving effective units from (*a*), actual issued quantity, total costs, and unit costs.

(*I.C.W.A. Final, Adapted*)

25. The following information is obtained in respect of Process 2 for the month of August:

Opening stock: 800 units valued at £352.

Degree of Completion:—

Material	60%
Labour	40%
Overheads	40%

Transfer from Process 1: 16,000 units at 4s. each.
Transfer to Process 3: 14,000 units.

	£	s.	d.
Direct material added in Process 2	1521	0	0
Direct labour amounted to	2240	5	0
Production overhead incurred	4480	10	0

Units scrapped: 1000

Degree of completion—

Materials	100%
Labour	70%
Overheads	70%

Closing stock: 1800 units

Degree of completion—

Materials	80%
Labour	60%
Overheads	60%

There was a normal loss of 5% of production.
Units scrapped realised 4s. each.

Prepare:

(a) Statement of Production;
(b) Statement of Cost;
(c) Statement of Evaluation;
(d) Process 2 Account.

(*Adapted*)

26. For the month ended May 31, 1958, the following particulars are submitted in respect of Process X:

	£
Raw materials used	27,690
Direct labour	14,625

Factory overhead, allocated at 100% on labour £14,625.

During the month 3800 units were begun and 3600 units passed to Finished Stores.

Certain losses were incurred in process, but are not to be regarded as part of the cost of production of the finished units.

Opening and closing work in progress were as follows:

	Units		£
May 1, 1958	200	25% complete	1955
May 31, 1958	250	80% complete	?

All works records are maintained on the F.I.F.O. basis.

It can be assumed that the material, labour, and overhead cost all accrue evenly over time, so that if a unit is half finished it can be assumed to have absorbed half its material cost, half its labour cost, and half its overhead cost. The F.I.F.O. principle is to be applied to partly finished units, *i.e.* all unfinished units in work in process at the beginning of the year are to be costed so far as the balance of the work on them is concerned on the basis of current unit costs.

Draft the Process Total Account, reconciling the quantities and money values, and bringing down the balances.

(*A.C.C.A. Final*)

27. Explain fully the principles you would adopt for the valuation of work in progress at the end of an accounting period.

(*I.C.W.A. Inter.*)

28. (*a*) What bases may be adopted in fixing the prices at which transfers from process to process are made?

(*b*) What bearing would these prices have on the value of the stock at the end of the accounting period?

(*C.A.A. Part 2*)

29. Cam, Curry, and Carfax are in partnership as manufacturers of a chemical product which passes through three consecutive processes. In the first process the raw materials are broken down and blended by heat treatment, and further blending is carried out in the second process, and the final— or warehouse—operation consists of packing into cartons for sale. Cam supervises the first process, Curry the second, and Carfax the third. There are no quantity losses in process. The output of Process 1 is charged to Process 2 at a figure which shows a profit of 10% on the transfer price, and that of Process 2 to Process 3 at a figure which shows a profit of 25% on such price. The stocks carried by Process 2 are valued at the cost of the year's production. The ultimate Net Profit as shown by the firm's annual accounts is divided between the partners in the ratio:

Cam $\frac{1}{5}$, Curry and Carfax $\frac{2}{5}$ each.

The following particulars are supplied for the year to March 31, 1949:

	Lbs	£
Process 1—		
Raw materials used	15,680	784
Wages: crushing and mixing		1372
Cam: management salary		400
Process 2—		
Transfer from Process 1		
Raw materials used	3,920	90
Coal and coke		100
Wages: furnace and mixing		1470
Curry: management salary		400
Process stocks—		
April 1, 1948 (subject to Stock Provision of £25)	1,500	325
March 31, 1949	1,100	
Process 3:		
Transfer from Process 2 including all opening stock	20,000	
Cartons		125
Wages		675
Carfax: management salary		600
Sales	18,000	9000
Selling expenses		1221

In respect of the year 1949 you are required:

(a) To write up the Process accounts in detail.

(b) To give the Profit and Loss Account, introducing such provisions as may be necessary to reduce stocks to cost, and show clearly how the ultimate net profit is divided between the partners.

(C.A. Final, May 1949)

Uniform Costing (Chapter 23)

1. Printing machines are made to print appropriate sizes of paper and usually cost more as the sizes increase. To meet the requirements of customers it frequently happens that a small sheet must be printed on a large machine. What procedures should be adopted when assembling the costs of the job?

(I.C.W.A. Final)

2. What information from a uniform Cost System would you suggest as *particularly* useful to manufacturers in the same line of business?

(I.C.W.A. Final)

3. What steps would you take to establish a system of uniform costing for fixing price standards in an industry controlled by a combine?

(I.C.W.A. Final)

4. What items of general expense would you expect to show most change per centum as a result of a combine? Indicate the direction of, and reasons for, these changes.

(I.C.W.A. Inter.)

5. Your firm propose making an amalgamation with another, and wish you, as Cost Accountant, to investigate and report. What especial features would you take into consideration for that report?

(I.C.W.A. Final)

6. The studio and design department of a printing business prepares ideas which are sometimes accepted by clients, but a large proportion of the work so produced is abandoned as unsuitable. How do you consider the cost of such a service should be recovered? Give your reasons.

(I.C.W.A. Inter.)

7. A proposal is being considered to amalgamate two factories at an estimated cost of £50,000. The savings expected to result therefrom are estimated at £20,000 per annum. State broadly the details of the savings, aggregating £20,000, that you would assume to follow on the amalgamation, and how you, as Cost Accountant, could contribute to the discussion of the proposal.

(I.C.W.A. Final)

8. How would you propose to deal with the following items in your costs:

(a) Warehousing expenses incurred in a printing business?

(R.S.A. Part of question)

9. State concisely your opinion as to the possibility of standardising costing systems in particular industries. Give reasons showing whether it is or is not desirable to attempt this task.

(*I.A. Final*)

10. From the following data prepare six prices per thousand for printing an art wrapper, viz.:

(*a*) First orders of 50,000; 100,000 and 250,000.
(*b*) Repeat orders for 50,000; 100,000 and 250,000.

Cost of sketch and lithographic work, £40. Making machines ready for printing, £20. All other work (per thousand), £2. Add for general overhead and profit, 25%.

(*I.C.W.A. Final*)

11. State as fully as possible what you consider are the advantages and disadvantages of uniform costing to:

(*a*) an individual firm;
(*b*) an industry;
(*c*) the public.

(*I.C.W.A. Final*)

12. As Cost Consultant to a trade organisation, you are requested to investigate the cost systems of various concerns with a view to the introduction of a uniform cost system. Describe the general lines upon which you would proceed, and indicate the principal preliminary difficulties to be overcome.

(*I.C.W.A. Final*)

13. A company has acquired a new undertaking. Because the accounting systems of the parent and subsidiary companies differ, results are not comparable. Uniformity of methods would render void for either company comparisons with previous periods. Suggest a compromise.

(*I.C.W.A. Final*)

14. Explain the objectives of uniform costing and outline the main causes of differences in costs between undertakings within the same industry.

(*I.C.W.A. Final*)

15. Design a form of Cost Statement suitable for a number of concerns engaged in the manufacture of the same standard product, adding a note as to the factors which you would consider in order to ensure that the results of the various concerns are strictly comparable.

(*C.A.A. Part 2*)

16. What is meant by "Uniform Costing"? What advantages would you expect to accrue from its adoption in an industry?

(*A.I.A. Final*)

17. The Chief Accountant of a group of companies in the same industry wishes to introduce uniformity of costing methods—and you are charged with investigating this objective. Tabulate the fundamental costing principles which need agreement and in respect of each give an example.

(*I.C.W.A. Inter.*)

Marginal Costing (Chapter 24)

1. "The technique of Marginal Costs can be a valuable aid to Management." Discuss this statement and give your views.

(*C.A.A.*)

2. It is a fundamental rule in cost accounting that "fixed" expense must be distinguished from "variable" expense. State the reasons for this rule, and give two examples of each type of expense.

(*C.A. Inter., November 1957*)

3. (*a*) Define Marginal Costing.
   (*b*) Present the following information to show clearly to management:

   (i) the marginal product cost and the contribution per unit;
   (ii) the total contributions and profits resulting from each of the following sales mixtures.

	Product	£ per unit
Direct materials	A	10
„	B	9
Direct wages	A	3
„	B	2
Fixed expenses		£800
(Variable expenses are allotted to products as 100% of direct wages)		
Sales price	A	20
„	B	15

Sales mixtures:

   (*a*) 100 units of product A and 200 of B
   (*b*) 150   „   „   150 „
   (*c*) 200   „   „   100 „

(*I.C.W.A. Inter.*)

4. Explain clearly what you understand by "contribution" in a cost accounting sense. How is it related to profit?

List three benefits that management can obtain from knowing the contribution from its cost units.

(*I.C.W.A. Inter.*)

5. Discuss the significance of the following terms in relation to marginal costing:

   (*a*) contribution;
   (*b*) policy costs;
   (*c*) key factor of production.

(*C.A.A.*)

6. What do you understand by the expressions "break even" and "margin of safety"? Outline a simple chart to illustrate the meanings you would attach to these terms, taking as your data assumed figures for fixed expenses, marginal profit, and normal sales.

(*C.A.A.*)

7. It has been said that Marginal Costs are used primarily in guiding decisions yet to be made. Choose two examples, and tabulate specimen figures with details for each to illustrate the statement quoted.

(*I.C.W.A. Final*)

8. What are the arguments for and against the inclusion of fixed overhead in the valuation of stock at the end of an accounting period?

What difference in profit for a period will result from the adoption of each method?

(*I.C.W.A. Inter.*)

9. What do you understand by the optimum production level of a business? Outline the matters you would consider to determine the optimum of a small concern with which you are familiar.

(*I.C.W.A. Final*)

10. A manufacturing company produced 10,000 units during the month of September 19... Direct Materials cost £10,000; Direct Labour amounted to £1000; and Variable Overhead Expenses to £2000. Fixed Overhead Expenses for the current financial year were estimated at £24,000. The whole production was sold at £2 per unit.

Prepare a statement showing the Marginal Cost and the profit or loss for the month, and calculate the break-even point.

(*C.A.A.*)

11. The following figures apply to a manufacturing company:

	£
Annual sales at 100% effective capacity	1,200,000
Fixed overhead	400,000
Total variable costs	600,000

It is proposed to increase the capacity by the acquisition of 30% additional space and plant. One result will be to increase fixed overhead by £100,000 per annum.

Plot the foregoing on a single break-even chart, and determine from the chart at what capacity-utilisation the same profit as before will be produced after the extensions have been made.

(*I.C.W.A. Final*)

12. The Makem Manufacturing Co. produces 10,000 units per annum by employing 50% of the factory capacity. The selling price of the unit is £5, and the total costs were:

	£
Materials	10,000
Wages	20,000
Fixed overhead	10,000
Variable overhead	4,000
	£44,000

Variable overhead maintains a constant ratio to the number of units produced.

The Company accepts an order for an additional 10,000 units at a selling price of £3 17s. 6d. each.

The increased volume of purchases reduces the material prices by $2\frac{1}{2}\%$. Wage-rates remain constant, but due to the employment of new workers there is a drop in labour efficiency of 5% on all production.

Prepare a statement showing the variation of net profits resulting from the acceptance of the order.

(I.C.W.A. Final)

13. The trading results of X Ltd. for the years 19.. and 19.. were as follows:

	Year A	Year B
	£	£
Materials consumed	50,000	66,000
Wages	30,000	33,000
Variable overheads	6,000	7,000
Fixed overheads	10,000	12,000
Net profit	4,000	8,500
	£100,000	£126,500

Material prices and wage-rates increased in year B by 10%, and sales prices were also increased by 10%.

What general factors have caused the increase in net profit? Prepare a statement showing how much each factor has contributed to the variation of profit.

(I.C.W.A. Final)

14. Two businesses AB Ltd. and CD Ltd. sell the same type of product in the same type of market. Their budgeted Profit and Loss Accounts for the year ending 19.., are as follows:

	AB Ltd.		CD Ltd.	
	£	£	£	£
Sales		150,000		150,000
Less: Variable costs	120,000		100,000	
Fixed costs	15,000		35,000	
		135,000		135,000
Net profit budgeted		£15,000		£15,000

You are required to:

(a) calculate the break even points of each business; and
(b) state which business is likely to earn greater profits in conditions of—

(i) heavy demand for the product;
(ii) low demand for the product.

Give your reasons.

(I.C.W.A. Inter.)

15. (*a*) Marginal income has been defined as selling value less variable cost. From the following tabulations plot a curve on a price–volume chart representing the marginal income for the three products; and another representing each product's marginal income in order of decreasing magnitude.

Product	Sales value	Marginal income	Cumulative marginal income
	£	£	£
A	1,000,000	300,000	300,000
B	500,000	100,000	400,000
C	2,000,000	200,000	600,000

(*b*) What conclusions do you draw from the chart?

(I.C.W.A. Final)

16. A manufacturing company concentrates its resources upon one single product which it sells to wholesale merchants at £4 16*s*. per unit. The following details apply:

Output (Units)	75,000	85,000	100,000
	£	£	£
Variable overhead (production)	40,000	48,000	55,000
Variable Selling and Administration overhead	15,000	17,500	22,000

Material costs £2 per unit, but quantity rebates of 10% and 15% apply to purchase contracts for 85,000 and 100,000 units respectively. Average wages cost is 10*s*. per unit. Fixed overhead is £70,000 (production); and £25,000 (Selling and Administration).

In order to sell the whole output selling price reductions of 5% and 10% are contemplated, for the output levels of 85,000 and 100,000 units respectively.

An offer to purchase 10,000 units at £4 per unit has been received from abroad.

    (*a*) Tabulate the necessary figures to show Marginal Costs and the increases in selling value for the three output levels, and indicate which of the three is the most profitable.

    (*b*) Prepare a simple statement to show Profit or Loss at each output level and indicate which of the three is the most profitable.

    (*c*) Prepare a statement showing the effect upon net income if the offer from abroad is accepted, assuming that other prices will not be affected, and the output level indicated in your answer to (*a*) is adopted.

(I.C.W.A. Final)

17. As a Cost Accountant operating a system of "Marginal Costing" you feel that the management regards the system of use mainly from a price-fixing point of view; you also feel that selling prices which are unnecessarily low— although higher than Marginal Cost—are often accepted. Explain how you would indicate to management the best use of the technique of Marginal Costing.

(I.C.W.A. Final)

18. The cost of a job is presented to management in the following form:

	s.	d.	s.	d.
Direct materials			12	0
Direct wages—				
Department A	4	0		
B	6	0		
C	2	0		
			12	0
Factory overheads—				
Department A	5	0		
B	9	0		
C	2	0		
			16	0
Factory cost			40	0
Administration, selling, and distribution expenses			8	0
Total cost			48	0

The Sales Manager states that the highest price he can obtain for this job is 45s., but that large orders can be obtained at this price.

Criticise the layout of the job cost, and, using any suitable additional figures, indicate how you would present the cost.

(*I.C.W.A. Final*)

19. A small jobbing foundry quotes for pattern equipment and castings on the basis of the following:

Pattern cost	£75
Labour cost	15s. per casting
Metal cost	65s. 4d. per cwt.
Variable overhead	16s. per casting.

Each casting weighs 84 lb, and the price quoted is £7 per casting, to include the cost of pattern equipment.

From the foregoing information, prepare a break-even chart and determine from it at what sales level contribution to fixed overhead will begin.

(*I.C.W.A. Final*)

Budgetary Control (Chapter 25)

1. In connection with budgetary control, enumerate and describe briefly the usual subsidiary budgets which make up the master budget.

(*C.A.A. Part 2*)

2. Explain the control of expense in relation to output by the method of flexible budgeting.

(*C.A.A. Part 2*)

3. "Standard costing is always accompanied by a system of budgeting, but budgetary control may be operated in businesses where standard costing would be impracticable." Discuss this statement, and indicate the method

s

and use of Budgetary Control systems in the type of business mentioned in the latter part of the question.

(*I.C.W.A. Final*)

4. (*a*) Name the three fundamental functions involved in operating a budgetary system, adding a concise note upon each.

(*b*) Indicate which of these three functions involve the Sales Manager and which the Works Manager. Show the contribution made by each.

(*I.C.W.A. Final*)

5. Describe the preparation of the direct wages element of a Production Cost Budget both with and without the advantage of a standard costing system. In establishing standard direct wages rates what information it required from the planning department and how would it obtain this information?

(*I.C.W.A. Inter.*)

6. Where would the following types of material be included in a production cost budget and how would the amounts to be included be assessed:

(*a*) direct material;

(*b*) supplies consumed directly in production processes;

(*c*) supplies consumed in supplying a service, *e.g.* coal for steam generation;

(*d*) consumable stores, *e.g.* oils, greases, waste;

(*e*) materials for repairs to buildings, plant, and machinery?

(*I.C.W.A. Inter.*)

7. "It has been found that budget and actual comparison statements are more effective when they are supplemented by explanatory notes, drawing attention to the more significant features of the results and providing explanations not readily apparent in the figures of the statement."

Using suitable figures, prepare such a statement for management in respect of one of the budgets used in a system of Budgetary Control.

(*I.C.W.A. Final*)

8. What do you understand by a master budget? Into what sections is it usually divided, and what are the purposes of the divisions? Explain with any necessary figures, how you would present to management a report on variances occurring on one of the sections.

(*I.C.W.A. Final*)

9. What difficulties would you expect to find in the compilation of a flexible budget? Give sufficient detail to justify any assumptions you make. How would such a budget be used?

(*I.C.W.A. Final*)

10. What is meant in a system of flexible budgeting by:

(*a*) budget overhead allowance;

(*b*) overhead incurred;

(*c*) absorbed overhead.

How are these costs related?

(*I.C.W.A. Inter.*)

11. What is a flexible budget?
Prepare a table showing in detail the relative variances arising out of the following:

	Standard	Actual
Output (units)	12,000	13,500
Overhead	£1,600	£1,750

Standard overhead for output of 13,500 units: £1700.

(*A.C.C.A. Final*)

12. The Costing Budget of a department for a year of normal activity of 50,000 hours is as follows:

	£
Fixed expenses	21,600
Variable expenses	12,000
	£33,600

During the first three months of the year for which the budget was prepared the expenses and activities of the business are as follows:

	Activities	Fixed expenses	Variable expenses
	Hours	£	£
January	2000	1570	750
February	4000	1865	875
March	5000	2060	1000

Show the variations in percentage form for each month as against the original budget, and prepare an amended budget for the remaining nine months to bring the year's figures to the original estimates.

(*C.A.A. Part 2*)

13. A manufacturing business has drawn up a budget for the current year, the proportion of the expected costs, etc., being as follows:

	%
Direct material	34·0
Direct labour	22·0
Variable factory overheads	16·5
Fixed factory overheads	12·0
Other variable costs	5·5
Other fixed costs	4·0
Profit	6·0
Total	100·0

After six months working it becomes apparent that the volume of business anticipated will not be obtained, and management considers that a figure of approximately 75% of budgeted sales will be obtained, *i.e.* £330,000 for the full year. As Cost Accountant of the business, present information to management at this stage, which will enable decisions to be made on matters of policy.

(I.C.W.A. Final)

14. The general manager of a manufacturing company asks you to examine a proposition to purchase some labour-saving equipment at a price of £7000. This will have the following effect:

    (*a*) Output will be increased by 15% p.a.
    (This can all be sold at present selling prices.)
    (*b*) Direct wages at the increased output level will be £3000 p.a. lower than at present.
    (*c*) The ratio of overhead to Prime Cost, which is 30% at present, will rise to 45%.

The general manager is worried about the increase in the ratio of overhead to Prime Cost that would result from the introduction of this equipment. Sales at present are £60,000 p.a., for which the Prime Costs are: direct material cost, £16,000; direct wages £24,000.

You are required to:

    (*a*) Prepare a simple budgeted Profit and Loss Statement for the year if the proposition is accepted.
    (*b*) State whether the general manager's worry about the increase in the ratio of overhead to Prime Cost is justified. Give brief reasons.

(I.C.W.A. Inter.)

15. A manufacturing company of which you are the Chief Accountant, produces three different products, X, Y, and Z. The processes by which they are produced are independent of one another, and in no case are the sales of any one product affected by prices or sales of the others. The following budgeted Profit and Loss Statement for the year ending November 30, 1958, is presented to you by your assistant:

	Total	*X*	*Y*	*Z*
	£	£	£	£
Sales	100,000	15,000	10,000	75,000
Variable production cost	60,000	8,000	4,000	48,000
Fixed production cost	20,000	1,000	3,000	16,000
(apportioned to products)				
	80,000	9,000	7,000	64,000
Gross profit	20,000	6,000	3,000	11,000
Variable selling cost	8,000	2,700	2,600	2,700
Fixed selling cost	2,000	700	700	600
(apportioned to products)				
	10,000	3,400	3,300	3,300
Net profit	10,000	2,600	—	7,700
Net loss	—	—	300	—

NOTE.—The basis of apportionment of fixed costs are known and acceptable to you.

Your assistant recommends that, to improve the profit position, product Y should be eliminated from the range of articles produced by the company, thus leaving only two articles to be produced.

You are required:

(a) To re-draft the budgeted Profit and Loss Statement to show the profit that would result if product Y were eliminated.

(b) To state whether or not you agree with your assistant's recommendation. Give brief reasons.

(I.C.W.A. Inter.)

16. In outlining a plan for a "Production" Budget, what main bases would you use?

(Com. A. Final)

17. Having completed budgets for all the functions of a company how would you ensure that they were put to use?

(Com. A. Final)

18. Production costs of a factory for a year are as follows:

	£
Direct wages	80,000
Direct materials	120,000
Production overheads, fixed	40,000
Production overheads, variable	60,000

During the forthcoming year it is anticipated that:

(a) the average rate for direct labour remuneration will fall from 3s. 4d. per hour to 3s. 1½d. per hour;

(b) production efficiency will be unchanged;

(c) direct labour hours will increase by 33⅓%;

(d) The purchase price per unit of direct materials and of the other materials and services which comprise overheads will remain unchanged.

Draw up a budget and compute a factory overhead rate, the overheads being absorbed on a direct wage basis.

(I.C.W.A. Inter.)

19. The XY Co. Ltd., manufactures two models, the "Hardy" and the "Luxury," in its London factory. It distributes them throughout the United Kingdom, which is divided into three sales areas. The budgeted Profit and Loss Account for the year ending November 30, 1958, is as follows;

Sales—

		£		£	*Total* £
Area A	"Hardy"	50,000	"Luxury"	100,000	150,000
„ B	„	100,000	„	150,000	250,000
„ C	„	150,000	„	250,000	400,000
		300,000		500,000	800,000

Production cost of sales—

"Hardy" (60% of sales)	180,000	
"Luxury" (70% of sales)	350,000	530,000

Gross profit   270,000

Direct selling and distribution costs—
Salesmen's Salaries and Commission

	£	£
Area A	14,500	
„ B	16,000	
„ C	7,500	38,000

Salesmen's expenses:

Area A	4,500	
„ B	3,000	
„ C	2,500	10,000

Sales office costs:

Area A	7,000	
„ B	6,200	
„ C	4,800	18,000

Advertising:

Area A	1,400	
„ B	3,400	
„ C	1,200	6,000

Carriage:

Area A	2,700		
„ B	2,400		
„ C	2,900	8,000	80,000

Indirect selling and distribution costs—

Advertising	24,000		
Carriage	4,400		
Warehousing	15,400		
Credit control and collection	8,800		
General administration	12,000	64,600	144,600

Budgeted net profit   £125,400

The budgeted analysis of sales is:

Sales area	"Hardy" Sales volume (machines)	No. of orders	"Luxury" Sales volume (machines)	No. o, orders
A	4,000	600	4,000	800
B	8,000	1000	6,000	1000
C	12,000	400	10,000	600

The cost manual of the Company states that indirect selling and distribution costs are to be apportioned to sales areas as follows:

	On basis of
Advertising	Sales values
Carriage	Sales volume
Warehousing	Sales volume
Credit control and collection	Number of orders
General administration	Sales values

The cost manual also states that selling and distribution costs of sales areas are to be apportioned to models on the basis of sales values.

You are required:

(a) to prepare a comparative statement showing an analysis of budgeted selling and distribution costs by sales areas;

(b) to prepare a comparative budgeted Profit and Loss Statement for each model by sales areas;

(c) to show the budgeted average net profit for each model sold in each sales area.

(I.C.W.A. Inter.)

Standard Costing (Chapters 26–28)

1. Explain, briefly, the term standard, as applied to standard costing.
(C.A. Inter., May 1957)

2. What advantages are likely to be obtained from the use, in appropriate circumstances, of Standard Costing as compared with other methods of costing?
(C.A. Final, May 1952)

3. Illustrate by means of examples, the significance of "variances" in relation to standard costing technique and discuss the interpretation of such variances.
(C.A.A. Final)

4. What are the most important variances you would expect to find in an operating statement of a manufacturing business using Standard Costs? Discuss the reasons for three types of variances and indicate any action you suggest should be taken to minimise such variances in future.
(A.I.A. Final)

5. Explain the meaning of the following terms in relation to Standard Costing:

(a) Capacity variance;
(b) Calendar variance;
(c) Efficiency variance.

(*A.I.A. Final*)

6. State what you understand by:

(a) efficiency ratio;
(b) activity ratio.

Illustrate your answer with a formula and an example of each, calculated from the following figures:

Budgeted production	88 units
Standard hours per unit	10
Actual production	75 units
Actual working hours	600

(*I.C.W.A. Inter.*)

7. To assist factory management it is usual to analyse Wages Cost Variances as to cause. Give two instances each of the causes of:

(a) Wages Rate Variance;
(b) Labour Efficiency Variance.

In each case show how the amount of the variance would be obtained and what corrective action factory management might take.

(*I.C.W.A. Inter.*)

8. Material Price Variance may be accounted for at one of two different stages in the accounting procedure. Set out simple Journal entries with suitable figures illustrating the two methods as far as the Work-in-progress Account.

How may the two methods be combined, and what advantage would there be when preparing annual accounts?

(*I.C.W.A. Final*)

9. The production of a certain unit is assumed to require 80 lb of material costing 3s. per lb and 18 hours labour at 2s. 6d. per hour. On the completion of the production of a unit it was found that 75 lb of material at 3s. 3d. per lb had been consumed and that the time taken was 16 hours at 2s. 8d. per hour. Prepare a statement showing the actual direct cost of producing the unit to the nearest penny, indicating the variances and explain what these variances are.

(*I.A. Inter., May 1957*)

10. Utopians Ltd. commenced business on January 1, 1955, and a system of Standard Costing was installed. The company manufactures one product of a standard type, and the Standard Cost was fixed:

Standard price of materials	6s. per lb
Standard quantity of materials	8 lb per unit
Standard direct labour cost	£10 per unit

Factory overheads were estimated at £60,000 for the year 1955. Normal operating time for the year was estimated at 2000 hours and standard time for the production of one unit is determined as 12 machine hours. The Company has twenty-four machines of a uniform type.

In January 1956 it was found that the actual total operating time for 1955 was exactly 2000 hours and all machines were fully employed for the whole of the time. The actual output for the year was 3600 units.

The actual quantity of materials used was 30,000 lb; and the cost £9150.

The actual direct wages for 1955 amounted to £40,000. Rates of pay did not vary from the estimated rate used in fixing the Standard Cost. The actual factory overheads for 1955 were £61,800. You are required:

(a) To compute the Standard Cost per unit and the Standard Cost of the output;
(b) To set out the variances.

(C.I.S. Final)

11. It sometimes happens that a favourable variance from one standard is directly related to an adverse variance from another, *e.g.* the purchase of processed materials may cause an adverse Material Price Variance but a favourable Labour Efficiency Variance. Give two examples other than the one given above, and explain how you would present and interpret the analysis of variances in such cases.

(I.C.W.A. Final)

12. A manufacturing company operates a Standard Costing system and showed the following data in respect of November 1957:

Actual number of working days	22
Actual man-hours worked during the month	4300
Number of products produced	425
Actual overhead incurred	£1800

Relevant information from the Company's Budget and Standard Cost data is as follows:

Budgeted number of working days per month	20
Budgeted man-hours per month	4000
Standard man-hours per product	10
Standard overhead rate per man-hour	10s.

You are required to calculate for the month of November 1957:

(a) the Overhead Variance;
(b) the Calendar Variance;
(c) the Volume Variance.

(I.C.W.A. Inter.)

13. Give the main bases used in building up a Standard Cost within the divisions of Material, Labour, and Overhead Costs.

(Com. A. Final)

14. The comment is sometimes made that Actual Costs are better than Standard Costs. How does a proper costing system give both Standard Costs and Actual Costs and consequently give the benefit of comparison?

(Com. A. Final)

15. Mass Production Ltd. manufactures one product of a standard type. A system of Standard Costing is in operation. The Standard Costs per hour were:

	£	s.	d.
Factory wages	2	5	0
Factory expenses	1	0	0
	£3	5	0

The standard output is 100 articles per hour. The normal working hours for a four-week period are 160. During the four weeks ended March 28, 1958 the actual factory wages paid amounted to £375, representing payments for 160 hours, of which 148 were working hours and 12 were idle hours. The actual factory expenses were £160. The output of the factory was 15,600 articles.

You are required to set out and complete a table in the following form:

Wages variances: Efficiency
                 Idle time
                 Rate   ———
                 TOTAL   £

Expense Variances: Efficiency
                  Volume   ———
                  TOTAL   £

(C.I.S. Final)

16. The Trading and Profit and Loss Accounts of A.B.C. Ltd. for the year ended March 31, 1956, are as follows:

	£		£
Materials	6,800	Sales (14,400 units)	14,400
Labour	4,280		
Direct charges	800		
	11,880		
General works charges	880		
Office charges	600		
Net Profit	1,040		
	£14,400		£14,400

The standard output for the year to March 31, 1956, was fixed at 20,000 units. Standard Costs per unit were as follows:

	s.	d.
Materials	9	0
Labour	6	0
Direct charges	2	0

General works charges are fixed at £600 per annum, the balance of expenditure being variable, with a standard of 6d. per unit.
Office charges are fixed at £600 per annum.
You are required to prepare a Profit and Loss Statement, showing the Standard Cost figures, actual costs and variances, suggesting reasons for the variances shown. Assume there were no opening and closing stocks.

(C.A.A. Part 2)

17. In Department X the following data is submitted for the week ended February 20:

Standard output for 40-hour week	1400 units
Standard fixed overheads	£140
Actual output	1200 units
Actual hours worked	32
Actual fixed overheads	£150

Compute the variances.

(A.C.C.A. Final)

18. From the following basic data calculate:

(a) efficiency variance;
(b) volume variance;
(c) calendar variance.

Item	Budget	Actual
Number of working days	20	22
Standard man-hours per day	8,000	8,400
Output per man-hour in units	1·0	1·2
Total unit output	160,000	221,760
Standard overhead rate per man-hour	2s.	

(I.C.W.A. Final)

19. For the six months ended June 30, 1957, the standard output and costs of three products A, B, and C were as follows:

	A	B	C
Output (units)	10,000	20,000	15,000
Cost: Materials	£1,500	£2,500	£3,375
Labour	£2,500	£3,000	£4,500
Standard labour time	1½ hours	1 hour	2 hours
Overhead: Variable	£500	£500	£750
Fixed	£750	£1,000	£1,875

Each product is made in a separate works department. Production and—except as stated below—production costs accrued evenly throughout the six-months period. Material prices (for product A only) were increased by 5% on May 1, 1957. As from April 1, 1957, a wage award of 2d. per hour was made as regards A and C only.

Actual output and costs for the six months were:

	A	B	C
Output (units)	9,600	18,400	14,200
Costs: Material	£1,560	£2,415	£3,550
Labour	£2,460	£2,875	£4,591
Overhead: Variable	£440	£460	£769
Fixed	£810	£1,230	£1,875

Prepare a statement showing clearly, in respect of each product Standard and Actual Costs, and the nature and amount of the variances that arise.

(A.C.C.A. Final)

20. The following information is extracted from the works records of A. Ltd. in respect of the three months ended May 31, 1956.

Output	5000 units
Raw materials used	£1085
Direct wages	£1690
Overheads: Fixed	£1120
Variable	£600

Work in progress is zero at the opening and closing dates.

Each unit of output requires 1 lb of raw material, the Standard Cost of which on March 1, 1956, was 4s. per lb, and at that date the stock was 2500 lb.

Raw materials used £1085 represent this opening stock at Standard Cost and the purchase cost of a further 2700 lb purchased in April, all of which were used in the period.

Standard labour rates and times per unit are 3s. 3d. per hour and 2 hours respectively.

There has been no change in labour rates during the period.

Fixed Overhead is estimated at £4000 p.a. and Variable Overhead at 2s. 6d. per unit. Assuming that there is no divergence between actual and standard output, prepare:

(a) Statement showing the total standard cost of ouput and the variances that emerge.

(b) A short explanation of the variances.

(A.C.C.A. Final)

21. (1.) Explain:

(a) Efficiency Variance;
(b) Capacity Variance;
(c) Expenditure Variance.

(2.) In a certain firm the planned overheads for a three-month period are £4000.

The hours actually worked (adjusted by average piece-work hours) and charged at the standard hourly rate are £4200. Actual overhead amounted to £4100, while standard overhead charged to production was £4300.

Compute the variances shown in (1) above.

(A.C.C.A. Final)

22. The Standard Cost Sheet for producing a job consisting of 100 articles for the Harem Manufacturing Co. showed:

Materials—
60 lb of A at 10s. per lb
50 lb of B at 12s. per lb

Direct wages
20 hours operation 1 at 9s. per hour
30   „   „   2 at 12s.   „
40   „   „   3 at 16s.   „

Overheads based on direct wages at 14s. per hour.

Actual costs of the job were:

Materials—
70 lb of A at 10s 6d. per lb
48 lb of B at 13s. per lb

Direct wages—
25 hours operation 1 at 8s.   per hour
28   „   „   2 at 12s.   „
40   „   „   3 at 16s. 6d.   „

Prepare a table to show:

(a) the Standard and Actual cost of the job;
(b) the variances analysed as between quantity and price.

(I.C.W.A. Final)

23. In Department X of A. Co. Ltd. a single product is manufactured. Departmental accounts are kept on a Standard Cost basis. On January 1, 1955, no stock of the finished product was on hand, but at that date raw materials were held as follows:

Materials: Stock: 3000 units £3750
Material price variance (Dr.: Stock: 3000 units £150)

For the half year to June 30, 1955, the budgeted output was 9600 units and the actual output 9000 units. Of these, 8800 were sold at £5 each. The standard cost per unit adopted on January 1, 1955, was:

	£	s.	d.
Raw material (1 unit)	1	6	0
Direct labour (14 hours at 3s. per hour)	2	2	0
Overheads (Fixed)		14	0
	£4	2	0

In respect of the half year to June 30, 1955, the following data are supplied:

Raw material—
10,000 units were bought costing £13,500
9300 units were drawn from stores

528   COST ACCOUNTING

Direct labour—

Clock hours paid were 131,560 at 3s. per hour. Of this total 520 hours were unproductive on account of temporary plant breakdown.

Actual overheads were £7050.

You are asked:

(a) to write up the following accounts: Raw Materials; Direct Labour; Overheads; Work in progress; Cost of Sales; Variance Accounts (clearly distinguishing each);
(b) to prepare from the above the Profit and Loss Account of Dept. X for the 6 months ending June 30, 1955;
(c) to draft a note to the Manager briefly explaining the nature of the several variances.

(A.C.C.A. Final)

24. The sales of Stancost Ltd. for the month of October 1957 was as follows:

Sales

Product	Quantity	Standard selling Price, each	Standard sales	Standard Profit on budgeted sales
		s. d.	£	£
A	1000	20 0	1000	100
B	400	30 0	600	100
		TOTAL	£1600	£200

The actual sales in October 1957 were:

Product	Quantity	Actual selling Price	Actual sales
		s. d.	£
A	1050	22 0	1155
B	500	34 0	850
			£2005

You are required to show the budgeted and actual sales for the month of October 1957, together with the related variances, as you would expect them to appear in the Costing Profit and Loss Statement of Stancost Ltd. for the month of October 1957.

(C.A. Final, November 1957)

25. A Sales Budget has been formulated using standard volumes and prices of five standard products. Since the preparation of the budget sales prices have increased and the Sales Manager has requested a monthly return which

will show him to what extent each product sale has fluctuated from the budget due to volume or price. You are required to:

(a) calculate the respective sales variances for each product from the following information for the month of May 1958.

Product	Budget Sales price £	Volume	Actual Volume	Value £
A	10	1000	1500	16,000
B	3	700	900	3,000
C	8	800	850	7,000
D	2	300	200	500
E	5	200	100	600

(b) design a form to meet the Sales Manager's request and insert the figures for May 1958.

(I.C.W.A. Inter.)

26. The standard cost of a certain chemical mixture is:

40% Material A at £20 per ton
60% Material B at £30 per ton

A standard loss of 10% is expected in production. During a period there is used:

90 tons Material A at a cost of £18 per ton
110 „ „ B „ „ £34 „

The weight produced is 182 tons of good production.
Calculate and present:

(a) Material Price Variance;
(b) Material Usage Variance;
(c) Material Mix Variance;
(d) Material Yield Variance.

(I.C.W.A. Inter.)

27. (a) Design a Materials Cost Analysis Form and enter suitable figures from the details given below:

Production for period   192 units

	Material X	Material Y
Standard price per ton	£24	£32
Actual price paid per ton	£22 16s.	£30 16s.
Actual usage	16 tons	13 tons

The standard production for the period represented by the above figures is 400 units, for which the standard quantity allowances for materials are 30 tons of X and 25 tons of Y.

(b) Using the appropriate four columnar totals from your entries on the form, show the Journal entries applicable to production, materials, and variance accounts.

(I.C.W.A. Final)

28. Common brass is an alloy consisting of 70% copper and 30% zinc. In melting and pouring it is expected that a 4% loss of metal will occur. Standard prices are £400 per ton for copper and £90 per ton for zinc. Using suitable figures for the purpose of illustration, show clearly how you would reveal:

(a) Material Price Variance;
(b) Material Mixture Variance;
(c) Yield Variance.

(*I.C.W.A. Final*)

29. The standard raw material mix for a ton of finished production is:

Material A 1200 lb at 3*d*. lb
„ B 500 „ 1*s*. 0*d*. „
„ C 500 „ 6*d*. „
„ D 100 „ 2*s*. 6*d*. „

Material used during an accounting period was as follows:

Material A 2900 lb at $3\frac{1}{4}d$. lb
„ B 1300 „ 1*s*. 1*d*. „
„ C 1350 „ $5\frac{1}{2}d$. „
„ D 260 „ 2*s*. 0*d*. „

Production during the period was 5600 lb. Identify and calculate the material cost variances.

(*I.C.W.A. Inter.*)

30. The standard mix of a compound of four materials is as follows:

Material	A	B	C	D
Percentage by weight	30	40	20	10
Price per lb	1*s*. 4*d*.	1*s*. 6*d*.	3*s*. 6*d*.	3*s*.

This compound should be used at the rate of 4 lb of compound per cubic foot of production. During a period in which 1000 cubic feet of finished product was made, actual usage was:

Material	A	B	C	D
Lbs used	1180	1580	830	440
Price per lb	1*s*. 3*d*.	1*s*. 8*d*.	3*s*. 4*d*.	3*s*.

Present these figures to the management of an undertaking where Standard Costing is used.

(*I.C.W.A. Final*)

31. A company manufacturing a special type of facing tile, 12 inch × 8 inch × ½ inch uses a system of Standard Costing. The standard mix of the compound used for making the tiles is:

1200 lb of material A at 1*s*. 5*d*. per lb
500 „ „ B „ 3*s*. 0*d*. „
800 „ „ C „ 3*s*. 6*d*. „

This compound should produce 12,000 square feet of tiles of $\frac{1}{2}$ inch thickness. During a period in which 100,000 tiles of the standard size were produced, the material usage was:

7000 lb of material A at 1s. 6d. per lb
3000 „ „ B „ 3s. 2d. „
5000 „ „ C „ 3s. 8d. „

Present the cost figures for the period showing:

(a) Material Price Variance;
(b) Material Mixture Variance;
(c) Yield Variance.

(I.C.W.A. Final)

Profitability (Chapter 29)

1. A business manufactures three quite different types of product, for all of which a steadily increasing demand arises. Capital, space, and technical knowledge are available for expansion of any one of the three.

Using suitable figures, present a report to the management on the profitability of the three products, and advise regarding the expansion of the most suitable product as revealed by your figures.

(I.C.W.A. Final)

2. An expanding business, making modest profits, finds its bank overdraft to be increasing. The Managing Director states that this indicates a need for the introduction of further capital, but a study of the figures indicates to you that with more efficient management, ample capital exists in the business. Using suitable figures, prepare a report to the Managing Director, indicating how the necessary capital can be found within the business.

(I.C.W.A. Final)

3. An item of plant costing £200,000 is estimated to have a life of 25 years. After about 15 years a substantial portion of the plant (original cost £100,000) is due for replacement in order to prolong the life of the plant to 25 years. Assume the annual production of the plant is 300,000 units and the estimated cost of replacement £120,000. Explain clearly how you would absorb the original and replacement costs of the rebuildable portion of the plant. Give reasons.

(I.C.W.A. Final)

4. Your directors are considering introducing additional capital into a business to:

(a) replace old machinery with modern equipment;
(b) build and equip a new department to manufacture a part of the final product which has hitherto been bought from outside.

Discuss the various factors you would consider to ascertain the additional profits which will result from this new capital expenditure.

(I.C.W.A. Final)

5. Using suitable figures, present a report to management, justifying the purchase of a very expensive machine requested and recommended by the Works Manager and other technical experts. You are to assume that a system of budgetary control is in operation.

(I.C.W.A. Final)

6. Your directors are contemplating the purchase of a new machine to replace a machine which has been in the factory for 5 years.

From the following information prepare a statement for submission to the board showing the effect of the installation on costs and profits and comment on the results shown. Ignore interest.

	Old machine	New machine
Purchase price	£4000	£6000
Estimated life of machine	10 years	10 years
Machine running hours p.a.	2000	2000
Units produced per hour	24	36
Wages per running hour	6s.	10s. 6d.
Power p.a.	£200	£450
Consumable stores p.a.	£600	£750
All other charges p.a.	£800	£900
Material cost per unit	1s.	1s.
Selling price per unit	2s. 6d.	2s. 6d.

(I.C.W.A. Final)

7. To increase productivity in Department X the works management are considering the complete replacement of the plant used. Present output is approximately 12,000 units p.a. selling at £2 per unit, and there is an unsatisfied demand at that price. Output after the replacement is estimated at about 50% more, retaining all existing labour but using no more labour. Selling prices will remain unaltered, for the time being at least. Present production costs p.a. (excluding depreciation) are:

	£
Raw material	12,000
Direct labour	3,000
Indirect charges (mainly fixed)	1,500

The plant in use cost £3000 and has a scrap value of £1400. The cost of new plant is £20,000, and depreciation would be provided at 10% p.a.

Draft a statement showing:

(a) present and prospective profit;
(b) the average yield (using simple interest) on the new capital outlay. You are expected to point out any factors that may qualify your figures.

(A.C.C.A. Final)

8. During a trade recession, production in a certain factory has fallen from an average of 8000 to 7000 units per week. In spite of this fall in production, the productivity of direct labour has increased.

Using suitable figures, present a report to management showing tne effects of the increase in productivity and the fall in production. The following figures for a normal average week may be used as a basis for your answer:

Production (units)	8,000
Labour hours	4,000
Production costs—	£
Direct materials	6,000
Direct labour	1,000
Factory overheads (variable)	2,000
„ „ (fixed)	1,000
Total Production Cost	£10,000

(I.C.W.A. Final)

9. A warehousing concern proposes to purchase electric high-lift trucks and auxiliary equipment to replace hand trucks now used. The new trucks would necessitate additional capital expenditure being made on buildings and fittings. The following appeared in last year's Profit and Loss Account:

	£		£
Management and clerical costs	32,000	Space rentals	250,000
Warehouse wages cost	104,000		
Rates and licences cost	18,000		
Power, light, and water cost	15,000		
Insurance cost	7,000		
Maintenance cost	3,000		
Depreciation—			
Buildings	10,000		
Hand trucks (final)	2,000		
	£191,000		£250,000

Proposed new expenditure:

Trucks, etc., £60,000, life 10 years, residual value £10,000.
Building and fittings, £50,000, to be written off over 20 years.
Estimated increased operating costs:

Management and clerical—estimated increase 10%	
Warehouse wages — „ „ 25%	
Power, etc.	—£3000
Insurance	—£2000
Maintenance	—£500

Rental income: increase of space available for renting 50%.
It is estimated that an overall reduction of charges of 10% will be possible.
From the above information present a forecast comparing the present Profit and Loss Account with the projected Profit and Loss Account when the scheme is in full working.

(I.C.W.A. Inter.)

10. Report to management on the relative profitability of the two products A and B.

Production cost per unit

	Product A (output 200 per week)	Product B (output 100 per week)
Materials	20	15
Wages	10	20
Fixed Overhead	35	10
Variable Overhead	15	20
	80	65
Gross profit	20	35
	£100	£100

Explain the variations disclosed by your statement.

(*I.C.W.A. Inter.*)

11. A certain factory producing packaging material has a 10-year-old plant, depreciated by the straight-line method, to which the following details apply:

Purchase price, including installation	£60,000
Estimated total life	20 years
Residual value after 20 years	£10,000
Output per minute	200 units

An offer is received to supply new plant to the value of £95,000. The offer also proposes a part-exchange provision of £20,000 in respect of the existing plant. The output of the new plant is 400 units per minute. It has an estimated life of 15 years, and residual value of £10,000.

The annual costs, etc., are to be taken as follows:

	Existing Plant	New Plant
Repairs and maintenance	£2,000	£2,500
Sundry indirect materials	£12,000	£15,000
Power and steam service	£6,000	£7,000
Proportion of general fixed cost	£1,500	£2,000
Wages of attendants	£2,500	£3,500
Running hours	2,500	2,500

The installation cost of the new plant will be £5000.

No change in the method of charging depreciation is proposed.

Disregarding direct materials cost, which is constant to both, prepare a Comparative Cost Schedule to show total and marginal costs per 1000 units of product produced by the new, and the existing plant.

(*I.C.W.A. Final*)

12. To increase productivity the works management are considering the complete replacement of the plant used in a particular department.

Present output is approximately 6000 units per annum, selling at £2 per unit, and there is an unsatisfied demand at that price.

Output after the replacement is estimated at 50% more, retaining all existing labour but using no more.

Selling prices will remain unaltered, for the time being at least.

Present production costs per annum (excluding depreciation) are:

	£
Raw material	6000
Direct labour	1500
Indirect charges (mainly fixed)	750

The plant in use cost £1500 and has a scrap value of £200. The cost of the new plant is £10,000, and depreciation would be provided at the rate of 10% per annum.

Draft a statement showing present and prospective profit and mention any factors that may qualify your figures.

(*Com. A. Final*

Auditing of Cost Accounts (*Chapter 30*)

1. In which direction are the costing records of value to the auditors of the Financial Accounts? To what extent do you consider an independent audit of the Cost Accounts is necessary?

(*I.C.W.A. Final*)

2. As Cost Auditor to a group of factories, describe the procedure you would adopt with regard to labour and material costs.

(*I.C.W.A. Final*)

3. What are your views on the suggestion that an Internal Auditor of an organisation with various branch offices should act in conjunction with the Chief Accountant in designing any new system?

(*C.A.A.*)

4. Give your reasons as to why a company or any large organisation should incur the expense of an Internal Auditor, when in fact it has to employ Professional Auditors to audit its accounts annually.

(*C.A.A.*)

5. In this age of electronics, clerical routine duties have been considerably reduced. What effect has this had upon the duties of the Internal Auditor?

(*C.A.A.*)

Mechanised Cost Accounting (*Chapters 31 and 32*)

1. Describe in detail a mechanical method of recording employees' starting and stopping times and state the advantages of such recording. In what circumstances may such reports be unnecessary?

(*I.C.W.A. Inter.*)

2. A company carries out a wide variety of contracts for engineering products. Certain components and sub-assemblies, however, are common to many contracts, and past costs are used in preparing estimates and tenders. What steps would you take in order to make use of punched-card accounting methods for the same purpose?

(I.C.W.A. Final)

3. The directors of Tightenup Ltd. are contemplating the introduction of mechanisation into the Company's wages office, which deals with the preparation and analysis of the payroll for 2500 weekly paid employees of the Company. This work is at present performed by manual methods.

Each employee is provided with a clock card on which is written his name and clock number and on which are stamped the times of arrival and departure. Space is provided on the card for entry of the following items:

(1) hourly rate;
(2) hours worked;
(3) calculation of the basic pay;
(4) addition of the overtime hours (where applicable);
(5) addition of the piece-work bonus (where applicable);
(6) totalling of gross pay;
(7) deduction of National Insurance contribution;
(8) deduction of P.A.Y.E.;
(9) net pay due;
(10) employer's contribution for National Insurance.

After all these items have been entered on the clock cards they are summarised in departmental sections in wages books and cast so that departmental total of each of the items (2) to (10) are provided. A final summary is then made.

Any machines which it is decided to use will have to be purchased, and there is no other office work which can be brought into the contemplated scheme of mechanisation.

The calculation of the piece-work bonus and the actual making up and distribution of the pay envelopes are to be excluded from the contemplated mechanisation.

You are required:

(a) to state the extent to which you consider the directors of Tightenup Ltd. would be well advised to mechanise the preparation and analysis of the payroll giving reasons for your opinion;
(b) to outline the scheme of mechanisation which you consider would be likely to prove the most satisfactory; and
(c) to state what modifications of the scheme would be required to allow for the production of a statement for each employee, showing the items (1) to (10) above applicable to him.

(C.A. Final, November 1957)

INDEX